Volume 8

The Broadman Bible Commentary

BROADMAN PRESS · **Nashville, Tennessee**

The Broadman Bible Commentary

Volume 8

General Articles
Matthew - Mark

4211–08

ISBN: 0–8054–1108–9

Dewey Decimal classification: 220.7
Library of Congress catalog card number: 78–93918
Printed in the United States of America

Advisory Board

Contributors

Clifton J. Allen, Baptist Sunday School Board (retired): *General Article*

Morris Ashcraft, Midwestern Baptist Theological Seminary: *Revelation*

G. R. Beasley-Murray, Spurgeon's College, London: *2 Corinthians*

T. Miles Bennett, Southwestern Baptist Theological Seminary: *Malachi*

Reidar B. Bjornard, Northern Baptist Theological Seminary: *Esther*

James A. Brooks, New Orleans Baptist Theological Seminary: *General Article*

Raymond Bryan Brown, Southeastern Baptist Theological Seminary: *1 Corinthians*

John T. Bunn, Campbell College: *Song of Solomon; Ezekiel*

Joseph A. Callaway, Southern Baptist Theological Seminary: *General Article*

Ronald E. Clements, University of Cambridge: *Leviticus*

E. Luther Copeland, Southeastern Baptist Theological Seminary: *General Article*

Bruce C. Cresson, Baylor University: *Obadiah*

Edward R. Dalglish, Baylor University: *Judges; Nahum*

John I Durham, Southeastern Baptist Theological Seminary: *Psalms; General Article*

Frank E. Eakin, Jr., University of Richmond: *Zephaniah*

Clyde T. Francisco, Southern Baptist Theological Seminary: *Genesis; 1, 2 Chronicles; General Article*

D. David Garland, Southwestern Baptist Theological Seminary: *Habakkuk*

A. J. Glaze, Jr., Seminario Internacional Teologico Bautista, Buenos Aires: *Jonah*

James Leo Green, Southeastern Baptist Theological Seminary: *Jeremiah*

Emmett Willard Hamrick, Wake Forest University: *Ezra; Nehemiah*

William L. Hendricks, Southwestern Baptist Theological Seminary: *General Article*

E. Glenn Hinson, Southern Baptist Theological Seminary: *1, 2 Timothy; Titus; General Article*

Herschel H. Hobbs, First Baptist Church, Oklahoma City: *1, 2 Thessalonians*

Roy L. Honeycutt, Jr., Midwestern Baptist Theological Seminary: *Exodus; 2 Kings; Hosea*

William E. Hull, Southern Baptist Theological Seminary: *John*

Page H. Kelley, Southern Baptist Theological Seminary: *Isaiah*

J. Hardee Kennedy, New Orleans Baptist Theological Seminary: *Ruth; Joel*

Robert B. Laurin, American Baptist Seminary of the West: *Lamentations*

John William MacGorman, Southwestern Baptist Theological Seminary: *Galatians*

Edward A. McDowell, Southeastern Baptist Theological Seminary (retired): *1, 2, 3 John*

Ralph P. Martin, Fuller Theological Seminary: *Ephesians*

M. Pierce Matheney, Jr., Midwestern Baptist Theological Seminary: *1 Kings*

Dale Moody, Southern Baptist Theological Seminary: *Romans*

William H. Morton, Midwestern Baptist Theological Seminary: *Joshua*

Barclay M. Newman, Jr., American Bible Society: *General Article*

John P. Newport, Southwestern Baptist Theological Seminary: *General Article*

John Joseph Owens, Southern Baptist Theological Seminary: *Numbers; Job* (with Tate and Watts); *Daniel*

Wayne H. Peterson, Golden Gate Baptist Theological Seminary: *Ecclesiastes*

Ben F. Philbeck, Jr., Carson-Newman College: *1, 2 Samuel*

William M. Pinson, Jr., Southwestern Baptist Theological Seminary: *General Article*

Ray F. Robbins, New Orleans Baptist Theological Seminary: *Philemon*

Eric C. Rust, Southern Baptist Theological Seminary: *General Article*

B. Elmo Scoggin, Southeastern Baptist Theological Seminary: *Micah; General Article*

Burlan A. Sizemore, Jr., Midwestern Baptist Theological Seminary: *General Article*

David A. Smith, Furman University: *Haggai*

Ralph L. Smith, Southwestern Baptist Theological Seminary: *Amos*

T. C. Smith, Furman University: *Acts; General Article*

Harold S. Songer, Southern Baptist Theological Seminary: *James*

Frank Stagg, Southern Baptist Theological Seminary: *Matthew; Philippians*

Ray Summers, Baylor University: *1, 2 Peter; Jude; General Article*

Marvin E. Tate, Jr., Southern Baptist Theological Seminary: *Job* (with Owens and Watts); *Proverbs*

Malcolm O. Tolbert, New Orleans Baptist Theological Seminary: *Luke*

Charles A. Trentham, First Baptist Church, Knoxville: *Hebrews; General Article*

Henry E. Turlington, University Baptist Church, Chapel Hill, North Carolina: *Mark*

John D. W. Watts, Serampore College, Serampore, India: *Deuteronomy; Job* (with Owens and Tate); *Zechariah*

R. E. O. White, Baptist Theological College, Glasgow: *Colossians*

Preface

The Broadman Bible Commentary presents current biblical study within the context of strong faith in the authority, adequacy, and reliability of the Bible as the Word of God. It seeks to offer help and guidance to the Christian who is willing to undertake Bible study as a serious, rewarding pursuit. The publisher thus has defined the scope and purpose of the Commentary to produce a work suited to the Bible study needs of both ministers and laymen. The findings of biblical scholarship are presented so that readers without formal theological education can use them in their own Bible study. Footnotes and technical words are limited to essential information.

Writers have been carefully selected for their reverent Christian faith and their knowledge of Bible truth. Keeping in mind the needs of a general readership, the writers present special information about language and history where it helps to clarify the meaning of the text. They face Bible problems—not only in language but in doctrine and ethics—but avoid fine points that have little bearing on how we should understand and apply the Bible. They express their own views and convictions. At the same time, they present alternative views when such are advocated by other serious, well-informed students of the Bible. The views presented, therefore, cannot be regarded as the official position of the publisher.

This Commentary is the result of many years' planning and preparation. Broadman Press began in 1958 to explore needs and possibilities for the present work. In this year and again in 1959, Christian leaders—particularly pastors and seminary professors—were brought together to consider whether a new commentary was needed and what shape it might take. Growing out of these deliberations in 1961, the board of trustees governing the Press authorized the publication of a multivolume commentary. Further planning led in 1966 to the selection of a general editor and an Advisory Board. This board of pastors, professors, and denominational leaders met in September, 1966, reviewing preliminary plans and making definite recommendations which have been carried out as the Commentary has been developed.

Early in 1967, four consulting editors were selected, two for the Old Testament and two for the New. Under the leadership of the general editor, these men have worked with the Broadman Press personnel to plan the Commentary in detail. They have participated fully in the selection of the writers and the evaluation of manuscripts. They have given generously of time and effort, earning the highest esteem and gratitude of Press employees who have worked with them.

The selection of the Revised Standard Version as the Bible text for the Commentary was made in 1967 also. This grew out of careful consideration of possible alternatives, which were fully discussed in the meeting of the Advisory Board. The adoption of an English version as a standard text was recognized as desirable, meaning that only the King James, American Standard, and Revised Standard Versions were available for consideration.

The King James Version was recognized as holding first place in the hearts of many Christians but as suffering from inaccuracies in translation and obscurities in phrasing. The American Standard was seen as free from these two problems but deficient in an attractive English style and wide current use. The Revised Standard retains the accuracy and clarity of the American Standard and has a pleasing style and a growing use. It thus enjoys a strong advantage over each of the others, making it by far the most desirable choice.

Throughout the COMMENTARY the treatment of the biblical text aims at a balanced combination of exegesis and exposition, admittedly recognizing that the nature of the various books and the space assigned will properly modify the application of this approach.

The general articles appearing in Volumes 1, 8, and 12 are designed to provide background material to enrich one's understanding of the nature of the Bible and the distinctive aspects of each Testament. Those in Volume 12 focus on the implications of biblical teaching in the areas of worship, ethical duty, and the world mission of the church.

The COMMENTARY avoids current theological fads and changing theories. It concerns itself with the deep realities of God's dealings with men, his revelation in Christ, his eternal gospel, and his purpose for the redemption of the world. It seeks to relate the word of God in Scripture and in the living Word to the deep needs of persons and to mankind in God's world.

Through faithful interpretation of God's message in the Scriptures, therefore, the COMMENTARY seeks to reflect the inseparable relation of truth to life, of meaning to experience. Its aim is to breathe the atmosphere of life-relatedness. It seeks to express the dynamic relation between redemptive truth and living persons. May it serve as a means whereby God's children hear with greater clarity what God the Father is saying to them.

Contents

General Articles

The Religious and Cultural Background of the New Testament

T. C. Smith

It is impossible to understand the origin and growth of the Christian movement apart from the religious and cultural background of the New Testament. Whether one believes that God prepared the events of history or created the need favorable for the dissemination of the gospel, we cannot view Christianity in any other way than in contact with its environment. It is with this truth in mind that we shall explore the political, religious, and cultural elements in Judaism and the Greco-Roman world in order to show how both of these influenced early Christianity.

I. *Political History of the Greco-Roman World*

The political history of the Greco-Roman world begins with Philip II, king of Macedonia and father of Alexander the Great. He found Greece, famous for its art, literature, and architecture, torn by strife and dissension between the city-states. By bribery, assuming the role of an arbiter and championing the Delphian god, he became the master of Greece in 338 B.C. and formed the Hellenic League. Philip dreamed of a united Greece that could dominate the world. Although the League was unwilling, he was chosen as the commander of the combined Greek forces to attack Persia. Before Philip could realize his dream, he was assassinated in 336. His son Alexander, at the age of nineteen, became the heir of his ambitions.

It took Alexander two years to prove to the Greeks his capability as a military leader. After the Hellenic League chose him as commander in 334 B.C., he crossed the Hellespont to engage the Persians in battle. Alexander routed the Persian army at Grannicus and Issus and moved south to Egypt, where he was hailed as a deliverer of the Egyptians. In 331 he advanced to the east and sealed the doom of Darius III and the Persians at the battle of Gaugamela. His exploits did not end with a decisive victory over the Persians but carried him farther eastward to the Indus River. When he died of fever in Babylon in 323, his realm extended from Greece to northern India. This fantastic military strategist achieved all this within 13 years.

History does not measure the greatness of Alexander in terms of the vast amount of territory that he won. His greatest achievement was bringing the East and West together through the propagation of Greek culture. The Hellenic spirit of individual liberty, emancipation from tyranny of custom and tradition, the free exercise of scientific and critical inquiry, a love for the beautiful in art and literature, and the development of mind and body extended to all parts of the world under his policy of Hellenization. From the babel of the Greek dialects there sprang a Greek language intelligible to all Greeks and usable by all conquered people.

Alexander broke down racial and national barriers by encouraging his soldiers to marry Asiatic women. His aim was to establish a mighty empire which disregarded the difference between Greek and barbarian, setting men free for international relationships. As his army advanced, he established Greek colonies which became centers for Hellenic culture. The intermingling of the races initiated a spirit of cosmopolitanism, a syncretism of religions, and an interest in the individual.

1. *Hellenistic Domination, 323–167 B.C.*

Upon the death of Alexander the vast empire was divided among his generals. Ptolemy seized Egypt and later laid claim to the land of Palestine. His seizure of this territory incurred the anger of Seleucus, another general of Alexander, who became ruler of Syria after the battle of Ipsus in 301 B.C. For more than a century the Seleucids of Syria and the Ptolemies of Egypt struggled for possession of Palestine. The Jews who inhabited the land were thus thrown into the middle of the conflict.

With the division of the empire of Alexander, Greece itself ceased to maintain its old position of leadership; but its culture spread and developed in the cities of the new kingdoms. While the Hellenists influenced the conquered people with their culture, they in turn were enriched by foreign cultures, including Judaism.

Under the rule of the Ptolemies something of tremendous importance occurred that swept the Jews into the main current of human progress. During the reign of Ptolemy Philadelphus (285–247 B.C.), the Old Testament was translated, at least in part, into the Greek language. It is doubtful that a translation was made of all the writings. Possibly nothing more than the Pentateuch was attempted at that time. At any rate, through this accomplishment, the Jewish religious writings were now available to the non-Jewish world in a language which they could understand. The religious beliefs of Judaism, which previously had been largely confined to the limits of the Jewish community, were now open for the world to consider.

Antiochus the Great, a Seleucid king, after three attempts to gain possession of Palestine from the Ptolemies, defeated the Egyptian army at the battle of Panium in 198 B.C. and wrested the land from Ptolemy V. The reign of Antiochus was significant for Jewish history, not only because Palestine ceased to be under Ptolemaic domination, but also because his reign witnessed the entrance of Romans in Asiatic politics.

Because of Antiochus' unsuccessful armed opposition to the extension of Roman domination, Rome imposed heavy war indemnities upon Antiochus and his political territory. In addition to tribute, the Romans compelled him to furnish hostages for the payment of indemnities.

The attitude of the Jews toward Antiochus the Great was favorable at first. The Jews were pleased to change their loyalty from the Ptolemies to the Seleucids. Antiochus favored the Palestinian Jews by relieving their taxation burden. He even went as far as to exempt the Temple personnel from taxation. However, when the Seleucid king was faced with war indemnities, he made heavy monetary demands, and the Jews felt that they had been betrayed.

Antiochus the Great was killed in the battle of Elam in 187, and his son, Seleucus IV (187–175), ascended the throne. As king, he followed an ill-advised policy in his treatment of the Jews. Seleucus sent his general Heliodorus to Jerusalem to seize the Temple treasure. A full account of this incident occurs in the apocryphal writing 2 Maccabees. Heliodorus was unsuccessful in his venture. In 175 B.C. Seleucus IV was killed.

Antiochus, the son of Antiochus the Great and brother of Seleucus IV, usurped the throne from Demetrius, the son of Seleucus IV and natural successor, and ruled from 175 to 163. Antiochus conceived the idea of reviving the Olympian gods of Greece and used them as instruments of unity for the empire. To maintain unification of the empire it was essential that there be only one religion. Thus he decided to make Zeus supreme again. Actually the statues of Zeus which he erected bore a striking resemblance to Antiochus. He became known as Theos Epiphanes (God Manifest) and demanded that he be counted among the gods. Halos found on his coins verify his claim of deification.

From the time of Alexander the Great until the accession of Antiochus Epiphanes, Hellenistic influences had gradually penetrated Palestine. The prevalence of Greek worship and Greek athletic festivals, coins bearing Greek inscriptions and emblems of Greek deities, plus evidence for many towns bearing Hellenic names, all bear witness to this fact. If Antiochus IV had not resorted to violent means for Hellenization of the Jews in Palestine, it is likely that they would have gradually submitted to Hellenism in a peaceful manner up to the limits of their acceptance.

This Syrian king was a man of violent impulses. When opposed he could become violent and cruel. His dream of overcoming the Romans and releasing the Syrians from the huge war indemnities inherited from his father became an obsession with him. He believed that the only course of action available to him was to force the people throughout his domain to accept Greek culture. Under the leadership of Jason, who, through influence with Epiphanes, had his brother Onias III deposed as high priest, the more influential Jews at first were rather sympathetic toward Hellenization.

The cheerful acceptance of Antiochus by the liberals began to wane when Jason was deposed and Menelaus replaced him. During an expedition by Antiochus Epiphanes against Egypt, Jason led an attack on Menelaus and captured the city of Jerusalem. Already halted by the Romans in his attempt to take Egypt and angered by the embarrassment of having to submit to Roman authority, Antiochus returned to have his rage augmented by the revolt of Jason. Antiochus was in no mood to tolerate any dissension in his empire. If he had any hope of defeating the Romans, he must have absolute unity. He saw that the real problem with the Jews was their religious beliefs. Therefore, he concluded that he must embark on a forced policy of Hellenization that would be complete in all details.

Antiochus decreed that the daily sacrifices in the Temple should be discontinued. An altar to Zeus Olympus was erected on the altar used by the Jews for burnt offering. Swine were offered as sacrifices in the Temple, and copies of the Law were destroyed. The penalty for possessing a copy of the Law or practicing the rite of circumcision was death. Antiochus also declared that sabbath observance was illegal. Most of these decrees came in the month of Kislev in 168 B.C. At first there was only passive resistance by those Jews who refused to submit. After the persecution of Epiphanes became more severe and many Jews were put to death, active resistance became inevitable.

2. *The Hasmonean Revolt, 167–142* B.C.

Leadership for the organization of active resistance came from the town of Modin near Lydda. There an aged priest by the name of Mattathias, who was of the lineage of a certain Hasmon, refused to perform sacrifices to the heathen gods. Mattathias killed an apostate Jew and the king's commissioner. He knew that this was the time to act and summoned all the Jews who were zealous for the Law to follow him and his five sons in a guerrilla war against the Syrians. This revolt occurred in 167 B.C. When Mattathias died, the leadership of the movement fell to his son Judas.

After several successful skirmishes against the Syrian forces, Judas took possession of Jerusalem with the exception of the garrison called Akra. On the twenty-fifth day of December (Kislev) in 165 or 164, he entered the Temple and destroyed the altar which had been dedicated to Zeus. He also renewed the sacrifices to Yahweh. This day was afterwards observed as an annual festival and continues to be observed to the present time by the Jews as the Festival of Hanukkah.

With religious freedom once more restored in Jerusalem, many of the Hasidim, the pious followers of Judas Maccabeus, decided that this victory was sufficient. However, Judas was not willing to settle for anything less than political independence. He was more convinced of this when the Jews of Gilead and Galilee appealed to him for help. His brothers, Simon and Jonathan, answered the call of these fellow Jews and brought them back to Judea. With this addition to his forces Judas dreamed of political power. His pious followers, the Hasidim, opposed the ambitious plans of Judas and forsook him. In order to maintain a fighting force, Judas had to resort to the hiring of mercenaries. He continued his skirmishes against the central government until finally, in 160, with only eight hundred men left in his army, his career came to an end at the battle of Elasa.

Jonathan, the brother of Judas, became the leader of the Jews after the death of Judas. This was a period of rival contestants to the Seleucid throne, and Jonathan gained some political vantage point for the Jews during the confusion.

3. *Rule of the Hasmoneans, 142–63* B.C.

After the death of Jonathan, Simon, his brother, became the recognized leader of the Jews. Simon achieved what was equivalent to political independence by supporting Demetrius II in his bid for the Seleucid throne. From the year 142 until 63, when Rome took over Palestine, Judea remained an independent state. After seven years of relative peace in Judea, while serving as high priest, Simon was assassinated, and his son, John Hyrcanus, succeeded him.

Even though Josephus, the Jewish historian, asserts that Aristobulus, the son of John Hyrcanus, was the first king of the Jews from the Hasmonean line, it is quite clear that John looked upon himself as the holder of the title along with the office of high priest. During the reign of John Hyrcanus, a period of approximately thirty years (135–105), the Jewish army overcame the Samaritans and destroyed their temple on Mount Gerizim in 127 B.C. Hyrcanus forced the Idumeans to submit to circumcision and become Jews.

From his conquests it appears that John intended to extend the borders of Judea to include the territory once held by David and Solomon. He was so successful in his campaigns that many of the Jews hoped he would be the anticipated Messiah.

Our first knowledge of the Pharisees and Sadducees comes from the time of John Hyrcanus. They appear before us as fully developed religious parties with conflicting views. John was a supporter of the Pharisees until they expressed opposition to his holding the office of high priest and to his absorption in worldly policy. He showed his resentment to their authority by abolishing certain religious regulations which the Pharisees had imposed upon the people. This was only the beginning of hostility and bitterness between the Hasmoneans and the Pharisees. The climax of this rift came under the rule of Alexander Janneus.

The successor of John Hyrcanus was Aristobulus, who was king and high priest for a little over one year. His only achievement was the defeat of the Galileans, whom he forced to submit to circumcision and the Jewish law. When he died, Salome his wife, released the brothers of Aristobulus from prison and married the eldest, Jonathan. Jonathan took the Greek name Alexander and was known as Alexander Janneus. He was an ambitious and warlike ruler who determined to possess Palestine from Dan to Beersheba.

The Pharisees opposed Alexander from the outset because he had married Alexandra Salome, his brother's wife. According to the Jewish levirate law it was legal for a man to marry his dead brother's wife, but this law did not apply to the priests. They were required to marry a virgin. The Jews openly demonstrated their hostility against Alexander by pelting him with citrons as he was officiating at the Feast of Tabernacles. In a fit of rage he ordered his soldiers to attack the people, and six thousand were massacred. He increased his crimes against the Jews by crucifying eight hundred Pharisees when they led a rebellion against him. The only sound advice that Alexander ever gave was to his wife just before he died. He advised her to make friends with the Pharisees.

When Alexandra Salome became queen of the Jews, she appointed Hyrcanus II, her elder son, to the position of high priest. Aristobulus II, the younger son, supported the cause of the Sadducees and waited for the opportune time to seize the priestly office and the throne. After the death of his mother, he moved against Hyrcanus II, who willingly submitted, since he was not favorably disposed toward the kingship or priesthood. Antipater, the governor of Idumea and adviser to Hyrcanus II, was not willing for him to give up so easily and solicited the aid of Aretas III, king of the Nabateans, to wage war against Aristobulus II. The settlement of this affair, much to their regret later, came through the intervention of the Romans.

From the days of Antiochus the Great the power of Rome was respected throughout the East, even though there was no attempt to follow up the victory at Magnesia by conquest. The Roman policy changed in the first century B.C. when Mithridates, the king of Pontus, waged three wars against Rome. In the third war, Pompey, who had previously made a reputation for himself in destroying the pirates on the Mediterranean and by making Cilicia a Roman province, commanded the Roman forces and invaded Pontus. Completely victorious, Pompey advanced against Syria and without any trouble annexed it as a Roman province. When he came to Damascus, he heard about the struggle between Hyrcanus and Aristobulus. In 63 B.C. Pompey entered Jerusalem and settled the dispute in favor of Hyrcanus, because he believed that Hyrcanus was weaker and could be used for his purposes.

The inability of the Jews to settle their own disputes was very costly. The independence that they had enjoyed from the time of Simon was swallowed up by Roman domination. All the extra-Judean territory gained through conquest by the Hasmoneans, with the exception of Idumea, was taken from them.

4. Roman Rule, 63 B.C.—A.D. 70

Hyrcanus II remained the ecclesiastical ruler of the Jews, but the political affairs of the country were managed by Antipater. It was fortunate for the Jews that they had a man like Antipater to lead them through the troublesome years of Roman civil wars. The Jews hated him in spite of the fact that he secured for them many privileges by playing it safe in politics and always coming out on the side of the victors. They despised him because he represented a foreign power in his administrative policy and also because he was an Idumean. Throughout the civil wars that began with Julius Caesar and Pompey and ended with the war between Octavian and Anthony at the battle of Actium in 31 B.C., Antipater and, after his death, his son Herod were always loyal to the Roman general who dominated the East.

In 42 B.C. after the battle of Philippi, Herod, who succeeded his father as governor of Judea, found himself in a very embarrassing position. He had supported Cassius, and—now that Cassius and Brutus suffered defeat in the battle—he had to gain the support of Anthony and Octavian. This he was able to do. In 40 B.C. Herod went to Rome to see Octavian and obtained the kingship of Palestine, but he was not able to establish himself on the throne until 37. He ruled over Palestine until his death in 4 B.C. It was during the time of his reign that Jesus was born in Bethlehem.

Herod the Great was by nature ambitious, passionate, sensual, and cruel; but despite these faults he was an energetic and capable, if unscrupulous, king. The Jews disliked him, partly because he was an Idumean and partly because of his oppressive taxation. He was indebted to Rome for his position as sovereign and was indisposed to permit the Sadducees to enjoy secular power along with their ecclesiastical power. Occasionally, Herod favored the Pharisees because they were more inclined to restrict themselves to religious affairs and leave politics to others. The Jews under the leadership of the Pharisees were displeased when Herod built a theater in Jerusalem and encouraged pagan worship in his kingdom. In his building program, which was an extensive one, he made provision for the reconstruction of the Temple. The Jews greeted this as a noble act. If the Jews had been willing to accept him as their king, Herod would have been less violent in his outbursts against them.

Following the death of Herod the Great, his territory was divided among three of his sons. Archelaus received Judea, Samaria, and Idumea and bore the title of ethnarch. In A.D. 6 he was deposed. From that time on, with the exception of a span of almost four years (41–44) when Herod Agrippa I was king, this area of Palestine was governed by Roman procurators. Herod Antipas became the tetrarch of Galilee and Perea. He was responsible for the death of John the Baptist, and it was during his rule that Jesus began and continued his Galilean ministry. When the Roman emperor Caius Caligula appointed Agrippa I, the brother of Antipas' wife Herodias, as the successor to Herod Philip, he gave him the title of king. The promotion caused Herodias to persuade Antipas to seek the same honor for himself. Agrippa did not like Antipas and accused him of treasonable negotiations with the Parthians. Caligula deposed Antipas and banished him to Gaul in A.D. 39. The emperor then awarded the region of Galilee and Perea to Agrippa I. Philip's share of the will of Herod the Great included Iturea, Trachonitis, Gaulanitis, Auranitis, and Panias. He ruled over this area until his death in A.D. 34. When Jesus withdrew from Galilee and came near Caesarea-Philippi, he was in the tetrarchy of Herod Philip.

From A.D. 6 to 66 no less than 14 procurators were sent by the Roman emperors to govern the province of Judea. Most of these men exercised poor administrative judgment and were often cruel in carrying out their assignments. Admittedly, the office of procurator was not one to be cherished because of the loyalty of the Jews to their religious faith and their stubborn resistance to alien control. Some of the procurators who come before us in the New Testament are Pontius Pilate (26–36), before whom Jesus was tried, Felix (51–60), who judged Paul's case, and Porcius Festus (60–62), the procurator before whom Paul made his appeal to Rome.

The reactionary groups increased in number to such extent, and the procurators became so ruthless in their policies, that open revolt against Rome broke out in A.D. 66. This uprising resulted in the destruction of Jerusalem and the Temple in A.D. 70, under the leadership of the Roman general Titus.

II. Religious Development in Palestine in the Hellenistic Age

Under the sway of Greek culture and the subsequent Roman political power, Judaism in Palestine slowly developed new religious teachings, institutions, and parties. These new forms of faith bore the marks of contact with Persians, Greeks, and Romans. The Jewish belief in demons and angels, the doctrine of the resurrection from the dead, the elaboration of apocalyptic eschatology, and the adaptation of the Law to everyday life resulting in rabbinism emerged during this period in Jewish history. The exclusivism of the Jews did not prevent them from borrowing from the Gentile world all that could bring enrichment to their religious beliefs and intellectual life. However much they may have assimilated from the neighboring cultures, Judaism possessed a vitality and strength which aided it in maintaining its central core and prevented it from sacrificing its identity.

1. Religious Doctrines

One of the most important doctrinal developments in Judaism of this age was the resurrection from the dead. Previous to this time the religion of Israel made provisions for a continued existence after death in some sense, yet it was a survival not too appealing to the Jews. When a person died, he went to Sheol, a subterranean abode similar to Hades among the Greeks. There he was confined, and his return to earth was impossible. The road to Sheol was a one-way trip, a place of silence, a land of no return. From the warm realities of life on earth a man moved to the cold semblance of a ghostly type of existence in the realm of the dead. Since this hope of after life lacked vitality, the religion of Israel stressed the doctrine of survival through the family. A man went on living in his children even after he was dead, so in reality their life was his own life. This is why it was so essential for the Jew to have many children.

When the Jews began to recognize the importance of the individual apart from his corporate relation to Israel, and when they observed that retributive justice did not come in this life, their dynamic faith in a just God led them to a belief in the resurrection from the dead. There are only two explicit affirmations of this teaching in the Old Testament. One occurs in Isaiah 26:19. This is embedded in the late section —according to the view of many scholars —of the book of Isaiah, containing chapters 24–27, referred to as the Isaiah Apocalypse. The date of this section of Isaiah is about the third century B.C. The other reference is Daniel 12:2—from a man of faith in the Maccabean revolt.

Some scholars disregard the passage in Isaiah because they say that it speaks of national restoration, not individual resurrection. If we accept this interpretation and discard the verse as a reference to a resurrection of the individual, the only clear and undisputed passage in the Old Testament is Daniel 12:2. The author of Daniel faced the sufferings of the Jews under the persecuting hand of Antiochus Epiphanes and believed that those who were loyal to God would live again. Those who suffered martyrdom would be raised to a life of happiness on earth, while those apostate Jews and Syrians who killed them would be raised to endure punishment.

When the doctrine of resurrection emerged in Judaism, the apocalyptists were the originators, developers, and propagators of it. We shall consider the apocalyptic literature later, but, suffice it to say, the book of Daniel is a representative of this type of thinking in the Old Testament. Speculations on the kind of body raised (whether physical or spiritual), divisions of the temporary abode in Sheol, and the final abode of the righteous and wicked occupied the interest of the apocalyptists from the Maccabean period to the second century A.D. The resurrection from the dead became a central tenet of the Pharisees, but their counterpart, the Sadducees, refused to accept the doctrine and promoted the skepticism displayed in Ecclesiastes.

Another teaching that entered Judaism by way of the apocalyptists during this period was the active role of angels and demons in the affairs of men. The Hebrews knew about angels long before the Exile, but it was not until they returned from the Babylonian captivity that angels became realities significantly influential in their daily religious life. The conception of divine transcendence and God's remoteness from the world and human life, noticeable in the Persian period, developed into a problem for the Jews of the Hellenistic age. They were forced to make use of angels to bridge the gap between them and God. Angels, who in pre-exilic days were nothing more than manifestations of God's majesty, became the channels by which God communicated to his people.

The new emphasis on angelic activity in the religion of Israel must have come through Persian influence. The angels ministered to the people in various ways. They were guardians of individuals and the nation, intercessors in behalf of men before God, communicators of God's message to individuals, and essential participants in the great eschatological drama. From apocalyptic literature we learn that archangels like Uriel, Raphael, Raguel, Michael, Gabriel, Remiel, and Saraquel functioned with specific assignments. Two of these, Michael and Gabriel, are mentioned in the New Testament.

As compared to the Old Testament, a marked feature of the New Testament is the appearance of demons and demon-possessed people. How do we account for the demons? When did they become realities with whom man must contend? We find our answers in apocryphal literature of the intertestamental period, especially in those works that are more apocalyptic in nature.

Before the Exile the Jews believed that

God was responsible for everything that happened, whether for good or evil. They did not think in terms of second causes. Only when they accepted a dualistic theory did they understand that the world was in the clutches of the demonic. This brought great relief to their minds. No longer did they hold to the view that all oppression came as a result of a vengeful God. The temporary rule of evil under the demonic powers brought the vast majority of suffering and misfortune to God's people, but evil could not stand against God's power.

A myth, based upon Genesis 6:1–4, was used in 1 Enoch and Jubilees to explain the origin of demons. The heavenly spirits descended to the earth and yielded to the seductions of women. From this unnatural intercourse a race of giants came into existence. These giants gave birth to evil spirits. Most of the evil spirits were bound by the angels of God, but the rest under the leadership of Mastema (Satan) led men astray and caused them to commit all sorts of sin and evil. Ultimately the demons and Satan, their leader, will be doomed at the final judgment; but in the meantime they are permitted to carry on their activities against men.

Heretofore we have been considering teachings that were introduced to Judaism in this era, but now we turn to a doctrine which was already established. This is the doctrine of Messiah. With the disruption of the united kingdom under Rehoboam, it appeared that the work of David and Solomon was in vain. Nevertheless, from that time on the prophets from the Northern Kingdom and the Southern Kingdom anticipated a reunification of the monarchy under the rule of a descendant of David. Out of this hope there arose a teaching concerning Messiah.

Messiah means "anointed." The word had been used in the past history of Israel to indicate the authority and close relation of the prophet, priest, and king to Yahweh. In the latter half of the first century B.C. Messiah had become a technical term related to a descendant of David.

In the Hellenistic age some of the Jews centered their hopes in a Davidic Messiah, while others were more concerned for a Golden Age in the future and did not stress the importance of a leader to accomplish this. They longed for a period of independence and power, peace and prosperity, rectitude and piety, and justice and brotherly love among men. Many of the apocalyptists who believed that Yahweh would intervene in history and relieve the people of oppression were not interested at all in a messiah. A few of the apocalyptists expected some sort of superhuman figure who would come and bring judgment upon the world along with God as is evidenced from 4 Ezra, 1 Enoch, and 2 Baruch.

Those Jews who anticipated a messiah did not entertain any notions that the messiah would suffer. No one but a man of extraordinary military strength could fulfil their hopes and aspirations for national restoration. Furthermore, there is no evidence that they expected anything other than a man as messiah. It is quite true that there were vague ideas of a superhuman figure as we have already noticed, but the normal Jewish hopes were in a man. Needless to say, Jesus did not measure up to their preconceived notions of Messiah since their standard of measurement was wrong.

Apocalyptic writings contained and emphasized the teachings we have examined thus far. The thought expressed by the authors of these works formed a definite element in Judaism, yet it is not clear how widespread the influence was. Some of the religious ideas were accepted by the Pharisees and found their way into rabbinical literature. Perhaps the writings were more popular among the people of the land than with the religious leaders. Apocalyptic literature grew out of a concern for the unfulfilled prophecies of the Old Testament. An attempt was made to rationalize and systemize the predictive side of prophecy. On the other hand, the scribes and their successors, the rabbis, stressed the importance of the commands of God found in the Law and the Prophets.

Apocalyptic literature was so varied that it is impossible to give characteristics that may apply to all the writings. Scholars who are specialists in this area have set forth distinctive features which we shall consider. The majority of these works were pseudonymous. The authors assumed the name of a worthy of the past to add authority to their message. Prophetic activity ceased when the scribes laid claim to prophetic succession through the interpretation of the Law. Therefore, if a man gifted with spiritual insight felt the call to proclaim a message from God, he was restricted by scribal authority. It became necessary, under such circumstances, for the apocalyptists to pretend that what they wrote was from Moses, Ezra, Enoch, or others.

In addition to being pseudonymous these writings portrayed a deterministic, dualistic, and pessimistic view of history. The real conflict between good and evil was staged in the heavens above. The forces of God engaged the forces of Satan in battle. God was victorious in the heavens, and this determined the outcome of the struggle between man and the demonic on earth. The present world was so evil that it was incapable of amendment. Man, even with the power of God on his side, was unable to bring about any change for the better in the society of which he was a part. All life was rotten and would become progressively worse. Yet with this pessimism the apocalyptists possessed an optimism. They believed that God would ultimately intervene in the affairs of men and clean up the world.

A further element of the religious background, though not strictly a doctrine, merits consideration. The oral law, which developed from the time of Ezra until its codification under Judah ha-Nasi toward the end of the second century A.D., played a vital role in Judaism. Ezra and a class of professional copyists and teachers of the Law who followed after him were responsible for this body of tradition. At first these scribes were priests, but eventually there arose a lay group who studied the Law and became its official interpreters. They transformed the Law from a written document that was losing in influence into a continuous revelation keeping step with the changes in society. These scribes set themselves to the task of expounding the Law in order to discover the will of God.

In the beginning this class of expositors deduced from exegesis of the Scriptures the rules applying to those cases for which no provisions had been made. Eventually, the rules and regulations were made without any scriptural basis. If the people became obedient to the Law, they must know the exact way to carry it out. The scribes sought this right way. The oral law was in a constant state of development. It was adapted, modified, and expanded from age to age to meet the practical needs of the people. This unwritten tradition passed into written form and was known as the Mishnah. The Mishnah in turn was interpreted and resulted in the Palestinian and Babylonian Talmuds. Repeatedly in the Gospels we notice that Jesus clashed with the "tradition of the elders." This means that he opposed the authority given to the oral law by the Pharisees.

2. *Religious Institutions*

Before the Seleucids ruled over Palestine, there is no clear indication that the Jews had any religious institution other than the Temple. After that time two institutions came into being, and both of these made significant contributions to the establishment of rabbinical Judaism.

One of these institutions was the synagogue. According to Josephus and Philo the synagogue originated with Moses. There is no real authority for determining the antiquity of the synagogue. Arguments for its origin range from the time of Josiah to the first century B.C. Synagogues existed in New Testament times throughout Palestine and wherever there were Jewish communities. Thus we are certain that they arose before the beginning of the Christian era. It seems that a more probable beginning would be shortly before the Hasmonean revolt.

The synagogue was a place of worship and study. It became a vital link between the Pharisees and the people. Here the expositors of the Law could instruct the people in the regulations governing their conduct in all walks of life. To do this they not only expounded the written Law but they also transmitted rules (halakoth) from the oral law. Some scholars believe that the Pharisees used the synagogue as a means of weaning the Jews from worship in the Temple. This is quite possible since Judaism under Pharisaic leadership continued to flourish without the Temple after A.D. 70.

The management of the synagogue was in the body of elders. A ruler was appointed, and his function was to maintain discipline. He also selected the speaker for the sabbath service. An attendant (hazzan) was in charge of the building and the copies of the Scriptures. It seems that he had the added responsibility of teaching in the synagogue.

A second institution that we shall consider is the Sanhedrin. Even though this was a judiciary system of the Jews, it was a religious organization. The Jews did not distinguish between civil life and religious life. All life was religious. Much doubt still remains as to the origin, method of selection of members, number of members, and functions of the Sanhedrin. Rabbis liked to boast about its antiquity and said that it grew out of the council of 70 in Numbers 16:16. It probably comes from the period of Antiochus the Great and was known at that time as the *gerousia*.

The rabbinical accounts are not in agreement with Josephus and the New Testament relative to the members who made up this body. From Josephus and the New Testament we get the notion that the chief priests, scribes, and elders were the administrators of justice and the high priest was the convener of the sessions. In the Mishnah we discover that the heads of the Great Court (*Beth Din ha-Gadol*) were Pharisees and all the members were of that party. Do the rabbinical accounts reflect the *Beth Din* at Jabneh after A.D. 70, or do they give an accurate story of the composition of this judicial body in the days before the destruction of the Temple? The decision is difficult to make.

There were five types of courts under the Sanhedrist system. Tradition has it that the supreme court sat in the Hall of Hewn Stone in the Temple. This court had jurisdiction over tribal affairs, false prophets, and priests. It had the authority to pass the death sentence with a quorum of 23 members. Also from rabbinical tradition it appears that this body had the power to legislate rules of conduct for all Jews.

3. *Religious Parties*

According to Josephus, there were four sects in Judaism of the first century A.D. They were the Sadducees, Pharisees, Essenes, and Zealots. All of these with the exception of the Essenes are mentioned in the New Testament. The Sadducees excelled in numbers, but the Pharisees had the greatest influence on the people. The origin of these parties remains in obscurity. However, we have already observed that the Pharisees and Sadducees were strongly established and powerful religiopolitical parties in the time of John Hyrcanus.

The Pharisees were probably the successors of the Hasidim, the Jews of the Hasmonean revolt who chose to die rather than violate the Law and the tradition of the elders. The word Pharisees in Hebrew and Aramaic means "separated ones." However, the question we face is from what or from whom were they separated? Varieties of opinions have been expressed on this matter. The best suggestion is that the name was given to them by their enemies, the Sadducees, because they separated themselves from priestly control and sought their own power. This seems likely, since there are very few references to Pharisees in Tannaitic literature.

The Pharisees considered themselves as the successors to the prophets. Their struggle with the Sadducees was the old struggle between prophet and priest. In religious outlook they were more liberal and more progressive than their rivals. The Pharisees tried to gain control of the cult and remove from it all the crude superstitions that had accrued through the years. They felt that they were responsible, as lay leaders, to transmit the oral tradition begun by the scribes, and in the end they made this body of tradition coeval with the written Law. In beliefs this party held to the resurrection of the dead, the existence of angels and spirits, divine Providence in the affairs of men and the world, and the extension of written authority to include the Prophets, Writings, and oral tradition, in addition to the Pentateuch.

The Sadducees busied themselves with the quest for political power, the administration of the Temple, and the preservation of the ritual. The general agreement is that their name was derived from Zadok, who was high priest during the reign of Solomon. The Sadducees attached little importance to any part of the Old Testament except the Law. Thus they were indisposed to share the messianic expectations found in the Prophets and Writings as well as the resurrection from the dead based on the book of Daniel. Furthermore, in opposition to the Pharisees, they did not believe in the existence of angels and spirits. How did the Sadducees reconcile such disbelief with the repeated allusions to angels in the Pentateuch? It could be that they opposed a highly developed angelology and demonology. Contrary to the Pharisees, this party advocated free will instead of Providence.

A third sectarian group in Judaism of the first century A.D. sprang up in Galilee out of a hotbed of revolutionaries. They were known as the Zealots. The founder of the movement, Judas the Galilean, was the son of Hezekiah, whom Herod executed in 47 B.C. Judas led a rebellion against Rome when Quirinius, the legate of Syria, tried to take a census of Palestine in A.D. 6. Later the Zealots became the followers of John of Giscala. John was one of the leaders in the revolt against Rome in A.D. 66, which terminated in the destruction of Jerusalem.

The intense nationalistic spirit of the adherents of this sect did not permit recognition of any ruler over them except God and his Messiah. The Zealots stood for a purely Jewish kingdom with the Messiah as head of the nation. These so-called patriots advocated a war to the finish against any foreign power over the land of Palestine. It is interesting to note that Simon, a Zealot, was one of the disciples of Jesus.

The last sect of Judaism—known from the writings of Josephus, Philo, and Pliny the Elder and more recently through the Qumran scrolls and the excavations of the community at Qumran—has sometimes been called "the Hasidim in seclusion." This sectarian party was the Essenes. They lived in communal disciplined brotherhoods and required their members to pass through periods of preparation for three years before they were finally admitted to the communal meal. The Essenes did not share in the sacrificial rites of the Temple, but they observed the sabbath scrupulously. The Law was held in high esteem by them, and from Josephus and discoveries near Qumran we know that they accepted books of the Old Testament outside the Pentateuch, plus apocryphal writings. Their teaching of immortality of the soul indicates a kinship with Greek thought. One group of the sect opposed marriage, while another section favored it in order to have sons as recruits for the community.

One of the leaders of the community was known as the Teacher of Righteousness. He suffered at the hands of a wicked priest and ruler. The wicked priest and ruler may refer to Alexander Janneus. From the Qumran materials it appears that this community anticipated a messiah who would represent the sacerdotal and royal dynasty in an eschatological setting.

III. The Jews of the Diaspora

The vast majority of Jews lived outside the land of Palestine. Out of approximately five million Jews who inhabited the world in the first century A.D., four million of these were known as the Diaspora. Before the Hellenistic period, Jews lived in Babylonia, Persia, and Egypt. They represented the descendants of those who did not wish to return to Palestine when the opportunity was afforded them. After the conquest of Alexander the Great, Jews migrated to all parts of the civilized world. The majority of them moved west and settled in centers of Greek civilization, primarily because of the greater freedom granted them.

Alexandria in Egypt became the most important center for Hellenistic Judaism. When Alexander founded the city, he allowed the Jews to have equal rights with the Greeks, but it is unlikely that at any given time they had full rights as citizens. Alexandria was divided into five districts, and two of these districts were known as the Jewish section, since the inhabitants were largely Jews. The Hebrew Scriptures were translated into Greek in this city during the rule of Ptolemy Philadelphus. This translation was valuable for the Jews since their language had become Greek, but it was more important as a means of communicating the faith of Israel to their pagan neighbors. According to Philo there were synagogues in all parts of the city. Philo, a contemporary of Jesus, lived in Alexandria, and his influence in the city was tremendous. Through his apologetic works and allegorical interpretation of Scripture, he was able to present Judaism in a manner that would not be too objectionable to the pagan world.

The Hellenistic Jews remained loyal to Jerusalem. They paid their Temple tax, and when possible they went to the feasts. The synagogue was the basis of their religion. They continued to worship on the sabbath and they practiced the rite of circumcision. The majority of them observed faithfully the requirements of the Law and the customs of their religion. Since the Hellenistic Jews were separated from the religious life of Palestine, they did not have the advantage of the juristic interpretations of the Law to show them how to adapt the Law to the changing conditions of life. It was essential for them to come into contact with the pagan world. They adopted the Gentile language, attended their public festivals, went to their amusements, joined their guilds for workers, engaged in business with them, and learned something of Greek philosophy and Roman law. When the Hellenistic Jews went to the homeland, fellow Jews in Palestine questioned their purity. Contact with the Gentile world meant a compromise of their religious faith.

The religion of the Jews made a strong appeal to the pagans. The pagans were attracted to Judaism because of its strict monotheism, ancient literature, salvation by observance of the Law, democratic worship, universalism, sabbath worship, and high ethical ideals. The missionary zeal of the Jews in various lands brought many Gentiles into the fold of Judaism. To become a Jew, a Gentile must submit to a proselyte bath, be circumcised, and make a sacrifice in the Temple. Later, when the apostle Paul made his trips to the cities in the Roman Empire and preached to the Gentiles, he was able to build on the foundation that was already laid by the Hellenistic Jews.

IV. General Characteristics of the Greco-Roman World

Gilbert Murray has characterized this period in history as "the failure of nerve." Nevertheless, this failure of nerve which permeated all of life was instrumental in producing a positive response to the glad tidings heralded by the Christians in the first and second centuries.

During this era the average man was overcome by the rapid advance of history. Old systems, traditions, and loyalties were swept away. The people rebelled against the tyranny of patriotism. The Greeks were cut loose from their allegiance to the city-state, and the citizens of Oriental lands severed their connection with despotism. In Rome ambitious leaders gathered a following and struggled for power. This led to civil wars. The state which once exploited the individual was now the object of exploitation. National patriotism gave way to cosmopolitanism. Men became citizens of the world. The people lost faith in their ancestral gods. Individualism asserted itself in art, literature, politics, society, morality, and religion. This was an age of change and upheaval. The changes brought with them a feeling of insecurity for the masses. It became increasingly difficult for them to adjust to this new order of life.

The expansion of the Roman Empire led to the augmentation of the number of slaves. This increase in slaves produced significant economic and moral effects upon society. Forced labor, being much cheaper, reduced the demand for freemen and also lowered the scale of pay. Unemployment increased idleness in the cities, and the idleness in turn led to a life of crime and immorality. The slaves, most of whom had once enjoyed freedom, took their revenge on their masters by corrupting their morals.

The two schools of popular philosophy that were influential in the life of this age were the Epicureans and the Stoics. Both of these philosophies were practical in their goals. To some they offered avenues of hope from a world engulfed by turmoil.

The highest good in life for the Epicureans was pleasure. Their definition of pleasure was not equivalent to the hedonists' notion to positive satisfaction, but rather a pleasure coming from the absence of pain, disturbing passions, and superstitious fears. Since fear was the cause of pain, especially the fear of gods and fear of punishment after death, they rejected immortality and taught that gods were unconcerned with the affairs of men.

The duty of man, according to the Stoics, was to harmonize his will with the universal will called reason or world soul. The virtuous person was he who understood what reason required of him and shaped his life according to the pattern. The Stoics also taught that all men were equal on the basis of their possession of a spark of the divine. When a man died, the spark of divinity went back to the world soul.

A second avenue of hope came from the Greco-Roman mystery cults. Increased contacts between East and West brought about a syncretism of religion. The old Greek mysteries blended with Oriental cults and fashioned something new that attracted people from all stations in life. These cults gave a satisfying message on suffering, answered the craving for immortality, promised communion with the god of the cult, offered a way of salvation, and presented a personal religion. Like the earlier Eleusinian and Orphic mysteries, they had their secret rites, esoteric doctrines, and initiation rites.

From Asia Minor came the worship of Magna Mater and the god consort, Attis. Introduced in Rome as early as 204 B.C., this religion became firmly established by the time of Augustus. The Isis and Osiris mystery religion had its origin in Egypt. Under Ptolemy I the cult was assimilated with the old Eleusinian mystery. The statue of Pluto was removed from Sinope in Pontus and brought to Alexandria where it was renamed Serapis. From that time on, the religion was known as Isis and Serapis. Isis with her god consort, Serapis, was introduced in Italy in the second century B.C., but later both Augustus and Tiberius resisted this form of worship. The mystery religion that proved to be the greatest rival of Christianity was Mithraism. It arose in Persia and spread westward after the fall of the Persian Empire. Plutarch says that Mithraism was brought to Italy by the Roman soldiers who were initiated into the religion by the Cilician pirates in 63 B.C.

A third avenue of hope was found in astralism. With the rapid rise and fall of rulers and kingdoms, men began to entertain the notion that chance or fate controlled their affairs and destinies. Astral religion has been classed as a "scientific theology of waning heathenism" that developed as a "learned superstition." Those who followed this religion believed that the stars determined the course of human events. This created a sense of helplessness, and no one could plan for the future. Therefore, ways to placate the forces in the planetary regions were sought. At first astralism was accepted only by the ruling class, but before long it became a live option for the masses. Astral ideas found their way into

Stoicism, Hermeticism, and Gnosticism.

Two other religions which were prevalent in the Greco-Roman world merit our attention. One was Gnosticism, an eclectic philosophical religion drawn from Zoroastrianism, Babylonian religion, Greek philosophy and religion, Christianity, and astrology. All Gnostics did not have the same beliefs, but they all claimed that a radical dualism governed God's relation to the world of matter. Man's spiritual nature was derived from a divine being. This spiritual nature had fallen out of the world of light into darkness. The human spirit, imprisoned in matter, could be released and restored into divine being only by the voluntary descent of a being who was equal or superior to man. Salvation came by knowledge, not intellectual understanding, but a supernatural gift of enlightenment to man. Through this knowledge a person could find his way back to God.

The other religion was emperor worship. The Roman emperors from the time of Augustus laid claim to deity following the pattern of Alexander the Great and Antiochus Epiphanes. Caius Caligula was the first ruler of the Roman Empire to press for divine honors among his subjects, but he died before he could force the people to submit. The open claim of being god and the demand to be worshiped as a god came under Domitian.

The many religions of this era reflect something of the spiritual unrest and great confusion in the minds of men. They were seeking some new hope and a reason for living in a world void of meaning and hope. Within the philosophical and religious thought of the day there were certain tendencies which were preparing the world to receive the revelation of God in Christ.

V. Conclusion

From this brief survey of the religious and cultural background of the New Testament we can readily see that the people were prepared by the conditions of the day to listen to the proclamation of the Christian faith. In an age when men were seeking for unity through one empire, one language, one civilization, one savior, Christianity came into being and gave a hope that was desperately needed by all men.

Our interest in the religions of this era comes not so much because they were symptomatic of spiritual emotions to which Christianity could appeal. Rather, our concern is the striking resemblances such as a new birth, union of the worshiper and deity worshiped, baptisms, and a communion with the deity. Nevertheless, in the midst of these similarities between Christianity and current religions, there was a noticeable difference. The mystery cults, founded on shadowy and mythical figures, had no historical basis. The Christian movement was firmly based in a historical person, Jesus Christ, whose life and teaching were sufficiently well known through reliable traditions transmitted by reliable witnesses.

Christianity gave what the world most needed—a God who was concerned for man so much that he was willing to suffer in man's behalf; a God able to overcome evil and death; a God who is Father and Redeemer; a God who is perfect truth and perfect love. The human sympathy in the historical life and death of Christ exceedingly overshadowed the human sympathy of the Oriental cults.

For Further Reading

Brandon, S. G. F. *Jesus and the Zealots.* Manchester: Manchester University Press, 1967.

Bultmann, Rudolf. *Primitive Christianity.* Translated by R. H. Fuller. New York: Meridian Books, 1957.

Grant, Frederick C. *Roman Hellenism and the New Testament.* New York: Charles Scribner's Sons, 1962.

Dana, H. E. *The New Testament World.* 3d ed. Nashville: Broadman Press, 1946.

Herford, R. T. *The Pharisees.* London: George Allen & Unwin, 1924.

Pfeiffer, Robert H. *History of New Testament Times.* New York: Harper & Bros., 1949.

Rowley, H. H. *Relevance of Apocalyptic.* New and revised ed. New York: Association Press, 1963.

The Text and Canon of the New Testament

James A. Brooks

Most readers take for granted both the wording and the content of the New Testament. Deeply embedded in Christian history, however, are the critical problems of text and canon. These problems were more acute during earlier centuries than they are now, but even today assurance that the correct text and canon have been determined must precede serious study of the New Testament itself.

The problem of the text arises because none of the original manuscripts or autographs has survived and because the existing copies differ from one another. Of the more than five thousand Greek manuscripts which have been studied no two are exactly alike! It is therefore no simple matter of translating from the Greek into English or some other modern language. An attempt must first be made to restore the original text of the New Testament. The literary science which attempts to do this is known as textual criticism.

The problem of the canon emerges from the fact that the twenty-seven books which now constitute the New Testament were not the only biblical type books which were written by the early Christians. During the second, third, and fourth centuries scores of gospels, acts, letters, and apocalypses were competing for recognition. At least a half dozen books which ultimately did not become a part of the New Testament were at one time given canonical status by some Christians even within orthodox circles. Likewise the canonical status of a similar number of books which are now in the New Testament was seriously questioned at one time by certain Christians. Therefore it was not self-evident which books would comprise the canon or that there would even be a New Testament canon. Eventually the church was forced to choose which books it would accept as authoritative.

The Text

The history of the text begins with the writing of each book of the New Testament and continues until the present time.

I. The Age of the Handwritten Text (prior to 1514)

1. The Period of Divergence of Manuscripts (Second-Third Centuries)

Most of the New Testament books began to be copied shortly after they were written. The process of copying soon resulted in a number of variations in the text. Each new manuscript produced additional variations so that throughout the period the manuscripts diverged further and further from the original and from one another. It is quite revealing that most of the variant readings known today appear to have been in existence by the year 300.

Several factors were at work to produce variation. Throughout the period the New Testament was usually copied by amateur rather than professional scribes, and such persons were especially prone to make mistakes. Many errors therefore were accidental. Other variant readings were deliberately introduced by scribes who thought they were correcting a previous error or who thought they were being led by God's Spirit to express the message in another way. Orthodox as well as heretical scribes were guilty of such practices. Another factor which produced variation was persecution. The wholesale destruction of manuscripts prevented the establishment of a stable textual tradition. It is also probable that the making of translations, which began around 200, and the common practice by the early Christian writers of quoting loosely from memory produced additional variant readings.

Only a small number of manuscripts have survived from the period prior to 300. Comparatively few were produced, and many of these were destroyed in the persecutions. Another factor is that the manuscripts of this period were written on papyrus, a highly perishable paper-like writing material which was manufactured from a reed that grew in the Nile Delta in Egypt.

2. *The Period of Convergence of Manuscripts (Fourth-Eighth Centuries)*

During this period the previous trend of divergence was reversed, and a larger amount of textual agreement began to be attained. By far the most important reason for the change was the absence of persecution. Christianity's new status resulted in an improved economic condition, the growth of learning, and an increase in ecclesiastical authority. These things indirectly led to a greater concern for an accurate text.

The convergence of manuscripts is discernible in the emergence of text-types, i.e., large groups of manuscripts which have much in common. The origin of text-types is probably to be traced to the local texts which began to appear about the year 200. It was natural that the manuscripts circulating in a given area would have more in common with one another than with the manuscripts circulating in other areas.

Four text-types have been identified. The earliest is the Western text, which despite the name is not confined to any particular geographical area. More and more contemporary textual critics, however, are questioning whether what has been called the Western text deserves the status of a text-type. Its representatives are comparatively few in number and lack homogeneity. It appears that the so-called Western text is really the popular, uncontrolled text of the second and third centuries. For this reason contemporary textual critics do not have a high regard for the Western text, even though it is of great antiquity.

Quite different is the case with the Alexandrian type of text. It is approximately as old as the Western text, and it appears to be the result of a definite editorial attempt extending over several centuries to restore the original text. The Alexandrian text is generally considered to be the best single text-type. It must be observed, however, that although the Alexandrian text represents a scholarly attempt to restore the original text, it is not the original text and is not correct in every instance. For this reason contemporary textual critics refuse to be bound to any one text-type but employ what is known as the eclectic method.

The Caesarean text-type has been identified only in the Gospels. For this reason, and because its representatives are somewhat lacking in homogeneity, it is doubtful whether it may properly be regarded as a text-type.

The Byzantine text is unquestionably the latest and poorest of the four types. It first appears in the Gothic version (fourth century), the writings of John Chrysostom (died 407), and Codex Alexandrinus (fifth century). Lateness alone, however, does not prove inferiority. Conclusive proof that the Byzantine text does not represent the original is seen in its practice of combining earlier variant readings.

Although papyrus continued to be used for several centuries, most of the manuscripts produced during this and the following period were written upon parchment or vellum, a more durable writing material made from animal skins.

3. *The Period of a Standardized Text (Ninth-Sixteenth Centuries)*

During the first half of the previous period the Byzantine text was but one of several text-types. During the second half of that period it more and more became the dominant text, and by the ninth century it had completely displaced the others. How did this late and inferior text prevail over the others? The answer is simple. It won by default. Use of the Greek language in Christian circles in the western portion of the Roman Empire had already begun to give way to Latin before that area was overrun by the barbarians in the fifth century. During the seventh century and following, Muhammadan armies overran much of the civilized world and destroyed Christianity in those areas. Constantinople, however, was able to survive until 1453. Inasmuch as it was the only major center of Greek culture during most of the Middle Ages, what was originally its local text became the dominant type of text. The vast majority of surviving manuscripts are of this type.

During the ninth century a major change took place in the way in which manuscripts were written. Prior to that time only the use of uncial script was considered proper in literary works. Uncial script may be compared to printing in all capital letters. During the ninth century, however, the cursive type of writing, which had been used since ancient times for nonliterary documents, was modified and began to be used even in literary works. This modified form of cursive script is usually referred to as minuscule script. All of the manuscripts produced after the ninth century employ minuscule script.

II. The Age of the Printed Text (Since 1514)

The first Greek New Testament to be printed was the Complutensian Polyglot in 1514. It was not actually published, however, until 1522, and it had little effect upon the later history of the text.

1. The "Received Text" (1516–1880)

The first Greek Testament actually to be published was that of Erasmus of Rotterdam in 1516, which incidentally was the year before the beginning of the Protestant Reformation. Erasmus' text was based upon about a half dozen manuscripts containing various portions of the New Testament. Of these he used no more than two or three for any one portion of his edition. For Revelation he had only one manuscript, and it lacked the last six verses of the book. Erasmus handled this problem by translating from the Latin Vulgate into Greek. In doing so he produced variant readings for which no manuscript attestation has ever been found. Elsewhere Erasmus made interpolations from the Vulgate.

Probably the most notorious example of interpolation from the Vulgate is the "heavenly witness" passage of 1 John 5:7–8. The passage did not appear in the first or second edition of Erasmus' work, for which omission he was severely criticized. Although doubting its validity, he later inserted it. Only three other Greek manuscripts have been found which contain the passage, and none of them is earlier than the twelfth century.

Erasmus did little more than stabilize in print the type of text that was found in current manuscripts. This was of course the Byzantine type of text. The various editions of the New Testament which were published during the century following Erasmus employed a text quite similar to that of his third edition. The result was the popularization of this text, which text came to be known as the "Received Text." It became so firmly entrenched that it reigned supreme until the nineteenth century, despite its inferior quality.

2. The Critical Text Period (since 1881)

During the seventeenth and eighteenth centuries more and more manuscripts were discovered, many of which were found to differ substantially from the "Received Text." These manuscripts provided the raw material out of which a critical text could be constructed. The first person to break completely with the "Received Text" and to produce an entirely new text by applying the principles of textual criticism was Karl Lachmann in 1831. Lachmann did not, however, claim to have recovered the original text of the New Testament but only that which was current during the fourth century. During the next four decades critical texts were also produced by Constantine von Tischendorf and S. P. Tregelles.

By far the most important work, not only of the nineteenth century, but probably in the entire history of textual criticism, is that of B. F. Westcott and F. J. A. Hort entitled *The New Testament in the Original Greek*, 1881–1882. Their text follows closely the Alexandrian type of text, which they themselves referred to as the Neutral text. Westcott and Hort did more than edit a text. They also wrote a lengthy volume in which they explained their textual theory. They proved conclusively that the Byzantine text was a late, inferior type of text. It is at this point that the true significance of Westcott and Hort is to be found: they exposed the inadequacy of the "Received Text." It is true that the "Received Text" has continued to have a few defenders until the present, but it is most significant that since 1881 it has not been used in new editions of the Greek New Testament or as the basis for new translations.

The reference to translations suggests a way in which textual criticism is of practical importance to the reader of the English Bible. The popular KJV is based upon the "Received Text," now known to lack trustworthiness at many points. Therefore practically any modern translation of the New Testament, including the RSV, is superior to the KJV from the standpoint of the Greek text upon which it is based.

The Canon

In tracing the history of the canon four things need to be distinguished: the mere use of apostolic writings, the collection of groups of related books, the ascription of biblical authority to individual books or groups of books, and the emergence of a concept of specific books comprising a New Testament canon. The history of the canon may be divided into three periods.

I. *The Period of Initial Collections and Use of New Testament Books (ca. 90–180)*

One of the first discernible steps in the long process of canonization is the collection of Paul's letters. This collection appears to have taken place even before the last New Testament books were written. Probably the first reference to at least a partial collection is 2 Peter 3:15–16, which also ascribes scriptural authority to the letters. Further evidence of a collection having been made prior to the beginning of the second century is that the Christian writers of the late first and early second centuries seem to be acquainted with most of the letters. The uniform textual tradition of the letters also points to a collection having been made at an early date.

It is more difficult to determine when the four Gospels were collected. The Gospels seem to have circulated separately at first. They do not display a uniform textual tradition, nor do any of the early Christian writers reveal a knowledge of all four of them. Papias (*ca.* 130) described the composition of Matthew and Mark but was silent about Luke and John (Eusebius, *Ecclesiastical History* III:39). Justin Martyr (*ca.* 155) unquestionably knew written Gospels, which he referred to by that name and by the term "Memoirs of the Apostles" (*Apology* I:66). He did not, however, indicate their names or number and therefore cannot be cited as evidence for the existence of a definite collection. It is certain that the collection was made prior to about 170, when Tatian composed his Diatessaron by interweaving the four Gospels into a single account of the life of Jesus.

The crucial question is whether the heretic Marcion (*ca.* 145), who accepted only Luke's Gospel, reduced a fourfold Gospel to a single Gospel or whether the fourfold Gospel was formed in reaction to Marcion's single Gospel. Although definite proof is lacking, the latter seems to be more probable. Therefore the collection of the four Gospels probably took place around 150–160.

Marcion was apparently the first to produce a canon list of New Testament books. He completely rejected the Old Testament and accepted only expurgated versions of Luke and ten of Paul's letters. Whether or not the concept of a canon of Christian books originated with Marcion, the growth of the canon in orthodox circles was certainly motivated by reaction to his heretical canon.

There is attestation for the existence and use during the period being considered of all the books of the New Testament except Acts, James, 2 Peter, 2 and 3 John, and Jude. Quotations, however, are comparatively few and inexact and are rarely introduced by the customary formulas used for citing Scripture. During the first half of the period there are few indications that Christian writings were being used as Scripture, i.e., as having authority equal to that of the Old Testament.

It has already been seen how Marcion exalted eleven Christian writings above the Old Testament. Although orthodox Christians were unwilling to follow Marcion in rejection of the Old Testament, they did begin shortly after his time to attribute scriptural authority to apostolic writings. For example the so-called 2 Clement (*ca.* 150) specifically cites a Gospel text as Scripture (2:4) and places the apostolic writings on the same level as the Old Testament (14:2). Justin indicates that the Gospels were read and commented on in public worship in the same way as was the Old Testament (*Apology* I:67).

By the year 180, therefore, most of the New Testament books were known and being used, separate collections of the Gospels and Paul's letters had been made, scriptural authority was beginning to be attributed to these books, and the concept of a canon was beginning to emerge.

II. The Period of the Emergence of a New Testament Canon (ca. 180–220)

At the very beginning of this period a clear concept of a New Testament canon appears within the context of orthodox Christianity. This concept is seen in the Muratorian Canon, a list of books used as Scripture by the church at Rome about 180. The manuscript is fragmentary, but the original list contained at least the following: the four Gospels, Acts, thirteen letters of Paul, at least two and perhaps three letters of John, Jude, and Revelation.

The Muratorian Canon gives some insight into the principles of canonicity. One is apostolic authorship. Another is orthodoxy. The Letters to the Laodiceans and the Alexandrians were rejected because they were forged in the name of Paul in order to support the heresy of Marcion. Another criterion is antiquity. The Shepherd of Hermas might be read privately but not in public worship because of its recent origin.

The concept of a New Testament canon also clearly appears in the three great writers of this period. The first is Irenaeus of Lyons in Gaul (died *ca.* 190). He was adamant in affirmation of the fourfold Gospel (*Against Heresies* III:11). He quotes as Scripture all of the books of the New Testament except Philemon, James, 2 Peter, 3 John, and Jude. The omission of several of these, however, might have been accidental because of their brevity. Irenaeus also knew Hebrews but gave it a subcanonical place. Hermas, however, was accepted as Scripture.

Clement of Alexandria (died *ca.* 215) clearly distinguished between the four Gospels and certain apocryphal gospels (*Stromata* III:93). He also cited the remainder of the New Testament books except James, 2 Peter, and 3 John. Eusebius, however, stated that Clement wrote a commentary on all of the General Letters (*Hist.* VI:14). Clement also regarded as inspired 1 Clement, the Didache, the Letter of Barnabas, Hermas, the Apocalypse of Peter, and the Preaching of Peter.

Tertullian of Carthage (died *ca.* 220) was the first of the Christian writers to employ Latin. He referred to or quoted from all of the New Testament books except James, 2 Peter, 2 and 3 John. He ascribed Hebrews to Barnabas and at best treated it as semi-canonical. Tertullian was apparently the first to use the term New Testament in the sense of a collection of books (*Against Praxeas XV*).

The importance of the Muratorian Canon, Irenaeus, Clement, and Tertullian for the history of the canon cannot be overestimated. Their testimony represents most of the Christian world of their day. They attest the existence and use of all of the books of the New Testament except James, 2 Peter, and perhaps 3 John. If, however, Eusebius' statement about Clement's commentary on all the General Letters may be accepted at face value, even these three are attested. The two most important portions of the canon, the four Gospels and the thirteen letters of Paul, were firmly established. Acts, 1 Peter, and 1 John had equally secure places. Although at this time Revelation was unquestioned, it later came under heavy fire in the East. Hebrews, James, 2 Peter, 2 and 3 John, and Jude were still disputed. Certain other books were strongly contending for a place in the canon. Irenaeus, Clement, and Tertullian frequently quoted from most of the New Testament books in such a way as to clearly indicate that they regarded these books as Scripture. By the beginning of the third century, therefore, the concept of a New Testament canon had clearly emerged. It remained only to define its exact limits.

III. The Period of Fixation of the New Testament Canon (ca. 220–400)

Origen (died 254) traveled widely and resided first at Alexandria and then at Caesarea. He was the first to display an awareness of the problem of the limits of the canon and to discuss the subject in a scientific way by classifying books as accepted, disputed, and rejected. He was also the first to reveal a certain knowledge of all of the books now in the New Testament including James, 2 Peter, and 3 John. Origen himself apparently accepted as canonical all of the twenty-seven plus the Didache, Barnabas, and Hermas. He was aware, however, that these patristic writings, Hebrews, James, 2 Peter, 2 and 3 John, and Jude were disputed.

Dionysius of Alexandria (died 264) denied that the apostle John wrote the Revelation (Eusebius, *Hist.*, VII:25). Although Dionysius himself did not deny the canonicity of Revelation, his view about the authorship provoked a long dispute about its status.

Eusebius of Caesarea completed his *Ecclesiastical History* about 325. In it he gave a comprehensive survey of prevailing views on the canon (III:25). Building upon the terminology first used by Origen, he classified Christian writings as follows. In the category of universally accepted books he placed the four Gospels, Acts, fourteen letters of Paul (including Hebrews, despite his awareness that the church at Rome did not accept the book as being a letter of Paul), 1 John, 1 Peter, and perhaps Revelation. Eusebius divided Origen's category of disputed books into those which were acknowledged by the majority and those which were spurious. In the former he placed James, 2 Peter, 2 and 3 John, and Jude; in the latter, the Didache, Barnabas, Hermas, the Gospel according to the Hebrews, the Acts of Paul, the Apocalypse of Peter, and perhaps Revelation. The ambiguity about Revelation was due to the fact that Eusebius himself would have rejected the book, but the tradition in its favor was too strong to permit such treatment.

Eusebius also mentioned a third category, that of books universally rejected, in which he placed various other apocryphal works. It is important to note that the category of universally accepted books plus that of disputed books generally accepted corresponds exactly to the twenty-seven-book canon now accepted. The problem of the canon was on the verge of being settled.

Cyril of Jerusalem (348) and Gregory of Nazianzus (died 390) both attested a canon of twenty-six books with only Revelation missing from the list and without any other books included. The first canon list to correspond exactly to the twenty-seven books now in the New Testament was that of Athanasius of Alexandria in his Easter Letter of 367. The Council of Hippo (393), the Council of Carthage (397), Jerome (died 420), and Augustine (died 430) also set forth such a canon.

Doubts continued to be expressed about Revelation for several centuries, and several patristic writings continued to linger on the fringe of the canon for a while longer. It is also true that none of the Syrian churches accepted a twenty-seven-book canon until the sixth century. In fact some of these churches accept only twenty-two books until this day. Furthermore, some of the Reformers revived the question of disputed books, and a few modern critics have questioned whether there should be any such thing as a canon. For the great majority of Christians, however, the canon has been irrevocably fixed since about the year 400.

Conclusion

Christian belief and practice are based in large part upon the New Testament. It is most important therefore to seek to determine whether the early church made the right decisions about the contents of the canon and whether modern scholars have been able to restore the original text of the books which properly constitute the canon.

Textual criticism is not an exact science. Mathematical certainty is not possible. In some instances the evidence is evenly divided, and the original reading must remain in doubt. It is for this reason that no two editions of the Greek New Testament and no two translations agree upon the choice of variant readings in every instance. Nevertheless, the portion of the text about which there are serious questions is quite small, and it may be confidently affirmed that for all practical purposes the original text has been recovered. Textual theory will no doubt continue to be refined as new discoveries come to light and as all of the evidence is further evaluated. It seems unlikely, however, that any major changes will be made.

An even larger measure of confidence is possible about the contents of the canon. Such confidence is created by two things. One is the fact that the canon which was established in the fourth century has not only survived but has rarely been seriously challenged for more than fifteen centuries. The other has to do with the way in which the particular books were chosen. It is most significant that pronouncements by church councils and ecclesiastical officials played a very minor role in the process of canonization. Such pronouncements did no more than ratify the decisions which had already been made somewhat unconsciously on the basis of common acceptance and use.

The books which were finally accepted as canonical were those which had proved to have spiritual value in the life of the church over a period of several centuries. The evidence which is derived from more than eighteen hundred years of Christian history is so strong that most Christians profess to believe in the working of divine Providence not only in the writing of the books of the New Testament but also in their selection.

For Further Reading

ALAND, KURT. *The Problem of the New Testament Canon.* London: A. R. Mowbray & Co. Ltd., 1962.

GREENLEE, J. HAROLD. *Introduction to New Testament Textual Criticism.* Grand Rapids: William B. Eerdmans Publishing Co., 1964.

GRANT, ROBERT M. *The Formation of the New Testament.* New York: Harper & Row, 1965.

FILSON, FLOYD V. *Which Books Belong in the Bible?* Philadelphia: Westminster Press, 1957.

KENYON, FREDERIC G. *The Text of the Greek Bible.* 2d ed. London: Gerald Duckworth & Co. Ltd., 1949.

METZGER, BRUCE M. *The Text of the New Testament: Its Transmission, Corruption, and Restoration.* New York and London: Oxford University Press, 1964.

SOUTER, ALEXANDER. *The Text and Canon of the New Testament.* Rev. C. S. C. Williams. London: Gerald Duckworth & Co. Ltd., 1954.

TAYLOR, VINCENT. *The Text of the New Testament: A Short Introduction.* London: The Macmillan Co., 1961.

WESTCOTT, BROOKE FOSS. *A General Survey of the Canon of the New Testament.* 7th ed. Cambridge and London: The Macmillan Co., 1896.

The History of Early Christianity

E. Glenn Hinson

Like the grain of mustard seed in Jesus' parable, Christianity sprouted in the soil of Palestine and became a tree whose branches spread across the civilized world. Small and almost unnoticed in its beginnings, within a century or two it reached from the British Isles in the west to the Tigris and Euphrates Valley in the east and from the Black Sea in the north to the upper Nile in the south.

Considering its inconspicuous beginnings, this story was remarkable. Christianity was the child of Judaism, born in a tiny corner of the far-flung Roman Empire. Its founder was an obscure Galilean whom the Roman governor, Pontius Pilate, allowed to be crucified, more for the purpose of preventing another riot among the rebellious Jews than because Jesus' activities bothered him. As far as this official was concerned, the impaling of Jesus on a cross ended a distasteful but necessary chore.

To many Jews, of course, Jesus *was* important, but for diverse reasons. Religious leaders, Sadducees and Pharisees, saw in him a threat to the established order. His teaching tended to undermine the twin foundations of first-century Judaism, Temple and Law. What was more dangerous still, he spoke and acted with an authority which they dared to ascribe to God alone. In the end they charged him with blasphemy and turned him over to the Romans as a threat to the peace of Judea. Many others, beginning with John the Baptist perhaps, saw in him the hope for a fulfilment of the Jewish expectations of Messiah. He sometimes did what they expected the coming ideal King to do, but in the end he disappointed them. Instead of gathering an armed band which, God helping, could repel the Romans and restore the kingdom of David, he himself ended up on a cross.

But beyond the cross something happened. Some of that motley band of followers during his earthly career perceived that their Teacher, though crucified and buried, had risen from the grave. Their experience transformed them into an army of witnesses to this dramatic event. "This Jesus whom you crucified," they testified to the Jews, "God has made him both Lord and Christ" (Acts 2:36). With boldness they proceeded from Jerusalem through Judea and Samaria to the farthest reaches of the civilized world. In the experience of Jesus' resurrection Christianity received the spark of life.

I. Into All the World

1. The Things of Caesar

Though born in Judaism, the church grew up in the vast domain of Rome. Beginning with its final conquest of Carthage about 200 B.C., this colossus had extended its sway over the entire area surrounding the Mediterranean before the birth of Jesus. After a century of relative independence under Greek influence, the Jews came under Roman rule in 63 B.C.

On the whole, Rome ruled its dependencies beneficently and efficiently. The Romans possessed a genius for administration. They structured the Empire in hierarchical fashion into a number of provinces and tied these to Rome through their administrators. They constructed a system of splendidly engineered roads which led to the capital and gave ready access to all parts of the Empire. They devised a speedy postal system which could keep lines of communication flowing to and from Rome. They boasted an army which had no peer in discipline, skill, and equipment.

Socially and economically Rome manifested vast contrasts. The ruling classes lived in great luxury, waited on hand and foot by their numerous slaves, the booty of extensive conquest. The masses eked out a minimal existence. They had no slaves to do their work, and the technological conveniences the Roman inventors contrived hardly filtered down to them. Problems of family, child-rearing, and securing daily bread generated a sense of futility. Their moral standards ran at a low level. Theft, adultery, infanticide, and all kinds of immorality were rife.

Yet, on the brighter side, many were seeking. The better educated found some satisfaction in philosophies like Platonism, Stoicism, Pythagoreanism, and Aristotelianism. Offering integrated systems of the world, man, and God, these satisfied even the religious craving of some. Platonism's accent on unity and its promise of union with the divine appealed especially to those who suffered from the distraction of a world always in conflict. Stoicism's ethical standards captured the fancy of those who loathed the moral deterioration of Roman society.

Many were attracted also to a kind of religiophilosophical movement now known as Gnosticism. Gnosticism was a hodgepodge of Oriental and Greco-Roman ideas. At its center was metaphysical dualism, a belief that matter is evil and the spirit good. Salvation in Gnostic thought involved being freed from the material, visible world and returning to the world of spirit or mind. To obtain this freedom required *gnosis*, i.e., knowledge, from which the name of the movement comes. This *gnosis* was not so much intellectucal as mystical, a knowledge of secret formulas by which one could get past the demonic powers which were believed to stand guard over the planetary spheres between heaven and earth and return to the world of pure spirit. Some Gnostics believed a redeemer descended from above to teach *gnosis*. The whole scheme of ideas formed a part of the early Christian world of thought and may have influenced the manner in which Paul and others expressed the gospel to the Gentiles. By the second century some Gnostics had entered the church and tried to develop within it a Christian Gnosticism.

The poorly educated masses, however, found their satisfaction in the Oriental religions which had established a strong claim in the West by this time. The old state cultus existed only in name. People still went through the rituals as required by ancient law, but this did not deter the more devout from seeking other remedies for their spiritual needs. And as long as they did not refuse the public duties, the officials did not mind. Only Christians and Jews, with their religious exclusiveness, caused any real anxiety.

What was attractive about the Oriental religions was their promise of salvation backed up by an impressive sacramentalism. With the help of baptism, sacramental meals, redemptive dramas, magical formulas, and various physical stimuli, these religions guaranteed a share in eternal life. The "bath in bull's blood" (*taurobolium*) of the Mithras cult gave an especially tangible guarantee, for the animal's life principle was thought to flow into the devotee and in this way to revitalize him. Its masculinity made Mithras a favorite in the Roman army, enabling it to give Christianity strong competition in capturing the allegiance of the masses.

2. *Christ and the Prince of Demons*

To compete with these Oriental cults, early Christianity had to meet the Roman citizen on his own grounds. Specifically it had to speak to his overpowering fear of demonic powers which he believed ruled his world. Demons, which even more sophisticated accepted without quibble, caused both good and evil happenings. One could not escape their influence on one's life. The secret of happiness was to find out how to placate the bad ones and to enlist the good ones on his side. Personal misfortunes, calamities, natural disasters, sickness—all were signs that someone had fallen into the wrong hands. The antidotes against such things included magical charms, secret formulas, household deities, and a multitude of superstitious habits.

Christianity answered the typical Roman's fears with a message of Christ's triumph over the prince of demons, the head of the whole demonic kingdom, Satan. In his lifetime, missionaries pointed out, Jesus had engaged the devil in combat and beaten him. Jesus had cast out demons and freed the helpless from their awful grip. But he registered his most magnificent triumph on the cross. Submitting voluntarily to death, he paid the price required to free men from their enslavement to the demonic Sin (cf. Rom. 5—8). God raised him from the dead, a triumphant sign that man's final enemy, Death, has fallen (cf. 1 Cor. 15:55).

The first Christians' life in the world involved a combat somewhat like Christ's. Although Christ had dealt Satan a heavy blow, he had not given the death stroke. Satan and the demons, Christians admitted, still held some grip on the world. None of them is good. Yet no Christian needs docilely to submit to their intimidations, as the average Roman believed. While living *in* the world, i.e., Satan's realm, one must display his allegiance to Christ in his manner of life, confident that Christ's Spirit will provide strength and keep him in peace.

Belief that the world is Satan's kingdom naturally raised some problems regarding pagan culture and the state. Some Christians went as far as to demand isolation from Greco-Roman society. But by and large they adopted the Pauline attitude of discrimination. Christ, Paul argued, rules over all things, even though we may not see it. So, to the Christian, "all things are permitted" (cf. 1 Cor. 10:23). However, not all things are good, for they may not serve Christ. Many things still belong to the Satanic realm, and, insofar as they do, the Christian should not indulge. Not accidentally, Christians often appeared to be "social snobs" on that account.

The Roman Empire itself held an ambiguous place too. In the ultimate sense, the first Christians believed, it is of divine origin and exists to fulfil a divinely ordained purpose—to preserve peace and order among men. It has contributed many things to the preparation for the gospel. Insofar as it serves its God-given purpose, then, it deserves the allegiance and commitment of all. But when it sets itself against the divine purpose, it serves Satan. For this reason John, the seer, warns of God's coming wrath upon "the harlot" Babylon. She who drank the blood of martyrs would fall along with Satan and his hosts when God pronounces his judgment (Rev. 14:8). In cases where Rome abided by God's will, the Christian submitted; where she set herself against it, he resisted passively.

3. *The World Turned Upside Down*

The cry of certain Jews from Thessalonica, as they dragged Paul and his companions before the magistrates, represents rather accurately what happened in the first century of Christianity's life. These early missionaries dreamed of a world in which every knee should bow and every tongue confess that Jesus Christ is Lord.

They had borrowed their vision from Jewish apocalyptic hopes like those expressed in the Qumran scroll, *The War of the Sons of Light and the Sons of Darkness*. The Essenes of Qumran conceived of themselves as a holy army being equipped and trained for the last great battle, when God's Messiah would lead them in vanquishing Satan and his hosts once and for all. The Christian hope differed from the Essene in a vital way, however. Whereas the Essenes looked forward to this day and waited in the desert in anticipation of it, the early believers actually engaged in a battle begun by Jesus. The Messiah of Jewish hope had already come and given them a command to march.

The mission did not proceed unhindered, however. The Jerusalem community seems to have split into two camps over the question of a mission to the Gentiles. Some, conservatively oriented toward their ancestral faith, insisted that Gentiles had to become Jews before they could become Christians. Others, whom Luke calls the Hellenists, followed the lead of Stephen in insisting that Gentiles could be Christians and still remain Gentiles, as long as they committed themselves to Jesus as Messiah and Lord. With Jewish officialdom concerned to preserve the integrity of the Temple and the Law, persecution hit the Hellenists. Stephen became the first Christian martyr (Acts 7).

Stephen's stoning, despite the tragedy of it, turned out to the advantage of the Gentile mission. The leader in that event, Saul of Tarsus, later called Paul, subsequently became a convert to the church and the leader of the very mission he attempted to halt. Teaming up with another Hellenistic Jew, Barnabas, he planted the seed of the gospel far and wide. Under sponsorship of the church at Antioch, they broadcast the seed in major cities of Asia Minor. Paul himself then proceeded to do the same on the Greek peninsula with the assistance of young converts like Timothy and Titus.

The old critics of the Gentile mission never relented, however. They plagued Paul wherever he went. Even the so-called Jerusalem conference of A.D. 49 did not resolve the issue, judging by Acts and Paul's letters. Although "the three pillars" (Peter, John, and James the half brother of Jesus) and other leaders in the Jerusalem church refused to impose the complete Jewish regimen upon Gentile converts, conservative Judaistic Christians refused to give in. They demanded circumcision and keeping of the ritual as well as the moral law. When Paul and his fellow missionaries did not capitulate, they attacked his apostolate as well as the mission and kept the vexed issue churning.

Paul persevered, nevertheless. After planting congregations in Antioch of Pisidia, Iconium, Lystra, and Derbe and returning briefly to Antioch, he launched out in a second campaign. Intending to head from the east directly through Asia Minor to Ephesus, he was constrained by the Spirit to go northward from Galatia. He and his party made their way to Troas on the Aegean Sea and crossed over into Macedonia. Following a brief term of work in Philippi, Thessalonica, Berea, and Athens, they stayed a year and a half in Corinth. In nearly all instances the Judaizers interfered with his work. They forced Paul to make the arduous trip to Jerusalem in order to confirm once again the validity of his endeavors (Acts 18:22). Subsequently, during his three-year stay in Ephesus (Acts 19), they kept causing trouble, both there and in other cities where Paul had established churches. This necessitated a hurried trip to Corinth, the writing of several letters, and finally Paul's return to Jerusalem for the last time (Acts 20—21), bearing the relief offering for the poor.

By the time Paul got to Jerusalem his opposition already had deadly intentions. Charging him with bringing a Gentile past the prohibited partition in the Temple, they nearly had him stoned on the spot (Acts 21:27 ff.). The presence of Roman soldiers alone saved him, for his attempted apology infuriated the crowd further. To save himself from a flailing, he had to appeal to his Roman citizenship and for a trial in Rome (Acts 22:22–29).

Before his arrest even, Paul had wanted to go to Rome, where he might set up a base of operations for the Gentile mission to Spain and the West. He wrote his letter to the Romans in part perhaps to pave the way for this. Already Rome had become a powerful center for Christianity in the West. But the Judaizers apparently tried to stop Paul even there, and in the end they secured his condemnation and death, after one or perhaps two trials.

By this time, A.D. 62–67, nothing they could do could halt the mission. The church, though spawned in Judaism, had become predominantly Gentile. By comparison with the Gentile wing the Jewish wing of the church looked insignificant. The locus of authority had shifted from Jerusalem to Antioch, Ephesus, and Rome. Some Palestinian Jewish Christians evidently got entangled in the revolt against Rome in A.D. 66–70, though clear evidence for this is lacking, and suffered along with their fellow Jews. The remnant that remained fled later to Pella in Transjordan, according to early Christian tradition. They continued to exist until the fourth century, but their conservatism kept them from flourishing. Having broken its Jewish bonds, the gospel became a universal gospel.

How and when universal? This is difficult to judge. Luke's naming of people from Mesopotamia, Asia Minor, Egypt, Libya, Rome, Crete, and Arabia in his Pentecost story may indicate his awareness of the establishment of Christianity in these areas when he wrote, late in the first century. We have evidence from the second century for vigorous colonies of Christians in almost all of those areas where the Jewish dispersion had prepared a seedbed. Where the Jews had a strong establishment, Christianity also became strong, despite harassment—in parts of Mesopotamia, Syria, Asia Minor, Greece, Rome, Alexandria, and later Carthage.

Like Judaism, which had laid a foundation for the Christian mission by regular meetings for worship and an apologetic in behalf of monotheism, Christianity had an impact of some depth on its converts. It did not tolerate adherence to Christ as one of many gods. It demanded different mores. Christians stood aloof from their neighbors. Nor could they accept invitations to the homes of pagan neighbors without qualms of conscience, when those neighbors insisted on paying homage to household deities. They had a King and a law which transcended the Roman. Their King had sent them to war against the principalities and powers which stood behind pagan fetishes and rites.

4. *The Fiery Trial*

Persecution among the first converts came from the Jews and the Judaizers. They (and their relationship is something of a mystery) caused damage mainly by stirring up the hatred of the Romans, according to early Christian sources. This may have had something to do with the brief pogroms of Nero in Rome and Domitian in Asia Minor.

The Neronian persecution (A.D. 64–68) seems to have been mainly a cover-up for the half-mad emperor's own folly. The rumor was, according to contemporary Roman historians, that in a fit of illusive dreaming Nero himself set fire to the old city, and large parts of it perished in the flames. In order to squelch the rumor about himself, he invented a scapegoat in the Christians. Their widespread unpopularity both with Jews and pagans allowed him to do with them as he wished. He used them mostly to satiate the bestiality of the masses. Tacitus reported that some Christians were sewn up in the skins of wild animals to be torn to death by dogs, others crucified, and others covered with pitch and used as human torches to light the arena at night.[1] In this brief reign of terror, according to an early Christian tradition, Peter was crucified and Paul beheaded. Hundreds of others died with them.

In the period of persecution which developed during the latter part of the reign of Domitian, *ca.* A.D. 91, the strictures apparently fell hardest on Christians in Asia Minor, where Paul's seed had sprouted and produced a healthy crop of devout disciples. The Jews or the Judaizers, the seer John tells us, again helped to instigate the persecution. The emperor and his officials probably had little direct hand in it. Among prominent martyrs were the emperor's cousin Flavius Clemens, his wife Domitilla, and an ex-consul named Acilius Glabrio, whose deaths attest Christianity's attraction for the upper classes by this time. Generally speaking, however, Christians suffered most from popular riots which destroyed property, injured persons, and sometimes killed them.

A third wave of persecution hit during the reign of Trajan, emperor A.D. 98–117, again in Asia Minor and again largely in the form of popular resentment. Provincial officials did take some action. But the emperor directed them not to receive anonymous accusations and to punish only

1 *Annals,* XV:44.

those proven to have Christian affiliation. Any who rejected their faith he ordered released. The famous letter of Pliny, governor of Bithynia, to Trajan about A.D. 112 reflects the genuine puzzlement of conscientious public officials concerning the new religion. Should Christians be punished for the name itself? he asked. Or only for a crime committed under the name? He could not find anything in their practices which merited the first. What offended him most was their obstinacy.

Pliny's letter furnishes a valuable clue to popular Roman resentment generally. Pagans hurled all sorts of charges at Christians—incest and cannibalism, hatred of the human race, social snobbery, and atheism heading the list. The charge of incest and cannibalism, of course, grew out of a misunderstanding of Christian observances. But the other three stemmed from a single source—Christian *exclusivism.* The Jews managed usually to escape the wrath of their neighbors by virtue of a privileged legal standing, though Alexandrian Jews did suffer a popular persecution during Caligula's brief reign (A.D. 37–41). But Christians enjoyed this legal protection only insofar as they remained identified with Judaism. When they made it clear that Christ had set them free, nothing could suppress the popular antipathy.

The charge of atheism possessed special importance and was symptomatic of the main grievance. Christians refused to worship the gods who had made Rome great. Hence, whenever calamities occurred—defeat in battle, earthquake, flood, famine, fire—the cry went up, "Christians to the lions!"[2] By their refusal to worship the ancestral deities, the Romans reasoned, the Christians had angered the gods and brought their wrath down upon the whole empire. With the Jews this charge was not so serious. They at least remained faithful to *their* ancestral deity. But Christians, former Romans as well as Jews, had betrayed *all* the gods for this one called Jesus. To the Roman mind they defied all reason by departing from ancient custom.

With religion connected so intimately with the health and welfare of the body politic it is not surprising to hear charges of treason. Octavian prepared the way for such charges by having the senate ascribe divine honors to Julius Caesar and was himself elevated to divine status in the provinces if not in Rome. Caligula, Nero, and others cultivated this adulation further in an attempt to enhance their power. Though the emperor did not officially receive the title of Dominus (Lord) until the reign of Diocletian (303–311), to all intents and purposes already in the first century he had begun to head up the Roman pantheon. This made the oath of allegiance to the gods an oath of loyalty to the state and vice versa. And when Christians refused to say, "Caesar is Lord!" they were considered traitors to the empire.

This spasmodic regional persecution and harassment of the first and early second centuries did not stop the Christian mission. The cruelty of Nero merely evoked popular sympathy and perhaps admiration. Notwithstanding a thinning of its ranks by death or defection, the church grew. About A.D. 197 Tertullian of Carthage even boasted, "The blood of the martyrs is the seed of the Church."

II. A Kingdom of Priests and a Holy Nation

The early church had an answer to the serious charge of novelty. In time they developed an extensive apologetic for their antiquity. They had not departed from the ancient faith at all, they insisted. On the contrary, they possessed the most ancient faith of all—that of Abraham and Moses. They were, in fact, the people whom God had elected in the beginning to fulfil his mission in and to the world.

In the strictest sense the earliest believers saw themselves as the true Israel, repudiating with vigor contrary views like Marcion's. With first-century Jews everywhere, they shared a belief in one God

[2] So Tertullian, *Apol.*, 40.

who had made a covenant with Israel, in his demand of holiness and righteousness, and in the coming of a Messiah-King according to the ancient promises. They differed with them principally in their strong conviction about the messianic hope. In this matter they stood nearer John the Baptist and the Essenes, both of whom sought to prepare the way for the Messiah's advent. But where even John and the Essenes looked forward, Christians believed this hope had begun to come to fruition in Jesus. They were themselves the messianic community!

This self-understanding set the pattern for early Christianity's dynamic thrust into the ancient civilized world. Like Israel under Moses and Joshua, they had fled the service of demons and dumb idols and marched triumphantly into the promised land. They trained themselves in holiness for their mission. They were, to employ the Old Testament phrase, "a royal priesthood, a holy nation" (1 Peter 2:9). In many respects this made them "a third race," as some second-century pagans labeled them in jest, for they possessed a distinctive manner of life and bore with pride the name Christian. Certainly in their fidelity to the one God revealed in Jesus Christ they stood apart from both Greeks and barbarians.

1. *Called Out of Darkness*

Against this background, "conversion" from Judaism entailed an acknowledgment of Jesus' messiahship and lordship. Accordingly, as C. H. Dodd has pointed out in *The Apostolic Preaching and Its Developments,* the early heralds of the gospel proclaimed: "The age of fulfilment has dawned through the ministry, death, and resurrection of Jesus. By virtue of his resurrection he has been exalted to God's right hand as messianic head of the new Israel. The Holy Spirit in the Church is a sign of his present power and glory. Shortly he will return and consummate the messianic age. Repent and believe the good news and receive salvation by participation in the messianic community."

To the average Roman, anyone who had not had a long association with Judaism, such a message sounded quite strange. The Christian missionary, therefore, needed first to teach him about the one God and how this God had revealed himself in historical events which culminated in Jesus. For him "conversion" amounted to a radical upheaval in his manner of thinking and acting. It involved a complete shift of allegiance—from many lords and gods to one Lord and God—which more often than not brought ridicule and harassment even from his own family.

In order to assist the conversion of pagans, the church soon developed an apologetic and instructional system like that employed by the Jews. Already in Paul's day, a special group of teachers concentrated on the instruction of new converts and inquirers, probably before baptism. By A.D. 200, experience had taught the church to extend this period up to three years. Some converts obviously needed considerable nurture before they were ready to break with Satan and be wholly subservient to Christ. In fact, to free them from the grip of demonic powers required more than instruction; it required exorcism. Just as Jesus had cast out demons, so also did the church. At least by the second century, conversion to Christianity entailed certain special rites by which the demonic hold could be broken. He who received the Holy Spirit could not be filled with malign spirits opposed to God.

2. *Putting on the Whole Armor of God*

The crux of conversion from paganism to Christianity was initiation into the messianic community. When a convert made this step, he committed himself irrevocably to Christ and set himself in opposition to his former masters. As a member of Christ's army, he had to be prepared for an attack from the latter. His only sufficient protection was the divine armament, which alone would enable him to stand against the intrigues of the devil (cf. Eph. 6:10–20).

The arming of the Christian was the

work of the Holy Spirit. The Spirit, according to Acts, had a special connection with baptism. For in that act a man declares that he puts off his old self and dons a new, as symbolized by the putting off of an old robe and donning of a new. The old self dies with Christ, as it were, and rises in a revivified form to live in a new manner. The grip of the tyrant sin has been broken, Paul said. One no longer can excuse himself from acting morally, for by sharing Christ's death he has become free (Rom. 6:1–8).

In practical terms the pledge made in baptism had immense import for the newly converted. Previously they had been accustomed to blaming their *mis*behavior upon the demons or fate. Baptism undermined this excuse. "Christ has freed you," Paul reminded Christians who lapsed back into the old ways. "Don't misuse your freedom. You who made a pledge to Christ in baptism henceforth must conduct your lives according to the Spirit, lest you again become slaves of Satan!" (cf. Gal. 5).

3. *Lifting Up Holy Hands*

Having become a part of the Christian community through baptism, the new Christian had to give constant and faithful attention to his spiritual development. Both private and public worship assisted him.

Privately Christians followed a prayer schedule somewhat like the Jewish. Three times daily—at 9:00 A.M., 12:00 noon, and 3:00 P.M.—they recited the Lord's Prayer (in place of the Jewish Shema). They also prayed upon arising in the morning and before going to bed at night. According to the Didache, probably composed as early as A.D. 100, Syrian Christians fasted on Wednesdays and Friday (rather than on the Jewish fast days, Tuesday and Thursday). The churches, insofar as buildings existed, were open for daily devotions.

Agape feasts were held regularly. Eventually, however, an abuse of these evidently led to a separation of them from the Lord's Supper meal (cf. 1 Cor. 11; 2 Peter 2:13; Jude 12). These provided an occasion for wealthier Christians to help the poorer. Christians frequently met at night, so that the slaves and laborers who belonged to the church could attend.

The major occasion for public worship was the first day of the week, the Roman Sunday, which Christians soon called "the Lord's Day" in commemoration of Jesus' resurrection (cf. 1 Cor. 11:20; Rev. 1:10, Did. 14:1, Justin, I *Apol.* 67). On this day, which already began to supplant the Jewish sabbath (Saturday) during the first century, they congregated in an appointed place to praise God and to seek direction for their lives. From the mid-second-century *Apology* of Justin Martyr one may see the basic outlines of Jewish synagogue worship still making their imprint upon the Christian liturgy.

The distinctively Christian feature of this service was the Lord's Supper or Eucharist. From earliest times apparently, members of the new Israel observed it every time they met. It possessed particular significance for them because in its observance "you proclaim the Lord's death until he comes" (1 Cor. 11:26). In this sense the Lord's Supper was the Christian Passover, as many early references tell us. Whereas for the Jews the Passover reminded them of God's mightiest act in their behalf, the exodus from Egypt, the Eucharist reminded Christians of an even greater act in their behalf, their redemption from bondage to Satan through the death and resurrection of Christ. In using the Greek word *anamnesis* with reference to the Supper, Paul meant more than "memorial," just as the Passover was more than that. The Mishnah, the codified oral tradition of Judaism, after setting forth the manner in which the Passover should be observed, commanded, "In every generation a man must so regard himself as if he came forth himself out of Egypt." [3]

Properly speaking, therefore, the first Christians thought of the partaking of bread and wine as a symbolic participation in the

[3] Mishnah, 10:5, trans. Herbert Danby (London: Oxford, 1933), p. 151.

death and resurrection of Jesus and whatever else that event connoted. The meal symbolized their participation in the messianic community through the Spirit, their sharing in Christ's victory over the principalities and powers, their union with Christ and with one another (cf. 1 Cor. 10:1–22; 1:18–34). For John and some second-century writers it denoted the reality of Jesus' human nature (cf. John 6: 1–14,26–71; Ignatius, *Eph.* 20:2; *Phila.* 4:1; *Smyrn.* 7:1). It also pledged that what God had begun in raising Jesus from the dead he would complete.

4. Speaking the Truth in Love

With its promise of salvation for all men without regard to previous life situation, the church loaded upon itself an imposing task. Its converts, some perhaps attracted by its charities, sometimes came from the very dregs of society. Paul reminded the Corinthians, for example, that some of them had been fornicators, idolators, adulterers, effeminate, pimps, thieves, embezzlers, drunkards, and slanderers (1 Cor. 6:9–11). The unconverted endangered the life of the church itself. So instruction and discipline "in the Lord" became a regular feature of early Christian community life.

Besides prebaptismal training, Christians received further instruction through the sermon and in daily church sessions. By the mid-second century there were also schools in which those who had the leisure and wished to could secure a higher level of theological understanding. But much education took place in the home.

Children received almost all their Christian training in the home, for Christianity did not produce special schools for them until the Middle Ages. Fathers and mothers taught their sons and daughters to pray, read the Scriptures to them, and inculcated "the fear of the Lord." Inasmuch as Christian children had to attend pagan schools for their liberal education, the burden of correcting pagan errors about the gods, etc., lay upon the shoulders of their parents.[4]

[4] Cf. Tertullian, *On Idolatry,* p. 10.

As a closely knit community of love, the early church also expressed concern for its members through discipline, "speaking the truth in love" (Eph. 4:15). The aim here was not vindictive, but redemptive. Some either failed to sever the ties with Satan, or they again fell under his sway. By words of encouragement or admonition they might reaffirm their allegiance to Christ and manifest it in their lives. Not unexpectedly, therefore, one encounters frequently in early Christian writings injunctions to encourage, admonish, rebuke, exhort, and instruct.

Regrettably some hardened cases required severer action. Those who did not respond to loving advice, the church "handed over to Satan" by cutting them off from the Christian koinonia. It was hoped that exclusion would seek both to restore the offender and to preserve at least the minimal standard of holiness in the body of Christ.

Two offenses merited this kind of discipline: gross immorality and faction or divisiveness. Both stood in antithesis to the nature of the church as the community of the Spirit and reflected the restoration of the demonic hold over the individual. In its action the church attempted to apply those measures which would restore and revitalize the one who had fallen. It was quick to pronounce God's forgiveness.

5. God Has Appointed

Like any other major movement, Christianity's success depended in large part on its leaders. At the outset, of course, the Jerusalem community could rely on apostolic leaders, the eyewitnesses and participants in the Christ event. But as the movement spread to the farthest parts of the empire, leaders like Paul, Barnabas, John Mark, Timothy, Titus, and hundreds who had not seen Christ in the flesh had to take charge. For a long time the Jerusalem community still furnished a checkpoint for other churches, like that at Antioch, for instance. But as the horizons of Christianity expanded, Jerusalem's influence waned, and other churches of apostolic foundation provided points of reference as well.

During this initial phase, hundreds served by spiritual appointment alongside the apostles, fulfilling the church's ministry in the world. In his earlier letters Paul named numerous functions which never solidified into offices—prophets, teachers, powers, gifts of healing, helpers, administrators, speakers in tongues (1 Cor. 12:28). Eventually, however, whatever functions these fulfilled were subsumed under the offices of bishop, presbyter, and deacon.

The office of presbyter (elder) probably was borrowed from the synagogue. As Christianity realized a line of separation from the latter, it installed its own presbyters. In the Greek world these presbyters were given the more descriptive title *episkopoi* or bishops, which means "overseers." The presbyters or bishops in a certain local area functioned as a board, with one member serving as "president" or "presiding presbyter." Eventually, although not at the same rate everywhere, the title bishop was reserved for the presiding presbyter. The churches in Syria and Asia Minor seem to have set the pattern for this structure, called the monarchical episcopate. Ignatius, Bishop of Antioch martyred about A.D. 110–117, urged its implementation with prophetic fervor, but his tone suggests that what he sought was not the pattern everywhere. Rome apparently retained the older structure until later in the second century.

Upon the presbyter-bishops and later the bishop alone rested the chief responsibility for directing and coordinating the total ministry of the church. They preached, administered baptism and the Lord's Supper, supervised the distribution of funds for the aid of the needy, taught new converts, and exercised a general pastoral watchcare over the flock. The deacons, on the other hand, discharged numerous functions connected with the church's ministry. They performed their multiple ministries at the direction of the presbyters or bishop.

Conclusion

Christianity's growth in these early centuries was remarkable, its impact even more remarkable. The church of the New Testament era laid the groundwork, so that in time the new Israel achieved a victory which outshone by far the conquests of the old. Breaking the bonds of one culture, they universalized the good news of God brought in Jesus Christ. They made remarkable adaptations to the political, social, economic, intellectual, and religious life of Rome. In the process they took risks. Sometimes perhaps they went too far. But their inventive courage, born of the confidence that the gospel is good news for all men everywhere, gave them a deserving triumph over dozens of competitors. Their sovereign Christ proved stronger than all the others combined.

For Further Reading

DAVIES, J. G. *The Early Christian Church.* ("History of Religion Series," ed. E. O. JAMES.) New York, Chicago, & San Francisco: Holt, Rinehart & Winston, 1965.

DODDS, E. R. *Pagan and Christian in the Age of Anxiety.* Cambridge: The University Press, 1965.

FREND, W. H. C. *The Early Church.* ("Knowing Christianity Series," ed. WILLIAM NEILL.) Philadelphia & New York: J. B. Lippincott Co., 1966.

———. *Martyrdom and Persecution in the Early Church.* Garden City, New York: Doubleday & Co., Inc., 1967.

GLOVER, T. R. *The Conflict of Religions in the Early Roman Empire.* Boston: Beacon Press, 1909; 1960.

HARNACK, ADOLF. *The Mission and Expansion of Christianity in the First Three Centuries.* Translated and edited by JAMES MOFFATT. New York: Harper & Bros., 1908; 1962.

LATOURETTE, KENNETH SCOTT. *The First Five Centuries.* ("A History of the Expansion of Christianity," Vol. I.) New York, Evanston & London: Harper & Row, 1939.

LIETZMANN, HANS. *The Beginnings of the Christian Church.* Translated by BERTRAM LEE WOOLF. London: Lutterworth Press, 1937.

NOCK, ARTHUR DARBY. *Early Gentile Christianity and Its Hellenistic Background.* New York, Evanston & London: Harper & Row, 1964 (reprint).

SCHLATTER, ADOLF. *The Church in the New Testament Period.* Translated by PAUL P. LEVERTOFF. London: S.P.C.K., 1955.

WEISS, JOHANNES. *Earliest Christianity: A History of the Period A.D. 30–150.* 2 vols. New York: Harper & Bros., 1959 (reprint).

The Theology of the New Testament

William L. Hendricks

New Testament theology is the study which emphasizes and spells out the content of the New Testament from a theological viewpoint. As such it is closely related to other theological studies, and it is often difficult to distinguish between them and New Testament theology.

New Testament theology differs from New Testament exegesis in concentrating on the larger themes and implications of New Testament materials. New Testament theology must, however, presuppose both the work of the exegete to provide the details of interpretation and the various meanings of a given passage.

New Testament theology also differs from systematic theology. Systematic theology deals more systematically and comprehensively with doctrines such as God, man, sin, and salvation. Systematic theology has as its sources the biblical materials; and it also uses historical insights in an intentional way to show the influence of culture and biblical interpretation on the shaping and formation of doctrine. Systematic theology is likewise concerned to relate both biblical and historical materials to the current setting. New Testament theology differs in the arrangement of material and the conscious exclusion of the concerns of classical historical theology. This means that New Testament theology is concerned to let the biblical materials speak first in their own setting, then to the contemporary setting.

New Testament theology differs from historical theology and church history. In one sense it is prologue and first chapter of these studies. In another sense it should provide the norms by which to evaluate historical theology and church history. A Protestant New Testament theologian presupposes the priority of the New Testament because of his view of the authority and significance of the biblical materials.

Since New Testament theology deals with the message of the New Testament in its own setting and in its theological dimensions, organization of the materials is important. The books of the New Testament are diverse in purpose and content. Their message is normative and practical in expression. The theological insights of the New Testament are not primarily systematic in structure. For example, the Gospels were written to tell the story of Jesus Christ and give direction and authority to the Christian witness. Paul did give a brief resumé of the Christian faith in Romans, but he more often spoke of specific problems as in Galatians and 1 and 2 Corinthians. It would be better to speak of theologies of the New Testament, for there are differences of emphases and insights in the various New Testament books.

By way of further introduction, let us note some major emphases in the current study of New Testament theology.

Understanding the historical background is important. New Testament theology expresses the theological insights of the New Testament. The Bible did not come in a vacuum. If modern man reads the New Testament only in the light of his experiences, he is likely to miss valuable biblical insight and distort the original meaning of the biblical materials. The emphasis on historical backgrounds is one of the most pronounced trends in the study of biblical theology today.

The New Testament is, however, more than a historical document. It is history interpreted by faith. There has been a strong reaction to the history-of-religion-emphasis to New Testament studies. This reaction asserted that history can never establish the facts of faith. Martin Kahler made this emphasis as early as 1892.[1] An important issue

[1] *The So-Called Historical Jesus and the Historic Biblical Christ,* trans. Carl Braaten (Philadelphia: Fortress, 1964).

rests in the faith and history debate. The issue is twofold: (1) What is the relation of historical happening and belief? (2) Granted that belief is not proved by events in history, can one commit himself to faith affirmations without any concern for their historical basis?

One of Kahler's most illustrious pupils is Rudolph Bultmann, who shared his teacher's insight that history cannot prove faith. However, Bultmann went much further than Kahler and denied that the historical aspects of the life of Jesus are important for faith. What we know of Jesus is mediated to us by the faith of the early church. One is saved by faith, not historical fact. This cleavage between history and faith has sparked one of the liveliest theological debates of the twentieth century. Bultmann and his school have been the predominant influence in New Testament studies for the past twenty years.[2]

The Bultmannian loss of history has not gone unchallenged in Germany and the English-speaking world. Bultmann's opponents have argued that a discriminating faith must ask about the historical basis for its belief. To ask only about the faith of the early church and about contemporary man's self-awareness makes Christ the unimportant factor and man's own being the all important one. So argues the opposition.[3]

There is no such thing as pure history. All reporting, writing, and editing is predisposed in some direction. It is obvious that we have, in the New Testament, accounts about Jesus and the early church which are greatly influenced by the faith and experience of the authors. Indeed, without the resurrection no faith account about Jesus of Nazareth would have been written. Conversely, if Jesus had not risen, there would have been no basis for faith. The New Testament involves both history and faith. The history of the New Testament is not recorded for its own sake. It is recorded for the promotion of faith. The faith of the New Testament is not without the occurrence in history which gave rise to believing hearts and faith-formed records.

Another area for consideration is hermeneutics. Students of the New Testament have long been aware that how one interprets the Bible determines what one declares to be the teaching of the Bible. Hermeneutics is the science of interpreting written records. Everyone who reads the Bible and relates it to life uses some principles of interpretation. Many use an experiential focus which relates all of the biblical materials to the life of the individual in terms of his own personal experience. Others stress a historical approach indicating what the Bible meant. The first approach lacks depth, the second lacks application.

The purpose of this article is to glean the basic theological insights of the New Testament. We seek to answer the question: What is the essential message of the New Testament? The answer may be found as we consider the affirmations set forth in the outline of this article.

1. God Has Concern and Care for His Creation.

The earliest Christians were Jewish. They were aware that Jehovah God had created the world and that he ruled it in power and love. It was of supreme importance that the God of Israel, the maker of heaven and earth, was also the Redeemer. The primary focus of the New Testament is that God has redeemed men in Christ. The redeeming work of God was the point of departure. New Testament thought moves from redemption back to creation.

Jesus' teaching reinforces the view that his Father is the Creator and sustainer of the world. God is concerned for the flowers of the field and the birds of the air (Matt.

2 See *Theology of the New Testament,* 3–62; James Smart, *The Divided Mind of Modern Theology* (Philadelphia: Westminster, 1967); and *Kerygma and Myth,* ed. by A. W. Bartsch (New York: Harper Torchbooks, 1961).

3 Cf. especially J. Moltmann, *Theology of Hope,* trans. James Leitch (New York: Harper, 1967), pp. 182–90; Paul Althaus, *Fact and Faith in the Kerygma of Today,* trans. David Cairns (Philadelphia: Muhlenberg, 1959); Alan Richardson, *An Introduction to the Theology of the New Testament* (New York: Harper, 1958).

6:28; 10:29–31). Paul accepts the Old Testament teaching that Creator and created are the two orders of existence. Men have erred in worshiping "the creature rather than the Creator" (Rom. 1:25). What God has created is basically good. It is men who have corrupted things (1 Tim. 4:3–4). James acknowledges that God is the originator of all things, especially the good that men receive (1:17–18). Peter encourages Christ's followers to commit themselves and their sufferings to God, who is "a faithful creator" (1 Peter 4:19).

The first chapter of the Gospel of John unites in its message the notion that God the Creator is also the Redeemer. John begins with the very words of Genesis. The parallel is intentional. The God of creation mentioned in Genesis 1 is further identified as he who was with the Word who became flesh. God's self-revelation is complete. The God who by the Word made all things (John 1:3) and gave the law to Moses (John 1:17) has fully revealed himself to men in Christ, the incarnate Word (v. 14).

In Christ God has acted for man's redemption (Rom. 3:24; Col. 1:14,20; 1 Peter 1:18–19). God sent Christ to the world (John 3:16; Luke 4:18). Since Christ effects our redemption, and Christ comes from God, no other conclusion can be drawn than that the God who redeems us in Christ is he who created the world.

Love is also a characteristic of God. God's love is seen in what he has done. He gave Christ for the world (John 3:16). He gives courage, hope, and grace to his people as evidence of his love (2 Thess. 2:16). He chastens his children as an evidence of his love (Heb. 12:6). God's love is especially bestowed upon his Son (John 3:35). God's essential nature is love (1 John 4:8). Love is the hallmark of God, and it is demanded of God's people as their identifying mark (1 John 4:11). Love for God and one's neighbor is the greatest command of God (Matt. 22:37–39).

Love is always a reminder of the possibility of God's wrath. Love and wrath are two sides of the same coin. God is not contradictory. His wrath grows out of his love. Wrath is love spurned. God's wrath abides on those who refuse to believe in Jesus (John 3:36). When men hold God's truth in false ways, his wrath abides on them (Rom. 1:18). Disobedience brings the wrath of God (Col. 3:6). Men who walk in the fleshly lusts of the world are by nature under God's wrath (Eph. 2:3). But it is not his final way with his children, rather they are appointed to salvation (1 Thess. 5:9).

God is called Father by Jesus Christ (Matt. 11:27; John 17:1). Christians assert a special relationship in Jesus' expression of God as his Father. This is the primary use of "father" in the New Testament; it is the fatherhood of God in relation to Christ the Son. A secondary, or derived use, is seen in Jesus' teaching his disciples to call God Father (Matt. 5—7). The early Christians called God Father because they were related to him through Jesus Christ the Son. The God and Father of our Lord Jesus Christ became almost a technical phrase to identify the God of Christians (2 Cor. 11:31). The benedictions and greetings of Christians are expressed in the name of the Father (Rom. 1:7; 2 Cor. 1:2; Philemon 1:3). The fellowship of the redeemed lies with the Father (1 John 1:3), and they bear the Father's name (Rev. 14:1).

II. Jesus Christ in His Life, Death, and Resurrection Is the Word of God.

The central focus of the New Testament is upon Jesus Christ. What is new in the New Testament is not its picture of God or its promise of man's deliverance. What is new is the affirmation that in Jesus of Nazareth God is clearly seen and man's salvation is fully accomplished.

1. Development of Christology

One of the earliest Christian confessions was that Jesus is the Christ (Matt. 16:16). Other early confessions of faith are: "Our Lord, come!" (1 Cor. 16:22); "Jesus Christ is Lord!" (Phil. 2:11). These were cries born of faith. The men of New Testament days were shaken by the impact of Christ on their lives. They began to reckon what Christ meant in terms of the God of Israel and the hope of all men. New Testament Christology may well have developed according to the following steps: (1) a full awareness that the crucified and risen Christ was indeed God's Messiah; (2) a continuation of fellowship with the risen Christ through the Holy Spirit; (3) the expectation of the return of Christ; (4) an evaluation of Jesus' life and teachings; and (5) an assertion of his preexistence with God from the beginning.[4]

The various New Testament authors approach the figure of Jesus from different perspectives. The New Testament gives a composite picture of Jesus Christ. Always he is central to the message. However, in order to perceive his fulness it is best to examine these pictures separately.

2. *Synoptic Christology*

The death and resurrection of Christ is the proper starting point for discussing how the early church saw Jesus. The Gospels are not biographies, in the traditional use of that term. More space is given to the final week and death of Christ than to any feature of his life (Matt. 21—27; Mark 11—15; Luke 19—23). In the death of Christ the life of the people of God began anew. Coupled with the death of Christ in humility is the triumph of his resurrection. The early believers were overwhelmed by the event of God's raising Christ. The death and resurrection of Christ shaped subsequent understanding of who Jesus was and how his mission was to be seen.

His Work. In biblical faith a man is known first by what he does rather than who he is. Even so the work of Jesus provided the focus from which his person and teachings were viewed. The death and resurrection were the primary stress of the Gospels. His mighty works (*dunameis*) were seen as significant acts of the Messiah. Just as the Synoptic Gospels give a large amount of space to the death and resurrection, so they also give much space to Jesus' mighty works or miracles. Nearly one-third of Mark (209 of 661 vv.) speaks of the miraculous. The mighty works are integral, not accidental to the fabric of the Gospels.

These works of Christ are not primarily signs to prove his credentials. Jesus asserted that his generation should have no sign but resurrection and judgment (Mark 8:11–12; Matt. 12:38–45; 16:1–5). At his trial Jesus performed no miracle for the curiosity of Herod (Luke 23:8).[5]

The miracles of Christ were basically of four types: healing, casting out demons, bringing the dead back to life, and using nature to meet the needs of his redemptive ministry. All of his miracles were closely connected with the kingdom of God.

The followers of the Baptist are told to recount the mighty works of Jesus as evidence that he is Messiah (Luke 7:22; Matt. 11:4 f.). "If it is by the finger of God that I cast out demons, then the kingdom of God has come upon you" (Luke 11:20; Matt. 12:28; cf. Mark 3:23–30). The question of the first century was not, Are miracles possible? Rather, "By what authority are you doing these things, and who gave you this authority?" (Matt. 21:23; cf. Mark 1:27; 11:28; Luke 20:2). Jesus evaded a direct expression of authority with the Jewish leaders. Yet his followers had already recognized in his mighty works the authority of God and the dawning of the kingdom.

The miracles were more than works of compassion or displays of strength. They were also promises of what God would ultimately do for his people when his kingdom is fully come. He will remove pain, death, evil, and the limitations of man's present existence (cf. Rev. 21:4).

In the fourth Gospel the miracles of Jesus

[4] For varying perspectives see R. H. Fuller, *The Foundations of New Testament Christology* (New York: Scribner's, 1965); and John Knox, *The Humanity and Divinity of Christ* (Cambridge: Univ. Press, 1967).

[5] See A. M. Hunter, *The Work and Words of Jesus* (Philadelphia: Westminster, 1950), pp. 54–59.

are called works and signs. The mighty works and signs were vital factors in the New Testament portrait of Jesus' life and ministry.

The events of Jesus' life are presented in the Synoptics as deeds of messianic fulfilment. His virgin birth is seen as the fulfilment of prophecy (Matt. 1:23; cf. Isa. 7:14; and Old Testament references in the pronouncements and "songs" related to Jesus' birth in Luke 1—2). His baptism is connected with the idea of the restoration of prophecy and the activity of the Spirit in the last day (Luke 3:16–22).[6] Both the descent of the dove and the heavenly voice at Jesus' baptism are to be interpreted messianically. That is, the last days have dawned. Messiah is here. The Spirit rests upon him. He is validated and confirmed by a heavenly voice. The formula of the heavenly voice is a combination of two Old Testament passages. "You are my son" (Psalm 2:7) "in whom my soul delights" (Isa. 42:1). In this combination of exalted Son of God and Suffering Servant of God lay the guidelines for Jesus' messianic task.

To be Messiah by way of suffering was the burden of Jesus' temptation (Matt. 4:1–11). The time of Christ's temptation was also a symbolic insight. The forty years of Israel's disobedient wanderings are relived and overcome in the forty days of obedience (cf. Ex. 16:35; Rom. 5:19). Likewise, the first lawgiver, Moses, was on Mount Sinai forty days and forty nights (Ex. 24:18). So the giver of the new law, a greater than Moses, experienced a period of temptation and revelation.[7] The crux of Jesus' temptation was to do God's will the devil's way: be a bread messiah, a spectacular messiah, a compromising messiah. The pressure of this trial of false ways to messiahship remained in Jesus' ministry.

The resurrection faith of the Gospel writers served as the springboard whereby his life and work were viewed in the full awareness that he was God's Messiah. The beginning of his life, his baptism, his temptation, and his mighty works were seen in the retrospective view of the resurrection.

His Teachings. The Synoptic Gospels present the teachings of Jesus from the messianic view. The stress was not on his method of teaching. Nor is he presented primarily as a religious genius. Jesus is the proclaimer of the kingdom of God. His message tells how men entering that kingdom must live and how the fulfilment of the kingdom lies in the hand of God.

Jesus' teachings were direct, intensely practical, and authoritative. He demands the radical obedience of men because God's kingdom confronts them. His use of parables was a device common in Judaism. The hiddenness of the parables provides opportunity for the Master (*rabban*) to develop the faith of the disciples.

The teachings of Jesus were born out of the relationships of his life. There were the chosen disciples whom Jesus gathered. It was these who both received and were responsible for transmitting Jesus' teachings (Matt. 4:18–22; Luke 6:12–16; Matt. 28:19–20).[8]

Those who sought to follow Jesus were given the requirement of leaving all and following him, despite the contingencies of life and the strict requirements of the kingdom (Matt. 8:19–22; Luke 9:57–62). Disciples were expected to serve in a climate of opposition (Matt. 9:37–38; 10:16; Luke 10:2–3) and with a sense of urgency and impending judgment (Luke 10:8–12; Matt. 10:15). The rewards of discipleship were largely intangible but of ultimate value. Discipleship gives a knowledge of God attained in no other way (Matt. 11:25–27; Luke 10:21 f.). Whatever the disciple

[6] The rabbis had taught that prophecy and the Spirit of God had left Israel after the last of the prophets and would return only with the coming of the Messiah. In the meantime God intervened directly in Israel by a heavenly voice. See W. D. Davies, *Paul and Rabbinic Judaism* (London: S.P.C.K., 1958), pp. 208–15.

[7] Christ as the New Torah (law) and the New Moses is a favorite motif of Matthew. See Alan Richardson, *An Introduction to the Theology of the New Testament*, pp. 166–69.

[8] See William Barclay, *The Master's Men* (New York: Abingdon, 1959).

needed would be given as long as he sought the kingdom of God first (Matt. 6:33; 7:7–11; Luke 11:9–13).

Not all men were related to Jesus in discipleship; many related to him in hostility and rejection. To these he responded by wise and measured words (Matt. 12:25–37; Luke 11:17–23). Jesus acknowledged that the claim of God was supreme and to do God's will was the standard by which God was pleased (Luke 11:21–28). Rejection in the face of confrontation of God in the teachings of Jesus brought greater responsibility and heavier judgment (Matt. 12: 41–42; Luke 11:31–32). As the scribes and Pharisees intensified their rejection of Jesus and assumed a censorious and persecuting attitude, he exposed and excoriated them (Matt. 23; Mark 12; Luke 11).

Jesus' relationship to God was determinitive for all other relationships. Jesus accomplished his work by the authority (*exousia*) of God (Matt. 9:8; 28:18). He provided the way of understanding God (Matt. 11:27). It is important not to be offended at the Christ (Matt. 11:6), to confess him before men (Luke 12:8), and not to be ashamed of the Son of man (Mark 8:38).

The God of Jesus Christ is actively concerned on behalf of man. His providential care extends to all that has life (Matt. 10:28–31; Luke 12:22–30). The world and its processes ultimately lie in his hands, "for he makes his sun rise on the evil and on the good, and sends rain on the just and on the unjust" (Matt. 5:45). God is especially the Father of peacemakers (Matt. 5:9), and the disciples of Jesus call upon him as "Our Father who art in heaven" (Matt. 6:9).

Jesus gave approval and respect to the Law of God. It abides and is fulfilled in him (Matt. 5:17–18). He perceived the spirit of the Law beyond its maze of specific requirements. The essence of the Law is love for God and one's fellow man (Matt. 22: 36–40). Jesus reverenced the Temple and the sabbath, but he did not hesitate to challenge their misuse or bring God's deeper intention to light against the interpretations and distortions of men (Matt. 21:13; Mark 2:23–24; Luke 6:2–9).

Jesus' teachings in relation to the Old Testament and the traditions of Israel are best summed up with the "you have heard that it was said . . . but I say to you" passages (Matt. 5:21–48). In what he taught and was and did the earliest witnesses knew that one greater than Moses was in their midst.

His Titles. In the New Testament days men were given titles according to their deeds. A man was what he did, how he acted, what he accomplished. The Gospel names given Jesus are reflections drawn from the messianic hopes of Israel and fulfilled by Jesus of Nazareth.[9]

The term prophet is used of Jesus by the crowds (Luke 7:16; Mark 6:15). In first-century Palestine this would mean that a spokesman for God has arisen. To some it meant the dawning of the messianic age. The Gospel writers do not themselves call Jesus prophet. Jesus intimates that he is a prophet (Mark 6:4; Luke 13:33–35). As Christianity grew beyond Palestine this designation of Jesus became less significant.

Christ is a favorite New Testament designation for Jesus. The term means anointed and is used by Matthew and Luke especially in connection with the birth and death of Jesus. The most memorable use of the term Christ is Peter's confession of Jesus as the Christ (Matt. 16:16 ff.) followed by Jesus' approval of the confession.

The term Lord (*kurios*) was widely used in the ancient world. It was as common as "sir" and in some instances was merely a polite form of address. In other uses it was a sacred word used instead of the divine name of God. There is an extensive use of the term in the Gospels, referring to God (Matt. 1:22; 9:38; 11:25) and to Christ (Matt. 12:8; 15:22; Luke 24:34). Since the term was widely used in both the Jewish and Gentile world, its exact meaning must be determined by the context in each

[9] See Oscar Cullmann, *The Christology of the New Testament,* trans. Guthrie and Hall (Philadelphia: Westminster, 1959).

case.

The most intriguing term applied to Jesus was Son of man.[10] He used it as a term to refer to himself: "The Son of man has nowhere to lay his head" (Matt. 8:20). It is used of an exalted figure coming on the clouds (Matt. 24:27–30). It is also used of the suffering Son of man (Mark 8:31; 9:12; 14:21). The term has a rich background in Old Testament and the intertestamental literature. In the Gospels it refers to Jesus as the one who has come to identify with man; to suffer for him; and as the future returning Redeemer at the "last day."

3. *John's View of Jesus Christ the Son of God*

The Gospel of John gives special stress to the sonship of Christ. The Son is "only Son"—unique, in a category by himself (1:14,18; 3:16,18). It sees the Son as the Word of God (1:1). The Word shares the divine nature and also becomes flesh (1:1,14). The incarnate Son is fully human. He grew weary at Jacob's well (4:6); showed concern for his mother (19:26); and demonstrated his obedience and dependence on the Father (5:19; 6:38). The close relationship of the Father and Son is stressed by the fact that the Father bears witness to the Son (5:17,37). The authority and power of God himself reside with Jesus. The Son is eternal; he was from the beginning (1:1; 8:58; 17:5) and goes to the Father after his death (16:17). The Son has come from the Father and returns to him (John 8; 14:1–3).

The Son goes out of the world by being lifted up on the cross. The term "lifted up" means both the crucifixion and glorification. For John it is in the crucifixion that Christ is glorified (3:14; 8:28). All the signs in John's Gospel are given to show that Christ by the power of God meets the needs of men.

4. *Paul's Christology*

Paul contributes much to the New Testament portrait of Christ. Paul speaks from his relationship with Christ the risen Lord. However, he knows that Jesus was a man "born of woman" (Gal. 4:4). Jesus was a Jew of David's seed (Rom. 1:3). Jesus was meek and gentle (2 Cor. 10:1). He showed endurance (2 Thess. 3:5) and obedience (Rom. 5:19). Paul's most frequent designation for Jesus is Lord. The confession of Jesus as Lord is necessary to salvation (Rom. 10:9–10). One can acknowledge that Jesus is Lord only by the power of the Spirit (1 Cor. 12:3). Because of Jesus Christ the Lord, grace effects eternal life for man (Rom. 5:21). Although the heathen speak of gods many and lords many (1 Cor. 8:5), there is but one Lord (Eph. 4:5). Christ the Lord was God's agent of creation and his instrument of redemption (Col. 1:13–17). Christ the Lord emptied himself to become the Servant-Saviour of men (Phil. 2:1–8). It is in Jesus the Lord that God will express God's own lordship over all creation and acknowledge the praise of all men (Eph. 1:10; Phil. 2:10).

5. *Other New Testament Writings*

The picture of Christ is given magnificent variety in other New Testament writings. The author of Hebrews stresses that Christ is the image of God (1:3). Christ formed the worlds and is the last and best—perfect in every way—of God's manifestations to men (Heb. 1:1–3). Christ is the sympathetic high priest on behalf of men (Heb. 8:1). Christ mediates God's new covenant with men and seals it with his death (Heb. (7:15–26). Peter speaks of Christ as the chief cornerstone of God's temple; the shepherd and bishop of our souls; the sinless lamb who brings men salvation as announced by the prophets (1 Peter 2:6,25; 1:19,10–12).

In James, Jesus Christ is viewed as the

[10] Bultmann denies that Jesus ever used this term of himself; he feels that the church applied the term to Jesus after his death. See H. Todt, *The Son of Man in the Synoptic Tradition*, trans. D. M. Barton (Philadelphia: Westminster, 1965); R. Fuller, *The Mission and Achievement of Jesus* (Chicago: Alec Allenson, 1956).

Lord of glory (2:1), who bears the honorable name (2:7) and comes to judge men (5:9). The Revelation brings a multifaceted expression of the triumph of Christ. The risen Christ is none other than Jesus (1:9), God's Messiah (Rev. 11:15). He is the Lamb of God, who gives a faithful witness for God's people (1:5); and he is the sovereign Lord of the churches (1:17–20). He is Alpha and Omega, the beginning and the end (Rev. 1:8).

The titles of Jesus emphasized who he was and what he did. He was a man who went about doing good (Acts 10:38), but he was also anointed by the Spirit of God. This Jesus was, in reality, Lord of all (Acts 10:36). In him dwelt the fulness of the Godhead bodily (Col. 2:9). The New Testament titles given to Jesus and the New Testament observations about him lead inevitably to the two affirmations that Jesus is both God and man.

6. *The Centrality of the Death and Resurrection of Christ*

The decisive event which was the climax of God's revelation in Christ was the cross-resurrection event. Without the shock of the cross, Jesus' life would have been incomplete, and his teachings would rank first in a long list of moral philosophies. Without the reality of resurrection the disciples would have remained in the tidewater of despair.

The death of Christ is given large space in all four Gospels. Paul knows only Christ and him crucified (1 Cor. 2:2). Peter reminds persecuted Christians that Christ's death is an example to them and a sacrifice—he bore our sins on the tree (1 Peter 2:21–24). Hebrews emphasizes the priestly ministry and the once-for-all sacrifice of Christ for men (8—10). His death was a brutal murder, but beyond the treachery of men lay God's predetermined plan for man's salvation (Acts 2:23). Generally Christ's death is interpreted in Old Testament sacrificial terminology. The cross, an instrument of Roman cruelty, is placed under the ancient Deuteronomic curse of God. The cross becomes the symbol of Christ's sacrifice, the highest sign of God's redemptive love for men, and the word to be proclaimed by the Christian church.

Connected with the humiliation of Christ's death is the exaltation of his resurrection. Each of the Gospels dwells fondly on the details. The tomb is empty (Matt. 28:6). The heavenly messenger proclaims the resurrection (Mark 16:6). Jesus himself appears to his disciples including two dispirited followers on the road to Emmaus (Luke 24). A scene from the Galilean seashore provides encouragement and instruction to a special group (John 21). Without Christ's resurrection our faith would be in vain, and the surety of man's resurrection would be void (1 Cor. 15). As the death of Christ, his resurrection also is related to man's salvation. Paul stresses the centrality of Christ's death and resurrection when he asserts that Christ "was put to death for our trespasses and raised for our justification" (Rom. 4:25).

III. *The Spirit of God Bears Witness to His Word and Draws Men to God.*

The term "word of God" has deep roots in Old Testament thought. When God spoke it was done (Gen. 1). The Greek term *logos* (word) also had rich and varied meanings in Greek soil. Perhaps one could best say that "word of God" means the instrument which accomplishes his purpose and will. In this light, Jesus Christ is God's first and last Word.

The words and message about Jesus became the word of God which is announced to men. When this message about Jesus the Word was put in written form it became for Christians the word of God, because it effectively tells and expresses God's intent in Jesus the Word. A threefold use of word is helpful. Jesus is the living Word; proclamation about Jesus is the spoken word; and the New Testament records are the written Word. In New Testament days the Spirit of God was related first and foremost to Jesus, then to the proclamation of the word.

The word comes to men today also in written form, and the contemporary church feels that the Spirit bears witness to this written word.

1. The Spirit in the Life of Christ

In the New Testament the Spirit of God bears vital witness to Jesus, the Word of God. His birth is by the coming of the Spirit upon Mary (Luke 1:35). His baptism is confirmed by the Spirit, symbolized by the dove (Matt. 3:16). The Spirit drives him into the wilderness to encounter temptation (Mark 1:12). His public ministry is begun with an Old Testament quotation claiming direction by the Holy Spirit (Luke 4:18). His mighty works are effected by the Spirit of God (Matt. 12:28), and he speaks of God's gift of the Holy Spirit to his people (Luke 11:13).

The Gospel of John, written with a view of adding theological insight to earlier details, speaks often of the Spirit and his relation to Christ. Christ will baptize in the Spirit (1:32–33). Christ informs Nicodemus he must be born of the Spirit to enter God's kingdom (John 3). Christ's presence is to be extended by the Spirit in a way analogous to a bubbling spring of living water (7:38–39). Jesus will send the Holy Spirit (15:26), who will bear witness to Christ and glorify him (John 16:14). The Spirit furthers the ministry of Christ by calling to mind Christ's words to the apostles (14:26; 16:14). The resurrected Christ breathes the Spirit upon the apostles (20:22).

2. The Spirit in the Life of the Church

Empowering God's People at Pentecost. The book of Acts tells of the coming of the Spirit at Pentecost. Pentecost was a historic festival in Judaism associated with the early grain harvest and, from rabbinic days, with the giving of the law to Moses. The Spirit came upon the followers of Jesus as they had assembled in Jerusalem (Acts 2). They were empowered (symbolized by the rushing winds) and cleansed for service (symbolized by the tongues of fire), and they proclaimed with joy the gospel to men representing every area of earth (symbolized by the tongues and the list of all nations). The message about Jesus (kerygma) was proclaimed in the power of the Holy Spirit, and the word was blessed with the gathering of new disciples (2:14–39; 3:12–26).

Shaping the Community of Faith. In keeping with the promise of Christ the Spirit came upon his followers to grant them comfort (John 14:16). The Spirit is the Spirit of truth (John 14:17), who will guide God's people. The Spirit as Comforter (Paraclete) is present to continue the fellowship of Christ (John 15:26) and to pass judgment on the world (John 16:8–11). The Spirit bears witness to men of God that Jesus was truly man (1 John 4:2). God's Spirit is a grace gift (charisma) to aid Christians in discerning the way of God (1 John 2:20,27) and to provide them assurance that they are God's own (1 John 3:24). The Spirit conducts the seer of Revelation through the mysteries and symbols of cosmic conflict and conquest (1:10; 4:2). The Spirit joins the church in issuing the invitation for all to come —"let him who desires take the water of life without price" (Rev. 22:17).

The Spirit of God bears witness to Christ and in so doing draws men to God. God's Spirit plumbs the depths of the divine inner being, even as man's own spirit interprets his innermost desires (1 Cor. 2:11). If one does not have Christ's Spirit, he is not Christ's (Rom. 8:9). The Spirit alone can enable man to confess Christ (1 Cor. 12:3). The Spirit makes God's people a living letter of testimony (2 Cor. 3:3), and the word they speak is about that living Word of God, for the Spirit and Christ are one in purpose (2 Cor. 3:17). Christians are to conduct their lives so that through the Spirit they may produce results that are recognizable as the "fruit of the Spirit" (Gal. 5:22–25).

The Spirit gives gifts to the people of God. These gifts come to individuals but are to be used for the good of the corporate body (1 Cor. 12–14). The gifts are for special purposes (1 Cor. 12:4–12; Eph.

4:4–12) and are granted to differing individuals. Each man does not possess every gift of the Spirit. However, all of God's people should be characterized by the three great and best gifts of the Spirit—faith, hope, and love (1 Cor. 13).

3. Spirit, Son, and Father

The New Testament reflects the dramatic movement of God toward men. The God of Israel spoke fully and finally in Christ (Heb. 1:1–3). Both God and Christ are extended to men by the Spirit (John 15:26–27). The Christian concept of God, of necessity, involves his threefoldness. The term trinity does not appear in the New Testament. It is a later historical expression. But the notion that lies behind the formulation of the doctrine of the Trinity is a primordial New Testament insight. This specific threefoldness of God (Father, Son, Spirit) arising from that particular era of world history (first-century Palestine) distinguishes in the most meaningful way Christianity from other religions and the New Testament from the Old.

The Christian concept of the Trinity has been often mistaken to mean that Christians worship three gods. Such tritheism is foreign to the New Testament. The oneness of God is a unity of purpose and common action. The threeness of God is his way of being God and of revealing himself in history. The New Testament did not reckon the Trinity from the viewpoint of philosophy or mathematics. Rather in the New Testament the threefoldness of God was a primary fact of experience. It was vocalized in benedictions and doxologies rather than systematic formulae (Rom. 15:33; 2 Cor. 13:14; 1 Peter 1:2).

7. God Has Chosen a Redeemed Community to Bear His Witness.

God reveals himself to men as Father, Son, Spirit. Every expression of the threefold movement of God to men is purposive. The purpose of God is one of his own choosing (election) and involves the redemption of man. In accomplishing this purpose God selects a people (the chosen or elect) to accomplish his purpose and to manifest it to all the world. The Old Testament community was intensely aware of being chosen of God to accomplish his purpose and to implement his revelation to men. The Christian Bible contains an Old Testament and a New Testament—two covenants. These covenants provide preliminary and final expressions of God's purpose. The constant feature of the Old and the New is the covenant of God and its redemptive purpose.

1. The Ongoing Purpose of God

Jesus placed himself consciously within the historic purposes of God. The beginning of his ministry was accomplished by his awareness of a prophet's task (Luke 4:18; cf. Isa. 61:1). His relation to the law of God was one of promise and fulfilment (Matt. 5:17). Both lawgiver and prophet appear at the transfiguration, which anticipates the death of Christ, God's decisive redemptive event (Matt. 17: 2 f.; Mark 9: 2 f.).

Jesus' selection of twelve apostles and the early church's insistence on maintaining that number shows a deliberate and conscious effort to portray the new Israel (Matt. 10: 1 f.; Mark 3:14; Luke 6:13; Acts 1:15–26). The great commandment for God's people is the same in the Old Testament (Deut. 6:5) and the New (Matt. 22: 37). The dimensions of the God of Israel have taken historical precision and enlargement in the coming of Christ (John 1:17). Jesus' intention to gather the new Israel was enacted in the calling of the disciples and expressed at Caesarea Philippi (Matt. 16:16–20). The empowering of God's people at Pentecost is interpreted as prophetic fulfilment (Acts 2:14–21). The New Testament authors interpreted the coming of Christ and his life in terms of fulfilment.

A brief history and philosophy of the purpose of God is found in Romans 9—11. In these chapters Paul introduces themes that exercise Christian faith in every age. Such themes are: the constancy of God's purpose; the relation of Israel and the church; God's final intentions for Israel; and the elective purpose and ways of God.

Paul interprets God's purpose for Israel and the Gentiles (Rom. 9—11). He is certain that God's purpose of redemption is constant (Rom. 9:4). What changes is man. This is illustrated by the refusal of God's people to do his will and accept his Christ (Rom. 9:31–33). Israel did not follow God's dramatic widening of his purpose in Christ. In the day of fulfilment, people are saved by calling on Christ (Rom. 10:9–13). Israel will be provoked to jealousy by the engrafted Gentiles (Rom. 11:17–24). One thing is sure, God's purpose to save extends to his original covenant community; but it can be effected only in Christ.

The relation of law and gospel is a Pauline concern. Law is a word of diverse uses. There is a law of conscience for Gentiles (Rom. 2:14). Law may refer to the entire Old Testament (Rom. 3:10–19) or just the Mosaic elements (Gal. 3:10–13). The Mosaic law and the Jewish traditions are personified into a legal system vying with the gospel for the affections of the Galatians. The law cannot save (Gal. 2:6), but the law itself was from God (Rom. 7:14). It reveals to man what is sin (Rom. 7:9). The law is good. It is men who are not (Rom. 9:12–25). The sum of the matter is that God's purpose to redeem is constant and the law serves within this purpose as a servant to conduct man to the teacher, who is Christ (Gal. 3:24).

2. *The Body of Christ*

The new Israel is a phrase which meant much in the framework of first-century Judaism. As the community of God spread into the world, carrying the salt and light of its witness, other terms were needed to express its existence. The body of Christ was used often by Paul to provide a living and organic analogy to describe the people of God.[11]

[11] Cf. J. A. T. Robinson, *The Body* (London: SCM, 1952).

The many individual Christians constitute one body in Christ (Rom. 12:5). Christians are baptized into the body of Christ and are nourished by his Spirit (1 Cor. 12:13). Each Christian is related to Christ as the various parts of a body to the head of that living organism (1 Cor. 12; Col. 1:18). Christians are to relate to Christ as members of a given body to the whole, or as the wife to the husband as they become one body (Eph. 4—5).

Church (*ekklesia*) is a widely used term for the people of God.[12] It has roots in the words used of Israelite assemblies. It is used in Matthew by Christ (16:18; 18:17). "Church" ordinarily refers to the specific local assembly of Christians. The plural form, churches, refers to congregations of a given locale (1 Cor. 1:2; Gal. 1:2). Church also refers to the larger congregation of all believers and is in such occurrences synonymous with the term the body of Christ (Eph. 1:22–23).

Many other expressions are used in the New Testament to speak of the ongoing purpose of God as embodied in the church.[13]

The church is to serve God. Special servants (ministers) in the church are called pastors, deacons, elders, teachers, bishops, and evangelists (Eph. 4:11–13; 1 Tim. 3:2; 1 Cor. 12:28–31). Various qualifications for those who oversee and minister to the flocks of God are listed (1 Tim. 3; Titus 1). The practical functions of ministry as deacon in the Jerusalem church are recorded (Acts 6).

All of the people of God are called by his Spirit. This must be so before they can become his people (John 1:12–13). Within this wider sense of calling, there is the special separation by the Spirit for specific redemptive tasks (Acts 13:2–3). This special calling is recognized and honored by

[12] Cf. J. R. Nelson, *The Realm of Redemption* (Greenwich, Conn.: Seabury, 1951).

[13] Cf. "Church," *Interpreter's Dictionary of the Bible*, I, 608–26. Men of the church are slaves of God (Rom. 1:1; 2 Peter 1:1; James 1:1). The church is the Israel of God (Gal. 6:16); the flock (Luke 12:32; 1 Peter 5:2-3); a holy nation; a peculiar people (1 Peter 2:9).

the congregations which give formal recognition and spiritual sanction to those who are called for particular redemptive service. This recognition took the form of laying hands upon the called (Acts 13:3). The differences in ministry were in function and not degree.

The New Testament is insistent that men are all responsible to God and are all guilty before him (Acts 17:26; Rom. 1—3). In Jesus Christ the man-made barriers existing between men are broken down (Gal. 3:28). All Christians are to be priests of God on behalf of a lost world. Special calling to ministry places one under heavy obligation and grants unusual grace for service. It does not mark the called as different or better than other children of God. The priesthood of all believers is a corollary to our sonship of God in Christ.

The churches, in addition to proclamation, observe the rites ordained by Christ which give symbolic witness to his redemptive event. These are baptism and the Supper. Baptism is commanded by the risen Christ (Matt. 28:20). It portrays the experience of dying and rising with Christ (Rom. 6:1–4). In his baptism Christ identified himself with men, became one with sinful humanity. He crossed the line of our imperfection to stand with us. In Christian baptism the believer in Christ consciously identifies himself with Christ. He confesses the name of Christ publicly (Rom. 10:9–10) and "puts on" Christ by his immersion (Rom. 6:3; Gal. 3:27).

The Supper was established by Christ and is taken by his followers both to remember his sacrifice for them and to reflect upon his ultimate coming for fellowship with them (Luke 22:19–30; Matt. 26:26–29; Mark 14:22–25; 1 Cor. 11:23–26). The cup and bread of the Lord's table provide fellowship and communion with him (1 Cor. 10:16–17). They remind the Christians of the need for separation in life and purity in conduct (1 Cor. 10:21). In the New Testament the Lord's Supper presupposed rigorous self-examination and much searching of the inner man (1 Cor. 11:28–33).

V. *The Redeemed Community Is Composed of Men Who Share the Weakness of Sin and the Experience of Salvation.*

1. Man in Sin

The New Testament view of man is neither pessimistic nor optimistic. It may be described as realistic. Man is God's creature and bears the image of God in a distorted way. Therefore, man is never to be despised by his fellows (James 5:9). In fact, man is the highest concern of the Creator, and his life is more valuable than that of other created beings (Matt. 10:29–31). Even the religious institutions ordained of God are for the good of men.

Parts of a man often stand for his total response or way of life. The heart is the organ of thought and response in the New Testament. A man is what he thinks in his heart (Matt. 12:34–35). The inner organs reflect compassion or deep emotion (Phil. 1:7; 2:1–2; Col. 3:12).[14]

The writings of Paul give much space to the reflection on man in sin. Man participates in a fallen race. Like the first Adam, all men have sinned (1 Cor. 15:21–22; Rom. 5:12–21). Righteousness is to be judged by God's standard, and by that criterion no man measures up (Rom. 3:21–23). Man is flesh. This means that there is an active principle in man which is evil and turns life in the direction of the demonic and the sinful (2 Cor. 7:1; 10:2).

Man has a body. Sometimes body and flesh are synonymous (Rom. 6:6; 7:24). Basically the body is the form of man. In this life it is chemical and earthly, and in the world to come it is spiritual (1 Cor. 15:39–40). Man has spirit which knows the depths of his being (1 Cor. 2:11); spirit is that sentient capacity of man that undergoes experience and relates it to all of man's existence (Rom. 7:6; 1 Cor. 2:12). Spirit is the opposite of flesh. It is the capacity of man to cooperate with the Spirit of God and order all of life toward the purpose of God (Rom. 8:1,4; 1 Cor. 6:20;

[14] Cf. C. Ryder Smith, *The Bible Doctrine of Man* (London: Epworth, 1949).

Gal. 5:16–17).

Man is a soul, a total being, a self. Soul may sometimes be a synonym for spirit and body (1 Thess. 5:23). Soul is the basic term for a man's self, all of a man, what man is (Rom. 12:1). Man in his present existence is sinful and in need of God.

Sin is described in many ways. It is missing the mark (*hamartia*); it is moral evil (*poneras*); it is unrighteousness (*adikos*); it is lawlessness (*anomos*); it is darkness (*skotos*). Sin is more than sins. It is the larger genus of which the various species or specific sins are born. Generic sin is characterized by lust or desire (*epithumeia*) and brings both death (James 1:15; Rom. 6:23) and separation from God (1 John 5:18). Sin produces its own fruit (Gal. 5:19); is a law working within a man (Rom. 8:2); and places man in bondage (Rom. 6:17).

Man as sinner needs a redeemer from sin. The New Testament asserts that sin is ingredient to the coming of Christ. Jesus' very name relates to deliverance from man's sin (Matt. 1:21). His blood cleanses from sin (1 John 1:7). He bears the sins of the world (John 1:29; Heb. 9:28).

The New Testament witness is unanimous that man is less than he was intended to be. Man, left to his own resources, has no hope of being really different from what he is. However, the essence of the New Testament message is that man may be different from what he now is and may, in Christ, become ultimately what he ought to be.

2. *Man as Redeemed*

Election and Response. The Christian life is a life undergoing experience and relating every experience to God through Christ. The possibility of the Christian life lies in God and his provision for man in Christ (2 Cor. 5:19). Men come to God because they are chosen to do so (1 Peter 2:4,9; Eph. 1:4). They are drawn to Christ by the proclamation of the gospel and the drawing of the Holy Spirit (Acts 2:14–47; Rom. 8:15; Gal. 4:6; Rev. 22:17).

Man's response to Christ through the Spirit is one of faith and repentance. Repentance is the divine requirement announced in the ministry of Jesus (Matt. 4:17; Luke 13:1–5). The injunction to repent framed the preaching of the early church (Acts 2:38; 3:19; 17:30). Genuine repentance is possible only because of faith.

Faith is the capacity God gives men when confronted with Christ to believe on him. Faith involves the total response of a man. It is intellectual, emotional, and volitional. Without faith it is impossible to come to God (Heb. 11:6). Without faith in Christ one is condemned because of his unbelief (John 3:36). This condemnation is impressed on the world by the Spirit of God, who convicts of sin on the basis of unbelief (John 16:8–9). In the gospel one finds the possibility of faith, and to live by faith is to live with God (Rom. 1:17). Man's salvation lies in faith and his possibility for faith lies in God (Eph. 2:8–9).

Man confronted by Jesus Christ is responsible for decision. During Jesus' earthly life a rich young ruler decided against Christ and "went away sorrowing" (Matt. 19:22). The Spirit of God convicts men of the sin of unbelief. It is failure to believe on Christ which condemns man (John 3:36; 16:9). The basis for belief and ability to believe are God's gifts to man. The decision and exercise of belief are man's obligations.

Expressions for the Christian Life. Many expressions are used in the New Testament to indicate what it means to be Christian. Most of the expressions are metaphors drawn from the diversities of life's experiences. Metaphors drawn from the family relationship stress that Christians are sons of God by adoption (Gal. 4:6). They are born anew (John 3:3–7); regenerated (Titus 3:5); become new creatures (2 Cor. 5:17); are heirs in the kingdom of God (Rom. 8:17). From the law court comes the analogy of justification or being pronounced right and thereby freed (Rom. 4:25; 3:24,28; 8:30). From the arena of personal relationships the term reconciliation is used to describe that cessation of estrangement between persons (Rom. 5:10 f.; Eph. 2:16).

The Christian, belonging to Christ, is set apart for the purpose of God, which relation is emphasized by a major group of terms for the Christian life: saint, holy, sanctify, sanctification. The vital relationship of husband to wife (Eph. 5:21–33) and of vine and branches (John 15:1–5) illustrate the status of Christians who are in Christ. These expressions connote an active, vital relationship. There is a vitality and joy about the relation of God's people to their Lord. This joy is well captured in the term redemption, which expresses release from the bondage of sin and the fetters of human disability (Rom. 3:24; 1 Cor. 1:30; Col. 1:14). The freedom of forgiveness is one of the chiefest blessings of the Christian life (Rom. 4:7–16).

VI. The Task of the Christian Community Is to Bear Witness to the Word.

This task carried forward by Christians results in mission, evangelistic concern, and ethical living on the part of the people of God.

1. Mission

The people of God are called in Christ to serve God. The primary service of the people of God is bearing witness to what he has done in the world. When Jesus was on earth he commissioned his followers to announce the kingdom of God by performing messianic signs. The proclamation of God's kingdom was in act as well as word (Matt. 10:1–11; Luke 10:1–16). The command of the risen Christ was to preach the gospel and minister to the needy (Matt. 28:19–20; John 20:21). The first Christians proclaimed the message (kerygma) about Jesus after they were empowered by the Spirit (Acts 2—5; 10). Christ indicated it was a sign of the kingdom that the gospel was preached by word and deed to the poor (Matt. 11:5). Paul stressed that he was sent to proclaim the message of Christ (1 Cor. 1:17); and this was his major effort (1 Cor. 1:23).

The message (preaching) of the gospel is God's chosen instrument to bear witness to the salvation (1 Cor. 1:21). The injunction to Timothy is to preach the word (2 Tim. 4:2). Preaching is more than saying words. It often refers to the vital content of the proclamation, the message not the means (2 Tim. 4:17; Titus 1:3; 1 Cor. 1:18). Other terms such as "show" and "proclaim" reinforce the relationship between telling the gospel and bearing witness to it in deeds and from a sense of compassion. In brief, preaching-mission, evangelism, and ethics are vitally related in the New Testament.

2. Evangelism

The Greek word for preaching provides the stem for our English words evangel, evangelize, evangelist, and evangelism. Evangelism in the New Testament is not a method but a calling. Some are called to be evangelists (Acts 21:8; Eph. 4:11; 2 Tim. 4:5). In the broad sense, all of Christ's followers participate in the calling to share the good news of Christ (1 Peter 2:9). Evangelism is a way of life characterized by compassion (Rom. 9:1–3; Mark 8:2; Luke 7:13); and spelled out by showing faith in Christ, the word and way of God (Acts 16:17).

The example of concern which characterizes evangelism is God himself. The parables of the lost coin, the lost sheep, and the lost boy (Luke 15) display the intensity of God's concern. The concern of God for man and his salvation is embodied in Jesus Christ who came to seek and to save the lost (Luke 19:10). Such compassion is contagious. It is found in Paul and his zeal for Israel (Rom. 9:3). It should characterize all the people of God.

3. Life

The community of faith is characterized by a style of life. Christians are so called because they are like Christ (Acts 11:26). They live out their professions in bodies dedicated to God (Rom. 12:1). They are under the mandate of love (John 13:34). Indeed, love is the identifying and noteworthy mark of the New Testament community (1 John 3:14). The life that does not produce Christian results is not Christian (Matt. 7:16). True faith produces right living. The profession of a Christian and the expressions of his life must be together (James 2:14–20). Specific rules change according to circumstance and situation (1 Cor. 8:1–9). General guides of conduct provide the norms for Christian living (Phil. 2:5; 1 Cor. 10:31; John 13:34; James 1:8). The Christian life is stable because it is rooted in soil larger than selfish purpose (Eph. 3:17 ff.). The Christian life is flexible and progressive because its goals are greater than any immediate situation (Phil. 3:12–14). Christian life is an abundant life now (John 10:10) and life with a face to the future (1 Peter 1:3; 1 John 3:3; 1 Cor. 15:19).

VII. God Has the Last Word with All of His Creation.

The Word of God in the flesh (Jesus Christ) is the first and last expression of God's way for man. He is Alpha and Omega (Rev. 1:11). There is an appropriate roundness to God's way with his creation. He begins his redemptive expressions in the garden of Eden (Gen. 2:8; 3:15) and concludes them in the garden of paradise (Rev. 22:1–5). Between these gardens of God lie the torturous paths of history and the revelation of God's redemptive plan for man. The biblical revelation is characterized by openness and an eye to the future (cf. J. Moltmann, *Theology of Hope*). The Old Testament looks beyond itself to the promise of the Messiah. The New Testament announces the arrival of the Messiah and anticipates his final coming (Rev. 1:7–8).

Christ as the fulfiller of God's purpose overcomes the evil one. In the New Testament the threat of evil is more pronounced than in the Old. Evil is projected on both a personal and cosmic scale. Satan (the adversary) tempts even the Messiah himself (Matt. 4:1–11; Mark 1:12–13; Luke 4:1–13). The evil one is a master of subterfuge appearing as an angel of light (2 Cor. 11:14). As prince of this world he exerts influence and power. But his doom is sure in Christ's conquering death (John 12:31; 14:30; 16:11).

One consistent affirmation in New Testament thought is that the adversary cannot ultimately harm man (1 John 5:18). For the dragon, the primeval serpent symbolizing opposition to God, will ultimately be overcome and cast into the lake of fire (Rev. 20:2,3,10). Christ's coming was to overcome the works of the devil (1 John 3:8). The defeat of the demonic has begun with the death of Christ, and it continues in the victory of the Christian life (John 16:11; 1 John 4:4). It will be fully accomplished at the last day (Rev. 20:10). The Christian will be cautious of the adversary and his strength (1 Peter 5:8). But one should fear God alone (Matt. 10:28).

1. Man's Ultimate Destiny

The fear of God is born of the awareness of judgment. The crisis (appropriately the Greek word for judgment) of the world is in God's hand. Christ is the instrument of judgment. The divisions between the good and bad, believers and unbelievers, heaven and hell are fixed (Matt. 24—25; Mark 13; Luke 16:19–31). But the decision of judgment is God's alone. Men must not judge (Rom. 2:1; Luke 6:37; 1 Peter 1:17).

Judgment means decision and a separation of bad and good. The destiny of men lies in God's hand is revealed in Christ. Those who persist in following the demonic are alienated and separated from God forever. Hell is their abode. The New Testament speaks about hell in terms borrowed from the Old Testament and intertestamental literature. Gehenna, or the valley of Hinnom, was associated with human sacrifice and the worship of Moloch. Hell reminds the church of the divisiveness and deadly outcome of sin and of the seriousness of the mission to proclaim the way of redemption from sin. All this is emphasized by the vivid description of hell: in terms of fire (Matt. 5:22), torment (Mark 9:43–47), and darkness (Matt. 22:13). Hell is separation from the presence of God in fellowship (Matt. 25:41) but is an awareness of his presence in judgment (Rev. 6:16).

The people of God are sojourners and pilgrims (Heb. 11:10,16; 1 Peter 2:11). They are in the world but not of it (John 17:9–18). They await the end of this age and the ultimate coming of Christ (Acts 1:11; Rev. 1:7). Their destiny is in heaven; their judgment is to enter into perfect fellowship wih Christ (Matt. 25:31–40).

Heaven is more than a geographical reference as to what is above the earth. It is the place of God. He is seated on his throne there (Rev. 4:2). It was into heaven that Jesus ascended, and from heaven he shall return (Acts 1:10–11). The promise to the Christian is that he shall ultimately be where Christ is (John 14). Heaven is the kingdom prepared from eternity for those who minister in the name of Christ (Matt. 25:34 f.). Heaven is like a great and perfect city. Earth's richest treasures describe it inadequately (Rev. 21). Man's imagination boggles at what God has promised for those who love him (1 Cor. 2:9–10).

2. *Cosmic Redemption*

God's last word is spoken in Christ who overcomes death, the last enemy, and delivers the kingdom up to God (1 Cor. 15:24–25). God brings all things to their intended completion in Christ (Eph. 1:10). The entire created order is the concern of God. Man is the foremost object of God's redemptive concern, but he is not the sum of God's concern (John 3:16). The created order also groans under a burden of being estranged from God. Deliverance is promised in the last day for all that God has made (Rom. 8:22–23). Only rebellious men and the demonic shall fail to share the completeness wrought in the redemption of Christ (Matt. 25:41–46; Rev. 20:10). The New Testament is permeated with an ultimate hope. Men of faith find their peace in worshiping God who made and redeems the world. His ways are past finding out (Rom. 11:33). Praises are sung unto him and unto the Lamb for ever and ever (Rev. 5:13).

Conclusion

The above paragraphs have attempted to perform the first task of New Testament theology. This task is to state descriptively what the New Testament said. It follows that the first focus of biblical theology is on what the Bible meant.

The second, and equally important, task of New Testament theology is to say what these descriptive materials mean today. Christians in every age must relate the essence of biblical faith to the times in which they live. This second task involves translation and interpretation (cf. appropriate articles in Volume 1), which include more than linguistic skills or putting words from one language into another. The mind-set of the biblical authors must become as familiar as a second and much used language is to a bilingual person. The first language of every person is the century and setting in which he lives. Spanning the gap of then and now is thus the second major task of biblical theology. Seeking the meaning of the New Testament for the time in which we live is the great challenge and open end of biblical theology.

For Further Reading

BULTMANN, RUDOLPH. *Theology of the New Testament.* 2 Vols. Translated by Kendrick Grobel. London: S.C.M. Press, 1952.

CONNER, W. T. *The Faith of the New Testament.* Nashville: Broadman Press, 1951.

GRANT, ROBERT. *Historical Introduction to the New Testament.* New York: Harper & Row, 1963.

Interpreter's Dictionary of the Bible. Vol 1. Articles on biblical theology. New York: Abingdon Press, 1962.

RICHARDSON, ALAN. *An Introduction to the Theology of the New Testament.* New York: Harper & Bros., 1958.

———. *A Theological Wordbook of the Bible.* New York: The Macmillan Co., 1950.

STAGG, FRANK. *New Testament Theology.* Nashville: Broadman Press, 1962.

Contemporary Approaches in New Testament Study

Ray Summers

Changing patterns of thought and of life demand changing approaches to the quest for ultimate truth. As Christians, we have committed ourselves to the belief that ultimate truth is to be found in, and in relationship to, Jesus of Nazareth as the Christ of God. We find, therefore, that our quest leads us to new approaches in the study of the New Testament—the book which expresses the faith and experience of those who first knew Jesus and the interpretation of that faith and experience.

Twentieth-century Christians agree with first-century Christians in confessing that "God was in Christ reconciling the world to himself" (2 Cor. 5:19). But we do not share the same kind of understanding, thought, language, and the many other elements of socioreligious life. We seek approaches in study which will make possible our better understanding of the New Testament and our applying it to our complex life.

I. The Intent of Biblical Language

The foremost task of the one who studies the New Testament is to determine the writer's intention. Interpretation has been defined as the effort of one mind to follow the thought processes of another mind through the medium of language. The main goal to be reached is the intention, the thought, which is being expressed through that medium. The only adequate goal is the discovery of the whole thought process and meaning of the writer—the entire state of consciousness which is expressing itself through this language. It follows, then, that the printed page is not the final objective in interpretation. The final objective is the meaning of that printed page to the writer, to the original reader, to subsequent readers in every age.

II. Historicocritical Interpretation

Basic to all competent contemporary approaches in New Testament study is the historicocritical method. Contemporary theological concern must be controlled by this method. It is the only method which keeps the exegete in continuous dialogue with the text he seeks to understand. To turn from this is to neglect the writer's theological intent. To qualify this leaves the interpreter in peril of being unconsciously influenced by his own background and theological milieu to the extent that he reads meaning *into* rather than *out of* the Scriptures.

Historicocritical interpretation is the determining of the meaning of a passage of Scripture in light of all the evidence provided by the phenomena of the original text and setting of the passage. The word critical is a transliteration of the Greek adjective *kritikos* from the verb *krino,* meaning to judge in the light of the evidence. The adjective pertains to tracing out and passing judgment on a matter; hence, to decide in the light of all the available evidence.

Such interpretation begins in an attempt to ascertain all the circumstances which in any way affect the meaning of a unit of Scripture. This includes a careful investigation of the details of the original text: lexical, grammatical, syntactical, comparative, and rhetorical. All this alone could be very dead apart from the life situation of the passage. Who is the speaker or writer? What is the nature of his religious experience? To whom does he address himself? What is the particular need to which he speaks? The Scriptures were addressed to men of deep spiritual needs and hungers. Under the Spirit's guidance, the biblical writer used the method and materials most effective for securing the interest and understanding of his readers. To fail to understand the religious experience, mental traits, and varied needs of both writer and readers is to be handicapped greatly in studying the message.

Historicocritical interpretation begins with the Scriptures, determines the intent of the Scriptures in the light of all available evidence, and moves forward to a statement of that intent in the form of teachings or doctrines. While it is the only valid method of study, it does not guarantee that every interpreter will come through with the same interpretation. Always there is the subjective element of value judgment. Many matters enter into the way one weighs evidences and forms conclusions. The sincere interpreter will strive for an objectivity which is free of prejudice; the honest interpreter will confess some degree of failure, whether in positive or negative results.

By this approach comes understanding, But only by reverent commitment of faith comes acceptance of this as indeed God's Word to man. Learning the meaning may be a group process; accepting remains an individual matter. And the sincere application of that which is learned and accepted is the ultimate goal of New Testament study. Only this delivers the student from sterility to fruitfulness.

Special attention is called to the fact that the subject of this article, "Contemporary Approaches in New Testament Study," suggests self-imposed limitations. By far the greatest thrust in contemporary approaches in New Testament study has related to Gospel study and, in the main, to the Synoptic Gospels. The Gospel of John shares with the Synoptics in the discipline of form criticism, but it is a limited sharing. The contemporary approach to John has been largely an examination of the theological intent. Nothing distinctive enough to be considered as contemporary approach has appeared in the study of the Johannine Epistles and the Revelation.

Strictly defined, "contemporary approaches" offer little in the area of Pauline study. Notable commentaries and theological works have been produced, but basically they follow the lines of earlier studies in the pattern of historicocritical interpretation, exegesis, and theological result.

III. Form Criticism

It is doubtful that any contemporary approach to New Testament study has had wider use than this instrument of literary criticism. The term is the commonly used translation of the German *Formgeschichte,* meaning literally "form history." It is a study of the history of how the materials of the Gospels came to be preserved and set in the form in which they appear in the written gospel. The main lines of the method were developed in Germany through the efforts of M. Dibelius (*From Tradition to Gospel*), R. Bultmann (*Jesus and the Word*), and K. L. Schmidt (*Die Rahmen der Geschichte Jesu*). To his first volume, Dibelius added *The Message of Jesus* as an extension of his views. Numerous works have been added by Bultmann and a multitude of other scholars—European, British, and American.

It is not possible to present the aims and methods of form criticism in one statement which will apply equally well to all scholars who employ it. Basically, the method of form criticism is twofold. First, by reconstruction and analysis, it seeks to explain the origin of the oral accounts of the words and works of Jesus by penetrating into the period before the materials were put in written form. Second, it seeks to make clear the intention and real interest of the earliest tradition about Jesus. By tradition is meant the oral account behind the written account. Form criticism wants to show why the first churches recounted stories about Jesus, why they collected these stories, and why they wrote them as "gospels."

Obviously, then, one important fact about form criticism is that it focuses attention on the earliest period of transmission of gospel materials, the first three decades after the death and resurrection of Jesus. This is a difficult period of study. No written records from the period are extant except, perhaps, the hypothetical *Logia* or *Quelle* (Q) source, isolated by source criticism a generation earlier than form criticism as a source possessed by Matthew and Luke but not by Mark.

Another feature of this method is the stress it places on the stage of oral tradition. It uses the written Gospels, recognizes written sources behind them, and capitalizes on the inestimable value of its predecessor, source criticism. But its main concern is not with written sources. Its interest is in the word-of-mouth handling of the deeds and sayings of Jesus. According to the form critic, it was by constant repetition during these years of oral use that the account received the "form" which it possesses in the written account.

Basic to the method is the view that the gospel materials were first circulated orally in small, independent units of teachings or actions of Jesus. For example, remove the eleven "straightways" which tie together the first chapter of Mark. A closely knit narrative disappears, and there remain multiple independent stories which could have been used separately, as needed, in varying situations. These units are called pericopes and may be classified in numerous categories, including: miracle stories, gnomic sayings, longer teaching sayings or paradigms, epic stories about some person, didactic dialogues, and exhortations.

Another trait of the form critical approach is the search for the background of the resulting written account in the life of the early church, the *Sitz im Leben* or "setting in life." The social situation in which the story or teaching under consideration was preserved must be envisioned. This offers a solution to the question as to why the particular material in our Gospels was preserved, used, and ultimately put in written form. Depending on the tricky question of the "Passovers" in the Gospel of John, the public ministry of Jesus is variously estimated as a bit less than one year, as a bit over two years, or as about three-and-one-half years. In either circumstance it is obvious that Jesus did and said much more than that which is represented in the fifty or fifty-one separate days which may be isolated in the Gospels.

Was it mere historical or biographical interest that governed the choice of what was preserved? The choice seems rather to have been determined by the usage and need of the early church. Four aspects of this need are identified.

One, the Christians preserved sayings and incidents which would give them guidance in matters of belief and conduct. What should be their attitude about the Law, forgiveness, tax payment, sabbath observance, and many social questions? What the oral account of Jesus' life and work offered by way of solution to these problems, the Christians kept, used, and eventually wrote.

Two, inquirers and converts had to have instruction as to the meaning of their faith and the character of their Lord. Applicable deeds and sayings of Jesus were treasured and used.

Three, at an early date the Christians found themselves not at home in Temple and synagogue. As they moved out, they established their own worship services. Retaining much from their synagogue cradle, they also added much of their own in worship forms. What they could gather from the practices and teachings of Jesus, they used. This is probably the motivating factor, for example, which led to the preservation of so much from Jesus on prayer, giving, and related elements of worship.

Four, there was controversy with the enemies of their faith. From the very first the Christians found themselves in the position where both apologetic and polemic were necessary. They had to face objection, criticism, and slander. Appeal to what Jesus had said and done gave them their best material. This they used, preserved and wrote down. Thus the materials which best served their needs of guidance, instruction, worship, and controversy were preserved.

The *form* of the material was affected by the practical concern; the oral account was shaped to serve the immediate end. It is the resulting product which appears in the written form.

A word of caution is in order. Some form critics hold that many of the stories and sayings attributed to Jesus were actually the creation of the early church, creations to meet their needs. It is at this point that the danger of extreme subjectivism comes into an otherwise helpful method of study. Avoiding this extreme subjectivism, other scholars who use the method (Manson, V. Taylor) insist that we travel too far and too fast if we say that the community created these stories to meet their needs. While granting the hand of the church in shaping the ultimate form of the written account, we must search not alone for the situation in the life of the early church but also for the situation in the life of Jesus himself.

To study the kerygma (the "thing preached") of the early church is to examine the early Christian conviction about Jesus. One thus discovers a single consistent story about Jesus, and it presents an important by-product of form criticism; i.e., as far back in oral account as one can trace Jesus (the preaching of the early church), he is a *supernatural* Jesus. It was the claim of the early church that in Jesus, God revealed himself in saving action. If God has revealed himself in history, it is in history that we must find him. If God did indeed speak redemptively through the life, death, and resurrection of Jesus it is vitally important to know as accurately as possible what sort of life, death, and resurrection constitute that medium. There is no escape from this inquiry, and there is no reason to be despondent about its prospect. Properly used, form criticism is a tool toward that goal.

IV. *Demythologizing*

Amos N. Wilder in his essay "New Testament Hermeneutic Today" (pp. 38–52 of *Current Issues in New Testament Interpretation*) notes that R. Bultmann's whole lifework testifies that he does not intend to substitute faith or piety for reason. Nowhere is this more evident than in his approach to New Testament study through demythologizing the language of the Gospels. The word "demythologizing" was first introduced by Bultmann in 1941 in an essay on the New Testament and mythology. Subsequently, practically everything written on the subject has been in dialogue—both support and denial—with his proposal that the New Testament be demythologized.

Bultmann's approach holds that the New Testament bears witness to the eschatological act of God in the history of Jesus of Nazareth. His view, however, is that this act is proclaimed in the New Testament in terms now obsolete, terms derived from Jewish apocalyptic and Greek Gnostic mythologies. He contends that an obsolete view of the world is presupposed in the New Testament kerygma: a three-storied universe (heaven, earth, hell) and the intrusion of spirits and demons from other spheres into the earth and into the affairs of men. The Son of man mythology of Jewish apocalyptic writing and the Gnostic redeemer-mythology furnish the terms used in the New Testament to describe and interpret the Christ event. These terms, Bultmann holds, are neither understandable nor acceptable to twentieth-century scientific man, so the New Testament account must be purged of the erroneous ideas suggested by this terminology. Nineteenth-century liberal scholars (such as F. C. Baur and D. F. Strauss) looked upon this language as mythological and solved the problem by eliminating the kerygma itself. Bultmann insists on retaining the kerygma but not the ideas suggested by the language.

Bultmann accepts what he understands to be the intended message of the New Testament, i.e., that the Christ event is God's act in which he has made available for man the gift of new life. Bultmann also wants modern scientifically oriented man to accept this. This goal he believes can be reached by interpreting the mythology. He states that the real purpose of mythological language is not to present an objective picture of the world as it really is but rather to express man's understanding of himself in the world in which he lives. It is better to interpret mythological language in terms of the understanding of human life which this language contains and to express that understanding of life in nonmythological terms. For example, in the Gospel story of Jesus' stilling the storm, the important matter would not be whether or not Jesus in the first century actually spoke to the winds and they obeyed his order to stop blowing. The important matter is Jesus' ability to calm the storms of life which man faces in his existential encounter in his social setting in whatever age.

To avoid the errors of earlier interpreters, who in eliminating the mythology had eliminated the proclamation of the eschatological act of God in Christ, Bultmann argues that any correct interpretation of the New Testament must be an existential one—one which confronts the interpreter with Christ in demand for response. Two examples may illustrate: the cross and the resurrection. The cross must be interpreted as an event which takes place within our own existence rather than outside of us. For Bultmann the important matter is not the preexistent, incarnate, sinless Son of God, offering his blood as an atoning sacrifice and thus overcoming demonic powers. Rather, the important thing is a man's own confrontation with evil and his death to it by identification with Christ. This Bultmann supports by Pauline references such as Romans 6:3 ff.; Galatians 5:24; 6:14; Philippians 3:10.

The resurrection must be interpreted not in terms of Jesus' body returning to life and experiencing transformation so as to transcend death. The important matter is what happened in the life of the disciples as they came to believe that even in his death the powers of evil had not overcome Jesus; only in this sense can he be spoken of as having "risen." Bultmann holds that in reality both cross and resurrection represent the same thing—faith in the saving significance of God's eschatological act in Jesus. To proclaim either cross or resurrection is to proclaim this. It is his view that this approach does better justice to the real meaning of the New Testament than that which accepts the language just as it stands.

Pressed to its logical conclusion this approach leads to historical skepticism. It is consideration of this which has led some students of Bultmann to observe that to follow Bultmann's view to its end is to find that one has only a mythical lord.

V. *The New Quest for the Historical Jesus*

Since Bultmann's demythologizing of the Gospels, when pressed to its extreme conclusion, results in a divorce from history in favor of the existential encounter, it was inevitable that a corrective methodology would arise. Significantly, this corrective arose through the effort of some of Bultmann's best-known students and out of their conviction that their teacher went too far. It is their view that it *is* important to know something of the "historical Jesus" who is behind the "Christ of faith" proclaimed in the kerygma and that it *is* possible to have such knowledge. This knowledge they find available through the teachings and actions of Jesus himself.

With varying emphases and working principles and with varying degrees of agreement, the new quest includes among its many advocates such names as Bornkamm, Conzelmann, Dinkler, Ebeling, Fuchs, Käsemann, and Robinson. Their work is an attempt to correct Bultmann and to make clearer the transition from the Jesus of history (the proclaimer) to the Christ of faith (the proclaimed) and to do so by securing the best possible knowledge of the former as he stands behind the latter. The end product will be that the two are one, since their method does not radically sever Jesus himself from the apostles' message about Jesus; they preached Jesus, not *about* Jesus. This approach emphasizes the concrete historical Jesus of apostolic faith.

The rather widespread twentieth-century lack of interest in the historical Jesus has been due to two major factors: one, the failure of the nineteenth-century quest of the historical Jesus; two, emphases such as that of K. Barth, whose dialectical theology insists on the importance of the "leap of faith"—the kind of faith which would not be faith if it required the absolute of historical verification.

The nineteenth-century quest, summarized in A. Schweitzer's monumental *The Quest of the Historical Jesus,* was doomed to failure from the beginning because of its erroneous approach to the Gospels themselves. It followed the standard view of the day that the Gospels were biographical portraits of Jesus, so an understanding of them should give the full record of Jesus—what he did and said. The historicocritical method proved that this was an erroneous view. It proved that even Mark—to say nothing of Matthew, Luke, and John—was kerygmatic in nature. It was not a biography of Jesus; it was a proclamation of Jesus. So were the others. A biography requires more than a knowledge of fifty days of one's life.

The theological emphasis of Barth was inadequate in this area. Even Bultmann's approach left open the way for a "new quest." It insisted that the kerygma of the apostles was really based on Jesus of Nazareth as a concrete figure in history, however slight the actual historical information about him in Bultmann's view.

This new quest originated in 1953, when E. Käsemann, appearing before a group of his Bultmannian fellow students, read an essay entitled "The Problem of the Historical Jesus." He asserted that we *can* know more and we *must* know more about the historical Jesus than Bultmann accepts. By taking this stand, Käsemann started one of the most vigorous movements in mid-twentieth-century New Testament study. He expressed firm belief that substantial information about Jesus is available and by careful scholarship can be isolated from the total text of the New Testament.

The most fruitful of American scholars engaged in the movement is James M. Robinson. Basic to his approach is the incentive of the relevance of history for faith. The importance of this in the New Testament is observable in the identification of the Jesus of humiliation (the cross) with the Christ of exaltation (the resurrection) in the proclamation of the church. In other words, for those who first proclaimed the Christ of faith, this Christ could not be separated from the Jesus of history. The message they proclaimed was that of good news of God's eschatological work of redemption in history. They were definitely interested in a Jesus who was a man in history, and they confessed him "born of woman, born under the law" (Gal. 4:4). He was the Son of God and through him men might become sons of God.

By what procedure do these scholars come to the Jesus of history? The procedure is twofold. First, they sift all the Synoptic sayings and events attributed to Jesus in order to sift out all those they regard as being created by the proclaiming church rather than by Jesus. This leaves only the sayings and events they, by their standards of judgment, accept as authentically those of Jesus. Second, with this body of accepted sayings and events, they work to grasp his own self-understanding of his role in the redemptive purpose of the God of Israel.

By what criteria do these scholars isolate what they accept as authentic? First, materials having parallels in contemporary Judaism or rabbinic literature are rejected. Second, all materials relating to the "post-Easter" situation in, or understanding of, the church are rejected, even though they appear as sayings of Jesus. Third, all materials possessing the "flavor" of kerygma are rejected as creations of the proclaiming church. This leaves two types of knowledge about the historical Jesus: what may be known by his own authentic historical life and sayings; what may be known through the reflective and creative preaching of the church.

Opponents of the approach are alert to point out basic weaknesses in the criteria.

For example, consider them in the order mentioned. First, Jesus was a man of the Judaism of his day. His teaching was rabbinical. Subsequently it will be observed that the parables, generally recognized as the very nearest to the elusive ipsissima verba of Jesus, are solidly rabbinic. It does not appear legitimate to reject them. Second, the "post-Easter" church identified the exalted Christ with the humiliated Jesus. It is more solid discipline to look for the "color" or "framing" imparted to the post-resurrection events as the church used them in their needs of proclamation and worship than to reject them totally as unauthentic. Third, if the churches understood the basic kerygma to be identified with the Jesus of history, their proclamation would necessarily involve the use of his sayings and actions—even though they imparted to these sayings a kerygmatic tone more applicable to their situation than to his.

It is in the area of these criteria that the scholars of this group show some disagreement. All in the group, however, hold to the same basic goal: *discovering whether or not there is an identifiable continuity between the Jesus of history and the proclamation by the church of the exalted Christ of faith.* Käsemann seeks evidence through the message Jesus preached—what are the similarities and differences in comparison to the message proclaimed by the church regarding the Christ of faith? Fuchs emphasizes the action of Jesus as more revelatory of identity or continuity, because he understands the action as foundation for the message. Even the most basic part of Jesus' message, the parables, is really a reflection of his action as redemptive in nature. The two views are complementary. In both the action and teaching of Jesus there is implicit an understanding of Jesus in his redemptive significance. This becomes explicit in the proclamation of the post-Easter church.

Conzelmann, in pursuit of the same goal as Fuchs and Käsemann, begins with those parables which are so clearly the product of Jesus that one does not become diverted by debate over genuineness of the text. He seeks for a characteristic inner unity in the teachings rather than a linking theme. He sees great importance in those teachings calling for decisive action *now*. He finds a Christology embedded in the eschatology and ethics in Jesus' teachings.

Bornkamm's *Jesus of Nazareth* was a first and major product of this movement. As he understands the problem, the Gospels both allow and demand search for the historical Jesus. The church proclaims Jesus as Lord after his resurrection, but the Jesus proclaimed is the one known as a man in history before the resurrection. Without this, the proclamation would be that of a myth with no anchor in history. Both Jesus' acts and his teachings are reflected in the proclamation of the church and underline the continuity of the Jesus of history and the Christ of faith.

If there is one central idea which serves as the center of the teaching of the historical Jesus and the proclamation of the early church, it must be the concept of the kingdom of God. Jesus understood that in his presence in the world the anticipated kingdom of God had broken into history. His work in casting out demons indicated the presence of the kingdom of God triumphing over the kingdom of evil. This was the understanding of the early church, even though it anticipated a future consummation of that kingdom. In Jesus' presence and the rule of God among men established by Jesus' presence, the old evil age and the future righteous age have overlapped. His once-for-all sacrifice of himself did indeed mark the "coming together of the ends of the two ages" (Heb. 9:26, author's translation).

How is the new quest for the historical Jesus to be evaluated? Both negative and positive evaluations are available. Forgetting the adverse views on details and concentrating on the unity of goal of the scholars involved, one may see positive values. J. B. Cobb does so. It is of value that the study puts Jesus solidly in the general sphere of "Christian faith" rather than that of Judaism, as Bultmann, Klausner, and others have insisted. Further, the message of Jesus is also effective as kerygma in that it conveys to man the redemptive grace of God, just as the kerygma of the early church did. From a weighing of all the involvements, one concludes that the purpose of the kerygma was to present the self-understanding of Jesus, and that was a matter definitely grounded in history.

On the other hand, an able scholar such as R. E. Brown finds the total result to be more negative, due to the methodology of the men making the quest. He sees the exegesis as too existential and standing in need of more objective or nonexistential exegesis after the order of O. Cullmann, J. Jeremias, and V. Taylor. He rejects the validity of eliminating from Jesus' teachings any which are kerygmatic or Jewish in tone; his rejection is for the same reasons voiced above in dealing with the "criteria" used. Refreshingly, he criticizes the movement for not taking seriously the Gospel of John, which affords positive and fruitful insight into the nature of the message of the historical Jesus. This omission of large bodies of Jesus' teaching as authentic is one of the handicaps under which these men work, as it is one of the areas of strength for those of the next "approach" to be evaluated.

VI. *Salvation-History*

Heilsgeschichte translates literally into English "salvation-history." That is the title of E. C. Rust's monograph on the subject. O. Cullmann's German title is *Heils als Geschichte*, "salvation as history." But he prefers the English rendering "salvation in history," and this is the title in the English publication. The term was first used by Bengel (1687–1752) in his affirmation that one can understand the historical books of the Bible only when he sees the divine purpose of redemption brought to reality in them. The historical events are not simply chronological accounting, but rather they follow a teleological principle: "God's redemptive purpose in history."

In relatively modern approach to New Testament study, this has become the organizing idea in the work of scholars in Europe, England, and America, such as: Cullmann, Rust, G. Beasley-Murray, R. H. Fuller, W. G. Kümmel, P. Althaus, E. Stauffer, A. M. Hunter, and O. Piper. Old Testament scholars of similar approach are F. Cross, W. Eichrodt, M. Noth, G. von Rad, and G. E. Wright.

The term salvation-history designates a principle of biblical interpretation and a theological theme as an organizer for understanding the full sweep of the Jewish-Christian Scriptures. It asserts that in history God has made a progressive revelation of his nature as redemptive. The biblical understanding of history is that the God of creation has involved himself in the affairs of his creation and that in a specific chain of events in earthly, human affairs, God has prepared salvation for his creation. This salvation is redemption from the totality of sin. The very core of the Scriptures is the history of this step-by-step process of salvation. Thus, as interpretive principle, this is an approach to the Scriptures from the viewpoint of how they view themselves. The Bible presents the successive unfolding of steps in the divine plan for man's salvation from sin as a part of history itself.

God is at work in historical events. Genesis 1–11 shows man's involvement in sin so that he needs salvation. The history of God's provision of this salvation begins in Genesis 12 with God's call of Abraham, and it continues in his raising up Abraham's descendants to the status of a people through the Exodus and subsequent events for God's redemptive purpose. Through this people God would bring his Redeemer-Saviour into the world and establish his kingdom, his spiritual rule among men.

In Jesus of Nazareth this redemptive purpose is brought to its realization. His presence in the world inaugurated the kingdom of God among men. By the once-for-all sacrifice of himself he brought to glorious climax the long, full sweep of the mighty redemptive acts of God in history.

The Synoptic Gospels report that as life ebbed away from Jesus on the cross he "uttered a shrieking cry" and yielded up his spirit to the Father. The mystic John reports that that cry was one word in Greek, *tetelestai.* In English this is rendered, "It is finished" (John 19:30). The Latin versions rendered it *consummatum est;* i.e., "It is brought to a consummation." All that God, in the call of Abraham, set in motion to re-create his lost creation was brought to a glorious reality in the historic event of the incarnation, crucifixion, and resurrection of Jesus, God's Redeemer.

In Romans 8:21–23, Paul viewed this as having such long reach that the total effect of sin, even in the material cosmos, would be effaced in relation to the anticipated release of man from sin in the resurrection. In Ephesians and Colossians, Paul viewed all this salvation-history as God's orderly administration of the affairs of his household so as to bring all of them once again and forever under one "captain," Jesus Christ. As in the Old Testament the Exodus-event spoke of God's redemptive act for the old Israel, so in the New Testament the climax of the Easter-event spoke of God's redemptive act for the new Israel, his new people of redemptive purpose. It was more than just history. It was "salvation-history." This is the nature of the Bible, a revelation of God's salvation-history.

VII. Parables

A review of contemporary approaches in New Testament study would be incomplete without a recognition of the attention which has been focused on one specific part of the New Testament, the parables. Today it is generally recognized that in this very down-to-earth type of wisdom material we are at our closest point in the search for the sometimes elusive ipsissima verba of Jesus. Such is the understanding represented in such writers as Denny, Dodd, Hunter, Jeremias, Linnemann, Summers, and Via. All this work is related to older works of A. Jülicher (*Die Gleichnisreden Jesu,* 1888–89) and P. Fiebig (*Altjudische Gleichnisse und die Gleichnisse Jesu,* 1904), which freed the parables from the paralyzing allegorical interpretation which had marked their use for fifteen hundred years. Jülicher and Fiebig brought the parables out so they could be seen in their true nature and purpose and started interpreters along the road of profitable exegesis, exposition, and vital application.

Dodd limited his study almost completely to one particular type of parable, the "kingdom parables," and limited the interpretation of these by a too rigid control of his view of realized eschatology. Jeremias' monumental work, *The Parables of Jesus,* has been one of the most fruitful current studies. It is the most complete one-volume analysis of the message of Jesus which has ever been written.

The beginning point (Fiebig's major contribution) is a recognition of the background of Jesus' parables in rabbinical teaching. While this form is almost completely absent from the Old Testament (Isa. 5:1–7; Judg. 9:7–15; and 2 Sam. 12:1–7 are examples of "near" parables but not true parables in the New Testament form), it abounds in the teaching of the rabbis. In the Talmud almost every religious and ethical concept is illustrated by a parable identical in form with parables in the New Testament. The force of these parables is in the comparison or "likeness" involved, and they were specifically to clarify or illustrate truth. It follows, therefore, that whatever the solution to the difficult saying of Jesus in Mark 4:11–12, it is simply nonsense to deny that Jesus' purpose in the use of parables was to make his message clear.

The next step is a very thorough analysis of the parables from the viewpoint of the purpose of the parable evident in its place in the New Testament—both the original setting and purpose of Jesus and the subsequent setting and purpose of the individual evangelist—Matthew, Mark, or Luke. The original and later settings and purposes may not be the same. Frequently the evangelist presents a parable of Jesus in a church setting and application of his own day rather than the day of Jesus. This may reflect coloration or application of the parable in a new setting.

Indispensable to this type of parable study is the relatively new technique which has come to be labelled *Redaktionsgeschichte,* which in popular terminology, means "editorial history." This is a phase of textual criticism and is addressed to the question of the nature of the text as received by the writer (or editor) of the Gospel and as altered by him in his own interpretation of what he received. An excellent analysis of the importance of this technique and its implications for the total study and understanding of the New Testament is Harold H. Oliver's "Implications of *Redaktionsgeschichte* for the Textual Criticism of the New Testament" (*Journal of the American Academy of Religion,* Vol. XXXVI, No. 1, March, 1968). He argues for the validity of the method and its far-reaching importance for the understanding of the New Testament.

The method proceeds along the same line as form criticism in recognizing theological creativity at both the level of oral transmission and of scribal transmission. Oliver points correctly to a complication of the problem of unravelling these varied strands—the theological perspective of the scholar involved in the process. Here, as in form criticism, the process may become prey to extreme subjectivism. This calculated risk must not, however, deter scholars in the use of the valuable tool.

One fruitful example of this approach has related to the study of the parables of Jesus. Such a study indicates that these parables were calls for action, challenges to response on the part of the hearers. This relates to the relevant application of the parables where first-century parable meets twentieth-century person. In this area Via writes convincingly of the "existential-theological interpretation" of the parables. At every point of contemporary experience, man in the parables confronts the realities of his own nature, the nature of his social environment, and the nature of God. Such confrontation is a demand to *consider,* to *decide,* to *act.* When the action demanded is drastic, character-changing, motivation-directing, energizing to response in relation to man's need and God's concern—when this is true, the parables will be realizing in the twentieth century that which was their purpose in the first.

Conclusion

As previously suggested, the length limitations of this article have precluded a detailed consideration of Johannine and Pauline materials. The contemporary approach to Johannine materials has been occupied chiefly with theological concerns, definitely more typical here than in the Synoptic Gospels. While opinion varies greatly, and is largely subjective, as to distinctives in Pauline studies, the contemporary approach seems to have focused on the church as the confessing and worshiping body of Christ. The heart of both confession and worship, as suggested by Schweitzer, may be seen in two Pauline creeds:

Christ died for our sins according to the Scriptures,
. . . He was buried,
. . . He was raised on the third day according to the Scriptures,
. . . He appeared. . . .

1 Corinthians 15:3–5, NASV

He who was revealed in the flesh,
Was vindicated in the Spirit,
Beheld by angels,
Proclaimed among the nations,
Believed on in the world,
Taken up in glory.

1 Timothy 3:16, NASV

The place of the Corinthian confession in the structure of the epistle is important. Beginning at 7:1, Paul has responded to a series of questions posed to him in a letter from the Corinthian church. One of these questions related to the Christian answer to the survival of death. In answering the question, Paul begins with a capsule statement of the gospel which he had preached and the Corinthians had accepted. That capsule is this confessional hymn. Paul builds his case for the resurrection of the dead on Christian faith in the resurrection of Jesus Christ, a faith confessed in the hymn.

The parallel use of "according to the Scriptures" in the two long lines does more than point to a Jewish milieu for this confession. It anchors the "two saving events" in the total redemption-history under God. Christ died according to the Scriptures; he was raised according to the Scriptures. That the early Christians believed that Jesus' death was prophesied in the Old Testament is everywhere clear (Gospels, Acts, Epistles, Apocalypse). That his resurrection from the dead was prophesied in the Old Testament is not so widely expressed, but it is clearly expressed in Peter's use of Psalm 16:11 in his sermon at Pentecost.

In each case a prepositional phrase joins the "according to the Scriptures" to the verb: Christ died *for our sins* according to the Scriptures. He was raised *on the third day* according to the Scriptures. "For our sins" is important because it relates the death of Christ to God's work of re-creation (redemption). "On the third day" must be equally important as a part of the confession that this "re-creation" of God was completed on the *first* day of the week (the day of Christian worship by the time this letter was written), just as his work of "creation" was finished on the sixth day of the week, the day of Jewish worship. The phrase is an apologetic for the Christian day of worship when in solemn assembly Christians confess through their hymns their faith in Jesus Christ.

The essence of Christian faith in Jesus Christ was also distilled in the confessional hymn in 1 Timothy. The two hymns differ in concepts and structure, but they agree on the centrality of Jesus worshiped as the Christ. In the Timothy hymn there is no specific reference to the death of Jesus, the resurrection of Jesus, the anchor in the Scriptures, the appearances to men. Still a confessing Christian cannot read (or sing) the hymn without sensing that all these features of the Corinthian confession are in the thought pattern of the Timothy hymn.

This is an incarnation hymn. In structure it has six lines arranged in three couplets:

The *fact* of the incarnation:
He was revealed in the flesh
He was vindicated in the Spirit

The *manifestation* of the incarnation:
He was beheld by angels
He was proclaimed among the nations

The *result* of the incarnation:
He was believed in the world
He was taken up in glory.

The confession begins with the invasion of the earthly realm by the incarnate Christ; it ends with his triumphant return to heaven. Heaven triumphs over earth in God's redemptive incarnation in Christ.

These creedal confessions focus on one supremely important fact, urgently significant for twentieth-century Christians. From the very beginning of the church, there has been but one center in the faith of the New Testament. That center is Jesus Christ, by virtue of his redemptive incarnation confessed and worshiped as the Lord of earth and heaven.

For Further Reading

Bornkamm, G. *Jesus of Nazareth.* New York: Harper & Row, 1956.

Butlmann, R. *Jesus and the Word.* New York: Charles Scribner's Sons, 1934.

Cullmann, O. *Salvation in History.* London: SCM Press, 1967.

Dibelius, M. *From Tradition to Gospel.* New York: Charles Scribner's Sons, 1935.

Funk, R. W. *Language, Hermeneutic, and Word of God.* New York: Harper & Row, 1966.

Jeremias, J. *The Parables of Jesus.* New York: Charles Scribner's Sons, 1953.

Neill, Stephen. *The Interpretation of the New Testament, 1861–1961.* New York: Oxford University Press, 1966.

Robinson, J. M. *A New Quest of the Historical Jesus.* Naperville, Ill.: A. R. Allenson, Inc. 1959.

Rust, E. C. *Salvation History.* Richmond: John Knox Press, 1962.

Summers, Ray. *The Secret Sayings of the Living Jesus.* Waco: Word Publishers, 1968.

Matthew
Mark

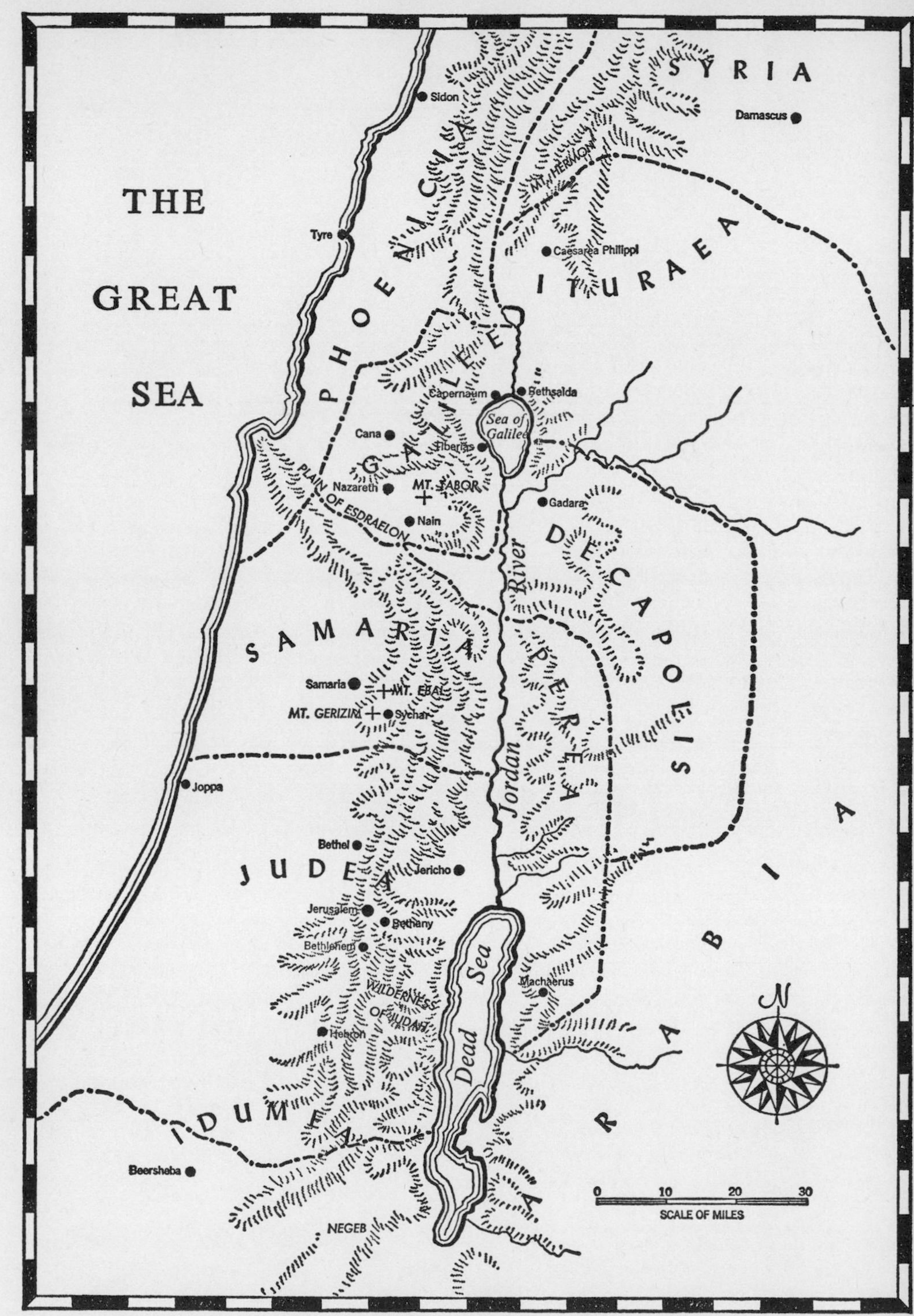

PALESTINE IN NEW TESTAMENT TIMES

Matthew

FRANK STAGG

Introduction

The Gospel of Matthew probably is best understood as a book written for a Jewish-Gentile church some years after the first Jewish-Roman War (A.D. 66–70). Jerusalem and its Temple had been destroyed, and the rupture between Judaism and Christianity was all but complete. What initially had been an all-Jewish church now was becoming increasingly Gentile. The church for which Matthew wrote was threatened on the side of its Jewish origins by Pharisaic legalism and on its Gentile side by antinomianism or libertinism (the view that in Christ the Law is no longer binding).

The legalism and antinomianism opposed by Matthew need not be understood as that of the Judaizers and antinomians of Paul's time but that which may emerge in religion at any time, growing out of the normal dispositions of mankind, with or without a promotional group.

Fighting on two fronts, Matthew points to a way which escapes, on the one hand, the pride, superficiality, and irrelevance of legalism and, on the other, the moral breakdown and ethical irresponsibility of the license which masquerades as liberty.[1]

Chiefly, Matthew wanted to convince or reassure his readers that Jesus is the Christ of Old Testament expectation and the creator of a new people, an indestructible church. This church is seen neither as a "new Israel" or "true Israel" but as God's people constituted of Jews and Gentiles (Hare, p. 170). Matthew saw the destruction of Jerusalem as a judgment upon Israel for its rejection of Jesus as the Christ. He saw Jesus as the fulfilment of the Law, both as its interpreter and as the one who actually lived up to the Law's intention.

The relevance of Matthew requires only to be found, not forced. How can one be free from outward rules and regulations and yet be morally upright and ethically responsible? How can one escape legalism on the one hand and license on the other? How can one know salvation as God's free gift and at the same time his absolute demand? How can religion be morally and ethically sensitive without becoming a hardened system of *do's* and *don't's*, a legal code "under cover of which the disobedient heart imagines that all is well" (Bornkamm, p. 25), or an indulgent religion which leaves one mired in moral and ethical failure? Matthew points us not to rules but to the rule of God. He uncovers the righteousness which exceeds that of the scribes and Pharisees (5:20) without becoming self-righteousness. He shows how salvation is offered in mercy to sinners without condonement of sin. He presents Jesus Christ as Lord and Saviour, as offering a yoke that is both heavy and light (11:28–30).

I. Life Situation and Purpose

In the decade or so after the first Jewish-Roman War, the church for which Matthew

[1] For variations of this view see Bacon, p. 348 *et passim;* Bornkamm, *et al.*, pp. 15 f., 94 f., 158 f., 162 ff., *et passim;* Davies; Hummel; and Hans Windisch, *The Meaning of the Sermon on the Mount* (Leipzig, 1929).

wrote stood somewhere between its Jewish origin and what later became a thoroughly Gentile church. This church was not yet ready to concede its separation from Judaism, although Judaism may have repudiated it. At least, Matthew's church was still interacting with Judaism (cf. 17:24–27; 23:1–12; 24:9). Christianity was rapidly becoming less Jewish and more Gentile. Jewish Christians needed to understand the meaning of the Law and the Temple (now in ruins) for themselves, as well as their relationship to Gentile converts. Gentile Christians needed to understand the nature of freedom with respect to God's law. Both needed to understand the relationship of Christianity with Judaism.

1. Distance and Interaction. Matthew's Gospel reflects both distance and interaction between synagogue and church. Matthew knows the synagogues as synagogues of Pharisaic Judaism (4:23; 9:35; 10:17; 12:9; 13:54; 23:34). Except for 4:23, each occurrence of the term "their synagogue" is redactional, Matthew's editorial work. Mark knows the expression (1:23,39), but Matthew stresses it. Where he does not speak of "their synagogues," he portrays them as synagogues of hypocrites or status-seekers (6:2, 5; 23:6). Only the book of Revelation goes further by referring to the "synagogue of Satan" (2:9; 3:9).

Although Matthew's church could probably no longer worship in the synagogues, he seems to avoid what would completely cut off the church from Judaism. He recognized at least in principle the authority of the scribes (23:2), and he omits Mark's "tradition of men" (Mark 7:8; Matt. 15:8–11) and Mark's "he declared all foods clean" (Mark 7:19; Matt. 15:17).

The debates with Pharisaism imply a continuing relationship, however strained. Matthew affirmed the continuing validity of the Law, so important to the Pharisees. What sets him off from them is his claim that in Christ is found a better understanding of the Law (5:21–48; 9:13; 12:3,5,7; 15:3–14; 16:6,11) and its true fulfilment, in contrast to Pharisaic misunderstanding and misuse of the Law (9:4; 15:12–14; 22:18; 23:2). Matthew sees Jesus as fulfilling the Law by uncovering its real intention and by giving it full obedience, expressed ultimately in the love that gives itself in sacrificial service.

Law is used in various ways in Judaism, the New Testament, and this Commentary. In the New Testament it generally means the law of God as revealed in the Old Testament. In the Old Testament law translates *torah* as well as other Hebrew words. *Torah* means instruction or direction, not just law in the restricted sense of commands or rules. The whole story of God's dealing with mankind is really Torah. But *torah,* translated *nomos* (law) in the LXX, came to designate the Pentateuch in particular, although it could yet refer to the whole Old Testament or in a larger sense to the whole revelation of God, written and oral. Matthew refers to "the law" eight times, designating the law of the Old Testament. In 5:17 and 11:13 "the law and the prophets" refers to the books of the Old Testament, with special reference to the two oldest divisions, the Pentateuch being designated as the Law.

2. Judaism's Struggle. The Jewish-Roman War was traumatic and far-reaching in consequences for both Judaism and Christianity. With the Temple destroyed, its elaborate cultic sacrifices and rituals had been ended. The once-powerful Sadducees, whose vested interests had been in the Temple and in the Sanhedrin, disappeared from the scene. The Essenes had suffered the loss of their center at Qumran, destroyed by the Tenth Roman Legion in A.D. 68. The Essenes were a priestly group who had withdrawn from the Temple in a double protest—one against the corrupt Sadducean priests and another against the Pharisees, laymen who had largely taken over the interpretation of the Law, formerly a priestly function.

The Zealots, fiery "right-wing" activists, whose zeal was for the liberation of their nation from Roman rule, had been crushed in the unsuccessful war which they had precipitated. The Pharisees remained the unrivaled leaders of Judaism. With schools at Jamnia and Babylon, they set about to rebuild the nation around the Law of Moses, codifying and expanding the oral tradition into what by A.D. 220 became the Mishnah (second law) based upon the Torah.

Around A.D. 85, a malediction against apostates, probably Christians and others, was added—or enlarged from an earlier form—to the Eighteen Benedictions, the daily synagogue prayer. The twelfth benediction is really a malediction, possibly introduced to exclude Jewish Christians from the synagogues. According to a form discovered in a Cairo Genizah it reads: "For persecutors let there be no hope, and the dominion of arrogance do Thou speedily root out in our days; and let Nazoreans [Christians?] and *minim* perish in a moment, let them be blotted out of the book of the living and let them not be written with the righteous." [2]

The inclusion of this benediction in the synagogue prayers made it impossible for Christians to continue to worship in the synagogues.

3. The Gentile Issue. Being Jews, the earliest Christians worshiped for some decades in the synagogues and the Temple. In addition to evidence throughout the New Testament, there is the story attributed by Eusebius (*Hist.*, II, 23) to Hegesippus (late second-century Jewish Christian in Palestine) to the effect that James was greatly respected by the Jews in Jerusalem and was daily in the temple until the time of his martyrdom, attributed by Hegesippus to the fears of the scribes and Pharisees that James would influence all the people to follow Jesus.

Tensions arose, not only because some followed Jesus as the Christ while others did not, but chiefly because men like Philip, Stephen, Paul, and to some extent Peter contended for the recognition of Gentile converts, even in table fellowship (cf. Acts; Gal. 2; Eph. 2:11—3:13). It was not Christology as such which split synagogue and church, for the Jews had many disagreements over their understanding of the function and identity of Messiah. What led to the split was the inclusion of uncircumcised Gentiles in the church, especially in table fellowship.[3]

The Jewish-Roman War apparently was the crisis which brought tensions to the breaking point. A war for national liberation and a gospel in which there is no "Jew or Greek" were incompatible. Judaism became more nationalistic and Law-centered, with a closed Torah (OT) and a growing Mishnah (second law). The Christian church moved deeper into the Gentile world.

Points of tension between Christian and non-Christian Jews are traceable within the New Testament. Many Christians questioned the central symbols of Jewish national solidarity: the Torah, Temple, holy city, purification rites, food laws, sabbath, and circumcision (Hare, pp. 3 f. *et passim*). In this they followed in principle a direction taken by Jesus. From the Jewish perspective, the "limits of tolerance" were exceeded; and, especially during and after the Jewish-Roman War, they resorted to public censure, social ostracism, and sometimes physical violence against Christian Jews.

4. Fulfilment. A major purpose of Matthew was to argue that true Judaism had its fulfilment in Christ and not in the Pharisaic Judaism centered in Jamnia. Jesus Christ is introduced as "son of David, the son of Abraham" (1:1), and Matthew shows how the covenants with Abraham and David were fulfilled in Jesus. The genealogy and the birth and infancy narratives (1—2) are so constructed as to show that Jesus is Son of David but also Son of God, in whom the covenants with Abraham and David are fulfilled.[4]

Abraham was promised that all the nations of the earth would be blessed in him

2 Translation and Hebrew text in Davies, p. 275.

3 Frank Stagg, *The Book of Acts, the Early Struggle for an Unhindered Gospel* (Nashville: Broadman, 1955), pp. 1–18 *et passim*.

4 Cf. Helen Milton, "The Structure of the Prologue to St. Matthew's Gospel," *Journal of Biblical Literature*, 81:175–181 (June, 1962).

(Gen. 12:2 f.; 18:18); and he was said to be known of God "to the end that he may charge his children and his household after him that they keep the way of Yahweh, to do righteousness and justice" (Gen. 18:19). So universalism, righteousness, and justice marked the covenant with Abraham. Matthew, accordingly, shows that Jesus came to establish a kingdom that is to include all nations under a rule of righteousness and justice (28:18–20).

David was promised that his throne would be established forever (2 Sam. 7:16). As Son of David (1:1), Jesus was given "all authority in heaven and on earth" (28:18); all nations were to be brought under his discipline (28:19); and they were to be taught obedience, with the assurance that Christ was with them (Emmanuel, "God with us!" 1:23) "unto the consummation of the age" (28:20). Thus in an eternal and universal reign, one in righteousness, the covenants with Abraham and David were fulfilled. Matthew would have Jews look to Jesus, not to Jamnia, for the fulfilment of the hopes of Israel.

5. Two Fronts. Matthew seems to have been fighting on two major fronts, finding it necessary to oppose Pharisaic legalism at Jamnia and the threat of antinomian libertinism within the church. The opposition to the Pharisees is unmistakable and constantly before the reader. Less obvious but clear enough is the other front. Among the Gospels, only Matthew (7:23; 13:41; 23:28; 24:12) employs the word lawlessness (*anomia*), reflecting his concern to resist antinomian libertinism.

Accordingly, to enter the kingdom of God one's righteousness must exceed that of the scribes and Pharisees (5:20). Not one smallest part of the Law or the Prophets is to be lost (5:18–19). In fact, Jesus came not to destroy but to fulfil the Law and Prophets (5:17). The demands of Christ are the highest possible, requiring not only that outward conduct be proper but that the inner man be clean and pure, free from hate, lust, or greed (5:21–42). Beyond that, one is to be so filled with love that he loves even his enemies (5:43–47). God's kingdom is so demanding that one is to be perfect even as the Heavenly Father is perfect (5:48).

A key to the Gospel may be found in Jesus' invitation to come under his yoke (11:25–30). It is a yoke, for there is demand. Yet the yoke is made easy, for the demand is based in love and mercy. Salvation is not indulgence nor legalism. The radical ethic of Jesus, epitomized in the Sermon on the Mount, is couched in the story of God's merciful acts; and the radical demand is made upon sinners who daily must forgive and ask forgiveness, be merciful and receive mercy (5:5,6,7,10; 6:12, 14 f.; 7:11). One is to live in the tension of God's gift and demand. God makes an absolute and ultimate demand upon his children (5:48; 28:20), yet salvation is a gift which can only be received. It belongs to the poor in spirit, those who mourn, the meek, those who hunger and thirst for righteousness, and those who seek forgiveness (5:3–7; 6:12).

The legalist seeks to achieve a standard which God must accept, usually outward performances which may be demonstrated, measured, and advertised. The antinomian libertine stresses salvation as the gift of God's grace, and he contends that he is free of all law. This can result in the surrender of moral and ethical values. Matthew opposes both.

Matthew made constant appeal to the Jewish Scriptures, showing from the Old Testament (cf. Micah 6:8; Prov. 14:22; Hos. 6:6) that God requires justice, mercy, and faith or faithfulness (23:23). The essence of the Law is shown to be love, directed toward God and man, and chiefly expressed in serving one's fellowman in the commonplaces of life, as where there is hunger, thirst, illness, or loneliness (25:31–46).

6. Gift and Demand. Matthew confronted his readers with a gospel of both gift and demand. The kingdom (sovereign rule) of heaven requires a righteousness which goes beyond that of the scribes and

Pharisees (5:20). The disciple is to hunger and thirst for righteousness (5:6). He is to make righteousness under the kingdom of heaven his first concern (6:33). By their righteousness are the true people of God under old covenant and new to be recognized (10:41; 23:34 ff.). The judgment at the end of the world will be concerned with whether or not God's will has been done (7:24–27; 24:37 ff.,42 ff.; 25:1 ff.,14 ff.). Practice, not just study of the Law, is God's requirement (23:3,5,23 ff.,28). Although outward "doing" can be superficial and hypocritical (7:21–23), Matthew does not hesitate to stress the importance of doing God's will (7:21; 23:3). Righteousness is a goal for fulfilment (3:15; 5:18). The Gospel closes with emphasis upon "keeping" or "guarding" all that Christ has commanded (28:20).

The standard is no less than the perfection which belongs to the Father in heaven (5:48). Matthew does not give one hint that this is to be explained away or watered down. God's demand is absolute and ultimate, that one be perfect. At the same time, it is declared that perfection is found only in God (19:17). Although perfect righteousness is the disciples' goal from the outset, it is to be realized only at the coming of the Son of man (13:43).

Salvation is also gift. Throughout Matthew, man is seen as sinner who daily requires forgiveness. Mercy and forgiveness belong necessarily to life within the church (5:7; 6:12,14–15; 18:15–17,21–35). The sons of the kingdom cannot escape this tension of living between gift and demand, salvation as God's free gift which can never be deserved or earned but only received and at the same time God's absolute demand which is never satisfied. Foreign to the true child of the kingdom is the legalist's pride that he has achieved and also the antinomian's easy escapism in the erroneous thought that mercy, forgiveness, and love are without demand.

But Matthew also shows that God's demands are always couched in love and mercy. Just as his merciful deliverance of the slaves from Egypt came before the awesome demands at Mount Sinai, so the heavy demands of the Sermon on the Mount are preceded by the good news that Jesus is Emmanuel, God with us (1:23), and that he came "preaching the gospel of the kingdom and healing every sickness and every malady among the people" (4:23). God always gives before he demands, and he gives what he demands. The righteousness which exceeds that of the scribes and Pharisees is real righteousness, but from beginning to end it is God's own creative work in man, not man's work offered to God. In Jesus Christ, God offers new standing to sinners who never deserve it, accepting them before they deserve acceptance; but in Jesus Christ he also is making man new. Salvation is release, cleansing, healing, renewal, righteousness, and peace. It is health, not merely a certificate of health.

Hans Conzelmann, in a discussion of God's demand, cogently observes that in the heavy demands that we love and be perfect, Jesus presupposes "that through the making known of his demand, God makes possible its fulfilment," for "the commanding One is at the same time the concerned One and the forgiving One." He further observes that "moral achievement does not bring man into relationship with God, but the relationship with God is God's own gift and first opens up the possibility for moral behavior." [5]

7. Many Concerns. The Gospel of Matthew is far too rich in its materials to be reduced to a one-factor analysis. It was a church book, seemingly designed to meet many needs: evangelism, missions, apology, teaching, discipline, and worship.[6] The stylistic improvements over Mark—self-contained stories and discourses, topical arrangements, and other factors—suggest that special care was given to produce a book suited to public reading. Worship and teaching may have been the two dominant

[5] *Grundriss der Theologie des Neuen Testaments* (München: Kaiser, 1967), pp. 137, 141.

[6] See both Kilpatrick and Stendahl for origin and purpose.

concerns. Even the Sermon on the Mount is set in a teaching situation and is suited for worship or instruction.

Of course, the basic purpose of Matthew is the one common to all the Gospels, to portray Jesus Christ: who he is, why he came, what he demands, and what he offers.

II. Structure and Plan

It is easier to recognize the main divisions of the Gospel of Matthew than its deliberate plan or design. The problem is to see to what extent the sources gave shape to the Gospel and to what extent the author consciously and deliberately shaped it. Since deliberate design reflects something of purpose, detecting an intended design would open up the Gospel to better understanding.

Everyone recognizes that there are five major discourses in Matthew: (1) Sermon on the Mount (5—7); (2) apostleship (10); (3) parables of the kingdom (13); (4) church discipline (18); and (5) last things (24—25). Each discourse is followed by a summary statement of almost uniform wording: "And it came to pass when Jesus had completed these words . . ." (7:28; 11:1; 13:53; 19:1; 26:1).

Artistic design, as in the genealogy, the Sermon on the Mount, and the parables of chapter 13, encourages one to look for careful design for the whole book comparable to that so obvious in smaller units. In 1930 Bacon (pp. 225–335, *et passim*), acknowledging debt to F. Godet, argued that Matthew developed a deliberate scheme of five books, a new Pentateuch, with narrative and discourse in each book: (1) discipleship (3—7); (2) apostleship (8—10); (3) the hiding of the revelation (11—13); (4) church administration (14—18); and (5) the judgment (19—25), calling chapters 1—2, "the preamble"; and chapters 26—28, "epilogue."

Although Bacon's thesis that Matthew was a neo-legalist is to be rejected, his penetrating insights are yet to be taken seriously. There are recognizable blocks of material, and some design may be seen within these blocks, as in the nine or ten miracles of chapters 8—9; but what falls short of demonstration is that one theme or design unifies each block of narrative material and relates it to the discourse which follows. Chapters 1—2 are too important to be designated "Preamble," and chapters 26—28 may by no means be reduced to an "Epilogue." If anything is to be considered Epilogue, it begins not sooner than 26:16, but even this is inadmissible (Walker, p. 146).

Although five major discourses and blocks of narrative material are obvious, it is not indicated that Matthew intended to create a new Pentateuch. Matthew opposed Pharisaic legalism, but he was not a neo-legalist. He saw the church as the true people of God and Jesus as its founder, but he did not present Jesus as a "new Moses" who gave a "new law." He drew some parallels between Moses and Jesus, whether consciously so or not; but he never presents Jesus as "the son of Moses." He does introduce him as "son of David, son of Abraham" (1:1).

"New law" is not the word for Matthew's concern. He does not and could not see Jesus as giver of a new law, for to him Jesus interprets and fulfils the Law (Bornkamm, pp. 35, 64). Matthew is concerned with continuity as well as fulfilment. Jesus fulfils the covenants with Israel as well as the Law (5:17–20). Matthew represents Jesus as both respecting and extending the Law (5:17 f.; 8:4; 19:17–19; 23:2 f.; 24:20; 26:18). In Matthew, Jesus does not oppose the Pharisaic emphasis upon the Law but the failure both to penetrate its depth to its intention and to practice it (23:3).

An older approach to the structure of Matthew featured geography and chronology, dividing the ministry of Jesus into preparation for the ministry (or early Judean), Galilean ministry, retirement from Galilee, journey to Jerusalem, and Jerusalem ministry. This approach has some validity in that Mark's chronological and geographical arrangements are to a great extent taken over by Matthew. But this is incidental to Matthew. Furthermore, the Gospels are not biographies, giving the life of Jesus in its chronological sequence, though there obviously is some adherence to sequence (birth, childhood, baptism, public ministry, death, resurrection, appearances).

III. Leading Themes

1. The Person of Jesus Christ. Jesus is unmistakably the dominant subject throughout the Gospel of Matthew. No discourse, event, or person has interest to Matthew except as related to Jesus, who alone holds the Gospel together and gives it meaning.

Matthew's primary concern is to present Jesus in terms of his human and divine origin, identity, mission, authority, gifts, demands, deeds, and teachings. Significant titles are employed: Son of David, David's Lord, King of the Jews, Emmanuel, Son of God, Servant of God, Son of Man, Lord, and Christ; but Jesus is set forth chiefly through his manner, his deeds, his words, and the responses of others to him. Matthew does not raise speculative questions about the nature of Christ. He chooses rather to present Jesus in terms of his function: fulfilling the Law, revealing the Father, saving men from their sins, creating the church, overcoming demons, sickness, and death.

Matthew shows Jesus to be human and divine. He was a real man: born of a virgin (1:18,23); son of Abraham and David (1:1); tempted (4:1–11; 16:23); denied knowing the time of the Parousia (24:36); prayed (26:39); felt forsaken (27:46). He was also divine. He was begotten of the Holy Spirit (1:18,20). His name Jesus meant "Yahweh [LORD] is salvation" (1:21). He was also called Emmanuel, "God with us" (1:23). He was worshiped as God (2:3; 28:9). Matthew knew Jesus as the eschatological or End-time Deliverer to whom was given the authority of God (7:29; 8:9; 9:6; 21:23–27; 24:30; 26:64; 28:18).

Matthew is interested in both the earthly Jesus of Nazareth and the risen Lord. The earthly Jesus cannot be understood apart from the risen Lord nor can the event of Easter or the risen Lord be understood apart from the earthly Jesus.[7] Matthew knows nothing of a merely human Jesus or of a "docetic" Christ to whom a real earthly existence is a matter of indifference. He writes of one whose earthly, human life was so real that he knew hunger, thirst, weariness, and temptation; and he writes also of him who already in this earthly life made claims for himself, made demands upon others, and walked among men in a manner proper only to one who was divine and who so understood himself.

Titles do not carry the full load of Matthew's portrayal of Jesus, but they are important. Jesus is called "Teacher" and occasionally used this term for himself (10: 24 f.; 23:8; 26:18), but he is presented as teacher even when the term is not employed. Matthew dislikes the term "rabbi," however. The disciples of Jesus are to avoid the term (23:7 f.), and only Judas uses it for Jesus (26:25,49).

As prophet (10:41; 13:57; 16:14; 21:11, 46) as well as teacher, Jesus spoke with the authority of God. Possibly Matthew saw him as the prophet of Deuteronomy 18: 15,18. Teacher and prophet do not set Jesus forth as divine; but with the authority of God claimed for his words as teacher and prophet, strong support is given to what elsewhere is explicit. In the "antitheses" (*but I say to you*) of the Sermon on the Mount (5:22,28,32,39,44; 7:29), Jesus makes claims for himself which set him above rabbi and prophet, for they set him above Moses. The only category which does justice to this claim is that ascribed to him in Matthew 16:16, "the Christ, the son of the living God" (Käsemann, pp. 37 f.).

Matthew sees Jesus as Christ and Lord, thus both uniting and separating Israel and church, Judaism and Christianity (Hummel, pp. 172 f.). He is the Messiah of Old Testament expectation, the true fulfilment of the Law, both as its interpreter and embodiment of its intention, thus achieving

[7] Cf. Ernst Käsemann, *Essays on New Testament Themes* (London: SCM, 1964), p. 25.

"the righteousness which exceeds that of the scribes and Pharisees." He is also the risen Lord of the church, rejected in the main by Israel but in his death and resurrection exalted as the Lord to whom is given "all authority in heaven and on earth" (28:18) and under whose discipline all nations are to be brought.

Jesus is both David's son (1:1; 9:27; 15:22; 20:30 f.; 21:9,15) and David's Lord (21:45). He is the lowly king prophesied by Zechariah (9:9) and also the risen, triumphant Son of man who already reigns upon earth (28:18). The lowliness, humility, and obedience of the Servant of Yahweh and the living presence and sovereignty of the Son of man are both strong emphases. Matthew likes to bring the two motifs together in the paradox of the lowliness and exaltation of Jesus.

In 3:17, Matthew adds "with whom I am well pleased" to Mark's quotation, drawing upon the Servant picture in Isaiah 42. In 8:17, he stresses Jesus' humble servant role, drawing upon Isaiah 53:4. In 12:15–21, he adds to Mark's narrative a quotation from Isaiah 42:1–4, picturing Jesus in a saving activity for the broken, proclaiming a judgment that is redemptive, giving victory and hope to the Gentiles. By his silence under oppression and his gentleness in dealing with the broken, Jesus is seen in his lowliness and humility. Matthew 21:4 f. adds to Mark's account of Jesus' entry into Jerusalem a blending of Isaiah 62:11 and Zechariah 9:9, thus making central the meekness or gentleness of "the king."

But to Matthew, Jesus is the enthroned risen one as well as the gentle Servant-King. The Gospel closes with the awesome picture of the risen Christ possessing "all authority in heaven and on earth," commissioning his followers to bring all nations under his discipleship and bind them to his commands (28:16–20). "All authority in heaven and on earth" (28:18) seems to echo Daniel 7:14, thus identifying Jesus as the Son of man (G. Barth, p. 133). The words "I am with you" probably look back to 1:23, Emmanuel or "God with us." In Jesus, God not only speaks and acts but is present. In his earthly ministry Jesus was the gentle, lowly, obedient Servant-King. The risen Christ is the Lord, the Son of man, God with us.

The term "Father" is used for God 45 times in Matthew, excelled only by John (107 times as compared with 4 in Mark and 15 in Luke). Jesus knew God as his Father and saw his work to be that of giving such knowledge to his followers (5:48; 11:27). Matthew traces Jesus' filial consciousness back to his baptism (3:17). Jesus is known to Matthew as Son of God (14:33; 16:16; 27:54; 28:18–20).

The term Christ appears 13 times in Matthew. Jesus accepted the title at Caesarea Philippi (16:16), but substituted for it the title "Son of man" (16:28) and interpreted both titles in terms of the Suffering Servant of Isaiah, without using the term itself (16:21). Jesus discouraged the use of the term Christ (16:20), presumably because in current usage it was closely tied to ideas of a national deliverer. In 26:63–64, Jesus neither denied nor fully accepted the title. To the Qumran community, "messiah" could stand for a priestly type from Aaron or a political type. The Zealots championed a national, political, this-worldly type. There were many false messiahs of this latter type (24:24). With this background, the title could be used only with caution.

Son of man is employed 31 times for Jesus in Matthew. This title was freer from political connotation and was more inclusive in meaning, suited to combining present (8:20) and future (25:31) aspects of Jesus' ministry as well as his suffering (17:22; 20:18) and also his exalted role of Sovereign and Judge (25:31). If 28:18–20 echoes Daniel 7:13–14, the very authority which the Ancient of Days promised to the Son of man was given to Jesus, the risen Lord. The promise to the Son of man was "dominion and glory, and a kingdom that all peoples, nations, and languages should serve him" and the assurance that his dominion is an everlasting kingdom that shall not be destroyed (Dan. 7:13–18). Precisely this is the claim for the risen Christ in 28:18–20. The term Son of man served further to indicate the concern of Jesus to create a community, the people of God, "the saints of the Most High."

The most direct Matthean reference to Jesus as the servant of God is 12:18, where Isaiah 42:1 is quoted: "Behold my servant, in whom I am well pleased." The Son of man is one who came not to be ministered to but to minister and to give his life a ransom for many (20:28). At his baptism came a voice from heaven declaring Jesus to be God's beloved son (3:17). This probably reflects both Isaiah 42:1 and Psalm 2:7. Reflected is Jesus' awareness of God as uniquely his Father, and of himself as God's Christ (Psalm 2:2) and God's Servant (Isa. 42:1). His messianic function was to be accomplished by sacrificial suffering, by giving life, not by taking the lives of Israel's Roman foes. To Matthew, Jesus is Christ, Son of God, and the suffering Son of man here on earth.

With Jerusalem in ruins, the Temple destroyed, Israel under the heel of Rome, and the Pharisees trying to rebuild Judaism around the Law, Matthew wrote to show that in Jesus Christ is the fulfilment of the Law, the prophets, and the Temple. In Jesus Christ the covenants with Abraham and David are fulfilled, the "throne of David" established forever in Christ, and his "authority" is to bring all nations under his righteous rule.

2. The Kingdom of Heaven. The term kingdom (*basileia*) appears about 100 times in Matthew, in 20 of the 28 chapters. Matthew prefers the term "kingdom of heaven" (32 times) over "kingdom of God" (4 times). He also speaks of "the kingdom," "kingdom of their Father," "my Father's kingdom," and "kingdom of the Son of man." The meaning is constant in these various formulations. Presumably, Matthew prefers "kingdom of heaven" either to avoid a political understanding of the kingdom of God or out of Jewish piety's avoidance of direct reference to God. There is no biblical basis for distinguishing between "kingdom of God" and "kingdom of heaven." In Synoptic parallels the terms are interchanged.

The kingdom of God is the sovereign rule of God. It means that God is king. The kingdom of God is not built or "brought in." It comes but does not become. God is king apart from man's obedience or disobedience. What man is and does affects man's standing under God's kingdom, but it does not determine the fact of God's kingdom. Other "kingdoms" oppose God's kingdom, but God remains king. The Old Testament already knows God as king, and it knows "one like a son of man" to whom "the Ancient of Days" has promised "a kingdom which shall know no end" (Dan. 7:13 f.).

Matthew knows Jesus of Nazareth as the Christ, God's anointed in whom the kingdom of God has already dawned. This means first of all that man must "repent," i.e., turn in submission to God (3:2; 4:17; 7:21). God is king and man is subject. Only when man accepts this relationship, his rebellion or indifference giving way to willing obedience, are new freedom and existence opened up to him.

The kingdom of heaven is good news. Matthew can speak of "the gospel of the kingdom" (4:23; 9:35; 24:14). In the terrible days of the mad king Herod, it was good news that God is the true King and that he has come in the "born king of the Jews" (2:2). It was good news when Matthew wrote, as Jerusalem lay in ashes and Rome seemed to rule the world. To the sick and sinful it was good news, for its breaking into the world anew in Jesus Christ was accompanied by healing every sickness and malady (4:23; 9:35) and freedom from the rule of evil forces (12:28).

Paradoxically, one reigns with Christ precisely when he surrenders all claim to sovereignty. The correlate of the kingdom of God is the freedom, not slavery, of the children of God (Käsemann, p. 47.). The kingdom belongs to those who do not try to snatch it. It belongs to the poor in spirit (5:3), those who suffer persecution for the sake of righteousness (5:10), and the childlike (18:1,3; 19:14). Publicans and harlots, who have no illusions about themselves, enter the kingdom before proud religionists (21:31). Unknowns from east and west enter the kingdom to sit with Abraham, Isaac, and Jacob at the messianic banquet, while the proud who think they merit it are cast out (8:11 f.).

The kingdom of heaven is both gift and demand. Inclusion or exclusion is not fate imposed but a decision to be made. It comes to one with the summons to repent, trust, obey. It demands a righteousness which exceeds that of the scribes and Pharisees (5:20), the doing of God's will (7:21), the bringing forth of fruit (21:43). One must sell all to possess this treasure or pearl of great price (13:44,45). Trust in riches excludes one from this kingdom (19:23 f.). It costs everything one has to enter the kingdom of heaven (6:33; 13:44,45), yet the kingdom is never earned; it is an inheritance, God's gift (25:34).

The kingdom of God comes as judgment as well as gospel. The judgment is seemingly delayed, yet it is certain and final. It is like the separation of the tares from the wheat in the harvest (13:24,36,41,44) or the separation of usable and worthless fish when the fishermen's net is drawn to the shore (13:47). Its judgment is easy on the merciful and forgiving but hard on the unmerciful and unforgiving (18:23). It judges one in terms of how he relates to Jesus Christ by relating to other people in situations of hunger, sickness, or imprisonment (25:31–46). Greatness in the kingdom is measured in terms of childlikeness (18:1–4), motive (20:1), and service (20:11,25 ff.).

The kingdom of Matthew is both present and future. Matthew apparently sees himself as a scribe of the kingdom (13:51 f.). The "keys of the kingdom" are a present reality (16:19; 18:18 f.). Both John and Jesus announce it as at hand (3:2; 4:17; 10:7). It already belongs to the poor in spirit and those persecuted for righteousness sake (5:3,10). It is already in conflict with the kingdom of Satan, and men try to take it by force (11:12; 12:28). It is to be sought now (6:33). The clearest and most conclusive recognition in Matthew of the present reality of the kingdom is seen in 12:28, "If by the Spirit of God I am casting out demons, then indeed has the kingdom of God come upon you." Already God's kingdom is overcoming Satan's kingdom. The risen Christ already has "all authority in heaven and on earth" (28:18).

But the kingdom is also future. The powers already at work in Jesus will only at "the end of the world" achieve their full victory. One is to watch, wait, and be prepared for that day (25:1). The kingdom in some sense had come; in a special sense (probably in the destruction of Jerusalem) it would come to the generation Jesus addressed (16:28); and it is yet to come in its fulness at the Parousia (24:27).

Contrary to the expectations of the Zealots, the kingdom would not come with the outward drama of war or catastrophe, as something to run to and watch (24:4–14). It comes as a tiny seed of mustard (13:31) or as a measure of leaven in a lump of dough (13:33).

3. The Church. The church and the kingdom are related but not identical. The kingdom is the sovereign rule of God, his absolute and ultimate claim over all that is, his sovereign rule which confronts the whole world in the person of Jesus of Nazareth, God's Christ whom he has anointed to rule. The church is that family of people yielded to the kingdom of God as it comes in Jesus Christ. The kingdom is wider than the church. It is God's rule over all, obedient and disobedient, church and world. The church is that part of creation which finds its existence in willing obedience to the kingdom of God. The church does not bring in nor build the kingdom. The kingdom creates and sustains the church.

The term church (*ekklēsia*) appears only three times in the Gospels, all in Matthew (16:18; 18:17). The concept of the people of God, expressed in various terms and analogies, is far more prominent in the

Gospels than those three occurrences of the word church may imply. Next in importance to the position given Jesus in the Gospels is that given to his followers. Jesus did call people to himself and formed a group about himself, by whatever term they may be called.

The presence of the term church in 16:18 and 18:17 is not traceable to Matthew's editorial interest, for it was seemingly in his source (R. Bultmann, *Synoptic Tradition*, 138 ff., 146). For Matthew, the more significant term for Jesus' followers is disciple (*mathētēs*), along with the terms slave (*doulos*) and house servant (*oikiakos*). These terms support Matthew's picture of Jesus as interpreter and fulfiller of the Law and as Lord of the church. The church is *his* church (16:18), just as the kingdom is also the Son of man's kingdom (13:41; 16:28). Matthew sees the church as the eschatological community, belonging to one who was both Israel's King Messiah and the Lord of the nations. He is the Teacher, his followers the disciples; he is Lord, they his slaves; he is the Master of the house, they the household servants (10:25).

"New Israel" is hardly the term for Matthew's conception of the church, although he does know Jesus' followers as the true children of Abraham (3:9). Matthew sees continuity between Israel and the church. The statement that many from the east and west, like the Gentile centurion from Capernaum (8:5), "will recline with Abraham and Isaac and Jacob in the kingdom of heaven" (8:11) looks two ways. Its chief concern is to include Gentiles, but it also recognizes that Abraham, Isaac, and Jacob belong to the people of God. Although Matthew sees the nation as a whole already judged in terms of the destruction of Jerusalem (23:37–39; 24:1–3), he nowhere hints that Jews as such are excluded from the people of Christ.

Matthew sees the church as bound to Judaism with respect to the Law and judgment. The Law is binding upon both, and both are to come under the same judgment. Fruit-bearing (7:16 ff.; 21:43), righteousness (5:20; 6:20), and perfection (5:48; 19:21) are the demands under which the church is to live, as was true of Israel. The outward church itself is to come under a judgment which separates the true people of God from those who are not (7:21 ff.; 13:24–30,36–43,47–50; 22:10,14; 25:31–46).

Matthew sees the Law as uniting the people of God under the old covenant and the new in that it is binding upon both. In both Israel and the church righteousness is demanded. As comparison with Lukan parallels shows, Matthew inserts "righteous" three times in 23:29–36. Only the righteous stand in the final judgment. The church, then, consists of the true people of God under both covenants, outwardly mixed now and sifted out from the untrue only in the last judgment.

4. The Dispute with the Pharisees. Evidence that Matthew was consciously interacting with the Pharisees of his time may be seen in that he consistently stresses their role as the opponents of Jesus. This does not mean that he invented the conflict, for it was historical; but more than Mark or Luke, he brought it out. In 3:7; 12:24,38, he writes "Pharisees" where Luke (3:7; 11:29) has "crowds." But in 3:7 and 12:38 Matthew inserts Pharisees into the material shared with Luke. Pharisees in 12:24 is redactional from Mark, who has "the scribes."

Especially in the debates do we see Matthew's interest in presenting the Pharisees as Jesus' opponents. In 12:24,38; 21:45; 22:34–35,41 Matthew has introduced the term Pharisees into his narrative (cf. Mark 12:12; Luke 20:19). His concern with the Pharisees is reflected in his emphasis upon the righteousness which must exceed that of the scribes and Pharisees (5:20), his emphasis upon the judgment which falls upon the Pharisees (15:12–13 and especially 23:1–36; cf. Mark 12:37*b*–40; Luke 20:45–47), his portrayal of the Pharisees as the opponents of John the Baptist (3:7), and the naming of the Pharisees as Jesus' opponents in the Passion narrative (21:45;

22:15; 27:62). In 22:15 he follows Mark, but in 21:45 and 27:62 Matthew alone names the Pharisees (Mark does not mention the Pharisees after 12:13).

Matthew did not invent the charge that the Pharisees plotted the death of Jesus, for Mark 3:6 preserves this tradition. Neither Mark nor the older tradition which he followed was interested in stressing the part played by the Pharisees. What is new is Matthew's interest in the Pharisees' guilt. That the tradition was earlier recorded without apparent motive argues for its historicity (Hummel, pp. 12–17). Matthew alone names the Pharisees as those who charged Jesus with casting out demons through the prince of demons (9:34). There are no parallels to 9:34, and the verse is missing in the Western text; but in 12:24 Matthew changes Mark's (3:22) "the scribes" to the Pharisees.

Matthew often refers to the scribes and Pharisees (5:20; 12:38; 23:2,13,15,23,25, 27,29), but he makes no distinction between them. A source behind Matthew and Luke may have distinguished between scribes and Pharisees (Luke 11:37,38,39,42, 43 and 12:1 have Pharisees; 11:45,46,52 have lawyers; 20:39,46 have scribes; and 11:53 has scribes and Pharisees). Most scribes were Pharisees, but there were Essene and some Sadducean scribes. The scribes were ordained scholars who stood above most Pharisees, but Matthew is not interested in this distinction (cf. 21:23 with 21:45).

IV. The Name Matthew

The Greek *Maththaios* or *Matthaios* is from a shortened form of a Hebrew or Aramaic word meaning gift of Yahweh. Matthew appears in four lists of the apostles of Jesus (Matt. 10:3; Mark 3:18; Luke 6:15; Acts 1:13). According to 9:9 and 10:3 he was a tax collector when Jesus called him. Whether or not he is to be identified with Levi is uncertain. Mark and Luke seem to distinguish between Levi and Matthew, but in Matthew they seem to be the same.

In Mark 2:14 a tax collector (*telōnēs*) who followed Jesus is called "Levi, the son of Alphaeus"; and in Luke 5:27,29, he is called Levi. It seems certain that Matthew 9:9–13, Mark 2:13–17, and Luke 5:27–32 are parallels, referring to the same tax collector. Thus the Matthew of 9:9 refers to the Levi of Mark 2:14 and Luke 5:27, 29. In each of the four lists of apostles (Matt. 10:2–4; Mark 3:16–19; Luke 6:13–16; and Acts 1:13) the name Matthew appears. The name Levi does not. Only in Matthew (9:9; 10:3) is Matthew called "the tax collector." Both Mark (2:14) and Luke (5:27,29) know a tax collector (*telōnēs*) named Levi. Whether or not Jews sometimes bore two names is debatable. Simon Peter is not a decisive example, for Peter is an epithet, not a true name.[8] There is substantial and early textual support for "James the son of Alphaeus" rather than "Levi" in Mark 2:14. This would agree with "James the son of Alphaeus" in 3:18. Heracleon (cf. Clement, *Stromata* 4:9) and Origen (*Contra Celsum* 1:62) distinguished between Levi and Matthew.

If Matthew and Levi the tax collector are the same, his office was under the authority of Herod Antipas, in the vicinity of Capernaum; and his assignment was to collect customs or tax on merchandise carried over the Damascus-Acre road and possibly to tax fishing and other businesses in his area. With the silence of Mark and Luke, the textual uncertainty in Mark 2:14 (Levi or James?), and the early patristic uncertainty, the scholar today is compelled to suspend judgment as to the identity of Levi and Matthew. Matthew is called a tax collector (9:9; 10:3), whatever the relationship between Matthew and Levi.

V. Authorship

Tradition has it that our Gospel was written by Matthew, one of the twelve apostles. The Gospel itself is anonymous. The superscription, "According to Mat-

[8] E. P. Blair, "Matthew," *The Interpreter's Dictionary of the Bible* (Nashville: Abingdon, 1962), III, 302.

thew," probably was added when the four Gospels were brought together under one cover. Scholars are far more convinced that Mark and Luke wrote the Gospels bearing their names than that the first Gospel was written by Matthew. What is at stake is a church tradition, not the genuineness or value of the Gospel of Matthew.

The truth seems to be that the authors of the four Gospels deliberately kept themselves in the background, covering up their tracks, as it were. The Gospels were written for the churches; and, in a real sense, they were products of the churches, even though there probably was an individual author behind each Gospel. How the author saw himself may be found in 13:52, a scribe who brings out of his treasure things old and new: the oldness in continuity with Judaism as reflected in the Old Testament and newness and fulfilment as found in Jesus Christ.

The tradition that Matthew wrote this Gospel and that it was the earliest, seems to go back to Papias of Hierapolis (d. A.D. 155) as quoted by Eusebius (III, 39): "Matthew compiled (*sunetaxato*) the oracles (*ta logia*) in the Hebrew language (*dialektō*), and each interpreted (*hermeneusen*) them as he was able." The passage contains several ambiguities. The Greek *sunetaxato* can mean both compile and arrange; *logia* can mean reports or oracles; and *hermeneusen* can refer to translation and/or exposition.

From this reference arose such views as that by *logia* Papias meant a life of Christ, our Gospel of Matthew, the sayings of Jesus, or a source now known as Q. Instead, Papias may have meant that Matthew compiled in Hebrew some Old Testament prophetic oracles and that each one in the early church interpreted them as he was able.[9] Later church fathers mistakenly assumed that Matthew wrote our earliest Gospel. Irenaeus (*ca.* A.D. 180) saw the Gospel of Matthew as the earliest of the four (*Against Heresies* III, 1; Eusebius, V, 8), as did Clement of Alexandria (*ca.* 200), according to Eusebius (VI, 14), Eusebius himself (III, 24), Jerome (Proem to the *Commentary on Matthew*, 5–7), and Augustine.

There must have been some substantial reason for ascribing the first Gospel to Matthew. That the apostle stood in some relationship to it is probable. Most likely it was as the compiler of the *logia* (cf. Papias), used extensively in this Gospel.

VI. Order of the Gospels

The present canonical order has been virtually uniform since Augustine (fourth century). Eusebius apparently understood Papias' reference to have been to the Gospel of Matthew, and from this came the view that Matthew's Gospel was the earliest. Augustine accepted this view and made it virtually standard until the modern critical period.

Overlooked by those who formed the tradition that Matthew was the earliest Gospel is the evidence that Papias discussed Mark before Matthew (Eusebius, III, 39), presumably dating Mark before Matthew.

Interestingly enough, Revelation 4:7 may well be a veiled reference to the order of the four Gospels: Mark, Luke, Matthew, and John. At least since the time of Irenaeus (III, 11), about A.D. 180, the four living creatures (lion, ox, creature with face of a man, and flying eagle) of Revelation 4:7 have been understood in exegesis and art as the four evangelists, identified respectively as Mark, Luke, Matthew, and John.[10] This is not to be pressed, for symbolism for the four Gospels seems to have varied in this early period.

Outside the Church of San Vitale at Ravenna, in the mausoleum of Galla Placidia, is a Roman mosaic (*ca.* 440) picturing the four Gospels in the following order: Mark, Luke, Matthew, and John. This mosaic may preserve a tradition antedating

[9] Cf. F. C. Grant, "Gospel of Matthew," *The Interpreter's Dictionary of the Bible*, III, 303. For the view that Papias had in mind our Gospel of Matthew, see W. G. Kümmel, *Introduction to the New Testament*, tr. A. J. Mattill, Jr., (Nashville: Abingdon, 1966), p. 85.

[10] Cf. F. C. Grant, 302, to whom this section is chiefly indebted.

the one which Eusebius and Augustine derived from a possible misreading of Papias. This order is also found in the Accademia in Venice, in the ceiling of the Sala della Presentazione, in a Spanish set of plaques now in the Metropolitan Museum, New York (M 167), and possibly elsewhere.

The strongest evidence that Matthew is later than Mark and roughly contemporary with Luke is internal, as will be seen under "Sources." In what is known as the Western text, another order prevailed, based upon a different principle: Matthew, John, Luke, Mark, placing the two apostles before the two non-apostles. This "Western order" is arbitrary and does not settle the question of authorship or order.

VII. Date and Place of Writing

There is no conclusive proof that the Gospels were not written early [11], as early as A.D. 60. Conversely, the probability is that Mark was written shortly after the Neronic persecution of Christians following the burning of Rome in A.D. 64, that Luke and Matthew were written after Mark, probably after the fall of Jerusalem in A.D. 70, and that John was written somewhat later. This cannot be demonstrated, but these approximate dates best satisfy the evidences and illumine the study.

The acknowledgment of sources by Luke (1:1–4) and their almost certain use by Matthew indicate that both of these Gospels belong to second-generation Christians. The statement by Papias that Matthew compiled the oracles in Hebrew and that each translated them as he was able indicates that by the early second century there may have been several Greek versions of what Papias referred to as Matthew's collection of oracles, possible Old Testament prophecies or proof texts. If the author of the Gospel of Matthew used these oracles or Old Testament verses, this would explain how the name of Matthew came to be associated with this gospel.

It is impossible to fix a date between A.D. 70 and A.D. 90, for there is no outstanding event in the seventies or eighties by which to be guided, sometimes called a "tunnel period."

The place of composition of Matthew is unknown and impossible to determine. The author wrote for a Greek-speaking community and seems to have been at home in a Greek-speaking environment. Palestine, especially Galilee, is not to be ruled out. Since the earliest certain witness to Matthew is Ignatius (*Smyrna* 1:1), Antioch or some place in Syria is the most probable place of origin, although Phoenicia (Kilpatrick) and Caesarea (Stendahl) have been cogently proposed.

VIII. Sources

Matthew makes no explicit reference to sources, but the evidences are so strong that he employed them that the burden of proof would fall upon the contrary view. Employment of sources, written and/or oral, does not call in question divine inspiration or the reliability of the Gospel of Matthew. The memory, interpretation, and faith of a community stand behind the Gospels, not just four men. The Spirit of God could work through this community as well as through an individual writer.

Although contested by some scholars, Matthew seems to have made Mark his basic narrative source. His only omissions of any length from Mark are: the healing of a demoniac (1:23–28), preaching in the synagogues of Galilee (1:35–39), the parable of the seed growing of itself (4:26–29), the healing of a deaf man (7:32–37), the healing of a blind man (8:22–26), an exorcism (9:38–40), and a widow and her alms (12:41–44).[12] Although Matthew used much of the organization of Mark, he freely transferred Mark's material as it

[11] R. M. Grant, *A Historical Introduction to the New Testament* (New York: Harper & Row, 1963), p. 107.

[12] W. C. Allen, p. xiii. See further pp. xiii–lxii for an exhaustive study of Matthew's use of sources. For the rejection of Matthew's dependence upon Mark, see W. R. Farmer, *The Synoptic Problem* (New York: Macmillan, 1964).

suited his purpose, with abbreviations, reformulations, stylistic changes, and the weaving in of new materials.

Matthew used about as much non-Markan material as Markan. About five-ninths of this non-Markan material, commonly called Q, is also found in Luke. The material peculiar to Matthew is usually termed M, just as that peculiar to Luke is called L. It is highly precarious to call Q a source. (Cf. A. M. Farrer, "On Dispersing with Q," *Studies in the Gospels*, ed. by D. E. Nineham; Oxford, 1957; pp. 55–86.) All that is really certain is that it represents a block of material common to Matthew and Luke and not found in Mark. Behind it may be written and oral sources. The same holds for M and L. Extensive agreements between Matthew and Luke suggests that Q represents at least some written material, but it is not likely that Q represents one written source. For all the talk about Q, M, and L, all that is actually known is that both Matthew and Luke contain almost all of the material in Mark and that in addition they have some non-Markan materials in common and others which are not common to both (R. M. Grant, p. 117).

One of the most remarkable characteristics of the Gospel is its extensive use of quotations (over 60) from the Old Testament. (See F. C. Grant, pp. 307–11.) Among them are eleven "formula quotations," i.e., introduced with a statement such as "in order that the word of the Lord through the prophet might be fulfilled, saying" (1:23; 2:6 f.,15,17 f.,23; 4:14–16; 8:17; 12:17–21; 13:35; 21:4 f.; 27:9 f.). Quotations which Matthew has in common with Mark and Luke are taken in Greek from his sources, and sometimes they are assimilated to the LXX.

Quotations found alone in Matthew and not having an introductory formula usually follow the LXX, with exceptions following the Hebrew text (11:29; 16:27 f.; 27:43). The formula quotations stand nearer the Hebrew, with some LXX influence. (Cf. Kümmel, pp. 78 f. for details.) That the author drew upon a collection of Old Testament quotations or prophetic utterances which had been in use in missionary preaching is likely. They may have been the *logia* referred to by Papias. The Gospel itself was not written in Hebrew (or Aramaic) but in Greek, as is clear from its use of Greek sources. One such source could have been a collection of Old Testament passages, first drawn up in Hebrew (possibly by Matthew) and then translated by various persons into Greek.

Behind all four Gospels and their written sources must certainly have been oral sources. Words spoken by Jesus were repeated during his lifetime and after his death. Things which he did would likewise be described by those who witnessed them. It is inconceivable that those who saw and heard Jesus would not have discussed these things among themselves and related them to others. To say the least, Jesus was by all evidences an unusal person, highly imaginative, daring, unconventional, controversial, winsome to some and a threat to others. He engendered the strongest feelings in people, both sympathetic and hostile. After all, he was crucified by some and worshiped by others. How could there ever have been a period of silence about him?

Besides this, the records indicate that Jesus not only called men to follow him but taught them and commissioned them to preach and teach. That there resulted a tradition (see 2 Thess. 2:15; 3:6) of the words and deeds of Jesus is not surprising. That this tradition began to take shape before the death of Jesus is highly probable. Following his death and resurrection, it would have been in keeping with all that we know about people for his followers to have shared these memories with one another. As new converts were sought and taught, they would have been instructed in things done and said by Jesus.

More than anything else, the resurrection of Jesus transformed Jesus' followers and made him the unrivaled center of their conversation and concern. His resurrection appearances excited their hopes for his future return, but their interest in a returning Lord was never divorced from their memory of an earthly Master. Selecting and shaping the tradition about Jesus was largely determined by community needs. This is not to exclude the fact that some things were remembered and repeated because they could not be forgotten or neglected (cf. Acts 4:20). Memory, lasting impressions, hopes and fears, disappointments and reassurances, and chiefly the loss and recovery of their Teacher and Lord made silence impossible. But beyond this were the daily needs in evangelism, instruction, and discipline.

The early Christians did remember, interpret, use, and thus shape the materials which ultimately found their way into the four Gospels. The Gospels, then, are sources for the life of the early church as well as for the works and teachings of Jesus.

Outline of the Gospel

I. The birth of Jesus and the beginning of his ministry (1:1—4:25)
  1. The genealogy of Jesus Christ (1:1–17)
  2. The birth of Jesus Christ (1:18–25)
  3. Rejection at home, reception from afar (2:1–23)
    (1) The Wise Men from the East (2:1–12)
    (2) The flight into Egypt (2:13–15)
    (3) Infants slain in Bethlehem (2:16–18)
    (4) From Egypt to Nazareth (2:19–23)
  4. The ministry inaugurated (3:1—4:25)
    (1) The message of the Baptist (3:1–12)
    (2) The baptism of Jesus (3:13–17)
    (3) The temptation of Jesus (4:1–11)
    (4) Withdrawal into Galilee (4:12–17)
    (5) Four fishermen called (4:18–22)
    (6) A threefold ministry (4:23–25)

II. The Sermon on the Mount (5:1—7:29)
  1. Introduction (5:1–2)
  2. The Beatitudes (5:3–12)
  3. Salt, light, and a city set on a hill (5:13–16)
  4. Jesus and the Law (5:17–20)
  5. The intention of the Law (5:21–48)
    (1) The essence of murder (5:21–26)
    (2) Lust and adultery (5:27–30)
    (3) The damage in divorce (5:31–32)
    (4) Teaching about oaths (5:33–37)
    (5) Overcoming evil with good (5:38–42)
    (6) Love for enemies (5:43–48)
  6. Motive in religious life (6:1–18)
    (1) Almsgiving (6:1–4)
    (2) Prayer (6:5–15)
    (3) Fasting (6:16–18)
  7. Freedom from tyranny of things (6:19–34)
  8. Judging others (7:1–6)
    (1) The speck and the log (7:1–5)
    (2) Pearls before swine (7:6)
  9. Ask, seek, knock (7:7–12)
  10. Perils to righteousness (7:13–27)
    (1) The two ways (7:13–14)
    (2) A tree known by its fruit (7:15–20)
    (3) Saying without doing (7:21–23)
    (4) Hearing and doing (7:24–27)
  11. Summary (7:28–29)

III. The authority of Jesus in work and word (8:1—9:34)
  1. A leper cleansed (8:1–4)
  2. A centurion's servant healed (8:5–13)
  3. The sick healed (8:14–17)

4. The cost of discipleship (8: 18–22)
5. A storm calmed (8:23–27)
6. Deranged demoniacs healed (8: 28–34)
7. Healing and forgiveness (9:1–8)
8. Matthew called (9:9–13)
9. New skins for new wine (9: 14–17)
10. A woman healed and a girl raised from dead (9:18–26)
11. Two blind men receive sight (9:27–31)
12. Pharisees protest a healing (9: 32–34)

IV. Compassion of Jesus and commission of the twelve (9:35—11:1)
1. Jesus' compassion for crowds (9:35–38)
2. The mission of the twelve (10: 1–4)
3. The twelve commissioned (10: 5–15)
4. The coming persecution: master and disciple (10:16–42)
   (1) Sheep in the midst of wolves (10:16–25)
   (2) Whom to fear (10:26–33)
   (3) Not peace, but a sword (10:34–39)
   (4) Rewards (10:40–42)
5. Summary (11:1)

V. Various responses to Jesus (11:2–30)
1. Uncertainty and confusion (11: 2–6)
2. Distortion and violence (11: 7–15)
3. Childish displeasure (11:16–19)
4. Wilful rejection (11:20–24)
5. Childlike trust (11:25–30)

VI. Growing opposition to Jesus (12: 1–50)
1. Above the sabbath (12:1–14)
   (1) Plucking grain on sabbath (12:1–8)
   (2) Healing on the sabbath (12:9–14)
2. The hope of the nations (12: 15–21)
3. The unpardonable sin (12: 22–32)
4. The inescapable judgment (12: 33–37)
5. The sign of Jonah (12:38–42)
6. The unclean spirit's return (12: 43–45)
7. Jesus' true family (12:46–50)

VII. Parables of the kingdom (13:1–52)
1. Sower and soils (13:1–23)
   (1) The parable given (13:1–9)
   (2) The purpose of parables (13:10–17)
   (3) The parable explained (13: 18–23)
2. Weeds among the wheat (13: 24–30)
3. Mustard seed and leaven (13: 31–33)
4. The use of parables (13:34–35)
5. Parable of weeds explained (13: 36–43)
6. Hidden treasure and a costly pearl (13:44–46)
7. Dragnet and the sorting of the fish (13:47–50)
8. Treasures new and old (13: 51–52)

VIII. Rejected at home but popular with crowds (13:53—14:36)
1. Rejection at Nazareth (13: 53–58)
2. The death of John the Baptist (14:1–12)
3. Five thousand fed (14:13–21)
4. Peter rescued from storm (14: 22–33)
5. Multitudes seek to be cured (14:34–36)

IX. Conflict with Pharisees, scribes, Sadducees (15:1—16:12)
1. Jesus challenges tradition (15: 1–20)
2. A Canaanite woman's faith (15: 21–28)
3. Multitudes healed and fed (15: 29–39)
4. Disciples warned against "leaven" of Pharisees and Sadducees (16: 1–12)

X. Christ, his church, and his cross

(16:13—17:27)
1. Christ and his church (16:13–20)
2. Jesus foretells death and resurrection (16:21–28)
3. Jesus transfigured: revelation and preparation for cross (17:1–13)
4. Faith to remove mountains (17:14–21)
5. Disciples again warned (17:22–23)
6. Temple tax paid, rights waived (17:24–27)

XI. Instructions for the church (18:1–35)
1. Greatness in the kingdom (18:1–14)
(1) Childlike humility (18:1–4)
(2) The sin of causing little ones to stumble (18:5–9)
(3) Concern that not one little one perish (18:10–14)
2. Church discipline, to correct and recover (18:15–20)
3. The forgiving alone able to receive forgiveness (18:21–35)

XII. Marriage, divorce, celibacy (19:1–15)
1. Introduction (19:1–2)
2. Marriage: sacred and indissoluble except by death (19:3–9)
3. Celibacy and its demands (19:10–12)
4. Children's access to Christ (19:13–15)

XIII. Rebukes to selfishness (19:16—20:34)
1. The peril of riches (19:16–30)
2. Workers in the vineyard: first last, last first (20:1–16)
3. Third reminder of coming death and resurrection (20:17–19)
4. Self-seeking disciples challenged to sacrificial service (20:20–28)
5. Jesus heals two blind men rebuked by the crowds (20:29–34)

XIV. Royal entry into Jerusalem (21:1—23:39)
1. The royal entry (21:1–11)
2. The Temple cleansed (21:12–17)
3. Lessons from a fruitless fig tree (21:18–22)
4. The question of the authority of Jesus (21:23—22:14)
(1) The authority challenged (21:23–27)
(2) Two sons: authority acknowledged in obedience, not words (21:28–32)
(3) Wicked tenants: crushed by spurned authority (21:33–44)
(4) Hardening of chief priests and Pharisees (21:45–46)
(5) Defiant guests and a king's wrath (22:1–14)
5. Abortive efforts to outwit Jesus (22:15–40)
(1) Paying taxes to Caesar (22:15–22)
(2) The question of the resurrection (22:23–33)
(3) The great commandment (22:34–40)
6. Jesus' question: David's son or David's Lord (22:41–46)
7. Scribes and Pharisees exposed and denounced (23:1–36)
(1) Warnings against their example (23:1–12)
(2) Seven woes and coming judgment (23:13–36)
8. Jesus weeps over Jerusalem (23:37–39)

XV. Judgment: immediate and ultimate (24:1—26:2)
1. Destruction of Temple foretold (24:1–2)
2. Woes before end of the age (24:3–14)
3. Fate of Judea and warning against false messiahs and prophets (24:15–28)
4. The coming of the Son of man (24:29–31)
5. Lessons from the fig tree (24:32–35)
6. Time of Parousia unknown (24:36–44)

7. On being prepared (24:45—25:13)
   (1) Faithful and unfaithful servants (24:45–51)
   (2) The ten maidens (25:1–13)
8. Parable of the talents: those who have and those who have not (25:14–30)
9. Final judgment: serving Christ in serving others (25:31–46)
10. Prediction of betrayal (26:1–2)

XVI. Arrest, crucifixion, and resurrection of Jesus (26:3—28:20)

1. Preceding events (26:3—27:26)
   (1) The plot (26:3–5)
   (2) Jesus anointed at Bethany (26:6–13)
   (3) Judas bargains to betray Jesus (26:14–16)
   (4) Passover with disciples (26:17–25)
   (5) Institution of Lord's Supper (26:26–29)
   (6) Jesus warns disciples of betrayal and Peter protests (26:30–35)
   (7) Gethsemane (26:36–46)
   (8) The betrayal and arrest (26:47–56)
   (9) Hearing before Caiaphas (26:57–68)
   (10) Peter's denial of Jesus (26:69–75)
   (11) Trial before Pilate (27:1–26)
2. The crucifixion (27:27–56)
   (1) Jesus mocked by soldiers (27:27–31)
   (2) Jesus crucified (27:32–44)
   (3) Jesus' death (27:45–56)
3. The burial of Jesus (27:57–66)
   (1) The burial (27:57–61)
   (2) The guard at the tomb (27:62–66)
4. The resurrection and appearances of Jesus (28:1–20)
   (1) Appearance to the women (28:1–10)
   (2) False report of the guards (28:11–15)
   (3) The commissioning of the disciples (28:16–20)

Selected Bibliography

ALLEN, W. C. *A Critical and Exegetical Commentary on the Gospel According to S. Matthew* ("The International Critical Commentary"). New York: Charles Scribners' Sons, 1907.

ARGYLE, A. W. *The Gospel According to Matthew* ("The Cambridge Bible Commentary"). Cambridge: University Press, 1963.

BACON, B. W. *Studies in Matthew.* New York: Henry Holt & Co., 1930.

BLAIR, E. P., *Jesus in the Gospel of Matthew.* New York: Abingdon Press, 1960.

BORNKAMM, GÜNTHER, GERHARD BARTH, and H. J. HELD. *Tradition and Interpretation in Matthew.* Tr. PERCY SCOTT. Philadelphia: Westminster Press, 1963.

BROADUS, J. A. *The Gospel of Matthew* ("An American Commentary on the New Testament"). Philadelphia: The American Baptist Publication Society, 1886.

DAVIES, W. D. *The Setting of the Sermon on the Mount.* Cambridge: University Press, 1964.

FILSON, FLOYD V. *The Gospel According to St. Matthew.* ("Harper's New Testament Commentaries"). New York: Harper & Bros., 1960.

HARE, DOUGLAS R. A. *The Theme of Jewish Persecution of Christians in the Gospel According to St. Matthew.* Cambridge: University Press, 1967.

HUMMEL, REINHARD. *Die Auseinandersetzung zwischen Kirche und Judentum im Matthäusevangelium.* 2d ed.: München: Chr. Kaiser Verlag, 1966.

JOHNSON, S. E. and G. A. BUTTRICK. *The Gospel According to St. Matthew.* ("The Interpreter's Bible," VII). New York: Abingdon-Cokesbury, 1951.

KILPATRICK, G. D. *The Origins of the Gospel According to St. Matthew.* Oxford: Clarendon Press, 1946.

LOHMEYER, E. and W. SCHMAUCK. *Das Evangelium des Matthäus.* 3d ed.; Göttingen: Vandenhoeck & Rüprecht, 1962.

MCNEILE, A. H. *The Gospel According to St. Matthew.* London: The Macmillan Co., 1915.

PLUMMER, A. *An Exegetical Commentary on the Gospel According to S. Matthew.* Reprinted; Grand Rapids: Wm. B. Eerdmans Publishing Co., 1963.

ROBINSON, T. H. *The Gospel of Matthew.* ("The Moffatt New Testament Commentary"). New York: Harper & Bros., 1927.

SCHNIEWIND, J., *Das Evangelium nach Mat-*

thäus. 9th ed.; Göttingen; Vandenhoeck & Rüprecht, 1960.

STENDAHL, K. *The School of St. Matthew.* Lund: C. W. K. Gleerup, 1954.

STRECKER, GEORG, *Der Weg der Gerechtigkeit, Untersuchung zur Theologie des Matthäus.* 2d ed., Göttingen: Vandenhoeck & Rüprecht, 1966.

TRILLING, WOLFGANG. *Das Wahre Israel, Studien zur Theologie des Matthäus-Evangeliums.* 3d ed., München: Kösel Verlag, 1964.

WALKER, ROLF, *Die Heilsgeschichte im ersten Evangelium.* Göttingen: Vandenhoeck & Rüprecht, 1967.

Commentary on the Text

I. *The Birth of Jesus and the Beginning of His Ministry* (*1:1—4:25*)

1. *The Genealogy of Jesus Christ* (*1:1–17*)

1 The book of the genealogy of Jesus Christ,
the son of David, the son of Abraham.
2 Abraham was the father of Isaac, and Isaac
the father of Jacob, and Jacob the father of
Judah and his brothers, 3 and Judah the father
of Perez and Zerah by Tamar, and Perez the
father of Hezron, and Hezron the father of
Ram, 4 and Ram the father of Amminadab, and
Amminadab the father of Nahshon, and Nah-
shon the father of Salmon, 5 and Salmon the
father of Boaz by Rahab, and Boaz the father
of Obed by Ruth, and Obed the father of Jesse,
6 and Jesse the father of David the king.
And David was the father of Solomon by the
wife of Uriah, 7 and Solomon the father of
Rehoboam, and Rehoboam the father of Abi-
jah, and Abijah the father of Asa, 8 and Asa the
father of Jehoshaphat, and Jehoshaphat the
father of Joram, and Joram the father of Uz-
ziah, 9 and Uzziah the father of Jotham, and
Jotham the father of Ahaz, and Ahaz the father
of Hezekiah, 10 and Hezekiah the father of
Manasseh, and Manasseh the father of Amos,
and Amos the father of Josiah, 11 and Josiah
the father of Jechoniah and his brothers, at the
time of the deportation to Babylon.
12 And after the deportation to Babylon: Je-
choniah was the father of Shealtiel, and Sheal-
tiel the father of Zerubbabel, 13 and Zerubba-
bel the father of Abiud, and Abiud the father
of Eliakim, and Eliakim the father of Azor,
14 and Azor the father of Zadok, and Zadok the
father of Achim, and Achim the father of
Eliud, 15 and Eliud the father of Eleazar, and
Eleazar the father of Matthan, and Matthan
the father of Jacob, 16 and Jacob the father of
Joseph the husband of Mary, of whom Jesus
was born, who is called Christ.
17 So all the generations from Abraham to
David were fourteen generations, and from
David to the deportation to Babylon fourteen
generations, and from the deportation to Baby-
lon to the Christ fourteen generations.

Jesus Christ, the son of David, the son of Abraham sets forth the theme of the whole Gospel, even though its closest tie is with the genealogy which follows. Matthew's theme is that Jesus is the Davidic Messiah in whom the covenants with Abraham (Gen. 12:2 f.; 18:18) and David (2 Sam. 7:16) are fulfilled (cf. Robinson, p. 2). The fulfilment theme is not explicit in the superscription, but it is unfolded in the Gospel and carried forward through the concluding verses of the book (28:18–20). Matthew begins with Israel's heritage and hopes which are fulfilled in Jesus Christ, and he closes the Gospel with a world outlook (Filson, p. 52).

Son of Abraham may have as antecedent either Jesus or David. There is no real difficulty, for both are sons of Abraham.

Book of the genealogy translates a word which literally means genesis. Probably Matthew deliberately follows a pattern in Genesis (2:4; 5:1; 6:9; 10:1; 11:10,27). Since 1:18 has a further introduction, ***the birth*** [genesis] ***of Jesus Christ took place in this way,*** it is likely that 1:1 formally introduces only the genealogy (1:1–17), but it has overtones for the whole Gospel.

In Matthew, the Davidic descent of Jesus is both affirmed (also Acts 2:30 ff.; 13:23; Rom. 1:3; 2 Tim. 2:8; Rev. 22:16) and clarified (22:41–43). Jesus is seen as the one in whom the promises to David are fulfilled, but he is more than just another David. He is David's Lord (22:41–43) as well as son. Matthew sees Jesus as Messiah but not in a political sense.

Matthew's artistic touch, so apparent throughout the Gospel, is clearly seen in the genealogy. According to his summary statement (1:17), the names fall into three groups of 14 each: from Abraham to David, from David to the deportation to Babylon, and from the Babylonian deportation to Jesus. That Matthew calls special attention to this point indicates the importance to him of the number 14.

The overriding concern of the genealogy is to trace the fortunes of God's people from the great expectations in Abraham to the seeming fulfilment in David (vv. 2–6), then the decline from David to the Babylonian exile, where all seemed to be lost (vv. 7–11), and finally from the hopelessness of the Babylonian exile to the true goal in Jesus Christ (vv. 12–16). What was promised to Abraham was seemingly fulfilled in ***David the king,*** under whom the Israelites attained what seemed to be their golden age, but what was gained in David was miserably lost in the Exile. The true fulfilment of what was promised to Abraham and David is found in Jesus Christ, the true ***son of David, the son of Abraham.*** What is gained in him will be guarded "to the close of the age" (28:20).

The genealogy may provide a cryptogram in the form of an acrostic for David. Fourteen may be a reference in code to Jesus as "David." Gematria was an ancient practice of assigning a number to a person (cf. Rev. 13:18), computed by totaling the number value of each letter in one's name. The first letter in the alphabet had the number value of one, the second letter two, etc. The name David in Hebrew would have the number value of 14 (DVD = 4 + 6 + 4). Matthew may have intended thus to have written "David" across each section of the genealogy.

Both Matthew and Luke trace the descent of Jesus through Joseph (the legal father), not Mary. The view that Luke traced the genealogy through Mary, advanced by Annius of Viterbo (*ca.* 1490), is to be rejected. The chief difference between Matthew and Luke is that Matthew traces the descent through the royal line of David and Solomon, whereas Luke traces it through David and Nathan. Luke's genealogy is concerned with Jesus' relation to the whole human race. Matthew's is more concerned with the royal descent and fulfilment of Israel's heritage and hopes.

The 14's clearly belong to Matthew's literary design and are not to be taken as an exact figure for the generations belonging to each period (cf. Broadus, pp. 4 ff). The names do not actually add up to 14 per division. Matthew has only twenty-seven names after David, whereas Luke has forty-two. In Semitic reckoning "son of" could designate line of descent as well as immediate parentage. Further evidence that fourteen is not intended to be understood literally is that there are omissions seemingly between Solomon and David (v. 5), clearly between Joram and Uzziah (Ahaziah, Joash, and Amaziah not appearing), and Jehoiakim omitted in verse 11 (cf. 2 Kings 8:24; 23:34; 24:6; 1 Chron. 3:11; 2 Chron. 22:1, 11; 24:27). These omissions make it clear that ***father of*** (and Luke's "son of") is to be taken "not literally, but as denoting progenitorship of descent in general" (Broadus, p. 6). Matthew deliberately sought to give symmetry to the literary style of the genealogy, and the fourteens may have symbolic value. One may safely follow Broadus in rejecting various attempts to harmonize the two genealogies and also the efforts to make the credibility of Matthew dependent upon a scientific analysis of the genealogy (pp. 5 ff.). His purpose is to relate Jesus to David and Abraham, not to give a literal and complete genealogical catalog.

Remarkable is the inclusion of four women (***Tamar, Rahab, Ruth,*** and the ***wife of Uriah***). Customarily, Jewish genealogies give only the names of men. Matthew not only passed over women like Sarah but included women who were involved in shameful acts or who were outside Israel. The widowed ***Tamar,*** posing as a harlot, tricked her father-in-law Judah into fathering her twin sons ***Perez*** and ***Zerah*** (cf. Gen. 38: 3–30). ***Rahab*** was a harlot of Jericho who assisted the invading Israelites (Jos. 2:1–7; 6:22–25). ***Ruth*** was a Moabitess, not of Israel. Bathsheba is not named but termed, the ***wife of Uriah*** by whom ***David was the father of Solomon.***

Matthew may intend to contrast Mary and these four women, but the poetic nature of the genealogy and birth narratives imply not so much a polemic against Jewish slanders against Mary as the church's confession of faith, for polemic seldom creates poetry (see Davies, p. 66).

Why did Matthew thus feature these women? Clearly, it was in no way to reflect adversely upon Jesus. It may have been to stress God's grace upon the sinful, the abused, and the unfortunate. Probably it was to show that salvation is God's act of grace, not dependent upon human merit. The inclusion of ***Rahab,*** a Canaanitess, and ***Ruth,*** a Moabitess, supports Matthew's universalism and portrayal of Jesus as one who came to bring all nations under his discipleship (cf. 15:22; 28:19). Jesus was ***son of David, the son of Abraham,*** but he also was related to the whole of mankind and came to create a new family of faith which transcends ties of flesh (12:50). Matthew's observance that Ruth was in the ancestry to ***David the king*** and to Jesus shows a disposition toward all people in striking contrast to the priestly denial of access to "the assembly of the Lord" to a "bastard . . . Ammonite or Moabite" unto "the tenth generation" (Deut. 23:2 f.).

Matthew's choice of the word genesis (*generation* in KJV and *genealogy* in RSV) seems to be a deliberate reflection of the book of Genesis. He obviously is concerned first of all to set forth the human (vv. 1–17) and the divine (1:18–25) sonship of Jesus. That he is also concerned to show a new beginning (genesis) which proceeds from Jesus Christ is an intriguing idea. Jesus is introduced in a long line of those who "begat" others. One might ask, "Whom did Jesus beget?" Did creation stop in Jesus? Jesus begat no one in the flesh, but in him creation continues on a new and higher level.[13] Matthew does not call Jesus the "second Adam" as does Paul (1 Cor. 15: 45), nor does he describe salvation as a new creation (2 Cor. 5:17) or as a "birth from above" as does John (3:3). In the genealogy are germinal ideas for seeing in Jesus a new "genesis," but the origin of Jesus, human and divine, is Matthew's first concern. Implicit may be the further idea that a new era and a new creation began with Jesus.

Although Matthew presents Jesus as a son of both Abraham and David, he is careful to point out that Jesus is also David's Lord (22:41–46) and that the true sons of Abraham share his faith and not just his flesh (3:9; 8:11; cf. 12:46–50). Matthew may see that the covenant promises to Abraham that in him all the nations would be blessed (Gen. 12:2 f.; 18:18) and to David that to him would be given an eternal and righteous kingdom (2 Sam. 7:16) are fulfilled in Jesus Christ (1:1; 28:18–20).

In Jesus is both a continuity and discontinuity with Israel. Jesus is the fulfilment of the Davidic-messianic hopes of Israel, but also in the virgin-born Jesus is the beginning of a new creation.

According to the generally accepted text, as followed here, verse 16 supports the story of the virgin birth of Jesus. However, an important fourth-century manuscript, Sinaitic Syriac, reads: "Joseph, to whom was betrothed the virgin Mary, begat Jesus, the one called Christ." A similar reading is found with variations in some Greek manuscripts (Theta and Family 13), the margin of Lectionary 547, some Old Latin manuscripts (a,c,d,g^1,q, and possibly b,k), and Ambrosiaster. These manuscript differences raise the question of traditions which may lie behind Matthew, but that Matthew accepts the virgin birth of Jesus is beyond

[13] Fritz Kunkel, *Creation Continues, A Psychological Interpretation of the First Gospel* (New York: Scribners, 1947), p. 22 *et passim.*

dispute. Joseph's fears (1:19) and plain statements in 1:18,23 place Matthew's position beyond doubt.

2. The Birth of Jesus Christ (1:18–25)

**18 Now the birth of Jesus Christ took place in
this way. When his mother Mary had been
betrothed to Joseph, before they came together
she was found to be with child of the Holy
Spirit; 19 and her husband Joseph, being a just
man and unwilling to put her to shame, resolved to divorce her quietly. 20 But as he
considered this, behold, an angel of the Lord
appeared to him in a dream, saying, "Joseph,
son of David, do not fear to take Mary your
wife, for that which is conceived in her is of
the Holy Spirit; 21 she will bear a son, and you
shall call his name Jesus, for he will save his
people from their sins." 22 All this took place to
fulfil what the Lord had spoken by the
prophet:
23 "Behold, a virgin shall conceive and bear a
son,
and his name shall be called Emmanuel"
(which means, God with us). 24 When Joseph
woke from sleep, he did as the angel of the
Lord commanded him; he took his wife, 25 but
knew her not until she had borne a son; and he
called his name Jesus.**

The same Greek word (*genesis*) is used for the genealogy (1:1) and the birth (1:18) of Jesus Christ. In vv. 1–17 is given ***the book of the genealogy;*** in 1:18–25 is given the birth story, with chief interest in the divine origin of Jesus: born of the virgin Mary and begotten of the Holy Spirit. With this primary emphasis on the divine origin is a second major concern in Matthew. All that took place in Jesus Christ was in fulfilment of prophecy as found in the Scriptures (v. 22). Jesus Christ is ***Emmanuel, God with us*** (v. 23); and the name Jesus indicates his purpose in coming, to save us from our sins (v. 21).

Matthew and Luke (1:26–38) alike feature the story of the virgin birth of Jesus. Neither shows dependence upon the other, indicating that the story is older than either Gospel. Each tells the story with a theological interest. Luke's concern seems to be to stress the divine power and grace. To Mary's question of how she could bear a son since she had no husband, the answer was, "With God there is no impossibility" (Luke 1:37). Mary of herself could not produce a son, but God could give her one. This is the gospel: man cannot produce his salvation, but God can accomplish it.

In Matthew the stress is upon the divine origin of Jesus, ***conceived . . . of the Holy Spirit.*** This is doubly emphasized by the name Emmanuel, Hebrew for ***God with us.*** Just as the genealogy traced the human origin of Jesus through Mary to David and Abraham, the birth narrative traces his divine origin through Mary to the Holy Spirit. Matthew does not attempt to explain how Jesus Christ could be both man and God; he simply affirms it. There is no disposition to distinguish "two natures" within Jesus. Matthew simply knows him as born of Mary (1:16) and conceived of the Holy Spirit (v. 20). He knows Jesus as a real man, not a seeming (docetic) one. He also knows him as ***Emmanuel, God with us.*** The name Emmanuel does not reappear in Matthew, but the equivalent recurs in the last verse of the Gospel: "and lo, I am with you always, to the close of the age" (28:20). As diverse in background and nature as are Matthew's Emmanuel and John's Logos, both make the same basic claim, that God himself is uniquely present in Jesus Christ.

Joseph is so introduced into the story as to reinforce the claim that Jesus had no human father. When he became aware of Mary's pregnancy, he concluded that she had been untrue to him, knowing that the child was not his own. Joseph resolved to divorce Mary and to do it privately. The word *dikaios* can mean just or righteous. If the former is intended, Joseph is to be understood as wanting to treat Mary justly. Probably what is meant is that he was righteous and in his understanding of righteousness could not consider continuing a relationship with one thought to be an adulteress. The conjunction can be translated "and" or "yet." "Being righteous" and, or yet, "not wanting to stigmatize her" probably refer to two different things. He wanted to do right, which to him meant that he must divorce her; but he had no desire to subject her to unnecessary shame or danger. An adulteress could be stoned to death (Lev. 20:10; Deut. 22:23 f.). Private divorce was a provision of Jewish law.

Betrothal was a legal arrangement, the betrothed being called husband and wife (Deut. 22:24), and could be dissolved only by divorce. Joseph and Mary legally were husband and wife, but they had not consummated the marriage through sexual relationship. Only the assurance that Mary's child was begotten of the Holy Spirit prompted Joseph to retain Mary as his wife.

Joseph ***knew her not*** until Mary ***had borne a son.*** "Know" is a biblical term frequently used for sexual relationship. Matthew clearly affirms that Joseph and Mary had no sexual relationship until after the birth of Jesus. There is not a hint that their abstinence from a normal marital relationship extended beyond the birth of Jesus. The dogma of the perpetual virginity of Mary is postbiblical and does not belong to the discussion here.

Although Matthew presents Jesus as virgin born, the emphasis is upon his being ***conceived of the Holy Spirit.*** He does not make the divinity of Jesus Christ depend upon Mary but upon the Holy Spirit. After Matthew and Luke, the next traceable reference to the virgin birth of Jesus is in Ignatius of Antioch (ca. 117), and his concern was to refute Gnostic or docetic views by stressing the human, carnal reality of the birth of Jesus.[14]

The virgin birth is not intended to explain Jesus' sinlessness. Significantly, it is precisely in Matthew and Luke, where the virgin birth stories appear, that the most direct attention is given to the temptations of Jesus. Mark's two verses on the wilderness temptations of Jesus (1:12–13) are considerably expanded by Matthew (4:1–17) and Luke (4:1–13). Both represent Jesus as severely tempted and both attribute to his own decision his complete victory over temptation. They credit Jesus, not Mary, with the victory over sin.

Later ideas that sin is transmitted through the male parent and through sex are foreign to Matthew's intention and contradict the biblical view of creation, sex, and sin. Sin belongs to personal, moral choice, not to biology. Neither sin nor salvation is biologically transmitted. Gnostic ideas which interpreted the virgin birth as God's way of overcoming sinful nature and speculations about Mary's "immaculate conception" and "perpetual virginity" are traceable to second-century writings like the apocryphal *Protevangelium of James,* not to the New Testament. That Jesus had no human father belongs to divine choice and not to Gnostic problems of sex.

Verse 23 follows the LXX rendering of Isaiah 7:14. *Parthenos* is the Greek term which normally translates the Hebrew *bethulah,* which generally means virgin but which can mean a young wife (Joel 1:8); but here it translates the Hebrew word *almah,* normally rendered in Greek by *neanis* (maiden).[15] *Parthenos* generally designates a virgin, although it is used occasionally for one not a virgin (Gen. 34:3 f.). The fact that the Hebrew text of Isaiah 7:14 does not go beyond designating a young woman (*almah* designates a young woman of marriageable age whether married or not) no more affirms nor excludes the further idea that the woman was a virgin than does Paul's statement that Jesus was "born of woman" (Gal. 4:4). Matthew's intention to affirm Jesus' virgin birth is to be found in the Matthean story, not in the ambiguities of Hebrew or Greek words.

It is untenable to hold that Isaiah 7:14 is the origin of the belief in the virgin birth of Jesus (McNeile, p. 10). The Lukan story makes no reference to Isaiah 7:14, and Luke's Gospel is independent of if not older

[14] Hans von Campenhausen, *The Virgin Birth in the Theology of the Ancient Church,* "Studies in Historical Theology No. 2" (Naperville: Allenson, 1964), p. 30.

[15] Broadus (p. 13) writes: "The Hebrew substantive signifies 'maiden.'" He continues: "No case has been found in which it [almah] *must* mean a married woman."

than Matthew's. The story of the virgin birth is older than both Gospels. Matthew appeals to Isaiah to support a story already believed.

The name Jesus is significant for Matthew (vv. 21,25). It is the Greek counterpart to the Hebrew Joshua and means "Yahweh is salvation." With some modification, Matthew sees the name as suggesting deliverance or salvation as springing from Yahweh. Jesus Christ came to save men ***from their sins.*** There may be the implied corrective to the Zealot notion that the Davidic Messiah would save Israel from Roman rule. Matthew may have the additional concern to reject and resist a libertine or antinomian threat within the Christian community which would make salvation gift without demand. To Matthew, salvation is both gift and demand. Salvation is ***from sins*** as well as from sin.

3. *Rejection at Home, Reception from Afar (2:1–23)*

Several of Matthew's interests are served in this chapter: the foreshadowing of Jesus' ultimate rejection at home and acceptance by the Gentiles, fulfilment of Old Testament expectations, Jesus' Davidic ancestry, Jesus' identity as King of the Jews yet as shepherd-king of God's people, and the persecution which he and his people were to suffer.

(1) *The Wise Men from the East* (2:1–12)

**1 Now when Jesus was born in Bethlehem of
Judea in the days of Herod the king, behold,
wise men from the East came to Jerusalem,
saying, 2 "Where is he who has been born king
of the Jews? For we have seen his star in the
East, and have come to worship him." 3 When
Herod the king heard this, he was troubled,
and all Jerusalem with him; 4 and assembling
all the chief priests and scribes of the people,
he inquired of them where the Christ was to be
born. 5 They told him, "In Bethlehem of Judea;
for so it is written by the prophet:**
**6 'And you, O Bethlehem, in the land of Judah,
are by no means least among the rulers of
Judah;
for from you shall come a ruler
who will govern my people Israel.' "**
**7 Then Herod summoned the wise men se-
cretly and ascertained from them what time
the star appeared; 8 and he sent them to Bethlehem, saying, "Go and search diligently for
the child, and when you have found him bring
me word, that I too may come and worship
him." 9 When they had heard the king they
went their way; and lo, the star which they had
seen in the East went before them, till it came
to rest over the place where the child was.
10 When they saw the star, they rejoiced exceedingly with great joy; 11 and going into the
house they saw the child with Mary his
mother, and they fell down and worshiped
him. Then, opening their treasures, they offered him gifts, gold and frankincense and
myrrh. 12 And being warned in a dream not to
return to Herod, they departed to their own
country by another way.**

The story of the visit of the Wise Men from the East would not seem strange to first-century readers and "violates no canon of historical probability" (Allen, p. 14). Throughout much of the world was the expectation of a world redeemer, and many Jews expected a messiah (or messiahs, as at Qumran). There were Eastern magi, variously considered as magicians, astrologers, or sages. Matthew intended to relate history, not legend. This is not to overlook the part played by the Old Testament in shaping the form of the story, but it is arbitrary to say that the story was invented to supply a fulfilment to Old Testament texts. It is more likely that the story came first and that Scripture texts were then found to support and illuminate the story.

To Matthew the Wise Men probably had a symbolical meaning, however historical. Their coming to Jesus foreshadows the coming of people "from east and west" (8:11) to bow before the ***King of the Jews.*** Like Paul, Matthew believes that the gospel must go to the Jew first and then to the "Greek" (cf. 8:10–12; 12:18–21; 15:24–28; 24:14; 28:19 with Rom. 1:16). Accordingly, the universalism which is explicit in Matthew's closing lines (28:18–20) is implied even at the outset as Jesus is presented as King of the Jews, the one who is to "shepherd" (*poimanei*) his people Israel (v. 6), but who receives homage from the East.

Bethlehem of Judea, five miles south of

Jerusalem, was the home of Ruth and David and the burial place of Rachel. There was also a Bethlehem in Galilee, seven miles northwest of Nazareth.

Matthew and Luke show no dependence upon or knowledge of each other. They follow different traditions, Matthew giving nothing of Luke's account of a previous residence of Joseph and Mary in Nazareth, and Luke giving nothing of Matthew's account of the flight into Egypt or departure from Judea because of Archelaus. Both, however, place the birth of Jesus in Bethlehem. This implies two independent traditions older than Matthew and Luke.

Herod the king was Herod the Great, son of the Idumean Antipater. He was given the title "king of Judea" by the Roman Senate, with the backing of Anthony and Octavius, in 40 B.C. He thus broke the Hasmonean or Maccabean dynasty which had been in power since about 142 B.C. When the Christian calendar was developed by Dionysius Exiguus of Rome (sixth century), he failed by at least four years to synchronize it with the older Roman calender. That Herod had the children of Bethlehem up to two years of age slain may imply that Jesus was in his second year at the time. Accordingly, the birth of Jesus seems to have been not later than 6 or 5 B.C.

That Herod would slaughter the infants of Bethlehem is in keeping with all facts otherwise known of this cruel man. He executed his favorite wife, the Maccabean princess Mariamne; his high priestly brother-in-law; several of his own sons; and others near him. This Idumean usurper of the throne lived in fear of intrigue or assassination, and especially did he distrust and fear the Maccabean family into which he had married. The Wise Men's inquiry about the one ***born king of the Jews*** would be enough to send the old king into a new fit of suspicion, fear, and jealousy. In Matthew's text "born" (*ho techtheis*) is not a verb but a participle, having an adjectival force. The question asked by the magi was, "Where is the born king of the Jews?" Herod was king by intrigue, maneuver, Roman appointment, and the constant use of the sword to eliminate Maccabean rivals.

When Herod was troubled, so was ***all Jerusalem.*** This is understandable. When the mad king was upset, no life was safe. Family, friends, and foe were easy victims of the cruel and unpredictable king.

The ***chief priests and scribes*** may refer to the Jewish Sanhedrin, highest court of the Jews, or to an informal gathering of priests and scribes. Herod reduced the influence of this court as long as he lived, but he did not abolish it. That he would call upon it when it suited his convenience is not unlikely. ***Chief priests*** (*archiereis*) may be translated "high priests." Traditionally, there was only one high priest at a time, an heir to Aaron, and he served his whole lifetime. But under the Syrians, from about 175 B.C., and under the Romans, from about 63 B.C., the high priests were appointed and changed at will. According to Josephus there were 28 high priests from 40 B.C. to A.D. 70, appointed by either the Herods or the Romans. By high priests or chief priests is probably meant the few aristocratic families from which the office of high priest was filled. The ***scribes*** in the time of Jesus were chiefly Pharisaic, with some among Essenes and Sadducees. Pharisaic scribes were "laymen," rather than priests, but they were ordained as the recognized interpreters of the Mosaic law.

The beautiful lines of verse 6 seem to come from Micah 5:2, supplemented by 2 Samuel 5:2. Bethlehem was a little village but not least in honor, being the birthplace of David and the expected origin of the Christ. Of great significance is the fact that the promised ***ruler*** (*hegoumenos*) was to ***govern*** his ***people Israel.*** Jesus was king but not in the familiar pattern. He was the shepherd king (govern translates *poimanei*, actually "to shepherd"). The supplement is Matthew's own editing and reflects his particular concern to picture Jesus as the shepherd-king of God's people Israel. A shepherd not only governs; he protects and feeds. Later Matthew depicts him as the lowly king (21:5, quoting Isa. 62:11 and

Zech. 9:9). Although Matthew often reflects the tension between Pharisaic Judaism and Christians, he also preserves expressions of strong affection for Israel, as in the words, "who shall shepherd my people Israel" (v. 6).

What time the star appeared could be rendered, "the time of the appearing star," a second manner of referring to the ***star in the East,*** literally, "the star at its rising." Kepler calculated that there was a conjunction of the planets Jupiter and Saturn in May, October, and November of 7 B.C., and some scholars see an allusion to this phenomenon. However, Matthew's word is star (*aster*) and not constellation (*astron*). Probably he had in mind a unique star which marked the birth of Jesus.

More important to Matthew than the star are the magi or ***wise men from the East.*** The word magi is Indo-European, its root appearing in many languages and carrying the meaning of greatness. The magi were originally a priestly caste among the Medes, later recognized as teachers of religion and science among the Medo-Persians, with special interest in astrology and medicine. That they were Gentiles is a credible deduction from their reference to *the Jews.* That they were three in number is a precarious deduction from the mention of gifts of ***gold and frankincense and myrrh.*** Three kinds of gifts may or may not imply three donors. The legend that they were kings may have been inferred from Isaiah 40:3. Medieval art and Christmas carols have popularized the notion that they were kings, a notion which contradicts every New Testament picture of the humble beginnings of Jesus. Schlatter's insight is sound in the observance that the whole Gospel would have been different had it begun with God's sending kings to do homage to Jesus.[16] The power structures of neither religion nor world were on the side of Jesus. Only one king (Herod) is mentioned, and he tried to kill Jesus. The names Saphar, Melchior, and Balthasar are legendary. That gold symbolizes royalty, frankincense (an odorous gum) divinity, and myrrh (a gum used for perfume, spice, medicine, embalming) humanity is also legendary and throws no light necessarily on Matthew's intention. These gifts were normal for the time, especially intended for a king. That the magi do represent for Matthew the recognition of Jesus on the part of Gentiles is in keeping with one of his major concerns. Matthew, interacting with a Judaism that had rejected Jesus, forcefully brings out his acceptance by these Wise Men from the East. The zeal of these foreigners in searching for Jesus, their joy over finding him, and the worship they gave him contrasts with the indifference and later hostility of his own people.

Matthew seems to see the star as leading the magi from Jerusalem to Bethlehem, specifically to *the place* (v. 9) or ***the house*** (v. 11) where Mary and the child Jesus were. Justin Martyr, Origen, and Jerome preserve the tradition that Jesus was born in a cave. Luke, alluding to the night of Jesus' birth, specifies a manger (2:7,12). Matthew seems to refer to a later stage when Jesus was more than a newborn baby, calling him a ***child*** (*to paidion*), possibly beyond his first year.

In this brief passage, Matthew's christological interest is emphatic as he represents Jesus as the King of the Jews, the Christ, ruler, and one to whom homage (or worship) is due. The homage of the Wise Men from the East points further to Jesus as the King of the whole world, not of Israel alone. Although ignored by some and rejected by others, he is the joy of those who, like the Wise Men, find him (v. 10; 28:8).

(2) *The Flight into Egypt* (*2:13–15*)

[13] Now when they had departed, behold, an angel of the Lord appeared to Joseph in a dream and said, "Rise, take the child and his mother, and flee to Egypt, and remain there till I tell you; for Herod is about to search for the child, to destroy him." [14] And he rose and took

16 Adolf Schlatter, *Das Evangelium nach Matthäus* (Stuttgart: Calwer, 1961), p. 15.

the child and his mother by night, and departed to Egypt, [15] and remained there until the death of Herod. This was to fulfil what the Lord had spoken by the prophet, "Out of Egypt have I called my son."

Egypt in the time of Jesus was a Roman province, outside Herod's authority. There was a strong Jewish colony in Egypt, nearly a million according to Philo; Egyptian Jews spoke Greek and by 150 B.C. had their own temple at Leontopolis. Although Egypt included the Sinaitic peninsula and reached almost to Bethlehem, Matthew probably had the Egypt of the Nile in mind.

There are traces outside Matthew of Jesus' sojourn in Egypt. Rabbi Eliezer ben Hyrcanus (A.D. 80–120) held that Jesus [Ben Stada] brought magic arts out of Egypt (*Shabbath* 104b), and Origen (*Contra Celsus* 1,38) had to answer a tradition that Jesus worked in Egypt as a laborer, learned magic arts there, and returned to Palestine claiming to be a god (cf. Justin, *Apol.* 1,30). These obviously prejudicial traditions may have been developed from Matthew's account, having no independent value. If independent, a part of Matthew's purpose may have been to counteract such adverse traditions by showing that Jesus was only a small child when in Egypt, not a grown man learning magic, and that he was taken there for protection from Herod and brought back under divine protection and guidance.

It is probable that the belief that Jesus spent some time in Egypt is older than the employment of Hosea 11:1 as a proof text in support of the story. Hosea referred to Israel as God's "son" whom he called out of Egypt in the time of Moses. Matthew applies this to Jesus, God's Son in whom a new people were to be constituted (or Israel reconstituted).

That the text must be somewhat strained or reinterpreted in order to apply to Jesus strengthens the case for the view that the belief in an Egyptian sojourn is older than the employment of the text. A parallel illustrating the working principle may be found in the later rabbinical application of Numbers 24:17 to Bar Cocheba, "son of the star." No scholar suggests that the story of Bar Cocheba and the second Jewish-Roman War (A.D. 132–135) were invented in order to supply a fulfilment to this obscure text. Many of Matthew's "proof texts" seem remote or strained in application. This very fact argues for the priority of the belief in the events over the employment of the proof texts. Texts were found to explain or justify beliefs already held.

Striking parallels between Jesus and Moses appear in this paragraph. Just as Moses had fled Egypt to escape the pharaoh and returned when the pharaoh was dead (Ex. 4:19), so Jesus was taken out of Palestine to escape Herod and returned after Herod's death. Just as God had called Israel out of Egypt, so Jesus is called ***out of Egypt*** to save his people. Despite these peripheral parallels, it does not follow that Matthew saw Jesus as a new Moses. In the antitheses, the "but I say to you" passages in the Sermon on the Mount (5:21–48) and elsewhere, Matthew puts Jesus above Moses, not in a sequence with him. Jesus came not as a new Moses but as "the son of Abraham, the son of David" and also the Son of God, whose role it was to fulfil the Law and the Prophets, not to give a new law.

Again, basic themes are clear: rejection of Jesus at home, forced withdrawal from his own people, God's guidance at every point, the foreshadowing of ultimate rejection and suffering, the creation of God's people, and the fulfilment in Jesus of Old Testament expectation. This paragraph, like the whole of chapters 1—2, is programmatic in that it points to a twofold development.[17] On one side are the humble surroundings of Jesus, his birth in a small village, his rejection and flight, foreshadowing the cross. On the other side is the hand of God, compelling men of all kinds—good and bad, friendly and hostile—to serve his ultimate purpose.

(3) *Infants Slain in Bethlehem (2:16–18)*

[16] Then Herod, when he saw that he had been tricked by the wise men, was in a furious

[17] Franz Lau, *Das Matthäus Evangelium* (Stuttgart: Oncken, n.d.), p. 25.

rage, and he sent and killed all the male
children in Bethlehem and in all that region
who were two years old or under, according to
the time which he had ascertained from the
wise men. 17 Then was fulfilled what was spo-
ken by the prophet Jeremiah:
18 "A voice was heard in Ramah,
wailing and loud lamentation,
Rachel weeping for her children;
she refused to be consoled,
because they were no more."

The massacre of little babies is almost incredible, but it has often been an ugly part of life. Herod had his own sons by Mariamne, Alexander and Aristobulus, put to death in 7 B.C., fearing that they were seeking his throne. This atrocious act prompted the Roman Emperor Augustus to say, with a play on Greek words, that it were better to be Herod's pig (*hus*) than Herod's son (*huios*). Five days before his own death, Herod had his son Antipater killed. Fearing that his own death would cause joy in the land, Herod left the command (understandably not carried out) that at his death the oldest child in each home be put to death, thus hoping to make the nation weep instead of rejoice.

Matthew changed his introductory formula in verses 16 and 17, employing the conjunction "then" (*tote*) rather than "that" (*hina*), possibly to avoid the implication that God willed the massacre of the infants (cf. Plummer, p. 18).

This story, like the others in Matthew 1—2, is told very simply, with no novelistic embellishments. Joseph is represented as obediently serving the divine directions for the care of the child and his mother. That the directives came through the medium of dreams is not so important to Matthew as the fact that they came.

Matthew's employment of Jeremiah 31:15 is characteristically free in its application, evidence that the story of the slaughter of the infants was not invented out of this passage but that it was made to serve the story. Rachel, according to tradition, was buried between Jerusalem and Bethlehem. Ramah was about eight miles north of Jerusalem, and Jeremiah's reference was to Rachel's weeping over the Ephraimites' going into Babylonian exile. Rachel was the mother of Benjamin and Ephraim. Matthew applies the verse to the sorrow at Bethlehem, near which Rachel was buried. It would require great imagination to invent the Bethlehem story out of Jeremiah 31:15. Christian thought could easily adapt the the verse to a belief already held or an event already known (cf. Robinson, p. 10). The poignant story points to the innocent suffering of the Saviour and his people.

Herod's order that ***all male children two years old or under*** be killed implies that Jesus at the time was beyond his first year or that the heartless king made his net wider than necessary, caring nothing for the number slain, as long as he reached his intended victim.

(4) *From Egypt to Nazareth* (*2:19–23*)

19 But when Herod died, behold, an angel of
the Lord appeared in a dream to Joseph in
Egypt, saying, 20 "Rise, take the child and his
mother, and go to the land of Israel, for those
who sought the child's life are dead." 21 And he
rose and took the child and his mother, and
went to the land of Israel. 22 But when he
heard that Archelaus reigned over Judea in
place of his father Herod, he was afraid to go
there, and being warned in a dream he with-
drew to the district of Galilee. 23 And he went
and dwelt in a city called Nazareth, that what
was spoken by the prophets might be fulfilled,
"He shall be called a Nazarene."

The purpose of this paragraph is to explain why Jesus, though born in Bethlehem, was known as ***a Nazarene*** (properly spelled Nazorean). Matthew derives the name from the town Nazareth. The fact that Jesus was known as a Nazorean and that he resided in Nazareth is well established, but the derivation and meaning of Nazorean (in Greek) and the origin of ***what was spoken by the prophets*** are problematic.

Jesus is called "the Nazorean" (*Nazoraios* in Greek, rendered *Nazarene* in RSV) in Matthew (2:23; 26:71), Luke (18:37; 24:19), John (18:5,7; 19:19), and Acts (2:22; 3:6; 4:10; 6:14; 22:8; 26:9). His followers are called Nazoreans in Acts 24:5. The problem arises out of the fact that Nazareth and Nazorean seem not to be cognates. How is "o" derived from "a" in

Nazareth? (Cf. Lohmeyer and Schmauch, pp. 31 f.) Some would derive the term Nazorean from Nazirite (*Nasiraios* or *Nazarios*), but Jesus was obviously not a Nazirite. John the Baptist had some affinities with the Nazirites (cf. Luke 1:15; Num. 6), but Jesus differed from John at this point (cf. 11:19). The suggestion has been made that the term Nazirite could have been applied first to John and then to Jesus as an early follower of John. Yet another possibility is that in a local dialect (Galilean-Aramaic) the term Nazorean and the name of the town (*Nas^{e}rath*) were related.

A further unsolved problem is the intention of the citation of ***what was spoken by the prophets.*** The phrase ***shall be called a Nazarene*** is not found in the Old Testament. Possible derivations are Isaiah 11:1; Judges 13:5; Jeremiah 23:5; and Leviticus 21:10–12. Some see an allusion to the branch (*netzer*) which grows out of what appeared to be a dead stump (Isa. 11:1). Against this is the fact that "branch" or "shoot" is not otherwise known as a messianic term.

What does emerge with clarity is that the elusive proof text did not give rise to the tradition that Jesus was from Nazareth or that he was known as the Nazorean. Matthew's interest was to explain current usage and belief. That Jesus grew up in the little village of Nazareth (unmentioned in the Old Testament, Josephus, and Talmud) in despised "Galilee of the Gentiles" (4:15) is no Christian invention.

Matthew accounts for the move of Jesus' family to Nazareth in terms of the Herodian threat. Herod the Great died in 4 B.C., and his last will designated his son Archelaus to be king of Judea, Samaria, and Idumea. Another son, Antipas, became tetrarch of Galilee and Perea. (For a third son, Philip, see Luke 3:1.) Augustus denied Archelaus the title king, holding out the prospect that as reward for proper conduct of his office he later might have the title. Augustus gave him the title "ethnarch," but banished him in A.D. 6. Archelaus was the worst of Herod's sons, although Antipas was little better. The plural form ***those . . . are dead*** refers to Herod the Great and was probably influenced by Exodus 4:19.

4. The Ministry Inaugurated (3:1—4:25)

At 3:1 Matthew reaches the point where Mark begins. In chapters 1—2 Matthew follows sources otherwise unknown, paralleled only slightly in Luke. From this point on Matthew seems to follow Mark as his chief narrative source, working other narrative and teaching materials into the Markan framework. Employing a topical or thematic principle, he breaks into or even reverses Mark's order when it serves this purpose. He often shortens and occasionally omits Markan material, presumably to make room for new material or to serve his own redactional or theological interests.

Some shaping of materials to make them intelligible and applicable to a given situation is valid and necessary. On the other hand, it cannot be made too emphatic that Matthew is working with materials which actually go back to the words and deeds of Jesus.

In chapters 3 and 4 are five main subjects: the preaching of John the Baptist (3:1–12), the baptism of Jesus (3:13–17), the temptation of Jesus (4:1–11), the move from Nazareth to Capernaum (4:12–17), and the calling of disciples (4:18–25). From the standpoint of sources, three categories of material are found: (1) material apparently from Mark, (2) non-Markan material common to Matthew and Luke, commonly called "Q," and (3) material found only in Matthew. Precisely what oral or written sources lie behind Matthew's usage is not in every case demonstrable.

(1) The Message of the Baptist (3:1–12)

1 In those days came John the Baptist,
preaching in the wilderness of Judea,
2 "Repent, for the kingdom of heaven is at
hand." 3 For this is he who was spoken of by
the prophet Isaiah when he said,
"The voice of one crying in the wilderness:
Prepare the way of the Lord,
make his paths straight."
4 Now John wore a garment of camel's hair,
and a leather girdle around his waist; and his

**food was locusts and wild honey. 5 Then went
out to him Jerusalem and all Judea and all the
region about the Jordan, 6 and they were baptized by him in the river Jordan, confessing
their sins.**

**7 But when he saw many of the Pharisees
and Sadducees coming for baptism, he said to
them, "You brood of vipers! Who warned you
to flee from the wrath to come? 8 Bear fruit
that befits repentance, 9 and do not presume to
say to yourselves, 'We have Abraham as our
father'; for I tell you, God is able from these
stones to raise up children to Abraham. 10 Even
now the axe is laid to the root of the trees;
every tree therefore that does not bear good
fruit is cut down and thrown into the fire.**

**11 "I baptize you with water for repentance,
but he who is coming after me is mightier than
I, whose sandals I am not worthy to carry; he
will baptize you with the Holy Spirit and with
fire. 12 His winnowing fork is in his hand, and
he will clear his threshing floor and gather his
wheat into the granary, but the chaff he will
burn with unquenchable fire."**

John the Baptist is introduced as one already known, evidence that Matthew wrote primarily for the church, whatever his hope that his Gospel would be read by people outside. The story is told with no special interest in John himself. Matthew's ***in those days*** seemingly refers to the days of Jesus, not of John, who is important only as he relates to Jesus.

Attention is focused on John's message, although Matthew describes his clothing and diet. His robe was made of ***camel's hair*** (not camel skins), gathered up by ***a leather girdle***, and his diet consisted of insects like ***locusts*** (not the fruit of a tree) and ***wild honey***, presumably deposited by bees in rocks or trees, likening him to the prophet Elijah (2 Kings 1:8; cf. Mal. 4:5 f.; Luke 1:17). It is possible that 11:18 may imply ascetic motivation behind John's diet, but the verse before us may imply no more than that John lived on what the desert afforded. Although in a priestly line, John was a prophet (11:9). His preaching as presented by Matthew was chiefly about the kingdom of heaven and the "coming one" in whom it had drawn near (vv. 2,11 f.).

The kingdom of heaven (interchangeable with kingdom of God) is the sovereign rule of God (see Introduction, pp. 69–70) which John sees to have drawn near in "the coming one." He sees the kingdom chiefly in terms of judgment (v. 7), set forth under the analogies of ***axe, fire***, and ***winnowing fork*** or shovel. The urgent call is to repentance, addressed first of all to Jews (vv. 5,9), including their Pharisaic and Sadducean leaders (v. 7). Matthew, unlike Mark and Luke, places the proclamation of the kingdom back into the ministry of John the Baptist.

John's ministry, according to Matthew, was ***in the wilderness of Judea***, seemingly west of the Dead Sea but reaching up to at least the lower Jordan River (v. 6). At some point he must have crossed over into Perea or have reached up into Galilee, otherwise he would not have come under the jurisdiction of Herod Antipas (cf. 14:1–12; John 1:28; 3:23; 10:40).

John probably was known as "the Baptist" or "the baptizer" (14:2,8) not only because he employed this initiation rite but because he baptized Jews. There was a Jewish proselyte baptism in the first century, and the likelihood is that it was practiced before John's time. There are Jewish traditions which possibly reflect its pre-Christian practice, as early as Hillel (*Tosephta Pesachim*, 7:13; *Jer. Pesach.* 8:8 or *Eduyoth*, 5:2). The Talmudic requirement of baptism, circumcision, and a sacrifice (*Kerithoth*, 81*a;* Jeb, 46*a*) implies a time before the destruction of the Temple (A.D. 70), after which time Temple sacrifices were impossible. It is not likely that orthodox Judaism would have adopted a Christian rite. Since Christianity was cradled in Judaism, no problem would be faced in the development of baptism from Jewish practice.

What was revolutionary in John's baptism was the baptism of Jews. This placed Jews on the same level as Gentiles, calling them to the same induction rite into the true people of God. John would not permit even Pharisees and Sadducees to base their hopes of inclusion in the people of God upon their descent from Abraham, with a probable play on Aramaic words, saying, ***God is able from these stones*** [*banim*] ***to raise up children*** [*abanim*] ***to Abraham.***

John called his hearers to repentance (v. 2). The Greek word by etymology means to change one's mind, but this includes far more than the rational. The term repent (*metanoeite*) is more adequately translated "be converted" or "turn," as in the Hebrew *shuv* or Aramaic *thuv.* In the presence of the kingdom of heaven, God's sovereign rule, one is to turn to God in submission. The basic relationship between God and man is acknowledged in repentance (conversion) as man takes his place as subject before God as king. The term Christ (1:1) designates the coming one as anointed of God to reign. The people of God are those who yield in submission to the kingdom of God as it confronts them in Christ. Matthew saw the kingdom as future with respect to its fulness, but already present in "the coming one."

Verse 3 not only supports Matthew's fulfilment theme (Isa. 40:3), but it points up a major presupposition in all biblical theology, i.e., God's initiative in the salvation of man. In Isaiah, God is pictured as coming to his people, exiled in Babylon, to deliver them and to lead them home. Matthew applies the passage to John and Jesus—John being ***the voice of one crying in the wilderness*** whose mission is to ***prepare the way of the Lord,*** Jesus being the Lord who is coming to save his people. In biblical perspective, initiative is with God in creation, revelation, and redemption. God creates; God reveals himself; and God comes to man to save him. In many religious systems, man is seen as discovering God and establishing himself before God, whether through ritual, works, goodness, asceticism, knowledge, or otherwise.

Great numbers of Jews from ***Jerusalem and all Judea and all the region about the Jordan*** went out to hear John. ***All*** is best understood as a hyperbole, with no claim that every individual person in these areas heard John. The sudden appearance of a man with the manner and message of a prophet, after many generations without one, created a sensation.

The middle voice of the verb *ebaptizonto* may best be rendered, "They were getting themselves baptized" (cf. v. 6). They were not passive. On the other hand it is not conclusive that they immersed themselves. Qumran ritual ablutions were repeated daily and were seemingly by self-immersion, but these do not form the background or model for John's baptism. His baptism was either an innovation or an adaptation of Jewish proselyte baptism.

That John's baptism was by immersion is not subject to serious debate. The word itself indicates a "dipping." Baptism is built upon the root *baph-*, akin to *bath-* in *bathus,* meaning "deep" (Curtius, *Greek Etymology*). The German *Taufe* (*tief* means deep) preserves this idea. Paul's whole analogy of being "buried" with Christ (Rom. 6:4) is meaningless apart from the picture in immersion. Whatever one may retain of the intention of baptism in any other mode, he loses the pictorial force of burial and resurrection except in immersion. More important than the form of baptism is its presupposition of repentance (vv. 2,8) and confession of sins (v. 6). Those whom John baptized in the Jordan River confessed their sins. That John did not view his baptism as having saving value follows from the fact that he denied it to Pharisees and Sadducees who failed to produce ***fruit*** (evidence) of ***repentance.*** Had John seen saving power in baptism itself, he would have been without excuse for denying it to those who by his own pronouncement were in the path of coming judgment (v. 7).

John excluded the hope that one's physical descent from ***Abraham*** would give him acceptance with God (v. 9). Being a Jew carried with it greater privilege (Rom. 2:17—3:2) and greater responsibility, but it did not guarantee acceptance with God. Sonship in the family of God is a matter of faith, not flesh. Verse 9 anticipates the inclusion of Gentiles among God's people.

John's baptism and that of Jesus differed in that John's water baptism could only outwardly signify a new situation for those who repented and confessed their sins, while Jesus offered a baptism ***with the Holy Spirit and with fire.*** Jesus is the bearer of the Spirit. The gift of the Spirit is not a special, "second blessing" for deluxe model Christians; it is that without which there is no newness of life. Every Christian receives the baptism (filling) of the Spirit. There are no non-charismatic Christians. The gift of the Spirit is not limited to a select few of the saved or to a special area of life in the saved. The Holy Spirit is God's coming into each of his children to give new direction, power, and meaning to the whole of life. "Spirituality" relates to each child of God and to all areas of life.

Baptism ***with fire*** apparently points to judgment, to be understood along with the analogies of ***axe*** and ***winnowing*** "shovel." Judgment belongs to salvation as surgery belongs to therapy. Judgment belongs essentially to the gospel. It is good news that God is against what is false and wrong, just as it is good news that he enters the world to bring right to victory over wrong. John's message seems to be weighted on the side of judgment, and only in Jesus is the balance between judgment and salvation fully attained. To see John's limitations is only to recognize what he himself and Matthew acknowledged (3:11; 11:11). John saw himself as ***not worthy to carry*** Jesus' ***sandals.***

Fire is interpreted as a symbol of judgment in verse 12, not of the Holy Spirit as in Acts 2. The ***winnowing fork*** was used to toss straw and grain into the air, the light chaff thus being blown aside and the heavier grain falling back to the ground. The chaff is burned and the grain preserved.

To argue from verse 12 for the ultimate annihilation of the wicked on the ground that they will be burned up (*katakausei*) is to press symbolism and logic beyond any intention apparent in Matthew. It would be just as "logical" to argue from unquenchable fire (*asbestō*) that the wicked would burn eternally or that there would be an inexhaustible supply of wicked people to keep the fire burning. Matthew's interest is not in such "logic" but to warn that Jesus comes with a salvation that involves judgment and that those who ***bear fruit that befits repentance*** will be separated from those who do not.

Matthew 3:7–10 is paralleled almost verbatim in Luke 3:7–9, reflecting a common source (probably Q) other than Mark, but there is a significant difference in verse 7. Matthew has ***Pharisees and Sadducees*** where Luke has "crowds." Since Matthew had no special concern with the Sadducees, it is likely that he retained what he found in his source, Pharisees and Sadducees. Luke, with other interests, substitutes "crowds." Matthew traces the conflict with the Pharisees, so sharp in his day, back to the time of John the Baptist. The strong feeling against the Pharisees is seen throughout Matthew, the ***brood of vipers*** charge reappearing in 12:34 and 23:33.

(2) *The Baptism of Jesus (3:13–17)*

**13 Then Jesus came from Galilee to the Jor-
dan to John, to be baptized by him. 14 John
would have prevented him, saying, "I need to
be baptized by you, and do you come to me?"
15 But Jesus answered him, "Let it be so now;
for thus it is fitting for us to fulfil all righteousness." Then he consented. 16 And when Jesus
was baptized, he went up immediately from
the water, and behold, the heavens were
opened and he saw the Spirit of God descending like a dove, and alighting on him; 17 and lo,
a voice from heaven, saying, "This is my beloved Son, with whom I am well pleased."**

Matthew is exceeded only by John (1:6–8,15,19–27,30; 3:22–30) in the concern to show the true relationship betwen Jesus and John the Baptist. The dialogue between John and Jesus over the appropriateness of Jesus' being baptized by John (vv. 14 f.) is not found in the Markan (1:9–11) and Lukan (3:21 f.) parallels. Traces of a movement centered around John the Baptist but not Jesus are explicit in Acts 19:1–7, and a sect of such disciples of John continued far beyond the New Testament period. Matthew is more concerned with the Pharisaic threat from without and the antinomian threat from within than with a rival sect of followers of John the Baptist, but his concern with the latter does appear (vv. 14 f.). It seems that what was known to Luke as an isolated movement (Acts 19: 1–7) was a more serious problem to Matthew and yet more so when the Gospel of John was written.

That John baptized Jesus is beyond question. This is not the kind of story that Christians would invent, for it posed problems to be solved. Followers of John could boast that he was not only prior to Jesus but baptized him. Matthew shows that the baptism took place at Jesus' initiative and insistence, over John's protest of unworthiness, and as Jesus' recognition of what was proper and right.

Matthew was concerned not only with the question of why the one who baptized with water only should baptize the one who baptized "with the Holy Spirit and with fire" but also with the question of why Jesus should submit to a repentance baptism at all, since he was without sin.

There is no record that John entered Galilee, but his influence and message reached into this region. Jesus presented himself to John at the Jordan River for baptism (v. 13). John tried to hinder him (*diekōluen*), protesting that he had need to be baptized by Jesus. John was very demanding upon all who came to him for baptism, requiring the confession of sins and the evidence of repentance (conversion). When Jesus appeared before him, he made no such demand, because he saw no sin in Jesus. He placed all under God's ultimate demand, the kingdom (reign) of heaven, without claiming perfection in himself or others. Only in Jesus did he find excellence.

Behind John's protest that he needed ***to be baptized*** by Jesus may lurk more than recognition of unworthiness. There may be also the implication that he needed the baptism of the Spirit which he had said the coming one would bring. This is not to overlook the fact that already the Spirit had been upon John, any more than it is to be overlooked that the one upon whom the Spirit came as a dove had himself been begotten of the Spirit (1:20; 3:16).

Against John's protest of unworthiness to baptize Jesus was Jesus' insistence that it was ***fitting*** (*prepon*) and that it was ***to fulfil all righteousness.*** Jesus recognized John's baptism as being from God (21:23–27) and that it was proper for Jews to respond to this baptism. That Jesus had no sin to confess, that he commanded John, and that John acknowledged his subordination to Jesus is clear. By taking his place among those who submitted to John's baptism, Jesus did endorse John's baptism and identify himself with those people who responded to John's call. Although without sin, Jesus did identify with sinners whom he had come to save (cf. Isa. 53:12). The ***for us*** (v. 15) may refer either to John and Jesus or to Jesus and the people with whom he associated himself. He became one with those who needed to repent, though he was without sin (Heb. 2:17). But Jesus' baptism was more than this; it was an open commitment to his mission.

That Jesus ***went up immediately from the water*** may describe his being raised out of the water after having been immersed in it, but probably it alludes to his walking out of the river and upon its bank. ***Immediately*** does not describe the quickness of the immersion but the fact that Jesus did not linger in the river following his baptism. Possibly some did linger, awaiting the baptism of others or to confess their sins.

When Jesus was baptized, ***the Spirit of God*** came upon him ***like a dove*** and ***a voice from heaven*** was heard, declaring him to be God's ***beloved Son*** in whom he was ***well pleased.*** Matthew differs from Mark in employing the more Jewish expression, ***the Spirit of God*** (cf. 12:28) for Mark's "the Spirit" (1:10), and in objectifying the voice as heard by others than Jesus. Mark's "thou art" is followed by Luke, but Matthew has ***this is.*** Matthew's "this is" is assimilated to the *this is* common to all Synoptics in the transfiguration narrative (Matt. 17:5; Mark

9:7; Luke 9:35). In the baptismal story, Mark and Luke follow the "you are" of Psalm 2:7. Luke is more objective than either Mark or Matthew in saying that the Spirit came "in bodily form, as a dove" (3:22). Apparent is the essential agreement in the witness of the Synoptics as well as independence and variation. They agree that Jesus on his own initiative was baptized by John, that John recognized his subordination to Jesus, that the Spirit came upon Jesus in a unique way, and that God was pleased with his beloved Son.

The dove is usually a rabbinical symbol for Israel, but it is also a symbol for the Spirit, possibly so implied in the "brooding" of the Spirit of God in the creation story (Gen. 1:2). John had preached in terms of an ax at the root of certain trees, of the winnowing shovel by which chaff and wheat were to be sifted, and of the baptism in fiery judgment. The coming of the Spirit as a dove afforded John a new revelation, for the dove is among birds what the lamb is among animals. John was correct in seeing that the kingdom of heaven comes in judgment, but that there was more to be said about the kingdom than John was privileged to know is explicit in 11:11. God's demands and judgments are always couched in prior acts of mercy. God gives before he demands, and behind his judgment is his mercy.

In verse 17 is given something of the self-understanding of Jesus. No scholar today wants to repeat the mistake of earlier generations in trying to "psychoanalyze" Jesus. We cannot look down into his heart and mind, trace out his growth in self-understanding, and describe it. But it is equally untenable to assume that Jesus had no self-understanding or that we are without clues as to how he saw himself. To assume that Jesus did not ponder the questions of his own identity and the work that was his to do is to assume that he was less than an average man, and it is to reject the plain teaching of the New Testament. It is ironical that some interpreters "know" so much about what Jesus did not and could not know! To say that Jesus could not have seen himself as Messiah or as Son of man is to claim knowledge which we do not have (for sober judgment, cf. McNeile, p. 32).

The Gospels represent Jesus in his boyhood (Luke 2:42–52), at his baptism, in the wilderness temptations, at the transfiguration, in Gethsemane, and elsewhere as struggling with the deep questions of his identity and mission. Apart from significant titles attributed to Jesus, the very manner in which he walked among men reflects an understanding of himself as one both identified with men and set apart from them, as one who could make promises and demands proper to God alone.

The voice from heaven, heard following the baptism of Jesus, seems to reflect Psalm 2:7 and Isaiah 42:1 (and possibly Gen. 22:2; Isa. 44:2). Significant titles and roles are in view here. In Psalm 2, reference is to God's Son who is anointed to reign, thus blending the pictures of Son of God and kingly Messiah. In Isaiah 42:1 is the picture of the Suffering Servant of God. Apparently Jesus pondered these passages and saw in himself their fulfilment, beginning with his filial consciousness, seeing himself as in a special way God's son (cf. 3:17; 17:5; Luke 2:49).

Not only did Jesus embody in himself the roles of divine Son and royal Messiah (Psalm 2) as well as that of servant of God (Isa. 42:1); but, according to the Gospels, it was he who first saw that the Messiah and the Suffering Servant were one and the same. Matthew later introduces the picture of the Son of man, also fulfilled in Jesus and interpreted in terms of the Suffering Servant. He will show that as Jesus set forth the Messiah or Son of man in terms of the Suffering Servant, he not only contradicted popular, political hopes but met with resistance in the inner circle of his own disciples (cf. 16:21–28). It was hard for them to see that the kingdom of God comes not with the outward trappings of a conquering army but like leaven, that it conquers not with a sword but a cross, not by taking life but by giving it. What is implicit in verse 17 will be expanded and made explicit in the unfolding of this Gospel.

(3) *The Temptation of Jesus* (*4:1–11*)

**1 Then Jesus was led up by the Spirit into
the wilderness to be tempted by the devil.
2 And he fasted forty days and forty nights, and
afterward he was hungry. 3 And the tempter
came and said to him, "If you are the Son of
God, command these stones to become loaves
of bread." 4 But he answered, "It is written,**

**'Man shall not live by bread alone,
but by every word that proceeds from the
mouth of God.' "**

**5 Then the devil took him to the holy city, and
set him on the pinnacle of the temple, 6 and
said to him, "If you are the Son of God, throw
yourself down; for it is written,**

'He will give his angels charge of you,'

and

**'On their hands they will bear you up,
lest you strike your foot against a stone.' "**

**7 Jesus said to him, "Again it is written, 'You
shall not tempt the Lord your God.' " 8 Again,
the devil took him to a very high mountain,
and showed him all the kingdoms of the world
and the glory of them; 9 and he said to him,
"All these I will give you, if you will fall down
and worship me." 10 Then Jesus said to him,
"Begone, Satan! for it is written,**

**'You shall worship the Lord your God
and him only shall you serve.' "**

**11 Then the devil left him, and behold, angels
came and ministered to him.**

All three Synoptics present the wilderness temptation of Jesus immediately following his baptism. Mark (1:12–13) states the fact without description. The stories in Matthew and Luke (4:1–12) are independent of Mark and of each other.

Matthew and Luke not only have some verbal differences but differ also in the order of the second and third temptations. Luke's order may be more primitive, Matthew's being a stylistic change so as to conclude with the climactic temptation. The verbal agreements point decisively to a common source which each utilized with redactional freedom or to two closely related sources.

In Mark, the temptations occurred during the forty days in the wilderness (1:13). Luke sees the temptations as occurring during the forty days (4:2) but also implies their resumption at "an opportune time" (4:13). Matthew seems to place the temptations at the end of the forty-day fast (v. 2). Luke's phrase implies that the wilderness temptations were typical, not isolated. Matthew shows their recurrence, as reflected in Jesus' reply to Peter, "Get behind me, Satan!" (16:23) and in the agony of Gethsemane (26:36–46).

The temptations of Jesus are to be taken at face value. They were not sham battles but real struggles. They probably reflect not so much uncertainty of mind as test of will (Schniewind, following Schlatter, p. 31). It is significant that the two Gospels which tell of the virgin birth of Jesus also emphasize his temptations. They are as certain of his real humanity as of his divine origin. They nowhere represent the choices made by Jesus as easy. Jesus *endured* the cross; he did not desire it. He did not relish his cup, but he did drink it (26:39).

Although Jesus was tempted in every way that we are (Heb. 4:15), the wilderness temptations were basically messianic, having to do with his mission. At his baptism he had seen himself as God's Son, God's chosen, understood as the kingly or "anointed" one of Psalm 2, and also as the lowly Suffering Servant of Isaiah 42:1. Later the disciples rebelled at the suggestion that the kingly Messiah (or glorious Son of man) should suffer and be crucified (cf. 16:21–28). It is not to be overlooked that it was precisely this that was not easy for Jesus.

Those who should have given Jesus support added to his burden. Jesus bore this burden alone. He alone saw and accepted all that is implied in the Suffering Servant role. He was without human companionship in the wilderness temptations. At Caesarea-Philippi they rebelled at his statement that he must suffer many things and be killed (16:21–23). As in the wilderness temptations, Jesus had again to fight off the satanic temptation to try to be "Christ" without being at the same time the Suffering Servant. In Gethsemane, as the inner circle of disciples slept, Jesus fought alone to victory over the recurrent temptation to escape his cup (26:36–46).

The wilderness temptations were mighty assaults upon Jesus, not only because he thus faced the almost unbearable demands of servanthood, but because what he was tempted to do was not unmixed with good. He was hungry and so were many people in the land. Man does not live by bread alone, but neither can he live without it. Then, too, the people did need a true leader who would deliver them from "blind guides" within Israel (23:24) and pagans from Rome. A tiny nation under the heel of Rome had the same claim to freedom belonging to any people.

The temptation was to take a short-cut to immediate goals yielding real benefactions or to employ the wrong means to achieve goals which at least in part represented valid human needs. But Jesus, who could offer only a narrow gate and an anguished way to his followers (7:13–14), could choose no easy way for himself.

Questions arise which do not represent the main interest of Matthew. What is meant by Satan? What is meant by fasting?

One may incline to the view that the more objective Satan is seen to be, the more seriously the idea is taken. Actually the opposite is true. The most objective view would be the one holding that Satan made a physical, visible appearance to Jesus. Would one conclude that Satan is present only where physically visible? He makes no such physically objective appearance to us. But one must go yet further. The more objectively concerned, the more remote Satan becomes and the farther the problem of sin is shifted from us. Our guilt at most would be in admitting him into our lives. Even so, one could plead, "Not I, but Satan."

It follows that the more subjectively conceived, the more seriously Satan is understood and the more fully man accepts the fact of his own sin and guilt. This is not to settle the question of the sense in which Satan is to be understood. It is to say that it does not follow that the objective view is the serious one and that the subjective one is the easy one. Whatever the meaning of Satan, it is unmistakable that Jesus found the essence of temptation to be deep in the human heart, and it is there that it must be confronted and overcome.

Matthew writes that Jesus ***fasted forty days and forty nights.*** One readily thinks of Moses' forty days and nights at Mount Sinai (Ex. 24:18; 34:28), Elijah's forty days of fasting (1 Kings 19:8), and Israel's forty years in the wilderness (Num. 14:33 f.; Deut. 8:2). Some see forty as a round number suggested by these Old Testament patterns or even a recapitulation of Israel's forty years, this time with a positive outcome. Nothing of this is explicit in Matthew. Either Jesus is to be seen as miraculously sustained through forty days of total abstinence from food and water, or it is to be understood that it was a real but not total fast.

Jesus' first temptation (vv. 3–4) was to use his power to turn stones into bread. Matthew connects the temptation with the hunger of Jesus (v. 2). ***Stones*** on the ground about him would easily remind one of loaves of bread (cf. 7:9). Although the temptation arose directly out of his own hunger, there was also the hunger of his people to be considered. Furthermore, the people expected that the Messiah would repeat the miracles of the time of Moses, especially the miracle of manna (cf. Ex. 16; John 6: 30 f.).

Jesus did want people to have bread. He fed the five thousand (14:13–21), and he made the giving of food to the hungry a basic test of one's relationship to himself (25:31–46). Jesus never found it easy to meet this human need. He was deeply concerned that men have bread, without which they could not live; but he was yet more concerned that they see and accept the fact that one cannot live by bread alone, but only ***by every word that proceeds from the mouth of God.*** The first temptation, then, cannot be written off simply as a temptation to selfishly employ powers at his command. The temptation was to take a short-cut to the meeting of an immediate need, whether for himself now or for his people later. The people wanted bread, with or without the word of God. Jesus saw that he must give them the word of God, preferably *with* bread but the word at all costs.

Satan's words, ***If you are the Son of God,*** were not necessarily calculated to cast doubt. Rather the design of the words (those heard at his baptism) was to prompt Jesus confidently to make certain demands upon God. But sonship is not manifested in demands but in obedience (cf. Rom. 5:19; Phil. 2:8; Heb. 5:8).

Jesus' second temptation (vv. 5–7) relates to the popular clamor for "signs and wonders." There was a tradition that the Messiah would dramatically appear at the Temple (Mal. 3:1–2). Jesus could gain an easy, popular following by providing signs and wonders but refused to build upon that foundation (16:1–4). He did employ "signs" and perform miracles but neither to gain followers nor to compel faith.

Jesus saw that true faith does not try to compel God to act, and true faith cannot be brought about by "compelling" signs and wonders. What Satan proposed, a leap from the Temple, would not be an act of faith but one of presumption and provocation. Satan represented such a leap as trust in God, who would send ***his angels*** to the rescue. Jesus saw it as tempting God. It would be the attempt to force God into certain action. True faith in God is reflected in a trust of his loving and wise will, not simply trust in his power to provide.

That Scripture may be used or abused is illustrated in this temptation narrative. Satan quoted Psalm 91:11 f. From the reply of Jesus, it may be seen that Scripture is best understood from Scripture (Deut. 6:16; Ex. 17:1–7). There are climactic texts which gather up basic biblical teachings, and they can stand alone (e.g., John 3:16); but it is highly precarious to use isolated texts as proof texts. Thus abused, they can be made to serve any interest, however removed from truth and right.

Matthew saw the third temptation from Satan (vv. 8–10) to lay claim to ***the kingdoms of the world*** as the climactic one. Jewish people in the time of Jesus believed that the Messiah would give Israel the rule over other nations. The Zealots constantly pressed for military revolt against the Romans, with the confidence that God would give the victory. Two bloody wars were fought with the Romans (A.D. 66–70 and 132–135) in the vain expectation that God would send the conquering Messiah to deliver Israel from Rome. Theudas and Judas (Acts 5:36 f.) and probably Barabbas (27:16–21) were messianic types or actual messiahs to some.

Jesus was forced to make a decision with respect to Jewish hopes for messianic deliverance from Rome. Without justifying Roman rule or denying the legitimacy of Jewish longings for national freedom, he refused to interpret the messianic function in political terms or to equate the kingdom of God with the kingdom of Israel. He recognized certain claims of "Caesar" upon the people (22:15–22) and bluntly rejected the employment of the sword in his interest (26:52).

The third temptation presumably is to be understood in terms of a vision, for there is no ***high mountain*** from which one can actually see all the kingdoms of the world. The devil's offer of ***the kingdoms of the world*** was on the condition that he be worshiped. Jesus rejected this short-cut to glory and power, probably to be understood as the temptation to follow the way of "kingdom building" as exemplified in David, Judas Maccabeus, or the Zealots. Jesus rejected this worldly way to worldly power. Matthew will show that "all authority in heaven and on earth" (28:18) was given to the one who refused to bow to Satan in the effort to grasp worldly rule. In the language of Revelation 11:15, "the kingdom [rule] of the world has become" that of "our Lord and of his Christ." To the one who refused to seek ***the kingdoms of the world*** was given "the kingdom of the world."

It is significant that the temptations came immediately after the baptism of Jesus. At his baptism the heavens were opened, the Spirit came, and a voice was heard to declare him to be God's beloved Son in whom he was well pleased (3:16 f). A higher moment of exaltation can hardly be imagined. The assaults upon his will followed soon after. Moments of great vision and exaltation are precisely those in which one is most subject to such assault. The higher life is keyed to the potentiality for truth and good, the more open it is to temptation. That Matthew had this in mind is not indicated. That Jesus on the threshold of his ministry was compelled to choose the road he would travel, against impulse and against popular expectation but in obedience to the will of God, is indicated.

(4) *Withdrawal into Galilee (4:12–17)*

12 Now when he heard that John had been
arrested, he withdrew into Galilee, 13 and leav-
ing Nazareth he went and dwelt in Caper-
naum by the sea, in the territory of Zebulun
and Naphtali, 14 that what was spoken by the
prophet Isaiah might be fulfilled:
15 "The land of Zebulun and the land of
Naphtali,
toward the sea, across the Jordan,
Galilee of the Gentiles—
16 the people who sat in darkness
have seen a great light,
and for those who sat in the region and
shadow of death
light has dawned."
17 From that time Jesus began to preach, say-
ing, "Repent, for the kingdom of heaven is at
hand."

Several implications arise out of the almost casual statement, ***when he heard that John had been arrested,*** as Matthew explains why Jesus ***withdrew into Galilee.*** The story of the imprisonment and beheading of John the Baptist is not related until 14:1–12, and then it is told almost incidentally in relation to Herod's reaction to reports about Jesus. In 11:2 the reader learns of John's imprisonment, and again John is brought into the narrative in a way that shows both his greatness and limitations as well as his subordination to Jesus. Matthew assumes in verse 12 that the reader knows who John is and about his arrest and execution. The Gospel is written first of all for the church, and it is assumed that the readers already know much of the story. Matthew no doubt intends to inform the reader, but chiefly he wants to interpret tradition that already belongs to the church. He holds John up for respect, but he also shows that his role was secondary to that of Jesus. John is never discussed except as he relates to Jesus.

The ***withdrawal*** of Jesus to Galilee was not an escape from Herod Antipas, for Antipas was tetrarch over Galilee as well as Perea. On the other hand the withdrawal motif is prominent in Matthew, as he shows that Jesus repeatedly was threatened from within his own nation and found better reception among the Gentiles (cf. 2:12,13,14, 22). This anticipates the movement into the Gentile world.

Matthew states simply that Jesus ***leaving Nazareth . . . dwelt in Capernaum by the sea, in the territory of Zebulun and Naphtali.*** But his word is not so much ***leaving*** as abandoning (*katalipōn*). Later he will tell of rejection at Nazareth (13:54–58). Luke (4:16–30) made this story foundational for his whole Gospel, showing how early amazement at "the words of grace proceeding out of his mouth" turned to anger and murderous intent when Jesus began to show from the stories of Elijah and Elisha that God had never limited himself to Israel but had always been concerned for other nations.[18]

Matthew's materials are not in strict chronological sequence, and it is significant that he connects the "abandonment" (*katalipōn*) of Nazareth and the settlement of Jesus ***in the territory of Zebulun and Naphtali . . . Galilee of the Gentiles,*** showing this to be in fulfilment of the words spoken in Isaiah 9:1–2. Thus he shows that the inclusion of Gentiles, already a part of the church known to Matthew, was of God. Matthew follows Mark in showing that Jesus worked almost exclusively among the Jews, his direct ministry to Gentiles being exceptional (8:5 ff.; 15:21–28); but already Matthew is pointing to the goal reached in

18 Cf. Stagg, *Studies in Luke's Gospel* (Nashville: Convention, 1967), pp. 41–44.

the risen Lord's commission that all nations be brought under his discipleship (28: 18 ff.). He had already hinted at this in the inclusion of certain women in the genealogy (1:2–16), in the appearance of the Wise Men from the East and the refuge in Egypt (2:1,13), and in John's word about the true children of Abraham (3:9). Matthew wrote about one who was "son of Abraham" and "son of David" but also Saviour of the world.

Galilee was not without reason called Galilee of the Gentiles. The territory in question once belonged to the tribes of Zebulon and Naphtali. Along with the Northern Kingdom of Israel, it had been captured by Assyria about 722 B.C. It remained basically Gentile until the second century B.C., when the Maccabees gave them the choice between "conversion" by circumcision or death. Many of those who were thus forced into Judaism were never more than nominal Jews.

Matthew saw Jesus as bringing light into a world of darkness. Although he does not explicitly call Jesus "the light" as does John (1:4–9; 8:12), he sees Jesus in that role. Matthew quotes Jesus as saying to his disciples, "You are the light of the world" (5:14); but he sees Jesus as the one in whom ***a great light*** comes to ***those who sat in darkness,*** in the ***region and shadow of death.***

Matthew's application of Isaiah 9:1–2 to Jesus' settlement in Galilee clearly illustrates how he used Scripture. That Jesus did settle in Galilee belongs to all early traditions (cf. Mark 1:14; Luke 4:14) and does not depend upon the quotation from Isaiah. Matthew did not invent situations as fulfilment for proof texts. Rather he drew upon the Old Testament to justify or illuminate what already was believed to have occurred.

(5) *Four Fisherman Called* (*4:18–22*)

18 As he walked by the Sea of Galilee, he
saw two brothers, Simon who is called Peter
and Andrew his brother, casting a net into the
sea; for they were fishermen. 19 And he said to
them, "Follow me, and I will make you fishers
of men." 20 Immediately they left their nets and
followed him. 21 And going on from there he
saw two other brothers, James the son of Zebe-
dee and John his brother, in the boat with
Zebedee their father, mending their nets, and
he called them. 22 Immediately they left the
boat and their father, and followed him.

Next to Jesus, interest in the Gospel of Matthew is focused upon his disciples. Jesus called people to himself. He did mighty works and he taught "as one who had authority" (7:29), but his chief concern was to make God known as Father and to bring people to God. Jesus left a great body of teachings, but he was not content simply to bind people to his teachings. He gave himself to his people and he bound them to himself. The first clear indication of this is seen in the calling of four fishermen.

Jesus called two pairs of brothers to himself: Simon and Andrew, then James and John. The Gospel of John indicates that Peter and Andrew were first followers of John the Baptist and that Andrew influenced his brother Simon Peter to follow Jesus (John 1:35–42). Matthew seemingly follows Mark (1:16–20) in his account of the calling of the four fishermen. There is no necessary conflict with the Gospel of John, for a following prior to this further step in discipleship is not necessarily to be excluded. At this point the men are asked to leave their nets, or both nets and father, in order to become ***fishers of men.***

That Jesus felt that he had the right to make ultimate demands upon men comes with force through all the traditions. He demanded the trust, love, obedience, and if necessary the lives of his followers. Of course, he gave himself to them in the same radical way, even to his life at Golgotha. He offered more than example and teaching. He offered himself. He demanded more than imitation and the acceptance of his teaching. He asked people to give themselves to him. That some were willing thus to yield to his claims is reflected in this story. This is paramount. In a radical way, Jesus bound himself to his people and bound them to himself—in life and in death. This theme will be recurrent in Matthew. The simple wording in verse 22 makes clear the abandonment required as Christ calls men to follow him (cf. 9:9; 10:37; 19:27).

The four fishermen were called to become ***fishers of men.*** Their new business was to take men alive for Christ. In rabbinical and Greek usage, this expression usually had a bad sense (cf. Jer. 16:16), but here a good sense.

Of the four disciples named, Peter and John are best known. Simon was called Peter or Cephas, Greek and Aramaic respectively for rock. James may have been an aggressive person, for he was the first of the twelve to be martyred (Acts 12:2). James and Jacob are the Greek and Hebrew respectively for the same name.

(6) *A Threefold Ministry* (*4:23–25*)

23 And he went about all Galilee, teaching in their synagogues and preaching the gospel of the kingdom and healing every disease and every infirmity among the people. 24 So his fame spread throughout all Syria, and they brought him all the sick, those afflicted with various diseases and pains, demoniacs, epileptics, and paralytics, and he healed them. 25 And great crowds followed him from Galilee and the Decapolis and Jerusalem and Judea and from beyond the Jordan.

Verse 23 brings together three terms which largely summarize the ministry of Jesus: ***teaching, preaching, healing.*** He taught in the synagogues. Wherever as many as ten heads of families were found, a synagogue was permitted. The synagogues (the Greek word means assembly) arose not later than the Exile, possibly earlier. During the Exile, as the Jews were cut off from the Temple, the synagogues became centers of worship, study, and discipline. They were under the control of laymen, not priests. Much of the activity of the synagogues centered around the study of the Mosaic Law, perhaps to compensate for neglect of the Law, considered a reason for the Exile. After the Exile the synagogues continued to function along with the restored Temple, so important had they come to be. After A.D. 70, with the Temple destroyed, the synagogues gained even greater importance and continue to this day to be centers of Jewish life. Jesus taught in the synagogues, clearly indicating that he was yet within the structure of Judaism.

Matthew repeatedly refers to the synagogues as ***their synagogues*** (cf. v. 23; 9:35; 10:17; 12:9; 13:54; 23:34) and in each case, except for 23:34, he has inserted "their" into his source, his redactional interest or historical situation thus being clearly reflected. When he wrote, Christians may have been expelled from the synagogues.

Preaching the gospel of the kingdom was a second major function in the ministry of Jesus. This proclamation of the reign of God was also a call to repentance. Jesus taught and preached inside the synagogue and out of doors. No sharp line can be drawn between his teaching and preaching. There could be proclamation of the kingdom of God without instruction, but teaching was built around the proclaimed event. What is called the Sermon on the Mount is introduced by Matthew as teaching (5:2) and summed up as teaching (7:28 f.), although it has a strong kerygmatic or preaching element throughout.

Healing constituted an important part of the ministry of Jesus. He was concerned for the total man, including body and mind. Compassion entered into his healing ministry, as did faith. On the other hand, as will be seen as healing narratives are studied, not all healing followed faith and there were concerns other than compassion. To a great extent the healing miracles were signs that the kingdom of God had already arrived, at least in its beginnings (cf. 12:28). The powers which ultimately would fully triumph were already at work in Jesus, overcoming disease, mental derangement, sin, and death.

The threefold formula of teaching, preaching, and healing (v. 23) is repeated in 9:35, thus bracketing the ministry of Jesus in word (5—7) and in deeds (8—9).

II. The Sermon on the Mount (5:1—7:29)

1. Introduction (5:1–2)

1 Seeing the crowds, he went up on the mountain, and when he sat down his disciples came to him. 2 And he opened his mouth and taught them, saying:

Probably 4:25 should go with 5:1–2 in forming the introduction of the Sermon. Mention of the "crowds" in 4:25; 5:1 f., and 7:28 f. supports this.

"Decapolis" is Greek for "ten cities," a league including among others Damascus, Gadara, Pella, Gerasa, Philadelphia (now Amman), and Scythopolis, all but the last being east of the Jordan River. The plural "crowds" alludes to the various groups from the different geographical sections named. Why Samaria, so prominent in Luke and John, is unmentioned is not apparent.

Those addressed.—Whether the Sermon on the Mount is addressed to the disciples alone (v. 2) or also to the crowds (4:25; 5:2; 7:28) cannot be fully resolved. The grammatical antecedent to ***them*** (he ***taught them***) in verse 2 can be either ***the crowds*** or ***his disciples*** or both (v. 1). In 5:1 may be the implication that Jesus withdrew from the crowds and addressed only his disciples who ***came to him***. However, to this point Matthew has named only four disciples (4:18–22), and special instruction for the twelve is first mentioned in chapter 14. Moreover, 7:28 is explicit to the effect that the crowds heard Jesus and marvelled at the authority with which he taught. Probably the sermon is addressed to all who follow Jesus, its promises and demands applying to all Christians and not to a select few.

Sermon or teaching?—What is universally termed the Sermon on the Mount appears under the caption of teaching: Jesus "taught them" as one having authority (7:28 f.). If the material is sermonic, Matthew places it in a teaching situation. Preaching (kerygma) and teaching (didache) may be distinguished—the former having to do fundamentally with the event at the center of which Christ stood, and the latter having to do primarily with its implications and applications. Kerygma was a proclamation to the world, and didache was instruction for the church. However, the distinction between kerygma and didache is not to be pressed. In all didache, as in the Sermon on the Mount, the kerygma is either explicit or implicit, the teaching presupposing the proclamation of the event. Matthew offers us Jesus Christ, never the preaching, teaching, or healing apart from him.

Origin and unity.—What Matthew gives in chapters 5–7 finds extensive parallels scattered through six chapters in Luke (chs. 6, 11, 12, 13, 14, 16). A much briefer discourse, somewhat paralleling Matthew's, is found in Luke 6:20–49, often called the Sermon on the Plain. The more extensive Lukan parallels to Matthew's sermon are found as follows: Luke 6:20–23; 14:34–35; 16:18; 6:29–30; 6:27–28,32–36; 11:2–4; 12:33–34; 11:34–36; 16:13; 12:22–34; 6:37–38,41–42; 11:9–13; 13:24; 6:43–44; 13:25–27; 6:47–49.

It is highly probable that Matthew here, as throughout his Gospel, follows the principle of gathering teaching and narrative materials around basic themes. This does not rule out a basic, pre-Matthean sermon, but it recognizes the liberty given the author in arranging materials so as to present Jesus and his message in the manner most meaningful to the readers.

The sermon's intention.—Apart from detailed exegesis is the question of how the sermon is to be heard. A dozen or more distinct approaches have been suggested.[19] Some sentimentalists boast that the only religion they want is the Sermon on the Mount. Have they read it? Others, awed or frightened by its heavy demands, give up in despair, concluding that it is unrealistic or impossible. A few have actually undertaken to follow it literally, even to self-mutilation (5:29 f.). Some have termed it

19 Cf. Harvey K. MacArthur, *Understanding the Sermon on the Mount* (New York: Harper, 1960) for a concise summary.

an interim ethic, intended for a brief period just before an expected end of the world. Others have held that the sermon applies only to the clergy and not to the laity or only to relationships within the church but not in the world, though Jesus never endorsed such double standards. The great danger is that less than justice be done to either the awesome demands or the merciful gifts or to both.

Our proposal is that the Sermon on the Mount is best understood when seen in its setting, seen as God's ultimate and absolute demand addressed to sinners who are also offered acceptance upon the basis of mercy and forgiveness.[20] The demands are not to be toned down or explained away, not even the awesome, "You, therefore, must be perfect, as your heavenly Father is perfect" (5:48). God's claims, i.e., the demands of the kingdom (reign) of God as it confronts us in Christ (anointed to rule), are ultimate and absolute. They are ultimate in that they are final. They are absolute in the sense that God does not divide his authority with any other. To enter into the kingdom of God is to acknowledge his right to rule as full and final.

This does not mean that any person, except Jesus, has lived up to this demand. But it does mean that to be a Christian is to live under that claim, however far he falls short of living up to it. God does not ask for 50 percent or 99 percent obedience. His will is that we be perfect.

On the other hand, the Sermon on the Mount is addressed to sinners (7:11) who are wholly dependent upon his mercy and forgiveness (cf. 5:3–7; 6:12,14 f.). At no point does the Sermon on the Mount assume that we are sinless or perfect. The sermon is in a setting of mercy. It is preceded by a summary statement of Jesus' ministry of teaching, preaching, and healing (4:23 f.), and it is followed by ten stories of merciful healing and care (8:1—9:34) and with a touching picture of the compassion of Jesus for the neglected multitudes (9:35–38). God's demands are always preceded by his gifts. Just as the Mosaic law arose out of the Exodus, God's merciful act of delivering Israel from Egyptian bondage, so the Sermon on the Mount is couched in God's merciful acts of deliverance. The high demand of Christ (5:1—7:28) comes from one who offers unlimited succour (4:23 f.; 8:1—9:34). The sermon is set in a framework of healing and pity (Davies, pp. 90, 96).

The Sermon on the Mount leaves us no hope except in the mercy of God, and at the same time it places us under moral, ethical, and other personal demands which are absolute and ultimate. The Christian cannot escape this "tension" between God's gift and his demand. Neither is to be blunted. A righteousness exceeding that of the scribes and Pharisees is demanded of sinners who daily are to forgive and seek forgiveness. The Sermon on the Mount takes seriously man's infinite need of mercy and his infinite moral and ethical possibilities. Of himself man can achieve nothing, but Christ can bring about a new kind of existence in those who are willing to be accepted on the grounds of mercy and to acknowledge God's right to rule. The Sermon on the Mount excludes the pride, superficiality, and deception of legalism and also the moral and ethical irresponsibility and escapism of antinomianism.

It is not moral achievement which brings man into proper relationship with God, but the new relationship is itself God's gift, offered on the basis of mercy; and this new relationship with God first opens to us the possibility for the moral behavior demanded (Conzelmann, p. 141). The one who commands is also the one who forgives, saves, and sustains. In a sense, the Sermon on the Mount confronts us with law and gospel, but it must be remembered that God's law itself is an expression of love and mercy, for what he demands belongs to our true needs and nature. His law consists not of arbitrary rules but of principles without which we miss our true existence. God's kingdom comes to us in Jesus Christ not as a set of

20 (Cf. Bornkamm, pp. 15–164, and Davies, pp. x, 14, 90 ff., 96, 119, 219, 440, *et passim*).

rules but as the rule of one who loves enough to give and demand.

The mountain.—Seeing the crowds, Jesus *went up on the mountain.* The mountain is not identified, but probably the reference is to a place west of Lake Galilee and in the vicinity of Capernaum (8:5). That Matthew sees a parallel between the Sermon on the Mount and the giving of the law at Mount Sinai is possible but far from conclusive. He draws no analogies between Moses' receiving the law at Sinai and Jesus' teaching *on the mountain.* Luke (6:12,17) comes closer to paralleling Exodus 19 than does Matthew, for Luke sees Jesus as descending from the mountain to teach, as did Moses. In Matthew, Jesus ascended to teach. To Matthew, Jesus is not a new Moses giving a new law but the fulfiller of the Law and the Prophets.

2. *The Beatitudes (5:3–12)*

3 "Blessed are the poor in spirit, for theirs is the kingdom of heaven.
4 "Blessed are those who mourn, for they shall be comforted.
5 "Blessed are the meek, for they shall inherit the earth.
6 "Blessed are those who hunger and thirst for righteousness, for they shall be satisfied.
7 "Blessed are the merciful, for they shall obtain mercy.
8 "Blessed are the pure in heart, for they shall see God.
9 "Blessed are the peacemakers, for they shall be called sons of God.
10 "Blessed are those who are persecuted for righteousness' sake, for theirs is the kingdom of heaven.
11 "Blessed are you when men revile you and persecute you and utter all kinds of evil against you falsely on my account.
12 Rejoice and be glad, for your reward is great in heaven, for so men persecuted the prophets who were before you.

Matthew seems to give nine Beatitudes. It is arbitrary to find ten by counting verses 11–12 as two Beatitudes. These verses are closely paralleled by Luke 6:22–23; and Luke quite clearly counts this as one, resulting in four Beatitudes (Luke 6:20–23) matched by four woes (6:24–26).

There is some argument that Matthew originally had only eight Beatitudes, 5:11–12 being an addition. The first eight are all in the third person, whereas the ninth is in the second person. Also, the first eight have parallelism and rhythm not found in the ninth. There is no manuscript evidence for the omission of the ninth Beatitude. Its stylistic difference is best accounted for in terms of differences in sources employed. Matthew's ninth Beatitude closely parallels Luke's fourth, and all of Luke's Beatitudes are in the second person.

Some see verse 5 as an addition, since certain manuscripts reverse the order of verses 4 and 5 (see below). Seven, a symbolic number, could be arrived at by eliminating verse 5 and either eliminating verses 11–12 or counting verses 10–12 as one. This is somewhat forced.

The word *makarioi* introduces each of the nine Beatitudes. It is a declaration of blessedness, an interjection not requiring a verb. It does not describe one's inner feeling about himself but his state of blessedness as seen by Jesus. The meaning intended may be expressed as "Oh, the happiness of," but the familiar "Blessed" is adequate.

The poor in spirit (v. 3). Luke's "you poor" (6:20) is likely to be more primitive than Matthew's "poor in spirit." Two views can be traced in ancient Judaism, one seeing wealth as a sign of God's favor, with adversity as a sign of divine judgment. The other view identifies wealth with wickedness and poverty with piety (cf. James 2:5; 5:1). Luke's Beatitude reflects the latter pattern, "the poor," possibly identified with "the people of the land." The Semitic term behind the Greek designates the pious in Israel, chiefly but not exclusively identified with the materially poor. Matthew removes the ambiguity by adding "in spirit," recognizing that material or social poverty alone is not a mark of faith or piety.

The Beatitudes stress the striking contrast between outward appearance and inner reality. The kingdom of heaven belongs not to those who by the world's standards are rich and mighty. They alone reign with God who surrender all claims to that end.

Neither material nor spiritual poverty is blessed, but one's honest and humble acknowledgment of his impoverishment (cf. Isa. 61:1) opens the way for the reception of God's blessings. It is precisely when man sees his own nothingness that God can give out of his own fulness. Lohmeyer (p. 83) argues that ***poor in spirit*** refers to those who voluntarily accept material poverty or even sell their possessions and give to the poor (19:21), thus finding in Matthew the same emphasis upon outward poverty as in Luke. So understood, Matthew stresses the blessedness of freedom from the tyranny of outward things, living under the rule of heaven rather than the rule of earthly goods (cf. 6:19–34).

Those who mourn (v. 4). Not all mourning is blessed and much sorrow finds no comfort. This Beatitude echoes Isaiah 61:1; and from the context, reference may be to the grief that follows one's realization of his spiritual impoverishment. But the meaning cannot be confined to sorrow over sin. Probably the reference is to the comfort that is found now and in the final judgment by those who mourn now, whether over the hurts and the hardships of life or over their sins and those of the world.

The meek (v. 5). This verse echoes Psalm 37:11. The meek are not the weak or cowardly. They are those who under the pressures of life have learned to bend their wills and to set aside their own notions as they stand before the greatness and grace of God (Lohmeyer, p. 86). They are characterized by humble trust rather than arrogant independence. The earth does not belong to the self-trusting or self-assertive who seek to possess it but to "the poor in spirit" who are willing to lose all for the kingdom. This paradox belongs to the larger teaching which sees that one lives by dying, receives by giving, and is first precisely when willing to be last.

Hunger and thirst for righteousness (v. 6). This Beatitude did not arise among people whose problem was overweight. It speaks of a craving for righteousness comparable to such physical hunger and thirst as is known only in lands where people die for want of food or water. Blessed are they who yearn for the victory of right over wrong, in their own lives and in the world. These are assured that God's righteousness will prevail.

The verse is eschatological, looking to fulfilment in the future consummation of the kingdom; but righteousness is also a goal for the present (3:15; 5:10,20; 6:1,33; 21:32). Righteousness and kingdom belong together (6:33). Where God reigns, he reigns in righteousness. Both kingdom and righteousness await eschatological fulfilment, but both are also present realities.

The merciful (v. 7). In mercy and forgiveness (6:12,14 f.; 18:21–35), receiving is bound up with giving. It is not that one earns mercy by being merciful, for then it would not be mercy but reward. It is not that one earns forgiveness by forgiving, for again that would be reward for merit. Neither is it that Jesus set up arbitrary requirements for receiving mercy or forgiveness. It is rather that in the nature of mercy and forgiveness there cannot be receiving without giving. The personal condition of the unmerciful or unforgiving is such that they are incapable of receiving. That in one which renders him incapable of being merciful or forgiving also renders him incapable of receiving mercy or forgiveness.

The pure in heart (v. 8). ***Pure*** translates *katharos*, the term for cleansing; and purity in heart contrasts with ritual cleansing of hands or body. By various groups within Judaism, a sharp distinction was made between what was ritually clean and what was unclean. Jesus brushed this aside in the interest of real purity, that of ***heart*** (cf. 15:1–20; 23:25). The heart stood for the whole inner self, mind as well as feeling. Purity of heart is simplicity or integrity as against duplicity. It is the concentration of the whole self upon God. The Beatitude seemingly draws upon Psalm 24:3 f., but also recalls Psalm 51:10. Although the emphasis here is upon inner purity or integrity as contrasted with outward, ritual cleansing, there is no indifference to the outward life of words and deeds. Purity of heart and wholeness go together, the outward life reflecting the inner purity.

The peacemakers (v. 9). Jesus is the "Prince of Peace" (Isa. 9:6). He is our peace (Eph. 2:13 f.). Peacemaking is positive and active, not passive. Jesus plunged into the midst of human life to bring order out of chaos, reconciliation out of estrangement, love in the place of hate. Israel had been designated "son" of God (Hos. 11:1). Jesus taught that God's sons are those who are joined together with him in his work of peacemaking. To ***be called*** is to be, for the name reflects the nature. Although peace includes the ending of war and strife, it is more. It is harmony with man through harmony with God.

Persecuted for righteousness' sake (vv. 10–12). Although two Beatitudes formally remain, they constitute one basic declaration. At some stage of transmission the Beatitudes may have concluded with verse 10, for the poetic rhythm does not continue in verses 11–12; and ***theirs is the kingdom of heaven*** in verse 10 looks back to the same in verse 3. With verse 5, the number would be eight, somewhat corresponding to Luke's four beatitudes and four woes. Without verse 5 (many manuscripts place it before v. 4), there would be seven, the number for completion. But as it stands, Matthew gives nine Beatitudes, the eighth and ninth being basically the same.

Although Matthew's eighth Beatitude (v. 10) is stylistically more like the first seven, the ninth (vv. 11–12) closely parallels Luke's fourth (6:22 f.). The verbal differences between Matthew's ninth and Luke's fourth are so great as to suggest different sources; yet their parallels are so striking, including Matthew's shift from third to second person, as to suggest a common origin, however far back in the tradition. Verses 11 f. cannot be accounted for as dependent on verse 10, as is often held. Verses 11–12 continue the thought of verse 10 but are independent in origin.

Persecution or abuse as such is not a blessing, but here is blessing for Christians in their suffering for Christ (Phil. 1:29). The blessedness holds only when one suffers in the service of Christ and righteousness and when the charges of evil doing are false. One may be opposed because he is wrong, wicked, or simply a disturber. For those who, like the prophets, suffer for truth and right, there is ***reward in heaven.*** There is no assurance of vindication or reward among men now. The reward belongs with certainty to the future, but even now as seen in heaven, those who thus suffer are in a blessed condition. The assurance belongs to those who suffer for what must ultimately prevail.

In Matthew Jewish persecution of Christians is linked with the view that Israel has always persecuted her prophets. This view did not originate out of Christian bias but is found in the Old Testament (cf. 2 Chron. 24:20 f.; 36:15 f.; Jer. 2:30; 26:20–23; 1 Kings 18:4; 19:10,14).

3. *Salt, Light, and a City Set on a Hill* (*5:13–16*)

13 "You are the salt of the earth; but if salt
has lost its taste, how shall its saltness be
restored? It is no longer good for anything
except to be thrown out and trodden under
foot by men.
14 "You are the light of the world. A city set
on a hill cannot be hid. 15 Nor do men light a
lamp and put it under a bushel, but on a stand,
and it gives light to all in the house. 16 Let
your light so shine before men, that they may
see your good works and give glory to your
Father who is in heaven.

The responsibility of Christians to the world is set forth in three closely related pictures: ***salt, light, and a city set on a hill.*** Ministry belongs not optionally but essentially to Christ's people. A mark of the redeemed is that they are redeeming. True Christians are not only saved but saving, not of themselves but as Christ lives in them.

Salt was a major food preservative as well as a seasoning. Apart from Christ we are corrupt and corrupting, but in Christ we are to be a saving factor in a perishing world. Pure salt, as we know it today, cannot lose its saltiness; but the salt taken from the Dead Sea in Jesus' time was a mixture of salt and other matter. Exposed to weather, the salt could be lost, leaving only what had the appearance of salt. Commercial salt could be adulterated, the weakened mixture having little or no taste. A strong possibility is that Jesus intended to picture the absurdity of "saltless" salt, physically impossible. No less absurd than saltless salt is savorless Christianity that is not a saving force in the world. Nothing is more despised.

It is possible that salt stands for wisdom. This would agree with the clause which literally reads, "If the salt [wisdom] should become foolish."

Apart from Christ we are darkness; he is the true light (4:16). But Christ declared his people to be ***the light of the world.*** Jesus taught that his followers ought to shine and would shine. He did not say that ***a city set on a hill*** (mountain) should not but could not be hidden. He did not say that men should not but do not ***light a lamp*** and then ***put it under a bushel.*** One lights a lamp that he may place it ***on a stand, and it gives light to all in the house.*** Apart from Christ, we are unlighted lamps; but he lights his lamps that they may give light to all men.

There is a possible allusion to the sectarian (Essene?) community at Qumran. They called themselves "the children of light," but they had withdrawn from the world, including most of Judaism. They were hiding in sectarian withdrawal what they called their light.

It is significant that Jesus commands us to let good works be seen and also warns against proud or self-seeking display in almsgiving, prayer, and fasting (6:4,6,18). He offers no easy way. The Christian is commanded to live in open goodness and service before the world, but he is warned against so doing except to the glory of God.

4. Jesus and the Law (5:17–20)

17 "Think not that I have come to abolish the law and the prophets; I have come not to abolish them but to fulfil them. 18 For truly, I say to you, till heaven and earth pass away, not an iota, not a dot, will pass from the law until all is accomplished. 19 Whoever then relaxes one of the least of these commandments and teaches men so, shall be called least in the kingdom of heaven; but he who does them and teaches them shall be called great in the kingdom of heaven. 20 For I tell you, unless your righteousness exceeds that of the scribes and Pharisees, you will never enter the kingdom of heaven.

These verses appear in Matthew alone and bring into focus opposition to the Pharisaic interpretation of the Mosaic Law and the antinomian evasion of the Law. That Jesus was actually charged by the Pharisees with destroying the Law and that others misconstrued his freedom from legalism as exemption from the Law is assumed here.

Verses 17–18 could be a reply both to Pharisaic charges that Jesus was destroying ***the law and the prophets*** (the two oldest parts of the OT) and the antinomian claim that freedom in Christ meant the abolishment of the Law. To both is the warning that one is not to begin to think (so the force of the Greek) that Jesus came to destroy Law or Prophets. He came not to destroy but to fulfil. By fulfilment is meant not just the carrying out of predictions but the accomplishment of the intention of the Law and the Prophets. In contrast to the Pharisees, Jesus brought out the true and deeper meaning of the Law, and he actually lived up to its intention.

The antinomians were warned that ***not an iota*** (smallest letter of the Greek alphabet) nor ***a dot*** (probably a stroke forming a part of a Hebrew letter) would pass away, but that the whole Law would be fulfilled. Verse 18 is not to be so interpreted as to contradict Jesus' own refusal to be bound by a wooden, literal reading of Scripture. This verse may best be understood as his protest against the disposition to set aside the Law. Jesus made what appears to be an extreme statement. His own actions and teachings demonstrate that he always took Scripture seriously but not always literally. To literalize may be to trivialize. Jesus is not a neo-legalist, making the letter of the Law supreme. His own ***I say to you*** shows that he stood above the Law, not it above him. Significantly, his first "I say to you" appears in this verse.

Verse 19 is directed chiefly against the antinomians, warning them not to discount any one of the Commandments. Salvation is God's gift in mercy and forgiveness, but his demands are not thus relaxed. License in the name of liberty is not to be tolerated.

Verse 20 may be directed against both Pharisees and antinomians. Pharisaic righteousnes fell short because of both inadequate understanding of the Law and failure to give real obedience to what was understood. Jesus fulfilled the Law and the Prophets both as final interpreter and in full obedience. Pharisaic "righteousness" is inadequate, and antinomians must be concerned for greater and not less righteousness than is found among the scribes and Pharisees. Matthew seems to make no distinction between scribes (the teachers of the Law) and the greater number of lay Pharisees.

Jesus accepted the Old Testament law in principle and as permanently binding, but he interpreted Scripture by Scripture, elevating the moral and ethical demands and the primacy of the personal above ritual laws. To him what ultimately mattered were God and man—not sabbath, purification of hands, and the like. The best commentary on this paragraph is what immediately follows, six illustrations of what Jesus meant by the fulfilment of the Law.

5. *The Intention of the Law* (*5:21–48*)

These six antitheses seemingly set Jesus' ***I say to you*** over against the Law. Actually, it is Jesus' interpretation of the Law which is set over against that of the Pharisees (Hummel, p. 50). Jesus did not give a new law, but rather he uncovered the intention of the old and brought it to its fullest expression.

(*1*) *The Essence of Murder* (*5:21–26*)

**21 "You have heard that it was said to the
men of old, 'You shall not kill; and whoever
kills shall be liable to judgment.' 22 But I say to
you that every one who is angry with his
brother shall be liable to judgment; whoever
insults his brother shall be liable to the council,
and whoever says, 'You fool!' shall be liable to
the hell of fire. 23 So if you are offering your
gift at the altar, and there remember that your
brother has something against you, 24 leave
your gift there before the altar and go; first be
reconciled to your brother, and then come and
offer your gift. 25 Make friends quickly with
your accuser, while you are going with him to
court, lest your accuser hand you over to the
judge, and the judge to the guard, and you be
put in prison; 26 truly, I say to you, you will
never get out till you have paid the last penny.**

Jesus traced sin back to disposition, attitude, or intention. The overt act of murder has its roots in anger, hostility, or contempt for another. Jesus cited anger ("without cause" in some manuscripts is probably a scribal gloss), insulting one's brother (*raca* is a term of contempt, but its exact meaning is uncertain), and calling another ***fool*** (*mōre,* also a term of contempt, may refer to one as stubborn or insubordinate) as being crimes for which one is brought before the ***court*** (local court of 23 persons), the Sanhedrin (highest ruling body of the Jews), or for which he is liable to Gehenna. No court seeks to convict a person on the grounds of feeling or attitude, but feelings of anger or contempt are as dangerous as are the outward crimes for which one is brought into the courts or considered liable to hell.

Jesus' words are not to be turned into a new legalism. They are to be understood as radical protests and warnings against wrong feeling toward another. This is not to say that it is just as bad to murder as to have ill feeling or ill will toward another. The victim would prefer being hated to being murdered, and it is better to bring hatred under control before it issues in murder than to let it run its course.

That Jesus had his own community in mind is reflected in the recurrence of ***his*** *brother,* a term reserved in Matthew for a Christian brother. Anger and contempt are not only self-destructive but destroy the fellowship of the church.

Verse 23 envisions not a synagogue but the Temple. It is better to interrupt or leave the Temple service in order to seek reconciliation than to try to worship God while estranged from one's brother. Jesus never permits one to isolate his relationship with God from that with his fellowman. One cannot compel his brother to join him in reconciliation before God's altar, but one has no access to God unless he seeks to come before God with his brother.

Verses 25–26 urge that reconciliation be sought outside the courts, with the warning that if one chooses otherwise, he can then only let the courts run their course. Christians are urged to work out their difficulties in direct relationship with one another (18:15–20; 1 Cor. 6:1–11).

(2) *Lust and Adultery* (*5:27–30*)

27 "You have heard that it was said, 'You shall not commit adultery.' 28 But I say to you that every one who looks at a woman lustfully has already committed adultery with her in his heart. 29 If your right eye causes you to sin, pluck it out and throw it away; it is better that you lose one of your members than that your whole body be thrown into hell. 30 And if your right hand causes you to sin, cut it off and throw it away; it is better that you lose one of your members than that your whole body go into hell.

The Ten Commandments forbade adultery and also the coveting of another man's wife (Ex. 20:17; Deut. 5:21). Upon this foundation Judaism built in two directions. It gave increasing attention to the lustful look as sin against one's own marriage. On the other hand, the rabbis tended to reduce the concept of adultery to sin against the property rights of another Jewish man, adultery being limited to illicit sexual relationship with the wife or betrothed of another Jew. In this view, seduction of a single woman or of a non-Jew's wife was not considered adultery.

Jesus saw adultery as sin against any woman, as something destructive to the offender, to the offended, and to marriage, and as first of all a matter of attitude or intention. Adultery may occur apart from the overt act. Jesus did not say that to look with lust is as evil as to commit the overt act, for the overt act continues the sin already in one's heart and extends the damage to other people. It is more destructive to all concerned to yield overtly to lust than to bring it under some measure of control. The point made is that it is not enough simply to refrain from the overt act. Freedom from lust is the divine demand.

The New Testament does not equate temptation with sin. Jesus was tempted but did not sin. The teaching is that sin begins at the point of consent, not with the temptation itself and not first in the overt act.

Obviously, lust cannot be controlled merely by plucking out the ***right eye*** or cutting off the ***right hand.*** Lust could be implemented through the remaining eye or hand or with no physical eyes or hands at all. Jesus is saying that not only is sexual lust a form of adultery but that the threat of lust is so strong and its dangers so great that a price comparable to the removal of eye or hand is not too great to pay as one seeks freedom from it. Implied, too, is that radical discipline is required for the life free of this evil.

"Gehenna" derives from Hinnom, a valley west of Jerusalem, scene of sacrifice to Molech and later the place where refuse from Jerusalem was burned. The term came to symbolize the place of judgment for the wicked. The description presupposes bodily existence after death.

(3) *The Damage in Divorce* (*5:31–32*)

31 "It was also said, 'Whoever divorces his wife, let him give her a certificate of divorce.' 32 But I say to you that every one who divorces his wife, except on the ground of unchastity, makes her an adulteress; and whoever marries a divorced woman commits adultery.

Discussion of this passage usually centers around the clause ***except on the ground of unchastity*** and ignores the real problem of the husband who first divorces his wife. Since the "except clause" is not in Mark 10:11–12 or Luke 16:18, it is widely held that Matthew has added the exception to make the teaching more workable in the church of his day. But the removal of this clause does not solve the problem of the passage. The real question is why, as commonly understood, the judgment falls on the divorced woman (who may be an innocent wife without the "except clause" and necessarily so with it) and the second husband, in the event of her remarriage. To say that the passage teaches that divorce is equated with adultery would make superfluous any reference to remarriage.

Freest from difficulty is the interpretation which retains the "except clause," fixes attention on the first husband as the person under judgment, and observes the passive voice of verbs employed. So understood, Jesus says that for a husband to divorce an innocent wife is to victimize her and her second husband should she remarry. It is to treat an innocent woman the way an adulteress is treated and to force a stigma upon her and her subsequent marriage.

What Jesus said may best be understood against the background of a man-centered world in which a husband could boast that in giving a rejected wife a bill of divorce he protected her rights. Jesus demolished these claims, showing that an innocent woman's rights are protected only if she is respected as a wife. A divorce certificate does not secure her against damage. The "except clause" recognizes that the guilty wife is responsible for her own ruin.

The Greek text does not justify the translation "causeth her to commit adultery" (KJV). The infinitive is passive (*moicheuthenai*), untranslatable in English. Something like "made adulterous" or "victimized with respect to adultery" approaches the idea. The RSV is little improvement over the KJV here. We know nothing about Jesus which would justify understanding him to say that an innocent wife (this follows necessarily if the "except clause" is retained, and is also assumed by those who strike the clause!) is an adulteress because her husband divorces her. Exegetes usually assume that she remarries, but this is only a deduction from the next clause.

The key to both Matthean passages on divorce (5:32 and 19:9) is to see that they concentrate upon the guilt of the husband, showing at least two circumstances under which he sins against marriage and is guilty of adultery. In 5:32 (retaining the except clause) the point may be that if a husband puts away an innocent wife and she remarries, he shares in the guilt of her second marriage, having created the situation for it (cf. Strecker, p. 131). In 19:9 (retaining the except clause) the husband who divorces an innocent wife is guilty of adultery if he remarries.

Retaining the except clause, these points appear in Matthew, chiefly concerned with the husband who divorces an innocent wife: (1) the husband is not guilty if he divorces a wife who already has committed fornication; (2) divorce without remarriage is not as such to be equated with adultery (this agrees with Mark 10:12; Luke 16:18; 1 Cor. 7:11); (3) either the husband who divorces an innocent wife automatically stigmatizes her as adulterous (having treated her as he would have treated an adulteress) or, by a less probable interpretation, he shares the responsibility for the subsequent guilt of his divorced (innocent) wife if she remarries (5:32); and (4) he is guilty of adultery if he remarries after divorcing an innocent wife (19:9). Thus understood, Matthew recognizes one valid ground for divorce and remarriage, that of the innocent party where the other has committed fornication. On the other hand, he is even severer than Mark or Luke on the husband who divorces an innocent wife (see further on 19:3–9).

(4) *Teaching About Oaths (5:33–37)*

33 "Again you have heard that it was said to the men of old, 'You shall not swear falsely,

**but shall perform to the Lord what you have
sworn.' 34 But I say to you, Do not swear at all,
either by heaven, for it is the throne of God,
35 or by the earth, for it is his footstool, or by
Jerusalem, for it is the city of the great King.
36 And do not swear by your head, for you
cannot make one hair white or black. 37 Let
what you say be simply 'Yes' or 'No'; anything
more than this comes from evil.**

This paragraph is a call for the simple honesty which makes oaths unnecessary and excludes casuistry (manipulation of an oath or of Scripture in such way as to mislead others and cover up one's own lack of integrity). The scribes found many ways to get around an oath while pretending to keep it. They made an oath binding or not, depending upon its wording. To swear by the gold on the altar was considered binding, but to swear by the altar itself was said not to be binding. Their idea was that an oath is binding if God is involved. The wording of the oath would involve God or not. But this overlooks the fact that the whole world is God's, and he is already concerned. We do not import him into our affairs. Jesus protests not so much against oaths as against the dishonesty which would hide behind legal fictions. Of course, he taught that for the honest person, one's word itself requires no oath, for his yes means yes and his no means no. This passage is not concerned with profanity or with civil oaths today but with perjury and casuistry, the dishonesty which tries to hide behind clever wording of an oath.

(5) *Overcoming Evil with Good* (*5:38–42*)

**38 "You have heard that it was said, 'An eye
for an eye and a tooth for a tooth.' 39 But I say
to you, Do not resist one who is evil. But if any
one strikes you on the right cheek, turn to him
the other also; 40 and if any one would sue you
and take your coat, let him have your cloak as
well; 41 and if any one forces you to go one
mile, go with him two miles. 42 Give to him
who begs from you, and do not refuse him who
would borrow from you.**

The law of ***an eye for an eye and a tooth for a tooth*** was introduced to restrain from greater evil. Just as a divorce certificate was required to give some measure of protection to the wife who otherwise would be defenseless, so the ***eye for an eye*** law first intended to restrict unlimited retaliation (cf. Ex. 21:23–25; Lev. 24:19–21; Deut. 19:21). But Jesus penetrated behind this law of controlled or equal retaliation and repudiated the whole idea of revenge.

"Not to resist with evil" may be a better translation than ***do not resist one who is evil.*** Jesus resisted evil, and that is the Christian's business. One is not to resist with evil but overcome evil with good (cf. Rom. 12:21). Few Christians today ever suffer a physical blow on the cheek, but the principle of "turning the other cheek" may be applied daily in terms of self-exposure to the insults, misunderstandings, resentments, or other harm as one tries to relate redemptively or constructively to others.

In Jewish law one could sue for another's ***coat,*** long undergarment with sleeves; but he could not sue for the ***cloak,*** an outer garment serving the poor as a cover by night (Ex. 22:26 f.). Roman soldiers and officers were permitted to force natives to carry their supplies or baggage for one mile (cf. 27:32, where Simon of Cyrene is compelled to carry the cross). Jesus admonished his followers to go beyond what could be taken or required by law, giving freely to undeserving people, and not to turn away from those who would beg or borrow.

One may protest that many do not deserve such generous treatment. But merit is not the basis for decision. If some do not "deserve" to be helped, neither do we deserve to be in position to help. The Christian's question is never, "Does the other deserve my help?" but "How can I help?" Love sometimes must withhold, but Christian response is to be controlled by the needs of the other, not his merit or one's own "rights." Although an enlightened conscience, must decide how to serve the other, love has already decided that one must serve.

(6) *Love for Enemies* (*5:43–48*)

**43 "You have heard that it was said, 'You
shall love your neighbor and hate your enemy.'**

44 But I say to you, Love your enemies and pray for those who persecute you, 45 so that you may be sons of your Father who is in heaven; for he makes his sun rise on the evil and on the good, and sends rain on the just and on the unjust. 46 For if you love those who love you, what reward have you? Do not even the tax collectors do the same? 47 And if you salute only your brethren, what more are you doing than others? Do not even the Gentiles do the same? 48 You, therefore, must be perfect, as your heavenly Father is perfect.

The Old Testament does not explicitly say, ***hate your enemy.*** There are passages which encourage hostility and retaliation. The Qumran *Manual of Discipline* (I, 4,10) commands love for all whom God has elected but hate for all whom he has rejected, including "all sons of darkness." The command to love one's neighbor (Lev. 19:18) would be understood by a Jew to refer to another Jew. The Pharisee would possibly restrict neighbor to another Pharisee (they called themselves *Haberim* or "neighbors").

Christians are seen to be ***sons of [their] Father who is in heaven*** when they embody his love. God's love does not discriminate but pours itself out upon friends and enemies alike. It is not motivated by our merit. It is governed by its own character, which is ever self-denying and self-giving. God's love seeks to relate to friend or foe for his good without counting the cost. The Greek word *agapē* does not of itself mean a certain kind of love. The ***tax collectors*** can also love. What is meant by ***love*** is not to be derived from a Greek word but from what we see of God revealed in Jesus Christ. The love commended is that which became incarnate in Jesus.

Some of God's gifts, like his sun and rain, can be given regardless of the character or attitude of the recipients. Higher gifts like forgiveness and newness of life can only be offered; in their nature they cannot be imposed. But God does not give as a bargainer, hoping to receive. Giving which is calculated to gain return is not God's love but rather is pagan.

The perfection demanded by Jesus (v. 48) is not the legalism of the Pharisees or the Qumranites but a deeper and radical understanding of the Law's intention. Matthew finds sinless perfection only in Jesus, but he does not flinch in representing Jesus as making radical, ultimate, and absolute demand upon his followers. ***You, therefore, must be perfect*** is grammatically in the future tense, but the force is that of an imperative. Jesus did not just predict future perfection. He held up God's perfection as the ideal or demand now. To interpret ***perfect*** (*teleios*) as "mature" becomes awkward when one extends it to read "as God is mature."

Bornkamm (p. 98) is exegetically sound in finding "wholeness" to be the Old Testament background to *teleios* (Hebrew *shalom* and *tamin*), citing 1 Kings 11:4 as the most illuminating example. In his old age, Solomon's heart was not "perfect" with the Lord his God as was the heart of David his father. By no test was David morally or ethically sinless. The point is that David the sinner had a heart which was given in "wholeness," undividedly to God, even though he contradicted that heart through his weakness and sin.

Even this exegesis must not weaken the demand in verse 48. God demands perfection, even though he accepts persons on the ground of mercy, not merit. Within the gift of salvation is absolute demand. Man rebels against this, preferring either the legalism in which he feels that he has earned his salvation or the libertinism in which he assumes that grace is all gift and no demand. Jesus calls us to the narrow way which escapes both legalism and antinomianism. Salvation is gift that is never earned, and the Christian is yet a sinner who needs daily forgiveness. One is never farther from goodness than when he thinks that he is good. On the other hand, following Jesus begins with conversion to the kingdom (rule) of God, submission to a claim that is ultimate and absolute. The demand for perfection is never met, but it is there to be met.

6. Motive in Religious Life (6:1–18)

The primacy of motive in religious life is illustrated in the areas of almsgiving, prayer, and fasting. Jesus esteemed all three and assumed that his followers would practice them. His point was that the motive behind religious expression gives it its meaning. Religion as performance designed to impress God, other people, or self is false and futile.

The proposition developed in the three illustrations is set forth in verse 1. ***Practicing your piety*** is to think of righteousness as outward performance. The fallacy stems from failure to recognize that moral, ethical, or spiritual value is not inherent in things done or said. Outward doing and saying can come from pagan motive as well as Christian. No deed or word is of itself good or bad; it takes on moral quality from motive, intention, context, and other factors. A shove, for example, may be of itself neither good nor bad. It may be a brutish act of self-assertion or a heroic act, as when one at the risk of his own life shoves another from the path of an oncoming car. A kiss may express love and trust, or cowardly betrayal as when Judas kissed Jesus. Almsgiving, prayer, and fasting may be significant expressions of authentic religion. They may also be performances calculated to gain selfish advantage.

(1) Almsgiving (6:1–4)

[1] "Beware of practicing your piety before men in order to be seen by them; for then you will have no reward from your Father who is in heaven.

[2] "Thus, when you give alms, sound no trumpet before you, as the hypocrites do in the synagogues and in the streets, that they may be praised by men. Truly, I say to you, they have their reward. [3] But when you give alms, do not let your left hand know what your right hand is doing, [4] so that your alms may be in secret; and your Father who sees in secret will reward you.

Alms translates the Greek *eleēmosunēn,* a term for acts of mercy more inclusive than almsgiving. Here the special reference is to charitable gifts. Whether or not Jesus meant that some literally blew a trumpet to call attention to their acts of charity, the ulterior motive is exposed through this picture. Trumpets were blown during fasts in times of drought. "Hypocrite" translates a word used in drama for an actor, one playing a part. God is not impressed by religious acts designed to impress him. If one performs religiously to win men's praise he may succeed, but this praise is the most for which he can hope. ***They have their reward*** (vv. 2,5,16) employs a commercial term for giving a receipt (*apechein*). Almsgiving, prayer, or fasting as a performance can attract attention; but when one is so recognized, he may as well turn in his receipt, for he has gotten all he will get from his performance.

The command, ***do not let your left hand know what your right hand is doing,*** is not to be interpreted apart from other teachings of Jesus, e.g., that one's light is to shine and his good works to be seen of men to the glory of God (5:16). Each verse is balanced by the other. To try to reduce these teachings to a rigid system is to miss their intention. From the presence of such verses as 5:16 and 6:3, side by side in the same sermon, emerges the important principle that Scripture is to be interpreted by Scripture. The whole truth can never be captured in a single statement. In 5:16 the teaching is that one is to share with others what he has received from God, doing it to man's good and God's glory. In 6:3 is the warning that self-seeking vitiates religious acts. The lamp is to give forth its light (5:16), but it is not to display itself (v. 3).

Reward is promised for almsgiving, prayer, and fasting done ***in secret*** (vv. 4, 6,18). The secrecy commanded is not to be absolutized. Jesus publicly did acts of mercy, prayed, and fasted. The warning is to be interpreted in context. Secrecy is prescribed for one whose temptation is to perform for others. Religious expression can be open and honest. To "do good" in secret can be an obsession as hypocritical and selfish as openly to parade one's religion. The promise of reward is itself both a blessing and a peril. Genuine service carries its reward, but the reward is proportionate to one's freedom from the seeking of reward. Those receiving the highest rewards in the judgment will be unaware that they had engaged in meritorious service (cf. 25:37 f.). The word "openly" after ***your Father who sees in secret will reward you*** (vv. 4,6,18) probably is spurious, although found in some early manuscripts.

(2) *Prayer* (*6:5–15*)

5 "And when you pray, you must not be like
the hypocrites; for they love to stand and pray
in the synagogues and at the street corners,
that they may be seen by men. Truly, I say to
you, they have their reward. 6 But when you
pray, go into your room and shut the door and
pray to your Father who is in secret; and your
Father who sees in secret will reward you.
7 "And in praying do not heap up empty
phrases as the Gentiles do; for they think that
they will be heard for their many words. 8 Do
not be like them, for your Father knows what
you need before you ask him. 9 Pray then like
this:
Our Father who art in heaven,
Hallowed be thy name.
10 Thy kingdom come,
Thy will be done,
On earth as it is in heaven.
11 Give us this day our daily bread;
12 And forgive us our debts,
As we also have forgiven our debtors;
13 And lead us not into temptation,
But deliver us from evil.
14 For if you forgive men their trespasses, your
heavenly Father also will forgive you; 15 but if
you do not forgive men their trespasses, neither
will your Father forgive your trespasses.

Three carefully balanced paragraphs of equal length and each ending with the promise of reward from the father (vv. 4, 6,18) may be seen if one for a moment sets aside verses 7–15. In other words, 6:7–15 seems to be inserted into an older structure of three balanced strophes on almsgiving, prayer, and fasting. The Model Prayer (vv. 9–13) is thus in a setting which warns against making prayer a babbling, as practiced in paganism (v. 7). So seen, verses 5–6 make up a unit on prayer, closely related to 2–4 and 16–18, three illustrations warning against the effort to impress men with one's religious life.

The unit 6:7–15 has to do with the danger of trying to use prayer as a means of impressing God or compelling him to bend to our wills. Further evidence that 6:7–15 is inserted into the threefold structure may be seen in the recurrence of ***hypocrites*** in verses 2,5, and 16, whereas in 6:7–15 the warning is against being like pagans (***Gentiles*** in RSV).

The strophe 6:5–6 develops with respect to prayer the same ideas brought out with respect to almsgiving: the bad example of the ***hypocrites,*** the temptation to display one's piety in the synagogues or on the streets, the desire to be seen of men, the warning that such motivation gains nothing more than men's praise for which a "receipt in full" may as well be given, and the admonition to pray in secret with the assurance of reward from the Father.

It follows, of course, that merely to ***go into your room and shut the door*** does not eliminate the possibility of hyprocrisy. It would eliminate other human auditors, but one could yet be his own auditor; and he could try to impress God with his praying. The word about secret prayer is to be taken in context. It is not a rule to govern all praying. Jesus prayed in public and so may we. This strophe deals only with the danger of praying to be heard by men.

Yet another problem is introduced in verse 7, that of trying through prayer to compel God to do our bidding. Jesus likened this to the babbling of pagans. Although this could serve as a warning against "tongues" such as occurred at Corinth (cf. 1 Cor. 14), it is likely that the warning is against the use of prayer to control God to gain selfish advantage. Jesus does not forbid sincere repetition in prayer. In Gethsemane he prayed three times for the possible removal of his "cup" (26:39,42,44). But God is not pressured into action when we ***heap up empty phrases.*** It is not the function of prayer to inform God, for he already ***knows what you need before you ask***

him. He does not have to be persuaded, for he already is concerned for our good.

Then why pray? Prayer's purpose is not to inform God or change his will but, as Georgia Harkness has it, to lay hold on his willingness. It is not that God needs to be asked but that we need to ask. Prayer is communion with God in which we are brought into new relationships and new attitudes, thus opening the way for blessings which God already purposed to impart. The English word prayer means to ask, and it reflects our unfortunate tendency to reduce prayer to asking. Prayer includes asking, but it is far more. It is more like opening oneself to God in trust and praise, that we may freely receive his gifts and yield to his demands.

The Model Prayer (*vv.* 9–13).—The Model Prayer in Matthew is paralleled by Luke 11:2–4. The Lukan form is shorter and on the whole more primitive, although Matthew may preserve some older forms in the petitions for bread and forgiveness. The simple address "Father" in Luke represents a most significant practice and teaching of Jesus. Judaism already knew God as Father, but the direct, childlike address (*Abba* in Aramaic) represents something new in the practice and teaching of Jesus. *Abba* (cf. Rom. 8:15 f.; Gal. 4:6) was a child's way of addressing his father, not the more formal "the father" or "our father," but the intimate and simple word "Father." Jesus knew God as Father and came to enable us so to know him. Matthew's ***our Father*** is adapted to congregational usage and stresses the fact that we cannot exclude others as we come before God (5:23 f.).

Matthew's ***who art in heaven*** preserves the balance between recognizing the nearness and transcendence of God. With the family-like intimacy, God may be addressed as Father, but he remains the transcendent God, always to be approached in awe and reverence. The paradox of nearness and transcendence is never lost in biblical revelation. God is in Christ and we meet Christ in other people (25:31–46), but he is other than the others in whom we meet him. To deism, God is distant and out of reach; to pantheism, God is everything and everything is God; to the sentimentalist, God may be "the man upstairs." To Jesus, God is none of this. He is Father and he is God, ever near and ever to be held in reverence.

The prayer that God's ***kingdom come*** looks both to the ultimate triumph of God's rule at the Parousia and to immediate and increasing submission to his rule on earth. Luke's simpler "thy kingdom come" preserves the primary eschatological stress, the final triumph of God's rule; but Matthew's ***on earth as it is in heaven*** preserves an authentic concern of Jesus for submission now to God's rule. The kingdom of heaven is both present and future, already being actualized but consummated only at the final coming of Christ.

Thy will be done relates closely to the prayer that God's kingdom come. "Will" translates a Greek noun with a result suffix (*thelēma*), stressing not the act of willing so much as what is willed. It is the prayer that what God has willed be fulfilled on earth as in heaven.

Matthew and Luke both have the phrase ***our daily bread.*** "Daily" attempts to translate *epiousion,* but the meaning is uncertain. "Our bread for the coming day" may be preferable, but even it is ambiguous, meaning either bread for the day in progress or bread for the morrow. Another possibility is bread "of necessity" or our "necessary" bread. No occurrence of the Greek word *epiousion* outside the model prayer has been established. Two examples have been claimed, but one is proved to have been mistaken and the other cannot be verified, having been cited in a now lost manuscript.[21] Luke's understanding of the word permitted the wording, "Keep on giving us day by day." He clearly saw this as a petition for literal bread for each day. Matthew's form may be more primitive: ***Give us this day.*** The aorist tense (*dos*) cannot legitimately be used to argue that

21 Bruce M. Metzger, "How Many Times Does 'Epiousios' Occur Outside the Lord's Prayer?" *The Expository Times,* LXIX, 2 (Nov., 1957), 52–54.

this must refer to a single action[22] or to a once-for-all giving of bread, as, e.g., for the messianic banquet at the end of the age. This is to misunderstand the Greek aorist tense, which only treats an action without description but does not tell whether the action itself was single, iterative, or extended (cf. the aorist tense in Luke 19:13—Carry on business while I am coming; and in John 2:20—the Temple was being built for forty-six years).

That *epiousion* refers to the ***bread for the morrow*** (RSV margin) is possible though not conclusive; but to argue that it refers to "the great Tomorrow, the final consummation" (Jeremias, p. 25), giving it an eschatological meaning, is to build upon a very shaky foundation. Matthew's ***this day*** and Luke's "each day" both understand the petition to be for literal bread for daily needs. To read eschatology into the petition is highly precarious. To exclude reference to material bread, tried at least as early as Origen, is to contradict the obvious concern of Jesus that people have bread, clearly expressed in his feeding of the five thousand (14:32–39) and probably reflected in the Model Prayer.

Matthew's ***our debts*** (v. 12) is probably more primitive than Luke's "our trespasses," for Luke also refers to "everyone who is indebted to us" (11:4). Luke has substituted a more familiar and interpretative word, "sins." This is the only petition upon which Matthew gives further comment, where he quotes Jesus as binding together forgiveness and forgivableness (vv. 14–15). As was said of mercy (5:7), so of forgiveness—one must be open to give if he is able to recieve. This is not to be explained away out of fear of a doctrine of "works" or merit. The requirement is not arbitrary. It belongs inherently and inescapably to forgiveness. It is not that God is unwilling to forgive the unforgiving but that the condition of the unforgiving is such that they are incapable of receiving forgiveness.

[22] As by J. Jeremias, *The Lord's Prayer* (Philadelphia: Fortress, 1964), p. 13.

When a door is closed, it is closed from both sides. What blocks the flow of mercy or forgiveness *from* us blocks its flow *to* us (cf. 18:21–35).

The petition, ***lead us not into temptation,*** does not imply that God tempts us (cf. James 1:13–15). This may be a poetic way of giving force to a positive statement, ***deliver us from evil,*** by setting the positive against the negative. A parallel would be: "Give us not darkness but light." The petition may be a deliberate contrast to the proud prayer of the self-righteous who invited God to test them and see their goodness. If so, Jesus was saying not to pray that prayer but, "Lord, do not test me; rather, deliver me from the temptations already about me." One theory holds that *peirasmos* (temptation and/or trial) refers to "the final great testing" and is thus a prayer for deliverance from apostasy as the Antichrist makes his final assualt. This view is forced and is to be rejected (cf. Jeremias, p. 30). *Peirasmos* may point to the fiery trial which ushers in the end of the world (cf. 2 Peter 2:9; Rev. 3:10), but the term may refer to trials or temptations at any time (cf. James 1:2). ***Evil*** translates a Greek word which may be either masculine or neuter—either the evil one or evil.

The beautiful and cherished doxology (v. 13, margin) is by all indications not original to Matthew. It is not in Luke. It appears as early as the *Didache* (early second century) in a short form, "For thine is the power and the glory forever." It also appeared in various manuscripts in other short forms and finally emerged in the long form widely known today, modeled apparently on 1 Chronicles 29:11 f.

(3) *Fasting (6:16–18)*

[16] "And when you fast, do not look dismal, like the hypocrites, for they disfigure their faces that their fasting may be seen by men. Truly, I say to you, they have their reward. [17] But when you fast, anoint your head and wash your face, [18] that your fasting may not be seen by men but by your Father who is in secret; and your Father who sees in secret will reward you.

Jesus sometimes fasted and expected his followers to do so. What he rejected was fasting for display. The Mosaic Law did not explicitly require fasting, but Leviticus 16:31 was understood to require it for the Day of Atonement. The Pharisees fasted twice a week (Luke 18:12) and made it a test of piety. Jesus refused to be governed by a calendar. He fasted as a normal thing in times of crisis (cf. 4:2), finding it meaningful when spontaneous in situations of sorrow or crisis (cf. 9:14–17). Abstinence may be a private means of freeing oneself of certain preoccupations (e.g., food, sleep, play, or work) in favor of concentration upon something which for the time at least represents a higher claim (cf. 1 Cor. 7:5). Anointing was a symbol of joy, forbidden on the Day of Atonement or other times of fasting or sorrow; but Jesus proposed that one ***anoint*** his head when he fasted, thus to avoid any display of "humility."

7. *Freedom from Tyranny of Things (6: 19–34)*

19 "Do not lay up for yourselves treasures on
earth, where moth and rust consume and where
thieves break in and steal, 20 but lay up for
yourselves treasures in heaven, where neither
moth nor rust consumes and where thieves do
not break in and steal. 21 For where your treas-
ure is, there will your heart be also.
22 "The eye is the lamp of the body. So, if
your eye is sound, your whole body will be full
of light; 23 but if your eye is not sound, your
whole body will be full of darkness. If then the
light in you is darkness, how great is the
darkness!
24 "No one can serve two masters; for either
he will hate the one and love the other, or he
will be devoted to the one and despise the
other. You cannot serve God and mammon.
25 "Therefore I tell you, do not be anxious
about your life, what you shall eat or what you
shall drink, nor about your body, what you
shall put on. Is not life more than food, and
the body more than clothing? 26 Look at the
birds of the air: they neither sow nor reap nor
gather into barns, and yet your heavenly
Father feeds them. Are you not of more value
than they? 27 And which of you by being anx-
ious can add one cubit to his span of life?
28 And why are you anxious about clothing?
Consider the lilies of the field, how they grow;
they neither toil nor spin; 29 yet I tell you, even
Solomon in all his glory was not arrayed like
one of these. 30 But if God so clothes the grass
of the field, which today is alive and tomorrow
is thrown into the oven, will he not much more
clothe you, O men of little faith? 31 Therefore
do not be anxious, saying, 'What shall we eat?'
or 'What shall we drink?' or 'What shall we
wear?' 32 For the Gentiles seek all these things;
and your heavenly Father knows that you need
them all. 33 But seek first his kingdom and his
righteousness, and all these things shall be
yours as well.
34 "Therefore do not be anxious about tomor-
row, for tomorrow will be anxious for itself.
Let the day's own trouble be sufficient for the
day.

This section seems to be governed by the theme of freedom from the tyranny of material things. The alternative is the kingdom of God (v. 33). One's choice is between finding his ultimate values in the treasures which perish or those which endure (vv. 19–21), between the stinginess which leaves one in darkness or the generosity which gives one light (vv. 22–23), between the worship of mammon or God (vv. 25–34).

Treasures in heaven (vv. 19–21).—The warning is twofold: (1) treasures on earth are perishable and (2) one shares the fate of that to which he gives his heart. There is no ultimate security in material things. ***Moth, rust,*** and ***thieves*** illustrate some of the threats to such "security." The warning against trust in the material is not given to the rich alone. The house "where thieves dig through" may be the poor man's house of mud brick.

The word rendered rust (*brōsis*) probably should be translated "eating," with a possible reference to the devouring of stored clothing or food by mice or other vermin.

One does not understand the teaching of Jesus unless he sees that he was both deeply concerned that people have the material necessities of life and that they be free from the tyranny of things. Jesus was not ascetic and required no withdrawal from corporal living. He healed the sick, fed the hungry, and made our attention to the material needs of other people the test of our relationship to him (25:31–46). At the same time, he warned against making material values the object of our trust or affection. Jesus gave bread to the hungry but warned that man cannot live by bread alone. One's **heart** is where his **treasure** is, and he shares the fate or destiny of that to which he gives himself—whether to the perishable or imperishable.

The lamp of the body (*vv.* 22–23).—This parable is built upon the analogy to the **sound** eye that can bring objects clearly into focus and the bad eye that cannot. The eye serves as a **lamp** for the body, giving it light or leaving it in darkness. Applied to the problem of material possessions, the lesson may be that if one divides his attention between God and the material, he may have neither in proper focus. **Sound** (*haplous*) means single, and is employed sometimes for generosity (cf. James 1:5, where God is said to give generously, *haplōs;* cf. also Rom. 12:8; 2 Cor. 8:2; 9:11,13). "Not sound" translates *poneros,* sometimes used for the grudging, stingy disposition (cf. 20:15, margin, "Is your eye evil [*poneros*], because I am good?" cf. also Deut. 15:9; Prov. 23:6). So understood, the parable teaches that the generous person (sound eye) walks in light but the stingy person (unsound eye) walks in darkness.

Another approach is to see the sound eye as representing openness or receptivity to God, the unsound eye representing the distrust which shuts one out of God's world of light. So understood, this parable agrees with that of the sower (see 13:1–9,18–23) in teaching that one with no openness to God is blind.

God and mammon (v. 24).—This parable can be understood only against the background of slavery, where a master held legal title to a slave and had complete authority over him and where experiments in dual ownership of a slave ran into the difficulty that a slave could not give himself totally to two owners. One cannot belong to God and mammon at the same time. **Mammon** is of uncertain derivation. It may designate something hidden or stored up or something trusted. Here it represents money or material possessions. Jesus warned in the parable of the rich farmer (Luke 12:13–21) that one may be owned by what he thinks he owns. So here, Jesus warns against the tyranny of things. The only escape from the rule of things is submission to the rule of God (v. 33).

Hate and **love** are best understood here as "reject" and "accept." The lesson is that God must have exclusive claim upon us. It is significant that Jesus makes money, not Satan, the rival to God's claim upon us (Schniewind, p. 92). Jesus was concerned about what we do with money (cf. 25:31–46), but his first concern was for what it does to us. It can blind (unsound eye), enslave (mammon), and thus destroy us. Money is not evil, for it can be made to serve God and man; but the love of money is the root of all kinds of evil (1 Tim. 6:10).

Distraction over things (*vv.* 25–34).—**Do not be anxious** is a better translation for *me merimnate* than "take no thought" (KJV), but "be not distracted" may be yet nearer its intention. Jesus did not prescribe indifference to material things nor encourage idleness (cf. 2 Tim. 3:1–12). Idleness is for neither the Christian nor the birds. Birds exemplify not idleness but freedom from anxiety. Far from being idle, Jesus' brief life was full and active. In John 4:6 he is pictured as being so wearied from a journey that he sat exhausted on the curb of a well at Sychar. Sometimes his concern was such that he went without sleep or food. His warning is against distraction or anxiety over things, not concern or effort with respect to legitimate problems and needs. The Greek word *merimnate* is built on a word for "a part," and it could be translated, "Don't go to pieces," or "Don't be distracted."

Anxiety over things like food and clothing is unnecessary, unprofitable, and evil. If God cares for the **birds of the air,** he can be trusted to care for us. If he gives life, he can sustain it. Anxiety is unprofitable, for thereby one does not **add one cubit to his**

span of life. Although cubit is a linear measure (about eighteen inches), the term may refer to length of life. Anxiety is more likely to shorten life than lengthen it. The heaviest charge against anxiety over food and clothing is not that it is unnecessary and unprofitable but that it is evil. It reflects lack of faith in God: ***O men of little faith!*** Striving for material things is "pagan," a better translation than Gentiles.

Escape from anxiety over things is found in giving first place to God's ***kingdom and his righteousness.*** Emphasis upon the kingdom (rule) of God and upon righteousness is characteristic of the whole Gospel of Matthew. The assurance that to those who ***seek first his kingdom and his righteousness*** will in addition be given ***all these things*** is to be balanced by the warning that sacrifice, privation, and even the cross belong to discipleship (10:34–39). Considering both the promise (v. 33) and the warning (10: 34–39), one may understand that the disciple's part is unconditional submission to the rule of Christ with the assurance that what one requires to fulfil his calling in discipleship will be provided. The disciple may in fact experience "fulness" or "hunger," but in Christ he will find his sufficiency (Phil. 4:11–13).

Verse 34 adds the warning against borrowing tomorrow's troubles for today. Jesus does not forbid foresight, but he does warn against burdening today with anxiety over the unknown problems of the future. One must not destroy himself by anxiety over a future which he cannot control. Along with legitimate foresight (not under discussion here) must be trust in God who alone knows the future. It may be noted that Jesus did not base the case for freedom from anxiety on grounds that the time was short before the end of the world. This is not an "interim ethic."

8. *Judging Others (7:1–6)*

[1] "Judge not, that you be not judged. [2] For with the judgment you pronounce you will be judged, and the measure you give will be the measure you get. [3] Why do you see the speck that is in your brother's eye, but do not notice the log that is in your own eye? [4] Or how can you say to your brother, 'Let me take the speck out of your eye,' when there is the log in your own eye? [5] You hypocrite, first take the log out of your own eye, and then you will see clearly to take the speck out of your brother's eye.

[6] "Do not give dogs what is holy; and do not throw your pearls before swine, lest they trample them under foot and turn to attack you.

Judgment is the dominant theme throughout chapter 7, although cohesiveness is less apparent than in chapter 5 or 6. Logical bonds are not always apparent as transition is made from one subject to another.

The speck and the log (vv. 1–5).— Forming judgments is an inescapable function of the mind, but expressing them is subject to control. One does not escape being judged by assuming the role of judge, but on the contrary makes certain the fact of his own judgment and determines its measure. Foremost in this teaching is the warning that when we presume to judge others, we bring upon ourselves the judgment of God. Further, when we engage in merciless judgment we deny to ourselves God's mercy. God is not arbitrary in this (cf. 5:7; 6:12,14 f.), but when we deny mercy to others, we deny it to ourselves. Either we take our stand on the mercy of God or we do not. We cannot have it both ways, mercy for ourselves but not for others. It is also true that one is judged in the very act of judging. In each judgment one reveals his own standards and values.

The hypocrisy of condemning in others what we tolerate in ourselves is set forth in the analogy of ***the speck*** and ***the log.*** Jesus deliberately drew the ludicrous picture of a man with a log in his eye trying to remove a speck from another's eye! Much of our judging of others is that absurd. If one is sincere, he will first bring himself under judgment, removing the log from his own eye.

Jesus is not saying that we are to ignore ***the speck*** in our brother's eye. It is our business to try to free a brother from the speck which impairs his vision. But one is in position for this ministry only after ***the log*** is out of his ***own eye.*** It is not a matter of speck or log. Both must be removed, but the log first. Only after one has known the shame or agony of coming under judgment and of having the log removed from his own eye will he understand the need and the feeling of the brother. Only then can he ***see clearly to take the speck*** from his ***brother's eye.***

Even so, God alone has the knowledge and integrity to render final judgment; and, happily, final judgment belongs to him and not us (1 Cor. 4:3–5). Although minds are so made that they cannot escape the function of judging, we can at least remember that we have not been appointed to the bench as judge; and we can remember our fallibility, marred by our own sins, never having all the truth about that which we judge, and always subject to bias or prejudice.

Pearls before swine (v. 6).—Dogs and swine were despised by the Jews, both considered unclean. Jesus is not alluding to Gentiles but to any person who is unable or unwilling to distinguish between ***what is holy*** and what is not, or between ***pearls*** and what is valueless. This saying sounds harsh, but it must be heard. Jesus did not arbitrarily exclude anyone, but he recognized that there were times when there was no opening for the gospel or for his ministry (cf. 26:63).

Although it is the Christian's business to share ***what is holy*** or his ***pearls*** with any who will receive, there are times when he can only remain silent or try to bring about a better climate for a later sharing. What is holy and pearls may here refer to one's discernments, judgments, or message. Three dangers threaten the Christian witness or minister who does not discern when to speak and when to keep silence: he may further damage the one he tries to help; he may try to force himself or his values upon another; and he may unnecessarily imperil himself and others.

9. *Ask, Seek, Knock (7:7–12)*

7 "Ask, and it will be given you; seek, and you will find; knock, and it will be opened to you. 8 For every one who asks receives, and he who seeks finds, and to him who knocks it will be opened. 9 Or what man of you, if his son asks him for bread, will give him a stone? 10 Or if he asks for a fish, will give him a serpent? 11 If you then, who are evil, know how to give good gifts to your children, how much more will your Father who is in heaven give good things to those who ask him! 12 So whatever you wish that men would do to you, do so to them; for this is the law and the prophets.

What may the Christian do in the face of the responsibility of removing the speck from his brother's eye and of sharing what is holy and his pearls, knowing his personal inadequacy for either ministry? He must look to higher wisdom and resources than his own. He must ***ask, seek,*** and ***knock.*** Surely, this admonition goes beyond the needs arising out of this ministry of judging and sharing, but this in included.

By ***ask, seek,*** and ***knock*** is meant primarily an openness to God for his instruction, guidance, or gifts. It does not follow that one may get what he wants simply by praying for it. Jesus prayed thrice for the possible removal of the cup awaiting him (26:39–44). He did not demand its removal and it was not removed. He did receive the strength to drink it. One may not receive what he requests, he may not find what he seeks, and the door upon which he knocks may not be the one opened; but the assurance is that where there is asking there will be receiving, where there is seeking there will be finding, and where there is knocking God will open a door.

God may not only be trusted to give, but to give ***good things to those who ask him.*** A father will not give ***a stone*** to a son asking for ***a loaf,*** or ***a serpent*** to a son asking for ***a fish.*** God will not give us stones or serpents when we ask for bread or fish, and he will not give us a stone or a serpent even when we are so confused or wayward as to ask no better! The need for persistent prayer is not because God is reluctant to give but because we need to be conditioned to receive.

If even evil men give ***good gifts*** to their children (v. 11), surely the ***Father who is*** *in heaven* can be trusted to *give good things to those who ask him.* Matthew does not indicate what the good things are. The Lukan parallel (11:13) has it that God gives the Holy Spirit. An old prayer happily has it: "Lord, give us not the object of our desire but the substance of what we require."

The Golden Rule (*v. 12*).—In a negative form, this proverb was widely known among Jews (Tobit 4:15; Philo; Hillel) and Gentiles. Jesus gave it positive form, and termed it the essence of the Law and the Prophets. The Golden Rule presupposes discipleship, submission to the rule of God. It is not a sufficient rule for everyone. In a pagan life the "rule" would be experienced in terms of pagan values, for pagan wishes come from a pagan heart. The intention of the Golden Rule, presupposing discipleship, is that one is to be as concerned for the other person's good as for his own (cf. 22:39 f.).

10. *Perils to Righteousness and Life* (*7: 13–27*)

It is difficult to trace the movement of thought or find the principle of cohesion for this large block of material. The danger of a neat outline is that it forces upon the material a system foreign to it. Some continuity may be seen in the warning against the easy way (vv. 13–14), the false prophets (vv. 15–20), profession without obedience (vv. 21–23), and building on the wrong foundation (vv. 24–27). There is also the positive side, stressing the way that leads to life, the good tree that produces good fruit, and the rock foundation which will not give way; but the strong warnings in verses 13,15,21,26 are so important that they cannot be over-emphasized. Matthew seems to have the antinomian threat in mind as he brings together these teachings of Jesus.

(*1*) *The Two Ways* (*7:13–14*)

13 "Enter by the narrow gate; for the gate is wide and the way is easy, that leads to destruction, and those who enter by it are many. 14 For the gate is narrow and the way is hard, that leads to life, and those who find it are few.

The Father who is in heaven gives good gifts to men who at best are yet evil (v. 11), and he offers the kingdom to the poor in spirit, the meek, and the merciful; but within the gift of salvation is also demand. Matthew knows no salvation through human merit, but neither a salvation which releases man from God's demands. ***The way*** which ***leads to life*** is entered through a ***narrow gate,*** and ***the way*** itself ***is hard,*** i.e., afflicted, anguished, or torturous. It is a way of decision, commitment, and obedience to God. In a wicked world it is a lonely road, traveled with a few companions. "Hard" translates *tethlimmenē,* normally rendered "afflicted." Reference may be to the cross, for Master and disciple (16:21, 24), persecution (5:10 ff.), temptation (6: 13; 26:41), self-denial (16:24), all characteristic of discipleship.

Although there is no explicit reference to either legalism or antinomianism, it may not be farfetched to think of the narrow, torturous way as running between the two, avoiding both. Religion easily becomes a rigid, legalistic system, stressing attainable goals or rules, whether ritual, doctrinal, ascetic, or whatever. It just as easily becomes a loose way of license in the name of liberty or grace, morally and ethically irresponsible. Jesus calls us to the narrow, hard way that is neither legalistic nor libertine.

(*2*) *A Tree Known by Its Fruit* (*7:15–20*)

15 "Beware of false prophets, who come to you in sheep's clothing but inwardly are ravenous wolves. 16 You will know them by their fruits. Are grapes gathered from thorns, or figs from thistles? 17 So, every sound tree bears good fruit, but the bad tree bears evil fruit. 18 A sound tree cannot bear evil fruit, nor can a bad tree bear good fruit. 19 Every tree that does not bear good fruit is cut down and thrown into the fire. 20 Thus you will know them by their fruits.

The ***false prophets*** who come in ***sheep's clothing*** but who ***inwardly are ravenous wolves*** are not Pharisees or Sadducees, for neither claimed to prophesy. These are persons within the Christian community who pose as prophets but who are false. In the next paragraph (v. 23), closely related to this one, may be found a clue in the employment of the word lawlessness (evildoers in RSV). These may be the antinomians who stress grace, the Spirit, and prophecy, but who prove to be false. Posing as sheep, they prove to be ravenous wolves who divide and destroy.

Fruit is a major term in the New Testament, never equated with outward works (see 3:8; John 15:1–10; Gal. 5:22). In verses 17 f., ***bad tree*** is a better translation than "corrupt tree" (KJV). *Sapron* does not designate a rotten tree, but the wrong kind. This word is used in the parable of the net (13:48). The bad fish are not diseased but the wrong kind, inedible. False prophets produce bad fruit, the wrong kind. What the fruit is, is not specified here; but in Galations 5:22 "the fruit of the Spirit is love, joy, peace, patience, kindness, goodness, faithfulness [or fidelity], gentleness, self-control."

(3) *Saying Without Doing* (*7:21–23*)

21 "Not every one who says to me, 'Lord, Lord,' shall enter the kingdom of heaven, but he who does the will of my Father who is in heaven. 22 On that day many will say to me, 'Lord, Lord, did we not prophesy in your name, and cast our demons in your name, and do many mighty works in your name?' 23 And then will I declare to them, 'I never knew you; depart from me, you evildoers.'

It may seem that this paragraph offers a simple choice between saying and doing, but that is not the case. Those rejected in the judgment were both sayers and doers! They said, "Lord! Lord!" and they did many religious works: prophesy, casting out demons, and mighty works. The doing required is the doing of ***the will*** of God and not merely religious deeds, however impressive.

To many who say "Lord! Lord!" and do impressive things (prophecy, exorcism, and miracles), the verdict in the final judgment (***on that day***, v. 22) will be ***I never knew you.*** They were not once known and then forgotten, but had never entered into a saving knowledge of Christ.

The "doing" that is required beyond "saying" is clearly not equated with orthodoxy, prophecy, exorcism, or miracles. Entry into the kingdom of heaven is promised those only who do the will of the Father who is in heaven (cf. 6:10). The Gospel of Matthew closes on this note, "teaching them to observe all that I have commanded you" (28:20).

The word lawlessness (*anomian*) in v. 23 is the key to those described. This is obscured by the RSV translation, ***evildoers.*** These seem to be antinomian libertines who claim that now that Christ has come, the Law is no longer in effect (cf. 5:17 ff.; 24:11 ff.). For works they seem to substitute what they probably would call the charismatic gifts of prophecy, exorcism of demons, and miracles (Barth, pp. 159–64). The Lukan parallel (13:27) has iniquity (*adikios*) where Matthew has *anomia* (v. 23), possibly reflecting Matthew's concern with the antinomian threat.

(4) *Hearing and Doing* (*7:24–27*)

24 "Every one then who hears these words of mine and does them will be like a wise man who built his house upon the rock; 25 and the rain fell, and the floods came, and the winds blew and beat upon that house, but it did not fall, because it had been founded on the rock. 26 And every one who hears these words of mine and does not do them will be like a foolish man who built his house upon the sand; 27 and the rain fell, and the floods came, and the winds blew and beat against that house, and it fell; and great was the fall of it."

Just as saying and doing were discussed in the preceding paragraph, hearing and doing are considered here. One ***who hears*** Jesus' words and ***does them*** is compared to ***a wise man who built his house upon the rock.*** One who ***hears*** but ***does not do them*** is like ***a foolish man who built his house upon the sand.*** One foundation holds while the other gives way.

Both Matthean and Lukan sermons conclude with the parable of the two foundations. The parable and its embodiment in some form of the sermon are earlier than both Gospels. For the Gospel of Matthew it represents a major concern, stressing the obedience indispensable to discipleship. It also reflects Jesus' sense of having the right to make ultimate claims upon men and his position that their destiny is bound up with their obedience to him.

11. Summary (7:28–29)

[28] And when Jesus finished these sayings, the crowds were astonished at his teaching, [29] for he taught them as one who had authority, and not as their scribes.

The summary statement here appears in basically the same wording at the end of each of Matthew's five major discourses (7:28; 11:1; 13:53; 19:1; 26:1). That Matthew has in mind a new Pentateuch is not likely (see Introduction, pp. 22–26), but it is clear that the five discourses represent a major distinctive of his Gospel.

The crowds were impressed with the ***authority*** with which Jesus taught. He made ultimate demands based upon his "I say to you." By contrast the scribes always appealed to former rabbis. But the authority in the teaching of Jesus is seen also in the depth, truth, and finality of what he said.

III. The Authority of Jesus in Work and Word (8:1—9:34)

This is a recognizable unit in that it consists largely of narrative material (ten miracles) preceded by Matthew's first of five great discourses, the Sermon on the Mount (chs. 5–7), and followed by his second great discourse, on apostleship (ch. 10). Further evidence for a major transition is seen in the almost verbal agreement of 4:23 and 9:35, each summarizing Jesus' ministry in terms of teaching, preaching, and healing and each marking a transition from one section to another. This "narrative" section also contains important discourse material (8:18–22; 9:10–17).

The authority of Jesus is a major theme in this section. Just as Jesus "*taught* them as one who had authority" (7:29), so his authority is recognized over disease, demons, death, nature, the forgiveness of sins, the calling of disciples, and the overriding of Jewish customs. The word authority is explicit in 8:9; 9:6,8, and implied throughout, especially in 9:28. Alongside the theme of Jesus' authority is stress upon "faith" (8:10,26; 9:2,22,29) and radical commitment to Jesus as Lord (8:18–22).

The mountain in 8:1 looks back to 5:1 and ***great crowds*** to 4:25 and 5:1. Matthew thus shows that the crowds who heard the Sermon on the Mount are also the ones who witnessed the mighty works. Not only does this tie together authority in word and work, but it further shows that the heavy demands of Jesus are couched in deeds of mercy, accessible to faith.

The number ten for the miracles brought together in this section may be by design, artistic and theological. Ten is a round number for completion and may correspond to the ten miracles in Egypt, ten at the Red Sea, and ten in the Temple claimed by Jewish tradition (*Pirke Aboth* 5:4–5).

The miracles of chapters 8—9 are sometimes subdivided into three groups of three each, 9:18–26 with the blending of the stories of the ruler's daughter and the woman with the hemorrhage counted as one. The three healing units would thus be interspersed by discourse material, 8:18–22 and 9:9–17. The ten miracles fall into three classes: exorcisms, cure of diseases, and nature miracles. More significant is the anticipation in the ten miracles of the summary statement of 11:5 f., characterizing the ministry of Jesus as one to the blind, lame, lepers, deaf, dead (some mss. omit this), and the poor (cf. Isa. 29:18; 35:5; 42:7).

The possibility of miracles was not questioned by Jesus' followers or foes. The age of rationalism, culminating in the nineteenth century, was very skeptical of "miracles." Both science and faith are less disposed today to set limits for man or God. The Pharisees did not question the fact of Jesus' miracles, only the source of his power and his right to it (9:34; 12:24).

Jesus was inclined toward miracles of mercy to meet human need, yet he drew back from the role of wonder-worker and from followers whose "faith" was dependent upon miracles. To Jesus the miracles were both acts of mercy and eschatological signs that the kingdom of God had come and its powers were already defeating the kingdom of Satan by overcoming sin, disease, demons, and death (cf. 12:28 f.).

"Miracle" means wonder and translates *teras*. This term is never used alone in the Greek New Testament. It remained for the Gospel of John to develop the idea that a "miracle" is a sign (*sēmeion*), having instructional and evidential value for faith. In the Synoptics faith is generally but not always (cf. 8:14–17) a precondition to healing miracles. Faith was not a condition for the expelling of demons or for nature miracles.

1. A Leper Cleansed (8:1–4)

[1] When he came down from the mountain, great crowds followed him; [2] and behold, a leper came to him and knelt before him, saying, "Lord, if you will, you can make me clean." [3] And he stretched out his hand and touched him, saying, "I will; be clean." And immediately his leprosy was cleansed. [4] And Jesus said to him, "See that you say nothing to any one; but go, show yourself to the priest, and offer the gift that Moses commanded, for a proof to the people."

The leprosy of the Bible included various skin diseases but, in the New Testament, not the leprosy now known as Hansen's disease. Leprosy could render a person, clothing, or house unclean. There were elaborate tests for its detection, provisions for isolating the diseased, and ritual procedures for those who recovered, all under the authority of the priests (cf. Lev. 13–14). Next to a corpse, leprosy was counted most defiling. The leper was required to wear torn clothing, let the hair of his head hang loose, cover his upper lip, and cry, "Unclean! Unclean!" when approached (Lev. 13:45). He was not to approach another person.

More significant than the fact that the ***leper*** approached Jesus, a violation of the law, is the fact that Jesus ***stretched out his hand and touched him.*** Jesus touched the untouchable! He did so as a deliberate act of will. The command that he ***say nothing to any one*** was probably to avoid letting healing miracles become the basis for a popular following. ***Show yourself to the priest*** reflects the legal requirement that recovery from leprosy be certified by a priest; otherwise, one could not mix socially. That Jesus told him to ***offer the gift that Moses commanded*** (Lev. 14:1–7) probably reflects Jesus' respect for the Jewish law (5:17).

For a proof to the people literally reads, "as a witness to them." The plural form "to them" may refer to the people rather than to the priest. More likely, the reference is to the priests and scribes, proof to them that Jesus was not destroying the Law or forsaking the Jews.

2. A Centurion's Servant Healed (8:5–13)

[5] As he entered Capernaum, a centurion came forward to him, beseeching him [6] and saying, "Lord, my servant is lying paralyzed at home, in terrible distress." [7] And he said to him, "I will come and heal him." [8] But the centurion answered him, "Lord, I am not worthy to have you come under my roof; but only say the word, and my servant will be healed. [9] For I am a man under authority, with soldiers under me; and I say to one, 'Go,' and he goes, and to another, 'Come,' and he comes, and to my slave, 'Do this,' and he does it." [10] When Jesus heard him, he marveled, and said to those who followed him, "Truly, I say to you, not even in Israel have I found such faith. [11] I tell you, many will come from east and west and sit at table with Abraham, Isaac, and Jacob in the kingdom of heaven, [12] while the sons of the kingdom will be thrown into the outer darkness; there men will weep and gnash their teeth." [13] And to the centurion Jesus said, "Go; be it done for you as you have believed." And the servant was healed at that very moment.

The centurion was a Roman officer over a hundred men. That he was not a Jew is explicit from Jesus' statement, ***not even in Israel have I found such faith.*** It probably is by design that Matthew places this story immediately after that of the cleansed leper. Luke does not join them (5:12–16; 7:1–10). Jesus' respect for the Jewish law and concern for the Jews is reflected in the story of the Jewish leper. The story of the centurion reflects his attitude toward the Gentiles and anticipates his mission to them.

Matthew's term *pais* could be rendered ***servant*** or "son." In the parallel, Luke has slave (*doulos*), so servant is probably correct here. English can hardly preserve the force of Jesus' reply, ***I*** [*ego*] ***will come and heal him.*** The pronoun is emphatic. Jesus indicated willingness to go personally to a Gentile's house, considered unclean by Jewish law. The suggestion that verse 7 should be read as a question rather than an assertion is grammatically possible but not likely (cf. Luke 7:6). If intended as a question, "Should I come?" it is best understood as testing the centurion's faith. That Jesus did not go but healed from a distance does not reflect an unwillingness to enter a Gentile's home but rather points up the matter of his authority, a main emphasis of the story. It may also be a veiled reference to the mission to the Gentiles, into which Jesus did not personally enter but which he later commanded.

As an army man, the centurion lived by the law of authority, having men over him as well as under him. He recognized the ***authority*** of Jesus, trusted and confessed it. It was this ***faith*** that Jesus praised, and this occasioned his far-reaching statement that ***many will come from east and west*** (i.e., Gentiles) ***and sit at table with Abraham, Isaac, and Jacob in the kingdom of heaven!*** Jesus had touched a leper, an "unclean" Jew, and he had offered to enter the house of an "unclean" Gentile. Superficial lines between clean and unclean and between Jew and Gentile were to fall, and Gentiles were to sit at the "messianic banquet" with Abraham, Isaac, and Jacob.

Such ***faith*** as manifested by the centurion was found ***not even*** in Israel; and many ***sons of the kingdom*** (Israelites) would be excluded from the company of Abraham, Isaac, and Jacob, presumably because they lacked faith. The warning is directed chiefly to those who presume on their place of privilege and ground their hopes in what they call their rights. The centurion's ***Lord, I am not worthy to have you come under my roof*** shows that his faith is in Jesus' goodness and power and not in his own merits or rights.

Outer darkness where men ***weep and gnash their teeth,*** expressions appearing six times in Matthew (13:42,50; 22:13; 24:51; 25:30), were early Jewish descriptions of Sheol (a pit), but they had come to characterize Gehenna. Obviously, logic finds difficulty with a picture of Gehenna as a place of fire (3:12) and darkness, a warning against reducing all biblical language to prose meaning. Symbolic and poetic language has its own logic, and its truth is no less true or serious because it employs such imagery. ***Sit at table*** is also imagery for the banquet-like joy of the coming age (cf. 22:1–14; 26:29; Rev. 19:9).

3. *The Sick Healed* (*8:14–17*)

[14] And when Jesus entered Peter's house, he saw his mother-in-law lying sick with a fever; [15] he touched her hand, and the fever left her, and she rose and served him. [16] That evening they brought to him many who were possessed with demons; and he cast out the spirits with a word, and healed all who were sick. [17] This was to fulfil what was spoken by the prophet Isaiah, "He took our infirmities and bore our diseases."

Matthew indicates that Jesus himself upon entering the house noticed the mother-in-law, possibly implying a one-room fisherman's house. Special importance may be attached to the remark that the healed woman ***served him.*** Is the lesson that healing and saving are with a view to service? Jesus enables one to fulfil his role in life.

Matthew passes over Mark's point that general healings took place at sundown (Mark 1:32), at which time the sabbath was past (Mark 1:21). Unlike Mark, Matthew had not introduced the sabbath reference, so had no reason to observe that it was ended. He was more interested in the fulfilment theme, translating the Hebrew text of Isaiah 53:4, ***He took our infirmities***

and bore our diseases. The Greek text makes the pronoun he (*autos*) emphatic. The term Suffering Servant is not used here but the idea is present. Although the emphasis is not upon his bearing man's sins but upon healing his sickness, this passage may remind us that though the redeeming work of Christ has its center in the cross, he already was Redeemer from sickness and sin during his earthly ministry.

4. *The Cost of Discipleship (8:18–22)*

[18] Now when Jesus saw great crowds around him, he gave orders to go over to the other side. [19] And a scribe came up and said to him, "Teacher, I will follow you wherever you go." [20] And Jesus said to him, "Foxes have holes, and birds of the air have nests; but the Son of man has nowhere to lay his head." [21] Another of the disciples said to him, "Lord, let me first go and bury my father." [22] But Jesus said to him, "Follow me, and leave the dead to bury their own dead."

Jesus' withdrawal from ***great crowds*** who had gathered ***around him*** and his reply to two would-be followers leave no doubt about the cost of discipleship. He turned from crowds of people whose interest apparently was only in the physical benefactions derived from miracles. Jesus' main concern was to enlist followers and give them new life, but he was unwilling to accept a following on just any basis. He fled from superficial popularity and compelled those who sought to follow him to consider the costs and consequences. Of course, he elsewhere warned the indifferent, the timid, and the rebellious of the terrible cost of not following.

The ***scribe*** who offered to follow Jesus may already have been a disciple, the second volunteer being introduced as ***another of the disciples.*** If so, this man was a Christian scribe.

The ***scribe*** who said, ***I will follow you wherever you go,*** did not know that Jesus was on his way to a cross (clearer in Luke 9:22,51–62). Jesus probably did not mean that he literally was without a bed in which to sleep. He lived in Capernaum (4:13), and he had just entered Peter's house. The Gospels indicate that he was offered hospitality in Bethany and even in homes of Pharisees. Possibly, Jesus meant what is explicit in John 1:11, "He came to his own home, and his own people received him not." ***Foxes have holes*** (dens) for refuge, and ***birds of the air have nests*** (actually "roosts" for the night, not nests), but he had no place of escape from a hostile world.

Jesus' word that he had ***nowhere to lay his head*** (*tēn kephalēn klinē*) may be echoed in John 19:30, where on the cross Jesus "bowed his head" (*klinas tēn kephalēn*). Robinson observes: "The only pillow on which he can claim to take his rest is the Cross" (p. 73).

The Son of man is introduced here and will become an increasingly important term in Matthew (see Introduction). The term is employed about 80 times in the Gospels, 31 times in Matthew. In the New Testament it is always a self-designation used by Jesus for himself. The term appears in Ezekiel more than 90 times for the prophet as a man. In Daniel 7:13 ff., it designates a heavenly man who receives from "the Ancient of Days" a universal and everlasting kingdom, and in 7:22,27 this son of man seems to be identified with "the saints of the Most High" who receive an everlasting kingdom.

According to the Gospels, ***Son of man*** became the favorite self-designation of Jesus. It was freer from political associations than was the term Messiah and also more inclusive, suited to stress future triumph and glory as well as his present ministry of humble service, suffering, and death. It was Jesus who blended with the term Son of man the picture of the Suffering Servant of Isaiah. In 8:20, we hear Matthew's first hint of this. The heavenly Son of man, destined to receive a universal and everlasting kingdom and to judge the nations, is on earth without a place ***to lay his head!*** Of course, in blending the two pictures necessary adaptations were made.

The second volunteer offered to follow Jesus, but he first wanted to ***bury*** his ***father.*** It may be observed that burial took place on the day of death and had the man's father already died, the son would have been there already. But the story has no interest in this point. To bury one's father was a sacred responsibility among the Jews, taking precedence over all other duties under the Law. Jesus demanded a loyalty which takes preference over even this significant family claim. He already had given up his Nazareth home (4:13) and soon would give his life for his people. He gave all and demands all. That Jesus insisted upon a son's loyalty to his father is clearly taught (15:3–6), but that is another story. ***The dead*** who are to ***bury their own dead*** are the spiritually dead.

5. *A Storm Calmed (8:23–27)*

23 And when he got into the boat, his disciples followed him. 24 And behold, there arose a great storm on the sea, so that the boat was being swamped by the waves; but he was asleep. 25 And they went and woke him, saying, "Save, Lord; we are perishing." 26 And he said to them, "Why are you afraid, O men of little faith?" Then he rose and rebuked the winds and the sea; and there was a great calm. 27 And the men marveled, saying, "What sort of man is this, that even winds and sea obey him?"

Matthew's story is an abridgement of Mark's more detailed narrative (4:35–41). The authority of Jesus over nature is driven home in the concluding question as to ***the sort of man*** whom ***winds and sea obey***. The teaching point, however, has to do with faith. Jesus' calmness in sleeping while the boat was being swamped stands in contrast to the fear and ***little faith*** of the disciples. The point is more forceful in Mark: "Why are you afraid? Have you no faith?" (4:40). Through the centuries Christians have legitimately applied this story to the perils and crises of life, gaining from it the assurance that Christ can deliver us from the "storms" of life.

6. *Deranged Demoniacs Healed (8:28–34)*

28 And when he came to the other side, to the country of the Gadarenes, two demoniacs met him, coming out of the tombs, so fierce that no one could pass that way. 29 And behold, they cried out, "What have you to do with us, O Son of God? Have you come here to torment us before the time?" 30 Now a herd of many swine was feeding at some distance from them. 31 And the demons begged him, "If you cast us out, send us away into the herd of swine." 32 And he said to them, "Go." So they came out and went into the swine; and behold, the whole herd rushed down the steep bank into the sea, and perished in the waters. 33 The herdsmen fled, and going into the city they told everything, and what had happened to the demoniacs. 34 And behold, all the city came out to meet Jesus; and when they saw him, they begged him to leave their neighborhood.

The ***other side*** is presumably the eastern side of Lake Galilee. ***Gadarenes*** is in Matthew the best attested reading in the manuscripts, with "Gergasenes" and "Gerasenes" also well supported. Gergasenes may have been the original reading in Mark and Luke. Possibly the town is to be identified with Kersa or Gersa, the ruins of which are on the eastern shore of Lake Galilee. Presence of swine, forbidden to Jews, implies a Gentile region.

The ***two demoniacs*** were men understood to be under the power of demons. Modern science would describe these as deranged, hostile, and suicidal. In the ancient world men lived in daily fear of evil spirits or demons. Although the Western world today is divided between those who substitute a psychological analysis for "demon possession" and those who retain the idea doctrinally, few Christians if any today live in daily dread of attack by demons.

Whatever is meant by demons, Jesus freed the world, or much of it, from that fear. The demon's question ***What have you to do with us?*** is really "What do we have to do with one another?" When Jesus comes, demons must go. Although Jesus did not deny the reality of demons, he turned men to a faith which is freedom from fear, including fear of demons. He also shifted the focus of attention to the evil thoughts, feelings, and intentions deep in the human heart and provided for victory over this stronghold of evil.

The modern reader is troubled over the fate of ***the herd of swine,*** either by the scientific question of how demons could affect swine or the moral question of the destruction of property. Neither question concerned Matthew. He rejoices over the salvage of two men, more important than a herd of swine. It does not necessarily follow that the townsmen asked Jesus to leave because of the loss of their swine. It may have been because they were afraid of the mysterious power at work in Jesus.

What the demons feared was ***torment before the time,*** i.e., before the final judgment. Jesus did overcome demons in history, not awaiting the end of history to do so.

In Matthew and Mark are two seemingly independent versions of a story which was first told in a Gentile territory in Galilee. Whereas the interest of Mark is in one man freed and restored, Matthew's interest is in the overcoming of the demons and the failure of the townsmen to accept a salvation which had drawn near, choosing to live in the tyranny of fear rather than in the freedom of faith.

7. *Healing and Forgiveness* (*9:1–8*)

[1] And getting into a boat he crossed over and came to his own city. [2] And behold, they brought to him a paralytic, lying on his bed; and when Jesus saw their faith he said to the paralytic, "Take heart, my son; your sins are forgiven." [3] And behold, some of the scribes said to themselves, "This man is blaspheming." [4] But Jesus, knowing their thoughts, said, "Why do you think evil in your hearts? [5] For which is easier, to say, 'Yours sins are forgiven,' or to say, 'Rise and walk'? [6] But that you may know that the Son of man has authority on earth to forgive sins"—he then said to the paralytic—"Rise, take up your bed and go home." [7] And he rose and went home. [8] When the crowds saw it, they were afraid, and they glorified God, who had given such authority to men.

Jesus' ***authority*** to forgive sins is the issue in this story. The ***scribes*** challenged Jesus' right to forgive sins, holding that to be God's right alone (Mark 2:7). The conflict between Jesus and the scribes is already taking shape, with other issues yet to be added to this one.

Jesus' ***own city*** is now Capernaum. The paralytic was brought in on ***his bed,*** probably a pallet. Not all Jesus' miracles were in response to faith, but in this case Jesus responded to the ***faith*** of those who brought in the paralytic. That Jesus began with the problem of the man's sins does not mean that he traced a direct causal connection between each case of illness and sin (Luke 13:1–5; John 9:1–3 refute this). On the other hand, Jesus did see sin as ultimately behind all human ill, and sometimes a direct causal connection can be traced.

Forgiveness is generally considered ***easier*** than healing. At least the latter is harder in that it is more open to testing. So understood, Jesus offered proof that he could heal and thus supported his claim to be able also to forgive sins. For us, forgiving is harder, for we have made more progress in healing diseases than in forgiving one another.

The crowds were amazed that ***authority*** was given ***to men*** to forgive sins. This authority belongs ultimately to God (Isa. 43:25), but here it is claimed by Jesus as the Son of man. In Jesus' teaching, forgiveness is also the responsibility of man (6:12, 14–15). In this story may be an approach to blending the ideas of the Son of man as an individual person (v. 6) and as a community (v. 8), in keeping with the picture in Daniel 7:13 f.,22. This idea is somewhat substantial but also difficult and elusive.

8. *Matthew Called* (*9:9–13*)

[9] As Jesus passed on from there, he saw a man called Matthew sitting at the tax office; and he said to him, "Follow me." And he rose and followed him.

[10] And as he sat at table in the house, behold, many tax collectors and sinners came and sat down with Jesus and his disciples. [11] And when the Pharisees saw this, they said to his disciples, "Why does your teacher eat with tax collectors and sinners?" [12] But when he heard it, he said, "Those who are well have no need of a physician, but those who are sick. [13] Go and learn what this means, 'I desire mercy, and not sacrifice.' For I came not to call the righteous, but sinners."

Although this story is occasioned by the call of Matthew, a tax collector, the real point is Jesus' rejection of the Pharisaic position with respect to ***the righteous*** and the ***sinners*** and his recognition of a community inclusive of ***tax collectors and sinners.*** The mission to ***sinners*** is defended as logical and right, by analogy to the ***physician*** who ministers to the ***sick*** and from Scripture, Hosea 6:6 being cited as teaching God's preference of ***mercy*** as over against ritual ***sacrifice*** (again in 12:7 and not outside Matthew). On the basis of what they have seen at Jesus' table, his eating with ***sinners,*** the Pharisees are to ***go and learn*** what Hosea 6:6 means. They need to restudy that Scripture in the light of Jesus' example and see that its intention is fulfilled in what Jesus is doing.

Matthew is possibly to be identified with the Levi in Mark and Luke (see Introduction, pp. 72). He was a tax collector, engaged in collecting export duties. Tax collectors were at least indirectly representatives of the Roman government; they were considered ritually unclean because of their dealing with people and things not clean; and they were often accused of extortion. For these reasons they were despised by the Pharisees and classed with *sinners.* The Pharisees considered themselves righteous and clean. Pharisee means separated, ones separated from "unclean" people and things. Socially and religiously, a great chasm separated the Pharisees from the ***tax collectors and sinners.*** Jesus bridged the gap; or, to change the figure, he destroyed the wall between the two. He ate with ***tax collectors and sinners*** as well as with Pharisees. The shared meal is universally recognized as a token of acceptance.

Jesus' acceptance of ***tax collectors and sinners*** foreshadowed the acceptance of Gentiles. It was legitimized from the Scriptures, as Jesus cited mercy as above religious sacrifices.

What the Pharisees rejected as evil, Jesus accepted as good. Jesus made table fellowship a virtue and duty where religious people had considered it an evil. Just as the physician does not wait until the sick are well before going to them, Jesus did not wait for bad people to become good before ministering to them, even through table fellowship. In denying any basic distinction between Pharisee and tax gatherer, Jesus in principle struck down all artificial and superficial walls between men; and he established relationship between man and man under God on the basis of God's mercy and not man's works.

Jesus not only received sinners, he sought them out! ***The house*** in which Jesus ***sat at table*** could be that of Matthew or Jesus, but the statement that ***many tax collectors and sinners came and sat down with Jesus and his disciples*** may imply that the house was that of Jesus. If so, he was the host. Strange it is that Jesus' followers, like the Pharisees, are often more exclusive than their Master.

9. *New Skins for New Wine (9:14–17)*

**14 Then the disciples of John came to him,
saying, "Why do we and the Pharisees fast, but
your disciples do not fast?" 15 And Jesus said to
them, "Can the wedding guests mourn as long
as the bridegroom is with them? The days will
come, when the bridegroom is taken away
from them, and then they will fast. 16 And no
one puts a piece of unshrunk cloth on an old
garment, for the patch tears away from the garment, and a worse tear is made. 17 Neither is
new wine put into old wineskins; if it is, the
skins burst, and the wine is spilled, and the
skins are destroyed; but new wine is put into
fresh wineskins, and so both are preserved."**

The contrast between the austerity of John the Baptist and the deep involvement of Jesus in life about him is reflected here, pointedly stated in 11:18 f., and supported by all that is known about both. There is no evidence of a clash between John and Jesus, although it is explicit that John was at least puzzled over the ministry of Jesus (11:2 f.), and for some time there were those who followed John and not Jesus (cf. Acts 19:1–7). Jesus held John in high esteem, but differed from him.

Jesus fasted on occasion and expected that his followers would, but for him fasting was governed not by religious customs or calendar but by the needs of the occasion (see 6:16–18). This he made clear in the analogy of the ***wedding guests.*** They do not fast during the joyous time the ***bridegroom is with them.*** Wedding participants and guests were freed from religious obligations, including fasting, during the seven days of the wedding celebrations.[23]

Presumably, Jesus alluded to his own death in referring to the days ***when the bridegroom is taken away.*** John's imprisonment (4:12) could well have been a factor in his anticipation of his own death.

The parables of ***the patch*** and the ***new wine*** apply not only to fasting but to the whole relationship between Jesus and Judaism. He had not come to destroy but to fulfil (5:17), and this meant respect for what had gone before him but also freedom for the creative work which was his to do. What he had come to do was dynamic and revolutionary and could not be contained in old forms like fasting and sabbatarianism.

Furthermore, Jesus refused to pour the ***new wine*** of the life he offered into the ***old wineskins*** of established religion, as illustrated by the fasting which the disciples of John and the Pharisees tried to impose upon him. To pour new wine into old, brittle skins would be to lose both, for as the wine fermented it would break the old skins. Although glass bottles were known (cf. 26:7), those commonly used were made from the skins of animals.

Jesus' concern was that we find new life together with one another and under the rule of God. For such life there must ever be freedom to develop new forms, vehicles or expressions for worship, fellowship, and service. Jesus did not reject forms as such, but rather implied that they are needed, just as skins were needed for wine, else it would be spilled on the ground. The point is that the skins only serve to conserve the wine and are not an end in themselves. They may be changed as required. The church needs forms but also freedom to develop new ones.

23 H. L. Strack and Paul Billerbeck, *Kommentar zum Neuen Testament aus Talmud und Midrash* (München: Beck, 1922), I, 506.

10. A Woman Healed and a Girl Raised from the Dead (9:18–26)

18 While he was thus speaking to them, be-
hold, a ruler came in and knelt before him,
saying, "My daughter has just died; but come
and lay your hand on her, and she will live."
19 And Jesus rose and followed him, with his
disciples. 20 And behold, a woman who had
suffered from a hemorrhage for twelve years
came up behind him and touched the fringe of
his garment; 21 for she said to herself, "If I
only touch his garment, I shall be made well."
22 Jesus turned, and seeing her he said, "Take
heart, daughter; your faith has made you well."
And instantly the woman was made well.
23 And when Jesus came to the ruler's house,
and saw the flute players, and the crowd mak-
ing a tumult, 24 he said, "Depart; for the girl
is not dead but sleeping." And they laughed at
him. 25 But when the crowd had been put out-
side, he went in and took her by the hand, and
the girl arose. 26 And the report of this went
through all that district.

Two healing narratives are blended, that of the woman who for twelve years ***had suffered from a hemorrhage*** being embedded in that of the raising from the dead of the twelve-year-old daughter (Mark 5:42) of ***a ruler.*** The fullest account is in Mark. At two points, at least, it seems that a non-Markan source was shared by Matthew and Luke. Both speak of "a ruler" where Mark has "one of the rulers of the synagogue" (5:22). More striking is their exact verbal agreement in saying that the woman ***came up behind him and touched the fringe of his garment,*** where Mark has it that she "came up behind him in the crowd and touched his garment" (5:27).

A hemorrhage rendered a woman "unclean," and this may account for her approaching Jesus secretly, hoping not to be detected as she violated Jewish law. ***The fringe*** of the garment was a tassel worn by Jews as a reminder of the commandments of God (Num. 15:37–39). It would serve Matthew's concern to mention this, showing that Jesus did not come to destroy but to fulfil the Law (5:17); but since the word is also in Luke, it belongs to his source and not to his editorial work.

The faith of the woman is the high point

of this story, all three Synoptics stating the climax with identical words, "Daughter, ***your faith has made you well.***" Her simple faith bordered on superstition, but Jesus saw the element of trust that was there. Faith calls for enlightenment and direction, but basically it is trust, not theological competence. Learning does not necessarily lead to faith, but trust can always be instructed. ***Made you well*** translates a Greek word often rendered "saved." Salvation in the New Testament relates to the whole self, including the body.

Matthew's term ***ruler*** may designate various kinds of officials, including Mark's "ruler of the synagogue" and community leaders. Mark's story leaves some question as to whether the daughter was actually dead or only thought to be (5:23,35,39), although the former seems to be Mark's intention. Matthew (and Luke) makes it explicit that she had actually died. The ***ruler*** reported to Jesus that his daughter had ***just died*** and expressed the faith that Jesus could make her live. When Jesus said, ***the girl is not dead but sleeping,*** he did not mean that death is no more than sleep. It is more than sleep! He meant that one can be awakened from death just as one can be awakened from sleep (cf. John 11:11–15). The story stresses the faith of the father and the authority of Jesus over death.

Flute players at a funeral were normal in Jewish life. For the burial of his wife, even a poor man would employ at least two flute players and one wailing woman. Professional mourners belonged to Jewish custom and were used at funerals. This accounts for the ease with which they stopped their ***tumult*** and ***laughed at him.*** These hired mourners seem not to have been in the house but in the court outside.

11. Two Blind Men Receive Sight (9:27–31)

**27 And as Jesus passed on from there, two
blind men followed him, crying aloud, "Have
mercy on us, Son of David." 28 When he entered the house, the blind men came to him;
and Jesus said to them, "Do you believe that I
am able to do this?" They said to him, "Yes,
Lord." 29 Then he touched their eyes, saying,
"According to your faith be it done to you."
30 And their eyes were opened. And Jesus
sternly charged them, "See that no one knows
it." 31 But they went away and spread his fame
through all that district.**

This passage is found only in Matthew, but it is strikingly similar to 20:29–34 (parallels in Mark 10:46–52; Luke 18:35–43). The significant title ***Son of David*** appears here, but with no apparent stress. The term is recurrent in Matthew (cf. 1:1; 12:23; 15:22; 21:9,15), and it supports Matthew's emphasis upon Jesus as Messiah. What is stressed in the story is the faith of the two blind men: ***Do you believe?*** and ***according to your faith.***

That Matthew retains but does not stress the title ***Son of David*** may be understood in terms of Jesus' stern command that the healing not be publicized. It is important to Matthew to present Jesus as "Son of David, son of Abraham" (cf. 1:1), but he also shows that Jesus was David's Lord (22:41–45). The terms Messiah and Son of David both represented authentic claims of and for Jesus, but both terms were of limited value to Jesus because of popular ideas of a political Messiah or Son of David. ***Sternly charged them*** (*enebrimēthē*) expresses strong feeling on the part of Jesus. His deep emotion may be understood in view of the fact that he had the compassion to heal yet did not want to be a mere wonder-worker, with a following of excited miracle seekers. He accepted the acclaim as Son of David, yet rejected the role of political Messiah.

12. Pharisees Protest a Healing (9:32–34)

**32 As they were going away, behold, a dumb
demoniac was brought to him. 33 And when the
demon had been cast out, the dumb man spoke;
and the crowds marveled, saying, "Never was
anything like this seen in Israel." 34 But the
Pharisees said, "He casts out demons by the
prince of demons."**

Dumb (*kōphos*) could be rendered "deaf," true to the Greek word and preferred by all "silent" people. The story sets in striking contrast the amazement of ***the crowds*** and the cynical attitude of the Pharisees, who could not deny the miracle but attributed it to ***the prince of demons.*** Important manuscripts in Greek, Latin, and Syriac omit verse 34, a possible addition from Luke 11:15. In any event, the identical charge appears in 12:24, where it will be discussed.

IV. Compassion of Jesus and Commission of the Twelve (9:35—11:1)

Matthew's second major discourse, the commission of the twelve, forms the greater part of this section, but it is best studied against the background of 9:35–38, a touching passage on the needs of the people and the compassion of Jesus. The inclusion of 11:1 in the unit follows from the fact that it explicitly looks back on the instruction of the twelve disciples and is a concluding formula for a major section of the Gospel (cf. 7:28; 13:53; 19:1; 26:1).

The materials of chapter ten are drawn from Mark and Q, with yet other material peculiar to Matthew. Consistent with his thematic arrangement of materials, Matthew makes no attempt to keep all units in their original setting or sequence. The reader who overlooks Matthew's working principle will be puzzled by the abrupt introduction of the twelve, the Beelzebul charge, and other matters; but Matthew's arrangement of material is well suited to his aim of giving the church of his day incentive, encouragement, warning, and instruction for the continuing ministry in word and work.

1. Jesus' Compassion for Crowds (9:35–38)

35 And Jesus went about all the cities and villages, teaching in their synagogues and preaching the gospel of the kingdom, and healing every disease and every infirmity. 36 When he saw the crowds, he had compassion for them, because they were harassed and helpless, like sheep without a shepherd. 37 Then he said to his disciples, "The harvest is plentiful, but the laborers are few; 38 pray therefore the Lord of the harvest to send out laborers into his harvest."

Verse 35 is a near duplicate of 4:23, summing up Jesus' threefold ministry of ***teaching, preaching,*** and ***healing.*** Matthew picks up Mark 6:6*b*, follows with a repetition of his own 4:23, next closely parallels Mark 6:34, and then apparently draws from Q (cf. Luke 10:2). This blending of materials continues through chapter 10.

Jesus saw ***the crowds*** as ***like sheep without a shepherd*** (cf. 1 Kings 22:17), ***harassed and helpless.*** Flock is a biblical picture for God's people. The word harassed (*eskulmenoi*) originally meant flayed or mangled, but it came to mean annoyed (cf. Mark 5:35; Luke 7:6; 8:49). "Helpless" (*errimmenoi*) pictures the people as being like sheep thrown down and lying helpless. ***The harvest,*** a biblical picture for judgment, introduces an eschatological note, pointing to the last judgment, although the emphasis falls upon the gathering of the grain which is about to be lost for want of harvesting. Jesus calls for prayer to ***the Lord of the harvest*** that he ***send out laborers into his harvest.*** "Send" (*ekbalē*) literally means to cast out but it had come to mean ***send*** or send forth (cf. 12:26). Why should men need to ***pray*** that God send laborers into his own harvest? Presumably the praying is not needed because of God's unwillingness to send but because of man's unwillingness to go. When one prays for the harvest he in some way becomes a harvester and may be among those sent.

The most striking feature of this paragraph is one easily overlooked. Palestine was crowded with religious leaders at the very time Jesus saw the crowds like sheep cast down and helpless and like a neglected harvest. By outward tests, religion was robust, with crowded Temple, synagogues in every village, six thousand Pharisees, twenty thousand lower priests, a small but powerful group of Sadducean priests, a sizable group of Essenes, and other sectarian groups. But with thousands of priests and laymen who made religion their chief business, the people were neglected, or even worse, thrown down and left helpless.

Although "shepherds" and "harvesters" were needed, the real need was more qualitative. Merely to have more religious leadership of the type by which the crowds already had been harassed would solve nothing. The need was for those whose concern was not so much for sabbath, fasting, purification rites, and the like, but for people.

2. *The Mission of the Twelve (10:1–4)*

1 And he called to him his twelve disciples and gave them authority over unclean spirits, to cast them out, and to heal every disease and every infirmity. 2 The names of the twelve apostles are these: first, Simon, who is called Peter, and Andrew his brother; James the son of Zebedee, and John his brother; 3 Philip and Bartholomew; Thomas and Matthew the tax collector; James the son of Alphaeus, and Thaddaeus; 4 Simon the Cananaean, and Judas Iscariot, who betrayed him.

The twelve disciples are introduced into the narrative as though the reader already knows about them (cf. 11:1; 20:17; 26:14, 20,47). That there were disciples known as the twelve is beyond any reasonable doubt. Paul is the earliest writer to mention the twelve (1 Cor. 15:5), and he referred to those who were apostles before him (Gal. 1:17). Paul was by some compared unfavorably with these apostles and was forced to defend his own authority as an apostle. Had there been any doubt about the existence of the twelve, he would have had no occasion or reason to defend his own apostleship.

That Jesus gave some symbolic value to the number twelve is clear from his word about their sitting on "twelve thrones, judging the twelve tribes of Israel" (19:28). The twelve dramatically symbolized the true Israel (twelve tribes) of God (cf. 3:9). Matthew seemingly saw the followers of Christ not so much as a new Israel as a renewed Israel, maintaining a continuity with Abraham, Isaac, and Jacob (8:11), as well as opening the way to a community which would ultimately include the Gentiles (28:19) as well as sinners in Israel (9:13).

The main point of this paragraph is the ***authority*** given the ***twelve disciples.*** The authority of Jesus, seen in word and work, is now shown to be extended to the twelve, through whom Jesus continues and enlarges his work. The disciples' work was to be that of their Master—healing (v. 1) and preaching (10:7). Teaching is not explicit here, but it may be assumed that these disciples (*mathētēs* means learner) also taught (cf. 28:20).

Matthew does not include Mark's datum that Jesus sent out the twelve "two by two" (6:7), but this arrangement is reflected in the fact that he lists the twelve in pairs, changing Mark's (3:16–19) order so as to put brothers together. Pairing the disciples may reflect the principle that two witnesses were required for establishing a matter (Deut. 19:15). Only in 10:2 does Matthew use the term ***apostles,*** elsewhere referring to them as disciples or as the twelve. The Greek word for "apostle" means sent, and this suits the context in which Matthew's lone usage appears. Behind the New Testament term is the Old Testament *shāliah,* an ambassador or one commissioned. The giving of ***authority*** is the nearest reflection of this idea in the paragraph before us. The term apostle is extended in the New Testament to include Paul and Barnabas (Gal. 1:1; Acts 14:14); Matthias (Acts 1:26); the brothers of Jesus (1 Cor. 9:5; Gal. 1:19), and Andronicus and Junias (Rom. 16:7).

Although the fact of the twelve is clear and a few of them are well known, the majority appear only as names in the New Testament. Even the names of some are not clear, as may be seen by comparing this list with the three others (Mark 3:16–19; Luke 6:14–16; Acts 1:13). Double names or some actual fluctuation in the twelve are possible but not certain explanations. That the majority are barely known may be traceable to their failure to move out into the larger mission to the nations (cf. Stagg, *The Book of Acts,* Introduction, *et passim*). In each of the four lists, there are three groups of four, Peter always heading the first four and Judas being the last in the third group. Except for these two fixed positions, there are variations within each of the three groups, both in order and in actual names.

Peter means rock, the Greek equivalent of the Aramaic *Kēphas* (Cephas). Peter is a nickname for Simon (Greek) or Symeon (Hebrew). ***First*** doubtless means foremost, not just first in the list. Peter's leadership among the twelve is generally recognized in the New Testament.

Andrew is a Greek name meaning manly. He is most prominent in John's Gospel (1:40–42). It may be surprising that ***James*** is named before ***John,*** but he may have been the more aggressive of the two, being the first known of the twelve to be martyred (Acts 12:2). ***Son of Alphaeus*** distinguishes him from others by that name. ***Philip*** is a Greek name, meaning "horse lover." ***Bartholomew*** is Semitic, son (*bar*) of Tolmai or Tolomai. ***Thomas*** means twin (John 11:16), possibly a Grecianized form of an Aramaic word.

For the discussion of ***Matthew*** and ***James the son of Alphaeus,*** see the Introduction. ***Thaddaeus*** is found as "Lebbaeus" in some manuscripts and is unknown except by name. ***Cananaean*** (not Canaanite) may be Aramaic for zealot, and he may once have belonged to the Zealots, hyper-nationalists who sought to free their country from Roman rule (cf. Luke 6:15; Acts 1:13). ***Iscariot*** is of uncertain derivation, but possibly means "man of Kerioth," a village in Judea (Dalman, *Words of Jesus,* pp. 51 f.). Possibly all twelve except Judas were from Galilee.

3. *The Twelve Commissioned (10:5–15)*

5 These twelve Jesus sent out, charging them,
"Go nowhere among the Gentiles, and enter no
town of the Samaritans, 6 but go rather to the
lost sheep of the house of Israel. 7 And preach
as you go, saying, 'The kingdom of heaven is
at hand.' 8 Heal the sick, raise the dead, cleanse
lepers, cast out demons. You received without
pay, give without pay. 9 Take no gold, nor
silver, nor copper in your belts, 10 no bag for
your journey, nor two tunics, nor sandals, nor a
staff; for the laborer deserves his food. 11 And
whatever town or village you enter, find out
who is worthy in it, and stay with him until
you depart. 12 As you enter the house, salute it.
13 And if the house is worthy, let your peace
come upon it; but if it is not worthy, let your
peace return to you. 14 And if any one will not
receive you or listen to your words, shake off
the dust from your feet as you leave that house
or town. 15 Truly, I say to you, it shall be more
tolerable on the day of judgment for the land
of Sodom and Gomorrah than for that town.

The restriction that the twelve were to ***go nowhere among the Gentiles*** and to ***enter no town of the Samaritans*** is one of the most difficult problems in Matthew, for it appears to contradict the concluding commission to "make disciples of all nations" (28:19). That Matthew wrote for a church already strongly Gentile makes what on the surface appears to be a nationalistic or particularistic view all the more strange. The suggestion that Matthew's own view is the universalistic one which prevails and that the nationalistic view merely belongs to one of his sources does not satisfy. Not only did Matthew not remove the apparent contradiction but he gives it what appears to be a deliberate prominence (cf. 15:24). It is better to try to understand both commissions, one restricted to Israel and one inclusive of the nations, as belonging to Matthew's intention. To Matthew presumably there was no problem.

Hummel (pp. 136–39) suggests that Matthew includes 10:5 f. and 15:24 because of christological, not missionary, interests, to show that Jesus was the "son of David," Israel's Messiah, and that only the risen Christ, after being rejected by Israel, commissions his disciples to go to all nations.

Probably the problem is best understood in terms of Paul's insight, "to the Jew first and also to the Greek" (Rom. 1:16). Jesus did offer himself first to Israel. The covenant with Abraham looked to the nations, but it also contemplated that God would reach the nations through Israel (Gen. 12:2 f.; 18:18). Isaiah is explicit in expecting the conversion of the nations, but he saw the conversion of Israel as coming first (2:2–4; 49:6 f.). What Jesus did in offering himself first to Israel and then to the nations is in keeping with Old Testament expectation.

Had Jesus gone first to the Gentiles or Samaritans, the Jews would have had more excuse to reject him. Jesus not only went directly to the Jews, but he attacked the problem of discrimination or exclusiveness where first he met it, within Judaism. In rejecting the superficial distinction between Pharisees and "sinners," Jesus opened the way for the ultimate rejection of any real distinction between Jew and Greek.

Luke-Acts traces the course of the gospel from Jew to Samaritan, to God-fearing Gentiles, and finally to pagans like the Philippian jailer (Acts 16:27–34). John (ch. 4) describes a ministry of Jesus to Samaritans, and Matthew also shows the beginnings of what later became a full mission to the Gentiles (8:5–13; 15:21–28).

By one approach, there is no favoritism at all for Israel, for the mission is one of mercy and hence of judgment. Israel is here considered a people in need of mercy, not a righteous people deserving reward but the ***lost sheep of the house of Israel.*** Before a gospel of mercy and grace is offered pagans, it is first offered to Jews who are equally sinners having no other hope (cf. Schlatter, pp. 154 f.).

Again it is shown that the ministry of the disciples is to be that of their Master. With his authority (10:1) they are to do his work of preaching and healing. The miracles of healing, raising the dead, cleansing lepers, and casting out demons would be eschatological signs that ***the kingdom of heaven*** was breaking in upon the world.

Without pay probably is a correct translation of *dōrean,* sometimes rendered "freely." Possibly the immediate reference is to the authority or power to heal. They did not pay for this power and are not to charge for it. Probably the reference is to the total ministry in word and work, for which they were not to receive pay. To reinforce this requirement, they were instructed to ***take*** no money in their ***belts.*** Take (*ktēsēsthe*) is really "procure." Belts translates *zōnas,* here referring to the purses carried on belts. A bag (*pēran*) was used for carrying food or other supplies. The tunic (*chitōn*) was a coat worn over the shirt (*sindōn*) and under the cloak (*himation*). ***Nor sandals*** reads as though they were to go barefoot (but see Mark 6:9). ***Staff*** (*rabdon*) refers to a stick, possibly for defense. That the disciples were thus to travel light may have been to speed them on their way, but probably it was both to safeguard them against desire for or trust in things and to encourage trust in God.

These are not a set of rules to be universally enforced. Luke gives the same basic restrictions in 10:4 but shows that Jesus later reversed the orders (22:35–38), presumably first giving a lesson in trust and later a lesson in commitment of all resources to the Master's work. Paul refused to accept pay for his work but defended the right to it (1 Cor. 9:4,15–18). For the most part the churches have found that a paid ministry makes it possible for ministers to become better prepared for and to give themselves more fully to their work. The price of this, however, is the danger of subsidy, that the minister will suit his message to those who support him or that those who support him will require that he do so. The disciples were not serving established churches but engaged in new missionary work. Integration into the lives of the community and the lesson in giving and receiving were some of the gains from the working plan Jesus gave them.

The disciples were to accept hospitality, ***for the laborer deseves his food.*** They were to seek out a ***worthy*** home, one open to the gospel, and remain in it until they departed that community. They were not to move about, seeking better quarters or keep. Their ***peace*** was thought of as more than a greeting, as something more substantial, a word clothed with power,[24] which could ***come upon*** a home or ***return to*** the disciples. To ***shake off the dust*** from one's feet was a Jewish practice when leaving Gentile soil, considered by them "unclean." Jews who reject the gospel are as "unclean" as those whom they thus classified. ***Sodom and Gomorrah*** were cities notorious for their wickedness, but they would receive lighter judgment than those who rejected the gospel. The greater the opportunity or privilege, the greater the accountability.

[24] Suzanne de Dietrich, *The Gospel According to Matthew* (Richmond: John Knox Press, 1961), pp. 62 f.

4. *The Coming Persecution: Master and Disciples (10:16–42)*

The remainder of chapter 10 is addressed to the disciples, intended to put them in the right frame of mind for their task. They are warned of the persecutions awaiting them, reminded that they answer ultimately to God and none other, impressed with the serious implications of acknowledging Christ or not under duress, warned of possible breaking of family ties, and assured of the rewards awaiting the faithful.

(1) Sheep in the Midst of Wolves (10:16–25)

**16 "Behold, I send you out as sheep in the midst of wolves; so be wise as serpents and innocent as doves. 17 Beware of men; for they will deliver you up to councils, and flog you in their synagogues, 18 and you will be dragged before governors and kings for my sake, to bear testimony before them and the Gentiles.
19 When they deliver you up, do not be anxious how you are to speak or what you are to say; for what you are to say will be given to you in that hour; 20 for it is not you who speak, but the Spirit of your Father speaking through you.
21 Brother will deliver up brother to death, and the father his child, and children will rise against parents and have them put to death;
22 and you will be hated by all for my name's sake. But he who endures to the end will be saved. 23 When they persecute you in one town, flee to the next; for truly, I say to you, you will not have gone through all the towns of Israel, before the Son of man comes.**

24 "A disciple is not above his teacher, nor a servant above his master; 25 it is enough for the disciple to be like his teacher, and the servant like his master. If they have called the master of the house Beelzebul, how much more will they malign those of his household.

Matthew introduced the twelve against a background picturing the people as like shepherdless ***sheep*** that had been beaten down to the ground and left helpless (9:36). The disciples themselves are sent out ***as sheep in the midst of wolves.*** The ***wolves*** will prove to be religious and civil authorities. ***Councils*** (*sunedria*) were local Jewish courts consisting of 23 men. In Palestine these were distinct from the synagogues, but in the Diaspora they generally were closely related to the synagogues (*Sanhedrin* 1:6). There were no state and church distinctions in local government, so trials could take place and those convicted could be flogged in the ***synagogues.*** To ***flog*** was to give one 39 stripes (Jewish law allowed 40, but they stopped at 39, lest by error in counting the law be exceeded.). Roman scourging was much more severe than Jewish flogging (cf. 2 Cor. 11:24 f.). ***Governors*** probably stands for Roman procurators of Judea, like Pilate. ***Kings*** could refer to Herodian princes like Antipas or Agrippa I. Reference to ***the Gentiles*** may anticipate a mission beyond Israel.

The disciples are plainly warned of rejection, persecution, and possible martyrdom, but they are in no way encouraged to seek martyrdom. To the contrary, they are instructed to avoid unnecessarily exciting opposition and on occasion to move away from hostility. They are to ***beware of men*** and are to be ***wise as serpents and innocent as doves. Wise*** (*phronimos*) refers to prudence and ***innocent*** (*akeraios*) to sincerity, i.e., pure or unmixed. This was probably a proverb. The disciples are to use the gumption which avoids unnecessary conflicts and to maintain integrity of motive and method in their missionary work. At times it will be best for all concerned, themselves and their enemies, to ***flee*** from one town to the next. This accords with the warning to avoid needless, unprofitable controversy (7:6) and with Jesus' own escape from his enemies until he could accomplish his basic task (4:12; Luke 4:29 f.).

Despite all precautions, there would be arrests and trials. The disciple's responsibility was to go about his work with diligence, wisdom, and integrity but not to ***be anxious*** in advance about how he would defend himself if brought to trial. What he was to say would be given him ***in that hour.*** This is not a promise of ready-made sermons for church services or a proof text against an educated ministry. This has to do with court trials, not pulpit preaching. The disciple will know what to say when that time comes. ***The Spirit of your Father*** refers to the Holy Spirit, the latter term never appearing in Matthew. ***The Spirit*** is God himself in his nearness to men.

The severest test for the disciple may come within the family, where the closest ties of flesh are severed and one may be ***hated*** or even ***deliver up*** his own kin to the authorities for trial. This refers in particular to the high price paid by many Jewish followers of Christ. Jesus himself lost his own family for a time and regained it only after his death (12:46–50). Endurance (*hupomenē*) is a basic New Testament term, denoting steadfastness or constancy. ***To the end*** (*eis telos*) may refer to the end of the age, but probably it means endurance even to martyrdom (cf. Rev. 2:10). This does not mean that only martyrs will be saved, but saving faith will endure even martyrdom. It is the constancy which reflects one's salvation, not the holding out which earns salvation.

Verse 23 is most difficult. The simplest reading seems to be that Jesus expected ***the Son of man*** to appear before the twelve had traveled through ***all the towns of Israel.*** If the reference is to the parousia, the coming of the Son of man on the clouds at the end of the age, it is strange that Matthew a generation later would have recorded it. The most difficult and likely approach is to assume that by Son of man Jesus referred to himself and that in some sense he would come in the disciples' time. In a real sense the Son of man came and comes in judgment in each crisis situation where man is compelled to choose his destiny, whether at Golgotha, at the destruction of Jerusalem, or otherwise.

It may be observed that the promised coming of the Son of man is here related to the persecution of the disciples. It was the role of Son of man to judge and to rule. Possibly the point is that as the disciples are being driven from town to town, judged and rejected by their countrymen, the Son of man is there judging those who condemn his own. The victory belongs to the Son of man and his persecuted disciples, not to those who drive them from town to town (cf. Schlatter, pp. 161 f.).

The ***disciple*** could expect no better reception than ***his teacher.*** Jesus sought followers but never let them forget what it would cost to follow him. Beelzebul is introduced here as though the reader already knows of the charge made against Jesus (see discussion of 12:24).

(2) *Whom to Fear (10:26–33)*

[26] "So have no fear of them; for nothing is covered that will not be revealed, or hidden that will not be known. [27] What I tell you in the dark, utter in the light; and what you hear whispered, proclaim upon the housetops. [28] And do not fear those who kill the body but cannot kill the soul; rather fear him who can destroy both soul and body in hell. [29] Are not two sparrows sold for a penny? And not one of them will fall to the ground without your Father's will. [30] But even the hairs of your head are all numbered. [31] Fear not, therefore; you are of more value than many sparrows. [32] So every one who acknowledges me before men, I also will acknowledge before my Father who is in heaven; [33] but whoever denies me before men, I also will deny before my Father who is in heaven.

The New Testament never teaches that one is to fear Satan, but to resist him (Eph. 6:11). ***Fear him*** refers to God, before whom ultimately one stands or falls. One is not to seek martyrdom, yet he is not to fear those who can ***kill the body*** but not ***the soul.*** The understanding of man here is not the Greek dualism which sees man as a soul imprisoned in a body. God made man in his bodily existence, and salvation is completed only in the resurrection of the body. The paragraph here simply refers to the distinction between the physical life which can be taken and the selfhood which is beyond the reach of physical death. ***Soul*** is often used for self.

Verse 26 consists of a Semitic parallelism as it declares that what is ***covered*** will be ***revealed*** and what is ***hidden*** will be ***known.*** Verse 27 also contains a parallelism, and it clearly means that what Jesus taught the disciples is to be openly proclaimed to all who will hear. Jesus had no secret or esoteric teaching as did the Essenes and rabbis. What verse 27 clearly says may be the intention of the more obscure verse 26, both teaching that the gospel is to be openly proclaimed. However, verse 26 may refer to the sufferings of the disciples. The hatred, insults, floggings, and other things suffered by them may take place secretly, at night, or in some remote place, but eventually all will be known, at once by God and eventually by the world. So understood, verse 26 is an encouragement to sacrificial ministry, and verse 27 is a command to open teaching and preaching, whatever the dangers.

The encouragement is reinforced by the assurance that God who observes even the death of a sparrow and knows the number of ***the hairs*** of one's head will surely watch over his own. The infinite value of man is stressed, contrasted by the market price of sparrows. ***Penny*** (*assarion*) was one-sixteenth of a denarius, the latter a day's wage for common labor (20:2). To suggest the equivalent in today's money is misleading, for that changes from day to day.

Promise and warning are combined in verses 32–33. The reference is to Christians under trial, either confessing Christ at the risk of life or denying him in order to escape punishment. This was a basic issue for the early church, its very existence being bound up with the willingness to die for Christ. The reference is not to confession of Christ before Christians (KJV) but to the acknowledgment that one is a Christian when under arrest or trial.

Christ's acknowledgment or denial of those who acknowledge or deny him is not arbitrary. Christ can but declare what one's true relationship is. He cannot confess as his own one who is not. Balancing the sober warning of this passage is Jesus' standing by Peter despite Peter's shameful denial of his Master (26:69–75; Mark 14:68–71). Presumably there is a distinction between wilful denial and human weakness which is not equal to the demands of a crisis situation. Matthew's obvious purpose is to warn the church of his day against denial of Christ under trial; thus he quotes the warning but does not include Mark's account of Jesus' special word to Peter (cf. 28:10 with Mark 16:7).

(3) *Not Peace, but a Sword (10:34–39)*

34 "Do not think that I have come to bring peace on earth; I have not come to bring peace, but a sword.
35 For I have come to set a man against his father, and a daughter against her mother, and a daughter-in-law against her mother-in-law;
36 and a man's foes will be those of his own household.
37 He who loves father or mother more than me is not worthy of me; and he who loves son or daughter more than me is not worthy of me;
38 and he who does not take his cross and follow me is not worthy of me.
39 He who finds his life will lose it, and he who loses his life for my sake will find it.

Either purpose or result can be intended by the grammar of verses 34 f. Of course, Jesus came to bring about the ***peace*** of reconciliation between man and man as well as man and God. This is his intention. The actual result is often the ***sword*** or division. In times of persecution, ***a man's foes,*** those who turn him in to the authorities, may be of his own family. Throughout this Gospel, basic kinship is a matter of faith rather than flesh (cf. 3:9; 12:46–50).

The deepest principle embodied in the teaching and life of Jesus is that of verses 38 f. The cross was a cruel means of execution which the Romans borrowed from the Carthaginians and employed for the humiliating and torturous execution of criminals, Roman citizens themselves being exempt from this manner of execution. A condemned man was required to carry the crossbeam, which at the place of his execution would be affixed to the upright piece. Jesus made the cross a symbol of victory. Its great paradox is that one ***finds his life*** by willingness to ***lose it,*** just as he inevitably ***loses his life*** by trying to save it. The ***cross*** is the utter self-denial and self-giving, first in Jesus himself and then as a transforming principle in those who trust him.

In this context, there is a special reference to martyrdom. The one who, under trial, seemingly saves his life by renouncing Christ actually loses it. The one who suffers martyrdom as the price of acknowledging Christ seems to lose but actually finds his life. For Jesus, and later for Matthew's church, the test was that of physical death, but in principle each accepts his cross or rejects it. Each one finds life by surrendering it to Christ or forfeits it by his self-trust, self-love, and self-assertion.

(4) *Rewards* (*10:40–42*)

[40] "He who receives you receives me, and he who receives me receives him who sent me. [41] He who receives a prophet because he is a prophet shall receive a prophet's reward, and he who receives a righteous man because he is a righteous man shall receive a righteous man's reward. [42] And whoever gives to one of these little ones even a cup of cold water because he is a disciple, truly, I say to you, he shall not lose his reward."

Another basic principle of the New Testament appears in this paragraph. One's true relationship to God is reflected in his relationship to Jesus, and his true relationship to Jesus is reflected in his relationship to his people (cf. 25:31–46). It is not that giving ***a cup of cold water*** to another makes one a child of God, but in a simple action like this one's true nature and relationship may be revealed. There is here the further dimension that one reveals his true relationship to God when he receives or serves a prophet, a righteous man, or a disciple because he is that, and not for some ulterior motive.

Special attention may be given to Jesus' concern for the ***little ones.*** These were not just children but also "little people," i.e., the ordinary people who are so easily taken for granted or overlooked. To Jesus there were no unimportant people, whatever their age, sex, or standing in the world. The ***reward*** is certain but it is not specified. Presumably the thought is that in receiving, one is received.

5. *Summary* (*11:1*)

[1] And when Jesus had finished instructing his twelve disciples, he went on from there to teach and preach in their cities.

Stephan Langton in 1228, in making our modern chapter divisions, could well have included this verse in chapter 10, for it belongs to the section of Matthew's five formulas indicating a major division of his work (cf. 7:28; 13:53; 19:1; 26:1).

V. *Various Responses to Jesus* (*11:2–30*)

Without forcing the material, one readily sees in this section at least five responses to Jesus: John's cautious approach (vv. 2–11), efforts to force the kingdom to serve man's goals (vv. 12–15), childish displeasure with all options (vv. 16–19), flagrant disregard or rejection of the gospel (vv. 20–24), and childlike trust (vv. 25–30).

1. *Uncertainty and Confusion* (*11:2–6*)

[2] Now when John heard in prison about the deeds of the Christ, he sent word by his disciples [3] and said to him, "Are you he who is to come, or shall we look for another?" [4] And Jesus answered them, "Go and tell John what you hear and see: [5] the blind receive their sight and the lame walk, lepers are cleansed and the deaf hear, and the dead are raised up, and the poor have good news preached to them. [6] And blessed is he who takes no offense at me."

John's arrest was mentioned in 4:12, and here his imprisonment is introduced as something already familiar to the reader. Not until 14:1–12 does Matthew describe the arrest itself in terms of causal factors and the result. From Josephus (*Antiquities*, XVIII, 5, 2) comes the information that it was at Machaerus, east of the Dead Sea, that John was imprisoned.

Grammar does not settle the question as to whether the problem of the identity of Jesus belonged to John himself or (as held as early as Origen) his disciples. The paragraph seems to imply that the question came from John himself. There is nothing to rule this out, and it is unlikely that Matthew would have left room for this interpretation had it not been the intended one. It seems best to assume that the question was John's. If so, it reflects both a measure of doubt and a measure of confidence. He did put his question directly to Jesus, an indication of trust, however puzzled.

A further ambiguity remains concerning John's question. Does it reflect growing doubt or newly awakened hope? This paragraph seems to favor the former, and other Gospel accounts support the view that this is not the beginning of John's faith that Jesus is the Christ but rather a period of uncertainty (cf. 3:14; John 1:29,35 f.). What John from prison heard about ***the deeds of the Christ*** caused him to send some of his disciples to ask Jesus if he was indeed ***he who is to come.***

John's uncertainty about Jesus grew out of the kind of ministry Jesus was pursuing. John had proclaimed the coming of the kingdom of heaven and had seen its coming in terms of judgment, symbolized by ax, winnowing fork, and fire (3:2,10–12). He seemingly expected the Christ to act dramatically in the overthrow of the wicked and in the vindication of the righteous. Outwardly, the signs for such a victory were not apparent, for he was in prison while Herod Antipas and Herodias were living in luxury and power (14:1–12).

John wanted to know if Jesus was ***he who is to come*** or if ***another*** was to be awaited. ***Another*** (*heteron*) can designate one of another kind, but this cannot be maintained from grammar alone. Context, however, supports the idea. What kind of Messiah was to be expected? "The coming one" is not a well established term, but seems to be messianic (cf. 3:11; Dan. 7:13; Heb. 10:37; Rev. 1:4). The Zealots clearly expected a military type messiah, and John seems to have expected at least a more militant one than Jesus' deeds seemed to reflect. Apparently he expected Messiah to take more direct and outward charge of the world about him. It may have seemed to him that Jesus was assuming too humble a role. It was at this very point that Peter and others stumbled (cf. 16:21–23; John 13:8).

It belongs to the strength of the New Testament that it presents the limitations of its heroes. Only Jesus is without fault. It is significant, too, that Jesus did not reject or belittle John, even though John's honest doubt or uncertainty was at the most crucial point, the identity of Jesus.

In reply, Jesus indicated that John would find his answer precisely where he found his question, in ***the deeds of the Christ.*** Jesus cited his works: sight for ***the blind,*** strength for ***the lame,*** cleansing for ***lepers,*** hearing for ***the deaf,*** life for ***the dead,*** and the gospel for ***the poor*** (cf. Luke 4:18 f. for a similar description of his ministry). Jesus' coming was an inevitable judgment; yet its intention was to heal, cleanse, restore, free, and empower all who would receive the salvation he offered. It is significant that Jesus made the preaching of the gospel to the poor, not miracles, his crowning work.

Verse 6 is decisive. This is another "beatitude," and the blessedness belongs to those who take no ***offense*** at Jesus because of the nature of his ministry. ***Offense*** translates a verb form built upon the Greek word *skandalon,* used first for the bait-stick of a trap and then as a metaphor for anything that trips one or causes him to stumble or fall. Jesus declares blessed those who do not stumble over the fact that his ministry is that of a servant rather than that of an outward "conqueror." Paul called this the "scandal [stumbling-block, RSV] of the cross" (1 Cor. 1:22–25). Even the apostles stumbled over the role Jesus declared to be his own (16:21–23).

2. *Distortion and Violence (11:7–15)*

[7] As they went away, Jesus began to speak to the crowds concerning John: "What did you go out into the wilderness to behold? A reed shaken by the wind? [8] Why then did you go out? To see a man clothed in soft raiment? Behold, those who wear soft raiment are in kings' houses. [9] Why then did you go out? To see a prophet? Yes, I tell you, and more than a prophet. [10] This is he of whom it is written,

'Behold, I send my messenger before thy face,
who shall prepare thy way before thee.'

[11] Truly, I say to you, among those born of women there has risen no one greater than John the Baptist; yet he who is least in the kingdom of heaven is greater than he. [12] From the days of John the Baptist until now the kingdom of heaven has suffered violence, and

men of violence take it by force. 13 **For all the prophets and the law prophesied until John;** 14 **and if you are willing to accept it, he is Elijah who is to come.** 15 **He who has ears to hear, let him hear.**

John praised (vv. 7–11).—Jesus exposed John's limitations and also paid him high tribute. John represented a dividing line between an age brought to its close and a new age begun. John was ***a prophet*** and ***more.*** He was the ***messenger*** announced by Malachi (3:1; 4:5). His function was to prepare the way for the Lord, here Jesus Christ. John stood at the end of a long line of prophets, yet he belonged to the age of promise, not fulfilment. The new age which Jesus brought in stood above the age which was passing away with John. "Its base stood higher than the other's summit" (Robinson, p. 101).

Grammar (*ti* can mean what? or why?) and the absence of punctuation marks in early manuscripts make possible the RSV translation or another. It could be rendered, "Why did you go out into the wilderness? To see a reed shaken by the wind?" In either translation, the intention is clear. Jesus is defending John against any suspicion that he is weak or vacillating. John may be puzzled or uncertain, but there is no question about his courage, dedication, or sincerity.

For all John's greatness, ***he who is least in the kingdom of heaven*** is greater. Some see the "least" to be Jesus himself; i.e., the one who "came after" (Jesus) actually "ranks before" the one who went before (John) as developed in John 1:15. More likely, the reference is to the followers of Jesus.

Jesus cast no doubt upon John's salvation, but he declared that John was not in position to see the true nature and manifestation of the kingdom. It was already breaking into history, but its great triumph in the death and resurrection of Jesus lay beyond John's span of life and experience. Ax, winnowing fork, and fire correctly symbolize the judgment which belongs essentially to the kingdom, but the cross is its supreme victory in both judgment and redemption.

Men of violence (vv. 12–15).—There are several possible interpretations of the statement that the kingdom of heaven has ***suffered violence*** and that violent men ***take it by force*** (McNeile, p. 155). The kingdom may be thought of in terms of its members seen as suffering persecution. This is unlikely, for the kingdom usually refers to God's ruling more than to the people under that rule. The kingdom may be seen as violently stormed by people eager to enter it, but this has no real support elsewhere in Matthew. The RSV gives the probable meaning. ***Men of violence*** try to take the kingdom and make it serve their own purposes.

The statement in verses 12 f. unmistakably goes back to Jesus, and in it he makes the claim that in himself the kingdom has already dawned but is being obstructed by men of violence. John's greatness is seen in that he stands at the turning point of the ages (aeons), yet Jesus himself is above John. The kingdom comes in Jesus and it is scorned by some while others try to distort it precisely because "it appears in the defenceless form of the Gospel" (Käsemann, pp. 42 f.).

Suffered violence (*biazetai*) pictures the kingdom as being assaulted. ***Take by force*** (*harpazousin*) can be what gramatically is known as "connative." If so, it describes effort or intention but not necessarily achievement. The connative force of a verb is not determined by its form but suggested by the context. The ***men of violence*** would include the Zealots and all the activists who thought of the kingdom of God in political terms and the role of Messiah as including the defeat of Roman rule through military force. The extremists sought through armed revolt to precipitate the messianic coming and to establish the kingdom of God. The moderates were content to wait for God to take the initiative. Both expected a kingdom which would take shape within a political structure. Jesus positively and repeatedly rejected this role.

That verse 12 may best be understood in the light of Qumran parallels is cogently argued by Betz.[25] He sees *biazetai* as a middle rather than passive verb form, and renders the passage, "From the days of John the Baptist until now the Kingdom of Heaven is breaking in by force, but violent men attack and plunder it." Thus interpreted, two movements are seen—the victorious inbreaking of the kingdom of heaven in the person of Jesus and the counterattack of men of violence, as exemplified in those who tried to turn men from Jesus by terming his work that of Satan. Betz sees 12:29 in this light, where Jesus is the warrior who breaks into Satan's house to plunder his goods.

Although the "connative" force of the verb is possible, as seen above, the picture may indeed be that of two kingdoms in such conflict that although the ultimate victory is assured for the kingdom of God, there are also casualties inflicted along the way by the kingdom of evil.[26]

Jesus couched his identification of John as Elijah in two significant statements: (1) ***if you are willing to accept it*** and (2) ***he who has ears to hear.*** The first recognizes the difficulty for Jews of the time of Jesus to identify Elijah with a man in prison. This would not correspond to their high hopes for national freedom and reconstruction. The second statement stresses the importance of the willingness to hear a claim which overrides popular, nationalistic hopes; and both statements may imply that John's identification with Elijah is to be taken seriously but not literally. John the Baptist and Elijah are two different men (cf. 17:3), but John the Baptist fulfilled the role associated with the name Elijah (cf. 17:12; Mal. 4:5).

John's denial that he was Elijah (John 1:21) does not contradict the intention of Jesus' claim (11:14). John's denial is in keeping with his refusal to make himself important, and Jesus' statement is to be understood in context, as indicated above. The passage does clearly recognize that John the Baptist stood on the dividing line between two ages, one giving way to the other. It was a time when the power of the kingdom of God was breaking into the world and being met by the violent efforts of some to oppose and defeat it and by others with strong effort to use or exploit it. ***The prophets and the law*** is the Jewish way of referring to what we know as the Old Testament, now finding fulfilment in the event and the person proclaimed by John.

Yet another interpretation of ***from the days of John*** is that which understands Jesus to say that the kingdom had already dawned in John, the latter being the initiator of the new aeon, Jesus thus drawing John to his side, even though he claimed for himself a mission yet higher than John's (Käsemann, p. 43). In this approach the kingdom may be seen as both having been inaugurated and as being obstructed by ***men of violence.*** The problem is not with the latter statement but with the relation of John to the kingdom. Elsewhere in the New Testament, the kingdom comes first in Jesus. If Käsemann's interpretation holds, Jesus here gives John a position next only to himself.

3. *Childish Displeasure (11:16–19)*

16 "But to what shall I compare this generation? It is like children sitting in the market places and calling to their playmates,
17 'We piped to you, and you did not dance;
we wailed, and you did not mourn.'
18 For John came neither eating nor drinking, and they say, 'He has a demon'; 19 the Son of man came eating and drinking, and they say, 'Behold, a glutton and a drunkard, a friend of tax collectors and sinners!' Yet wisdom is justified by her deeds."

Jesus likened his generation to disagreeable and faultfinding children. Usually this analogy is understood to refer to children who find fault with any game proposed. They would play neither wedding nor fu-

25 Otto Betz, "The Eschatological Interpretation of the Sinai-Tradition in Qumran and in the New Testament," *Revue de Qumran*, VI, 21 (Février, 1967), 89–107.

26 Norman Perrin, *Rediscovering the Teaching of Jesus* (New York: Harper & Row, 1967), p. 77.

neral. They would neither ***dance*** nor ***mourn.*** Another reconstruction is possible.[27] The disagreeable children may be ones who while ***sitting*** expected the other children to do the more strenuous parts of the game. They merely played their pipes but expected other children to dance, or wailed and left the mourning (beating of breasts) to other children. When the others refused to dance or mourn, those who piped and wailed blamed them for spoiling the game.

John was criticized for being too stern and ascetic. ***Neither eating nor drinking*** is of course an exaggeration, for he did have a simple diet. The charge that he had a demon may have been intended in its literal sense, although sometimes this was an expression similar to the popular charge, "he is crazy" (cf. John 10:20).

Jesus was criticized for the opposite reason, because he came ***eating and drinking.*** The charge, as that against John, was exaggerated, for Jesus was not ***a glutton and a drunkard.*** On the other hand, it is clear that Jesus did plunge deeply into life, often offending religious leaders by the freedom and joy with which he moved among people of all kinds and by his refusal to let superficial rules or customs take priority over people.

We probably tend to underestimate the extent to which Jesus entered into joyous table-fellowship with people who had known only exclusion but who now knew the joy of forgiveness and acceptance. This was the background to the *koinōnia* so important to the early church. It foreshadowed the Lord's Supper and the ultimate "messianic banquet" (cf. Acts 2:42; Rev. 3:20). This table-fellowship with such people probably more than anything else aroused the wrath of the Pharisees.

The proverb that ***wisdom is justified by her deeds*** probably means that Jesus' manner and ways are vindicated by their results. Jesus was willing to endure criticism, persecution, and death as he followed a way which would ultimately prevail and be vindicated. There is possible reference to John as well as to Jesus. The proverb may say that the wisdom and will of God worked through both the sternness of John and the freedom of Jesus.

This generation does not refer to all of the Jews of a given time, as is borne out by verse 25. ***Generation*** (*genea*) is always used by Jesus in rebuke (except in 24:34 and parallels and in Luke 16:8). It never refers to the whole Jewish race but to those addressed at the time as representative of it (cf. 12:39,41 f.; 16:4; 17:17; 23:36).

4. Wilful Rejection (11:20–24)

20 Then he began to upbraid the cities where most of his mighty works had been done, because they did not repent. 21 "Woe to you, Chorazin! woe to you, Bethsaida! for if the mighty works done in you had been done in Tyre and Sidon, they would have repented long ago in sackcloth and ashes. 22 But I tell you, it shall be more tolerable on the day of judgment for Tyre and Sidon than for you. 23 And you, Capernaum, will you be exalted in heaven? You shall be brought down to Hades. For if the mighty works done in you had been done in Sodom, it would have remained until this day. 24 But I tell you that it shall be more tolerable on the day of judgment for the land of Sodom than for you."

The main lesson of this unit is that the severity of judgment is determined by the extent of privilege. The greater the privilege the greater is the responsibility. It is no mere play on words to say that responsibility is measured by ability to respond. One is accountable for no more and no less than that which has come within the range of his opportunity and competence. The cities where so many of his ***mighty works*** were done were condemned ***because they did not repent*** (for repent, see 3:2).

Chorazin is possibly to be identified with the ruin Keraze, just over two miles northwest of Tel Hum, probably Capernaum. It has the unhappy distinction of being remembered only for its failure to respond to Jesus. That Jesus did many works there makes explicit the fact that we know only a small part of what Jesus did and said

[27] E. F. F. Bishop, *Jesus of Palestine* (London: Lutterworth, 1955), p. 104.

(cf. John 20:30; 21:25). Capernaum seems to have been for a time the residence of Jesus (8:5); and with Bethsaida, on the north shore and about a mile from the Jordan, are linked such names as Philip, Andrew, and Peter (John 1:44). These cities made some response to Jesus, but not comparable to their privilege. ***Tyre and Sidon*** were Gentile cities, often denounced by the prophets for their wealth and wickedness (cf. Amos 1:9 f.; Isa. 23:1 ff.; Jer. 25:22; *el al.*). ***Sackcloth and ashes*** were symbols of mourning and repentance. ***Sodom*** was a city of the Dead Sea, destroyed for its sins and proverbial for its wickedness. From it has come the term sodomy.

Verse 23, condemning ***Capernaum,*** is adopted from what originally was directed against Babylon (Isa. 14:13–15). The first part is in the form of a question, introduced by a particle (*mē*) expecting a negative answer. The second part probably should be translated, "Unto Hades you shall go down," rather than as in the RSV. Manuscripts vary between the active and passive voice of the verb, but the active (*katabēsēi*) is best attested. It is not that proud Capernaum, aspiring to heaven, will be sent down or ***brought down*** but that she will "sink" or "go down." The most serious fact about sin is that it is like a disease, it carries within itself the seeds of self-destruction. That God judges the sinner is clearly taught, but Scripture also teaches that sin carries ruin within itself. The seriousness of sin, like a malignancy, is not that it will be discovered but that it is there.

Hades, like Sheol in the Old Testament, refers to the grave or place of the dead. It seems to have gradually taken on more of the meaning of Gehenna or hell, although originally Hades simply referred to the realm of the dead (the Greek term means unseen).

It may be observed that the moral response of repentance, not merely curiosity or seeking after temporal gains, is the proper reaction to the miracles of Jesus.[28]

[28] George E. P. Cox, *The Gospel According to Saint Matthew* (New York: Macmillan, 1952), p. 87.

5. *Childlike Trust* (*11:25–30*)

**25 At that time Jesus declared, "I thank thee, Father, Lord of heaven and earth, that thou hast hidden these things from the wise and understanding and revealed them to babes;
26 yea, Father, for such was thy gracious will.
27 All things have been delivered to me by my Father; and no one knows the Son except the Father, and no one knows the Father except the Son and any one to whom the Son chooses to reveal him. 28 Come to me, all who labor and are heavy laden, and I will give you rest.
29 Take my yoke upon you, and learn from me; for I am gentle and lowly in heart, and you will find rest for your souls. 30 For my yoke is easy, and my burden is light."**

Verses 25–27 are known as the Johannine passage in Matthew, because in both thought and style it bears such resemblance to the Gospel of John. Its presence here may well serve as a call to reassess the origin of the tradition preserved in the Gospel of John.[29] This is best understood as a Greek translation of an Aramaic saying that goes back to Jesus.

This paragraph is unsurpassed with respect to the nature and meaning of revelation. Knowledge of God is not the achievement of ***the wise and understanding.*** It is God's gift ***to babes.*** By the ***wise and understanding,*** Jesus probably referred primarily to the scribes who were so certain of their knowledge. The judgment would apply to any who are "shut up to their own wisdom" (Dietrich, p. 72). The ***babes*** are the "little people," the humble and receptive. Man does not discover God, but God reveals himself to those who trust him. Paul, in a similar vein, wrote that in the wisdom of God it is not through wisdom but through faith that we know God, self-disclosed chiefly through the cross (1 Cor. 1:21).

Revelation is concerned with facts, for God's supreme revelation took place in a person in a concrete event in history. Hence, revelation is concerned with ***these things,*** i.e., those concerning the coming of the kingdom of heaven in Jesus Christ. Yet its essence is not in propositions but in what is personal. God comes to us not as a propo-

[29] Cf. C. H. Dodd, *Historical Tradition in the Fourth Gospel* (Cambridge: University Press, 1963).

sition to debate but as a person to trust, know, love, and serve. Salvation is to know the Father through the Son (John 17:3). Jesus came to enable us to know God as Father. To "know" as used here is not to have intellectual knowledge. Were that the case, the scholar would have the advantage. To "know" God is to meet him in trust and love. It is to know him as a person is known.

The uniqueness and the loneliness of Jesus in the world are both reflected in the statement that only the Father ***knows the Son.*** Not even John knew him with adequacy. Jesus repeatedly was misunderstood by those nearest him. Only the Father truly knows him. The Father himself is known in the Son. God not only spoke and acted in Jesus, but he was uniquely present in Jesus. God is self-disclosed in all that he has done and in all that he has made, but he is supremely revealed in Jesus Christ alone (cf. John 1:1,14; Rom. 1:19 f.; Heb. 1:1–3).

Knowledge of the Father is possible to those to whom the Son ***chooses to reveal him.*** This may sound arbitrary, as though Jesus selected some for salvation and withheld it from others. The preceding paragraph rules out such an interpretation. The cities of privilege are condemned because they rejected the light offered them. Human responsibility and divine determination cannot be harmonized, and our passage does not ask us to do this. The biblical doctrine of election is that God takes the initiative in revelation and redemption. God comes to man; man does not make his way to God. God reveals himself to man; man does not discover God. Not only does Jesus reveal the Father to us, but he ***chooses*** to do so. Knowing God as Father is the ultimate goal of revelation and redemption.

Verse 18 makes it clear that none is arbitrarily excluded from salvation. Jesus' gracious invitation is to ***all who labor and are heavy-laden.*** Special reference probably is to those who labor to keep the Law and bear its burdens as taught by the scribes (cf. 23:4; Acts 15:10). The ***rest*** which Jesus offered is not escape from work or other demands of life. "I will refresh you" is another way to translate his promise. Jesus himself did not escape the toil, pain, conflicts, and all that makes life hard. In it all, he had that which enabled him to live abundantly, joyfully, and triumphantly. He found ***rest*** in the midst of such a life and offers that rest to any who come to him. For us the ***rest*** is more than Stoic fortitude in the face of adversity. It is the overcoming of fear, anxiety, uncertainty, and meaninglessness in the joy and peace of God's very presence in Jesus Christ. It is the security of one who knows the forgiveness of sins and acceptance into the family of God.

Jesus offers a ***yoke*** as well as rest. The rabbis spoke of the Jewish law as a yoke, and although they spoke of it as a joy they had made it a burden for the people. Jesus offers a ***yoke*** that is ***easy*** and a ***burden*** that is ***light.*** This catches up the deep paradox that runs throughout Matthew's Gospel. Salvation is gift and demand. It is gospel and law. God gives all and demands all. Jesus can be known as awesome Lord and as the judge who separates "the sheep" from "the goats" (25:31 f.), and he can be known as the ***gentle and lowly*** Master. He places his yoke upon us and it is not without heavy demand (cf. 5:20; 10:38; 16:24), but it is also easy and light. ***Easy*** (*chrēstos*) means kind and good. It is well-fitted and does not gall the neck. ***Light*** (*elaphron*) means that his burden is not burdensome (cf. 1 John 5:3). A yoke is made for two, never for one alone. Jesus never imposes upon his disciple a yoke which he himself does not also bear.

VI. Growing Opposition to Jesus (12:1–50)

Matthew traces a new stage in the opposition to Jesus. The Pharisees began to make plans to destroy Jesus as they felt that their system and its values were being threatened. Two radically different approaches to religion are seen here. Jesus' interest was always strictly personal. No law, no religious practice, nothing mattered except as it related to God and to man. The Pharisees, on the contrary, made sabbath, purification rites, and the like ends in themselves. This chapter will trace the widening gap between Jesus and the Pharisees, and even between himself and his own mother and brothers. It will point to a new family of faith and obedience to the will of God, one in which the Gentiles may be included.

1. *Above the Sabbath* (*12:1–14*)

The sabbath was almost a national emblem for Israel, along with its initiation rite of circumcision. Jesus shook the foundations of Pharisaic religion when by word and deed he asserted his lordship over the sabbath, placed man above it, and reminded men that God prized mercy above the whole cultic system.

The sabbath is a religious division of time, not a natural one as the year, seasons, lunar month, days, and nights. God gave the sabbath as a day of rest. Jewish legalism became almost idolatrous in its elevation of the sabbath above man. On the other hand, it was with strong conviction that the Jews kept the sabbath, as evidenced by their willingness to be slaughtered rather than wage war on the sabbath (cf. 1 Maccabees 2:31–38). Jesus offered a true rest, himself as the fulfilment of what was foreshadowed in the weekly sabbath (cf. 11:28; Heb. 4:9 f.). He is our "sabbath" as he is our "temple."

(*1*) *Plucking Grain on the Sabbath* (*12:1–8*)

**1 At that time Jesus went through the grain-
fields on the sabbath; his disciples were hungry, and they began to pluck ears of grain and
to eat. 2 But when the Pharisees saw it, they
said to him, "Look, your disciples are doing
what is not lawful to do on the sabbath." 3 He
said to them, "Have you not read what David
did, when he was hungry, and those who were
with him: 4 how he entered the house of God
and ate the bread of the Presence, which it was
not lawful for him to eat nor for those who
were with him, but only for the priests? 5 Or
have you not read in the law how on the
sabbath the priests in the temple profane the
sabbath, and are guiltless? 6 I tell you, something greater than the temple is here. 7 And if
you had known what this means, 'I desire
mercy, and not sacrifice,' you would not have
condemned the guiltless. 8 For the Son of man
is lord of the sabbath."**

The law permitted one to pluck grain by hand but not by sickle as he passed through a neighbor's standing grain (Deut. 23:25). Jewish tradition listed 39 major kinds of work which were forbidden on the sabbath, including the plucking and rubbing out of grain. Jesus defended his disciples on the principle that human need and comfort are more important than sabbath observance. He cited the example of David, who ate "the bread of the Presence" during his flight from Saul (1 Sam. 21:1–6). This special bread was placed upon the table in the tabernacle on the sabbath and kept until replaced the next sabbath; the replaced bread then was eaten by the priests alone (Ex. 25:30; Lev. 24:5–9). Even the priests were permitted to set aside sabbath laws in order to carry out the ritual sacrifices (Num. 28:9–10).

To the arguments of precedent (David and the priests) and of human need, Jesus added his own authority over the sabbath and God's desire for ***mercy*** above ***sacrifice***. Jesus did not repudiate the Temple or the sacrifices, but he contended for the priority of other claims. ***Something greater*** properly translates the neuter form of *meizon* in verse 6. Specific reference is to the kingdom of heaven, which has come in Jesus, or simply to the authority of Jesus. God's concern for mercy (Hos. 6:6) was Jesus' constant stress (cf. 5:7; 9:13). This is one expression of the "easy yoke" (11:30).

Son of man is here interpreted in terms of sovereignty, ***lord of the sabbath***, and also in the form of the Suffering Servant, whose identity is with needy humanity. Mark may see Son of man referring both to Jesus and to his people (2:27 f.), but the community idea in Son of man is elusive. What is clear is that Jesus claimed authority over the sabbath and above the Temple.

(*2*) *Healing on the Sabbath* (*12:9–14*)

**9 And he went on from there, and entered
their synagogue. 10 And behold, there was a**

**man with a withered hand. And they asked
him, "Is it lawful to heal on the sabbath?" so
that they might accuse him. 11 He said to them,
"What man of you, if he has one sheep and it
falls into a pit on the sabbath, will not lay hold
of it and lift it out? 12 Of how much more
value is a man than a sheep! So it is lawful to
do good on the sabbath." 13 Then he said to the
man, "Stretch out your hand." And the man
stretched it out, and it was restored, whole like
the other. 14 But the Pharisees went out and
took counsel against him, how to destroy him.**

The Pharisees saw their whole theology and authority threatened, and they began to develop their case against Jesus. In the ***synagogue*** they put him to the test with respect to healing ***on the sabbath*** a man ***with a withered hand.*** The Pharisees held that only emergency cases could be helped on the sabbath. Jesus favored any ministry to human need regardless of the day. Jesus reminded the Pharisees of their law which permitted the rescue of an animal on the sabbath or festival day. Because ***a sheep*** had value to them, they would set aside normal sabbath restrictions to save it. Jesus could not have placed their system under heavier indictment than when he had to remind them that ***a man*** is worth more than ***a sheep.*** Before we unduly condemn the Pharisees, we may well ask what things we tend to place above the value of human personality.

The fury of the Pharisees as they plotted to ***destroy him*** was their own unintentional acknowledgement of Jesus' complete moral victory over them (Cox, *op. cit.*, p. 89). He contended for the value of a man and for the lawfulness of doing ***good*** (*kalōs* means what is proper) at any time, while they contended for the observance of a day. In effect, Jesus placed the love commandment above the sabbath. Unable to meet him even on their own ground, they resorted to external force, the persecutor's unwitting confession of defeat. Mark informs us that they even called upon the Herodians for help (3:6).

2. *The Hope of the Nations (12:15–21)*

**15 Jesus, aware of this, withdrew from there.
And many followed him, and he healed them
all, 16 and ordered them not to make him
known. 17 This was to fulfil what was spoken
by the prophet Isaiah:**

18 "Behold, my servant whom I have chosen,
my beloved with whom my soul is well pleased.
I will put my Spirit upon him,
and he shall proclaim justice to the Gentiles.
19 He will not wrangle or cry aloud,
nor will any one hear his voice in the streets;
20 he will not break a bruised reed
or quench a smoldering wick,
till he brings justice to victory;
21 and in his name will the Gentiles hope."

This paragraph contrasts the gentle ministry of Jesus with Pharisaic fury as well as with current messianic expectations, and it contrasts rejection of Jesus by his own people with his ultimate acceptance by ***the Gentiles.*** Matthew continues to develop the themes of Jesus' forced withdrawal from Israel and the fulfilment of Old Testament prophecy.

Matthew recognizes that because of the Pharisaic plot Jesus ***withdrew.*** The time had not come for a final confrontation with the leaders of the nation. Jesus yet had work to complete. Jesus withdrew not only from Pharisaic hostility but also from publicity based upon miracles, commanding those healed ***not to make him known.*** Matthew's greater interest here, however, is in the quiet nature of Jesus' ministry, seeing him in terms of the Suffering Servant of Isaiah (42:1–4). This is the longest Old Testament quotation in Matthew, and it does not fully follow either the Hebrew or LXX texts known to us.

The servant picture in Isaiah was first understood by the Jews as referring to Israel, but the figure came to be understood messianically. To Jesus and the early church it was a basic messianic source. The Greek term *pais* can mean ***servant*** or "child." With the addition of ***beloved*** it approaches the idea of son. In the passage, however, the basic role of servant is uppermost. The ***servant*** is God's Servant, ***chosen*** and ***beloved.*** He is the bearer of God's ***Spirit,*** and his ministry is to be quietly extended to the *Gentiles*.

Justice (*krisis*) translates a word usually rendered "judgment." Probably the basic idea of judgment is to be retained here. Jesus goes about his work in a gentle manner, but this does not exclude judgment. In fact, judgment belongs necessarily to redemption. Judgment's goal is not negative but positive, not simply to condemn but to correct and save. Jesus brings justice or "judgment" ***to victory*** as judgment leads to repentance, a turning to God in submissive faith.

Probably Matthew's interest in the long quotation from Isaiah falls equally upon the quiet manner of Jesus, contrasted with the outward show expected by the people, and the inclusion of ***the Gentiles***. Although Jesus comes in "judgment," he deals gently with each ***bruised reed*** and ***smoldering wick***. Instead of crushing people, he seeks to heal the morally wounded and to fan each spark of faith into a flame.

3. *The Unpardonable Sin* (*12:22–32*)

22 Then a blind and dumb demoniac was
brought to him, and he healed him, so that the
dumb man spoke and saw. 23 And all the people were amazed, and said, "Can this be the
Son of David?" 24 But when the Pharisees
heard it they said, "It is only by Beelzebul, the
prince of demons, that this man casts out
demons." 25 Knowing their thoughts, he said to
them, "Every kingdom divided against itself is
laid waste, and no city or house divided
against itself will stand; 26 and if Satan casts
out Satan, he is divided against himself; how
then will his kingdom stand? 27 And if I cast
out demons by Beelzebul, by whom do your
sons cast them out? Therefore they shall be
your judges. 28 But if it is by the Spirit of God
that I cast out demons, then the kingdom of
God has come upon you. 29 Or how can one
enter a strong man's house and plunder his
goods, unless he first binds the strong man?
Then indeed he may plunder his house. 30 He
who is not with me is against me, and he who
does not gather with me scatters. 31 Therefore I
tell you, every sin and blasphemy will be
forgiven men, but the blasphemy against the
Spirit will not be forgiven. 32 And whoever says
a word against the Son of man will be forgiven; but whoever speaks against the Holy
Spirit will not be forgiven, either in this age or
in the age to come.

As Jesus restored speech and sight to a ***demoniac***, the crowds asked if this could not indicate him to be ***the Son of David***, but the Pharisees charged Jesus with casting out demons only by ***Beelzebul, the prince of demons***. As Jesus ministered in their midst, a blind man saw and religious leaders went "blind." It is against this background that "the unpardonable sin" is to be understood. The sin described is one of deliberate, arrogant blasphemy, calling what unmistakably is God's work the devil's work.

Beelzebul (*Beelzeboul*) is the proper spelling of the term employed here. "Beelzebub" entered English translations from the Latin Vulgate, influenced by "Baalzebub" in 2 Kings 1:2. ***Beelzebul*** may mean "the exalted one," either exalted in the temple or in heaven (McNeile, pp. 143 f.). What is important for usage here is not the derivation of the term but its employment for ***the prince of demons*** (v. 24) and presumably also for ***Satan*** (v. 26). In brief, Jesus is accused of getting his power from Satan.

In reply, Jesus first showed the absurdity of the charge. Exorcism of demons cannot be the work of Satan, for Satan would not be so foolish as to destroy his own kingdom. What Jesus is doing represents God against Satan, not Satan against Satan. The second point was that the Pharisees condemned their own ***sons***, i.e., their disciples, in condemning Jesus, for they also cast out demons. Incidentally, this implies that in Jewish thinking exorcism of demons was not limited to or a necessary sign of the Messiah.

Verse 28 is climactic, one of the most important in this Gospel. Not only does Jesus affirm that his power is through ***the Spirit of God***, but that this is evidence that ***the kingdom of God has come***. This is the clearest statement in Matthew that the kingdom of God has already arrived in Jesus. The Greek verb for ***has come*** (*ephthasen*) indicates not only nearness but presence. Of course, the whole point is that the casting out of demons means that the kingdom of God is now overcoming the kingdom of Satan. The consummation of the kingdom is future, but it is already realizing itself in Jesus. ***The strong man*** is already being bound and men are being freed from the power of evil.

Matthew's usual "kingdom of heaven" (32 times) appears here and three other times (19:24; 21:31,43) as ***kingdom of God.*** This may be due to his source, but it also suits well the phrase, ***the Spirit of God.*** The Spirit of God is the Holy Spirit; i.e., the very presence of God. Luke has "the finger of God" (11:20), an Old Testament expression for God's work in creation (Psalm 8:3), delivering the Israelites from Egypt (Ex. 8:19), and giving the Law (Deut. 9:10), i.e., God as creator, revealer, and redeemer. The Spirit of God is not another God or only a part of God. The Spirit of God is God himself, here uniquely present in Jesus Christ.

Before Jesus, man is called to decision. One may not remain neutral. One who is not positively with Jesus is ***against*** him. One who does not ***gather*** the flock (possible reference to harvest as in 9:37) ***scatters*** it.

The sternest warning attributed to Jesus appears in verses 31 f. ***Blasphemy against the Spirit*** is unforgivable (see the interchange of the terms Spirit of God, Spirit, and Holy Spirit in vv. 28,31,32). This must be understood in context. Jesus had restored sight and hearing to a demoniac. Unable to deny the deed, trusted religious leaders attributed its source to Beelzebul. They looked upon an obvious work of God and called it the work of Satan. Their problem was not one of the head but of the heart. This is wilful blindness, for which there can be no excuse. The ignorant may be informed and the weak may be strengthened, but by wilful rejection of God's Spirit one denies himself his only help toward repentance and faith.

This passage seems harsh, but it is to be taken in all seriousness. Jesus is not saying that God is ever unwilling to forgive but that man can render himself unforgivable. This has to do with a condition in man. A parallel to this is found in John 9:1–41, where it is shown that the price of rejecting God's light is blindness. To close one's eyes is not to put out the light, but it is to put out one's sight. This is the principle behind "the unpardonable sin."

To speak against ***the Son of man*** is forgivable, but to speak against ***the Holy Spirit*** is not. Possibly Jesus means that the problem is not with himself, ***the Son of man;*** for he is ever ready to forgive (cf. Broadus, pp. 271 ff.). But to speak against the Holy Spirit, as the Pharisees have done in a wilful act of disbelief and disobedience, is to deny oneself his only hope. It is for one to cut himself off from the one who alone can lead him to repentance.

4. The Inescapable Judgment (12:33–37)

33 "Either make the tree good, and its fruit
good; or make the tree bad, and its fruit bad;
for the tree is known by its fruit. 34 You brood
of vipers! how can you speak good, when you
are evil? For out of the abundance of the heart
the mouth speaks. 35 The good man out of his
good treasure brings forth good, and the evil
man out of his evil treasure brings forth evil.
36 I tell you, on the day of judgment men will
render account for every careless word they
utter; 37 for by your words you will be justified,
and by your words you will be condemned."

This paragraph makes explicit what is implied above, that Jesus found the center of evil in the human heart, not in forces outside it. Even the words of blasphemy would not be ultimately serious were they only sounds from the mouth or throat. But words are serious as they come from ***the heart,*** reflecting what one is as well as what he says. By analogies of ***fruit*** and ***treasure,*** Jesus drives home the point that it is as words and deeds reflect character, what one is, that they are significant.

A tree can bear fruit only in terms of its kind or species. ***Good*** and ***bad*** (cf. 7:16–20) refer not to states of health but to kinds of fruit, whether edible or not. One can bring out of his ***treasure*** only what he has, whether good or evil. Jesus does make a distinction between a good (*agathos*) man and an evil (*ponēros*) man, using moral terms. One is judged even for ***every careless word.*** Careless translates *argon* (contraction of *a-ergon*), i.e., what is "workless," to no purpose.

The harsh words about a ***brood of vipers*** are directed to those who out of wilful blindness call God's work the work of Satan. Their words are not accidental. They reflect the nature of the source from which they come. Of course, words do not always reflect what one is, as in the case of the hypocrite (cf. 7:21–23); but words and deeds may actually reveal what one is, especially habitual words which show patterns and unpremeditated ones by which one unconsciously discloses his thoughts, feelings, and values. Jesus is not saying that good and evil are inherent in words themselves, but that the good or evil is in the heart out of which the words come. The ugly charge made by the Pharisees against Jesus could come only out of ugly hearts. In the very act of presuming to judge Jesus, they judged themselves.

5. *The Sign of Jonah* (*12:38–42*)

38 Then some of the scribes and Pharisees said to him, "Teacher, we wish to see a sign from you." 39 But he answered them, "An evil and adulterous generation seeks for a sign; but no sign shall be given to it except the sign of the prophet Jonah. 40 For as Jonah was three days and three nights in the belly of the whale, so will the Son of man be three days and three nights in the heart of the earth. 41 The men of Nineveh will arise at the judgment with this generation and condemn it; for they repented at the preaching of Jonah, and behold, something greater than Jonah is here. 42 The queen of the South will arise at the judgment with this generation and condemn it; for she came from the ends of the earth to hear the wisdom of Solomon, and behold, something greater than Solomon is here.

The request for a sign is for something dramatic and compelling. True faith does not come this way. Moreover, those who asked for such a sign were not sincerely open to the evidence already before them. Their problem mainly was one of the heart, not the head. They needed a willingness to believe, not more evidence for faith. This is the point of the story before us.

Matthew's special interest in the opposition of the Pharisees may be seen by comparing this section with its parallel in Luke 11:29–32. Luke does not mention the ***scribes and Pharisees.*** Calling this generation ***adulterous*** parallels Old Testament usage of the term for unfaithfulness to God, as in the analogy of Israel as God's bride who proved unfaithful (cf. Jer. 2:1–5,32; Hosea 2:16–23; Ezek. 16:1–63).

Jesus offered these insincere people only ***the sign of the prophet Jonah.*** Ninevites ***repented,*** although they had as their evangelist only a reluctant prophet who really did not want them to be spared. ***Something greater than Jonah*** refers to the kingdom of heaven which came in Jesus. This generation stood in the presence of Jesus, in whom the powers of the kingdom were already at work, yet they asked for more!

The ***queen of the South*** is the queen of Sheba or southern Arabia (1 Kings 10:1–13). She disbelieved the reports about Solomon when she first heard them; but to her credit, when she heard him she acknowledged her error and his wisdom. Like the Ninevites, she accepted the evidence as she confronted it. Jesus' generation stood condemned because in the presence of one greater than Jonah or Solomon, it asked for more. It needed not more light but rather sight, not something to see but eyes willing to see.

Verse 40 develops another idea. It is not in the Lukan parallel. In Matthew the Jonah analogy serves the further purpose of pointing to the resurrection of Jesus. ***Three days and three nights*** are not to be taken in a literal sense as applied to the resurrection of Jesus. In Jewish counting, a part of a day was counted a full day; and the expression here is like a round number, not a scientific one. Of course, the resurrection of Jesus is the climactic "sign," yet even it did not convince many.

6. *The Unclean Spirit's Return* (*12:43–45*)

43 "When the unclean spirit has gone out of a man, he passes through waterless places seek-

ing rest, but he finds none. 44 Then he says, 'I
will return to my house from which I came.'
And when he comes he finds it empty, swept,
and put in order. 45 Then he goes and brings
with him seven other spirits more evil than
himself, and they enter and dwell there; and
the last state of that man becomes worse than
the first. So shall it be also with this evil
generation."

The immediate reference of this warning may be against undue interest in exorcisms, healings, and other such benefactions. It is not enough simply to expel the demons or remove physical ailments like blindness. God must dwell in one, making him God's temple. It is not enough to receive God's outward gifts; one must receive him.

Applied more widely, the judgment falls upon Israel for her great attention to "reforms," in which her house was outwardly ***swept and put in order*** but left ***empty.*** Since the time of Ezra, Israel had given attention to the Law, working out an elaborate system to govern every situation in life. Nothing was left to chance. There was a rule for everything: home, business, worship, dress, diet, etc.

But with all the attention to the things of religion and life, the greatest neglect was in terms of the personal: God and man. Old gods had been banned, and there was no more outward idolatry as before the Exile. Baal, Chemosh, Molech, and other such gods were no longer a threat to Israel. But new "gods" had moved in—worse than the old ones: mammon, pride, provincialism, sabbath, fasting, purification rites, and the like. These "gods" are more subtle and more dangerous than the crude, outward gods of paganism.

7. *Jesus' True Family (12:46–50)*

46 While he was still speaking to the people,
behold, his mother and his brothers stood out-
side, asking to speak to him. 48 But he replied
to the man who told him, "Who is my mother,
and who are my brothers?" 49 And stretching
out his hand toward his disciples, he said,
"Here are my mother and my brothers! 50 For
whoever does the will of my Father in heaven
is my brother, and sister, and mother."

At this point Matthew returns to Mark's narrative order (Mark 3:31–35). Mark presents in sequence three groups and their reactions to Jesus: "his friends" who said, "He is beside himself" (3:21); the scribes who said that he was "possessed by Beelzebul" (3:22); and Jesus' mother and brothers who, "standing outside," sent for him, presumably to remove him from the public eye (3:31). Matthew has no parallel to Mark 3:21, but he does point up the reactions of the Pharisees and Jesus' family.

Neither Mark nor Matthew explicitly declares the attitude of Jesus' ***mother*** and ***brothers,*** but the response of Jesus implies that they were not sympathetic with what he was doing. The best that could be said for them was that they feared that he would suffer harm from those hostile to him. It seems, however, that the relationship was more strained, and that it was not until after the resurrection that the family of Jesus began to understand and support him. Jesus had to lose his mother and brothers before he regained them on a new and more meaningful basis (cf. John 2:4 f.; 7:5; 1 Cor. 9:5).

Jesus left no room for doubt that faith and not flesh was the basis of true kinship. More precisely, ***whoever does the will*** of Jesus' Heavenly ***Father*** is his ***brother, sister,*** or ***mother.*** This stresses not only the true basis for kinship but also the importance of doing God's will. It may be observed that although Jesus calls others his mother, brother, and sister, he calls only God his Father.

Verse 47 is strongly supported in the Western type text but is not supported by the best manuscripts of the Alexandrian text type. It probably is not original to this context.

III. Parables of the Kingdom (13:1–52)

The parable was a major teaching method for Jesus, but it was not new. The Old Testament has many parables, and they were widely used outside Judaism. In the LXX, *parabolē* translates the Hebrew term *māshal* about 45 times. Parable literally means something "cast alongside," as illustration or analogy, but etymology does not go far in indicating meaning or usage.

The Old Testament *māshal* could be an oracle, riddle, or "dark saying," intelligible to the initiated but unintelligible to outsiders. Psalm 78:2 speaks of "a parable" and "dark sayings from of old," national secrets passed down from family to family. But generally the parable is to be understood by all addressed, not only to enlighten but to judge and to evoke a moral response. This is well illustrated in Nathan's parable of "the one little ewe lamb" taken from the poor man by the rich man (2 Sam. 12:1–14). This parable is drawn from real life; it teaches by analogy or illustration; it instructs or enlightens; it judges and calls for moral response.

Parables are many and varied in the New Testament. By the most restricted understanding of what constitutes a parable, there are dozens in the New Testament. The number increases when parables are understood in a wider and more flexible sense. For example, "Physician heal yourself" is explicitly termed a parable in Luke 4:23 (proverb in RSV but *parabolē* in Greek).

In both Old and New Testaments the *māshal* or parable is best understood as including a wide variety of types and forms: simile, maxims, or pithy sayings (cf. 1 Sam. 10:12), a proverb, metaphor, stories from real life and imaginary ones, and even an occasional allegory or approach to the allegory. A simile likens one thing to another. A metaphor is more direct, calling one thing another, as "You are the salt of the earth" (5:13). An allegory may personify abstract things. Some New Testament parables approach the allegory, as is true of the parable of sower and soils (13:3*b*–23). However, it follows that comparison is "the hallmark of a parable" while hidden identity is "the hallmark of an allegory," for it requires a key to be understood (Perrin, pp. 84, 86).

A parable usually has one main point and one only, but this is not always true. Two extremes are to be avoided: the allegorical approach which seeks to make every word or phrase teach something, but also the restriction of all parables to one meaning. The first pattern was followed by early interpreters like Origen and Augustine, who could let the imagination run wild in reading anything they wanted into a parable.

This fallacy was thoroughly exposed and refuted by Adolf Jülicher.[30] Unfortunately, Jülicher erred on the other side, understanding the nature of parables in terms of some pagan Greek usage rather than Old Testament usage and thus limiting each parable to one meaning only. A happier balance was soon recovered as reflected in works like those of Paul Fiebig[31] and McNeile (pp. 185 f.). In this understanding, New Testament parables are seen in terms of their wide variety of type and form, usually having one meaning only, but sometimes having secondary meanings or even approaching the allegory.

A major step forward in the understanding of New Testament parables came in the modern period, as closer attention was given to the settings of parables. There was, of course, the original setting as Jesus taught in parables. Where possible, this setting should be recovered in order to see the original thrust of the parable. But there may be the further setting of the church in which the parable was preserved or of the evangelist who repeated it. It was valid and necessary to adapt the parables to the new situations which arose in the life of the church.

Two errors may well be avoided: the failure to distinguish between the original setting and that of the church and also the exaggeration of the change from the original setting to that of the later church. It is as untenable to say that the setting is always changed as to say that it is never changed. Matthew, e.g., understandably and properly so reported the parables of Jesus as to give them maximum relevance to the church of his day. This does not mean that he was indifferent to their original intention. The same principle holds for employment of parables today. We must necessarily adapt and apply them to our problems and needs.

30 *Die Gleichnisreden Jesu* (2d ed.; Tübingen: Mohr, 1899).

31 *Die Gleichnisreden Jesu im Lichte der rabbinischen Gleichnisse des neutestamentlichen Zeitalters* (Tübingen: Mohr, 1912).

but this does not justify violation of their original intention. It is proper to ask what a parable may say to us today, but it must never be made to contradict what it originally intended to say.

The most difficult question relating to the parables of Jesus concerns purpose. Verse 13 seems to say that parables intended to conceal truth from some rather than reveal it. On the other hand verses 34 f. represent parables as disclosing "what has been hidden" since the beginning of the world. Verse 13 will be studied in context, and its point must be taken seriously; but it is clear that the overriding purpose of Jesus was to give light and not withhold it, to reveal and not conceal. He came as the "Word . . . made flesh" (John 1:14, KJV), to be the understood Word of God.

The seven parables in chapter 13 constitute Matthew's third major "discourse," concluded with his recurrent formula in 13:53 (cf. 7:28; 11:1; 19:1; 26:1). Two of the parables are from Mark (sower and mustard seed); these two and that of the leaven are shared with Luke; and in addition Matthew has four parables not found elsewhere (weeds, hidden treasure, pearl of great price, and the dragnet). This may reflect three sources (Mark, Q, and M); all that it necessarily means is that Matthew has two of the seven in common with Mark, three in common with Luke, and four peculiar to himself.

Although parables relate to various themes, these seven have to do with the kingdom of heaven. They teach its presence in the words and works of Jesus, its judgment, its call to repentance, its nature, and its ultimate triumph and significance in striking contrast to its seeming smallness and weakness as it first appears in the person and method of Jesus.

1. Sower and Soils (13:1–23)

(1) The Parable Given (13:1–9)

**1 That same day Jesus went out of the house
and sat beside the sea. 2 And great crowds
gathered about him, so that he got into a boat
and sat there; and the whole crowd stood on
the beach. 3 And he told them many things in
parables, saying: "A sower went out to sow.
4 And as he sowed, some seeds fell along the
path, and the birds came and devoured them.
5 Other seeds fell on rocky ground, where they
had not much soil, and immediately they
sprang up, since they had no depth of soil,
6 but when the sun rose they were scorched;
and since they had no root they withered
away. 7 Other seeds fell upon thorns, and the
thorns grew up and choked them. 8 Other seeds
fell on good soil and brought forth grain, some
a hundredfold, some sixty, some thirty. 9 He
who has ears, let him hear."**

Jesus drew most of his parables from everyday life and told them in such a simple way that the intended truth was transparent to the ordinary person. "Parables were not meant to be decoded in the study; they were intended to be understood, heeded, and acted upon." [32]

Farmers sowed seed upon unplowed ground and then plowed in the seed (cf. a similar practice to this day in America, as reflected in the phrase "plow in oats"). That some seed would fall upon unproductive soil and be lost was a calculated risk. The farmer sowed in the expectation of a harvest which would give him an increase over the seed planted. ***The path*** was the hard-packed footpath that ran by or through one's field. ***Rocky ground*** refers to thin soil over a rock stratum, not to rocks mixed up with soil. The thin soil would be soon warmed by the sun, and quick germination of the seed would follow. Lacking depth, the soil would not have the moisture to sustain growth. ***Thorns*** grew on the "head land" and in the corners of the field. These would choke out the new plants. ***Good soil*** yielded varying amounts, ***some a hundredfold, some sixty, some thirty.*** An increase of twenty-five to one is good. A ratio of a hundred to one would be phenomenal. In rice farming, e.g., one grain can produce two hundred grains, yet any farmer is pleased with forty pounds harvested to one pound sowed.

Verse 9 points to the proper function of ears. They are to hear with. Responsibility

32 Harold S. Songer, "Jesus' Use of Parables: Matthew 13," *Review and Expositor*, LIX (October, 1962), 495.

for hearing belongs to the one who has ears. Ears are God's gift to man, but hearing becomes man's responsibility.

(2) *The Purpose of Parables (13:10–17)*

10 Then the disciples came and said to him,
"Why do you speak to them in parables?"
11 And he answered them, "To you it has been
given to know the secrets of the kingdom of
heaven, but to them it has not been given.
12 For to him who has will more be given, and
he will have abundance; but from him who has
not, even what he has will be taken away.
13 This is why I speak to them in parables,
because seeing they do not see, and hearing
they do not hear, nor do they understand.
14 With them indeed is fulfilled the prophecy
of Isaiah which says:
'You shall indeed hear but never understand,
and you shall indeed see but never perceive.
15 For this people's heart has grown dull,
and their ears are heavy of hearing,
and their eyes they have closed,
lest they should perceive with their eyes,
and hear with their ears,
and understand with their heart,
and turn for me to heal them.'
16 But blessed are your eyes, for they see, and
your ears, for they hear. 17 Truly, I say to you,
many prophets and righteous men longed to
see what you see, and did not see it, and to
hear what you hear, and did not hear it.

Inserted between the relating of the parable and its explanation is a discussion of the purpose of parables. Thus the parable of the sower serves as an introduction to all parables, in addition to its immediate application.

Matthew makes more emphatic what already is in Mark 4:10–12, that the disciples understand but the outsiders do not. In Mark the question is simply about the parables, but in Matthew it is the question of why Jesus speaks in parables "to them," presumably non-disciples. Jesus replies that understanding ***the secrets of the kingdom*** is something ***given,*** not achieved. This is consistent with the teaching that revelation is always God's self-disclosure and not man's discovery, the gift of God's grace, not the result of man's work (cf. 11:25–27). This does not necessarily carry the implication that God arbitrarily reveals himself to some and withholds revelation from others. If so, man would be reduced to passive, nonmoral being, without virtue or blame. Determinism excludes responsibility for all except the one making the determination. Jesus does not say that God withholds his ***secrets*** from some, but that man can hear only because God has spoken.

Matthew at times seems to approach a doctrine of divine determination, but he backs away from it, holding man responsible for his own guilt (Hare, p. 150). Matthew sees a "voluntarism" given man, whereby he may enter the kingdom of God (19:17) or refuse to do so (23:37).

Jesus distinguishes between those to whom ***it has been given to know*** and those to whom ***it has not been given,*** restated in terms of ***him who has*** and ***him who has not.*** To one ***who has,*** more can be given, and from one who ***has not*** is taken even what he has. Clearly this cannot be taken literally, for it is impossible to take what one does not have. The principle taught is that God can impart his higher gifts to those alone who are open to receive. Those not having this openness sink deeper into their deafness and blindness. They are like the hard ground of the path, where seed cannot penetrate and bear fruit. In popular idiom some "have it" and some do not. God is in the speaking business, but not all are in the hearing business. The price of refusing to hear is that one becomes deaf, just as the price of refusing to see is blindness (cf. John 9:39–41).

In verse 13 Matthew has somewhat eased Mark 4:12, employing the conjunction ***because*** (*hoti*) rather than Mark's "so that" (*hina*). He also omitted Mark 4:12, "lest they should turn again, and be forgiven." The difference may not be as great as appears, for both *hina* and *hoti* may denote either result or purpose (18:16). Although Matthew omits Mark 4:12*c*, the equivalent appears in the long quotation from Isaiah in 13:14 f. Mark echoes Isaiah 6:9 f., and Matthew quotes it, following the LXX version.

The Isaiah quotation and its treatment,

especially by Mark and to a less extent by Matthew, is open to the meaning that God deliberately closes the ears and eyes of some in order that they be unable to hear or see. This position would go against the major biblical thrust which pictures God as offering light to all who will receive it. A deterministic view would relieve man of all responsibility, virtue, or guilt; but this view is not sustained in the major thrust of Mark or Matthew.

This difficult passage is best understood as stressing God's initiative and sovereignty in dealing with man. If God did not open the way for man to hear and see, man could not do so. God reveals himself to man; man does not discover God. But the passage goes a step further in its understanding of human blindness in terms of divine providence, intended not to excuse man but to declare God's sovereignty.

Logic requires the conclusion that when one determines another's condition, the whole responsibility rests with the one (subject) who determines and not with the one (object) determined. Logic cannot escape this. But Isaiah 6:9 f. and its employment by Matthew are to be understood in terms of intention, without forcing the logic of the statement. The parable does not intend to excuse man for being deaf or blind, for it calls him to responsible hearing and seeing.

The quotation from Isaiah stops short of explaining man's deafness and blindness as due to God's will. It describes people who ***hear*** words but who do not ***understand*** and who ***see*** yet do not ***perceive.*** Hearts that have ***grown dull*** and ears that are ***heavy of hearing*** describe man's lack of receptivity to God's revelation. It is not said that God closed the eyes of certain people but that ***they have closed*** their own eyes. This is man's rejection of God's light, not a divine predestination which fixes man's fate.

Verses 16–17 stress the great privilege of the disciples, for they now see the fulfilment of all that the ***prophets and righteous men longed*** for. ***Your*** (*humōn*) is emphatic in the Greek text. Matthew's concern for righteousness is reflected in his choice of the word righteous where Luke 10:24 has "kings."

Behind Matthew 13:10–15 stands Mark 4:10–12, and possibly the most able study of this passage is that of Joachim Jeremias.[33] He sees Mark 4:11 f. as preserving an early Palestinian paraphrase of Isaiah 6:9 f., similar to the Targum (oral translation of Hebrew texts into Aramaic). To the disciples is given the secret (*mustērion*) of the kingdom of heaven, a gift of the pure grace of God. To outsiders everything comes in parables, i.e., in mystery (*mustērion*). Here "parable" is used in the sense of a riddle, one employment of the Hebrew *māshal* (cf. the antithesis between *paroimia*, wayside saying, and *parrēsia*, openness [plainly, RSV] in John 16:25). For the time, everything is in riddles or parables to the outsiders. Mark's *hina* (v. 12), "so that," may be understood as an abbreviation for "in order that it may be fulfilled," referring to Isaiah 6:9 f. This could mean "with a view to" or "with the result that" the prophecy of Isaiah 6:9 f. be fulfilled. Mark's *mēpote* (v. 12), usually rendered "lest" can be translated, in keeping with rabbinical exegesis of Isaiah 6:10 (cf. Strack and Billerbeck, I, 662 f.), "that it may be that" they turn and God forgive them. Rabbinical exegesis understood Isaiah 6:10 not as a threat of final stupor but as a promise of ultimate conversion and forgiveness. So approached, Mark 4:12*b* is seen as understanding Isaiah 6:10*b* as a promise, not a threat. Matthew, with some softening or clarifying, builds upon Mark 4:10–12.

(3) *The Parable Explained* (*13:18–23*)

18 "Hear then the parable of the sower.
19 When any one hears the word of the kingdom and does not understand it, the evil one comes and snatches away what is sown in his heart; this is what was sown along the path.
20 As for what was sown on rocky ground, this is he who hears the word and immediately receives it with joy; 21 yet he has no root in himself, but endures for a while, and when tribulation or persecution arises on account of the word, immediately he falls away. 22 As for what was sown among thorns, this is he who

33 *The Parables of Jesus* (rev. ed.; New York: Scribners, 1963), pp. 12–18.

hears the word, but the cares of the world and the delight in riches choke the word, and it proves unfruitful. [23] As for what was sown on good soil, this is he who hears the word and understands it; he indeed bears fruit, and yields, in one case a hundredfold, in another sixty, and in another thirty."

Two basically different interpretations of this parable are possible. It may be seen as ***the parable of the sower,*** as here, or as the parable of the soils. The former stresses the successful harvest, despite all hazards and opposition. Many scholars understand the parable initially to have had this emphasis. So understood, Jesus gives assurance that the kingdom of heaven will prevail over all opposition. Despite hard ground, birds, rocky soil, and thorns, there will be an abundant harvest.

As the parable stands, it seems to place the emphasis upon the different kinds of soil, even though it is yet known as "the parable of the sower." So understood, the stress is upon man's responsibility to hear. Ears are to hear with (13:9). The "have nots," i.e., those who are not open to God's word, lose their capacity to hear. The "haves," i.e., those who are like the ***good soil,*** open to the word of God, grow in their capacity to receive.

In this second approach, seemingly developed by all Synoptics, four kinds of hearers are pictured. There are the hardened, impenetrable ones. Minds, ears, and eyes are closed to God's words and deeds. A second group is like the ***rocky soil.*** They are those who follow Jesus in a superficial way, quickly attracted by outward benefactions but basically uncommitted to the Servant of God whose pillow is a cross. The third group is like the seed among the ***thorns.*** They have sincere interest but also ***cares of the world.*** Thus divided and distracted, they make no basic commitment to Jesus as Lord. The ***good soil*** typifies those who make a genuine response to God's word. Even here are differences, some being more productive than others.

Matthew's interest in portraying the disciples as "understanding" is reflected in his introduction of the term in 13:19,23,51. This is especially clear in 13:23, where Matthew's ***he who hears the word and understands*** replaces Mark's those who "accept" (4:20). One of Matthew's purposes is to stress the disciple's understanding of God's word in contrast to Pharisaic misunderstanding, although the latter are not brought in here.

2. *Weeds Among the Wheat (13:24–30)*

[24] Another parable he put before them, saying, "The kingdom of heaven may be compared to a man who sowed good seed in his field, [25] but while men were sleeping, his enemy came and sowed weeds among the wheat, and went away. [26] So when the plants came up and bore grain, then the weeds appeared also. [27] And the servants of the householder came and said to him, 'Sir, did you not sow good seed in your field? How then has it weeds?' [28] He said to them, 'An enemy has done this.' The servants said to him, 'Then do you want us to go and gather them?' [29] But he said, 'No; lest in gathering the weeds you root up the wheat along with them. [30] Let both grow together until the harvest; and at harvest time I will tell the reapers, Gather the weeds first and bind them in bundles to be burned, but gather the wheat into my barn.' "

This parable is peculiar to Matthew, appearing in the place of Mark's parable of the seed growing of itself (4:26–29). One may observe the careful wording to the effect that the kingdom of heaven ***may be compared to,*** not that it is actually like a man sowing a field (cf. 11:16; 18:23; 22:2; 25:1). The kingdom is not like a man, a field, etc., but something about it may be compared with the farmer's experience with wheat and weeds (but see 13:31,33,44,45, 47; 20:1).

Weeds (*zizania*) were one of the various kinds of tares or bearded darnel (*lolium temulentum*) which grew in Palestine. They grew along with the wheat and closely resembled it. They would be most clearly distinguishable when they "headed out," i.e., when the grain appeared at harvest time. But the chief reason for letting ***weeds*** grow along with ***wheat*** was that to pull up the one would uproot the other. Farmers did then, as now, "weed" their crops; but the farmer here ruled this out, presumably because of the great number of weeds deliberately sown by an enemy.

The *man* who sowed the field and *the householder* are the same. The appearance of *weeds* (tares or darnel) among the good grain is a perennial threat, but deliberate sabotage is unusual. Since the farmer had sown *good seed,* i.e., "clean" or free of *weeds,* it was concluded that *an enemy* had sown the bad seed. At the harvest the weeds were to be *burned* lest they seed or "poison" the land for its next crop. The servants are not blamed because they slept; the point is that the enemy took advantage of this time for his evil work. The interpretation of the parable follows in verses 36–43.

3. *Mustard Seed and Leaven (13:31–33)*

31 Another parable he put before them, saying, "The kingdom of heaven is like a grain of mustard seed which a man took and sowed in his field; 32 it is the smallest of all seeds, but when it has grown it is the greatest of shrubs and becomes a tree, so that the birds of the air come and make nests in its branches."

33 He told them another parable. "The kingdom of heaven is like leaven which a woman took and hid in three measures of meal, till it was all leavened."

These parables seem to be paired, contrasting the magnitude and might of the kingdom of heaven with its seemingly small and unpromising beginning in Jesus.

In Jewish expectation the kingdom of God would come with awesome power and catastrophic results, striking down the wicked and vindicating the righteous. That it came in a tiny baby and manifested itself in one who rejected all militaristic means and who saw himself as the Suffering Servant of God was contrary to the extravagant ideas of many. But so came the kingdom of heaven! It came in one who gave himself to tax gatherers and sinners and who began his mission with a handful of ordinary people. The parables reflect Jesus' joy and confidence in the work he is doing.

The two parables were seemingly joined in Q, a source common to Matthew and Luke. Mark has only the parable of the mustard seed, not the leaven. Verbal agreements between Matthew and Luke where they differ from Mark indicate that they knew the parable of the mustard seed in Q as well as in Mark.

Grain of mustard seed instead of simply "a mustard seed" is a tautologous translation preserved from Tyndale (McNeile, p. 198). The contrast between the smallness of the mustard seed and the greatness of the plant it produced was proverbial. It is not necessary to press the matter of the actual size of either.

Whether or not symbolism is to be found in the details of the parable of the mustard seed, branches, and birds is uncertain. Possibly they serve only to make more vivid the picture of a large plant derived from a tiny seed. On the other hand, some careful scholars find the main point just here, observing that in Judaism birds nesting in tree branches symbolized the coming of the Gentiles into the blessings of the kingdom (Ezek. 17:3; 31:6; Dan. 4:12). As birds flock to the shade of the tree for shelter, so the blessings of the kingdom of God are seen to be now available to all men.[34] If this is valid, the main point still holds. The parable is one of contrast, from small beginnings with a little band of ordinary people to a universal fellowship.

The parable of the leaven also draws a lesson in contrast, although the amount of leaven is not specified. ***Three measures of meal*** would make about four and a half bushels, or about 40 to 50 pounds of bread. The greater emphasis, however, is probably upon the inner and transforming way leaven penetrates and changes the dough. The kingdom does not come with outward show or with worldly powers. It does come with revolutionary force, changing from within. Both parables, mustard seed and leaven, stress the miraculous power of God's kingdom, the wonder of God's creative power, out of the most unpromising beginnings, bringing about so great a result (Jeremias,

34 C. H. Dodd, *The Parables of the Kingdom* (rev. ed.; New York: Scribners, 1936), p. 190 f. cf. T. W. Manson, *Teaching of Jesus* (Cambridge, 1935), p. 133, n. 1.

Parables, p. 148).

In the Old Testament and elsewhere in the New Testament, leaven is a symbol for evil (cf. 16:6,11 f.), but that seems impossible here. In this parable leaven conquers the whole lump of dough, and Jesus did not teach the triumph of evil. It is the kingdom of heaven, not evil, which works like leaven.

4. *The Use of Parables* (*13:34–35*)

[34] All this Jesus said to the crowds in parables; indeed he said nothing to them without a parable. [35] This was to fulfil what was spoken by the prophet:
"I will open my mouth in parables,
I will utter what has been hidden since the foundation of the world."

The concluding formula indicates that at one stage a collection of parables ended here, verse 51 being a second formula to mark the conclusion of Matthew's larger collection. That there were early collections of the sayings as well as works of Jesus is explicit in Luke 1:1–4 and is reflected in passages like this one. There was no period of silence between the time of Jesus and the completed Gospels. There was rather an unbroken tradition—oral, then written—in which the materials were remembered, shaped, and preserved.

That Jesus ***said nothing*** except in parables must apply to a given situation only, as here, not to his whole teaching ministry, for he often taught without parables. Although parable can represent a "dark saying," something understandable only to the initiated (cf. 13:11–13; John 16:25, although the word here is *paroimia,* not *parabolē*), in verses 34 f. it implies something understandable. Things that have been hidden are now proclaimed, not concealed. This would support the evidence elsewhere that Jesus taught in parables to be understood, not to veil his teaching.

The prophet may refer to the psalmist, for verse 35 is from Psalm 78:2. The superscription for Psalm 78 is "A Maskil of Asaph," and in 1 Chronicles 25:1, the sons of Asaph were set apart to "prophesy with lyres, with harps, and with cymbals." Jerome seems to have known manuscripts which had the name "Asaph," but no such manuscripts are extant. Many early and weighty manuscripts have "through Isaiah," persuading Hort of the reading's originality. ***The prophet,*** meaning the psalmist, is probably the correct reading, but the matter is not decisive.

5. *Parable of the Weeds Explained* (*13:36–43*)

[36] Then he left the crowds and went into the house. And his disciples came to him, saying, "Explain to us the parable of the weeds of the field." [37] He answered, "He who sows the good seed is the Son of man; [38] the field is the world, and the good seed means the sons of the kingdom; the weeds are the sons of the evil one, [39] and the enemy who sowed them is the devil; the harvest is the close of the age, and the reapers are angels. [40] Just as the weeds are gathered and burned with fire, so will it be at the close of the age. [41] The Son of man will send his angels, and they will gather out of his kingdom all causes of sin and all evil-doers, [42] and throw them into the furnace of fire; there men will weep and gnash their teeth. [43] Then the righteous will shine like the sun in the kingdom of their Father. He who has ears, let him hear.

The parable is interpreted and applied point by point, in an allegorical manner. The style throughout is typically Matthean.[35] The main teaching is that the separation of ***evildoers*** and ***the righteous*** will take place ***at the close of the age*** and not before. Judgment thus seems to be delayed, but it is certain. This is a reminder to impatient disciples that God has his own way of judging the wicked and vindicating the righteous, and he will not be pressured into adopting some other method or timetable for either.

The contrast between ***evildoers,*** actually "the lawless" (*anomia;* cf. also 7:23; 23:28; 24:12), and ***the righteous*** supports Matthew's great concern to show that Jesus rejected not only Pharisaic legalism but also antinomianism or lawlessness. Moral demand is not sacrificed by a gospel of salva-

[35] Cf. Jeremias, *Parables* (pp. 81–85), for style and significance.

tion as the gift of God's mercy.

It may be observed further that for Matthew ***the world*** is the field for missionary work, not the nation Israel alone (cf. 28:19 as well as 10:5; 15:24). ***The close of the age*** (cf. 28:20) is the consummation of the age, when history is brought to its goal. Both judgment and salvation are present realities, but the completion of each belongs to the consummation of the age.

It is possible that this parable served to caution the church against rashly expelling questionable members from its fellowship. Jesus did not expel Judas from the twelve, although he knew his treachery before Judas acted to betray him. More likely, however, the parable's concern is with the impatience of those who wanted God to act immediately in outward and final judgment of the wicked and reward of the righteous. Two reasons are given for delaying the "weeding" until the harvest: (1) lest the good be uprooted with the bad and (2) because God has appointed an end-time for the separation. When man tries to assume God's function as judge, he both disobeys God and risks confusing the good with the bad.

6. *Hidden Treasure and a Costly Pearl (13: 44–46)*

44 "The kingdom of heaven is like treasure hidden in a field, which a man found and covered up; then in his joy he goes and sells all that he has and buys that field.

45 "Again, the kingdom of heaven is like a merchant in search of fine pearls, 46 who, on finding one pearl of great value, went and sold all that he had and bought it.

These twin parables have the same basic teaching, the joy occasioned by the inbreaking of the kingdom of God (Jeremias, *Parables,* p. 201). Along with the joy are closely related lessons. The privilege of living under God's rule, the kingdom of heaven, is a ***joy*** worth the surrender of all else. Not only is this joyous privilege worth all, it costs all. Paradoxically, salvation is free yet costs everything (cf. 10:37–39). One must sell all to possess the ***treasure*** or the ***pearl of great value.*** The parables are a call to decision. The kingdom has come in Jesus and it is the highest good. One may have this joy if he is willing to leave all and follow Jesus.

There is possibly a further teaching through the difference between the accidental finding of the hidden treasure and the finding of the valuable pearl only at the end of a long search. This may suggest that some encounter the kingdom without seeking it while others first search for it. Whether or not the parables are to be pressed this far cannot be determined. Priceless worth, the joy of possession, willingness to surrender all else for the kingdom, and call to decision seem to be the lessons of the parables. The parable of the hidden treasure is not concerned with the ethics of the man who bought the field without informing the owner of its hidden treasure.

Jülicher (II, 581–85) long ago showed the danger of trying to draw moral lessons from the details of every parable.

7. *Dragnet and the Sorting of the Fish (13: 47–50)*

47 "Again, the kingdom of heaven is like a net which was thrown into the sea and gathered fish of every kind; 48 when it was full, men drew it ashore and sat down and sorted the good into vessels but threw away the bad. 49 So it will be at the close of the age. The angels will come out and separate the evil from the righteous, 50 and throw them into the furnace of fire; there men will weep and gnash their teeth.

This parable may be paired with that of the weeds among the wheat, each teaching that judgment is outwardly delayed yet certain. The ***net*** (*sagēnē*) is a seine or dragnet. It was pulled between two boats or taken out into the water by a single boat and drawn to shore by ropes. In this kind of fishing, all kinds are taken together, the sorting taking place only after the net is drawn to the shore. ***Good*** (*kala*) and ***bad*** (*sapra*) fish are edible and unedible, as determined by taste or Jewish law. Jews were forbidden to eat things from the water unless they had fins and scales (Lev. 11: 9–12).

In application, it is to be seen that the kingdom does not outwardly separate the good and the bad in this life. God sends the sun and rain upon both alike (5:45), and their material and physical circumstances may not reflect their true standing with God. Only ***at the close of the age*** is the outward separation made. At that time both judgment and redemption will be brought to completion.

Immediate application may have been made to the church in Matthew's time. The Qumran community had considered itself a living sanctuary, a sphere of holiness in sharp contrast to the rest of the world, which it thought to be defiled (Betz, p. 98). Jesus called for purity and righteousness far beyond that of Qumran yet did not force Judas out of the circle of the twelve.

Dodd sees the point of the story to be that just as in fishing with a dragnet one cannot select his fish but must expect a mixed catch, so the "fishers of men" must be prepared to cast their nets widely over the whole field of human society, the mission of Jesus involving an undiscriminating appeal to men of every class and type (*Parables*, p. 188).

8. *Treasures New and Old* (*13:51–52*)

[51] "Have you understood all this?" They said to him, "Yes." [52] And he said to them, "Therefore every scribe who has been trained for the kingdom of heaven is like a householder who brings out of his treasure what is new and what is old."

This little paragraph catches up much of the emphasis of Matthew. The disciple is seen as a Christian scribe (cf. 8:19; 23:34). Just as Jesus came not to abolish the Law and the Prophets but to fulfil them (5:17), so his disciples are to conserve the treasures found in the teaching of Jesus. It has been suggested that Matthew may reflect here his understanding of his own role (Bacon, p. 131).

In the analogy, the ***householder*** is seen as one who is prepared to care for his family or guests by drawing upon both old and new goods. The Christian scribe is expected to be able to meet the needs of his hearers with truths drawn from the heritage of Israel and from Jesus.

VIII. *Rejected at Home but Popular with Crowds* (*13:53—14:36*)

1. *Rejection at Nazareth* (*13:53–58*)

[53] And when Jesus had finished these parables, he went away from there, [54] and coming to his own country he taught them in their synagogue, so that they were astonished, and said, "Where did this man get this wisdom and these mighty works? [55] Is not this the carpenter's son? Is not his mother called Mary? And are not his brothers James and Joseph and Simon and Judas? [56] And are not all his sisters with us? Where then did this man get all this?" [57] And they took offense at him. But Jesus said to them, "A prophet is not without honor except in his own country and in his own house." [58] And he did not do many mighty works there, because of their unbelief.

In verse 53 is the third appearance of Matthew's five summary formulas, each marking the end of a major discourse (cf. 7:28; 11:1; 19:1; 26:1). At this point Matthew returns to Mark's order and follows it to the end of Mark.

His own country (*patris*) probably refers to Nazareth, although this is not explicit here nor in the parallel in Mark 6:1–6. Luke (4:16–30) identifies the place as Nazareth and makes this the basic narrative against which he sets forth the nature of Jesus' ministry and the grounds for his conflict with his people. In all three Synoptics the experience of rejection in the synagogue at Nazareth foreshadows the ultimate rejection and crucifixion of Jesus (17:12).

Any Jewish man could be invited to teach in a synagogue. ***Taught*** (*edidasken*) translates a Greek imperfect tense and may imply that Jesus taught on more than one occasion in this synagogue. This point of grammar is not to be pressed, for it could describe nothing more than the process of teaching in a single service. The townspeople were not prepared for such ***wisdom*** in one who had grown up among them. The ***mighty works*** may have been those done elsewhere (cf. chaps. 8–9 and of which they had only heard (Luke 4:23), for in Nazareth he did not do many mighty works (v. 58).

The villagers ponder the source of Jesus' wisdom and power, thinking of him only as ***the carpenter's son,*** whose humble family lived in their midst. "Carpenter" translates *tektōn,* a term which may refer to one who works with wood or stone. In Mark (6:3) Jesus is called "the carpenter, the son of Mary." Matthew reports the villagers as calling him ***the carpenter's son.*** Both Joseph and Jesus could have been "carpenters." In terming Jesus the carpenter's son, Matthew does not thus contradict his account of Jesus as virgin born (1:23). It was not the Jewish custom to identify a son in terms of his mother.

There is no reason for understanding ***brothers*** and ***sisters*** in any sense but the normal one. After the birth of Jesus, Mary lived with Joseph and bore sons and daughters to him. Theological bias in the second century began to develop stories which made these Joseph's children by a former marriage, thus seeking to build a case for the perpetual virginity of Mary (cf. *The Protevangelium of James*). These were not foster brothers and sisters or cousins. They were half brothers and sisters.

The family of Jesus, as well as the villagers, seem not to have supported him in his ministry. Only after his death and resurrection did they begin to understand him (12:46–50; John 7:5). The villagers ***took offense at him,*** with apparent jealousy and resentment. Luke brings out the fact that Jesus' description of his mission moved them even to throw him out of the synagogue and to try to kill him (4:16–30).

Because of ***unbelief*** in Nazareth, Jesus ***did not do many mighty works there*** (this preserves the ambiguity of the Greek). Matthew softens Mark's "could do no," leaving open the question of whether Jesus was unable or unwilling to do mighty works in the face of unbelief. If unwilling, it was because he did not do miracles in order to compel faith or to satisfy curiosity. "He did not make God's might serve man's unbelief or seek to overcome this unbelief with force" (Schlatter, *op. cit.*, p. 226).

2. *The Death of John the Baptist (14:1–12).*

**1 At that time Herod the tetrarch heard
about the fame of Jesus; 2 and he said to his
servants, "This is John the Baptist, he has been
raised from the dead; that is why these powers
are at work in him." 3 For Herod had seized
John and bound him and put him in prison, for
the sake of Herodias, his brother Philip's wife;
4 because John said to him, "It is not lawful for
you to have her." 5 And though he wanted to
put him to death, he feared the people, because they held him to be a prophet. 6 But
when Herod's birthday came, the daughter of
Herodias danced before the company, and
pleased Herod, 7 so that he promised with an
oath to give her whatever she might ask.
8 Prompted by her mother, she said, "Give me
the head of John the Baptist here on a platter."
9 And the king was sorry; but because of his
oaths and his guests he commanded it to be
given; 10 he sent and had John beheaded in the
prison, 11 and his head was brought on a platter and given to the girl, and she brought it to
her mother. 12 And his disciples came and took
the body and buried it; and they went and told
Jesus.**

The death of John is related not for its own sake but because of its bearing on the actions of Jesus and as foreshadowing Jesus' fate. Even the story of John's martyrdom is made to serve the Gospel's primary interest in Jesus. The ***fame of Jesus*** reminded Herod Antipas, tetrarch of Galilee and Perea (4 B.C. to A.D. 39), of John the Baptist. The parallel was in their prophetic message, for John did no miracles (John 10:41). Herod may have believed that John had literally arisen from the dead, but probably he meant that Jesus' prophetic message was like hearing John once more.

The execution of John by Herod Antipas (son of Herod the Great and his Samaritan wife Malthace) is related by Josephus (*Antiq.* XVIII:5) as well as by Mark (6:14–29) Luke (9:7–9) and Matthew. At insignificant points, no one has been able to correlate fully these accounts. Chief difficulty arises in connection with the relationship between Herodias and Herod Philip.

Josephus says only that Herod Antipas married the wife of his brother Herod. Mark and Matthew call him Philip, although some important manuscripts do not have the name Philip in Matthew 14:3. Josephus has it that Salome, daughter of Herodias, married Philip, half-brother to Antipas.

This much, at least, is clear from all accounts. Herod Antipas married Herodias, the wife of one of his brothers, and later he executed John the Baptist (at Machaerus, near the Dead Sea, according to Josephus). Antipas' first wife was the daughter of Aretas, king of Nabataea. On a visit to Rome, he fell in love with Herodias, wife of his brother (Philip according to Mark; Boethus elsewhere). He divorced his first wife and married his brother's wife, contrary to Jewish law (Lev. 18:16; 20:21).

John condemned the king's adulterous marriage and did so to his face. Possibly Antipas had summoned John to appear before him, thinking that he might then back down from what he had been saying (tense in v. 4 indicates repeated charges). John did not waver. Antipas wanted to kill John but feared the people. Josephus (XVIII, 5.2) wrote that Antipas wanted to kill John because he feared that John would instigate a revolt. Antipas could have feared both to let John live and to execute him.

At a birthday celebration, probably after heavy drinking and watching a seductive dance (cf. Dietrich, p. 86), Herod under oath made a rash promise to the daughter of Herodias. When the demand came from mother and daughter that they be given the head of John on a ***platter*** (i.e., dish from the table), he found himself trapped. Filled with fear and suspicions, he regretted an oath made in the presence of his guests. Herod's fears were many. He feared John; he feared the people who saw John as a prophet; he feared to break his unholy oath; he feared to back down before his guests; and he feared his scheming wife Herodias (Filson, p. 169). The weak king kept his oath and had John beheaded, although Jewish law prohibited the execution of a man without a trial and did not permit beheading. Herod followed Roman custom, not Jewish. Memories of John continued to haunt the old king.

Historical and inconsequential problems and gory details about actions of the Herodian family should not detract us from lasting lessons from this passage: the prophetic integrity of John and Jesus under severest pressure, the sanctity of marriage which can never be compromised with impunity, and the relationship between disciple and Master in both life and death.

3. Five Thousand Fed (14:13–21)

**13 Now when Jesus heard this, he withdrew
from there in a boat to a lonely place apart.
But when the crowds heard it, they followed
him on foot from the towns. 14 As he went
ashore he saw a great throng; and he had
compassion on them, and healed their sick.
15 When it was evening, the disciples came to
him and said, "This is a lonely place, and the
day is now over; send the crowds away to go
into the villages and buy food for themselves."
16 Jesus said, "They need not go away; you
give them something to eat." 17 They said to
him, "We have only five loaves here and two
fish." 18 And he said, "Bring them here to me."
19 Then he ordered the crowds to sit down on
the grass; and taking the five loaves and the
two fish he looked up to heaven, and blessed,
and broke and gave the loaves to the disciples,
and the disciples gave them to the crowds.
20 And they all ate and were satisfied. And they
took up twelve baskets full of the broken pieces
left over. 21 And those who ate were about five
thousand men, besides women and children.**

This is the only miracle story appearing in all four Gospels (cf. Mark 6:35–44; Luke 9:10–17; John 6:1–14). Mark (8:1–9) and Matthew (15:32–38) also have a similar story about the feeding of four thousand people. That Jesus fed the multitudes was of primary importance to early Christians. This is attested by the fact that these stories are so deeply embedded in the tradition and so often told. For John's Gospel, this is a major sign, followed by an extended discourse on Jesus as the Bread of life (6:1–71).

The ***compassion*** of Jesus for hungry people is the most obvious concern behind the miracle and its report. Although Jesus refused to use miracle power to satisfy his own hunger (4:2–4), he was actively concerned for the material and physical needs of other people. Whatever else this miracle may imply, this compassion of Jesus may not be obscured without grave injustice to the intention of the story.

The nature miracles are more difficult for the modern mind than are the healing miracles, for psychological factors are ruled out. The basic question with respect to nature miracles does not have to do with God's power for such miracles. Faith can put no limit on God's power. The more difficult question has to do with the incarnation.

A question often raised is, "Do such miracles imply that the Word did not really become flesh?" Two observations may be made in reply. First, the mystery of the incarnation is beyond explanation. Christian faith may simply affirm, not explain him who was fully man and yet "God with us." Secondly, Jesus' employment of powers beyond those otherwise known to be human were for the sake of other people, not to escape the limits of incarnation for himself.

The meaning of the feeding of the five thousand goes beyond the ***compassion*** of Jesus, basic as that is. Clear indication of the symbolism found in the miracle is found in Mark 6:52; 8:17–21; and in Matthew 16:8–11. In the Gospel of John (6:1–71) this is made primary in the discourse on Jesus as the Bread of life. Just as Jesus gave material bread for the body, so he came to impart the higher bread for life eternal.

In Matthew, as in the other Gospels, language suggestive of the Lord's Supper is employed. The words ***taking, blessed, broke,*** and ***gave*** belong also to the language of the Lord's Supper. Although there may be some hint in Matthew, and a stronger one in John, of the Lord's Supper and the "eschatological banquet" beyond that, this has been greatly exaggerated in New Testament study. The Synoptics do not put the emphasis there, and it is highly questionable that John does. All Jewish meals were sacred, and the terms taking, blessed, broke, and gave are normal ones for a host at any Jewish meal.

When Jesus said that one must "eat the flesh of the Son of man and drink his blood," the disciples found this to be "a hard saying" and many "drew back and no longer went about with him" (John 6:53,60,66). They were not turned back by the requirement that they eat the Lord's Supper or the messianic banquet! It was the cross from which they shrank. The "Eucharist" is not to be read into John 6 and then read back from John into Matthew 14:13–21.

Twelve baskets full of the broken pieces stress the abundance of food provided by Jesus. Twelve probably reflects the serving of the multitude by the twelve apostles, each with a basket. After all were served, each basket was yet full. Another possibility is that no baskets were actually used, but the quantity of bread remaining was equal to twelve baskets full. The ***broken pieces*** were not scraps left over from eating but the pieces which fell from the hands of Jesus as he broke the loaves.

4. Peter Rescued from Storm (14:22–33)

**22 Then he made the disciples get into the
boat and go before him to the other side, while
he dismissed the crowds. 23 And after he had
dismissed the crowds, he went up into the hills
by himself to pray. When evening came, he
was there alone, 24 but the boat by this time
was many furlongs distant from the land,
beaten by the waves; for the wind was against
them. 25 And in the fourth watch of the night
he came to them, walking on the sea. 26 But
when the disciples saw him walking on the sea,
they were terrified, saying, "It is a ghost!" And
they cried out for fear. 27 But immediately he
spoke to them, saying, "Take heart, it is I; have
no fear."**

**28 And Peter answered him, "Lord, if it is
you, bid me come to you on the water." 29 He
said, "Come." So Peter got out of the boat and
walked on the water and came to Jesus; 30 but
when he saw the wind, he was afraid, and
beginning to sink he cried out, "Lord, save
me." 31 Jesus immediately reached out his hand
and caught him, saying to him, "O man of little
faith, why did you doubt?" 32 And when they
got into the boat, the wind ceased. 33 And those
in the boat worshiped him, saying, "Truly you
are the Son of God."**

Only John tells of the abortive effort of the disciples to take Jesus "by force to make him king" (6:15), but Matthew reflects this in saying that Jesus ***made the disciples get into the boat*** and precede him to the other side of the lake (Galilee), while he ***dismissed the crowds.*** Apparently the crowds found in the miraculous feeding encouragement to believe that Jesus would become their national deliverer—Messiah in a political sense. Since the feeding took place as the Passover was at hand (John 6:4), the annual celebration of deliverance from Egypt, hopes for a new deliverance from Rome would be high. It appears that the twelve were encouraging the crowds to press their claims upon Jesus. This is why he first had to force them into the boat, to get them away from the crowds, whom he then dispersed. Misunderstood by the crowds and the twelve, Jesus then ***went up into the hills by himself to pray.***[36]

The fact that the disciples were caught in the middle of the lake in a storm during the ***fourth watch of the night*** (by Roman time, 3:00–6:00 A.M.), suggests that they lingered long near the scene of the miracle before starting to row across the lake. This may imply that they were upset by Jesus' refusal to become "king." The lake was about four and a half miles wide.

The disciples' ***fear*** and Peter's rash request, subsequent fear, and ***little faith*** are not complimentary. This picture of the weakness of the disciples and even of Peter underscores the integrity of the Gospels. The apostles, and in particular Peter, are esteemed, yet the accounts do not obscure their failures and faults. Jesus was ***worshiped*** as ***the Son of God.*** In Matthew this title articulates the highest faith of the disciples (cf. 16:16) and is used by Jesus for himself (26:63 f.; cf. 11:27; 24:36). Although perfection is the demand upon all (5:48), it is found alone in Jesus. ***It is I*** (*egō eimi*) is the same Greek expression so often used for deity (Ex. 3:14; John 6:35; 8:12,58; *et al.*).

[36] Cf. William Hersey Davis, *Davis' Notes on Matthew* (Nashville: Broadman, 1962), pp. 59 f.

Matthew's intention is to describe a miracle or a cluster of miracles: Jesus' walking on the water, Peter's walking on the water, and the calming of the storm. ***Walking on the sea*** is not to be explained as walking on the shore near the sea. It is true that the Greek phrase employed in verse 26 (*epi tēs thalassēs*) could of itself refer to Jesus' walking by or at the edge of the sea, but evidence otherwise is far too strong to allow this interpretation. The whole story and its many details imply something other than mere walking on the shore. One may believe or disbelieve the story, but competent exegesis cannot explain it away as intended to be understood as other than a miracle.

From earliest times the church has drawn from this story the lesson that Christ comes to his people in the storms of life to deliver them. Matthew seems to have had a collection of stories about Peter. They show his weaknesses and recovery. The "Rock" was not rocklike, yet he was Christ's, as are all who accept his care. Matthew does not mean to teach that failure does not matter, but that Christ does not fail even those who fail him. This is in keeping with the position strongly taken throughout this Gospel, that salvation is gift and demand, grace and law at the same time.

5. *Multitudes Seek to Be Cured (14:34–36)*

34 And when they had crossed over, they came to land at Gennesaret. 35 And when the men of that place recognized him, they sent round to all that region and brought to him all that were sick, 36 and besought him that they might only touch the fringe of his garment; and as many as touched it were made well.

Gennesaret was a fertile plain northwest of Lake Galilee, between Capernaum and Tiberias. Sometimes the lake was called by this name (Luke 5:1). This paragraph reflects the great popularity of Jesus with the crowds. It also shows the patience of Jesus with the common people, even though their interests were often secondary, physical and material, and though their faith sometimes bordered on superstition, as in thinking that to ***touch the fringe of his garment*** would put them in touch with his power. Jesus was concerned for their physical and material needs, even though he taught that "man does not live by bread alone" (4:4). ***Made well*** (*diesōthēsan*) could be translated "saved." The same word is used for "saving" at all levels, physical and spiritual.

IX. Conflict with Pharisees, Scribes, Sadducees (15:1—16:12)

If anything emerges with clarity from the Gospels, it is that Jesus lived within Judaism with true piety and at the same time maintained freedom to differ radically with its strongest leaders and exponents. Critical scholarship today is nowhere more convinced by clear Gospel teaching than that Jesus was characterized by deep piety and at the same time was considered a dangerous liberal by the religious world to which he belonged.[37] This was a major factor in the Pharisaic determination to have him put to death. Jesus did live in freedom and independence of religious customs for which many were prepared to give life or take life.

A gulf separating Jesus from both the Pharisaic laymen and the Sadducean priests became increasingly apparent as by word, deed, and manner of life Jesus made clear his intention. He differed with both Pharisees and Sadducees, but for different reasons. His conflict with the Pharisees was basically over the ritual law, which for the Pharisees distinguished between Jews and non-Jews and even between the "righteous" and "sinners" within Judaism. In the passage before us may be seen Jesus' rejection of the Pharisaic basis for these distinctions. The Sadducees opposed Jesus because of his stand with respect to the Temple and because they thought Jesus would disturb their comfortable alliance with Rome. Matthew is not greatly interested in pursuing the difference between Pharisees and Sadducees. He tends to combine them as the leaders of Israel, those chiefly responsible for Israel's rejection of Jesus and the nation's fall (cf. 3:7; 16:1,6,11,12; 18:6).

1. Jesus Challenges Tradition (15:1–20)

**1 Then Pharisees and scribes came to Jesus
from Jerusalem and said, 2 "Why do your disciples transgress the tradition of the elders? For
they do not wash their hands when they eat."
3 He answered them, "And why do you transgress the commandment of God for the sake of
your tradition? 4 For God commanded, 'Honor
your father and your mother,' and, 'He who
speaks evil of father or mother, let him surely
die.' 5 But you say, 'If any one tells his father
or his mother, What you would have gained
from me is given to God, he need not honor his
father.' 6 So, for the sake of your tradition, you
have made void the word of God. 7 You hypocrites! Well did Isaiah prophesy of you, when
he said:**

8 'This people honors me with their lips,
but their heart is far from me;
9 in vain do they worship me,
teaching as doctrines the precepts of men.'"

**10 And he called the people to him and said
to them, "Hear and understand: 11 not what
goes into the mouth defiles a man, but what
comes out of the mouth, this defiles a man."
12 Then the disciples came and said to him,
"Do you know that the Pharisees were offended when they heard this saying?" 13 He
answered, "Every plant which my heavenly
Father has not planted will be rooted up. 14 Let
them alone; they are blind guides. And if a
blind man leads a blind man, both will fall into
a pit." 15 But Peter said to him, "Explain the
parable to us." 16 And he said, "Are you also
still without understanding? 17 Do you not see
that whatever goes into the mouth passes into
the stomach, and so passes on? 18 But what
comes out of the mouth proceeds from the
heart, and this defiles a man. 19 For out of the
heart come evil thoughts, murder, adultery,
fornication, theft, false witness, slander.
20 These are what defile a man; but to eat with
unwashed hands does not defile a man."**

The tradition of the elders was the Jewish oral tradition which ultimately formed the Talmud. The tradition was a body of material which grew through many generations, being transmitted orally from one generation to another, each generation adding to it. This material represented rabbinical interpretation of the Torah, oldest part of the Old Testament, and its application to all aspects of life. Between A.D. 70 and

[37] Ernst Käsemann, *Der Ruf der Freiheit* (Tübingen: Mohr, 1968), pp. 29, 33 f.

around 200 there were several collections of this tradition, all built around six major subjects, called orders. The one ascribed to Judah the Patriarch prevailed. This was known as the Mishnah, or second law. By the sixth century this had been extended in Babylon to include the Gemara, commentaries on the Mishnah. Together, the Mishnah and Gemara constituted the Talmud. Another Gemara was produced in Palestine, but it was never completed.

The Pharisees gave the oral tradition a value as great as that of the written Law. They held that Moses received the oral law at Mount Sinai and passed it on to the prophets, who in turn passed it down to the men of the Great Synagogue (*Pirke Aboth* 1:1). Thus they gave Mosaic sanction to traditions which were actually under development at the time of Christ. Jesus rejected the authority of this oral tradition and thus alienated the Pharisees.

The issue of washing hands before eating was one of ritual concern rather than hygiene. This was not required by the Old Testament, but the Pharisees considered it a mark of piety. To touch a Gentile was one of the many ways one could become ritually unclean, in their teaching. Jesus rejected outright this ritual distinction between clean and unclean. The term ***defile*** (*koinoi*) was used by Jews to designate one as "common," i.e., ritually disqualified for religious acts.

Jesus charged the Pharisees with elevating their tradition above ***the commandment of God,*** by which he meant the Scriptures. Jesus reversed this, recognizing the authority of the Scriptures but rejecting the oral tradition. He exposed their tendency to elevate tradition above Scripture, giving as example their failure to observe the intention of the fifth of the Ten Commandments (cf. Ex. 20:12; 21:17). He illustrated the point by citing their rule known as "corban," Aramaic for ***given to God.*** According to this rule, if one said corban with respect to his property, it was thus dedicated to God. This could result in a son's inability to help his parents, and it offered a selfish son an escape from helping a needy parent.

Although by the end of the first century the rabbis ruled that one was not required to keep a vow if it conflicted with his duty to his parents (*Nedarim* 9:1), this practice was current in the time of Jesus. But Jesus refused to put religion above man. Religion is not to be confused with God. The practice of corban dishonored God as well as man. This was "lip service" to God, as denounced by Isaiah (29:13). ***Precepts of men*** is made to apply here to the Jewish oral tradition, although Matthew does not make it so explicit as Mark's "tradition of men" (7:8).

Jesus not only rejected the authority of the oral tradition in favor of the Scriptures, but he introduced a far-reaching principle for interpreting the Scriptures. He recognized the authority of the Scriptures as ***the commandment of God,*** but he stressed the intention of the Law, not the letter of the Law. Jesus showed an independence of the Law but with a different result from that of the scribes. His concern was to fulfil it, bring its intention to realization, not to empty it or obscure it. He did not stop with repudiating the Pharisaic rule about unwashed hands, but he swept away the whole idea that moral defilement or cleansing was dependent upon any form of legalism. He rejected the idea that evil is in nature or things, tracing the root of evil to the human heart (Schlatter, p. 239). He appealed to this as something which man ought to ***see*** (v. 17), not as something belonging to hidden or esoteric wisdom.

In declaring defilement to be a condition of the heart rather than the result of ***what goes into the mouth,*** Jesus repudiated much of the foundation of Pharisaic Judaism (cf. Rom. 14:14; Titus 1:15). Jesus found the fountain of evil in ***the heart*** of man, out of which come evil thoughts, impulses, and feelings which can become outwardly expressed as ***murder, adultery, fornication, theft, false witness, slander*** (this modeled after the Ten Commandments). He refused to find evil in terms of ritual concerns, as eating with ***unwashed hands.*** He categorically denied that an act of eating or drinking is as such an evil thing. He described it as a physiological process (v. 17). He even went behind all outward action to find the origin of evil, tracing it to the intention or condition of the inner self (cf. 5:8). Heart includes feeling and thinking in biblical usage.

Matthew leaves no doubt about the wide gulf between Jesus and the Pharisees with respect to the relative authority of the Scriptures and the oral tradition and also with respect to the nature of evil. Even so, Matthew does not include Mark's most forceful statement, "Thus he declared all foods clean" (7:19). Matthew is sometimes charged with being overly harsh with the Pharisees, but in this section, he twice softens Mark's stronger language (omitting Mark 7:8,19). Matthew does show the basic conflict between Jesus and the Pharisees, but he did not make the gulf between Jesus and the Pharisees greater than it was. In fact, from the earliest disciples until today, it has been difficult for any followers of Jesus to accept him in the full force of his rebellion against ***the precepts of man.*** This is said reverently, but in his break with established religious beliefs and practices, Jesus was more radical than any of his followers have been. Even the disciples were frightened, and Peter found Jesus' teaching to be puzzling (vv. 12,15). Peter and the other disciples were ***still without understanding.*** We all tend to "water down" or explain away his teaching. Do we not today tend to tone down such far-reaching statements as ***not what goes into the mouth defiles a man, but what comes out of the mouth?*** Do we not hedge at his teaching, ***For out of the heart come evil . . . ,*** choosing rather to center it in more outward things?

By ***every plant*** not planted by God, Jesus' immediate reference may have been to the oral tradition, as illustrated by the ritual law about washing hands. Of course, the principle relates to any of our religious laws, practices, or teachings which contradict God's commandments. ***Plant*** is a familiar biblical figure for God's people. Here it could refer to the Pharisees as those who consider themselves to be the "core" of God's community (Schniewind, *op. cit.*, p. 183; McNiele, *op. cit.*, p. 227). The ***blind guides*** against whom he warned were religious leaders who considered themselves the authorities in interpreting God's law. The blindness which he declared would cause leaders and followers to ***fall into a pit*** was the religious blindness best termed legalism. This legalism was not simply that of some village extremists. The battle was joined between Jesus and ***Pharisees and scribes*** who came ***from Jerusalem.***

2. *A Canaanite Woman's Faith (15:21–28)*

21 And Jesus went away from there and with-
drew to the district of Tyre and Sidon. 22 And
behold, a Canaanite woman from that region came out and cried, "Have mercy on me, O Lord, Son of David; my daughter is severely possessed by a demon." 23 But he did not an-
swer her a word. And his disciples came and begged him, saying, "Send her away, for she is crying after us." 24 He answered, "I was sent only to the lost sheep of the house of Israel."
25 But she came and knelt before him, saying, "Lord, help me." 26 And he answered, "It is not fair to take the children's bread and throw it to the dogs." 27 She said, "Yes, Lord, yet even the dogs eat the crumbs that fall from their master's table." 28 Then Jesus answered her, "O woman, great is your faith! Be it done for you as you desire." And her daughter was healed instantly.

It is striking that this story follows the account of Jesus' rejection of external tests for what is clean or unclean. On the surface, this story of at least a momentary rejection of a Canaanite woman on the basis of her being non-Jewish seems to contradict the principle just given, namely, that the condition of the heart, not externals, determines whether one is defiled or not. The story is also in seeming conflict with the Great Commission with which the Gospel closes (28:19).

Matthew even more than Mark points up wide differences which are finally overcome. ***Canaanite*** is almost archaic (Mark 7:26 identifies the woman by language as "a Greek" and by birth as "a Syrophoenician"). Canaan was the name of the heathen land given to Israel. This story places side by side the claims of a ***Canaanite woman*** and ***the lost sheep of the house of Israel.*** Wide differences also appear in the comparison of ***the children*** and ***the dogs.*** The latter is not so harsh in Greek as in English and is not necessarily a term of contempt, for the diminutive term is used for dogs, possibly referring to the children's pets. So children and "little dogs" are related as well as distinguished. The Canaanite woman does not contest Jesus' mission to the lost sheep of the house of Israel, and she it is who observes that the dogs eat the crumbs falling from ***their master's table*** (Mark has it that the little dogs under the table eat "the children's crumbs," as though the children fed them). How are these problems to be resolved?

First, it may be observed that Jesus did not turn his back on the Jewish people, even as he rejected Pharisaic legalism and brought his people under heavy judgment. His mission was to ***the lost sheep of the house of Israel.*** He went to Israel not to reward righteous people but to rescue lost people. Had Jesus turned from the Jews and gone at once to the Gentiles, this would almost certainly have closed all doors between himself and the Jews. The larger world was from the first included in his mission, even as the nations were included in God's covenant with Abraham. But there were important reasons for offering himself "to the Jew first" and then to the Gentiles (Rom. 1:16). The Jews were best prepared to receive and understand him; they could have received him and shared him with the world; and there were no major barriers to Gentiles' accepting from Jews a Jewish Saviour.

It may be observed further, that in offering himself first to the Jews, Jesus did so in a way which repudiated the basic distinction between Jew and non-Jew. This follows from the section just studied. Jesus kept faith with a certain (chronological) priority to the Jews, "to the Jew first." But he did so in such a way as to discount ultimate distinctions between Jew and non-Jew. ***The Canaanite woman*** and ***Israel*** at first appear to be poles apart, but they actually are brought together in the story. The ***lost sheep*** of ***Israel*** and the ***Canaanite*** crying for ***help*** are joined together in their common need. "Israel" and "Canaan" have one hope for union—the confession of their lack, their need.

There are at least three different approaches to the problem of Jesus' response to the Canaanite woman. He may have been testing her faith, compelling her to put aside her non-Jewish pride or prejudice. The fact that she hailed him as ***Son of David*** seems either to rule out any such problem in her or to show that in her great need she bridged the gap between Jew and non-Jew. It was her ***great faith*** which deeply moved Jesus. Her faith, like that of the centurion (8:10), stood out in contrast to its lack in Israel.

A second possibility is that Jesus took this means of instructing the disciples. They showed impatience with the woman and ***begged*** Jesus to ***send her away,*** for her crying bothered them. Whether or not they meant for Jesus first to heal her is not clear. Jesus may have assumed their position only to repudiate it as a rebuke to them and to point them to a better attitude.

A third and more difficult approach is one which finds a struggle within Jesus himself. His great compassion for all people is too well established to be overlooked, even as we hear such seemingly harsh words as, it is not ***fair*** (*kalon* means fitting) to give ***children's bread*** to ***dogs*** (or "little dogs"). Was it that Jesus struggled between his desire to give himself at once to the larger world and his purpose to give his own people every opportunity to receive him? To have turned from the Jews would have been to seal their fate, and the Gentiles did not have the background of preparation to receive and proclaim him most meaningfully. To this day, we read a Jewish New Testament (with the possible exception of Luke–Acts). They were Jews who first received, best understood, and proclaimed him.

Matthew shows that Jesus did not reject his nation, although it ultimately rejected him. He also shows that Jesus offered himself to the Jews on a basis which discredited any essential difference between Jew and non-Jew. The risen Lord commissioned his disciples to bring all nations into discipleship. Whatever the hesitation and words of Jesus may imply, the fact remains that he did commend the woman and heal her daughter. Israel denied him, but he did not deny Israel. From his bread he fed both the children and the "little dogs" (Schlatter, *op. cit.*, p. 245).

Although the restriction to Israel in this passage and 10:5 f. seems to be the very opposite to the world commission of 28:19, they are correlated in Matthew's Gospel. Those commissioned to make disciples of all nations have solid ground under their feet. Jesus did keep faith with Israel, and Israel's rejection of Jesus could not be excused on the grounds of an early Gentile mission. A Gentile church could proclaim as Christ one who was "son of David, son of Abraham," and who had kept faith with his people (cf. Hummel, p. 138).

3. *Multitudes Healed and Fed (15:29–39)*

29 And Jesus went on from there and passed
along the Sea of Galilee. And he went up into
the hills, and sat down there. 30 And great
crowds came to him, bringing with them the
lame, the maimed, the blind, the dumb, and
many others, and they put them at his feet, and
he healed them, 31 so that the throng wondered,
when they saw the dumb speaking, the maimed
whole, the lame walking, and the blind seeing;
and they glorified the God of Israel.
32 Then Jesus called his disciples to him and
said, "I have compassion on the crowd, be-
cause they have been with me now three days,
and have nothing to eat; and I am unwilling to
send them away hungry, lest they faint on the
way." 33 And the disciples said to him, "Where
are we to get bread enough in the desert to feed
so great a crowd?" 34 And Jesus said to them,
"How many loaves have you?" They said,
"Seven, and a few small fish." 35 And com-
manding the crowd to sit down on the ground,
36 he took the seven loaves and the fish, and
having given thanks he broke them and gave
them to the disciples, and the disciples gave
them to the crowds. 37 And they all ate and
were satisfied; and they took up seven baskets
full of the broken pieces left over. 38 Those
who ate were four thousand men, besides
women and children. 39 And sending away the
crowds, he got into the boat and went to the
region of Magadan.

Paralleling Mark's account of the healing of a deaf mute (7:31–37), Matthew gives a general summary statement, describing a healing ministry to the multitudes somewhere near the Sea of Galilee. Presumably, this ministry was to Gentiles as was the feeding of the four thousand. The crowds praised ***the God of Israel.*** This could refer to praise offered by Jews, but it probably is Gentile praise of the God of Israel.

The feeding of the ***four thousand men*** is set forth as a ministry of ***compassion.*** Jesus was unwilling to send away hungry people, ***lest they faint.*** Some see this as a variant or doublet for the feeding of the five thousand. Both Matthew and Mark see the two feedings as distinct (16:9 f.; Mark 8:18–20). In many details the stories differ: number of loaves and fish, kinds of baskets (*sphuris*, a fisherman's flexible mat basket for carrying fish or fruit, is used here), and the number fed.

Probably the four thousand were Gentiles, the five thousand having been Jews. If so, this is a Gentile ministry paralleling that to the Jews. This would trace back to Jesus a concern for the larger world, even though he concentrated his ministry upon "the lost sheep of the house of Israel."

Matthew has Magadan where Mark has "Dalmanutha" (8:10). Each refers to the ***region*** of the city named, not to the city itself. Neither city has been identified. Some late manuscripts have "Magdala," a well-known town on the western side of the lake. Whatever the town, the region of which he entered, the feeding of the four thousand had been on the eastern side, possibly in the Gentile Decapolis (cf. Mark 7:31). The locality of the two feedings was practically the same, but the five thousand were Galileans who were following Jesus.

4. *Disciples Warned Against "Leaven" of Pharisees and Sadducees (16:1–12)*

1 And the Pharisees and Sadducees came, and to test him they asked him to show them a sign from heaven. 2 He answered them, "When it is evening, you say, 'It will be fair weather; for the sky is red.' 3 And in the morning, 'It will be stormy today, for the sky is red and threatening.' You know how to interpret the appearance of the sky, but you cannot interpret the signs of the times. 4 An evil and adulterous generation seeks for a sign, but no sign shall be given to it except the sign of Jonah." So he left them and departed.

5 When the disciples reached the other side, they had forgotten to bring any bread. 6 Jesus said to them, "Take heed and beware of the leaven of the Pharisees and Sadducees." 7 And they discussed it among themselves, saying, "We brought no bread." 8 But Jesus, aware of this, said, "O men of little faith, why do you discuss among yourselves the fact that you have no bread? 9 Do you not yet perceive? Do you not remember the five loaves of the five thousand, and how many baskets you gathered? 10 Or the seven loaves of the four thousand, and how many baskets you gathered? 11 How is it that you fail to perceive that I did not speak about bread? Beware of the leaven of the Pharisees and Sadducees." 12 Then they understood that he did not tell them to beware of the leaven of bread, but of the teaching of the Pharisees and Sadducees.

Matthew joins the Pharisees and Sadducees five times (3:7; 16:1,6,11,12; 22:34). To him they represent the teachers and leaders of Israel, and he has little interest in distinguishing between them (Walker, p. 13). Mark has "Pharisees" and "Herod" (8:15) where Matthew has ***Pharisees and Sadducees.*** Mark and Luke mention the Sadducees only once each (Mark 12:18; Luke 20:27).

Verses 2*b*–3 are not found in the oldest manuscripts in Greek, Syriac, Coptic, and Armenian. They were also omitted by Origen and in manuscripts known to Jerome. These verses seem to have been added by Western type texts, apparently modeled after Luke 12:54–56. The meaning of these verses is clear enough. Men who can anticipate the weather by color of the sky or direction of the wind are strangely blind to the signs of coming judgment upon their nation. The ***signs of the times*** possibly allude to the growing influence of the Zealots, the increasing tensions with Rome, and the nation's unwillingness to hear its true deliverer. In A.D. 70 the nation, having followed its false "Messiahs," was crushed by the Romans. Textual evidence, however, weighs against the originality of these verses at this point.

The Pharisees and Sadducees, testing Jesus, asked for ***a sign from heaven.*** What they demanded of Jesus was some miracle so overpowering that it would compel faith. Jesus refused to give such a performance. The only sign he offered ***an evil and adulterous generation*** was ***the sign of Jonah.*** Adulterous is a familiar Old Testament term for unfaithfulness to God. The ***sign of Jonah*** has already been interpreted (cf.12:38–42). Jonah preached judgment and the Ninevites repented. Jesus' generation had greater privilege than the Ninevites, and they would come under heavier judgment. This warning is doubly attested in gospel tradition, being drawn from Mark and Q; and it appears not only in Mark 8:11–13 and Luke 11:29 but twice in Matthew (12:39; 16:4). It is the greatest irony of history that Jesus, who tried so hard to turn his nation from its collision course with Rome and who repeatedly rejected the role of political Messiah, was crucified under the charge of rebellion; and the nation, having followed its false "messiahs," followed its collision course to ruin.

Verses 5–12 reflect not only the threat of Pharisaic and Sadducean teaching but also the dullness of the disciples as Jesus sought to teach them. ***Leaven*** has its normal biblical symbolism here, symbolizing evil or corruption. The disciples had forgotten to take bread as they entered the boat for a lake crossing. When Jesus warned them against the ***leaven of the Pharisees and Sadducees*** they took literally what he intended to be figurative. They understood Jesus to be warning them against literal bread of thei opponents. Jesus had reference to their teaching (Luke 12:1 calls it "hypocrisy").

Verses 8–10 may give a double rebuke and warning to the disciples. They are called ***men of little faith,*** for they should have learned from the two miraculous feedings that they need not have anxiety over food. But the real emphasis falls upon the danger of the teaching of the Pharisees and Sadducees. The miracles of feeding were given not only to nourish bodies but for the teaching value of their symbolism. They were evidence that the teaching of Jesus was adequate and that they did not need the teaching of these false leaders (Johnson, p. 447).

X. *Christ, His Church, and His Cross (16:13—17:27)*

The themes belonging to this section are the central ones of the gospel: Christ, his church, and his cross. Peter's confession of Jesus as the Christ and Jesus' response with respect to the creating of his church and the cross as the way of triumph for himself and his church mark the turning point in all three Synoptics. In brief, the gospel is the proclamation of what God has done in the person of Jesus Christ, climaxed in his death and resurrection and embodied in the people whom he has created and is creating, the church.

1. *Christ and His Church (16:13–20)*

13 Now when Jesus came into the district of Caesarea Philippi, he asked his disciples, "Who do men say that the Son of man is?" 14 And they said, "Some say John the Baptist, others say Elijah, and others Jeremiah or one of the prophets." 15 He said to them, "But who do you say that I am?" 16 Simon Peter replied, "You are the Christ, the Son of the living God." 17 And Jesus answered him, "Blessed are you, Simon Bar-Jona! For flesh and blood has not revealed this to you, but my Father who is in heaven. 18 And I tell you, you are Peter, and on this rock I will build my church, and the powers of death shall not prevail against it. 19 I will give you the keys of the kingdom of heaven, and whatever you bind on earth shall be bound in heaven, and whatever you loose on earth shall be loosed in heaven." 20 Then he strictly charged the disciples to tell no one that he was the Christ.

The Christ (vv. 13–17).—The confession of Jesus as Christ took place in ***the district of Caesarea Philippi,*** not in the town itself. This is the farthest north Jesus is known to have traveled, with the possible exception of the withdrawal into the district of Tyre and Sidon (cf. 15:21). ***Caesarea Philippi*** is not to be confused with the coastal city of Caesarea. The ancient Paneas (modern Banias) was refounded by the tetrarch Herod Philip and named Caesarea in honor of the emperor Tiberius. It came to bear the double name to avoid confusion with other cities named Caesarea. It was located far above the Sea of Galilee, at one of the sources of the Jordan, and received its earlier name from the Greek god Pan.

There were many assessments of Jesus, ranging from intense fear and hatred to love and adoration. Jesus' first question brought out some of the current assessments. By many, Jesus was seen to be a prophet. Some saw him as ***John the Baptist*** brought back to life or as a second John the Baptist (cf. 14:1–2). ***Elijah*** was not only a great prophet, but he was expected to be sent before the day of judgment in a ministry of reconciliation (Mal. 4:5 f.). ***Jeremiah*** is not elsewhere identified with Jesus, and Matthew alone of the Gospels quotes him (2:17; 27:9). ***One of the prophets*** is indefinite. Some thought John the Baptist to be "the prophet," presumably the prophet of Deuteronomy 18:15 (cf. John 1:21), but that is not envisioned here.

Although Jesus was seen in the role of a prophet and accepted that designation (cf. 13:57), this term was not adequate. Jesus could not build on that alone, and he saw himself in a higher role. He saw himself above Moses, above John, and above all the prophets. This is reflected not only in what he said, but especially in the promises he made, in the demands he made (e.g., that one love him above parents, wife, or children and that one leave all to follow him), and in the very manner in which he moved among men.

Käsemann is profoundly right in saying, "The only category which does justice to his claim (quite independently of whether he used it himself and required it of others) is that in which his disciples themselves placed him—namely, that of Messiah" (*Essays,* p. 38). The "but I say to you" antitheses of the Sermon on the Mount (5:21–48); placing himself above Moses, unheard of by prophet or rabbi, by reinterpreting the law (15:10–20; Mark 7:19); and his assuming the same authority over the sabbath that God has (12:8; John 5:17) are among the evidences that Jesus saw himself as having the authority which belongs alone to God.

Comparison of the Synoptics (16:16; Mark 8:29; Luke 9:20) demonstrates that there was no one fixed, authorized formulation of Peter's confession at Caesarea Philippi. But "the Christ," "the Christ of God," and ***the Christ, the Son of the living God*** all point to the same basic recognition of who Jesus was. That basic recognition, not verbal agreement, is what is important. The very fact that among the charges made against Jesus at his trial was that of being a pretender to the Jewish throne (Johnson, p. 448) is irrefutable evidence that in his lifetime Jesus was thought of in messianic terms, however misunderstood by friend or foe. Jesus was the Christ, the one whom God anointed to rule. The term was accepted by Jesus, but it was inadequate and required better interpretation because it was variously understood by Jews and Romans.

Peter is called ***Simon Bar-Jona.*** Simon was his Jewish name. Bar-Jona is "son of Jonah." In John 1:42 he is "Simon the son of John." But Simon's understanding did not come from his earthly father or from ***flesh and blood,*** i.e., humanity. It was a revelation from God, Jesus' Heavenly Father, not a discovery of human insight (cf. 11:25–27).

The church (*vv. 18–20*).—This is probably the most controversial passage in the Bible among Christians. The very atmosphere of controversy is a major barrier to its proper interpretation. One confessional group claims far too much from the passage, and this tempts others to find too little in it. No interpreter can boast that he is without bias as he reads the passage. "Pure objectivity" is not only a false boast, but it would be an improper approach if attainable. The Bible does not open its secrets to "pure science," only to devoted faith. But the devotion of faith does require the discipline of scientific method. Chiefly, one must honestly want to hear the intention of Scripture, if it is to be heard.

Peter is a Greek noun for "rock," corresponding to the Aramaic "Cephas" (cf. John 1:42). This was a nickname given Peter by Jesus. Peter was not rock-like. He was often impulsive, unpredictable, and undependable (cf. 14:28–31; 16:22 f.; 26:33–35; 26:69–75; Gal. 2:11–14). Did Jesus call him "rock" with affectionate irony? More likely it was a name given as a promise of what he was to become, not for what he was. He became a bulwark of strength, especially under physical persecution (cf. Acts 3:11—4:22).

Peter's relation to the church is highly controversial. Some play on the word *rock* is apparent. In the Greek text, two forms appear in ***you are Peter*** [***Petros***], ***and on this rock*** [*petra*]. Both mean rock, the masculine form, *Petros,* being proper when applied to a man. The feminine form, *petra,* corresponds to the feminine form of the Aramaic *kepha.* That Jesus spoke in Aramaic rather than Greek is almost certain. Among the evidences is the parallel in John 1:42, "So you are Simon the son of John? You shall be called Cephas." As far as is known, no play on words for "rock" was possible in Aramaic, the same Aramaic word standing behind *Petros* and *petra.* The Aramaic statement would be "You are *Kepha* and upon this *kepha.*"

The antecedent to ***this rock*** upon which Christ promised to build his church cannot be demonstrated with finality. Possibilities are Peter himself, the faith of Peter, the confession of Peter, Christ himself, or a combination of factors. On the surface, the reference seems to be to Peter himself; but if he is the rock, it is strange that the impersonal ***this rock*** follows the personal ***you are.*** It is not only impossible to isolate precisely what Jesus meant but it may be pursuing the wrong course to narrow it down to one thing. In the answer to his first question, as to who men said him to be, Jesus found nothing upon which to build. In Peter's answer he found that upon which he could build his church. An ordinary man, anything but rock-like, illumined by the Spirit of God, recognized and confessed Jesus as the Christ, the Son of the living God. In contrast with those who confused Jesus with some prophet, Peter recognized him as the Christ, the Son of God. Jesus is not John, Elijah, Jeremiah, or anyone but himself. Jesus, too, accepts Peter as he is and without confusing him with any other. ***You are the Christ . . . you are Peter.*** On this Jesus can build his church, each committed to the other and each accepted by the other.

Although Peter was an individual and unique disciple and apostle, he may also be seen by Matthew as a type for early Christians. Matthew gives much attention to Peter, extending the Markan emphasis by further Petrine tradition peculiar to himself (cf. 14:28–31; 15:15; 17:24–27; 18:21), but he has no special biographical interest in Peter. He is neither pro-Petrine nor anti-Petrine. Matthew presents the positive and negative factors relating to Peter, showing not only his inconsistencies but holding him up as a type for the disciples, with all their self-contradictions, a perennial problem within the church (cf. Strecker, pp. 198–206).

The most natural understanding of the passage is to see some special importance attached to Peter (see Broadus, pp. 355–61, for this position). The New Testament clearly gives him a certain primacy. In every list of apostles, he is named first. He was always in the innermost circle around Jesus. He it was who made the confession at Caesarea Philippi. He was among those to whom the risen Christ appeared, named first by Paul (1 Cor. 15:5). He called together the company of about one hundred and twenty in Jerusalem following the ascension of Christ (Acts 1:15). He preached the sermon on the day of Pentecost (Acts 2:14).

On the other hand, there is no indication that Peter had singular authority among the twelve or among early Christians. He did not send other apostles but was sent by them (Acts 8:14). James soon emerged as the leader of the Jerusalem church (Acts 21:18). Paul could openly rebuke Peter in the church in Antioch (Gal. 2:11). There is not a shred of biblical evidence that Peter was made bishop over the whole church or that any special office was transmitted from him to another.

Although there are traditions traceable through literary and archaeological evidences which link the names of Peter and Paul with the Roman church, for Peter these do not go back earlier than the later second century; and even so, they relate both to Paul and Peter.[38] The meaning of our passage with respect to Peter has no valid reference to claims made by the Roman Church. It is unfortunate that this statement, a conclusion inescapable to competent biblical and historical study, must be made in a context of controversy.

Although Peter and all the apostles (Eph. 2:20; Rev. 21:14) were in some sense the foundation upon which the church was built, the New Testament never allows this in an absolute sense. Jesus himself is "the rock" upon which the church is built. This needs no "proof-texting." The New Testament is about Jesus, not about Peter. There could be a church without Peter, none without Christ. Peter is neither the head nor foundation of the church. Jesus founded it; it stands or falls with him; and he is yet its living Lord and head.

The ***church*** which Jesus promised to build is his church. ***Church*** translates the Greek *ekklesia,* which in turn translates the Hebrew term *qahal* in the LXX. Both Hebrew and Greek words literally designate a calling out. *Qahal* can designate Israel as a whole or assembled as a congregation, and *ekklesia* can designate the church in a universal

[38] For the best study of traditions linking Peter with Rome, cf. Oscar Cullmann, *Peter: Disciple, Apostle, Martyr,* tr. F. V. Filson (Philadelphia: Westminster, 1953).

sense or in a local assembly. In 18:17 the reference is obviously to a local assembly, met to discipline its members. In 16:18 the reference is just as clearly to the universal church. The passage would lose all validity if restricted to a local church. Jesus was not in Jerusalem and certainly not in Rome when he spoke these words. No local assembly in the region of Caesarea Philippi or Jerusalem has survived from the time of Jesus. The church of which he spoke has survived, and it is indestructible even by ***the powers of death.***

The fact that the word ***church*** appears only here and 18:17 in Matthew and not at all in the other Gospels leads some interpreters to conclude that Jesus did not intend to create the church and that this passage does not go back to Jesus. The evidence that Jesus intended to create what we know as the church goes far beyond the word church. This is but one of many terms employed in the New Testament for the people of God, traced through the Old Testament and reconstituted by Jesus. Jesus called people to himself and bound them together by bonds of trust, commitment, and love. They were bound together by a common life, task, and destiny.

Conzelmann argues not only from the rare occurrence of the word ***church*** but also that "the historical Jesus did not separate one group as a band (*Shar*) of the elect out of the Jewish people; he called the whole nation" (pp. 49 f.). He repeatedly equates church with an "organization." It is quite clear that Jesus did not "organize" a church, but he did call and create a people of God, known as the church and by other terms. Conzelmann correctly observes that Jesus had followers and that they were not organized. He is also correct in his view that "the Twelve" represented Jesus' claim upon all Israel. But this does not warrant the conclusion that Jesus did not create a church. He did seek to win all Israel, and there is no evidence that he organized anything; but there is irrefutable evidence of his primary purpose to call to himself people whose kinship to him and to one another would be one of faith and spirit, not flesh or nationality. This is the church in its primary sense. Its existence is bound up with the resurrection, without which no church is likely to have survived. But its beginnings were around "the historical Jesus," not for the first time around the risen Christ.

It is only a confusion to argue that "Jesus expected the kingdom of God . . . the church came" (Loisy). Jesus not only expected the kingdom but declared its arrival. It was not kingdom or church but both. The kingdom came in Jesus Christ, and he created the church.

Powers of death is a valid translation of what literally reads "the gates of hades." Hades (like Sheol) was a term for the realm of the dead (cf. Isa. 38:10). Jesus was soon to die, and many of his followers would suffer martyrdom. But death for Master or disciples, by crucifixion or natural causes, cannot overcome the church. Had Jesus yielded to pressures to become a political Messiah, what he would have built would have been as vulnerable as were the kingdoms of David and the Maccabees. He came to create the church under the kingdom (ruling) of God. He would build by a cross and not a sword, by giving life and not by taking it. His church would be indestructible for all time.

Otto Betz (*Was Wissen Wir von Jesus?*, p. 38) correctly finds the biblical background to this passage in Isaiah 28:15–18. Proud rulers in Jerusalem boasted that they had made "a covenant with death," and "an agreement with Sheol." They thought that they were insured against death. But God's prophet declared that this "covenant with death will be annulled" and their "agreement with Sheol will not stand." That is, they would be defeated and die. Over against this false security of the proud rulers of Jerusalem was the assurance that the Lord God was "laying in Zion for a foundation a stone, a tested stone, a precious cornerstone, of a sure foundation" (v. 16). On this foundation one could trust. This foundation would be true, for in constructing it God would make "justice the line, and righteousness the plummet" (v. 17).

This passage seems clearly to have been

in the mind of Jesus as he pointed to the creation of the church, built upon a sure foundation, and indestructible by death or Hades (Sheol). The passage in Isaiah is beautifully poetic, to be taken in all seriousness but not with crude literalism. The words attributed to Jesus also have their poetic symbolism, to be taken in all seriousness but not spoiled by crude literalism, and certainly not to be made to serve any confessional group's selfish and ambitious claims. Such promises as are contained in Isaiah 28:15–18 and Matthew 16:18–20 are fulfilled in Jesus Christ alone.

The keys of the kingdom symbolize authority. Here they are given to Peter; in 18:1 the power to bind and loose is given to all the disciples. Here the application seems to relate primarily to teaching; in chapter 18 to church discipline. ***Bind*** and ***loose*** were rabbinical terms for forbidding and permitting (cf. *Terumoth* 5:4).

Shall be bound (*estai dedemenon*) and ***shall be loosed*** (*estai lelumenon*) may not be precise translations of the Greek tenses behind them. In each case the Greek tense is a periphrastic form of the future perfect passive. Possibly they should be rendered "shall have been bound" and "shall have been loosed," although many grammarians would call this pedantic. If the force of the future perfect tense holds here, the meaning would be somewhat altered. This would suggest not that the action on earth would be ratified in heaven but that it is anticipated in heaven. In other words, earth thus follows heaven, not the reverse.

The charge that the disciples ***tell no one*** that Jesus is the Christ, is in keeping with Jesus' avoidance of the role of a popular, political king. Since Messiah was variously understood, and especially since to many Jews and Romans it carried political implications, Jesus discouraged the open use of the term. He accepted it but only as ***he*** interpreted it.

2. *Jesus Foretells Death and Resurrection (16:21–28)*

21 From that time Jesus began to show his disciples that he must go to Jerusalem and suffer many things from the elders and chief priests and scribes, and be killed, and on the third day be raised. 22 And Peter took him and began to rebuke him, saying, "God forbid, Lord! This shall never happen to you." 23 But he turned and said to Peter, "Get behind me, Satan! You are a hindrance to me; for you are not on the side of God, but of men."

24 Then Jesus told his disciples, "If any man would come after me, let him deny himself and take up his cross and follow me. 25 For whoever would save his life will lose it, and whoever loses his life for my sake will find it. 26 For what will it profit a man, if he gains the whole world and forfeits his life? Or what shall a man give in return for his life? 27 For the Son of man is to come with his angels in the glory of his Father, and then he will repay every man for what he has done. 28 Truly, I say to you, there are some standing here who will not taste death before they see the Son of man coming in his kingdom."

The question raised and answered at Caesarea Philippi had to do with the identity of Jesus. Having accepted the disciples' confession of him as the Christ, Jesus moved next to indicate the way which was his and theirs to follow. Matthew records that Jesus thrice declared that it would be the way of the cross, the way of utter self-denial and self-giving (cf. also 17:22 f.; 20:18 f.). The deepest paradox of the gospel is set forth here. One saves life only by losing it. He lives only by dying. The only true triumph is through the cross. Paradoxically, the cross is a way of death, but it is for Jesus and his followers the way of life through death.

Jesus began to show that his going to Jerusalem to suffer and die was something that he must do. It was a necessity within freedom, not from outward compulsion but inner. Moved by redeeming love, this was something that he "had to do." It was not an inescapable fate, for the door of escape remained open to the last (cf. 26:53), but his complete devotion to human need and to the Father's will drove him onward to the cross and the glory beyond.[39]

Jesus saw ***Jerusalem,*** the center of the Jewish world, as the city where he must offer himself to his nation. There he would

39 Cf. Eduard Lohse, *Die Geschichte des Leidens und Sterbens Jesu Christi* (2d ed.; Gütersloh: Mohn, 1967), p. 27.

call his nation to decision. It must receive or reject him. This was not a fate imposed upon his nation. The offering of himself was a real offer. But Jesus foresaw for himself rejection and execution at the hands of the leaders of Israel. By ***the elders and chief priests and scribes*** is meant the Sanhedrin. This body of priests and laymen would have him put to death. But Jesus saw not death but life as the last word. ***On the third day*** he would be ***raised*** from the dead. Matthew's "on the third day" and Mark's "after three days" were understood to mean the same thing. (Cf. Deut. 15:12, "in the seventh year" and the Hebrew text of Jer. 34:14, "at the end of six years.")

Peter spoke for the group in refusing to consider the suffering and death as the lot of the Messiah. They shared the Jewish expectation that the Messiah would defeat the enemies of Israel and restore the kingdom to Israel (cf. Acts 1:6). Peter presumed to correct Jesus for what to him was unnecessary pessimism and a contradiction of accepted ideas of the Messiah. ***Took him*** (*proslabontes*) may describe an action in which Peter drew Jesus aside or drew Jesus to himself, implying intention to offer protection or even protective custody. ***God forbid*** translates what literally is "[God] be merciful to you." Possibly Peter meant, "May God be merciful to you for saying such a thing" (cf. Filson, p. 188).

Jesus found it necessary to rebuke Peter more severely than Peter had rebuked him. Having earlier attributed Peter's confession to divine revelation, he now brands Peter's protest as Satanic. The Aramaic behind the Greek words rendered ***Get behind me*** could mean "Get back" or "Get away" (Robinson, p. 143). Probably Jesus felt the force of the wilderness temptations come to expression again in Peter's contention for a Messiah without suffering and death. Peter was wrong, and Jesus again had to put behind him this suggestion of political messiahship (cf. on 4:8–10). Peter's suggestion was a ***hindrance*** to Jesus, i.e., something over which to stumble (*skandalon*). The messianic goals envisioned by Peter belonged to man's purposes and not God's.

Jesus insisted upon the necessity of the way of the cross, not only for himself, but also for his followers. The cross could prove to be literal for disciples as well as Master. Whether literal or not, it represents a real way of life through "death to self" for each disciple.

That the follower of Jesus ***deny himself*** is not optional within discipleship. There is no following without this principle. To follow is to take up one's cross and deny self. Denying self is not to be confused with denying something to oneself, whether material things, pleasure, or whatever. Wicked people often deny themselves many things in order to achieve their selfish goals or conquer their enemies. Denying things to oneself may be an expression of what Jesus meant by "denying oneself," but it may be just as much a self-discipline for anti-Christian goals. Every warrior, to go no farther, disciplines himself in order to win over his opponents.

What Jesus meant by self-denial is far more radical than denying something to oneself. He meant that one must say no to oneself. He meant the opposite of Adam's yes to self and no to God. He meant a yes to God and no to oneself. All man's sin and self-destruction centers in self-love, self-trust, and self-assertion. The cross means the opposite. It means trust in God, the love of God, commitment to God, and no to self. Paradoxically this no to self is yes to the true self. One for the first time becomes what he was made to be when he denies himself.

One ***saves*** his life only when he ***loses*** it to Christ. He ***loses*** his life when he tries (selfishly) to save it. ***Life*** and ***soul*** translate the same Greek term (*psuchē*). Thus one may save himself only by losing himself. He loses himself when he tries to save himself. This is a law of life, stated in the New Testament in many ways. It was not only stated; Jesus saved his own life (self) precisely in losing it on the cross (cf. 27:41–44).

Verses 26–28 are concerned with judgment. After warning that one may lose himself in the very act of trying to save himself, Jesus then indicated how great and how irretrievable is that loss. Even should one gain ***the whole world,*** it would be worthless to one who ***forfeits his life.*** By forfeiting life, Jesus did not refer to physical death, for that comes to all. He referred to one's missing his true destiny, failing to become the self he was designed to be. For the ***return*** of his life, or in exchange for his lost selfhood, one would gladly give the world, could that be done. To state it more simply, as one pursues his goals in life, he may miss the true life which can be known alone in proper relationship with God. Could such a one live his life over, he would give the world in exchange for the life that lasts.

The Son of man was promised a kingdom both universal and everlasting (cf. Dan. 7:13 f.). Although his positive purpose is to save mankind, he also comes to judge. Judgment belongs to redemption just as surgery belongs to therapy. But judgment proves to be not redeeming but only condemnation to those who reject the rule of the Son of man. Jesus spoke of judgment as a payment; it is to "repay" (*apodosei*) each ***for what he has done,*** for his "practice" (*praxis*). One is saved as a free act of God's grace, but he is judged according to his deeds.

Jesus foretold a ***coming*** of ***the Son of man*** of his ***kingdom*** during the lifetime of some of those who heard him speak. This coming seems to relate specifically to judgment.

The limit, that this judgment would come in the lifetime of some who heard him speak, is most congenial to a fulfilment either in the events surrounding his death or to the judgment which overtook the nation in A.D. 70. The former may be more natural to the context. In his death and resurrection, Jesus triumphed and also brought man into the crisis of judgment (cf. John 3:18–21). Not to be ruled out is a reference to the destruction of Jerusalem and the nation in A.D. 70. Jesus repeatedly tried to turn the nation from its collision course with Rome. The ruin which overtook the nation as it was in the very act of trying to save itself was a real coming of the Son of man in judgment.

The most obvious reference in verses 27 f. is to the Parousia or ***coming*** of the Son of man at the end of the age (cf. 10:23), but this understanding runs into difficulties. The reference is to an event to be witnessed by contemporaries of Jesus. When Matthew wrote, almost a full generation had passed. Matthew seems elsewhere clearly to anticipate an extended period of waiting and of missionary activity throughout the world prior to the end (cf. 24:48; 25:5,19; 28:20). Then, too, he records Jesus as saying "that day and hour" were known to the Father alone (24:36).

Verses 27 f. are best understood in terms of Matthew's paraenetic or instructional interest, here heightened by its position in an eschatological context. Matthew gives us no systematic formulation or picture of the "end-time." What is assured is that the death of Jesus was not to be his defeat, for he would come again as Judge and as King! With this are both warning and encouragement to each that ***what he has done*** will soon be judged by the Son of man who will come in his kingdom. Thus Matthew's concern is not to fix a date for the Parousia, but to heighten present demands by placing them in an eschatological context.

3. *Jesus Transfigured: Revelation and Preparation for Cross (17:1–13)*

**1 And after six days Jesus took with him
Peter and James and John his brother, and led
them up a high mountain apart. 2 And he was
transfigured before them, and his face shone
like the sun, and his garments became white as
light. 3 And behold, there appeared to them
Moses and Elijah, talking with him. 4 And
Peter said to Jesus, "Lord, it is well that we are
here; if you wish, I will make three booths
here, one for you and one for Moses and one
for Elijah." 5 He was still speaking, when lo, a
bright cloud overshadowed them, and a voice
from the cloud said, "This is my beloved Son,
with whom I am well pleased; listen to him."
6 When the disciples heard this, they fell on
their faces, and were filled with awe. 7 But
Jesus came and touched them, saying, "Rise,
and have no fear." 8 And when they lifted up
their eyes, they saw no one but Jesus only.**

**9 And as they were coming down the moun-
tain, Jesus commanded them, "Tell no one the
vision, until the Son of man is raised from the**

dead." [10] And the disciples asked him, "Then
why do the scribes say that first Elijah must
come?" [11] He replied, "Elijah does come, and
he is to restore all things; [12] but I tell you that
Elijah has already come, and they did not
know him, but did to him whatever they
pleased. So also the Son of man will suffer at
their hands." [13] Then the disciples understood
that he was speaking to them of John the
Baptist.

It is now commonplace to call this a resurrection appearance read back into the life of Jesus. This is unwarranted. Matthew terms it a ***vision,*** stressing the subjective. A real experience in the lives of Jesus and his disciples is intended. That this experience was better understood by the disciples after Jesus' resurrection is to be assumed. Translation of *metamorphōthē* as "transfigured" is due to the Latin Vulgate. The word normally is rendered "transformed," as in Romans 12:2 or "changed" as in 2 Corinthians 3:18 (RSV).

That ***Peter and James and John*** formed an inner circle about Jesus is well attested (cf. 26:37; Mark 5:37; 13:3). James was an early martyr (Acts 12:2), and for a time may have been more prominent than John. The ***high mountain*** is identified by a late tradition as Tabor, but Hermon is more likely, nearer Caesarea Philippi and rising to a height of 9,100 feet.

The transfiguration of Jesus may have served to strengthen him for the ordeal ahead, but this is not explicit. The concern made explicit relates more to the needs of the disciples. They are to be reassured by the ***voice from the cloud*** that Jesus is God's ***beloved Son,*** with whom God is ***well pleased.*** Peter had just expressed displeasure over what Jesus had said about suffering and death (16:22). Peter had shown more disposition to instruct Jesus than to be instructed. He and his companions now witness an awesome glorification of Jesus and they are told to ***listen to him.***

Luke alone tells what Moses and Elijah discussed with Jesus (9:31). They spoke of his departure, literally "exodus" (*exodon*), which Jesus was "to accomplish at Jerusalem." ***Moses and Elijah*** may represent the Law and the Prophets, showing the relationship between the old and the new covenants. Possibly the important point is the triumphant manner in which each completed his life. Elijah was taken up into heaven "by a whirlwind" and presumably in a chariot of fire (2 Kings 2:11). One tradition had it that Moses had not died but ascended into heaven (cf. The Assumption of Moses in pseudepigraphical writings). The conversation about his departure would strengthen Jesus for his cross, and it was especially upon this subject that the disciples needed to ***listen to him.***

The disappearance of Moses and Elijah from the vision, leaving ***no one but Jesus only,*** serves to exalt Jesus and to emphasize the command to the disciples that they were to hear him. If Moses and Elijah typify the Law and the Prophets, the message is that Jesus is their fulfilment. He alone is sufficient. The command to tell no one of the vision until after Jesus is raised from the dead, would serve several purposes. The disciples were not yet prepared fully to interpret the vision and the people would tend to read the fulfilment of popular nationalistic hopes into it. ***Raised from the dead*** preserves the earliest way of describing the resurrection. What was stressed was not that he arose but that he was raised (Acts 2:24)

On the basis of Malachi 3:1 and 4:5, it was expected that Elijah would come before the Messiah, to prepare his way. Jesus identified Elijah with John the Baptist. Although Jesus would experience a triumphant death he also would suffer rejection and execution at the hands of wicked men, as had John. Verse 11 is unclear in saying that Elijah ***is to restore all things.*** John the Baptist, the "Elijah" who came, was killed. If punctuated as a question, less difficulty would follow: "Elijah comes, indeed; but does he restore all things?" This would recognize that the work of restoration remained for Jesus to accomplish.

4. Faith to Remove Mountains (17:14–21)

[14] And when they came to the crowd, a man
came up to him and kneeling before him said
[15] "Lord, have mercy on my son, for he is an
epileptic and he suffers terribly; for often he

**falls into the fire, and often into the water.
16 And I brought him to your disciples, and
they could not heal him." 17 And Jesus answered, "O faithless and perverse generation,
how long am I to be with you? How long am I
to bear with you? Bring him here to me."
18 And Jesus rebuked him, and the demon
came out of him, and the boy was cured
instantly. 19 Then the disciples came to Jesus
privately and said, "Why could we not cast it
out?" 20 He said to them, "Because of your
little faith. For truly, I say to you, if you have
faith as a grain of mustard seed, you will say
to this mountain, 'Move hence to yonder place,'
and it will move; and nothing will be impossible to you."**

Matthew follows Mark in making this story serve as a contrast to the transfiguration experience. Raphael, in a great painting, captured the contrast between the glory of the transfiguration upon the mountain and the suffering and frustration below. There is also the contrast between the power of Jesus and the helplessness of the disciples.

The afflicted boy is called an *epileptic* (literally, "moon-struck") and also said to have had a *demon.* This is within the New Testament itself some indication that the same malady may be described both scientifically or medically and theologically. The employment of the term *demon* implies some relationship between human ills and evil, but the relationship is not as direct as when the term Satan is employed. One's own guilt is clearly implied when his attitudes or actions are attributed to Satan. However, when one is said to be possessed of a demon, as in the case of this epileptic boy, what is stressed is not guilt but one's being overpowered or victimized by destructive forces or factors, resulting in physical and psychological (mental and emotional) disturbances.[40]

Jesus' charge that his *generation* was *faithless and perverse* reflects Deuteronomy 32:6. The disciples' failure to heal the boy was charged to their *little faith,* not to unbelief, as in the KJV. *Mustard seed* was proverbially the smallest of the seeds (cf. 13:32). The point is that any amount of faith should give one victory over ordinary limitations and conditions in life. The reference to the removing of mountains is proverbial and to be taken as a hyperbole, not in a literal sense. For the literal removal of mountains, earth-moving equipment is sufficient.

Verse 21 has wide support among the manuscripts, but it is absent from the most reliable manuscripts of the Alexandrian and Caesarean text types. It seems clearly to be an addition in Matthew. It is better attested in Mark 9:29, but even there, its originality is not certain. It shifts the emphasis from faith to prayer (and also to fasting, in an even later textual development). The absence of the verse in the best texts of Matthew and Luke may mean that it was not original to Mark.

40 Cf. Ragnar Leivestad, *Christ the Conqueror* (New York: Macmillan, 1954).

5. *Disciples Again Warned (17:22–23)*

**22 As they were gathering in Galilee, Jesus
said to them, "The Son of man is to be delivered into the hands of men, 23 and they will kill
him, and he will be raised on the third day."
And they were greatly distressed.**

Jesus seems often to have tried to prepare his disciples for his rejection and death. Matthew follows Mark in bringing this into focus three times. The first prediction followed Peter's confession of Jesus as the Christ (16:21). The second announcement was made in Galilee. The third took place as Jesus approached Jerusalem shortly before his death (20:17–19).

It seems strange that the disciples were so unprepared for Jesus' death when it came. This demonstrates the extent to which one can be tone-deaf to what he does not want to hear. Ears are to hear with, but they do not always hear (13:9; 17:5). The disciples do not yet understand, but on this second occasion they at least do not rebuke Jesus. They were greatly distressed, hearing the word about death but not resurrection.

6. *Temple Tax Paid, Rights Waived (17:24–27)*

**24 When they came to Capernaum, the
collectors of the half-shekel tax went up to
Peter and said, "Does not your teacher pay the
tax?" 25 He said, "Yes." And when he came
home, Jesus spoke to him first, saying, "What**

do you think, Simon? From whom do kings of the earth take toll or tribute? From their sons or from others?" 26 And when he said, "From others," Jesus said to him, "Then the sons are free. 27 However, not to give offense to them, go to the sea and cast a hook, and take the first fish that comes up, and when you open its mouth you will find a shekel; take that and give it to them for me and for yourself."

This story is found in Matthew only, possibly the strangest of the miracle stories. Some have made sport of it, a miracle for a shekel (roughly an American half-dollar)! A further problem arises out of the fact that Jesus normally refused to employ miracle power for his own convenience. Serious scholars have asked if this seemingly insignificant, almost bizarre, miracle may actually be attributed to Jesus.

But this fails to appreciate the great principle involved. This strange story teaches the primary principle of relinquishing personal rights where this can serve the interests of others. The point is that Jesus did what he had the right not to do. He paid a Temple tax from which he was rightfully exempt.

The ***half-shekel tax*** (one-third shekel according to Neh. 10:32) was a Temple tax, to be paid annually, six weeks before Passover, by every male Jew "from twenty years old and upward" (Ex. 30:11–16). When Matthew wrote, the Temple tax was paid to Rome, not Jerusalem, and could serve to warn against refusal to pay a tax to the Romans; but in its earlier application it exhorted Christians not so to use their freedom as to offend the Jews (Hare, p. 142). The tax collectors asked Peter if his ***teacher*** did not ***pay the tax,*** wording the question so as to expect an affirmative answer. Peter impulsively answered for Jesus, possibly expecting later to clear the matter with Jesus.

In the house later (the home of Jesus, Peter, or some other), ***Jesus spoke to him first,*** i.e., anticipated (*prosephthasen*) him. Jesus established the point that the ***sons*** of kings ***are free*** from ***toll or tribute,*** these taxes being levied upon ***others,*** i.e., aliens. ***Toll*** (*telē*) refers to local taxes or customs, and ***tribute*** (*kēnsos*) was a poll-tax or "head" tax. As the Son of God, Jesus declared his freedom from the Temple tax. None the less, he paid the tax, lest ***offense*** be given others. This willingness to relinquish personal rights in the interest of others is basic to the way of Christ (cf. 1 Cor. 8:13; 9:12: 10:28). The human family never moves ahead significantly to more meaningful life except where someone is willing to surrender personal rights for the good of others. This principle found its ultimate expression in Jesus Christ, especially in his cross.

The resort to a miracle (it seems to be implied yet not actually declared or described) may have been designed as an immediate demonstration to support Jesus' claims that he was indeed the Son to whom the Temple belonged and who thus was exempt from paying its tax. Its purpose was not to serve personal convenience but to set the stage for driving home a basic principle. To sum it up, Jesus declared his unique sonship, his freedom from the Temple tax (with the implication of his freedom and that of his disciples from the temple itself) and his willingness to pay the tax in consideration of others. Especially does the passage keep in balance two cardinal principles: (1) the freedom of Jesus and his followers from the Temple and from Jewish law and (2) the concern for others as limiting one's freedom. One may say that one's faith makes him free and his love sets the limits within which that freedom is to be exercised.

XI. Instructions for the Church (18:1–35)

Here begins the fourth of Matthew's five major discourse sections (cf. 5—7; 10; 13; 18; 24—25). This collection of sayings is built around the theme of the relationship of disciples to one another within the church (Lau, p. 134). Proud ambition is rejected in favor of humble service.

Acceptance of Christ's people is a basic test of discipleship. To cause another to fail, whether through the bad example of proud ambition, indifference, or otherwise, is a deadly sin. The importance of the "least" and the last is sufficient to lead to all-out effort at recovery of the lost. Church fellowship requires self-discipline, but the goal of discipline is salvage or recovery. Reconciliation is the business of the church. Forgiveness is bound up inseparably with forgivableness and is to know no limits.

1. *Greatness in the Kingdom* (*18:1–14*)

Mark (9:33–37) indicates that the disciples had been discussing the question of who was the greatest. After entering a house in Capernaum, possibly Peter's, Jesus asked them what they had been discussing. Their silence betrayed their realization that their interest would not please Jesus. Mark quotes Jesus as laying down the great principle in paradox, that greatness belongs to the willingness to be last and to be servant of all.

Matthew shortens Mark's treatment but preserves the essential point. He also omits Mark's (9:38–41) story of the disciples' hostility toward an exorcist who worked outside their group, with Jesus' rebuke of the disciples' prejudice against this outsider. Thus Matthew concentrates upon the threat of pride, whereas Mark treats the twin threats of pride and prejudice. Possibly Matthew's omission of Mark's story of the outsiders whom Jesus sanctioned is to be understood in terms of his concern to focus attention upon the church. His readers could have used the story to justify splinter movements.

(*1*) *Childlike Humility* (*18:1–4*)

1 At that time the disciples came to Jesus, saying, "Who is the greatest in the kingdom of heaven?" 2 And calling to him a child, he put him in the midst of them, 3 and said, "Truly, I say to you, unless you turn and become like children, you will never enter the kingdom of heaven. 4 Whoever humbles himself like this child, he is the greatest in the kingdom of heaven.

Jesus answered the disciples' question about greatness by means of an acted parable, placing a child in their midst. He first jolted their interest in greatness in the kingdom by affirming that unless they had a different spirit they would not even *enter* the kingdom. They must ***turn*** (*straphēte*) ***and become like children.***

Two familiar analogies are employed here: conversion and renewal. Turn is the idea of conversion, a reversal of life's basic attitudes and course. Concern for personal greatness is the direct opposite of the concern of true discipleship. It is also the opposite of the submission required by the kingdom of God. As already observed, the kingdom is the rule or the ruling of God. Ambition for greatness ill suits that demand. The disciples' struggle for power or primacy among themselves also betrays their confusion of the kingdom of heaven with an earthly, political type of kingdom which provides for positions of power (cf. 20:20–28).

The requirement that those entering the kingdom ***become like children*** closely parallels the "birth from above" analogy in John 3:3. To ***enter the kingdom*** means that one must start life over, with basically new attitudes, values, trust, and commitment.

Childlikeness is made the measure of greatness within the kingdom as well as the condition of entrance. The greatest is the one who ***humbles himself.*** The child's sense of dependence, based in his awareness of his smallness, may be considered, but Jesus stresses humility as the opposite to the disciples' proud ambitions (cf. 23:12).

(*2*) *The Sin of Causing Little Ones to Stumble* (*18:5–9*)

5 "Whoever receives one such child in my name receives me; 6 but whoever causes one of these little ones who believe in me to sin, it would be better for him to have a great millstone fastened round his neck and to be drowned in the depth of the sea.

7 "Woe to the world for temptations to sin! For it is necessary that temptations come, but woe to the man by whom the temptation comes! 8 And if your hand or your foot causes you to sin, cut it off and throw it from you; it is better for you to enter life maimed or lame than with two hands or two feet to be thrown into the eternal fire. 9 And if your eye causes you to sin, pluck it out and throw it from you; it is better for you to enter life with one eye than with two eyes to be thrown into the hell of fire.

Acceptance of one another, and especially the receiving of the ***little ones,*** is a basic test of discipleship. Jesus so identified himself with the *little ones* that to receive them in his *name* is to receive him (cf. 25:40). By *little ones* Jesus meant both children and the people who are commonly overlooked, neglected, or exploited—the "little people" of the world. Comparison of verses 5, 6, 10, and 14 bears this out.

One has to consider contemporary attitudes toward children and "little people" to appreciate the attitude and teaching of Jesus. The Jews were far more considerate of children than were pagans, but even they fell short of the example of Jesus. The disciples' impatience with children stood in contrast to Jesus' openness to them (19:13–15). Little girls suffered more than boys in Jesus' world. Pagans often exposed to death unwanted girl babies. This is explicit in a first-century papyrus fragment with a letter of Hilarion to his wife Alis, instructing her about their expected child, if a boy to keep it, if a girl to let it die.[41]

In Judaism a daughter was property to be given another in a contract of marriage. Jesus lifted children as well as women, "little people," and "outsiders" to the status of precious persons who were to be accepted, cared for, and loved.

The "little people" have been neglected or exploited in every age. There were millions of slaves in Jesus' time, and even the Jewish leaders despised the *'am ha' arez*, "the people of the land" (cf. *Pirke Aboth* 2:6; John 7:49). To Jesus there were no unimportant people. *Little ones* may be his term for all his disciples.

The insistence that one receives or rejects Jesus in receiving or rejecting his people is a recurrent theme in the New Testament. One's true attitude and relationship to Jesus is reflected in that toward his people. One cannot divorce the "vertical" relationship with God from the "horizontal" relationship with one's fellowman (cf. 5:7, 23 f.; 6:14 f.; 25:40; 1 Cor. 8:12; 1 John 4:20 f.).

To cause a little one, literally, child or ordinary person, ***to sin*** (*skandalisēi* is "to stumble") is worse than to die. It would be better to be drowned in the sea than to cause a little one to go wrong. The ***great millstone*** was the upper of two millstones, so large that it had to be turned by an ass. Causes of stumbling may be varied, but the one in mind here is proud ambition such as just manifested by the disciples. Mark brings in also the poisonous effect of prejudice (9:38–41).

The inevitable ***temptations*** (*skandala*) against which Jesus warned are occasions for stumbling. In saying that these are ***necessary*** (*anagkē*), Jesus did not mean that God decrees them or that they are indispensable to us. He meant that life being as it is, one may count on the recurrent problem of temptation. Wherever life is free it is hazardous. To give man the option of good is to give him the option of evil. That does not mean that there can be no good without evil, for that is a "dualism" foreign to the Bible. It does mean that God has given us real freedom and real choices and that life is filled with pitfalls. But the warning is chiefly against causing another to stumble.

A sudden turn is made in verses 8 f. One must not only guard against causing another to stumble; he must put himself under whatever discipline is necessary to safeguard against his own stumbling. Of course the literal sacrifice of ***hand, foot,*** or ***eye*** would not solve the problems of temptation and sin, but the illustration is clear. Just as one would sacrifice an organ of the body to save physical life, so it is that any discipline, however severe, is not too great a price to pay for victory over ***temptations to sin.***

In 5:27–30 a similar surgical analogy is employed with respect to the problem of carnal lust. Here the same surgical analogy is applied to the deep-rooted problem of pride (and prejudice in Mark). Man's real problem is within himself, and victory over his deep-seated egocentricity (pride, prejudice, lust, or whatever) comes only with

[41] Cf. W. H. Davis, *Greek Papyri of the First Century* (New York: Harper, 1933), pp. 1 f.

the radical "surgery" of repentance, conversion, birth from above, and daily discipline.

(3) *Concern that Not One Little One Perish (18:10–14)*

10 "See that you do not despise one of these
little ones; for I tell you that in heaven their
angels always behold the face of my Father
who is in heaven. 12 What do you think? If a
man has a hundred sheep, and one of them has
gone astray, does he not leave the ninety-nine
on the hills and go in search of the one that
went astray? 13 And if he finds it, truly, I say to
you, he rejoices over it more than over the
ninety-nine that never went astray. 14 So it is
not the will of my Father who is in heaven that
one of these little ones should perish.

Matthew seems to have drawn the story of the lost sheep from Q, its parallel being found in Luke 15:3–7. Stressed is the importance of the least and the last. God does not will the loss of even ***one of these little ones,*** but rather he ***rejoices over*** the recovery of even one. To have ninety-nine in safety does not satisfy the shepherd if there is yet one sheep that ***has gone astray.*** It is not that he loves the ninety-nine less but that there is no joy like that of recovering the one that was lost. God's joy in recovering the lost was probably the chief point in the story as Jesus told it (cf. Luke 15:7,10, 22–24).

Jesus warned against the sin of despising a little one. That ***their angels always behold the face*** of God reflects the view that each person has his heavenly counterpart or angelic representative in heaven (cf. Esther 1:14; Dan. 10:13; Acts 12:15; Rev. 1:20). That Jesus meant to endorse the belief in guardian angels is not clear. The concern is not with that doctrine as such. It is only incidental to the real point. Jesus' concern is to say that children and "little people" are important to God and so they must be important to us.

Manuscript evidence both for and against verse 11 is strong. The verse is probably not original with Matthew, but borrowed from Luke 19:10. Had it been original, scribes would have had no reason to drop it in the early Greek, Latin, Syriac, and Coptic manuscripts.

2. *Church Discipline, to Correct and Recover (18:15–20)*

15 "If your brother sins against you, go and
tell him his fault, between you and him alone.
If he listens to you, you have gained your
brother. 16 But if he does not listen, take one or
two others along with you, that every word
may be confirmed by the evidence of two or
three witnesses. 17 If he refuses to listen to
them, tell it to the church; and if he refuses to
listen even to the church, let him be to you as
a Gentile and a tax collector. 18 Truly, I say to
you, whatever you bind on earth shall be bound
in heaven, and whatever you loose on earth
shall be loosed in heaven. 19 Again I say to
you, if two of you agree on earth about anything they ask, it will be done for them by my
Father in heaven. 20 For where two or three are
gathered in my name, there am I in the midst
of them."

This paragraph provides the model for church discipline, including motive, spirit, and basic procedure. Absent from it are all traces of legalism or penal motive. The concern is to salvage and strengthen, not to expose or dispose of erring ones.

Jesus placed major responsibility for reconciliation upon the one sinned against. It is not that the offender is without responsibility (cf. 5:23 f.) but that the very fact of sin impairs the sinner. The wronged person is in better position to initiate reconciliation than is the wrongdoer (cf. Gal. 6:1). Jesus was further concerned that reconciliation be effected without unnecessary public exposure of the wrongdoer. Excluded is any disposition to punish, to embarrass, or to hold one up for scorn. Only where all private efforts fail is it necessary to call the offender before the church.

Jesus outlines four possible steps in church discipline. First, ideally, reconciliation should be attempted by those immediately concerned. The objective is that the brother be ***gained*** or reclaimed. In the event of failure, the second effort should be through a committee. This follows the principle of Deuteronomy 19:15, to the effect that disputes should be settled in the presence of two or three witnesses. One word against another may lead only to a deadlock, and no person should be indicted upon the word of one witness. Should the second step fail, the offender is to be called before ***the church.*** Concerned discipline is not antithetical to the nature of the church but proper to it. It is to be assumed that the same motive and spirit would govern the church as should govern the individual or committee in seeking to gain the brother. A fourth step may be found necessary, where one ***refuses to listen even to the church.*** In this event, it is not so much that he is excluded as self-excluded. It is not that the church "withdraws fellowship" but that it learns sadly that there is no fellowship there.

The statement that the one who ***refuses to listen to the church*** is to be ***as a Gentile and a tax collector*** sounds harsh. It clearly reflects a Jewish-Christian situation, not a Gentile setting. The harshness is not so sharp when all factors are considered. First of all, three steps seeking reconciliation are presupposed. Next, it is not so much exclusion as refusal to "belong" to the church. Further, Jesus was always kind and open to the Gentiles and tax collectors. For the church to recognize that one who refused to listen is already an outsider does not close the door to his reception when he is willing to be received as a brother. The paragraph teaches that each disciple is responsible for his brother, that the whole church is responsible for each member, and that each member is answerable to the church (cf. Schniewind, p. 200).

The authority to ***bind*** and ***loose,*** given to Peter in 16:19, is here extended to the whole church. In 16:19 it seems to relate primarily to instruction, what conduct is permitted and what not. Here it relates primarily to church discipline. The periphrastic future perfect passive tense is used for bind and loose as in 16:19 (which see). If this tense distinction may be pressed, the church is assured that its action in receiving one who listens or excluding one who refuses to listen has already been anticipated in heaven. Understood as a simple future tense, the assurance is that heaven will validate the action of the church. Either way, agreement between heaven and church is pictured. This, of course, presupposes that in undertaking the discipline of a member the church has been governed by the motive and spirit prescribed.

The disciples are further assured of Christ's blessing and presence wherever they are found together in prayer or agreement. This is not a "blank check" for selfish people. In context this is to be understood as assurance of divine presence and help as Christ's people undertake the difficult work of the care of one another, even to the extent of corrective and redemptive discipline for the erring. For example, to receive back an erring brother without subjecting him to shame or punishment could leave the church open to the criticism that it is indulgent. To exclude a member who refuses to listen is most painful to a conscientious church. In either case, the church has a difficult task. It needs the comfort of reassurance when it so functions.

Jesus promised all of this. He promised to be there when ***two or three*** meet together in his name. A rabbinical teaching (*Aboth* 3:2) spoke of the Shekinah, the presence of God, as being with those occupied with the words of the Torah (Law). The church is assured of God's presence when it truly acts as the church.

3. *The Forgiving Alone Able to Receive Forgiveness* (*18:21–35*)

**[21] Then Peter came up and said to him,
"Lord, how often shall my brother sin against
me, and I forgive him? As many as seven
times?" [22] Jesus said to him, "I do not say to
you seven times, but seventy times seven.**

**[23] "Therefore the kingdom of heaven may be
compared to a king who wished to settle accounts with his servants. [24] When he began the
reckoning, one was brought to him who owed
him ten thousand talents; [25] and as he could
not pay, his lord ordered him to be sold, with
his wife and children and all that he had, and
payment to be made. [26] So the servant fell on
his knees, imploring him, 'Lord, have patience**

with me, and I will pay you everything.' [27] And out of pity for him the lord of that servant released him and forgave him the debt. [28] But that same servant, as he went out, came upon one of his fellow servants who owed him a hundred denarii; and seizing him by the throat he said, 'Pay what you owe.' [29] So his fellow servant fell down and besought him, 'Have patience with me, and I will pay you.' [30] He refused and went and put him in prison till he should pay the debt. [31] When his fellow servants saw what had taken place, they were greatly distressed, and they went and reported to their lord all that had taken place. [32] Then his lord summoned him and said to him, 'You wicked servant! I forgave you all that debt because you besought me; [33] and should not you have had mercy on your fellow servant, as I had mercy on you?' [34] And in anger his lord delivered him to the jailers, till he should pay all his debt. [35] So also my heavenly Father will do to every one of you, if you do not forgive your brother from your heart."

Questions can be as revealing as answers. Two questions appear in chapter 18, each reflecting the disciples' serious lack both in understanding and in spirit (vv. 1,21). Who is the greatest? Must I always forgive? Jesus answered the first by showing God's concern for children and "little people." He answered the second by showing God's unlimited mercy toward sinners (cf. Schlatter, p. 289).

Reconciliation is the Christian's business, even as it is that of Christ, and it knows no limits (cf. 2 Cor. 5:18–20). Peter undertook to ask a good question but asked it in a wrong way. He was right in considering the matter of forgiving an erring brother but wrong in thinking of limits beyond which responsibility ended. ***Seven times*** may have seemed generous to him, but it is not. Forgiveness is not so much an act as an attitude (Robinson, p. 156), and the disposition or willingness to forgive is to be limitless.

The reading ***seventy times seven*** is uncertain at an insignificant point. The Greek possibly should be translated "seventy-seven times" rather than "seventy times seven."[42] The problem arises out of the LXX version of Genesis 4:24 which stands behind the passage here. The point is unimportant, for the intention is not to say literally 77 or 490. To keep count would betray the lack of the real spirit of forgiveness, however few or many times one presumed to forgive another.

The real significance of Jesus' reply is found only when one sees it as his reversal of the old law of vengeance as expressed by Lamech (Gen. 4:23–24). Lamech is quoted as having said to his two wives, "I have slain a man for wounding me, a young man for striking me. If Cain is avenged sevenfold, truly Lamech seventy-sevenfold." Jesus reverses Lamech's law of revenge. Instead of endless revenge, the disciple is to practice endless forgiveness (cf. 5:38–48). The parable contains both a promise and a warning. It promises God's forgiveness of man's debts, however enormous. It warns that forgiveness is impossible to the unforgiving.

The parable of the unmerciful servant, found alone in Matthew, serves well to drive home the nature and principle of forgiveness. It contrasts man's enormous debt to God with the smallness of what we tend to consider the debts of others to us. Our debt to God is so great that we can never pay it. We are utterly dependent upon his mercy, which alone can free us from our debt. It is not only absurd for us to demand payment from others under threat of vengeance against them, but it is to deny the only ground upon which we may hope to stand before God. The unforgiving must remain unforgiven, because in denying forgiveness to others they show themselves to be unforgivable.

Jesus deliberately painted an absurd picture of a man who owed his king an enormous sum sending another to prison because of a trifling debt. Money values change from day to day, and it is impossible to arrive at a sum in today's money which would be the equivalent of the ***ten thousand talents*** owed by one debtor and ***a hundred denarii*** owed by the second. Amounts of ten million dollars and twenty dollars would at least

42 Cf. E. J. Goodspeed, *Problems of New Testament Translation* (Chicago: University, 1945), pp. 29–31.

suggest the contrast. The illustration is taken from the pagan world, where such punitive actions against a debtor were possible. In Judaism an Israelite could be sold only for theft and in such cases where the sum was not less than the price for which the thief could be sold and where the thief could not make restitution. The sale of a wife and torture of a debtor were forbidden by Jewish law (cf. Jeremias, *Parables*, 211). The story could be told in Palestine from a Jewish perspective but drawing upon non-Jewish practices for illustration.

The story is so clear and detailed that its point can hardly be missed. It is consistent with a principle often repeated by Jesus. The principle is not arbitrary. Real forgiveness is from the heart. It is an attitude as well as an act. To be unforgiving shows that one has not accepted the principle of forgiveness.

To base one's relation to others on a merit basis is to deny mercy and grace. This is to deny one's only hope as he stands before God. To be unforgiving and vengeful is a condition. One in such condition has no openness to receive or offer forgiveness (cf. 6:14 f.). There is no surer sign that one has known what it is to see himself a sinner before God and to have known the joy of forgiveness than is seen in his own mercy toward others. One who is unmerciful shows that he has never known what it is to receive mercy before God.

Forgiveness is to be from the ***heart.*** The disciple's obligation to forgive is unconditional and unlimited. It is governed not by mathematics but by a disposition which comes from Christ.

XII. Marriage, Divorce, Celibacy (19:1–15)

1. Introduction (19:1–2)

[1] Now when Jesus had finished these sayings, he went away from Galilee and entered the region of Judea beyond the Jordan; [2] and large crowds followed him, and he healed them there.

Matthew's fourth formula marking the end of a discourse appears here (cf. 7:28; 11:1; 13:53; 19:1; 26:1). There is no complete separation between discourse and narrative materials, for much discourse or discussion immediately follows the formula. In verse 2 Matthew characteristically calls attention to Jesus' healing ministry, although his Gospel is loaded with teaching material. Mark, in the parallel (10:1), characteristically calls attention to Jesus as teacher, although he includes more action material than teaching. For all their difference in emphasis, both recognize the importance of Jesus' deeds and words.

Matthew marks a significant transition as Jesus begins his final approach to Jerusalem. Jesus left ***Galilee and entered the region of Judea beyond the Jordan,*** i.e., Perea. The reference is not clear, for Perea was a political district under Herod Antipas, as was Galilee. Perea was separate from Judea, but Matthew apparently reflects a popular way of referring to it as a part of Judea. The recent divorce of Herod Antipas sharpens the reference to the question of divorce.

Much of the material in chapters 19 through 25 is under the theme of judgment (cf. Bacon, pp. 308–25). The story moves toward the judgment of Jesus, but the Pharisees and the nation are themselves under the judgment of the one whom they presume to judge. This longer section will trace the widening gulf between Jesus and the nation's leaders and point to his judgment and theirs.

2. Marriage: Sacred and Indissoluble Except by Death (19:3–9)

[3] And Pharisees came up to him and tested him by asking, "Is it lawful to divorce one's wife for any cause?" [4] He answered, "Have you not read that he who made them from the beginning made them male and female, [5] and said, 'For this reason a man shall leave his father and mother and be joined to his wife, and the two shall become one'? [6] So they are no longer two but one. What therefore God has joined together, let no man put asunder." [7] They said to him, "Why then did Moses command one to give a certificate of divorce, and to put her away?" [8] He said to them, "For your hardness of heart Moses allowed you to divorce your wives, but from the beginning it was not so. [9] And I say to you: whoever di-

vorces his wife, except for unchastity, and marries another, commits adultery."

This is Matthew's second treatment of the question of marriage and divorce (see comments on 5:31 f.). Each passage contains the much debated "except clause." The two related passages do not have the same emphasis, for the earlier one focuses attention upon the enormous injustice done in divorcing an innocent wife, where the "except clause" is necessary to the point under consideration. In verses 3–9 the whole question of marriage and divorce is approached more directly, although it focuses attention upon the guilt of the husband who divorces an innocent wife and then remarries.

Striking differences appear between Matthew and the Markan parallel (10:2–12). In Mark the phrase ***for any cause*** does not appear in the Pharisees' question, and the words ***except for unchastity*** do not appear in Jesus' reply (cf. Luke 16:18; 1 Cor. 7:10 f.). Did Jesus completely rule out divorce, or did he recognize one ground for it? Scholars are almost unanimous in holding to the priority of Mark (reinforced by Luke and Paul) and in holding that Matthew incorporates a later church modification which sought to adjust the ideal to a workable rule. They argue that not only do Mark, Luke, and Paul preserve the stricter position but that even in Matthew the appeal of Jesus to God's purpose in creation makes no room for the ***except for unchastity*** modification. Can a better case for Matthew's "except clause" be made? The least that can be said is that more support can be claimed for Matthew's clause than the above implies.

Background to the Matthean form of the Pharisees' question is easily found. The schools of Shammai and Hillel in the time of Jesus debated the grounds for divorce, taking different positions in their interpretation of Deuteronomy 24:1 (cf. *Gittim* 9:10). The passage in Deuteronomy assumes the practice of divorce and seeks to regulate it. It assumes the right of a husband to divorce his wife "if then she finds no favor in his eyes because he has found some indecency in her."

The schools of Shammai and Hillel debated the meaning of "some indecency." The phrase in Hebrew is of uncertain meaning, but it appears also in Deuteronomy 23:14 and literally reads, "the nakedness of a thing." [43] The school of Shammai stressed the word for "nakedness" and interpreted it as implying adultery, making that the sole grounds for divorce. The school of Hillel chose to base its exegesis upon the word "thing" and thus found a proof text for making anything serve as the ground for divorce. To the school of Hillel the "thing" could be, for example, the wife's burning of the food, the husband's seeing a woman who pleased him better, or the wife's causing her husband to eat something that had not been tithed.

The phrase in Deuteronomy apparently refers to "immodest or indecent behavior" but not to adultery, else it would have come under a severer penalty than divorce by the first husband (Driver, p. 271). Whatever its intention, it is certain that in the time of Jesus the school of Shammai took the strict view that divorce is permissible only on grounds of the wife's adultery and that the school of Hillel took the liberal view that a man could divorce his wife for any cause. There is no evidence that the Pharisees of the time questioned the right of divorce as such.

In both Matthew and Mark, Jesus went behind Deuteronomy 24:1 and built upon the intention of God in the creation of man (Gen. 1:27; 2:24). He observed that ***from the beginning*** God ***made*** mankind ***male and female***, prescribing that for the sake of marriage a man should ***leave his father and mother and be joined to his wife, and the two*** thus becoming ***one***. This joining together he recognized as God's work, not to be undone by man. Putting ***asunder*** is man's work, not God's.

[43] S. R. Driver, *Deuteronomy*, "The International Critical Commentary," (3d ed.; Edinburgh: T. & T. Clark, 1902), pp. 269 ff.

By saying that the *two . . . become one,* Jesus did not mean that individuality is lost in marriage any more than it is lost in redemption as a disciple is made one with Christ (cf. 25:40). Individual selfhood is brought to fulfilment in marriage, but paradoxically the two become one. The outward physical union is hallowed by a personal, spiritual union which is to be indissoluble except by death.

The Pharisees appealed to the *command* of *Moses* (Deut. 24:1). Jesus put the command in its true perspective, affirming that Moses *allowed divorce* because of their *hardness of heart* (see Mark 10:2–8 for reverse order in reference to Moses and creation).

Divorce was commonly practiced, and the ruling in Deuteronomy sought to control it, affording the wife some protection. A wife had been considered man's property. The bill of divorce would at least prove that the husband had released his legal claims upon the wife he sent out of his home. This meant that the dismissed wife could seek a new home or relationship. Without the divorce certificate, another man could be charged with stealing or violating the property rights of the first husband, should he take the woman as wife or servant. Thus the writing of divorce was intended to place some limits upon the husband and to afford the wife some protection. Jesus cut behind all of this, basing the nature and indissolubility of marriage on God's intention in creating man.

B. H. Streeter argues that Matthew's section on divorce is "more naturally told and more closely related to Jewish usage than the parallel in Mark."[44] He observes that the question of divorce *for any cause* was actually debated at the time but that the right to divorce as such was not. He suggests that Matthew may have employed a source independent of Mark, a parallel version in what Streeter termed "M," material peculiar to Matthew. In finding Matthew at this point more primitive than Mark, Streeter followed R. H. Charles,[45] who argued forcefully for the originality of Matthew's account.

The debate will continue among interpreters as to whether Jesus simply took the side of the school of Shammai against that of Hillel or that he disallowed divorce altogether. It is at least clear that in going back to creation, he affirmed unambiguously that God's intention for marriage is fulfilled only in the life union of husband and wife, not to be dissolved by divorce. In terming the marriage union God's act of joining two together, Jesus did not say that some marriages are not of God's making and therefore may be dissolved. There may be "marriages" which God has not made, but this passage does not authorize us to dissolve any marriage on the claim that God did not make it. There are commitments and obligations in every marriage which may not be renounced without damage to all concerned.

It is significant that Jesus discussed marriage without subordinating women to a secondary role. The two become one. Jesus recognized no double standard for man and woman, husband and wife. Judaism allowed men to divorce their wives but did not allow the wife to divorce her husband, as was permitted in the Roman world. Jesus contended for the permanency of monogamous marriage, honoring husband and wife alike. The Romans gave husbands and wives equal right to divorce; Jesus gave husbands and wives equal right (and responsibility) for permanency in marriage.

The word rendered *unchastity* (*porneiai*) is usually translated "fornication," and it may denote premarital unchastity. Etymologically the term refers to the sale of one's body in sexuality. Thus for a time at least, *porneia* designated either prostitution or premarital unchastity, whereas *moicheuai* designated adultery, illicit sexuality within and against marriage. The two words came to be used interchangeably. Whether *porneia* in Matthew retains its early meaning or not is uncertain. If so, the "except clause"

44 *The Four Gospels, A Study of Origins* (London: Macmillan, 1924), p. 259.

45 *The Teaching of the New Testament on Divorce* (London: Williams & Norgate, 1921), pp. 85 ff.

refers to premarital ***unchastity*** making possible what today would be called annulment. In Jesus' time it was called divorce, for even betrothal was a legal (and often financial) contract which could be broken only by divorce (cf. 1:18 f.).

It is possible, then, that even the "except clause" relates to what we would term a case of annulment, not divorce, and even on the basis of Matthew it is not absolutely certain that Jesus may be cited as authorizing remarriage after divorce. If Jesus may be appealed to at all for a second chance in marriage it is more likely to be in terms of his mercy and grace, not his explicit statement. Jesus clearly held up one ideal alone, monogamous marriage that is not to be broken. For the broken in any and every sense he offered forgiveness and redemption. But this is to go beyond our text.

3. *Celibacy and Its Demands* (*19:10–12*)

10 The disciples said to him, "If such is the case of a man with his wife, it is not expedient to marry." 11 But he said to them, "Not all men can receive this precept, but only those to whom it is given. 12 For there are eunuchs who have been so from birth, and there are eunuchs who have been made eunuchs by men, and there are eunuchs who have made themselves eunuchs for the sake of the kingdom of heaven. He who is able to receive this, let him receive it."

The disciples found Jesus' standard for marriage so high that they questioned the wisdom of marriage. Not only were they frightened by the demands of marriage but saw it from a man's perspective only. They said that marriage was not ***expedient*** if such is ***the case of a man*** with his wife. Apparently they meant that ***a man*** should not get into a marriage from which he could not escape. They said nothing about the danger that a woman might get trapped with a sorry husband. They speculated that it might be better for a man to remain single than for him to risk the entanglement of marriage.

The alternative to marriage is celibacy. Jesus made room for both as honorable and proper to discipleship. He warned, however, that the demands upon celibacy are high, just as they are upon marriage. Some are incapacitated for marriage because of physical impotence or impairment. They are those who are ***eunuchs who have been so from birth*** or those ***who have been made eunuchs by men.*** In royal courts, especially, there were slaves who were made eunuchs through surgery so that they would not be a threat to their masters' household. Those who ***made themselves eunuchs for the sake of the kingdom of heaven*** are those who forego marriage with a view to a life given more fully to the service of Christ. As Jesus spoke of marriage and celibacy he did not say that one was morally higher than the other or that one offered greater opportunity for discipleship. Each is an honorable choice to be made on an individual basis.

Celibacy is a valid vocational choice of the follower of Christ, but it is for the one ***who is able;*** i.e., equal to its demands. Marriage is not an evil to be shunned but something good to be surrendered by those who fulfil discipleship in celibacy. Celibacy is sanctioned as a vocational choice but not for ascetic reasons. Monogamous marriage as a life union and celibacy for the sake of the kingdom are both honorable and high in their demands.

4. *Children's Access to Christ* (*19:13–15*)

13 Then children were brought to him that he might lay his hands on them and pray. The disciples rebuked the people; 14 but Jesus said, "Let the children come to me, and do not hinder them; for to such belongs the kingdom of heaven." 15 And he laid his hands on them and went away.

This beautiful picture of Jesus tenderly receiving little children is a happy conclusion to a section on marriage, divorce, and celibacy. It is marred only by the impatience of the disciples who ***rebuked the people*** for bringing their children to Jesus. Jesus gave place to little children, just as he did to the women, the poor, the sick, tax gatherers and sinners, Jews and non-Jews. Children were to be permitted to ***come*** to him, and no one must ***hinder*** their coming.

The passage cannot validly be used as a proof text for infant baptism. It was not until ***the kingdom of heaven*** was confused with the church that this text was applied to baptism (cf. McNeile, p. 277). The text says nothing of church or baptism; and it speaks of children (*paidia*) who are to be permitted to ***come,*** not to infants brought for baptism.

XIII. Rebukes to Selfishness (19:16–20:34)

Comparison of 19:30 and 20:16 discloses that the story of the rich young man and the parable of the workers in the vineyard are intended by Matthew to be read together. Each concluded with the "first last and last first" principle. Sequence and connections are not so obvious with respect to the other units of this section. Our outlining or blocking out of materials does not in every case necessarily reflect Matthew's own sense of order. Our own study needs compel us to look for order, and the warning against various expressions of selfishness seems to be a motif throughout this section.

1. The Peril of Riches (19:16–30)

16 And behold, one came up to him, saying, "Teacher, what good deed must I do, to have eternal life?" 17 And he said to him, "Why do you ask me about what is good? One there is who is good. If you would enter life, keep the commandments." 18 He said to him, "Which?" And Jesus said, "You shall not kill, You shall not commit adultery, You shall not steal, You shall not bear false witness, 19 Honor your father and mother, and, You shall love your neighbor as yourself." 20 The young man said to him, "All these I have observed; what do I still lack?" 21 Jesus said to him, "If you would be perfect, go, sell what you possess and give to the poor, and you will have treasure in heaven; and come, follow me." 22 When the young man heard this he went away sorrowful; for he had great possessions.

23 And Jesus said to his disciples, "Truly, I say to you, it will be hard for a rich man to enter the kingdom of heaven. 24 Again I tell you, it is easier for a camel to go through the eye of a needle than for a rich man to enter the kingdom of God." 25 When the disciples heard this they were greatly astonished, saying, "Who then can be saved?" 26 But Jesus looked at them and said to them, "With men this is impossible, but with God all things are possible." 27 Then Peter said in reply, "Lo, we have left everything and followed you. What then shall we have?" 28 Jesus said to them, "Truly, I say to you, in the new world, when the Son of man shall sit on his glorious throne, you who have followed me will also sit on twelve thrones, judging the twelve tribes of Israel. 29 And every one who has left houses or brothers or sisters or father or mother or children or lands, for my name's sake, will receive a hundredfold, and inherit eternal life. 30 But many that are first will be last, and the last first.

This story is found also in Mark (10:17–31) and Luke (18:18–30), with variations in each Gospel. Matthew calls the inquirer a ***young man*** and Luke identifies him as "a ruler," possibly a synagogue ruler. All three Gospels describe him as ***rich*** and find the problem there. In Judaism there were two views of wealth, one holding it to be a sign of piety and divine favor, the other seeing it as a sign of wickedness. Jesus did not find evil in wealth itself, but he saw it as a major threat to the one who had it. Although he was deeply concerned for the poor and made concern for the poor a test of kinship to himself (cf. 25:31–46), that is not the burden of this passage. Jesus was first of all concerned for what money does to the one who has it, and next for what a man does with it.

Jesus based discipleship on utter dependence upon God. This is why the poor, the "little people," children, tax gatherers, and "sinners" have the advantage. They know their lack, their need, and their absolute dependence upon God. Possession of money tends to give one a false sense of security and less disposition to trust God. Jesus sought to free man from the tyranny of things by bringing him under the sovereignty of God, in which alone is freedom and life.

The rich young ruler was far from ***eternal life*** even though he sincerely sought it. He felt confident that he had ***observed,*** literally "guarded" (*ephulaxa*) all the commandments. Actually he was a bargainer, seriously seeking eternal life; but as a bargainer he was unwilling to pay more than he thought it was worth. His egocentric or self-centered approach is the very opposite of self-denial, the way of the cross, apart from which one cannot follow Jesus (cf. 16:24 f.). He came to Jesus for eternal life, to the right one for the right thing; but he ***went away*** without what he sought. He was possessed by his ***possessions.*** Chiefly, he was possessed by himself and failed in his unwillingness to surrender all to follow Jesus. He failed to learn that all gain begins with loss.

The translation ***to have*** blunts the force of the question in verse 16. The young man asked, "What must I do that I may get (*schō*) eternal life?" Likewise the translation, ***What then shall we have?*** blunts Peter's question. He asked, "What then is for us?" Both questions are egocentric. What's for me? This contradicts the basic principle of the cross and moves from rather than toward the quality of life found in Jesus. Paradoxically, ***eternal life*** belongs to the one who loses his life for Christ, not to the one who seeks "to get" it. Jesus rebuked the bargaining spirit which persisted in Peter and which triumphed in the rich young ruler.

Matthew avoids the Markan address, "Good Teacher," and reply, "Why do you call me good?" (10:17 f.). Possibly this was to prevent the readers from understanding Jesus to be denying that he was good. In neither Mark nor Matthew does Jesus imply that he is not good. The point is that goodness is found in God alone and not in what man does. Goodness may be reflected in doing, but it belongs essentially to being, i.e., to what one is. First of all, it belongs to what God is.

In two ways Matthew seems to go beyond Mark in his emphasis upon deeds, in quoting Jesus as saying to the young man that he must ***keep the commandments*** if he would ***enter life*** (v. 17) and in setting forth the conditions under which he ***would be perfect*** (v. 21). In Mark the man is simply reminded that he knows the commandments and is told that he yet lacked one thing (10:19,21). In part, this reflects the great emphasis in Matthew upon the demand as well as the gift in salvation. The demand is implied in Mark but is not so explicit. In Matthew as well as Mark, eternal life is determined finally not by keeping the commandments but by the willingness to surrender all and to follow Jesus.

Although perfection remains the demand (v. 21), goodness is found only in God, so it is beyond man's attainment (cf. Lohmeyer, p. 286). Here again we meet in Matthew, side by side, the absolute demand of God (vv. 17,21), yet man's utter dependence upon God in whom alone is goodness (v. 17) and who alone has the power to save (v. 26).

The clause ***if you would be perfect*** may imply that in Matthew there are two grades of disciples, those who have eternal life and those who are ***perfect*** (*teleios*). This is not borne out elsewhere in Matthew, and in 5:48 the demand that one "be perfect" is made of all disciples. Jesus did not separate his followers into two groups, the ordinary and the perfect. He did emphasize perfection as the ideal for all but the attainment of none. Matthew's ***if you would be perfect*** is the counterpart of Mark's "you lack one thing." Neither Matthew nor Mark represents the man as having eternal life. No disciple is held up as being perfect.

The commandments listed are basically those of the second table of the Decalogue, those concerned primarily with man's relation to man. Matthew follows Mark 10:19 but drops "do not defraud," which is not found in the Old Testament. Matthew's wording is closer to the Hebrew text of Exodus 20:12–16, with the added commandment to ***love*** one's ***neighbor*** being drawn from Leviticus 19:18.

Which (*poias*) may bear the meaning "which kind," but this seems not to be the intention in verse 18.

The command to ***sell*** and ***give*** obviously reflects concern for the poor, but that was not the basic concern of Jesus here. It was to free the rich young man from the clutches of riches. Jesus did not exact the surrender of property from every would-be follower. Peter seems to have owned a house (8:14) and a boat (John 21:3), and Joseph of Arimathea was a rich man and disciple of Jesus (27:57). It is significant that Jesus had no stereotyped way in approaching people. Each was an individual, and he went to the heart of each one's problem.

The key to the rich young ruler's life problem was money, and Jesus challenged him at that point. It was by this test that the young man could discover whether or not he really wanted the life available in following Jesus.

Jesus astonished the disciples by declaring that it is ***hard for a rich man to enter the kingdom of heaven. It is easier for a camel to go through the eye of a needle.*** All effort to interpret ***camel*** as confusion with the word for a ship's cable or rope and ***eye of a needle*** as reference to a little gate in the wall at Jerusalem is pure fancy with no supportive evidence. Jesus used a deliberate hyperbole. The intention was to represent the salvation of a rich man as nothing short of a miracle, possible only with God. It would be a miracle for a camel, largest animal in Palestine, to go through the eye of a sewing needle.

Only God's power can free a man from the tyranny of things and bring him into the true freedom known under the kingdom (ruling) of God. This passage has to do not only with man's need of salvation but also with God's demand for righteousness, so prominent throughout this Gospel. Matthew shows that both salvation and righteousness are possibilities only to God's power.

Jesus did not indicate a fixed sum marking the difference between a rich man and a poor one. This is a relative matter. The same person is rich by the standards of one community and poor by the standards of another. A poor man can be enslaved to his pennies, but the greater the wealth the more likely one is to give it his heart of love and trust.

Peter confidently pointed to sacrifices which he and his fellow disciples had made in order to follow Jesus. He then asked a question which betrayed his great distance from Jesus (cf. 26:58). ***What then shall we have?*** is literally, What then is for us? What do we get out of this? Peter was "being saved" (cf. 1 Cor. 1:18), but most of his pilgrimage was yet ahead. His question is more pagan than Christian. It is egocentric. Jesus gave a patient answer, yet one which was weighted with both judgment and promise, warning and assurance.

Jesus first assured Peter that God would amply reward his people. ***In the new world*** (*paliggenesiai*) the disciple could be assured of gains ***a hundredfold*** greater than the costs of discipleship. The word *paliggenesia* carries the idea of renewal or rebirth. ***The new world*** is apocalyptic language for this world either as transformed or replaced by another after its destruction (cf. Isa. 65:17; 66:22; Rom. 8:18–22; Gal. 6:15; 2 Peter 3:13; Rev. 21:1–5). It is not the intention of this passage to describe or discuss this new world as such but to assure the disciples of the great blessings in store for them.

The promised new world is one in which ***the Son of man*** sits ***on his glorious throne*** and in which the disciples, presumably the apostles, ***sit on twelve thrones, judging the twelve tribes of Israel.*** Although the intention is serious, this is not to be pressed in its literal sense. Elsewhere, all followers of Jesus are assured that they will reign with Christ (Luke 12:32), and the saints will judge the world (1 Cor. 6:2). This is no promise that the original ***twelve tribes of Israel*** will be revived, for Jesus came to create the true "children of Abraham" out of faith, not flesh.

There are interpreters who envision a literal kingdom in Palestine with literal thrones there for Jesus and the twelve apostles. This or any other literal approach may well reckon with the whole passage. If these terms are to be taken literally, does the same hold for the promise of ***a hundredfold*** increase in parents, brothers and sisters, children, and land? Luke includes "wife" in his list! Surely Jesus did not promise a hundred wives for each one left. To literalize is obviously to trivialize and to miss the intention of Jesus. His reply was a dramatic and forceful way of assuring his disciples that God is far more generous in his rewards than man deserves. One cannot outgive God. A ***new world, eternal life,*** and rewards far beyond the costs of discipleship are certainties for those who are willing to surrender all to follow Jesus.

But Jesus had more to say in reply to Peter. Although the rewards of discipleship are certain and generous, there will be many surprises. Many standings in the ***new world*** will be a reversal of those of the present. Many who seemed to be ***first*** will prove to be ***last,*** and many ***last*** ones ***first.*** The parable to follow closes with the same principle and is its explication. Rewards will be greatest to those not seeking reward, least to those most concerned for reward. One will "get" all that he deserves; but if his concern is over, "What's for me?" his reward will be small.

2. *Workers in the Vineyard: First Last, Last First (20:1–16)*

1 "For the kingdom of heaven is like a house-
holder who went out early in the morning to
hire laborers for his vineyard. 2 After agreeing
with the laborers for a denarius a day, he sent
them into his vineyard. 3 And going out about
the third hour he saw others standing idle in
the market place; 4 and to them he said, 'You
go into the vineyard too, and whatever is right
I will give you.' So they went. 5 Going out
again about the sixth hour and the ninth hour,
he did the same. 6 And about the eleventh hour
he went out and found others standing; and he
said to them, 'Why do you stand here idle all
day?' 7 They said to him, 'Because no one has
hired us.' He said to them, 'You go into the
vineyard too.' 8 And when evening came, the
owner of the vineyard said to his steward, 'Call
the laborers and pay them their wages, begin-
ning with the last, up to the first.' 9 And when
those hired about the eleventh hour came, each
of them received a denarius. 10 Now when the
first came, they thought they would receive
more; but each of them also received a denar-
ius. 11 And on receiving it they grumbled at the
householder, 12 saying, 'These last worked only
one hour, and you have made them equal to us
who have borne the burden of the day and the
scorching heat.' 13 But he replied to one of
them, 'Friend, I am doing you no wrong; did
you not agree with me for a denarius? 14 Take
what belongs to you, and go; I choose to give
to this last as I give to you. 15 Am I not
allowed to do what I choose with what belongs
to me? Or do you begrudge my generosity?'
16 So the last will be first, and the first last."

Stephen Langton in 1228, in making out modern chapter divisions, could well have avoided separating 20:1–16 from 19:16–30. The parable explains the principle that the first will be last and the last first. The reward motive is solidly based in the teaching of Jesus, but it is important to see that for the followers of Jesus "reward becomes increasingly the crown rather than the motive of service, nor is it the sort to attract the self-centered man" (Cox, p. 125). The parable teaches the bearing of motive and attitude on the matter of rewards.

The "first last and last first" saying was probably a proverb employed in various situations (cf. 19:30; Mark 10:31; Luke 13:30). That Matthew intends to relate the parable and the proverb to the discussion with Peter may be seen from the introduction of the parable by the word ***for*** (v. 1) and the introduction of the second employment of the proverb (v. 16) by the word ***so*** (*houtōs* is an adverb meaning "thus").

There was in the time of Jesus a wide use of a "first last and last first" proverb to stress equality, and this has sometimes been applied to Matthew's usage, finding the meaning to be that rewards are all alike in the kingdom of heaven. In Fourth Ezra 5:42, judgment is likened to a "round dance," a circle in which no one is first or last.

It is true that in the parable all laborers received the same wage, but that is not its point. It points up the freedom and generosity of the ***householder*** in giving a full wage to laborers who had worked but one hour. It is a defense of the free grace of the gospel against the protests of those who stumble over this (cf. Jeremias, *Parables*, pp. 33–38). Just as some laborers ***grumbled at the householder*** for paying the ***last*** the same as they received, so Jesus was constantly criticized for receiving sinners (cf.

Luke 15:1 f.).

Although the parable in its first setting probably stressed the generosity of Jesus over against his critics, in Matthew it serves a further purpose. It is a rebuke against the bargaining spirit, found in the rich young ruler, yet a problem even for Peter, and characteristic of the laborers who ***grumbled at the householder.*** The first laborers had a bargain with the householder, *agreeing* with him ***for a denarius a day.*** That the fact of a bargain is important to the story is clear from the householder's reminder to one of them that his was a bargain, that it was kept, and that he could now *go* (v. 14). Only the last workers, those who worked only one hour, had no bargain at all. They simply answered the call to work in the vineyard.

The first laborers agreed to work a full day for ***a denarius.*** This was the average daily wage for common labor, low by our standards, yet more substantial than the money equivalent of about fifteen or twenty cents would imply (four *denarii* would buy a lamb). The second group was employed at ***the third hour*** by Jewish time, counted from sunrise to sunset. These were promised ***whatever is right,*** presumably a fair percentage of a day's wage. The same bargain was agreed upon with the workers employed at ***the sixth hour*** [noon] ***and the ninth hour.*** The last workers were employed at ***the eleventh hour,*** just an hour before sunset. They explained their idleness as due to no opportunity to work. The householder said, ***You go into the vineyard too.*** Late manuscripts add the promise given the middle group of workers (KJV); but this is not found in the best manuscripts, and the addition obscures a main point of the parable. These last had no bargain and asked for none.

At evening the ***owner of the vineyard*** instructed ***the steward*** (identical with the householder) to pay the laborers, ***beginning with the last*** and ending with ***the first. Each received a denarius.*** Seeing the generosity of the owner, the first eagerly anticipated a greater sum, for they had worked through the long hours and heat of the day. They were not only disappointed in not getting more but ***grumbled*** because those who worked only an hour were ***made equal*** with them. The householder reminded them of their bargain, ***a denarius a day.*** The bargain had been kept on both sides and was fulfilled. The householder defended his freedom and right to be generous with those who had worked with no bargain.

A striking contrast is drawn between those who begrudge and the one who exercised generosity. "Begrudge" translates Greek which reads literally, "Is your eye evil?" Evil eye was a term for envy or stinginess (cf. 6:23; Mark 7:22).

Applied to the rich young ruler and to Peter, this would say that motive and attitude bear upon reward. Jesus called for followers who asked for no "bargain," and whose concern was not for what he would "get." The disciple, like the bargainer, will "get" all that is due him, but the bargainer will always be dissatisfied with what he gets. The greater rewards are for those who seek no reward. Jesus seeks those who ask only the opportunity to work in his vineyard. His generosity is far greater than the wages guaranteed by any bargain. Jesus offers himself to us without measure and calls us to himself on the same basis. Our relationship with him is to be one of trust and love, with generous giving and receiving. Bargaining is utterly foreign to this kind of relationship.

3. *Third Reminder of Coming Death and Resurrection* (*20:17–19*)

17 And as Jesus was going up to Jerusalem, he took the twelve disciples aside, and on the way he said to them, 18 "Behold, we are going up to Jerusalem; and the Son of man will be delivered to the chief priests and scribes, and they will condemn him to death, 19 and deliver him to the Gentiles to be mocked and scourged and crucified, and he will be raised on the third day."

For the third time Jesus sought to make his disciples understand what awaited him and them (cf. 16:21–23; 17:22–23). This time, Jesus was on his way ***to Jerusalem,*** Awaiting him there were betrayal, mockery, torture, and death by crucifixion, as well as resurrection.

This third prediction indicates that the initiative against Jesus was taken by the Jewish leaders and that the Gentiles, Roman officials, were enlisted for the execution of Jesus. Despite modern protests that the death of Jesus was initiated by the Romans and that the Gentile Christian church subsequently shifted the blame from Romans to Jews, Matthew's position is supported by the evidence. Paul was not anti-Jewish, yet just after A.D. 50 he wrote that "the Jews" killed the Lord Jesus (1 Thess. 2:14 f.). Matthew is not anti-Jewish. His heroes as well as villains are Jews. Jesus himself is "Son of David, Son of Abraham" as well as "Son of God."

On each occasion the twelve are shown to fail to grasp what Jesus tells them. Each time, their response is one of refusal to hear or absorption in their own selfish ambitions. Matthew does not explain the disciples' failure to understand Jesus in terms of a "messianic secret" but rather in terms of their refusal to hear Jesus. Even Mark, to whom the "messianic secret" is most prominent, pictures Jesus as clearly proclaiming his death to his disciples (10:32–34), showing such strong feeling that those journeying with him to Jerusalem were "amazed" and "afraid."

3. *Self-seeking Disciples Challenged to Sacrificial Service (20:20–28)*

20 Then the mother of the sons of Zebedee
came up to him, with her sons, and kneeling
before him she asked him for something. 21 And
he said to her, "What do you want?" She said
to him, "Command that these two sons of mine
may sit, one at your right hand and one at your
left, in your kingdom." 22 But Jesus answered,
"You do not know what you are asking. Are
you able to drink the cup that I am to drink?"
They said to him, "We are able." 23 He said to
them, "You will drink my cup, but to sit at my
right hand and at my left is not mine to grant,
but it is for those for whom it has been pre-
pared by my father." 24 And when the ten heard
it, they were indignant at the two brothers.
25 But Jesus called them to him and said, "You
know that the rulers of the Gentiles lord it over
them, and their great men exercise authority
over them. 26 It shall not be so among you; but
whoever would be great among you must be
your servant, 27 and whoever would be first
among you must be your slave; 28 even as the
Son of man came not to be served but to serve,
and to give his life as a ransom for many."

Matthew specifies the ***mother of the sons of Zebedee,*** i.e., James and John, as speaking to Jesus in behalf of her sons. Mark has it that James and John made the request for themselves (10:35). Whether Matthew is removing some of the blame from the two disciples or simply supplying further detail to Mark's account, both Matthew and Mark show that the disciples themselves were responsible for the selfish and benighted request. This is clear from Jesus' reply in verses 22 f., directed to the disciples themselves, not to the mother.

The request for the positions of honor, at the ***right*** and ***left*** of Jesus in his ***kingdom*** (probably the same as Mark's "in your glory," 10:37), reflects the disciples' selfish interest and also their misunderstanding of the nature of Jesus' kingdom. The pattern which they envisioned was strikingly like the kingdoms of this world. They saw the messianic kingdom as basically political, expecting Jesus to overthrow Roman rule at Jerusalem. The seat at the right of a king's throne was that of first honor, and the one to the left was second in honor. The disciples' desire for honor and their understanding of greatness were essentially pagan, as Jesus charged.

The disciples did not realize what they were asking, in seeking the places next to Jesus in his kingdom. They did not yet understand that his throne would be the cross. ***Cup*** is one figure Jesus used for the death which awaited him. In the Markan account (10:38) "baptism" is also used as a figure for the suffering and death that awaited him. These are not direct references to the Lord's Supper and water baptism but powerful, figurative language for death.

Verse 22 places the responsibility for the selfish request squarely upon James and John and charges them with failure to understand what they were asking. This means that they did not understand what awaited Jesus.

To Jesus' question about their ability ***to drink the cup*** which he was to drink, the disciples glibly answered, ***We are able.*** How unable or unwilling they proved to be! When Jesus was arrested, all the twelve "forsook him and fled" (26:56). Ironically, the positions at the right and left of Jesus in his hour of greatest triumph were occupied not by James and John but by two robbers (27:38).

Jesus predicted that James and John would drink his ***cup,*** i.e., enter into his sufferings. James proved to be the first of the twelve to suffer martyrdom, being executed by Herod Agrippa (Acts 12:2). Neither of the conflicting traditions about John, one to the effect that he suffered martyrdom and a stronger one that he lived to old age in Ephesus, can be verified. John 21:22 seemingly supports the latter. Although ***to drink*** Jesus' ***cup*** may well look to physical martyrdom, in New Testament thought such commitment to Christ that one stands ready to die for him is thought of as martyrdom in principle (cf. 16:24 f.; Gal. 2:19 f.). In this sense John did ***drink the cup,*** whether or not he suffered physical martyrdom.

The places at Jesus' right and left hand are by nature not such as may be arbitrarily assigned or awarded. Jesus himself could not "grant" them, for they belonged to ***those for whom*** they had ***been prepared.*** Jesus will show that greatness is measured by sacrificial service. The greatest is the one who is ***servant;*** the ***first*** is one who is ***slave.*** In the pagan world the *Gentiles* measure greatness by domination, the greatest being the one who exercises most control over the most people. Jesus reversed the pagan pattern, but the disciples were yet to learn this lesson. Presumably those for whom the chief seats were prepared are those who give themselves most fully in sacrificial service. This is another statement of the "first last, last first" principle (19:30; 20:16).

The indignation of ***the ten*** showed that they were no freer from selfish, worldly interests than the two brothers, possibly not as bold. There are traces in the New Testament of rivalry between Peter and John, and the request of James and John may reflect this (cf. John 20:2–6; 21:20–22). If such rivalry appeared at all, at least they later were found working together in harmony (Acts 3:1–4).

The words concerning the contrast between the world's false standards of greatness and Jesus' principle of sacrificial service were addressed to all the disciples. In their world the ***slave*** was considered at the very bottom of the social order. Jesus took the terms ***servant*** and ***slave*** for patterns of greatness. The one who became a voluntary slave, renouncing all claims to rights and pretensions of merit or greatness, was ***first among*** them.

Verse 28 is among the most important in Matthew. Jesus interpreted the role of ***the Son of man*** in terms of sacrificial service, presumably drawing upon the Servant passages in Isaiah (cf. 53:12). In combining these figures or roles, Jesus moved far beyond contemporary Judaism and his own disciples. ***The Son of man,*** to whom dominion and glory and a kingdom, both universal and everlasting, were given (Dan. 7:13 f.) had come in the lowly form of a servant and would ***give his life as a ransom for many.*** Not only were these roles blended in Jesus, but it was he who first declared it, not the disciples or the church. The earliest disciples and the early church resisted this strange way, just as we do today.

The word ***ransom*** (*lutron*) is built upon a Greek word, the root of which means to loose or free. It carries the idea of cost and of liberation. Through the giving of his ***life,*** Jesus would set many at liberty. ***Life*** (*psuchē*) can mean self or physical life. Jesus gave both. He gave his physical life on the cross, but he gave more. He gave himself in complete self-denial and self-sacrifice.

The term ***ransom*** is not a cultic term used

in connection with a sin-offering (cf. Robinson, p. 168, and Hummel, p. 101). It is a term used in connection with the rescue of a person or animal, but never in Jewish thought for the substitution of a sin victim for a sinner. Jesus was speaking of something far more demanding, more personal, and more significant. He came to free man from the clutch of sin (1:21), and this he could accomplish only by giving his life (himself) and by working that miracle of conversion in those who trusted him, by which they too drank ***his cup,*** endured his "baptism" (Mark 10:38), and followed their Master in self-denial and the way of the cross (16:24).

Ransom for many does not imply a limited number for whom Jesus died or to whom salvation is possible. Many is a Jewish way of saying "all" (cf. Isa. 53:12). The preposition ***for*** (*anti*) carries no necessary implication of "in place of," as study of this word in its frequent New Testament usage demonstrates. Jesus gave his life ***for*** us, but he did so to enable us in a real sense to give ours. This is the whole point in his rebuke of the self-centered and self-assertive ambition of the disciples. They can find life only by "losing" it and live only by "dying." This is not an "example theory of atonement," far from that. It is not that man saves himself by following the example of Jesus. It is a rescue, as Jesus Christ becomes a transforming presence in his follower, delivering that one from the death that looks like life to the life that takes the shape of death.

5. *Jesus Heals Two Blind Men Rebuked by the Crowds (20:29–34)*

29 And as they went out of Jericho, a great crowd followed him. 30 And behold, two blind men sitting by the roadside, when they heard that Jesus was passing by, cried out, "Have mercy on us, Son of David!" 31 The crowd rebuked them, telling them to be silent; but they cried out the more, "Lord, have mercy on us, Son of David!" 32 And Jesus stopped and called them, saying, "What do you want me to do for you?" 33 They said to him, "Lord, let our eyes be opened." 34 And Jesus in pity touched their eyes, and immediately they received their sight and followed him.

This story is strikingly like that in 9:27–31. In each story ***two blind men*** cry out for ***mercy*** to Jesus as ***Son of David.*** In the earlier story they are questioned about their faith, and upon being healed they are told not to report it. In this story the ***pity*** or compassion of Jesus is contrasted with the crowd's rebuking of the men. At this point Jesus is moving openly toward Jerusalem for his final confrontation there, and he no longer requires silence from those healed.

The motive of the crowd in telling the blind men to be silent can only be surmised. Whether a reflection of their indifference to the men's needs or fear that their public acclaim of Jesus as ***Son of David*** might arouse hostility is not clear.

Son of David is an important and recurrent title in Matthew (cf. 1:1; 9:27; 12:23; 15:22; 21:9,15). It emerged late as a messianic title in Judaism, but popular Jewish messianic hopes were centered on a Davidic king. ***Lord*** (*kurios*) can be used all the way from a polite "Sir" to a title for God. Its force here is not clear, but ***Lord*** came to be a major title for Jesus in the New Testament. The one who is on his way to Jerusalem as the Suffering Servant, there to suffer mockery, scourging, and crucifixion, and to whom even the twelve are yet so blind, is here acclaimed by ***two blind men*** in the majesty of the ***Son of David.***

XIV. *Royal Entry into Jerusalem (21:1—23:39)*

Jesus was first of all sent to "the lost sheep of the house of Israel" (10:6), and at this point Matthew shows how Jesus openly pressed his messianic claims upon Jerusalem and legitimized those claims by his miracle works. The royal entry into Jerusalem, his acceptance of the people's acclamation of him as ***Son of David,*** the cleansing of the Temple, and the messianic signs in Jerusalem all point up the fact that Jesus is the ***Son of David*** sent to Israel (cf. Hummel, pp. 138 f.). Jerusalem's hour of decision has come. Israel must receive or reject her King. No third course is open to her.

1. The Royal Entry (21:1–11)

**1 And when they drew near to Jerusalem and
came to Bethphage, to the Mount of Olives,
then Jesus sent two disciples, 2 saying to them,
"Go into the village opposite you, and immediately you will find an ass tied, and a colt with
her; untie them and bring them to me. 3 If any
one says anything to you, you shall say, 'The
Lord has need of them,' and he will send them
immediately." 4 This took place to fulfil what
was spoken by the prophet, saying,
5 "Tell the daughter of Zion,
Behold, your king is coming to you,
humble, and mounted on an ass,
and on a colt, the foal of an ass."
6 The disciples went and did as Jesus had
directed them; 7 they brought the ass and the
colt, and put their garments on them, and he
sat thereon. 8 Most of the crowd spread their
garments on the road, and others cut branches
from the trees and spread them on the road.
9 And the crowds that went before him and
that followed him shouted, "Hosanna to the
Son of David! Blessed is he who comes in the
name of the Lord! Hosanna in the highest!"
10 And when he entered Jerusalem, all the city
was stirred, saying, "Who is this?" 11 And the
crowds said, "This is the prophet Jesus from
Nazareth of Galilee."**

This is a messianic act, more accurately designated a royal entry than a triumphal entry. Jesus deliberately presented himself as King, but not as a worldly, political king. He employed no symbol of worldly power. He entered upon a lowly beast of burden, not upon a white horse, like a victorious militarist. This is seen as fulfilment of the promise in Zechariah 9:9, the stress being upon Jesus as Israel's King and as being humble. The line from Zechariah reading "triumphant and victorious" is not quoted (cf. Mark 11:3–10; Luke 19:31–38; John 12:12–19). Of course, Jesus did triumph in Jerusalem, through the strange way of the cross, but any likeness to the world's pattern of "triumph" is avoided. According to John, the arrival at Bethany took place six days before Passover (12:1) and the entry into Jerusalem the next day (12:12).

Bethphage is mentioned here for the first time. Its precise location is unknown, but it was near Bethany (Mark 11:1), about two miles southeast of Jerusalem. Its meaning, "house of young figs," may have some bearing on its being mentioned, since the story of the barren fig tree soon follows (21:18–22).

Although supernatural knowledge may be implied, a previous arrangement for the ***colt*** (or colt and its mother) may have been made. If so, Lazarus of Bethany may have made the arrangement. Thus understood, ***the Lord has need of them*** may have been a password. Such plans would have provided for maximum secrecy until the time for the dramatic entry into Jerusalem; otherwise, it may have met with interference or the surprise element would have been lost. That such arrangements were made in advance is admittedly presupposition, but it is not inherently inadmissible nor does it reflect adversely upon the story. It would explain the willingness of the owners to surrender the colt (and its mother) without resistance.

Matthew clearly refers to two animals, ***an ass*** and her ***colt.*** He reads Zechariah 9:9 as referring to two animals. The other three Gospels mention only the ***colt.*** The Greek conjunction *kai* may be translated "and" or "even." The poetic lines are generally understood to contain Hebrew parallelism, "upon an ass, even on a colt, the foal of an ass." *Autōn* in verse 7, rendered ***thereon*** by the RSV, is most naturally rendered "on them," meaning that Jesus sat either upon the two animals or upon the garments. Even if the garments are meant, the statement is yet unclear, for the reference is to the ***garments on them.*** There is no obvious escape from the problem.

It is clear that Matthew has in mind two animals and that this is his reading of Zechariah 9:9. What is most significant is that he has not invented the story of the entry of Jesus into Jerusalem, riding upon a lowly animal. Matthew made much of the theme of the fulfilment of prophecy, and he employed the language of his Old Testament citations in his stories. But as has been insisted upon throughout this commentary, he did not create the stories to match proof texts, but he interpreted by the Scriptures what already were recognized as events in the life of Jesus. Even the sometimes strained relationship between Scripture text and event argues *for* the priority of the story, not *against* it.

The first line of verse 5 comes from Isaiah 62:11, a promise to ***the daughter of Zion,*** i.e., Jerusalem, that her salvation comes. Matthew sees the fulfilment of this in Jesus, the lowly king who thus entered Jerusalem. The crowd's greeting echoes Psalm 118: 25 f., the last of the Hallel songs, sung at the Passover. ***Hosanna*** meant "Save, we pray thee." It formerly was a prayer for help but seems here to be a shout of praise. Both ***Son of David*** and ***he who comes*** are messianic titles. The crowds also acclaimed Jesus as ***the prophet,*** probably more than just *a* prophet. There was a Jewish expectation of a prophet like Moses (Deut. 18:15, 18), apparently messianic.

For the third time Matthew has shown that as Jesus is proclaimed ***Son of David*** by the common people, two blind men (9: 27–31), the crowds (12:22 ff.), and here, he is rejected by the leaders (Walker, p. 131).

2. *The Temple Cleansed (21:12–17)*

[12] And Jesus entered the temple of God and drove out all who sold and bought in the temple, and he overturned the tables of the money-changers and the seats of those who sold pigeons. [13] He said to them, "It is written, 'My house shall be called a house of prayer'; but you make it a den of robbers."

[14] And the blind and the lame came to him in the temple, and he healed them. [15] But when the chief priests and the scribes saw the wonderful things that he did, and the children crying out in the temple, "Hosanna to the Son of David!" they were indignant; [16] and they said to him, "Do you hear what these are saying?" And Jesus said to them, "Yes; have you never read,

'Out of the mouth of babes and sucklings
thou hast brought perfect praise'?"

[17] And leaving them, he went out of the city to Bethany and lodged there.

The cleansing of the Temple was a prophetic act. It was not a protest against the Temple itself but against the abuses there. The high priestly families, particularly that of Annas in the time of Jesus, exercised great control of the Temple through their collaboration with the Romans. By ***temple*** (*hieron*) is meant not the sanctuary proper (*naos*) but the thirteen-acre complex which included various courts and buildings. Not being a priest, Jesus was barred from the Temple proper (*naos*). The sale of sacrificial animals and the changing of money took place in the Court of the Gentiles. The practice initially served the needs of the people, for Jews coming from distant places could not conveniently bring sacrificial animals with them and would also need to change Greek, Roman, or other coins for the required half-shekel. It seems that salt, wine, and oil were also sold in the Temple court. The money changers set up their tables from the Jewish month Adar 25 until Nisan 1 (roughly March–April).

Possibly exorbitant rates were charged by the money changers, but there are no known Jewish protests against them. There were protests against the sale of animals and birds. It could be that Jesus' action was directed primarily against those selling the doves and animals and that ***the tables of the money-changers*** were ***overturned*** in the confusion (Johnson, p. 504). Robinson finds the most serious offense to be reflected in the words ***den of robbers*** (cf. Jer. 7:11). The Temple served as a sanctuary for any Jew who wronged a Gentile, and he sees the Temple authorities to be allowing the Temple to shelter wrongdoers or fugitives from justice, with whom were identified some of the traders (pp. 171 f.). This possibility cannot be verified. The simplest and most probable explanation is that Jesus saw the Court of the Gentiles in such confusion that prayer was almost impossible there and that he saw the people being exploited in the name of religion. Against this he protested.

Jesus' declaration that the Temple was God's house and ***a house of prayer*** reflects the language of Isaiah 56:7 and Jeremiah 7:11. The phrase "for all the nations" is found in Mark 11:17 (cf. Isa. 56:7). It has been suggested that Matthew omitted it because he saw the Temple as the house of prayer for Israel only, but this would not account for its absence from Luke (19:46) whose theme of a gospel for all nations it would so well have served. The explanation may be that Matthew and Luke followed a text other than Mark at this point, or the words may be a scribal addition in Mark.

Although earlier Jesus had avoided the encouragement of popular acclaim, because of its many dangers to his mission, he now openly healed ***the blind and the lame,*** even ***in the temple.*** What pleased the crowds and caused even the ***children*** to cry out their praises made ***the chief priests and the scribes*** indignant. As the ***children*** praised Jesus as ***the Son of David,*** these religious leaders made protest to Jesus. Praise from children and protests from Temple and synagogue authorities seems to be a strange pattern, but it was not new. Jesus found in Psalm 8:2 an anticipation of ***perfect praise*** from ***babes and sucklings.***

Leaving the Temple, Jesus went ***to Bethany, and lodged there. Lodged*** (*ēulisthē*) may indicate that he spent the night in the open, but the term is not limited to this meaning. Probably for safety, Jesus spent the night in the open or with friends at Bethany, home of Lazarus, Mary, and Martha (John 11:1 f.; 12:1 f.).

Specific dating of the cleansing of the Temple is problematic. John introduces the cleansing of the Temple at the outset of the ministry of Jesus (2:14–17). The Synoptics all place it after Jesus' royal entry into Jerusalem—Matthew and Luke on the day of the entry, and Mark on the day following (11:11–15).

That Jesus did register such protest against the abuses of the Temple is solidly based in all four Gospels. That he spoke of a true temple, himself and his church, that would replace the one "made with hands" is featured by John (2:19) and constituted a major charge at his trial (26:61; Mark 14:58; cf. Eph. 2:18 ff.). More than anything else, this action and these words aroused the Sadducean high priests to action, for Jesus' protest was against them, not just against the merchants and money changers. The Pharisees had long since determined to destroy Jesus, because he had challenged the foundations of their system and their distinction between God's "clean" and "righteous" people and those who were not. At this point the two most powerful groups in Judaism, Sadducees and Pharisees, joined forces against their common foe.

3. *Lessons from a Fruitless Fig Tree* (*21:18–22*)

18 In the morning, as he was returning to the city, he was hungry. 19 And seeing a fig tree by the wayside he went to it, and found nothing on it but leaves only. And he said to it, "May no fruit ever come from you again!" And the fig tree withered at once. 20 When the disciples saw it they marveled, saying, "How did the fig tree wither at once?" 21 And Jesus answered them, "Truly, I say to you, if you have faith and never doubt, you will not only do what has been done to the fig tree, but even if you say to this mountain, 'Be taken up and cast into the sea,' it will be done. 22 And whatever you ask in prayer, you will receive, if you have faith."

That Jesus ***was hungry*** the morning after he lodged (v. 18) at Bethany suggests that he may have spent the night in the open. The verb for lodged (*ēulisthē*) may indicate this. If he spent the night in the open, he may have had no food.

Figs appear at the same time as the leaves on a fig tree, the buds actually appearing before the leaves. The leaves mature before the figs, but a few figs are edible before the main crop. Foliage would arouse hopes in the hungry that the tree might have edible figs. Finding ***leaves only*** meant that this tree would bear no figs that season.

If Jesus used the fig tree as an object lesson, as a dramatic sign, or as prophetic symbolism for the fate of fruitless Israel, all is clear enough. The fig tree was a familiar figure for Israel, and that seems to be the lesson in the parable of the barren fig tree in Luke 13:6–9. The sacrifice of a tree by the wayside would be justified could that awaken the twelve and they the nation to its dire peril (cf. 21:41,43). The lesson could likewise be applied as a warning against fruitlessness in the individual life (cf. John 15:2–6).

The discourse on ***faith*** and ***prayer*** is not obvious in its relationship to the withering of the fig tree. That one is to pray and to pray in faith is clear enough. But what is meant by causing yet other fig trees to wither or a ***mountain*** to be ***cast into the sea?***

Some parallel may be found between the passage here and John 15:1–11. In both the Matthean and Johannine passages the discussion moves from the importance of fruit to the matter of asking. It is fatal for nation or individual to be fruitless, but this is not necessary. There are divine resources which can save either from fruitlessness and its consequent destruction. In John these resources are open to one who "abides" in Christ and "asks." In Matthew these resources are open to the one who prays in faith.

4. The Question of the Authority of Jesus (21:23—22:14)

Authority is the key word giving unity to this section. The question is raised by the recognized Jewish authorities, and Jesus met it head-on. He first exposed the hypocrisy of those who asked him for his credentials. Then he set forth the nature, significance, and tests of authority and the consequences of the disrespect of authority.

(1) The Authority Challenged (21:23–27)

**23 And when he entered the temple, the chief
priests and the elders of the people came up to
him as he was teaching, and said, "By what
authority are you doing these things, and who
gave you this authority?" 24 Jesus answered
them, "I also will ask you a question; and if
you tell me the answer, then I also will tell you
by what authority I do these things. 25 The
baptism of John, whence was it? From heaven
or from men?" And they argued with one
another, "If we say, 'From heaven,' he will say
to us, 'Why then did you not believe him?'
26 But if we say, 'From men,' we are afraid of
the multitude; for all hold that John was a
prophet." 27 So they answered Jesus, "We do
not know." And he said to them, "Neither will
I tell you by what authority I do these things.**

The ***chief priests and the elders*** were the recognized authorities in Judaism. The ***chief priests*** included the high priest, who was also president of the Sanhedrin, highest court of the Jews. ***The elders*** (*presbuteroi*) were the laymen, Pharisees or scribes, who also were represented in the Sanhedrin. These men had the right to ask Jesus for his credentials, especially in view of the liberty he had taken in the interpretation of the Law, assessing the oral tradition, and in cleansing the Temple. Jesus had boldly spoken and acted within areas of what was recognized as their sphere of authority. Jesus did not challenge their right to question him. They would have been negligent of their duties had they been indifferent to what was being taught and practiced.

Jesus challenged the "authorities" at another point, that of their sincerity. He exposed their hypocrisy by putting them to test. Had they honestly inquired into his authority, Jesus would have respected their inquiry. But it was not evidence that they needed. It was a willingness to assess honestly evidence already before them. Jesus exposed their hypocrisy by asking them about ***the baptism of John.*** Was it from God or man? Seeing their dilemma, they became evasive. Unwilling to acknowledge John's commission from God and fearing the people who recognized John as a prophet, they claimed that they did not know.

Jesus refused to give further answer to their question, not because the question itself was improper but because they were not open to the truth. Jesus had no word for hypocrisy except judgment. If they were not competent to judge John, whose life was completed, how could they judge Jesus? It was not that they could not but that they would not fairly judge John or Jesus.

(2) Two Sons: Authority Acknowledged in Obedience, Not Words (21:28–32)

**28 "What do you think? A man had two sons;
and he went to the first and said, 'Son, go and
work in the vineyard today.' 29 And he answered, 'I will not'; but afterward he repented**

**and went. 30 And he went to the second and
said the same; and he answered, 'I go, sir,' but
did not go. 31 Which of the two did the will of
his father?" They said, "The first." Jesus said
to them, "Truly, I say to you, the tax collectors
and the harlots go into the kingdom of God
before you. 32 For John came to you in the way
of righteousness, and you did not believe him,
but the tax collectors and the harlots believed
him; and even when you saw it, you did not
afterward repent and believe him.**

The main point is clearly that authority is respected by obedience, not by lip service. The chief priests and elders, in asking Jesus about his authority, implied that they had respect for authority. Jesus first exposed their hypocrisy by questioning them about John, and then he pinpointed the matter of what constitutes respect for authority. Obedience, and nothing short of that, is the answer.

The only problem in this parable is textual. Extant manuscripts give three different readings. (1) In that followed by the RSV, the first son says no but repents, the second son says yes but does nothing. The first son is approved for having done his father's will. This reading has fairly good manuscript support and is probably correct. (2) What usually are highly reliable manuscripts reverse the order, having the first son saying yes but doing nothing, the second saying no but obeying. The second son is approved. (3) The Western type manuscripts have the surprising reading. The first son says no but repents; the second says yes but does nothing, yet the second is approved. This clearly is not the point Jesus intended. The choice is between readings (1) and (2), both approving the son who obeyed, even though he first said no.

Following the RSV, the first son typifies ***the tax collectors and harlots,*** while the second son typifies Israel or the leaders of Israel who promise God obedience but fail to obey his commands. The former enter the ***kingdom of God before*** the Jewish rulers. The kingdom is the ruling of God. It calls for submission, not mere lip service. ***Tax collectors and harlots*** are more aware of their sin and more readily ***repent and believe.*** The guilt of the religious authorities is compounded in that they not only ignored John but were unmoved when they saw even ***the tax collectors and harlots*** being brought into ***the way of righteousness*** under God's kingly rule through John's preaching.

In praising ***tax collectors and harlots*** above chief priests and elders, Jesus gave no sanction to libertine or antinomian tendencies. What he censored the leaders for was failure to respond to John, who came in ***the way of righteousness.*** The kingdom of God makes righteous demands such as John proclaimed, yet opened its doors to ***tax collectors and harlots*** who ***repent and believe.*** That is Matthew's emphasis, and in this he correctly represents the position of Jesus. Radical demand and limitless mercy are brought together in the teaching and manner of Jesus.

(3) *Wicked Tenants: Crushed by Spurned Authority (21:33–44)*

**33 "Hear another parable. There was a
householder who planted a vineyard, and set a
hedge around it, and dug a wine press in it,
and built a tower, and let it out to tenants, and
went into another country. 34 When the season
of fruit drew near, he sent his servants to the
tenants, to get his fruit; 35 and the tenants took
his servants and beat one, killed another, and
stoned another. 36 Again he sent other servants,
more than the first; and they did the same to
them. 37 Afterward he sent his son to them,
saying, 'They will respect my son.' 38 But when
the tenants saw the son, they said to themselves, 'This is the heir; come, let us kill him
and have his inheritance.' 39 And they took him
and cast him out of the vineyard, and killed
him. 40 When therefore the owner of the vineyard comes, what will he do to those tenants?"
41 They said to him, "He will put those
wretches to a miserable death, and let out the
vineyard to other tenants who will give him the
fruits in their seasons."**

**42 Jesus said to them, "Have you never read
in the scriptures:**

**'The very stone which the builders rejected
has become the head of the corner;
this was the Lord's doing,
and it is marvelous in our eyes'?**

**43 Therefore I tell you, the kingdom of God
will be taken away from you and given to a
nation producing the fruits of it."**

Authority is the continuing theme in the parable of the wicked tenants. This is a story of rebellion against authority and its consequences. The parable is in the form of an allegory, largely patterned on Isaiah 5:1–7. The ***vineyard*** is a familiar figure for Israel, and that is its symbolism here. God is the owner of the ***vineyard,*** and the ***tenants*** are the rulers of Israel or Israel itself. The ***servants*** are the prophets, and the ***son*** is Jesus. The ***other tenants,*** to whom the ***vineyard*** is given, are the Christian leaders or the church itself.

The description of the ***vineyard*** and its provisions is clear and true to the times. ***Hedge*** is a fence, a protection against wild beasts. The ***wine press*** consisted of two parts, the upper part where the grapes were crushed and the lower part in which the juice was collected. The ***tower*** served as a shelter for the workers and as an observation tower for the guards. These features belong only to the color of the story and have no symbolic value, except to suggest the careful provision which God made for his people, as the owner did for his vineyard.

A major point of the parable is that in rejecting the ***servants*** and the ***son,*** the wicked ***tenants*** were really rejecting the authority of the ***owner.*** It was with him that ultimately they had to reckon. Likewise, Israel or her leaders had killed the prophets and would soon kill the ***son,*** but they would not thus succeed in gaining ***his inheritance*** for themselves. In killing prophets and ***son,*** they were defying the authority of God and would have to answer to him.

A further point, indicating the guilt of the ***tenants,*** is that they killed the prophets and the ***son*** knowing who they were. It was not done in ignorance. Jesus is thus driving home the charge that the high priests and elders who question his authority are insincere. They ask for more evidence but are not open to it. It is their wilful rejection of ***the son*** which constitutes their great sin.

One of the most moving and instructive verses is the thirty-seventh. The ***son*** was sent even though the servants had been abused and killed. God sent his Son into a world which already had killed his prophets. This was love's calculated risk. The ***tenants*** did not have to kill the ***son,*** and the ***owner*** did not send his ***son*** so that he would be killed. The ***owner*** sent his ***son*** to prevail upon the ***tenants*** to yield the ***fruit.***

God did not force Israel to crucify Jesus, and he did not want Israel to reject and crucify him. God sent his Son to convert people, to save them. The New Testament condemns what the Jews and Romans did as rejection (21:42; John 1:11; Acts 4:11; Rom. 9:32; 1 Peter 2:7), betrayal (Mark 8:31; 9:31; 10:33; 14:41), and murder (Acts 7:52). God gave his Son and Jesus gave his life, and in that giving is redemption; but man took life and that is man's guilt (cf. Acts 2:23).

Verses 42 f. reflect Psalm 118:22 f., a passage very prominent in its application to Jesus by early Christians (cf. Acts 4:11; 1 Peter 2:7). Jesus is the ***stone which the builders rejected.*** But the rejected stone is made ***the head of the corner,*** presumably the chief foundation stone. The cornerstone was more than an ornamental stone or depository for mementos, as is true today. It actually bore much of the weight of the building (McNeile, p. 312).

Some see the stone to refer to the capstone, but this is not likely. Whatever the function of the stone, it is the most important in the building. Israel is about to cast Jesus aside, but he is the very foundation to the "building" which God erects. Favored Israel, having forfeited her stewardship, will lose the kingdom to another ***nation,*** i.e., to the church, the believing community (cf. 1 Peter 2:9–10).

Verse 44 is of uncertain authenticity. It is not found in the Western type manuscripts and may be borrowed from Luke 20:18. Its warning seems to be that those who oppose Christ will be broken and that under his ultimate judgment they will be crushed. The destruction of Jerusalem and the nation in A.D. 70, after Israel followed its false warlike messiahs, was at least in part the fulfilment of this fate.

(4) *Hardening of Chief Priests and Pharisees (21:45–46)*

**45 When the chief priests and the Pharisees
heard his parables, they perceived that he was
speaking about them. 46 But when they tried to
arrest him, they feared the multitudes, because
they held him to be a prophet.**

This paragraph looks back to 21:23, except the elders are now identified as Pharisees. It indicates also that the parables of the two sons and of the wicked tenants belong to Jesus' reply to the high priests and Pharisees (the elders of 21:23). It is further indicated that their minds were already made up, closed to the evidences which led the multitudes to hold Jesus ***to be a prophet,*** one who spoke for God.

(5) *Defiant Guests and a King's Wrath (22:1–14)*

**1 And again Jesus spoke to them in parables,
saying, 2 "The kingdom of heaven may be compared to a king who gave a marriage feast for
his son, 3 and sent his servants to call those
who were invited to the marriage feast; but
they would not come. 4 Again he sent other
servants, saying, 'Tell those who are invited,
Behold, I have made ready my dinner, my
oxen and my fat calves are killed, and everything is ready; come to the marriage feast.'
5 But they made light of it and went off, one to
his farm, another to his business, 6 while the
rest seized his servants, treated them shamefully, and killed them. 7 The king was angry,
and he sent his troops and destroyed those
murderers and burned their city. 8 Then he
said to his servants, 'The wedding is ready, but
those invited were not worthy. 9 Go therefore
to the thoroughfares, and invite to the marriage
feast as many as you find.' 10 And those servants went out into the streets and gathered all
whom they found, both bad and good; so the
wedding hall was filled with guests.**

**11 "But when the king came in to look at the
guests, he saw there a man who had no wedding garment; 12 and he said to him, 'Friend,
how did you get in here without a wedding
garment?' And he was speechless. 13 Then the
king said to the attendants, 'Bind him hand
and foot, and cast him into the outer darkness;
there men will weep and gnash their teeth.'
14 For many are called, but few are chosen."**

This parable may not be as closely connected with the question of authority posed in 21:23 as are the parables of the two sons and the wicked tenants, but Matthew may have intended it to be the climactic parable in the development of that theme. The lesson would closely parallel that in the parable of the wicked tenants. Here ***a king*** is the central figure, and it is his authority which is defied but not escaped.

The ***king*** issued invitations to many to become guests at the ***marriage feast*** for his son. Although issued as an invitation, a king's invitation is more than just a social courtesy. To spurn a king's invitation is to reject his authority. This cannot be done with impunity. In the parable, the ***king*** has reference to God. God invites men to his table. If he did not invite, man could not sit at that table, just as a subject cannot attend a king's banquet unless invited. God does invite, but he does not compel one to eat of his banquet. One may refuse, but in so doing he defies the authority of God and thus chooses the alternative, destruction in ***outer darkness.***

One must understand ancient customs to get the point in the servant's being sent ***to call those who*** had been ***invited.*** The invitations went out in advance; and when the banquet was ready, the servants were sent to those invited to tell them that the banquet was ready and it was time to come. This meant that those who refused to attend had received their invitations earlier and had less excuse for declining.

Those invited first refused to come and later ***made light*** of the invitation as they made too much of other interests. But there was not only indifference to the king's invitation; some showed hostility. When for a second time servants were sent, some of the invited scoffed, and others abused and killed the servants. The conduct of those invited is almost too shocking to believe. It was rude, crude, and cruel. But this is the point. More amazing than God's gracious invitation to men to sit at his table is man's indifference, refusal, and even defiance.

Verse 7 is difficult to fit into the story

The king sent out ***his troops*** to destroy the ***murderers*** and burn ***their city*** (presumably an allusion to the destruction of Jerusalem, fulfilled in A.D. 70), yet the ***wedding is*** still ***ready*** (v. 8) for the guests. It is forced to speak of a *Blitzkrieg* which could be completed before the meal cooled. It is best simply to remember that this is a parable. The lessons are clear enough, even though the details of the story are hard to envision. Although a banquet does not remain ***ready*** while a war is fought, the "messianic banquet" to which the parable refers does continue to stand ready.

When the ones first invited proved to be ***not worthy,*** servants were sent out into ***the thoroughfares*** (*diexodous* may mean the roads leading out of the city or the crossroads) to invite any who could be found, ***bad and good.*** The reference may be to the Gentile mission following Israel's rejection of Jesus, but first of all it referred to the tax gatherers and "sinners" within Israel. Calling or election roots in God's grace, not in man's merit. The ***wedding hall*** will be filled, whether or not those most privileged respond.

A parable within a parable is found in verses 11–14. One guest was found to have ***no wedding garment.*** The conjecture that the host provided his guests with wedding garments may be correct, but it derives solely from this passage (unless, as seems unlikely, such is reflected in Gen. 45:22; Judges 14:12 f.). We are not told why the man was considered guilty. When asked to explain what right he had to enter (not *how* he got in) without the garment, ***he was speechless.*** Presumably he had no excuse. The point may be that his defiance of authority was greater even than that of the men first invited. They defied the king's authority by refusing to attend the feast. This man defied that authority in a more arrogant way, by trying to attend on his own terms.

The puzzling passage about the man without the ***wedding garment,*** as well as the closing statement that ***many are called, but few are chosen,*** may be designed to serve warning to the last group invited, whether tax gatherers and harlots (21:32) or Gentiles, that they too are in danger of being presumptuous. Just as the first group invited represents the Jewish leaders, so the second group, to which the man without the wedding garment belongs, represents Gentiles, or the outside group in Israel. By presumption on privilege, either can be rejected. The ***wedding garment*** is a reminder that even within the grace of divine calling or election there is moral demand (cf. Lau, p. 157).

Jeremias holds that by ***wedding garment*** no particular garment used only for celebrations is meant but that the reference is to the condition of the garment, washed clean and white for the banquet (*Parables,* pp. 187–89). God's free gift of salvation is often pictured as "garments of salvation" or a "robe of righteousness" (Isa. 61:10). In rabbinical interpretation of Ecclesiastes 9:8, "let your garments be always white," the festal garment stands for repentance. In Revelation a white robe is symbolic of purity or repentance (3:4,5,18; 19:8). So here, the ***wedding garment*** may symbolize God's gift of salvation, or specifically repentance and righteousness. Salvation is offered to tax gatherers, harlots, and Gentiles, but it is not indulgence. It is gift and demand.

The price of rejecting God's invitation is rejection. ***Many are called*** [*klētoi*], ***but few are chosen*** [*eklektoi*]. This seems to mean that many are invited, but not all approved. The teaching here somewhat parallels that of the parables of the weeds (13:24–30,36–43) and the dragnet (13:47–50). The "good" and the "bad" are found together until the judgment, but in the final judgment they are separated.

Matthew differs from Paul in the employment of the terms "called" and "chosen" or "elected." Paul restricts the terms to those who have responded in faith to God's invitation. For him, the opposite to "the called" are not the "uncalled" but those who have refused or disobeyed. Matthew employs "called" for God's invitation, extended to all, and "elected" for those who are found to have properly responded.

5. *Abortive Efforts to Outwit Jesus* (*22: 15–40*)

Matthew now follows Mark in presenting three attempts by the Jewish authorities to outwit Jesus, either to draw him into making statements on some controversial issue or to embarrass and discredit him before the people. The Pharisees with the help of the Herodians made the first attempt. They were followed by the Sadducees and then tried yet another time to entangle Jesus in the area of the Law, where they thought themselves to be authorities.

(*1*) *Paying Taxes to Caesar* (*22:15–22*)

15 Then the Pharisees went and took counsel how to entangle him in his talk. 16 And they sent their disciples to him, along with the Herodians, saying, "Teacher, we know that you are true, and teach the way of God truthfully, and care for no man; for you do not regard the position of men. 17 Tell us, then, what you think. Is it lawful to pay taxes to Caesar, or not?" 18 But Jesus, aware of their malice, said, "Why put me to the test, you hypocrites? 19 Show me the money for the tax." And they brought him a coin. 20 And Jesus said to them, "Whose likeness and inscription is this?" 21 They said, "Caesar's." Then he said to them, "Render therefore to Caesar the things that are Caesar's, and to God the things that are God's." 22 When they heard it, they marveled; and they left him and went away.

Questioning Jesus about paying ***taxes to Caesar*** was a deliberate plot, designed to force upon him a dilemma from which he could not escape. The Pharisees opposed the payment of this tax to Caesar, although it remained for the Zealots to plunge the nation into war with the Romans (A.D. 66–70). ***The Herodians*** (cf. Mark 3:6) were political partisans, supporting the heirs of Herod the Great. Since the Herods were dependent upon the Romans for their offices, they supported the payment of the tax.

The tax (*kēnson*) in question was a capitation or head tax, called poll tax today, levied equally upon all males over fourteen years of age and upon all females over twelve years, up to the age of sixty-five in provinces like Judea that were directly under the rule of Rome. This personal tax was in addition to a property tax and customs on produce. The tax was paid with a special silver denarius, bearing the picture and name of the reigning Caesar. The tax was doubly hateful to patriotic Jews, for it forced them to acknowledge their subordination to a foreign ruler, and the Caesar's image violated their law and conscience against idolatry. It was this tax which was the occasion for the revolt of Judas of Galilee in A.D. 6 (Josephus, *Antiq.* 18.1; and *Wars* 2:8).

Hoping to ***entangle*** Jesus ***in his talk,*** i.e., to trick him into saying something which would either alienate Jewish patriots or give the Herodians grounds for charging him with revolutionary tendencies or treason, the Pharisees first tried to throw Jesus off guard by flattery. They addressed him as ***Teacher,*** a title of honor among them; and they praised him as ***true*** and impartial. The phrases ***care for no man*** and ***do not regard the position of men*** are ambiguous in English. What was meant was that Jesus did not show partiality and that he did not judge men by outward appearances. In this context they asked what they thought would leave Jesus no escape: ***taxes to Caesar, or not?*** They used the word give, not the word pay. In Mark 12:14 it is more pointed, "Should we pay them, or should we not?" The question as to whether or not it was ***lawful to pay*** the tax was asked from the standpoint of Mosaic law.

Jesus did not evade the question, but he gave a surprising answer, both devastating to the Pharisaic position and far-reaching in its direction for all people. The alternative to "straddling the fence" is not necessarily to fall off on one side or the other. It may be to demolish the fence. Jesus was ***aware of their malice*** and called their hand as ***hypocrites.*** He replied to the question by calling for ***the money*** [*nomisma*] ***for the tax*** [*kēnsou*], i.e., the special coin for the census or head tax.

The very fact that they possessed the coin proved that they already had acknowledged Caesar. In accepting his coin they had assumed certain obligations. He compelled them to acknowledge that it bore Caesar's ***likeness*** (literally "image") ***and inscription*** (name). Jesus then charged them to "give back" (*apodote*) ***to Caesar*** what is ***Caesar's and to God*** what ***is God's.*** He changed their "give" to give back, to stress their debt to Caesar and to God.

Jesus implicitly refused to support what proved to be Israel's hopeless and devastating war with Rome, nor did he say that Rome had the right to rule the Jews. He taught the validity of human government and recognized Roman rule as a fact. In recognizing debt to Caesar and to God, Jesus was not making a complete separation between the two, making Caesar independent of God or isolating secular and sacred. "Caesar" or state has valid claims, but "Caesar" remains valid only as he is submissive to God, who alone is sovereign and who is always over Caesar. Whenever government (Caesar) seeks to be totalitarian or independent of God, then it becomes idolatrous.

Likeness (*eikōn*) may have additional reference to the biblical teaching that man is made in the "image" of God (Gen. 1:27). What man must "give back" to God is first of all himself.

(2) *The Question of the Resurrection* (*22: 23–33*)

23 The same day Sadducees came to him,
who say that there is no resurrection; and they
asked him a question, 24 saying, "Teacher,
Moses said, 'If a man dies, having no children,
his brother must marry the widow, and raise
up children for his brother.' 25 Now there were
seven brothers among us; the first married, and
died, and having no children left his wife to
his brother. 26 So too the second and third,
down to the seventh. 27 After them all, the
woman died. 28 In the resurrection, therefore,
to which of the seven will she be wife? For
they all had her."
29 But Jesus answered them, "You are wrong,
because you know neither the scriptures nor
the power of God. 30 For in the resurrection
they neither marry nor are given in marriage,
but are like angels in heaven. 31 And as for the
resurrection of the dead, have you not read
what was said to you by God, 32 'I am the God
of Abraham, and the God of Isaac, and the
God of Jacob'? He is not God of the dead, but
of the living." 33 And when the crowd heard it,
they were astonished at his teaching.

The Sadducees (the name possibly from Zadok) are mentioned here for the sixth time by Matthew (cf. 3:7; 16:1,6,11 f.), but for the first time as acting alone. In Mark and Luke, they are mentioned only in this story (Mark 12:18; Luke 20:27). The Sadducees were wealthy aristocrats, few in number, but very powerful. They emerged from the "Grecians" or "Hellenists" who in the time of Antiochus Epiphanes (*ca.* 175 B.C.) collaborated with the Syrians, adapting to Grecian ways. Under the Romans (60 B.C. onward), they were the collaborationists, accepting the high priesthood as an appointive office by the Romans. They were the priestly party, the Pharisees being laymen.

Neither liberal nor conservative adequately describes the Sadducees. If either term applies, they were politically and socially conservative (status quo) and were biblical (Pentateuch) literalists. There is no conclusive evidence that they rejected any part of the Scriptures, but they built only upon the Pentateuch. They rejected the oral tradition of the Pharisees. They rejected the doctrines of resurrection, angels, fate and providence, emphasizing man's free will (cf. Acts 23:8; Josephus, *Antiq.* 13:5; 18:1; *Wars* 2,8). The doctrine of resurrection emerged rather late in the Old Testament (cf. Isa. 26:19; Dan. 12:2 f.; Habakkuk; Job; Psalm 73), and the Sadducees did not accept it. It is significant that Jesus went back to Exodus 3:6,15 f. to find a biblical basis for the doctrine of resurrection.

The intention of the Sadducees was chiefly to embarrass Jesus, but there were to them and the Romans some political overtones in the doctrine of resurrection. The doctrine was eschatological and could suggest a national Israel restored to sovereignty and freedom from Rome. But since the powerful Pharisees strongly believed in a resurrection, the Sadducees could make little of this as a political charge against Jesus. They probably intended only to ridicule both Jesus and the Pharisees.

The story of the ***seven brothers*** who in turn married one wife was probably a stock joke used by the Sadducees in derision. It alludes to the Levirate doctrine of Deuteronomy 25:5 (implied in Gen. 38:8), which required that where brothers lived together and one died without a son, the surviving brother was to take ***the widow*** as wife ***and raise up*** a son to his deceased brother. The Sadducees quoted the LXX version, which omits the condition that the brothers had lived on the same estate and which refers only to ***no children*** (*sperma*, seed) rather than "no son." The Sadducees' story also assumed a material resurrection, where the risen life would be like this one.

Jesus corrected the Sadducees at two points. They were ignorant of the ***scriptures*** (even of the part they acknowledged) and also of what God can do. Resurrection is continuing personal life but not in material expressions like the physical side of marriage. Jesus and Paul (1 Cor. 15:35–44) taught that the resurrection body would be spiritual, body but not "flesh and blood." In the analogy of the "seed," Paul found both continuity and discontinuity between the body now and the risen body. Jesus does not go into detail, but this seems to be implied in his answer to the Sadducees.

The New Testament doctrine of resurrection avoids two extremes, the crudely literal view of the Sadducees and the so-called "Greek" view of an immortal soul. The material view was widely held in the ancient world, as evidenced, e.g., in the burial customs of the ancient Egyptians and the early American Indians. They expected life in the next world to be physical and material. The "Greek" view (held by many non-Greeks) of the immortality of the soul, held that the body was only the tomb or prison of the soul and that death was the friend which freed soul from body. This contradicts the biblical doctrine of creation, which sees body as essential to what man is, and the doctrine of redemption, which sees the whole man as the object of redemption. But the body is seen as undergoing change, comparable to the renewal beginning with the inner self.

It is significant that Jesus appealed to the Pentateuch (Ex. 3:6), the older part recognized by the Sadducees, in affirming God is ***the God of Abraham, the God of Isaac, the God of Jacob,*** and the God ***of the living.*** First of all, this affirms the eternal importance of individuality. He is not only God of Israel but of individual persons. We are distinct individuals in creation, redemption, and in the future world. Jesus affirmed that God now, presently, is the God of Abraham, Isaac, and Jacob. These are ***not dead*** but alive. They are alive as individual persons. They are not dead or asleep. Whatever further dimensions belong to the resurrection at the Parousia of Jesus, already those who have died are living persons (cf. 17:3). Belief in continuing life for man is bound up with belief in a living God.

The statement that in the resurrection men are ***like angels*** is not to be pressed beyond one point: ***they neither marry nor are given in marriage.*** The popular idea that men become angels in heaven has no biblical support.

(3) *The Great Commandment* (*22:34–40*)

34 But when the Pharisees heard that he had silenced the Sadducees, they came together. 35 And one of them, a lawyer, asked him a question, to test him. 36 "Teacher, which is the great commandment in the law?" 37 And he said to him, "You shall love the Lord your God with all your heart, and with all your soul, and with all your mind. 38 This is the great and first commandment. 39 And a second is like it, You shall love your neighbor as yourself. 40 On these two commandments depend all the law and the prophets."

The ***great commandment*** appears in all three Synoptics, based upon Deuteronomy 6:5. There are minor variations in each statement of it. The Synoptic differences seem to point to two basic traditions, one preserved in Mark 12:28–34 and another in Q. In Luke, the "lawyer" is credited with combining Deuteronomy 6:5 and Leviticus 19:18, bringing together the commandments to love God and man. Luke seems to preserve the Q tradition. In Mark the two commandments are brought together by Jesus (12:29 f.), and then they are restated by the "scribe" (12:32 f.). Matthew follows Mark in attributing the summary statement to Jesus. In Mark the great commandment is introduced against the declaration of the oneness of God (Deut. 6:4), and the story is conciliatory. In Luke the second of the great commandments is expounded through the story of the good Samaritan. In Matthew the hostility between the Pharisees and Jesus is prominent.

The Pharisees had found the laws to be 613 in number—365 prohibitions and 248 positive commandments. They had also discussed the relative importance of the laws. Lawyer (*nomikos*) is an alternate term for scribe—copyist and student of the Mosaic law.

The key word in the ***great commandment*** as well as the ***second*** that is like it, is ***love*** (see discussion of 5:43–48). Love is the basic disposition of one's whole being to relate to God for his glory and to man for his good. ***Heart*** in Jewish thought was the seat of thinking and feeling. ***Soul*** (*psuchē*) may refer to life, mind, or self. ***Mind*** (*dianoia*) refers to the rational element.

When comparison is made of all passages involved, it becomes clear that the terms vary in number and order. The Hebrew text of Deuteronomy 6:5 has heart, soul, and might. The LXX has the same in Codex Alexandrinus but mind, soul, and might in Codex Vaticanus. In Mark, Jesus speaks of heart, soul, mind, and strength, while the scribe mentions heart, understanding, and strength. In Luke, the lawyer names heart, soul, strength, mind. What is intended in each passage is the whole self given to God and to others. Mechanical precision is not a goal important to biblical writers.

Jesus makes love not only ***the great commandment*** but also the essence and fulfilment of ***the law and the prophets*** (cf. 5:17). All the Scriptures ***depend*** upon ***these two commandments.*** Literally translated, ***the law and the prophets*** "hang" (*krematai*) on these two love commandments, like a door on its hinges. This means that the twofold love commandment is the principle of interpretation for the whole of ***the law and the prophets*** (our Old Testament). It also means that in the performance of the law of love toward God and neighbor all God's laws are performed, for it is the essence of the Law.

Jesus and the rabbis were seemingly together in this understanding of the Law, but there was a major difference which separated them. Although the rabbis occasionally recognized a summary of all the laws in one or in a few commandments, they held firmly to the principle that each commandment is as important as the others, the "light" commandments being as important as the "heavy" ones (cf. *Aboth* 2:1*b*., Jerusalem *Kiddushin* 1:61*b; Tanhuma* 5*b;* Babylonian Hagigah 5*a*). Jesus, however, found love to be the fulfilment of all the laws, not just one law alongside the others (cf. Bornkamm, pp. 75–78, 85). Matthew shows that Jesus recognized the validity of the whole Law, this against the antinomians. He showed that Jesus had a deeper understanding of the Law than the rabbis. This opposes all legalism. This is not to place us under lighter but heavier demand, for the demands of love are heavier than all legalism. Love both liberates and binds. It freely gives and yet requires the whole of oneself for God, neighbor, and oneself.

To a Pharisee his ***neighbor*** would be another Pharisee. The name Pharisee, meaning separatist and alluding to their purpose to separate themselves from ritually "unclean" people and things, was a nickname given them by others. They called themselves Haberim, meaning neighbors. Jesus taught that the true neighbor is the one who acts in love toward anyone whom he might serve (cf. Luke 10:29–37).

Although the emphasis is upon loving God and neighbor, one is also to love himself. There is a self-love which is the essence of depravity, but there is also a godly love which necessarily includes oneself. When one sees that he belongs to God and neighbor, he finds that he must be true to himself also. Love cannot be divided, and the true self cannot be isolated from God or neighbor. Either one loves God, neighbor, and himself or he loves neither.

6. *Jesus' Question: David's Son or David's Lord (22:41–46)*

**41 Now while the Pharisees were gathered
together, Jesus asked them a question,
42 saying, "What do you think of the Christ?
Whose son is he?" They said to him, "The son
of David." 43 He said to them, "How is it then
that David, inspired by the Spirit, calls him
Lord, saying,
44 'The Lord said to my Lord,
Sit at my right hand,
till I put thy enemies under thy feet'?
45 If David thus calls him Lord, how is he his
son?" 46 And no one was able to answer him a
word, nor from that day did any one dare to
ask him any more questions.**

After answering various test questions posed by the Pharisees and Sadducees, Jesus took the initiative in posing a question which not only silenced his opponents but also brought into focus the basic question as to his identity. Who is Jesus? The answer is that he is both David's son and David's Lord.

Matthew began by calling Jesus "son of David, son of Abraham," and he shows that Jesus accepted the title "son of David" (20:31; 21:9,15). But he is infinitely more than David's son. He is truly human, "descended from David according to the flesh" (Rom. 1:3); but he is also "Son of God" and David's Lord. He is not a political, Davidic Messiah as understood in current Judaism.

This passage does not mean to deny that Jesus is "son of David," but it corrects or interprets the statement. It is significant that the discussion, quoting Psalm 110:1, ends with the question "How?" The uniqueness of Jesus Christ as both David's son and David's Lord, as truly man and truly God, is a fact to be affirmed but not one which can be reduced to logical explanation. Christian faith stands securely before the mystery of the incarnation and does not remove the mystery.

7. *Scribes and Pharisees Exposed and Denounced (23:1–36)*

A major section beginning here and continuing through chapter 25 could be recognized. The denunciation of the scribes and Pharisees led to Jesus' lament over Jerusalem (23:37–39) and this in turn to his judgments upon Jerusalem and the world (24–25).

The section immediately before us, 23:1–36, has some parallels in Mark 12:37–40 and extensive parallels scattered through several chapters in Luke and in a different order (especially chs. 11 and 20). The discourse in Matthew falls into two parts: warnings against the example of the scribes and Pharisees (23:1–12) and judgment upon the scribes and Pharisees (23: 13–36). The scribes and Pharisees as the religious leaders represent Israel as a whole, not just one party.

(1) Warnings Against Their Example (23:1–12)

**1 Then said Jesus to the crowds and to his
disciples, 2 "The scribes and the Pharisees sit
on Moses' seat; 3 so practice and observe whatever they tell you, but not what they do; for
they preach, but do not practice. 4 They bind
heavy burdens, hard to bear, and lay them on
men's shoulders; but they themselves will not
move them with their finger. 5 They do all their
deeds to be seen by men; for they make their
phylacteries broad and their fringes long, 6 and
they love the place of honor at feasts and the
best seats in the synagogues, 7 and salutations
in the market places, and being called rabbi by
men. 8 But you are not to be called rabbi, for
you have one teacher, and you are all brethren.
9 And call no man your father on earth, for you
have one Father, who is in heaven. 10 Neither
be called masters, for you have one master, the
Christ. 11 He who is greatest among you shall
be your servant; 12 whoever exalts himself will
be humbled, and whoever humbles himself will
be exalted.**

Scribes and Pharisees are not identical. Most scribes were Pharisees, but not all Pharisees were scribes. The scribes were the recognized interpreters of the Jewish law. Their origins are traced to the time of Ezra. The earliest scribes were priests, but the later ones were laymen. The Pharisees in the time of Jesus consisted of about six thousand Jewish laymen who scrupulously sought to carry out the scribal rulings. Luke preserves the distinction between scribes and Pharisees, recording three woes against each (11:42–52), but Matthew was not interested in this distinction (cf. Introduction). When he wrote, the Pharisees were the almost unrivaled leaders of Judaism. To him they represent Israel as a whole.

Moses' seat seems to refer to an actual chair in a synagogue, symbolizing the origin and authority of scribal teaching. The scribes traced all their teachings back to Moses. The charge that ***the scribes and Pharisees*** did not ***practice*** what they ***preach*** is not to be taken in an absolute sense, as verse 5 indicates. Jesus did not endorse everything they taught, and he recognized that they practiced *some* of their teachings, at least outwardly. At this point the charge is against their motive and manner which rob their actions of value, for paradoxically they did not in God's sight actually practice what they appeared to do (McNeile, p. 330).

This passage reflects a relationship between Jesus' disciples and the synagogue, with no suggestion of a complete break between them (Lohmeyer, p. 335; Bornkamm, pp. 21 f.).

The ***burdens*** which the ***scribes and Pharisees bind*** upon the people are the meticulous rules about purification rites, food laws, sabbath observance, tithing of even garden produce, and the like. ***Bind*** is the technical term for forbidding. The school of Hillel was more liberal than that of Shammai, but in many matters the latter seems to have prevailed in the time of Jesus. Religion had come to be too much a burden to be borne and not a power to bear one up (cf. 11:28–30).

The charges here are sweeping ones, but they reflect the extent to which reform was needed. Milder charges would not have been heard. Although there were exceptions among the teachers and the teachings, one need only to read through long sections of the Talmud to see the extent to which burdens of trivialities had been thrust upon the people. Jesus called for the displacement of rules by basic commitments of love to God and neighbor. He called for more liberty for individual conscience and less regulation of every area of the individual's life by the scribal lawyers.

A major charge was that of acting to be seen of men. This led to extreme acts of ostentation, parading or dramatizing one's piety. ***Phylacteries*** were leather cases worn upon the forehead and left arm (Ex. 13:9; Deut. 6:8–9), containing the words of Exodus 13:1–10,11–16 and of Deuteronomy 6:4–9; 11:13–21, written on strips of vellum (skins) in literal fulfilment of Exodus 13:16 and Deuteronomy 6:8; 11:18. Some made these leather cases unduly large to call attention to their piety. The ***fringes*** were tassels worn on the four corners of the outer garment (cf. Num. 15:38 f.; Deut. 22:12). Jesus himself wore such tassels (9:20; 14:36). His protest was not against the custom but against ostentation, lengthening the tassels so as to appear pious.

Along with public display of piety through dress was the desire for special privileges and honors. The chief ***place of honor*** at a feast was the couch next to the host and to his right. It seems that the chief seats were on a platform facing the congregation. ***Salutations*** were not hasty greetings, as in the Western world, but more formal recognitions. Jesus found two faults with the desire for special titles, claiming what belongs to God alone or his Christ and the denial of the basic principle that service is the measure of greatness.

Rabbi means "my master" (teacher). After the time of Jesus the pronoun lost its force, and the term meant "master." In the community of Christ, he is the ***teacher***, and we are ***brethren***. "Abba" (father) was a term used for rabbis and great men of the past, and apparently it now was being applied to living persons. ***Master*** (*kathēgētēs*) translates another term for teacher, found here only in the Bible. Like *hodēgos* in verse 24, it stresses a leadership role, not administrative. There is no distinction between *teacher* in verse 8 and *master* in verse 10, the two Greek words apparently representing the Hebrew *rab* (teacher, master). True greatness as measured by service and humility is a recurrent New Testament teaching. Christians are to be brothers, learners, and servants (*diakonos,* deacon or servant).

(2) *Seven Woes and Coming Judgment (23:13–36)*

13 "But woe to you, scribes and Pharisees, hypocrites! because you shut the kingdom of heaven against men; for you neither enter yourselves, nor allow those who would enter to go in. 15 Woe to you, scribes and Pharisees, hypocrites! for you traverse sea and land to make a single proselyte, and when he becomes a proselyte, you make him twice as much a child of hell as yourselves.

16 "Woe to you, blind guides, who say, 'If any one swears by the temple, it is nothing; but if any one swears by the gold of the temple, he is bound by his oath.' 17 You blind fools! For which is greater, the gold or the temple that has made the gold sacred? 18 And you say, 'If any one swears by the altar, it is nothing; but if any one swears by the gift that is on the altar, he is bound by his oath.' 19 You blind men! For which is greater, the gift or the altar that makes the gift sacred? 20 So he who swears by the altar, swears by it and by everything on it; 21 and he who swears by the temple, swears by it and by him who dwells in it; 22 and he who swears by heaven, swears by the throne of God and by him who sits upon it.

23 "Woe to you, scribes and Pharisees, hypocrites! for you tithe mint and dill and cummin, and have neglected the weightier matters of the law, justice and mercy and faith; these you ought to have done, without neglecting the others. 24 You blind guides, straining out a gnat and swallowing a camel!

25 "Woe to you, scribes and Pharisees, hypocrites! for you cleanse the outside of the cup and of the plate, but inside they are full of extortion and rapacity. 26 You blind Pharisee! first cleanse the inside of the cup and of the plate, that the outside also may be clean.

27 "Woe to you, scribes and Pharisees, hypocrites! for you are like whitewashed tombs, which outwardly appear beautiful, but within they are full of dead men's bones and all uncleanness. 28 So you also outwardly appear righteous to men, but within you are full of hypocrisy and iniquity.

29 "Woe to you, scribes and Pharisees, hypocrites! for you build the tombs of the prophets and adorn the monuments of the righteous, 30 saying, 'If we had lived in the days of our fathers, we would not have taken part with them in shedding the blood of the prophets.' 31 Thus you witness against yourselves, that you are sons of those who murdered the prophets. 32 Fill up, then, the measure of your fathers. 33 You serpents, you brood of vipers, how are you to escape being sentenced to hell? 34 Therefore I send you prophets and wise men and scribes, some of whom you will kill and crucify, and some you will scourge in your synagogues and persecute from town to town, 35 that upon you may come all the righteous blood shed on earth, from the blood of innocent Abel to the blood of Zechariah the son of Barachiah, whom you murdered between the sanctuary and the altar. 36 Truly, I say to you, all this will come upon this generation.

Seven woes (23:13–32).—These verses have been often criticized as too severe to go back to Jesus and have been attributed to the later church in a period of bitter conflict with Judaism. On the one hand, it is to be recognized that the discourses and deeds of Jesus were preserved and proclaimed by different Christian communities and writers with sufficient freedom to allow for different stress and application. This follows inescapably from any comparison of Synoptic parallels. Something of the experience and character of each community and writer is stamped on each transmission of the Gospel. But when due allowance is made for the church's part, justice must be done to the clear picture of Jesus himself which shines through. The passage before us does preserve a judgment of Jesus upon the trusted religious leadership of his day.

First of all, it may be observed that the outright rejection of basic scribal and Pharisaic foundations comes to more forceful expression in Mark than in Matthew. For example, in 15:6, Matthew softens the stronger Markan (7:8) expression, "the tradition of men." In 15:18 he omits the far-reaching "thus he declared all foods clean" of Mark 7:19. Matthew did write at a time of great tension between church and synagogue, but he also sought to keep the channels open between the two. The New Testament contains strong evidence that Jesus was actually more "radical" in his rejection of teachings, practices, and goals of Pharisaic Judaism than was the church. It continued to cling to elements in current Jewish practice from which Jesus offered full freedom (cf. Acts, Gal., Heb.).

Yet further, it is easy to misconstrue the intention and spirit of Jesus as he pronounced these "woes" upon the ***scribes and Pharisees. Woe*** (*ouai*) is not a curse, and it is not simply a denunciation. The word may express anger or pity. Although it carries a judgment, it is here a cry or lamentation. It could be translated "Alas!" Jesus wept over Jerusalem, and the seven woes are lamentations over, as well as condemnations of, religious leaders who were misleading those who trusted them. It is not to be overlooked that these woes were not directed against "little people," tax gatherers, or harlots, but against those who were in position to know better and to do better. They were directed against privileged leaders who ***shut the kingdom of heaven against men.***

The woes were spoken by one who thus exposed his own life and actually gave it up in the effort to turn the leaders and the people from death to life, from bondage to freedom, from the things of religion to God himself. Jesus was not anti-Jewish. He was, according to the flesh, a Jew who loved his people enough to expose their false values and misplaced trust and point them to their only hope. It was out of love, not hate, that these strong denunciations came. Although judgmental, they were redemptive in intention.

It does not follow from verse 13 that no scribe or Pharisee is saved. Joseph of Arimathea, e.g., was a disciple of Jesus as well as a member of the Sanhedrin (27:57; Mark 15:43; Luke 23:50–53; John 19:38) and presumably a Pharisee. The point is that the Pharisees were not giving the world a fair chance at salvation, a most serious charge (Robinson, p. 188).

Verse 14 is properly omitted by the RSV and all modern texts, for it has support only in late manuscripts. It is borrowed from Mark 12:40 by manuscripts behind the KJV.

First-century Judaism was open to proselytes, Gentiles who were inducted into Judaism as both a religion and a nation by circumcision for men (in the ancient world there was a circumcision for women, but not in Judaism) and also baptism and the offering of ritual sacrifice for men and women. Often a ***proselyte*** to a religion is more extremely partisan than those who win him to their religion. Probably, Jesus meant that the plight is worsened for a Gentile who is led to trust legal and ritual values for salvation.

The third woe has to do with casuistry, a legal distinction between oaths found binding and those not. In making some oaths valid and some not, the way was opened for legalizing perjury, i.e., pretending to bind oneself by oath yet leaving oneself a technical or legal loophole. Behind this casuistry was the idea that an oath is not binding unless made in the presence of God, as though God were more present and involved if the oath was by the ***gold*** of the Temple than ***by the temple*** itself. In 5:33–37 Matthew shows that Jesus taught that no oath at all is necessary for honest people. It is sheer folly and blindness to seek to hide behind such legal fiction as that the particular wording of an oath binds one to his word or not.

The fourth woe exposes the fallacy of scrupulous attention to minor matters in the face of the neglect of basic principles and values. The tithing (a tenth) of grain, wine, oil, fruit, flocks, and herds was prescribed in the Scriptures (cf. Lev. 27:30; Deut. 14:22), but the scribes had extended this to include even the herbs from the garden. ***Mint and dill and cummin*** were herbs or spices for seasoning, and the latter two were also used as medicine. The greater failing was not the misplaced emphasis on the minor but the failure to give proper attention to the more important ***matters of the law. Justice and mercy and faith*** are somewhat reminiscent of Micah 6:8 and Proverbs 14:22. ***Faith*** (*pistin*) can mean either trust or faithfulness, faithfulness to God probably being the thought here.

The parable of the ***gnat*** and ***camel*** is deliberately grotesque, to point up the blindness of meticulous attention to such small matters as tithing garden herbs while neglecting basic matters of character and conduct. To strain out is to filter. The strange "strain at a gnat" in the KJV is due to a printer's error made in 1611 and never corrected.

The fifth woe is a warning against an outwardly regulated life that conceals an inner uncleansed self. ***Extortion*** (*harpagēs*) ***and rapacity*** (*akrasias*) are heavy charges. *Harpagēs* is robbery, and *akrasias* is lack of self-control or unrestrained desire (cf. 1 Cor. 7:5). Jesus was concerned that both the ***inside and*** the ***outside*** of cup and platter ***be clean.*** He made the inner self primary but also taught that inner renewal will be reflected or expressed in the outer life.

The ***whitewashed tombs*** of the sixth woe probably refer to the Jewish custom of whitewashing tombs a month before Passover so that they could be seen readily and avoided. To touch a tomb was considered defiling. Whitewashing made the tombs ***appear beautiful,*** but everyone knew their condition within. This woe is directed against ***hypocrisy.*** Legalism easily becomes a cloak underneath which may lurk an unredeemed heart. Jesus here and elsewhere warned against religion designed for show, to be seen of men. Matthew, resisting antinomianism as well as legalism, may have a special interest in the contrast between the righteousness Jesus demanded and the practice of ***iniquity*** (*anomias* is lawlessness or antinomianism).

The seventh woe uncovers the contradiction between praise for the ***prophets*** now conveniently dead and the rejection of ***prophets*** who make us uncomfortable by their presence. This is dishonesty. First of all, one thus pretends to be better than his forebears, implying that he would have respected the prophets of old. Then it is dishonest because one rejects in his day the very prophetic witness which he presumes to honor from the past. Would we listen responsively to Amos, Micah, or Jeremiah if they were to appear in our day? All of us like to identify with the prophets or the Saviour, safely locked up in the past. ***Sons of those who murdered the prophets*** is a proverbial way of saying "like father like son." Verse 32 is correctly translated as an imperative, built upon the best attested Greek reading. Jesus employs sad irony here, "Go ahead and complete what your fathers began!" The sons of those who killed the prophets would soon crucify him.

Coming judgment (*23:33–36*).—These words sound like the harshest ever attributed to Jesus. Many interpreters hold that Jesus would not have said these things. But careful reading may throw a different light upon them. Let it be noted that Jesus never remotely suggested that his followers persecute other people. He did not even allow his disciples to defend him in Gethsemane. He is denouncing persecution, and at the same time pleading with those who are so disposed to turn from such ways.

Who can deny that every form of hatred and persecution denounced here has come to active expression countless times in Judaism of old as well as in other religions? Who can deny that men have murdered one another "in the name of God" and even "in the name of Christ"? Jesus was not fighting a straw man. He hated no one, and he never once sanctioned persecution. In these strong words he is denouncing any religion in which man tries to "play God" in dealing with other people. The words of Jesus may shock us. Are we less shocked by those who ***kill, crucify, scourge*** others even in a religious assembly, or ***persecute*** people ***from town to town?***

It is to be remembered that these words were uttered against the piety of religious authorities who insisted upon their piety and authority. At stake was their destiny as well as that of their nation. The devastation of A.D. 70 was but a part of what was to ***come upon this generation.***

The murders of ***Abel*** and ***Zechariah*** reflect the order of the books of the Hebrew Bible, beginning with Genesis and concluding with 2 Chronicles. Jesus simply called attention to the trail of bloodshed or murder of righteous men from the first mentioned (Gen. 4:8) to the last mentioned (2 Chron. 24:20 ff.) in the Hebrew Bible. ***Barachiah*** (absent from Luke 11:51) was actually the father of the Zechariah of Zechariah 1:1, Jehoiada of the Zechariah of 2 Chronicles 24:20 ff. At what point this exchange of names occurred is unknown and in itself unimportant.

8. *Jesus Weeps over Jerusalem (23:37–39)*

37 "O Jerusalem, Jerusalem, killing the prophets and stoning those who are sent to you! How often would I have gathered your children together as a hen gathers her brood under her wings, and you would not! 38 Behold, your house is forsaken and desolate. 39 For I tell you, you will not see me again, until you say, 'Blessed is he who comes in the name of the Lord.' "

This deeply moving lament over Jerusalem throws further light on the woes of the preceding passage. It was deep sorrow and active concern which prompted Jesus to plead with and warn his people. ***Jerusalem*** was the unrivaled center of the Jewish world. It was there that the destiny of the nation was decided. For all her record of ***killing the prophets and stoning*** (Jewish manner of execution) ***those sent to*** her, Jesus went to her, offering himself for acceptance or rejection.

How often may imply support to the Gospel of John's record that Jesus made several trips to Jerusalem during his ministry (John 2:13; 5:1; 7:14; 10:22 f.; 12:12). ***Hen*** (*ornis*) may refer to any mother bird, and the analogy of a mother bird gathering ***her brood under her wings*** may reflect passages like Psalm 36:7 and Isaiah 31:5. Jesus intended no harm to Jerusalem or to her people. He gladly would have shielded them with his own person, gathering them to himself in love, to shelter and shield.

But Jerusalem ***would not!*** No doctrine of predestination (determinism) can survive between Jesus' I ***would*** and Jerusalem's ***would not.*** Jerusalem remained ***forsaken and desolate,*** but the fate was chosen, not imposed. Special reference may be to the ruin of the Temple, the city, the nation, or all. Verse 39 is eschatological, referring to Jesus' Parousia. He would come again in judgment, hailed by his own as the blessed one ***who comes in the name of the Lord.*** But then would be too late for those who have rejected him.

XV. Judgment: Immediate and Ultimate (24:1—26:2)

The long discourse contained in chapters 24–25 is eschatological in nature and practical in purpose. It is the fifth major discourse in Matthew. Eschatology is a view of the world and history in which God is seen as moving them toward a goal, a consummation of both judgment and salvation. The practical purpose of the discourse is to awaken or sustain an expectation that Jesus will return to earth to bring the world to its goal, to warn against being misled by false prophets or christs, to encourage readiness for Christ's return, and to remind the followers of Jesus of their world mission.

The literary method found here has some but not all the features of apocalyptic. Just as eschatology is the view that history has a goal (*eschaton*) in judgment and salvation, so apocalyptic is a method of declaring this. Apocalyptic is Greek for "revelation" or "unveiling." The poetic symbolism employed in this discourse belongs to the apocalyptic method; but other apocalyptic features are absent, like the imparting of secret knowledge through dreams, visions, and auditions (cf. Johnson, p. 542). It is not an apocalypse like Daniel or Revelation.

Matthew's concern is for a balanced eschatological faith: on the one hand, seriously expecting the imminent return of Christ and, on the other, careful attention to personal readiness, faithfulness to sacred trust, obedience to the commission to preach the gospel to all nations, and refusal to be misled by false prophets or christs or to engage in speculations about the time of Christ's return.

The question of the origin of the "apocalyptic discourse" (24:1—26:2) has found no completely satisfactory answer. Almost all scholars recognize that Mark 13 stands behind Matthew 24:1–36. Mark's conclusion (13:33–37), urging the need of watchfulness, is considerably expanded by Matthew. Of Matthew's conclusion, 24:37–51 is largely drawn from Q (cf. Luke 17:26–27, 34–35; 12:39–40, 42–46). The rest consists of the parable of the ten maidens (25:1–13), that of the talents (25:14–30), and a teaching about the final judgment (25:31–46). Of these three units, only the second is paralleled, Luke's parable of the pounds (19:12–27).

That Jesus shared the eschatological view of history, that it is ultimately under the control of God and is being brought to its goal in redemption and judgment, is clearly indicated. Jesus disclaimed knowledge of any timetable for its fulfilment and warned against any effort to determine this. His concern was to urge moral commitment rather than speculation about the time of the end. He discouraged the fanatical nationalism which expected the kingdom of God to come as a national deliverance from Rome, and the extravagancies of apocalypticism seem not to go back to him.

Mark 13 is concerned with the Parousia of the Son of man (13:24–27) as well as with the destruction of Jerusalem; but Matthew heightens Mark's concern for the former (cf. 24:3 with Mark 13:4, and see his additional pericope on the Parousia of the Son of man in 24:26–28). Whether there is also a heightening of apocalyptic interests in sources behind Mark or in Mark over these sources cannot be determined. If so, Jesus was less apocalyptic than the church came to hold.

1. Destruction of the Temple Foretold (24:1–2)

[1] Jesus left the temple and was going away, when his disciples came to point out to him the buildings of the temple. [2] But he answered them, "You see all these, do you not? Truly, I say to you, there will not be left here one stone upon another, that will not be thrown down."

A clue to the interpretation of the eschatological discourse is given at the outset. It has to do first of all with the destruction of the ***temple*** in Jerusalem. That the discourse looks beyond this catastrophe to the greater event which it foreshadows, the return of Christ, becomes equally clear as the discourse unfolds.

The ***temple*** was the third Jewish Temple to stand on Mount Moriah in Jerusalem. The first was built by Solomon (1 Kings 6:1 f.) and destroyed in 587 B.C. The second was built under the leadership of Zerubbabel (Ezra 2:68 f.), and the third was begun by Herod the Great in 20–19 B.C. as a replacement of the smaller one. The magnificence of the complex of ***buildings*** which constituted ***the temple*** (hieron) amazed the disciples (Mark 13:1; Luke 21:5). The buildings were of white marble and were decorated with gold, precious stones, and rich tapestries. The Temple was one of the wonders of the world.

Jesus foretold the destruction of the Temple, carried out by the soldiers of Titus when Jerusalem was conquered and destroyed in A.D. 70 (Josephus, *Wars* 7.1). The stones which were to ***be thrown down*** included some granite blocks about 36 by 12 by 18 feet in size (Josephus, *Antiq*, 15.11). In *Wars* 5.5, Josephus writes of stones 60 feet long. Part of the foundation of the great outer wall, known today as the "wailing wall," as well as stones at the southeast and southwest corners yet stand. Obviously, "not one stone" is not to be pressed in a literal sense. The language is not scientific but popular (cf. Broadus, p. 481).

2. Woes Before End of the Age (24:3–14)

[3] As he sat on the Mount of Olives, the disciples came to him privately, saying, "Tell us, when will this be, and what will be the sign of your coming and of the close of the age?" [4] And Jesus answered them, "Take heed that no one leads you astray. [5] For many will come in my name, saying, 'I am the Christ,' and they will lead many astray. [6] And you will hear of wars and rumors of wars; see that you are not alarmed; for this must take place, but the end is not yet. [7] For nation will rise against nation, and kingdom against kingdom, and there will

be famines and earthquakes in various places:
8 all this is but the beginning of the sufferings.
9 "Then they will deliver you up to tribula-
tion, and put you to death; and you will be
hated by all nations for my name's sake. 10 And
then many will fall away, and betray one
another, and hate one another. 11 And many
false prophets will arise and lead many astray.
12 And because wickedness is multiplied, most
men's love will grow cold. 13 But he who en-
dures to the end will be saved. 14 And this
gospel of the kingdom will be preached
throughout the whole world, as a testimony to
all nations; and then the end will come.

The Mount of Olives stands across the deep Kedron Valley, eastward from the Temple. Looking across at the Temple, the disciples raised a cluster of questions. They asked ***when*** these things (plural) were to be and ***what*** would be ***the sign*** of Jesus' ***coming*** (*Parousia*) ***and of the close of the age.*** The question implied that a number of things were bound together in one bundle: the destruction of the Temple, the Parousia, and the end of the age. Jesus broke the bundle, and indicated that at least the destruction of ***the temple*** and ***the end*** were distinct, however much related. The catastrophe of the destruction of the ***temple*** would foreshadow the judgment at ***the close of the age,*** but it would not coincide with it.

Your coming translates the technical term "your parousia." *Parousia* is Greek for coming or presence. Here the idea of coming seems to be intended. The expression "second coming" does not appear in the New Testament, the nearest approach being found in Hebrews 9:28, "Christ . . . will appear a second time." The ***close of the age*** could be rendered "the consummation [*sunteleias*] of the age [*aiōnos*]." This is a frequent expression in Matthew, forming the very last words of this Gospel (28:20). The emphasis is not upon termination so much as completion or consummation. At the Parousia this age gives way to the ultimate age in which the kingdom of God is asserted in its fulness, bringing all men and nations to their final judgment or reward.

The introductory ***take heed*** sets the tone for the discourse. It is weighted on the side of warnings against such preoccupation with end-time speculations that leaves one vulnerable to false prophets or false christs and which results in neglect of the mission to preach the gospel to the nations. Contrary to many interpreters of this passage, the burden is not to revive faith in the Parousia. This is one concern, but not the only one. The discourse plainly affirms the destruction of the Temple and the subsequent return of Christ in judgment. It further assures that the end of the Temple is not the end of the world.

A major concern is to affirm a period of indefinite length between the destruction of the Temple and the return of Christ at the end of the age. Matthew's concern is with the life of the church during this period between the two catastrophic events: refusal to be misled, attention to personal readiness for Christ's return, endurance of persecution, and the preaching of the gospel. The emphasis is captured in words like ***take heed,*** wait, watch, endure, work.

During the first and second centuries there were many who claimed to be ***the Christ.*** These were Zealots whose goal was to liberate the nation from Roman rule. There were many local uprisings, leading to two Jewish-Roman wars (A.D. 66–70 and 132–135). In the second war, Bar Cocheba was actually acclaimed "Messiah" by Akiba, the leading rabbi of the time. Jesus warned against the futility of such wars and plainly taught that they were not truly messianic. The ***wars and rumors of wars*** against which he warned were "messianic" wars, not the usual wars which take place in the world. This text is sometimes misapplied, as when one is resigned to the fact of international wars as inevitable. Jesus was not teaching that nothing can be done to prevent wars. His particular concern was to warn his followers against being drawn into "holy wars" which claimed to be messianic.

See that you are not alarmed may seem to be an impossible command, for all wars are alarming. "Frightened" better translates the Greek, but the thought is that ***wars and rumors of wars*** are not to frighten one into believing that the end of the age has come.

The beginning of the sufferings or beginnings of travail are the "birth pangs" of the Messiah (cf. Isa. 26:16–19; Micah 4:9–10; Rev. 12:1–5). These are the sufferings of Christ's people, which is continuing the suffering of Christ himself (cf. Col. 1:24). Not only will Christ's people live in a world where there are wars and natural disasters like ***famines and earthquakes,*** but they will suffer actual persecution. ***Deliver you up*** refers to their being handed over to the ruling authorities, whether Jewish or Roman. As early as A.D. 64 Christians were persecuted by the Roman Emperor Nero, who falsely charged them with arson—burning the city of Rome. A common charge came to be atheism, because they did not acknowledge the gods of the Roman Empire.

That they would ***betray*** and ***hate one another*** seems to reflect a period when the followers of Jesus were yet a Jewish-Christian congregation, not yet separated from Judaism (cf. Mark 13:9). The ***many false prophets*** could be either Jewish proclaimers of false christs or nominal Christians who sought to turn their fellows to false hopes, particularly with respect to ***the end.***

Verses 10–13 reckon with the problem of a "mixed church," i.e., true and false disciples within the church. This is a major concern in the Gospel of Matthew. That the church will come under the same judgment as the world is a recurrent emphasis (cf. the parables of the tares, dragnet, the ten maidens, the sheep and goats, etc.). Special warnings are directed against those who desert or betray the church under persecution. ***Many will*** fail the test and ***fall away.*** The Greek term *skandalisthēsontai* means to be scandalized or to stumble. Some will become informers and ***betray one another*** to the authorities, whether of the synagogue or the Roman government. Under the pressures of persecution some will actually ***hate one another. False prophets*** could include those who turn messianism into political revolt or those who ***lead many astray*** into libertinism or antinomianism. Probably the latter is intended here (cf. Bornkamm, p. 75). ***Wickedness*** translates *anomian,* which seems to be the lawlessness of the antinomians who confused the liberty of grace with freedom from law. The outgoing concern of ***love*** is thus chilled by the egocentric concern for self-assertion in militant, political messianism or for self-indulgence in antinomianism. Probably the latter is in view here, for love is the opposite of *anomia* (lawlessness) in Matthew.

Those alone are ***saved*** who endure ***to the end.*** This clearly implies that not all nominal disciples will be saved. To conclude that one can or cannot lose salvation once possessed is to go beyond anything explicit in verse 13. Most interpreters understand actual apostasy to be implied, but this is not explicit. What is explicit is that the test of salvation is endurance to the end (whether the end of the period of persecution or of one's life). What chiefly is condemned is the desertion or betrayal of the church in its times of persecution (cf. 10:16 f.,22,33). The test of salvation is not verbal profession but faithful obedience to God's will (7:21–23).

The gospel of the kingdom, i.e., the good news of the ruling of God through the Christ, is to be ***preached throughout the whole world as a testimony*** or witness ***to all nations. Nations*** usually stands for Gentiles. This is the task of the disciples (cf. 28:19). Only then will ***the end*** of the age come. An early coming of ***the end*** seems to be anticipated, yet no date is fixed, only an order of events. Although the weight of emphasis falls upon the obligation to preach the gospel to the whole world, there is also assurance, by implication at least, that the ***gospel will be preached*** until ***the end*** (Schniewind, p. 242).

3. *Fate of Judea and Warning Against False Messiahs and Prophets (24:15–28)*

[15] "So when you see the desolating sacrilege spoken of by the prophet Daniel, standing in the holy place (let the reader understand), [16] then let those who are in Judea flee to the mountains; [17] let him who is on the housetop

not go down to take what is in his house;
18 and let him who is in the field not turn back
to take his mantle. 19 And alas for those who
are with child and for those who give suck in
those days! 20 Pray that your flight may not be
in winter or on a sabbath. 21 For then there
will be great tribulation, such as has not been
from the beginning of the world until now, no,
and never will be. 22 And if those days had not
been shortened, no human being would be
saved; but for the sake of the elect those days
will be shortened. 23 Then if any one says to
you, 'Lo, here is the Christ!' or 'There he is!'
do not believe it. 24 For false Christs and false
prophets will arise and show great signs and
wonders, so as to lead astray, if possible, even
the elect. 25 Lo, I have told you beforehand.
26 So, if they say to you, 'Lo, he is in the wilder-
ness,' do not go out; if they say, 'Lo, he is in the
inner rooms,' do not believe it. 27 For as the
lightning comes from the east and shines as far
as the west, so will be the coming of the Son
of man. 28 Wherever the body is, there the
eagles will be gathered together.

In this paragraph there is unmistakable reference to the destruction of Jerusalem (A.D. 70). Luke removes all doubt of this as he pictures the city under siege, suffering vengeance of the sword, and being trampled by the Gentiles (21:20–24). The discourse will move on to equally clear reference to the end of the age, but the point of transition is not clear. Some references are intelligible only in their reference to an event within history, some only with respect to an event at the end of history, and some are not clear as to their reference.

The ***desolating sacrilege*** or abomination of desolation is a phrase from Daniel (9:27; 11:31; 12:11). In Daniel it refers to the replacement of the sacrificial offerings in the Temple by "the abomination that makes desolate." This is generally understood to refer to the atrocious act of Antiochus IV (Epiphanes), the Syrian ruler who in 168 B.C. sacrificed a hog on the altar and set up in the Temple an altar to the Greek gods (cf. Josephus, *Antiq.* 12.5 and 1 Macc. 1:54–64). This became a symbol for the most arrogant and atrocious affront conceivable to the Jews. The term is here applied to the Roman desecration and destruction of ***the holy place*** or Temple in A.D. 70. The parenthesis, ***let the reader understand,*** follows verbatim the Markan parallel (13:14). Either Matthew (following Mark) is alerting the reader to a hidden meaning in his text, or Jesus himself alerted his hearers to a hidden meaning in Daniel.

Christians in ***Judea*** were to ***flee to the mountains*** in order to escape the murderous onslaught of the destroyers of Jerusalem. In A.D. 70 they actually fled to Pella in the Jordan valley. Had this text been composed after A.D. 70, it seems that it would have read differently. It may be best understood as spoken before the event. In order to escape with their lives, it would be necessary to leave behind their belongings. Even to go from the flat roof of a house to gather belongings from within the house might cost life. Special hardship would be worked upon expectant mothers and those with little babies. ***Winter*** flight would be hard upon all, and ***sabbath*** scruples or restrictions upon travel would add to the hardships of some. A Jewish, Palestinian situation is envisioned. Also, an event within history, not at its end, is implied by the details in the instructions for flight. At the end of the age, the location of one's ***mantle,*** the season of the year, or the day of the week would have no bearing on one's needs or behavior.

Although verse 21 may have overtones for the end of the age, its primary reference is to the destruction of Jerusalem. The ***tribulation*** or affliction of Jerusalem during the long siege and after the Romans broke through the walls of the city is almost indescribable (cf. Josephus, *Wars* 5:10). It is understandable that to Matthew's generation it seemed to be the worst possible event. Some hyperbole is to be allowed, but had the slaughter continued, the whole Jewish nation would have been destroyed.

Jesus repeatedly warned his followers against the false hopes held out to them by ***false Christs and false prophets.*** During the long siege of Jerusalem, there were assurances given to the people that they would have a messianic deliverance before the Romans prevailed. Jesus' followers were warned to discount any claims by or for a messianic deliverer who had appeared ***in the wilderness*** or in some ***inner rooms,*** even if these claims were supported by dramatic ***signs and wonders.***

Verses 27–28 may refer to either the destruction of Jerusalem or the end of the age, but the latter seems to be indicated. There is a real sense in which ***the Son of man*** did come in judgment upon Jerusalem in A.D. 70, and this may be implied here. If so, there are overtones for the judgment at the end of the age. Probably the reference is directly to that latter judgment. The passage is strongly eschatological. When ***the Son of man*** comes at the end of the age there will be no secrecy about it. His coming will be as apparent as the ***lightning*** that flashes across the sky. Further, his coming in judgment is as inevitable as is the gathering of the vultures where there is a carcass. ***Eagles*** is the literal Greek word, and there may be but probably is not a veiled reference to the coming of the Roman "eagles" upon Jerusalem. The Greek word *ptōma* normally designates a corpse or carcass, not a living body. The word for ***the coming of the Son of man*** is Parousia, an apparent reference to his coming at the end of the age.

4. The Coming of the Son of Man (24:29–31)

29 "Immediately after the tribulation of those days the sun will be darkened, and the moon will not give its light, and the stars will fall from heaven, and the powers of the heavens will be shaken; 30 then will appear the sign of the Son of man in heaven, and then all the tribes of the earth will mourn, and they will see the Son of man coming on the clouds of heaven with power and great glory; 31 and he will send out his angels with a loud trumpet call, and they will gather his elect from the four winds, from one end of heaven to the other.

The ***tribulation*** of verse 29 apparently looks back upon that of verse 21. The great tribulation just described pertained to the sufferings and temptations of men. The days following the tribulation are marked by cosmic upheavals, described in typical apocalyptical language. There is nothing in the context to require other than a literal understanding of the darkening of the ***sun*** and ***moon*** and the falling of the ***stars,*** but normally such language is poetic in apocalyptic writing. A glance at Acts 2:16–20 provides rather conclusive evidence of this use of symbolism, for it is not likely that Peter meant that the ***moon*** had literally turned into blood on the day of Pentecost. The ***powers of the heavens*** include the sun, moon, and stars. The ***sign of the Son of man*** is of unknown meaning, although it is more directly related to Jesus than are the astronomical signs. The Greek genitive allows for the idea that the ***Son of man*** is himself the sign, i.e., "the sign, which is the Son of man."

The coming of the Son of man ***on the clouds of heaven*** is his return to earth in ***power*** and ***glory.*** During his earthly ministry, he took the form of a servant, suffered, and died. His coming now is in judgment, but stressed is his coming to ***gather his elect*** from all parts of the world. Where they will be gathered is not indicated (cf. 1 Thess. 4:17). Two Old Testament passages are brought together in verse 30: Zechariah 12:10–14, which tells how the people of the earth ***mourn*** over one whom they have pierced, mourning like that over an only child or a firstborn, and Daniel 7:13 f., which pictures the triumphant ***coming*** of the Son of man. In Daniel the coming is "to the Ancient of Days," but here it clearly is a coming to earth. That the blending of these two passages is primitive is seen in the fact that they are brought together also in Revelation 1:7.

5. Lessons from the Fig Tree (24:32–35)

32 "From the fig tree learn its lesson: as soon as its branch becomes tender and puts forth its leaves, you know that summer is near. 33 So also, when you see all these things, you know that he is near, at the very gates. 34 Truly, I say to you, this generation will not pass away till all these things take place. 35 Heaven and earth will pass away, but my words will not pass away.

This parable admonishes alertness to the signs which point to a forthcoming event.

The rise of the sap in a fig tree, indicated by tender buds and then leaves, is a sure sign *that summer is near. These things* in verse 33 point to the signs of the previous paragraph. *He is near* could also be translated, "*It* is near," for the Greek text has no expressed subject at this point. The meaning is that either the Son of man is near or the end is near. The former is probably intended.

The meaning of *this generation* is much disputed. Efforts like those of Jerome, to make it mean the Jewish race, or of Origen and Chrysostom, to refer it to all Christians, are arbitrary and are to be rejected. *This generation* refers to the contemporaries of Jesus, as does the phrase in 11:16 and elsewhere. If first used to refer to the destruction of Jerusalem and the Temple, its fulfilment is clear. If the things to *take place* in this generation refer to *the coming of the Son of man,* that too had a fulfilment in the judgment upon Israel in A.D. 70.

The harder interpretation is the one which seems more natural here, the reference being to the end of the age. This would see a dual reference, first to the destruction of Jerusalem and then to the end-time judgment which it foreshadowed. If this is the intention, the obvious problem arises out of the fact of continuing history. Verse 36 may supply the solution, for Jesus denied that he knew the time of the end, declaring only the fact of its approach. (Cf. comments on 16:27 f.)

6. *Time of Parousia Unknown (24:36–44)*

**36 "But of that day and hour no one knows,
not even the angels of heaven, nor the Son, but
the Father only. 37 As were the days of Noah,
so will be the coming of the Son of man. 38 For
as in those days before the flood they were
eating and drinking, marrying and giving in
marriage, until the day when Noah entered the
ark, 39 and they did not know until the flood
came and swept them all away, so will be the
coming of the Son of man. 40 Then two men
will be in the field; one is taken and one is left.
41 Two women will be grinding at the mill; one
is taken and one is left. 42 Watch therefore, for
you do not know on what day your Lord is
coming. 43 But know this, that if the householder had known in what part of the night the
thief was coming, he would have watched and
would not have let his house be broken into.
44 Therefore you also must be ready; for the
Son of man is coming at an hour you do not
expect.**

Various expressions are used for the end of the age, the concern of this paragraph. It is *that day and hour,* and it is also referred to as *the coming* [Parousia] *of the Son of man* as well as the *day your Lord is coming.* The point is that for all the certainty of its coming, the time is known to *the Father only.* Its coming will take men by surprise, finding them preoccupied with normal and universal interests like *eating and drinking, marrying and giving in marriage,* working *in the field,* and *grinding at the mill.*

In the expression *that day and hour,* the addition of "and hour" is rhetorical, day and hour having the same meaning (McNeile, p. 356). Knowledge of *that day and hour* belongs to *the Father only.* Greek grammar permits the idea that it is not the time but the nature of that day and hour which is known only to the Father, but the context heavily favors the generally accepted interpretation that the time is meant.

Nor the Son is a disputed reading in Matthew, the KJV omitting it on the basis of late Byzantine manuscripts. The inclusion has the overwhelming support of Alexandrian, Western, and Caesarean manuscripts. The reading is certain in Mark 13:32, and it is implied in the undisputed *the Father only* in Matthew. The saying undoubtedly goes back to Jesus, for no disciple would have suggested that he had limited knowledge. The statement does support the solid claim of the New Testament that Jesus Christ was truly human as well as divine.

Christian faith can only stand before this mystery of the full reality of the incarnation. God came uniquely in one who was a real man, not just a seeming (Gnostic) man. Not only does this verse demand the full recognition of the human limitations of Jesus, but it also demands that we acknowledge our human limitations, one being that we do not know the time of the end of the world or ***the coming of the Son of man.*** The Christian must accept the necessity of living in the tension between knowing the certainty of Christ's coming and not knowing when.

The Parousia will be like ***the days of Noah*** in that men will be found unprepared. There is nothing wrong with ***eating and drinking, marrying and giving in marriage,*** working ***in the field,*** or ***grinding at the mill.*** What is fatal is such preoccupation with those normal and necessary matters that one neglects to ***watch*** for the coming of the Lord and to ***be ready*** for it. The illustration of ***the householder*** teaches that the Lord will come ***at an hour*** we ***do not expect,*** just as a ***thief*** comes without announcing in advance the particular "watch" of the night in which he intends to come. Just as the householder ***must be ready*** for any coming of the thief, so ***must*** we ***be ready*** for the coming of the Lord at any time (cf. 1 Thess. 5:2).

The separation between those ***taken*** and those ***left*** will not follow conventional lines such as race or nationality. The lines will run through families and neighbors, separating those who had known ties so close as daily work (Luke 17:34 includes reference to "two men in one bed," presumably of the same family). The ***one taken*** is probably the good man and the other the ***one left*** to his fate, although the reverse idea of one taken for punishment and one left in safety is possible but not probable (McNeile, p. 357). What is clear is the fact of separation and the contrast in fates, determined by readiness for ***the coming of the Son of man*** and not by national or family identity. In Matthew the dual emphasis is expressed in ***watch*** (v. 42) and ***be ready*** (v. 44).

7. *On Being Prepared* (*24:45—25:13*)

Grouping the parable of the faithful and the unfaithful servants with that of the ten maidens serves to point up the demand for preparedness. This theme is already apparent in the foregoing paragraph but receives special emphasis in these two parables.

(*1*) *Faithful and Unfaithful Servants* (*24:45–51*)

[45] "Who then is the faithful and wise servant, whom his master has set over his household, to give them their food at the proper time? [46] Blessed is that servant whom his master when he comes will find so doing. [47] Truly, I say to you, he will set him over all his possessions. [48] But if that wicked servant says to himself, 'My master is delayed,' [49] and begins to beat his fellow servants, and eats and drinks with the drunken, [50] the master of that servant will come on a day when he does not expect him and at an hour he does not know, [51] and will punish him, and put him with the hypocrites; there men will weep and gnash their teeth.

The followers of Jesus are not only to watch for his coming, but they have work to do. ***The faithful and wise*** (*phronimos* means prudent) ***servant*** will be found ***doing*** what he was told to do. As throughout this Gospel, nothing short of actual obedience or the ***doing*** of God's will is demanded of the disciple. One is not saved by his works, but he is judged by them. ***Servant*** translates *doulos,* slave. One shows that he belongs to God by obeying him. The reward of obedience is not retirement to rest but promotion to a greater task. The faithful servant is placed ***over all his*** master's ***possessions.***

The ***wicked servant*** misinterprets his master's delayed return. ***Delayed*** translates *chronizei,* tarries. The warning is against assuming that since the Son of man has not already come he will not come, or at least the coming is so remote that it does not concern us. ***Punish*** translates *dichotomēsei* (our dichotomize), a strong term for "cutting one down." The parable has a special warning for Christians who have responsible assignments for the care of others but who use their position for personal advantage, trying to be masters instead of servants, exercising a tyranny over those who do not support them and indulging with those who do. It may be observed in passing that Jesus warned his would-be followers as severely as he did the scribes and Pharisees. This severity is born of concern, not contempt.

The Qumran scrolls may shed further light on verse 51, where ***punish*** translates *dichotomēsei,* literally to cut in two (dichotomize). Betz finds a close parallel to the *Rule of the Community* (1 QS II, 16 f.), where the hypocrite who enters the Qumran covenant only to gain the eschatological blessings but with no intention of changing his ways is "cut off from the Sons of Light" and is given "his allotted portion in the midst of those accursed forever."[46] He sees "cut in two" as translating the Hebrew *karath,* a word that can mean to cut, to cut off, to make (cut) a covenant, or even to cut in two (cf. Josh. 3:13; 4:7). To cut in two is a more literal and dramatic rendering of the Greek word in verse 51 which originally meant "he shall become cut off," i.e., from the midst of God's people. The second part of the judgment, ***put him with the hypocrites,*** is literally "He will place his lot with the hypocrites." This parallels the second part of the Qumran passage, where the hypocrite is the one who enters the community for the eschatological blessings only. Verse 51 thus says that the wicked servant shall be cut off from God's people and be assigned his proper lot with those accursed forever. Psalm 37 stands behind the Qumran passage and the parable of 24:45–51 and illumines the study of each.

(2) *The Ten Maidens (25:1–13)*

[1] "Then the kingdom of heaven shall be
compared to ten maidens who took their lamps
and went to meet the bridegroom. [2] Five of
them were foolish, and five were wise. [3] For
when the foolish took their lamps, they took no
oil with them; [4] but the wise took flasks of oil
with their lamps. [5] As the bridegroom was de-
layed, they all slumbered and slept. [6] But at
midnight there was a cry, 'Behold, the bride-
groom! Come out to meet him.' [7] Then all
those maidens rose and trimmed their lamps.
[8] And the foolish said to the wise, 'Give us
some of your oil, for our lamps are going out.'
[9] But the wise replied, 'Perhaps there will not
be enough for us and for you; go rather to the
dealers and buy for yourselves.' [10] And while
they went to buy, the bridegroom came, and
those who were ready went in with him to the
marriage feast; and the door was shut.
[11] Afterward the other maidens came also, say-
ing, 'Lord, lord, open to us.' [12] But he replied,
'Truly, I say to you, I do not know you.'
[13] Watch therefore, for you know neither the
day nor the hour.

This parable takes over features of an allegory with several points of comparison. Its chief concern is to admonish readiness or watchfulness for the Parousia, the exact time of which is unknown. Jesus is the bridegroom, the ***ten maidens*** are the people (possibly but not necessarily the church) awaiting his return, the bridegroom's delay is the time of waiting for the Parousia, the bridegroom's sudden coming is the Parousia, and the rejection of the foolish maidens is the judgment upon those not prepared when Christ returns.

The kingdom of heaven is not like ***ten maidens*** but is ***compared*** to the experience of the ***ten maidens.*** It comes offering salvation but also judgment. There is a time for preparation and a time when it is too late to prepare. This is the point of emphasis. ***The day*** of the Lord's return may be a joyous one in which one enters into ***the marriage feast.*** The "messianic banquet" is a familiar analogy for the joys of salvation (cf. Rev. 3:20). Those not prepared are left outside as ones unknown. The translation ***I do not know you*** misses a part of the meaning. The perfect tense of the verb (*oida*) may imply, "I have not known you and do not now know you." It is not that they were once "known" and then forgotten, but never known.

Lamps (*lampas*) usually mean torches, possibly lamps attached to poles, our flambeaux. The term is sometimes used for a lamp as in Acts 20:8. Who the maidens were, whether from the village or the bride's house, is not divulged. Neither is the house identified, whether that of the bride's father (if the bridegroom is coming for her) or that of the bridegroom (if,

[46] Otto Betz, "The Dichotomized Servant and the End of Judas Iscariot," *Revue de Qumran,* 5:17 (October, 1964), pp. 43–58.

according to many manuscripts, she is already with him). There is strong manuscript support for the inclusion of "the bride" along with ***the bridegroom*** in verse 1. The idea of the church as the bride of Christ (cf. 2 Cor. 11:2) is not present in the story. The five ***foolish*** maidens knew the need of ***oil,*** for they had oil in ***their lamps.*** Their folly was in not reckoning with a delay which could make an extra supply necessary. They had failed to take along ***flasks*** with extra oil.

The story is told vividly, although some of these details belong only to the scenery of the story and are not to be pressed for meaning. ***Was delayed*** (*chronizontos*) could as well be rendered "tarried." All ***ten maidens, wise*** and ***foolish, slumbered and slept,*** i.e., dozed off and then kept sleeping. The foolish ones are not censured for sleeping, only for not having provided necessary oil. That they ***trimmed their lamps*** means that they removed the burned portions from the wicks and lighted them. The lamps of the foolish maidens began to go out, the oil exhausted. If a lesson is to be derived from verse 9, it is that preparation for the Parousia cannot be borrowed, but this is probably not intended. The real point is that the five ***foolish*** maidens waited until it was too late to prepare for ***the bridegroom.***

Many interpreters object that verse 13 does not suit the intention of the parable and that it is a later addition. Jeremias (*Parables,* pp. 51–55) argues that the parable was originally not an allegory and that the admonition to ***watch*** shifts the emphasis from the original issue of preparedness, holding that the ***foolish*** virgins were not judged because they ***slept*** but because they had ***no oil.*** The ***wise*** were no less asleep than the foolish. He finds the more primitive form of the story in Luke 12:35–38; 13:22–30 and Matthew's use of ***watch*** in verse 13 to be borrowed from Mark 13:35. This may follow, but another case can be made for Matthew's usage.

It is true that one would logically expect verse 13 to admonish the reader to "be ready" (cf. 24:44) rather than to ***watch.*** But this is to insist upon a logical consistency which probably was of no concern to Matthew. A study of Luke 12:35–38 discloses a virtual equating of the ideas of readiness and being awake. Luke 12:35 admonishes that "loins be girded" and "lamps burning" (preparation), yet those declared blessed are the ones found "awake," literally watching" (v. 37). The logic Jeremias requires of Matthew would require that Luke 12:37 read, "Blessed are those servants whom the master finds *ready* when he comes." Again, in Luke 12:39–40, in the reading found in most manuscripts, there is a clear equation between watching and readiness. The same interchange between "watch" and "be ready" is found in Matthew 24:42,44. It follows, then, that although verse 13 may shift the emphasis and may be a later addition, there are no compelling reasons for this conclusion. It is to insist upon a science more modern than ancient to require "be ready" instead of "watch" as the conclusion to the parable before us.

8. *Parable of the Talents: Those Who Have and Those Who Have Not* (*25:14–30*)

**14 "For it will be as when a man going on a
journey called his servants and entrusted to
them his property; 15 to one he gave five talents, to another two, to another one, to each
according to his ability. Then he went away.
16 He who had received the five talents went at
once and traded with them; and he made five
talents more. 17 So also, he who had the two
talents made two talents more. 18 But he who
had received the one talent went and dug in
the ground and hid his master's money. 19 Now
after a long time the master of those servants
came and settled accounts with them. 20 And
he who had received the five talents came
forward, bringing five talents more, saying,
'Master, you delivered to me five talents; here I
have made five talents more.' 21 His master said
to him, 'Well done, good and faithful servant;
you have been faithful over a little, I will set
you over much; enter into the joy of your
master.' 22 And he also who had the two talents
came forward, saying, 'Master, you delivered
to me two talents; here I have made two
talents more.' 23 His master said to him, 'Well
done, good and faithful servant; you have been**

**faithful over a little, I will set you over much;
enter into the joy of your master.' 24 He also
who had received the one talent came forward,
saying, 'Master, I knew you to be a hard man,
reaping where you did not sow, and gathering
where you did not winnow; 25 so I was afraid,
and I went and hid your talent in the ground.
Here you have what is yours.' 26 But his master
answered him, 'You wicked and slothful servant! You knew that I reap where I have not
sowed, and gather where I have not win-
nowed? 27 Then you ought to have invested my
money with the bankers, and at my coming I
should have received what was my own with
interest. 28 So take the talent from him, and
give it to him who has the ten talents. 29 For to
every one who has will more be given, and he
will have abundance; but from him who has
not, even what he has will be taken away.
30 And cast the worthless servant into the outer
darkness; there men will weep and gnash their
teeth.'**

There are striking parallels between Matthew's parable of the talents and Luke's parable of the pounds (19:11–27). The principal lesson of each is the same, that God can and does impart greater gifts to those who are faithful while those who distrust him can only lose what they have.

Verse 29 embodies the parable's principle, applied to different situations in the Gospels (cf. comment on 13:12). More can be given to ***every one who has,*** but (paradoxically) from the one who ***has not will be taken away*** even ***what he has.*** The unused gift or unused opportunity is lost. The life given to God in trusting service is made richer. The truth here parallels that in the great principle that to lose one's life is to find it, whereas to try to save it is to lose it (cf. 16:25).

The differences between the parables in Matthew and Luke are almost as striking as are their parallels. They were not drawn from the same source. Either Jesus gave two distinct but similar parables or the Matthean and Lukan versions took shape in different church situations with adaptations to somewhat different needs. The story in Matthew is simpler than that in Luke. Jeremias (*Parables,* pp. 61 f.) holds that the parable originally was directed against the scribes as an indictment of their poor stewardship of God's Word which had been intrusted to them. He sees that it then became eschatological, with special reference to the Parousia. His argument is based chiefly on a comparative analysis of the stories in Matthew and Luke as well as one in a later development in the apocryphal gospel of the Nazareans. However one may assess Jeremias' theory, the parable in Matthew clearly relates to the Parousia, such references as the ***joy of your master*** (v. 21) and the banishment to ***outer darkness*** (v. 30) being unmistakably eschatological.

Beyond the main principle of the parable are several lessons. All of man's gifts and opportunities are from God. What is required is faithfulness. God's gifts and their corresponding responsibility are imparted ***to each according to his ability.*** It is not the amount of the gift that is important but one's faithfulness to it, as seen in the fact that the man who gained ***two talents*** for his master received the identical praise received by the man who gained ***five talents.*** The reward for faithful service is greater opportunity to serve. Faithfulness over a ***little*** opens the way for one to be entrusted with ***much.*** The reward for faithful service is also known in terms of entry into ***the joy of*** one's ***master.***

The servant who received but ***one talent hid*** it ***in the ground.*** He tried to justify himself when the time came to settle ***accounts.*** He tried to excuse himself by attacking the character of his master, accusing him of being a ***hard man,*** exploiting the labors of others. He did not trust his master, and he said that he was ***afraid*** of him. He clearly did not love him, else he would have risked personal loss in the effort to serve his master. He tried to "save his own life" and thus lost it. The least he could have done was invest his master's ***money with the bankers*** for a sure rate of ***interest.*** Instead of knowing the ***joy*** of his master, the ***worthless*** (unprofitable) ***servant*** is ***cast into the outer darkness,*** symbol for rejection or of Gehenna, where men ***weep and gnash their teeth,*** the painful and "unprofitable" expressions from one victimized by an unlived life.

That the *one talent* was given to the man with *ten* may best be interpreted by a metaphor used by Johannes Weiss, "The gifts of God are not given like money, but like plants, which need a suitable soil for their growth" (Robinson, p. 207).

The term *talent* first represented a measurement of weight and then came to designate a certain amount of silver or gold. Money values vary from day to day and cannot be compared across the centuries. A thousand dollars may suggest the equivalent of a *talent,* but only as a very rough estimate. The use of the word for personal capabilities or "gifts" arose from this parable.

9. *Final Judgment: Serving Christ in Serving Others (25:31–46)*

**31 "When the Son of man comes in his glory,
and all the angels with him, then he will sit on
his glorious throne. 32 Before him will be gathered all the nations, and he will separate them
one from another as a shepherd separates the
sheep from the goats, 33 and he will place the
sheep at his right hand, but the goats at the
left. 34 Then the King will say to those at his
right hand, 'Come, O blessed of my Father,
inherit the kingdom prepared for you from the
foundation of the world; 35 for I was hungry
and you gave me food, I was thirsty and you
gave me drink, I was a stranger and you
welcomed me, 36 I was naked and you clothed
me, I was sick and you visited me, I was in
prison and you came to me.' 37 Then the righteous will answer him, 'Lord, when did we see
thee hungry and feed thee, or thirsty and give
thee drink? 38 And when did we see thee a
stranger and welcome thee, or naked and
clothe thee? 39 And when did we see thee sick
or in prison and visit thee?' 40 And the King
will answer them, 'Truly, I say to you, as you
did it to one of the least of these my brethren,
you did it to me.' 41 Then he will say to those
at his left hand, 'Depart from me, you cursed,
into the eternal fire prepared for the devil and
his angels; 42 for I was hungry and you gave
me no food, I was thirsty and you gave me no
drink, 43 I was a stranger and you did not
welcome me, naked and you did not clothe me,
sick and in prison and you did not visit me.'
44 Then they also will answer, 'Lord, when did
we see thee hungry or thirsty or a stranger or
naked or sick or in prison, and did not minister
to thee?' 45 Then he will answer them, 'Truly, I
say to you, as you did it not to one of the least
of these, you did it not to me.' 46 And they will
go away into eternal punishment, but the righteous into eternal life."**

Although the section which began at 24:1 is concerned with the fate of Jerusalem as well as the world, the former emphasis gives way completely to the latter in this paragraph. It includes the parable of the sheep and the goats, but it is more than a parable. In its wholeness it is a prophetic picture of the final judgment awaiting all people. Emphasis falls upon the standard or principle of judgment, which is one's true relationship to Christ as reflected in his ministry to the least of his people, especially in their situations of need.

This passage unmistakably goes back to Jesus and preserves some of the deepest and most far-reaching teaching (cf. Jeremias, *Parables,* p. 209). It is found only in Matthew, probably preserved by Jewish Christians. It has striking affinity with passages like Luke 10:30–37 and James 1:27; 2:14–17. It sees *all the nations,* church and world, to be judged by the same standard —love reflected in ministry to others. This is not just a humanitarian spirit, for it is something that one has in his relationship with Christ.

The passage is strongly christological. Jesus never explicitly refers to himself, but there can be no doubt that by *the Son of man, the King,* and *Lord* Jesus himself is meant. The one who took the lowly form of a servant and who was scorned, rejected, and crucified will ultimately return as the glorious *Son of man, the King,* to declare the judgment of God upon all men.

Appearing *on his glorious throne* as King, the Son of man will judge *all the nations.* At that time he will separate *the righteous* from the *cursed* in the manner that a shepherd separates *sheep from the goats.* As in the parables of the weeds and the dragnet and elsewhere in Matthew, it is taught here that the good and the bad live together in the same world and even in the same structures of religion. In Palestine, sheep and goats were often mixed in a single flock. At night they were separated, the goats requiring more protection from the cold than the sheep. The sheep and goats are easily distinguished by the shepherd, but ***the righteous*** and the ***cursed*** do not always recognize their own true identities, and they are distinguished with certainty by God alone.

In a sense, Jesus does not so much judge as declare judgments already made by the Father. Those on the ***right hand,*** usual place of honor and power, are the ***blessed*** who belong to his ***Father.*** The word ***blessed*** (*eulogēmenoi*) designates them as the objects of God's blessing. It is not the word introducing the Beatitudes (*macharioi*), where a state of happiness is meant.

The blessed are to ***inherit the kingdom.*** Precisely those who come under the rule of God are the ones who enter into that reign. Paradoxically, these self-giving persons who seek only to serve and not rule are those who reign with Christ (cf. 5:3; Luke 12:32; Rom. 5:17; Rev. 1:9; 5:9 f.; 22:5). This blessed inheritance is one *prepared* for them from creation. It is not a gift imposed, an accident, nor something traceable to human initiative. It is the realization of something traceable to God's deliberate provision.

The emphasis of the paragraph is upon the standard by which all men are judged. This is the "final examination," and the questions are announced in advance! It would be less than clever to prepare for the wrong set of questions when those to be given on the final examination are posted in advance. ***The King*** was ***hungry, thirsty, a stranger, naked, sick,*** and ***in prison;*** and the righteous ministered to him! The identity of Jesus with his people is a major New Testament teaching (cf. Acts 9:4 f.; 1 Cor. 1:13; 8:12). In ministering to the needy, one ministers to Christ. It is significant that those recognized as having thus ministered to Christ did not realize that they were doing so. That is the point. They were not religious acts calculated to be good, to please God, or to gain reward. They were spontaneous acts, their normal response to another human being in need. Place a mouse before a cat and one sees what a cat is; place a person in need before a true child of God and one sees what a child of God is.

It does not follow that goodness is in deeds themselves. Selfish motives which veil hypocrisy may prompt one to feed the hungry, give water to the thirsty, give hospitality to the stranger, clothe the naked, or visit the sick and the imprisoned. It is the doing which reflects what one is that is significant. What ***the righteous*** are is traceable to their relationship to the very one whom they served in serving his people.

Although ministry to the needs of other people is unmistakably the criterion of judgment emphasized here, Jesus' omission of other demands does not exclude them (McNeile, p. 370). This passage does cut through to what basically discloses one as a child of God, and we dare not neglect its plain implication. Never did Jesus place such weight upon cultic (religious) practice or creedal orthodoxy as upon the kindness to others which reflects kinship with him.

The ones who must ***depart*** as ***cursed*** are judged by the same standard. They are not ones who have committed what are normally considered gross sinful acts, but their guilt is in what they failed to do (and be). They were unaware that they were passing up the ***Lord.*** Their answer implies that had they recognized him in the person of those ***least*** ones of his ***brethren*** they would have ministered to him. But their defense was their condemnation. If one has to ask who is in need, he shows himself not to belong to the one whose love is indiscriminate, who offers his gifts to good and bad alike (cf. 5:45).

The contrasting fates are ***eternal punishment*** and ***eternal life.*** The former is the ***eternal fire prepared*** not for man but ***for the devil and his angels.*** The latter is the destiny intended and prepared for man. God does not will the loss of any person; he does will the salvation of each (cf. 18:14; 2 Peter 3:9). ***Eternal fire*** or ***eternal punish-***

ment represents man's self-chosen fate, not God's will for man. The standard by which ***all the nations*** are judged is not one beyond the reach of any. The "fruit" by which each is known (cf. 7:20 f.) is that which is formed in each one who is receptive to God, having the faith which is openness to him to receive his gifts and to yield to his claims.

Eternal punishment is a term from which most people shrink and which many either refuse to attribute to Jesus or explain as meaning something other than is apparent. (See Broadus, pp. 511–15 for a thorough and cogent review of linguistic, metaphysical, and moral arguments.)

Punishment translates the Greek *kolasis,* first used for pruning (a tree or vine) and then for checking or chastisement. In classical Greek it differed from *timoria* in that the latter stood for vindication or vengeance. Aristotle held that *kolasis,* punishment, is for the sake of the sufferer but that *timoria* is for the satisfaction of the one who inflicts it. In the New Testament *timoria* is used only in Hebrews 10:29. *Kolasis* does take on the idea of penalty in some New Testament usage (cf. Acts 4:21; 22:5; 26:11). It cannot be maintained, then, that *kolasis* in our text must be understood only as chastisement and not as penal. The word itself will not decide that issue.

Eternal translates the Greek *aiōnios,* the identical word being used for ***eternal fire*** (v. 41), ***eternal punishment*** (v. 46), and ***eternal life*** (v. 46). There is nothing to suggest anything other than that in each usage the same meaning is intended. It is true that *aiōnios* may be used more qualitatively than quantitatively in connection with "life," but here the durative idea is never lost and seems to be intended here. There is uncertainty about the root meaning behind *aiōnios,* but the same root underlies *aiōn* (aeon or age) as *aiei* and *aei* (always). The Latin equivalent is *aevum* from which comes *ae(v)ternus* (eternal), as are the German *ewig* (everlasting) and the English ever (cf. forever). In verse 46 both ***punishment*** and ***life*** are described by the same term, apparently, as everlasting (cf. Dan. 12:2).

In the LXX *aiōnios* corresponds to the Hebrew *holam* and could be used of things which had existed for a long time in the past. When used of the future it seldom implied the full idea of everlasting, denoting rather perpetuity, permanence, or inviolability. As Jewish thought began to center more on the future life, the idea of "everlasting" became more prominent, whatever the root meaning of *aiōn.* In the New Testament, as "eternal life" is seen to be a present reality, *aiōnios* came to give more stress to the spiritual or qualitative aspect of that life (cf. McNeile, pp. 262 f.). The durative idea sometimes fades into the background; but it is never lost, and sometimes it moves to the fore, as is seemingly the case in the passage before us.

Only a sick mind can find pleasure in the thought of such a fate as everlasting punishment, even if *kolasis* is understood in its milder sense. But displeasure with a reality does not remove the reality. God himself takes no pleasure in the fate of the wicked; and it represents his rejected will, not his intention for man. But this is not the point. To be free to trust God, man must be free to distrust him. To be free to find life by losing it, man must be free to lose it by trying to save it. God made man free, free enough to turn from God and to go his own way. God does everything short of compelling man to do otherwise, yet he will not compel man. To compel would itself be to destroy man, for it would rob man of a freedom without which he cannot be truly man. That man may choose a way that leads to self ruin is a terrifying thought, but it is no less real because terrifying.

It may be asked what is meant by ***fire*** in the term ***eternal fire.*** The fact that ***fire*** is employed in various nonliteral ways in the New Testament leaves open the question of its usage here. Broadus (p. 511) soberly observes, "Whether eternal punishment involves any physical reality corresponding to fire, we know not; there will be something as bad as fire, and doubtless worse, for no earthly image can be adequate." To understand *fire* in a nonliteral sense is neither to reject what it symbolizes nor to reduce its seriousness any more than to understand streets of transparent gold (Rev. 21:21) to be symbolism for the splendor of heaven robs it of meaning. Whatever in particular is meant by ***eternal fire*** or ***eternal punishment,*** a fate is meant that is the very opposite of the ***eternal life*** or the inheritance of the kingdom which God has prepared for man. That there will be degrees of punishment as of reward is clearly taught in the New Testament (cf. 11:22; Luke 12:47, and 2 Cor. 5:10), but this is not a part of the discussion here.

10. *Prediction of Betrayal* (*26:1–2*)

[1] When Jesus had finished all these sayings, he said to his disciples, [2] "You know that after two days the Passover is coming, and the Son of man will be delivered up to be crucified."

This is Matthew's final summary colophon, marking the close of the fifth major discourse (cf. 7:28; 11:1; 13:53; 19:1). It also marks the transition to the great passion and resurrection section, the climax of the Gospel. The ***Passover*** was the annual feast of the Jews commemorating their deliverance from Egyptian bondage. It fell on the fourteenth day of Nisan (March–April). The paschal lamb was slain at the Temple on the fourteenth and eaten between sundown and midnight on the fifteenth, the new day beginning at sundown.

Jesus' fourth prediction of his death (cf. 16:21 ff.; 17:22 f.; 20:17 ff.) relates it to ***the Passover.*** Jesus did not seek death but anticipated and accepted it. He did not hold his enemies to be mere instruments selected for a part, for he judged their act as a betrayal. Jesus marched to his death, offering himself to his people for acceptance or rejection, and did so as something that he must do. On the other side, what wicked men did to him is called "rejection" (21:42; John 1:11; Acts 4:11; Rom. 9:32; 1 Peter 2:7), "betrayal" (26:2; Luke 6:16), and "murder" (1 Thess. 2:14 f.; Acts 7:52). In the giving of his life is redemption, behind which is God's love and will. The taking of that life is man's wickedness in its ultimate expression (cf. Acts 2:23).

XVI. *Arrest, Crucifixion, and Resurrection of Jesus* (*26:3—28:20*)

The passion narrative was probably the earliest part of the gospel tradition to take shape. The death of Jesus came as a severe blow to Jesus' closest followers, despite his efforts to prepare them for it. Death on a cross at the hands of the Romans meant that outwardly he died the way a criminal dies, especially an enemy of the state.

The death of Jesus would require explanation both for the followers of Christ and their enemies. This would call for a full statement in which it would be shown historically how Jesus came to his death, showing his innocence and the guilt of those who joined together to crucify him. Theologically, Christians would need for themselves reinterpretation of Jesus' death. They were able to reinterpret Jesus' death in the light of the resurrection and of the Scriptures, to which they turned again for guidance. In fact, they not only interpreted Jesus by the Scriptures but came to a new understanding of the Scriptures through Jesus (Lohse, p. 16). Matthew especially sees rabbinical interpretation of the Scriptures as thus superseded.

Matthew follows Mark very closely, supplementing his account with a few additions (cf. 26:52*b*; 27:3–10,19,24 f.,51*b*–53, 62–66) and allusions to the Old Testament (26:54; 27:34,43).

1. *Preceding Events* (*26:3—27:26*)

(*1*) *The Plot* (*26:3–5*)

[3] Then the chief priests and the elders of the people gathered in the palace of the high priest, who was called Caiaphas, [4] and took counsel together in order to arrest Jesus by stealth and kill him. [5] But they said, "Not during the feast, lest there be a tumult among the people."

The chief priests and the elders were the Sadducean and Pharisaic representatives of the Sanhedrin. Joseph Caiaphas was high priest (*ca.* A.D. 18–36) and thus president of the Sanhedrin (Josephus, *Antiq.* 18:2). The Sanhedrin met informally ***in the palace,*** literally "court" (*aulē*), ***of the high priest.***

Although the Pharisees had been the first to oppose Jesus, because of conflicts over the Law, the Sadducees seem to have taken the lead at the last. Their opposition to Jesus was more political than religious, for they saw not only their authority over the Temple challenged but their whole relationship with the Romans threatened. As collaborationists with Rome, depending on Rome for their appointment to office, they feared anything that even appeared to be potentially revolutionary.

They hastily ***took counsel,*** not to decide upon goals, but means. They had already decided to kill Jesus. Their problem was to achieve it with minimum risk of excitement on the part of the crowd. Since Jerusalem was crowded with Jewish worshipers during ***the Passover,*** and since patriotic feelings ran high at the time, they planned to avoid the action during the Passover. They were agreed on two things: Jesus must be killed but not during Passover. They seem not to have found a suitable plan until Judas offered them unexpected help.

(2) *Jesus Anointed at Bethany (26:6–13)*

6 Now when Jesus was at Bethany in the house of Simon the leper, 7 a woman came up to him with an alabaster jar of very expensive ointment, and she poured it on his head, as he sat at table. 8 But when the disciples saw it, they were indignant, saying, "Why this waste? 9 For this ointment might have been sold for a large sum, and given to the poor." 10 But Jesus, aware of this, said to them, "Why do you trouble the woman? For she has done a beautiful thing to me. 11 For you always have the poor with you, but you will not always have me. 12 In pouring this ointment on my body she has done it to prepare me for burial. 13 Truly, I say to you, wherever this gospel is preached in the whole world, what she has done will be told in memory of her."

The story in Matthew is almost identical with that in Mark 14:3–9. The parallel in John 12:1–8 is so striking that, despite differences, it is to be recognized as describing the same incident. John names Mary, sister to Martha and Lazarus, as the woman who anointed Jesus. John does not say that the anointing took place in Mary's home, and he may imply otherwise. The chief problem arises out of the dates given, John placing the event six days before the Passover whereas in Mark and Matthew it is within two days of the Passover. Broadus (pp. 517 f.) probably is correct in preferring the date in Matthew and Mark. In John, Mary anoints Jesus' feet, while in Matthew and Mark the unnamed woman ***poured*** (no word for "it" in Greek text) ***on his head,*** leaving the possibility that it was also upon his feet. The story in Luke 7:36–50 differs so extensively as to suggest a separate incident.

Simon is known as ***the leper,*** but presumably the leprosy had been healed, else Jewish law would have prohibited his presence in table fellowship. Of course, specific reference is only to ***the house of Simon,*** leaving open the question of his presence. Mark fixes the value of the ***ointment*** at three hundred denarii, about a year's wages for a common laborer (cf. Matt. 20:2, where laborers were paid a denarius per day). The disciples protested the ***waste,*** arguing that it could have served ***the poor.*** Jesus rebuked the disciples, reminding them that there were always poor people at hand for them to serve, whereas he would not be with them always.

The story serves to balance the emphasis of 25:31–46, where ministry to the needy is made paramount. This woman's extravagant act also had its place. She had ***done a beautiful thing.*** Not all Christian service must be "practical" or directed ***to the poor.*** Lavish expression of gratitude or love has its place too.

Jesus affirmed that the woman had poured the ointment upon his ***body to prepare*** him ***for*** his ***burial.*** Matthew does not disclose the woman's motive, but Jesus indicates the effect. He did receive it as an act of love as he approached his death, yet more meaningful at a time when one of the twelve was about to betray him, another deny him, and all forsake him. The story has been told wherever the gospel is preached, just as Jesus foretold.

(3) *Judas Bargains to Betray Jesus* (*26:14–16*)

[14] Then one of the twelve, who was called Judas Iscariot, went to the chief priests [15] and said, "What will you give me if I deliver him to you?" And they paid him thirty pieces of silver. [16] And from that moment he sought an opportunity to betray him.

Judas received ***thirty pieces of silver*** (shekels worth about 120 denarii) for the betrayal of Jesus (see Zech. 11:12) and later returned them and committed suicide (27:3–10). The full motive behind his act is not disclosed. Perhaps Judas followed Jesus in the expectation that Jesus would become the ruler of Israel as a political Messiah. If so, he was the first of the twelve to take Jesus at his word as Jesus rejected that role.

Were Mary of Bethany and Judas the first to realize that Jesus would actually die? If so, they reacted in opposite ways, one lavishing costly ointment upon her Lord, the other betraying him for about 120 denarii, the price of a slave (Ex. 21:32). Possibly Judas hoped for greater reward, but found himself at the mercy of the high priests, once he became an informer.

What Judas betrayed ("deliver" and "betray" translate the same Greek word) was the place Jesus could be taken with least public notice. He would lead them to Jesus during the night. This unexpected help caused the ***chief priests*** to make their move sooner than they had planned. The phrase ***one of the twelve*** reflects the continuing feeling of the church concerning this betrayal from a trusted apostle. The story is also a part of the church's honesty in refusing to hide from the world its shame.

(4) *Passover with Disciples* (*26:17–25*)

[17] Now on the first day of Unleavened Bread the disciples came to Jesus, saying, "Where will you have us prepare for you to eat the passover?" [18] He said, "Go into the city to such a one, and say to him, 'The Teacher says, My time is at hand; I will keep the passover at your house with my disciples.'" [19] And the disciples did as Jesus had directed them, and they prepared the passover.

[20] When it was evening, he sat at table with the twelve disciples; [21] and as they were eating, he said, "Truly, I say to you, one of you will betray me." [22] And they were very sorrowful, and began to say to him one after another, "Is it I, Lord?" [23] He answered, "He who has dipped his hand in the dish with me will betray me. [24] The Son of man goes as it is written of him, but woe to that man by whom the Son of man is betrayed! It would have been better for that man if he had not been born." [25] Judas, who betrayed him, said, "Is it I, Master?" He said to him, "You have said so."

Passover and ***Unleavened Bread*** were originally two distinct but closely related feasts (cf. Ex. 12:1–8,18–20; Lev. 23:5 f.; Num. 28:16–25). The Passover fell on the fourteenth of Nisan (March–April, but the first month for Israel), the lamb being slain on the afternoon of the fourteenth (cf. Num. 9:3) and the Passover meal being eaten from evening on into the night. Hence the Passover overlapped the fourteenth and fifteenth of Nisan. The Feast of Unleavened Bread continued for seven days. The two feasts were so closely related that they came to be referred to as one eight-day feast, called by either or both names (cf. Josephus, *Antiq.* 2,15; 3,10; *Wars* 5,3; Mark 14:1,12; Matt. 26:17; Luke 22:7).

There is an apparent conflict between the Synoptics' explicit claim that Jesus ate the Passover and what seems to be John's implication that Jesus was under arrest before the Passover was eaten (John 13:1; 18:28; 19:14). There may also be an implication by Paul that Jesus was crucified at the time the Passover lamb was slain (cf. 1 Cor. 5:7). But if "Passover" in John's Gospel is used for the eight-day feast, Passover and Unleavened Bread, there is some possibility of reconciling it with the Synoptics.[47]

Previous arrangements seem to have been made for a room for Jesus' observance of ***the Passover*** with the twelve (cf. Mark

[47] Cf. Jeremias, *The Eucharistic Words of Jesus*, tr. Norman Perrin (rev. ed., New York: Scribner's, 1966), pp. 15–88 for description of Passover.

14:13 f.). ***The Teacher says*** is a simple formula which arose out of the same circle of hearers in which the "I say to you" carried absolute authority, like the "thus says the Lord" of the Old Testament (cf. Lohmeyer, p. 352). Jerusalem was always crowded with Jewish pilgrims on the occasion of the Passover, and the paschal meal had to be eaten within the walls of the city. Because of the problem of housing, all inhabitants of the city were obligated to open their houses to the visiting worshipers (Lohse, p. 45). It was required that the Passover lambs be slaughtered at the Temple in the afternoon and then be prepared and eaten in the homes. The word ***time*** (*kairos*) does not necessarily mean "season of crisis" in distinction to the merely chronological idea (*chronos*), but that seems to be intended here. The disciples completed the preparations for the meal, which if actually a Passover meal included a roasted lamb, unleavened bread, bitter herbs, and wine. However, no reference is made to the lamb, bitter herbs, or other distinctives of the paschal meal in the description of the Last Supper. Silence concerning these paschal distinctives does not prove that the Last Supper was not a Passover; nor can it be argued from the bread and cup that it was a Passover, for these belonged to ordinary meals. In the observance of the meal the participants reclined on couches. ***Sat at table*** mistranslates the text.

Jesus' announcement that one of their number would betray him shocked and saddened the twelve. That eleven did not suspect Judas and that they were not absolutely certain of their own loyalty is reflected in the question posed by each, ***Is it I, Lord?*** The negative particle does give the question a softened tone, "It is not I, is it?" Jesus did not designate the guilty one so clearly as to unveil him to the others, even when he referred to the one whose hand was with him ***in the dish.*** All dipped into the common bowl, and several may have dipped at a time. The identification of the betrayer moves in three steps: one of the twelve, one who was dipping in the dish, and then Judas (Lohmeyer, p. 353).

Verse 24 has two very carefully formed and balanced statements, one saying that the ***Son of man*** (the Greek particle *men*, suggesting "on the one hand") ***goes as*** the Scriptures foresaw, but (the Greek particle *de* suggesting "on the other hand") ***woe*** (alas!) ***to that man by whom the Son of man is betrayed.*** No life at all would have been better than the one he lived. Judas asked the same question as did the eleven, ***Is it I, Master?*** Jesus' reply is somewhat enigmatic, literally reading, "You said it." This seems to be idiomatic for "Yes" (compare v. 64 with Mark 14:62).

(5) *Institution of Lord's Supper* (26:26–29)

[26] Now as they were eating, Jesus took bread, and blessed, and broke it, and gave it to the disciples and said, "Take, eat; this is my body." [27] And he took a cup, and when he had given thanks he gave it to them, saying, "Drink of it, all of you; [28] for this is my blood of the covenant, which is poured out for many for the forgiveness of sins. [29] I tell you I shall not drink again of this fruit of the vine until that day when I drink it new with you in my Father's kingdom."

There are four accounts of the Lord's Supper in the New Testament, somewhat differing in emphasis (cf. Mark 14:22–25; Luke 22:14–23; 1 Cor. 11:17–34). Matthew closely follows Mark in stressing the covenantal aspect of the Supper. The text is disputed in Luke, so the full emphasis is uncertain. Paul has the earliest account in the New Testament, and it has the fullest presentation: memorial, covenant, communion (*koinōnia*), and eschatological hope. The prominence of the Supper in early Christian life is strong evidence that Jesus foresaw his death and pointed to its significance for his followers.

Although it is not explicit that Jesus ate and drank with the twelve, he clearly served as the host. The shared meal for most of the world has always been a bond of fellowship, and this was especially true for the Jews. The Lord's Supper does not bear one dominant name in the New Testament, as is true for baptism; but terms like

blessed and ***thanks*** (vv. 26 f.), ***covenant*** (v. 28), "communion" (1 Cor. 10:16, margin), and "remembrance" (1 Cor. 11:24 f.) are employed within the narratives of the Supper. The Supper is a memorial or remembrance of Jesus, especially of his death. It is the expression of a hope, anticipating his triumphant return. It is a covenant with Christ and with one another through his shared life (blood). It is a communion with Christ and his ***body,*** the church (1 Cor. 10:16).

As the host, Jesus took a loaf of ***bread, blessed*** it, and ***gave it to the disciples*** to eat, saying, ***this is my body.*** The ***bread*** first of all symbolizes Jesus' own body given on the cross. Beyond this it symbolizes his church, the body of Christ, although it is in the Pauline writings that one finds the explication of the doctrine of the church as the body of Christ (cf. Rom. 12:4 f.; 1 Cor. 10:16; 12:12–27; Col. 1:18,24; 2:16–19; 3:15; Eph. 1:22 f.; 4:1–16).

Of course, the ***bread*** does not actually become the body of Christ. It remains bread in essence and accidence (appearance, taste, etc.). But although the bread remains bread and as such is a symbol, it symbolizes that which is itself beyond symbolism. Jesus is not a symbol, nor is his church, the body of Christ. Eating together in trust, love, acceptance, grateful remembrance, and hope is more than symbolism. The Supper employs symbols, ***bread*** and ***cup;*** but if genuine, it is more than symbolism. It is not magic nor mere symbol. It is a grateful act of worship, memory, hope, fellowship, and proclamation, employing symbolism.

Broke points to an act necessary for the eating and sharing of the loaf. The idea that it stresses the "broken body" of Jesus comes from a late addition to 1 Corinthians 11:24, where the true reading is, "This is my body which is for you." John 19:33–36 makes a point of the fact that not a bone was broken. The loaf symbolizes the whole body of Christ, given at Golgotha and continuing as he is embodied in his church. To "break bread" is a way of saying "to eat together," with no special attention to tearing apart a loaf of bread.

The RSV properly translates verse 27, showing that ***all*** refers to the disciples and not to the wine. The KJV is ambiguous in its, "Drink ye all of it." The Greek can only mean ***all of you*** and not "all of it." That Judas remained through the Supper (Luke 22:21) does not mean that he deserved the privilege, but it reflects the fact that Jesus left open to Judas a door for repentance until the last (John 13:26–30).

The cup of wine symbolizes Jesus' ***blood of the covenant.*** Several Old Testament passages form the background to this saying. The covenant given Moses at Sinai was sealed as blood of oxen was thrown upon the altar and upon the people, symbolizing the bond between God and Israel (Ex. 24:4–8). Jeremiah declared a new covenant, with the law written not upon tablets of stone but upon the hearts of men who come to know God in the forgiveness of sin (31:31–34).

The cup symbolizes the blood of Jesus poured out in realization of the new covenant of which Jeremiah wrote. ***Blood*** stands for the life itself poured out or given (Gen. 9:4). The reference is not primarily to the blood of a sacrificial animal, as though Jesus is seen as the Passover lamb, but the emphasis is upon the giving of his life for and to mankind. It means not the appeasement of the Father but new life for man in ***the forgiveness of sins*** (cf. Lohse, pp. 55 f.). That Jesus' followers are to ***drink*** the cup symbolizes the further idea that the new covenant must be "within, written on the hearts." Jesus died for us, but we must "die" with him if his death is to become saving in us, as is taught in passages like Mark 10:38; Luke 12:50; John 12:24 ff.; Romans 5:1–11; Galatians 2:20; Colossians 2:20 (cf. Stagg, *New Testament Theology,* pp. 122–48).

That Jesus' death is ***for many*** does not mean that it is limited to some only. This is biblical language for all. Jesus' whole ministry was one of reconciliation and this takes place in ***the forgiveness of sins*** (Eph.

2:13–16).

The Lord's Supper is a foretaste of the "Messianic Banquet" at the end of the age. The Last Supper was not a farewell but a pledge that the ***Father's kingdom*** would prevail and that Jesus' people would be reunited in the messianic banquet under that sovereign rule. The Supper ends with a triumphant note. Jesus' death is not defeat but victory. Although Jesus will no longer drink of the ***fruit of the vine*** (wine) in this life, he will ***drink it new*** (literally "fresh") with his people ***in*** his ***Father's kingdom.*** There he will drink a new kind (*kainon*) of wine, the fulfilment of that foreshadowed in the Lord's Supper.

The term "Eucharist" is derived from the Greek rendered ***given thanks*** (*eucharistēsas*) in verse 27. It is a "thanksgiving" as well as a grateful memory, a confident hope, and a communion in a new covenant of people who in Christ have experienced forgiveness. It is one of the ironies of history that Christians are most divided over the Supper which was most concerned for their oneness.

In Matthew and Mark there is no command to repeat the rite. Such command is explicit in Paul's account and in the disputed text of Luke 22:19.

(6) *Jesus Warns Disciples of Betrayal and Peter Protests* (*26:30–35*)

30 And when they had sung a hymn, they went out to the Mount of Olives. 31 Then Jesus said to them, "You will all fall away because of me this night; for it is written, 'I will strike the shepherd, and the sheep of the flock will be scattered.' 32 But after I am raised up, I will go before you to Galilee." 33 Peter declared to him, "Though they all fall away because of you, I will never fall away." 34 Jesus said to him, "Truly, I say to you, this very night, before the cock crows, you will deny me three times." 35 Peter said to him, "Even if I must die with you, I will not deny you." And so said all the disciples.

The ***hymn*** sung at the close of the Supper was probably the last half of the Passover Hallel (praise, as in Hallelujah, "praise God") consisting of Psalms 115—118. The ***Mount of Olives*** was across the Kedron Valley, northeast of Jerusalem, in sight of the Temple. ***Fall away*** (*skandalisthēsesthe*) means here to stumble. The disciples would fail Jesus, but except for Judas they would later rally to him (cf. Luke 24:33 f.). In Matthew this is seen as fulfilment of Zechariah 13:7 ff. The ***flock*** would be tested and ***scattered,*** but it would also be "refined." Jesus' death would be a shattering experience for his followers, but beyond his death was his resurrection which would rally them. Matthew and Mark stress ***Galilee*** as the scene of the risen Lord's appearances to his disciples, although ***go before*** could mean that Jesus will lead his disciples into ***Galilee,*** implying prior appearance in Jerusalem.

Peter boasted that he would not falter, even though all others should. Jesus warned him that he would ***deny*** him ***three times before the cock crows.*** That ***three*** goes with the denials and not with the crowing of the cock is clear from Mark 14:30. The expression "cock crow" was idiomatic for the third watch of the night, roughly midnight until 3:00 A.M. in the Roman system of dividing the night into four watches (cf. 14:25), although an actual crowing of the cock is implied in 26:74. What Peter denied was that he was even acquainted with Jesus (cf. John 13:38). Peter had boasted further, as did all the disciples, that he would ***die*** for Jesus before he would ***deny*** him. He failed miserably that night and the day following, but according to Acts he later risked his life for Christ, and according to the Gospel of John and later tradition he actually gave it (cf. John 21:18 f.).

(7) *Gethsemane* (*26:36–46*)

36 Then Jesus went with them to a place called Gethsemane, and he said to his disciples, "Sit here, while I go yonder and pray." 37 And taking with him Peter and the two sons of Zebedee, he began to be sorrowful and troubled. 38 Then he said to them, "My soul is very sorrowful, even to death; remain here, and watch with me." 39 And going a little farther he fell on his face and prayed, "My Father, if it be possible, let this cup pass from me; nevertheless, not as I will, but as thou wilt." 40 And he came to the disciples and found them sleep-

**ing; and he said to Peter, "So, could you not
watch with me one hour? 41 Watch and pray
that you may not enter into temptation; the
spirit indeed is willing, but the flesh is weak."
42 Again, for the second time, he went away and
prayed, "My Father, if this cannot pass unless
I drink it, thy will be done." 43 And again he
came and found them sleeping, for their eyes
were heavy. 44 So, leaving them again, he went
away and prayed for the third time, saying the
same words. 45 Then he came to the disciples
and said to them, "Are you still sleeping and
taking your rest? Behold, the hour is at hand,
and the Son of man is betrayed into the hands
of sinners. 46 Rise, let us be going; see, my betrayer is at hand."**

Gethsemane is probably Aramaic for "olive press," but no allusion to the idea of being trodden is explicit (Isa. 63:3–6, sometimes cited here, is about a wine press and reflects another mood). The humanity of the Son of God is clearly expressed in his longing for human companionship and support in his supreme ***hour*** of trial, sorrow, and loneliness. His trusted friends failed him, including Peter, James, and John. The church would never have invented such a story of the failure of these chief apostles at the time of their Lord's greatest sorrow and trouble. The ***place*** was possibly a private garden, and the three may have been asked to remain at the entrance to watch. Its precise location is now unknown.

Matthew describes Jesus' intense emotional state as ***sorrowful and troubled.*** Mark has a stronger term, "distressed." Jesus cried out that he was in sorrow almost to the point of death or as great as the sorrow of death. The request of his disciples that they ***watch*** may refer to watching for the enemy, but the phrase ***with me*** suggests rather that they give him support in his agony. Had his intention been to escape the enemy, it would have been a time to flee, not to ***pray*** and ***watch.*** He wanted their help not to scout the oncoming enemy but to have strength to meet the demands of the ***hour.***

The burden of Jesus' prayer concerned his ***cup,*** but its heart was for the doing of his Father's ***will.*** The ***cup*** is not explained. It seems to refer to his death and all that surrounds it: the failure of his disciples; the new release of selfish, cowardly, and angry passions in the very people whom he had come to save; all this and far more than any but he could know. We simply cannot fathom his sorrow, nor know the extent of his trial, nor understand all that his ***cup*** meant.

The submission of his will to that of his Father is Jesus' great victory in Gethsemane. Everything about his ***cup*** or his ***hour*** gave him reason to shrink back. Death was no beautiful friend to liberate "soul" from body as with Socrates. It was an ugly enemy to be conquered. At stake was Jesus' submission to the Father, and this in turn was the basic question of whether he would save himself or save others (cf. 27:41 f.). Had he acted to save himself, he would have followed the self-centered principle at the heart of the world's way. But he did not let this principle prevail. He was tempted in Gethsemane, even as following his baptism. The ***temptation*** was real and the victory was real (cf. Heb. 5:7–10). Under the supreme test, he committed himself to the way of self-denial and self-sacrifice and rejected the way of self-preservation. In his ***thy will be done*** is an echo of the Model Prayer. What he taught others to pray he practiced. He had no doubt that all things were possible to his Father, to remove or retain the cup, but his will was to do the Father's will. Out of his suffering came his triumph and glory (cf. John 12:20–28).

Jesus' added admonition to the disciples that they ***pray*** as well as ***watch*** was for their security. He asked that they ***watch with*** him, to bear his burden with him. He urged them to pray for themselves, that they have the strength to meet their test. The conflict between the willingness of ***spirit*** and weakness of ***flesh*** is that between sincere devotion and human weakness. ***Flesh*** is not to be taken in a literal sense, but as representing the whole man in his weakness and distance from God. The ***flesh*** which failed included will and emotion.

The command to ***watch*** and ***pray*** is preserved here not only as it was applied first to the needs of the disciples in Gethsemane but as the course proper to Christians in their continuing trials and temptations. In such watching and praying, and not in the world's reliance upon the sword, are the true armaments for Christian warfare (cf. 2 Cor. 10:3 f.).

The contrast between the willingness of ***spirit*** and the weakness of ***flesh*** is similar to that in Paul's thought (cf. Rom. 7.7–25) but not identical with or dependent upon it. To Paul, flesh stands for the natural man, hopelessly striving to achieve his own salvation, either as Jew through the law or the Greek through wisdom. Man as spirit is the man in Christ, God's spirit alone being able to deliver man as "flesh" from sin and death. In Matthew (cf. Mark 14:38) ***flesh*** and ***spirit*** represent struggles within man himself, similar to man's inner struggles as depicted in the Qumran literature (1 QS iv, 23–25; xi, 9 ff.). To Paul the flesh is weak in that it cannot free itself from sin and death but it is strong in its rebellion and can be overcome only by the Spirit of God.[48]

The verbs in verse 45 may be indicative or imperative. The RSV probably is correct in taking the verbs as indicative and translating the sentence as a question. Seeing or hearing the approach of a band of men, he declared ***the hour*** to be ***at hand.*** His ***betrayer*** likewise was at hand. For Jesus the real victory was already accomplished (cf. John 16:33). Until this moment he had the option of escape, but he had refused it. A full moon at Passover time and torches carried by the enemy (John 18:3) would make the approach of the crowd easily visible. Even at this point Jesus seized the initiative: ***Rise, let us be going!*** He did not seek crucifixion. The cross came to him, yet he met it face to face, not fleeing.

A more poignant charge could hardly have been given than that ***the Son of man is betrayed into the hands of sinners.*** The latter were the Gentiles, called sinners by the Jews. The Son of man's own people have not only rejected him but turned him over to ones they despise as "sinners." He was crucified by sinners, but he was rejected and betrayed by his own people. This is history, not the fiction of theology.

[48] Cf. R. G. Kuhn, "Jesus in Gethsemane," *Evangelische Theologie* 12, 1952–53, pp. 260–85).

(8) *The Betrayal and Arrest* (*26:47–56*)

[47] While he was still speaking, Judas came, one of the twelve, and with him a great crowd with swords and clubs, from the chief priests and the elders of the people. [48] Now the betrayer had given them a sign, saying, "The one I shall kiss is the man; seize him." [49] And he came up to Jesus at once and said, "Hail, Master!" And he kissed him. [50] Jesus said to him, "Friend, why are you here?" Then they came up and laid hands on Jesus and seized him. [51] And behold, one of those who were with Jesus stretched out his hand and drew his sword, and struck the slave of the high priest, and cut off his ear. [52] Then Jesus said to him, "Put your sword back into its place; for all who take the sword will perish by the sword. [53] Do you think that I cannot appeal to my Father, and he will at once send me more than twelve legions of angels? [54] But how then should the scriptures be fulfilled, that it must be so?" [55] At that hour Jesus said to the crowds, "Have you come out as against a robber, with swords and clubs to capture me? Day after day I sat in the temple teaching, and you did not seize me. [56] But all this has taken place, that the scriptures of the prophets might be fulfilled." Then all the disciples forsook him and fled.

Judas knew where to find Jesus in the night. John tells us that Jesus often met there with his disciples (18:2). The armed group led by Judas was sent under the authority of ***the chief priests and the elders.*** They probably consisted of Temple guards and slaves of the high priest. Judas had arranged ***a sign*** by which the officers would know whom to arrest; indicating that the Sanhedrin was primarily interested in arresting Jesus, not his followers, mistakenly thinking that to kill the leader would end the movement. Luke points up the irony of betrayal by a kiss, normally expressive of love, trust, and loyalty. It was normal for a disciple to greet his master with a kiss. Matthew follows Mark in employing a strong form of the verb for ***kissed*** (*katephilēsen*), indicating that Judas made a strong outward show of affection in the ***kiss*** of betrayal.

Friend (*hetaire*) could be rendered "comrade." It is normally used as a kindly term, but in each usage in Matthew the one so addressed has wronged the speaker (cf. 20:13; 22:12). The question directed to Judas is of uncertain meaning. Jesus knew why Judas was there. Possibly the question was asked not for information but to compel Judas to face up to what he was doing. The question may have been a last appeal to Judas to repent.

It was too much for Peter to bear when the men ***laid hands on Jesus.*** Only John identifies the ***one*** who drew his sword and severed an ear from the high priest's slave (18:10). Luke and John report that it was the right ear, causing some to speculate that Peter was left-handed or that the slave ducked his head just in time to avoid more serious damage. Peter's intention was doubtless to do more than ***cut off*** an ***ear.***

Jesus rebuked Peter, and Luke reports that Jesus healed the man (22:51). Matthew stresses Jesus' rejection of the sword and his warning that those who resort to ***the sword perish by the sword.*** As he had done earlier, Jesus rejected the world's weapons. He would conquer with a cross, not a sword. He would conquer by giving life, not taking it. This was his way, and it is to be ours. Not only did Jesus reject the sword, but he declined to call upon his Father for the aid of ***more than twelve legions of angels.*** The victory which he must win was to be through inner commitment to the Father's will, not by seeking deliverance through the swords of men or the intervention of the angels of God.

Jesus yielded to arrest but protested the false implications of the ***swords and clubs*** with which the crowd was armed. He was no robber or man of violence. ***Robber*** translates a word used by Josephus for insurrectionists who combined armed revolt and banditry (*Antiq.*, 20:8). He had taught openly in the Temple where he had left himself open to seizure. ***Day after day*** may imply more visits to the Temple than the Synoptics record, giving support to the Gospel of John, which records several visits to Jerusalem.

Although Peter was prepared to fight and probably would have given his life in physical combat, he and ***all the disciples fled*** when their Master gave himself up to his enemies, neither fighting nor permitting them to fight. Jesus was left alone.

(9) *Hearing Before Caiaphas (26:57–68)*

**57 Then those who had seized Jesus led him
to Caiaphas the high priest, where the scribes
and the elders had gathered. 58 But Peter followed him at a distance, as far as the courtyard
of the high priest, and going inside he sat with
the guards to see the end. 59 Now the chief
priests and the whole council sought false testimony against Jesus that they might put him to
death, 60 but they found none, though many
false witnesses came forward. At last two came
forward 61 and said, "This fellow said, 'I am
able to destroy the temple of God, and to build
it in three days.' " 62 And the high priest stood
up and said, "Have you no answer to make?
What is it that these men testify against you?"
63 But Jesus was silent. And the high priest said
to him, "I adjure you by the living God, tell us
if you are the Christ, the Son of God." 64 Jesus
said to him, "You have said so. But I tell you,
hereafter you will see the Son of man seated at
the right hand of Power, and coming on the
clouds of heaven." 65 Then the high priest tore
his robes, and said, "He has uttered blasphemy. Why do we still need witnesses? You
have now heard his blasphemy. 66 What is your
judgment?" They answered, "He deserves
death." 67 Then they spat in his face, and
struck him; and some slapped him, 68 saying,
"Prophesy to us, you Christ! Who is it that
struck you?"**

Caiaphas already has been introduced to the reader (cf. 26:3). The disciples fled when Jesus submitted to arrest, and it is not known how far they went. Peter turned back and ***followed him at a distance, as far as the courtyard of the high priest.*** The high priest's palace was apparently built on Roman style, with an open court in the middle. Peter sat with the servants or subordinates (*huperetōn*) to the high priest. ***Guards*** may be a proper understanding of these men, but that is not the necessary meaning of the term used. Peter waited ***to see the end,*** i.e., the outcome, which by every indication could be expected to be execution. John 18:15 reports that another disciple also followed into the palace, presumably John.

Hearing rather than trial probably best describes the appearance of Jesus before the Sanhedrin. Its function was to formulate charges to be presented to the Roman court, the latter having the final authority. It is not clear as to what powers were left to the Sanhedrin by the Romans in the first century (cf. Josephus, *Antiq*. 14,9; *Wars* 6,2). John 18:31 indicates that the Sanhedrin could not give the death sentence.

The powers of the Sanhedrin had been restricted under the Hasmonean rulers (*ca.* 166–40 B.C.). Under Herod the Great (37–4 B.C.) these powers were further limited. In A.D. 6 Judea became a Roman province, governed under a Roman procurator. Since the procurator had his official residence in Caesarea, some local powers were left to the Sanhedrin in Jerusalem. It seems that in one exceptional case, where the Temple was desecrated by a Gentile, even if he were a Roman, the Sanhedrin had the power of capital punishment (cf. Lohse, p. 78).

There is no conclusive evidence that the Sanhedrin's powers of capital punishment went beyond this one concession. Alleged cases are questionable. The case of a priest's daughter stoned on the charge of unchastity (*Sanhedrin* 7:2) probably and that of the execution of James the brother of John (Acts 12:2) certainly occurred under Herod Agrippa 1 (A.D. 41–44). Herod had the title of king with sovereign powers for a brief period. The execution of James, the brother of Jesus, occurred in a chaotic period between the death of Porcius Festus and the appointment of his successor, the Sanhedrin seizing power in the interval (Josephus, *Antiq*. 20:9). The stoning of Stephen (Acts 7:54–60) is best understood as a mob lynching, not formal action of the Sanhedrin.[49]

All four Gospels describe aspects of the trial of Jesus. It is impossible to reconstruct the whole scene, even though the basic procedure, motives, and charges are clear enough. Luke and John contain materials not in Mark and Matthew. According to Luke, the trial was not held until morning, Jesus being kept through the night in the high priest's courtyard, where he was insulted and brutally handled by the guards and where he heard and saw Peter thrice deny him. John records a hearing before Annas, former high priest and father-in-law to Caiaphas. The story may be telescoped in Mark and Matthew, the hearing before the Sanhedrin appearing to be held in the middle of the night.

The question of irregularities in the trial of Jesus could be pursued and demonstrated. For example, according to a second-century ruling which was possibly but not certainly in force in the first century, criminal cases coming before the Sanhedrin were to be tried in the daytime; and where the verdict was "guilty," the trial could not be concluded until the second day (*Sanhedrin* 4:1). But it is pointless to pursue such matters. The real indictment of the Sanhedrin is that its decision was reached before the trial. The trial was a mere formality to make the execution appear legal and right. False witnesses were sought, and their testimony was accepted, even where it did not agree. Reports on the trial could have come from Joseph of Arimathea (Mark 15:43; Luke 23:50–53) and from the unnamed disciple in John 18:15.

A major charge against Jesus revolved around something that he had said concerning ***the temple.*** Although his precise statement cannot be recovered, Jesus undoubtedly said something about the destruction of the Temple and his rebuilding it in three days (cf. 24:2; John 2:19–22;

[49] Paul Winter, *On the Trial of Jesus* (Berlin: Walter de Gruyter, 1961), pp. 62–90, argues that the Sanhedrin retained the authority of capital punishment until A.D. 70. He cites no conclusive evidence, basing his argument chiefly upon alleged implications from Mishnah Sanhedrin 7.1 and Acts 5:33; 6:12; 22:4; 25:9; 26:10.

Acts 6:14). Jesus predicted the destruction of the Temple; and by his rebuilding of it, he probably meant two things: first of all his own resurrection and then the creation of the church as the true temple of God (cf. 1 Cor. 3:16 f.).

Matthew avoids Mark's (14:58) contrast between a temple "made with hands" and one "not made with hands." Matthew has ***the temple of God.*** Where Mark has "I will destroy," it appears as ***I am able to destroy*** in Matthew. This may be further evidence that Matthew sought to avoid a complete break with Judaism or anything that would appear to question the legitimacy of the Temple for Judaism. His emphasis would be upon fulfilment of what legitimately was foreshadowed in Judaism. On the other hand, the portrayal of Jesus by the false witnesses as able to destroy what God has built was well suited to the Sanhedrin's search for a major charge (here blasphemy) against Jesus.

Jesus was silent before some of the questioning, knowing that there was no openness to the truth. The high priest seemed eager to have the full agreement of the Sanhedrin, so sought to get Jesus to furnish additional grounds for conviction, the witnesses being in obvious conflict with one another. He placed Jesus under oath, ***I adjure you,*** to say unambiguously whether or not he was ***the Christ, the Son of God.*** According to Matthew, Jesus' answer was literally, "You said it." In Mark 14:62 it is a simple, "I am." The Matthean form no doubt means "The statement is yours, and it is true."

Jesus' confession of messiahship gave the Sanhedrin an issue which could be made to interest the Roman court, especially if messiahship were interpreted politically. This is what the Sanhedrin wanted.

Incidentally, Mark's unambiguous "I am" seems less primitive in form than either Matthew's ***You have said so*** or Luke's altogether different stress (22:67). This is but another of many evidences that the relationship of the Gospels to one another is far from settled (cf. Lohmeyer, p. 367).

Verse 64 combines Daniel 7:13 and Psalm 110:1. In verses 63 f. Matthew follows Mark in bringing together three major titles: ***Christ, Son of God,*** and ***Son of man*** and also in tying together the ministry, passion, and Parousia of Jesus. The Suffering One and the Coming One are the same.[50]

The claim made by Jesus technically was not blasphemy, for there was nothing said against the name of God. The high priest arbitrarily ruled it ***blasphemy,*** probably reflecting his own opposition against messianism in principle and Jesus in particular. Tearing ***his robes*** was expressive of real horror or was a symbolic act in accordance with the Law that one who heard blasphemy was supposed to tear his garments.

The prejudiced verdict of the Sanhedrin in ruling that Jesus deserved ***death*** gave the rough guard sufficient excuse to insult and abuse Jesus. To spit in one's face is universally recognized as a degrading insult. They ***struck*** Jesus with their fists (*ekolaphison*) and ***slapped him,*** possibly with sticks (*rapis*). Mark 14:65 supplies a datum necessary to understanding the taunt, ***Prophesy to us, you Christ!*** They had blindfolded Jesus and were either playing a cruel game of "blindman's bluff" or they were testing him to see if he had supernatural knowledge.

(10) *Peter's Denial of Jesus* (26:69–75)

69 Now Peter was sitting outside in the courtyard. And a maid came up to him, and said, "You also were with Jesus the Galilean." 70 But he denied it before them all, saying, "I do not know what you mean." 71 And when he went out to the porch, another maid saw him, and she said to the bystanders, "This man was with Jesus of Nazareth." 72 And again he denied it with an oath, "I do not know the man." 73 After a little while the bystanders came up and said to Peter, "Certainly you are also one of them, for your accent betrays you." 74 Then he began to invoke a curse on himself and to swear, "I do not know the man." And immediately the cock crowed. 75 And Peter remembered the saying of Jesus, "Before the cock crows, you will deny me three times." And he went out and wept bitterly.

50 Conzelmann, "Historie und Theologie in den synoptischen Passionsberichten," *Zur Bedeutung des Todes Jesu* (Gütersloh: Mohn, 1967), p. 47.

All four Gospels tell of Peter's denial of Jesus. The church's honesty in exposing the failings of its heroes is a healthy self-criticism. The saints are yet sinners and concede it. No effort is made to excuse Peter's failure. His denials of Jesus are fully exposed against the background of his proud boasts of loyalty unto death. He was forgiven, first by Jesus and then by the church. He was accepted, not his sin. To put it in the perspective of the "gift and demand of grace," his sin was condemned but he was forgiven and received.

In minor details the variants among the four Gospels are apparent, although the essential agreement is clear. Matthew refers to two maids, Mark twice to the same maid. Both refer to ***bystanders*** who questioned Peter. Luke refers to a maid and two men, while John refers to a maid, bystanders, and a kinsman of the slave whose ear Peter had severed. Matthew and Mark see Peter as moving from the ***courtyard to the porch*** or gateway. Luke and John are silent about any change of place. There are verbal differences in conversations reported. In all essential points the story is clear. Under oath Peter denied knowing Jesus and did so in an emotional outburst which included the evoking of a curse upon himself. He then ***wept bitterly,*** knowing both his sincere love and also his failure. This is the Christians melancholy and security: to live under demand never fully met, yet to know himself to be "accepted though not acceptable" (Paul Tillich's beautiful phrase).

Peter's first denial was in the form of an evasion, ***I do not know what you mean,*** or literally, "I do not know what you are saying." His second reply was a categorical denial under oath, ***I do not know the man.*** The man had been designated as ***Jesus the Galilean*** and then as ***Jesus of Nazareth,*** first use of this title since 2:23. The first maid's ***you also*** is ambiguous. There could be an implication that she already had seen another disciple in the courtyard (cf. John 18:15 f.) or the ***also*** could mean that he was not only in the courtyard but also a disciple.

The ***bystanders*** pointed to Peter's ***accent*** as betraying his Galilean origin. Peter repeated his denial and invoked curses upon himself, presumably on condition that he was lying. That he continued this for some time, possibly to one and then another, is implied by ***began*** as well as by the present infinitives which follow, ***to invoke*** and ***to swear.*** Although "cock crow" was a technical term for the third Roman watch of the night (12:00–3:00 A.M.), it seems here to imply the actual crowing of a cock.

(11) Trial Before Pilate (27:1–26)

a. Jesus Delivered to Pilate (27:1–2)

[1] When morning came, all the chief priests and the elders of the people took counsel against Jesus to put him to death; [2] and they bound him and led him away and delivered him to Pilate the governor.

Their minds already made up to have Jesus put to death, but apparently not having the legal authority to do it themselves, the priests and elders ***delivered*** Jesus over ***to Pilate the governor.*** Pontius Pilate was appointed procurator (governor) of the Roman province of Judea (including Samaria) in A.D. 26 and was recalled to Rome in A.D. 36. Josephus (*Antiq.* 18:3; *Wars* 2:9) and Philo (*Ad Gai,* 38) both picture him as anti-Jewish and a bad ruler.

Allowing for Jewish prejudice against him, his recall by the Romans is clear evidence of their displeasure with him. He offended the Jews once by bringing soldiers into Jerusalem without first removing the emperor's picture from their insignia (pictures were considered images) and once for seizing Temple funds to build an aqueduct. His recall was occasioned by his brutality in putting down a small revolt in Samaria. That he was left in office for ten years speaks something in his favor.

b. Judas' Suicide (27:3–10)

[3] When Judas, his betrayer, saw that he was condemned, he repented and brought back the thirty pieces of silver to the chief priests and the elders, [4] saying, "I have sinned in betraying innocent blood." They said, "What is that to us? See to it yourself." [5] And throwing down the pieces of silver in the temple, he departed;

and he went and hanged himself. [6] But the chief priests, taking the pieces of silver, said, "It is not lawful to put them into the treasury, since they are blood money." [7] So they took counsel, and bought with them the potter's field, to bury strangers in. [8] Therefore that field has been called the Field of Blood to this day. [9] Then was fulfilled what had been spoken by the prophet Jeremiah, saying, "And they took the thirty pieces of silver, the price of him on whom a price had been set by some of the sons of Israel, [10] and they gave them for the potter's field, as the Lord directed me."

The death of Judas is recorded by Matthew alone in the Gospels. Luke tells the story in a somewhat different form in Acts 1:16–20. At each mention, Judas is branded as the ***betrayer.*** The church felt deeply about this betrayal on the part of one who had been so close to Jesus. The full motive of Judas in betraying Jesus is not known, but that he ***repented*** when he saw Jesus condemned gives some support to the theory that his intention had been to create a crisis situation in which Jesus would act positively to seize the power in Jerusalem, becoming a political Messiah. If so, this misguided act failed, and Judas committed suicide when he saw that Jesus would not fight but would submit to execution. This is a possible interpretation, but at best it is only an implication and highly precarious.

Repented (*metamelētheis*) is not the term normally used for repentance in the New Testament, and "remorse" may be a better translation. Judas did not experience the repentance of conversion. He knew only frustration and a sense of guilt leading to suicide. He had ***sinned*** against Jesus and betrayed ***innocent blood.***

The ***chief priests and the elders*** show up even worse than Judas. Their indifference to Judas comes out in their calloused question, ***What is that to us?*** They had used him and were now prepared to drop him. Judas flung the silver into the Temple, apparently expressing his resentment against the religious leaders who had used him and also in an effort to free himself of some of his guilt. The religious leaders' only concern was for the meticulous observation of the ceremonial law. They were willing to shed blood but could not accept ***blood money*** into the Temple treasury, so they used it to buy a field for the burial of strangers.

Matthew tells the story in the language of Zechariah 11:12 f., influenced by Jeremiah 18:2 f.; 32:6–15. This is in keeping with his principle of stressing fulfilment of Scripture. Again, it is clear that the event was believed before it was told in the language of Scripture. Imagination would never have created the story from the obscure language of Zechariah and Jeremiah, but these passages could serve to clothe the story with biblical language. The very fact that the relationship between text and event seems to be strained argues for the priority of the belief over the employment of the proof text. The early church formulated the whole passion narrative in the language of Scripture, the only language suited to the story, but it was only by the events in the life of Jesus that they were able to gain a new understanding of the Scriptures (cf. John 2:22; 12:16). It was not that a certain understanding of the Scriptures first enabled them to understand the events, and certainly they did not invent the stories in order to create "fulfilment" of Scripture.[51]

c. *Trial and Sentence (27:11–26)*

[11] Now Jesus stood before the governor; and the governor asked him, "Are you the King of the Jews?" Jesus said to him, "You have said so." [12] But when he was accused by the chief priests and elders, he made no answer. [13] Then Pilate said to him, "Do you not hear how many things they testify against you?" [14] But he gave him no answer, not even to a single charge; so that the governor wondered greatly.

[15] Now at the feast the governor was accustomed to release for the crowd any one prisoner whom they wanted. [16] And they had then a notorious prisoner, called Barabbas. [17] So when they had gathered, Pilate said to them, "Whom do you want me to release for you, Barabbas or Jesus who is called Christ?" [18] For he knew that it was out of envy that they had delivered him up. [19] Besides, while he was sitting on the judgment seat, his wife sent word to him, "Have nothing to do with that right-

[51] Eduard Lohse, "Die alttestamentlichen Bezüge im neutestamentlichen Zeugnis vom Tode Jesu Christi," *Zur Bedeutung des Todes Jesu* (2d ed.; Gütersloh: Mohn, 1967), pp. 111 f.

eous man, for I have suffered much over him
today in a dream." 20 Now the chief priests and
the elders persuaded the people to ask for
Barabbas and destroy Jesus. 21 The governor
again said to them, "Which of the two do you
want me to release for you?" And they said,
"Barabbas." 22 Pilate said to them, "Then what
shall I do with Jesus who is called Christ?"
They all said, "Let him be crucified." 23 And he
said, "Why, what evil has he done?" But they
shouted all the more, "Let him be crucified."

24 So when Pilate saw that he was gaining
nothing, but rather that a riot was beginning,
he took water and washed his hands before the
crowd, saying, "I am innocent of this man's
blood; see to it yourselves." 25 And all the
people answered, "His blood be on us and on
our children!" 26 Then he released for them
Barabbas, and having scourged Jesus, deliv-
ered him to be crucified.

Jesus was sentenced to death by the Roman governor Pilate on a charge of treason against the state (cf. Luke 23:2). Of course the charge was false, and Pilate did not believe it. The chief blame must rest upon the high priests and elders, who for different reasons pressed the charges. Since only a political charge would interest a Roman court, they were forced to center their charges in that area. The crowds were fickle and could easily be aroused.

It has become fashionable, almost a dogma, to hold that the initiative for the execution of Jesus was with the Romans and that the church shifted the blame to the Jews after its break with Judaism. This is to charge the church with a major crime, exonerating the guilty and condemning the innocent. But this charge is false, and it is time that it be dropped. Certainly the anti-Semitism which feeds off passages like verse 25 is to be deplored, but the evil of anti-Semitism is not to be overcome by denying or rewriting history. Paul plainly affirmed that the Jews "killed . . . the Lord Jesus" (1 Thess. 2:14 f.), and he was not anti-Jewish. The very Gospels which point to Jewish guilt in the crucifixion of Jesus also extoll Jews: Jesus, the prophets, and others, as well as the Jewish Scriptures.

The story as the Gospels have it is credible. Although Christian tradition for generations did tend more and more to exonerate Pilate, the balanced story in the Gospels, showing his guilt as well as some effort to free Jesus, is not to be dismissed as fiction. Pilate's conduct is understandable in the light of all else that is known about him. His efforts to free Jesus may be traced in part to Roman justice and to the severity of Emperor Tiberius with governors who mistreated his subjects. Pilate may have resented the pressure brought upon him by the Jewish leaders. This tension between the Jewish rulers and Pilate is clearly reflected in John 19:6 f.,12. Pilate's resentment of being pressured into executing an innocent man was offset by fear that to release Jesus may have left him open to the charge in Rome of being lenient with one accused of being a rebel against the state.

Pilate's asking Jesus if he were ***king of the Jews*** presupposes Jewish charges that Jesus had made such a claim. Jesus' answer, ***You have said so,*** was an acknowledgement with the implication that more needed to be said. Jesus accepted the title of Christ but not in a political sense. Jesus was silent before the chief priests and elders because he knew that nothing he could say would change minds made up already.

Release of a prisoner at Passover was a political move calculated to ease national unrest. To serve the purpose, the one released would have to be of nationalist sympathies. ***Barabbas*** was just such a man, a rebel who had taken up arms against Rome (cf. Mark 15:7). ***Notorious*** could be rendered "notable." There is substantial manuscript evidence (Greek, Latin, Syriac, Armenian, Georgian, and patristic) that "Jesus Barabbas" was his name. Origen knew manuscripts in which he was called Jesus, but he rejected the reading on prejudiced grounds, for to him Barabbas was not worthy of the name. It is less likely that the name would have been supplied than deleted.

If the name Jesus is original for Barabbas, Pilate's question is pointed. Which Jesus did they want released? Jesus means savior (1:21), and each offered himself as a savior, Jesus the Christ as the Saviour from sins and Jesus Barabbas as a savior from Rome. The crowd, stirred up by the chief priests and elders, chose ***Barabbas.***

Matthew alone tells about the dream of Pilate's wife. She recognized him as a ***righteous man.*** Pilate recognized that Jesus was not guilty as charged. To his repeated appeal, the clamor of the people was that Jesus ***be crucified.*** To Pilate's question ***Why?*** the answer was only, ***Let him be crucified.*** Pilate yielded to pressure, fearing ***a riot.*** To have permitted a riot to develop would have jeopardized his position as governor, for it was his responsibility to keep order.

Washing one's hands as a symbolic act is Jewish (cf. Deut. 21:6 f.). Pilate tried to exonerate himself, but of course he was criminally guilty in abdicating his authority and in permitting the execution of one whom he had found not guilty. His ritual act and protest that he was ***innocent*** removed none of his guilt. Having Jesus ***scourged*** was a part of Roman custom when one was crucified. This was a cruel beating with a leather whip, loaded with pieces of bone and metal.

Matthew clearly saw the sufferings of the nation, including the destruction of Jerusalem, as traceable to the rejection of Jesus. It is demonstrably true that the fatal wars with Rome resulted from following the type of messianism that Jesus rejected. Verse 25 has unfortunately been used in anti-Semitism, and such use is to be deplored. Jesus was crucified by Romans at Jewish initiative, but not all Jews then supported the crime, and Jews today are no more guilty than any other people. Jesus died on account of the sins of the world, not of the Jews alone.

2. *The Crucifixion* (*27:27–56*)

(1) *Jesus Mocked by Soldiers* (*27:27–31*)

**27 Then the soldiers of the governor took
Jesus into the praetorium, and they gathered
the whole battalion before him. 28 And they
stripped him and put a scarlet robe upon him,
29 and plaiting a crown of thorns they put it on
his head, and put a reed in his right hand. And
kneeling before him they mocked him, saying,
"Hail, King of the Jews!" 30 And they spat
upon him, and took the reed and struck him on
the head. 31 And when they had mocked him,
they stripped him of the robe, and put his own
clothes on him, and led him away to crucify
him.**

The mocking of Jesus by Pilate's soldiers is not to be confused with that by the servants of Caiaphas (26:67 f.). The soldiers probably were a part of a cohort stationed in Palestine. The ***praetorium*** was the official residence of the governor when in Jerusalem, his permanent headquarters being in Caesarea. The soldiers saw Jesus only as an impostor who thought of himself as King of the Jews. They had only scorn for his seeming weakness. The ***scarlet robe*** was probably a soldier's coat. The ***crown*** (*stephanon*) was in imitation of a victor's wreath. A ***reed*** or cane served as a scepter. The huge joke was further implemented by mock allegiance, hailing him as ***King of the Jews.*** This gave way to undisguised hatred as ***they spat upon him*** and repeatedly ***struck him on the head*** with ***the reed.***

The soldiers ridiculed the idea that one like Jesus could be king. Their criterion of power was altogether different. Pilate had been more reserved, but he too seemed amazed that one like Jesus could be thought of as a king. Matthew would have us see that precisely this one, so despised and seemingly unkingly, is indeed the ***King of the Jews*** and of us all.

(2) *Jesus Crucified* (*27:32–44*)

**32 As they were marching out, they came
upon a man of Cyrene, Simon by name; this
man they compelled to carry his cross. 33 And
when they came to a place called Golgotha
(which means the place of a skull), 34 they
offered him wine to drink, mingled with gall;
but when he tasted it, he would not drink it.
35 And when they had crucified him, they divided his garments among them by casting
lots; 36 then they sat down and kept watch over
him there. 37 And over his head they put the
charge against him, which read, "This is Jesus
the King of the Jews." 38 Then two robbers
were crucified with him, one on the right and
one on the left. 39 And those who passed by
derided him, wagging their heads 40 and saying, "You who would destroy the temple and
build it in three days, save yourself! If you are**

the Son of God, come down from the cross."
41 So also the chief priests, with the scribes and
elders, mocked him, saying, 42 "He saved
others; he cannot save himself. He is the King
of Israel; let him come down now from the
cross, and we will believe in him. 43 He trusts
in God; let God deliver him now, if he desires
him; for he said, 'I am the Son of God.'"
44 And the robbers who were crucified with
him also reviled him in the same way.

It was customary for the condemned to carry the cross beam (*patibulum*), not the upright beam; and Jesus seems to have carried this until he staggered, apparently exhausted from the scourging (cf. John 19:17). ***Simon*** of Cyrene was conscripted by the Romans to ***carry*** the ***cross*** beam the rest of the way. Mark 15:21 identifies him as "the father of Alexander and Rufus," apparently well-known Christians when Mark wrote (cf. Rom. 16:13). It is noteworthy that the impetus for the great revival and missionary thrust in Antioch of Syria came through "men of Cyprus and Cyrene" (Acts 11:20). Although no such connection is traceable, it is altogether possible that Simon of Cyrene became a disciple and introduced Christianity to Cyrene, a major force behind the revival which embarked Barnabas and Paul on a great missionary campaign (Acts 13:1–3).

Golgotha is Aramaic for ***skull*** or head. It probably designated a skull-shaped hill, not an old burial ground, for in that case skeletons and not just skulls would have been there. The location is not known. Hebrews 13:12 makes a point of Jesus' suffering "outside the gate." It is not likely that the present Church of the Holy Sepulcher marks the spot. The "Garden Tomb" or "Gordon's Calvary" no doubt presents a view similar to that described in the Gospels, but that it is actually the place of the crucifixion and burial cannot be verified.

It was customary to give the one crucified a narcotic to lessen the pain. Jesus refused the mixture of ***wine*** and ***gall*** (*cholēs*), a bitter drink of some kind (cf. Psalm 69:21). Why Jesus refused it is not disclosed, although his determination to retain consciouness to the last is quite plausible.

Jesus' hands were nailed to the cross beam, and apparently his feet were nailed to the upright beam, for there were nail prints in his hands (John 20:25) and apparently also in his feet (Luke 24:39; Psalm 22:16). The feet of the one crucified were probably only a few feet above the ground, making it easy for the spectators to see and speak to the victim. The Gospels exercise great restraint with respect to the physical sufferings of Jesus on the cross, giving far more attention to the callousness of those who mocked and Jesus' sense of utter abandonment as he suffered alone. "The eternal value of the cross does not lie in its physical tortures" (McNeile, p. 418). Physical torture has been suffered by many. No other has suffered as did Jesus, the sinless one who bore the sins of the world.

By custom, the garments of the victim belonged to the executioners. They cast ***lots*** for the spoils. The soldiers ***kept watch*** to prevent friends of the condemned man from rescuing him from the cross.

The caption over the head of Jesus is most significant, although the exact words are not known (cf. Mark 15:26; Luke 23:38; John 19:19). By all accounts, the essence of the caption was ***the king of the Jews.*** This probably represents Pilate's way of striking back at the high priests and elders, but it also represents the formal charge under which the Romans executed Jesus, that of high treason. It unintentionally proclaimed the true identity of Jesus as the ***King of the Jews,*** although he was far more. The execution of ***two robbers,*** probably insurrectionists, helped to emphasize the charge that Jesus had aspired to be a political Messiah, a charge which neither Jew nor Roman had more than superficial grounds to believe.

The derision of ***those who passed by*** as well as that of the ***chief priests, scribes and elders*** was based upon a mixture of truth and error, distortions of things Jesus had said and of what he was. Through all the distortion, basic truths come through. Jesus had spoken of the destruction of ***the temple*** and of its reconstruction in a new and significant way. The clamor for a dramatic sign, like a miraculous descent from the cross, echoes the earlier demands for messianic signs, as following his baptism (cf. 4:6 f.).

The very heart of the gospel shines through the taunts of the high priests, scribes, and elders. It was profoundly true, in a way missed by his tormentors, that Jesus could not ***save himself*** if he was to save ***others.*** The deepest principle in the life and death of Jesus is that salvation is based upon the giving of life, not upon taking or guarding it. Had Jesus elected to ***save himself*** he would but have embraced the egocentric way which has plagued mankind from Adam until now. The greatest lie of all is that one can find life by "saving it." The greatest truth of all is that one finds life only in giving it up (cf. 16:24 f.; John 12:24 f.; Rom. 6:3–11; Gal. 2:20).

Another basic tribute to Jesus, intended in scorn and sarcasm but profoundly true, was that ***he trusts in God.*** This characterized the life of Jesus from beginning to end. Even in the death from which he shrank, his trust was in God. He leaned heavily upon his disciples and craved their understanding and support, but in the Father alone did he find that understanding and support. ***If he desires him,*** i.e., "if he wishes to have him," was uttered in bitter sarcasm. Unwanted by men, they assumed that God too would reject him. How little did they know that the one so despised among men was not only desired by the Father but was the Father's "beloved Son."

(3) *Jesus' Death* (*27:45–56*)

45 Now from the sixth hour there was dark-
ness over all the land until the ninth hour.
46 And about the ninth hour Jesus cried with a
loud voice, "Eli, Eli, lama sabach-thani?" that
is, "My God, my God, why hast thou forsaken
me?" 47 And some of the bystanders hearing it
said, "This man is calling Elijah." 48 And one
of them at once ran and took a sponge, filled it
with vinegar, and put it on a reed, and gave it
to him to drink. 49 But the others said, "Wait,
let us see whether Elijah will come to save
him." 50 And Jesus cried again with a loud
voice and yielded up his spirit.

51 And behold, the curtain of the temple was
torn in two, from top to bottom; and the earth
shook, and the rocks were split; 52 the tombs
also were opened, and many bodies of the
saints who had fallen asleep were raised, 53 and
coming out of the tombs after his resurrection
they went into the holy city and appeared to
many. 54 When the centurion and those who
were with him, keeping watch over Jesus, saw
the earthquake and what took place, they were
filled with awe, and said, "Truly this was the
Son of God!"

55 There were also many women there, look-
ing on from afar, who had followed Jesus from
Galilee, ministering to him; 56 among whom
were Mary Magdalene, and Mary the mother
of James and Joseph, and the mother of the
sons of Zebedee.

That "Christ died for our sins in accordance with the scriptures" belongs to the earliest traceable Christian preaching, being pre-Pauline (1 Cor. 15:3). The earliest Christians saw the death of Jesus as saving and interpreted it by the Scriptures as well as the Scriptures by it. They saw it not as a drama enacted upon a stage but as a real death followed by a real resurrection, not automatically saving, but saving to those who by faith receive the living Christ into their lives as a transforming, saving presence.

Psalm 22 shines through this paragraph and much of the passion narrative. It should be read in its entirety and kept in mind as one reads Matthew's account of the crucifixion. Many of its utterances are reflected or actually recited. This psalm was in the mind of Jesus, and some of its language came to expression on his lips. The snatches from the psalm are better understood in the light of the whole psalm, a picture of one forsaken, beleaguered, and who has unshaken confidence in the goodness of God and in his ultimate dominion over all nations.

The psalm first pictures an individual person as suffering alone. This is followed by praise to God for his act of deliverance, first for that individual and then extended as an act of deliverance for all mankind and for all time. It is a song in praise of the inbreaking of the kingdom of God in a mighty act of deliverance.[52]

The sixth hour and ***the ninth*** represent Jewish time, counted from rising to setting of the sun, i.e., noon until 3:00 P.M. The ***land*** means the country of Judea. The ***darkness*** was not due to an eclipse, for such was not possible during the full moon at the time of the Passover. Other natural phenomena may be implied, as a storm or black sirocco, but the Synoptics seem to mean that even nature bore witness to the magnitude of the event at Golgotha.

Matthew and Mark record only one utterance by Jesus from the cross. Luke records three others (23:34,43,46) and John yet three more (19:26 f.,28,30), but the beautiful and cherished prayer for the forgiveness of his enemies in Luke 23:34 seems to be a scribal addition to the Lukan text. There can be no doubt that the cry recorded by Matthew and Mark goes back to Jesus, even though uncertainty remains as to its linguistic form.

My God, my God, why hast thou forsaken me? is an Aramaic rendering of Psalm 22:1, except that Matthew has the Hebrew *Ēli* ("My God") where Mark has the Aramaic *Elōi.* Even so, the manuscripts differ in Matthew, but *Ēli* is probably correct. An Aramaic Targum on Psalm 22:1 also has the Matthean form *Ēli.* This form may more readily account for its confusion with ***Elijah*** by ***the bystanders.*** Matthew's version, including the Greek translation of the Aramaic, is independent of Mark. Whatever may have been the original form, the cry goes back to Jesus and ultimately to Psalm 22:1.

We cannot fathom the cry of Jesus. It is often observed that Psalm 22 is a cry of despair that ends on a triumphant note, and this may be a clue to its meaning to Jesus. Käsemann insists that this cry not be understood as an expression of doubt, but as evidence that Jesus died as he lived, with God's word on his lips and with unshaken trust in him who alone and always is one's true help.[53]

Broadus may be near the truth in saying: "If it be asked how he could feel himself to be forsaken, we must remember that a human soul as well as a human body was here suffering, a human soul thinking and feeling within human limitations (Mark 13:32), not psychologically unlike the action of other devout souls when in some great and overwhelming sorrow" (p. 574).

The Son of God was also truly human, and he was overwhelmed by his loneliness, yet his faith in God was affirmed in the very cry of loneliness. God did not turn his back on Jesus, as some theology has it. God was never nearer than at Golgotha as Jesus gave himself in full obedience to the Father's will (cf. Argyle, p. 215). God was there! "God was in Christ reconciling the world to himself" (2 Cor. 5:19).

Possibly the one act of kindness to Jesus while on the cross came from a Roman soldier. The unidentified bystander who offered him ***vinegar*** (a sour wine) was probably a soldier. However, the statement may echo Psalm 69:21 and intend to represent the giving of ***vinegar*** to one who was thirsty as a further abuse. Others were moved only by curiosity, waiting to see if ***Elijah*** would come to deliver Jesus. That Jesus did not die of slow exhaustion as was usual for those suffering crucifixion is evidenced by the fact that he had strength to cry out ***with a loud voice*** just before he died. John records it that Jesus died with a triumphant shout, "It is finished!" Matthew says that Jesus ***yielded up his spirit,*** possibly stressing a voluntary action. Those crucified sometimes lived for days before they died. That Jesus died within a few hours was a surprise to all.

Of the portents attending the death and resurrection of Jesus, the two most significant were the rending of ***the curtain of the temple*** and the raising of ***many bodies of the saints.*** There were two veils in the tem-

52 Hartmut Gese, in a 1967–68 Tübingen seminar, demonstrated the extensive impact of the Aramaic form of Psalm 22 upon early Christian understanding of the death of Jesus and the Lord's Supper.

53 Ernst Käsemann, "Die Gegenwart Christi: Das Kreuz," *Christus Unter Uns* (2d ed.; Stuttgart: Kreuz-Verlag, 1967), p. 6.

ple, one before the holy place and the other before the holy of holies. Although the reference could be to either, it is most likely that ***the curtain*** was the chief one, that before the holy of holies. That it was rent ***from top to bottom*** implies that it was a divine act, not man's. Symbolism is to be seen, with two major possibilities. This could be seen as a judgment upon the Temple because of Israel's rejection of Jesus (cf. Hummel, pp. 83 f.). The interpretation more generally followed is that the holy of holies is now open to all men, not just to the high priest; for in Jesus Christ every man has direct access to the presence of God (cf. Eph. 2:18; Heb. 9:1–14; 10:19–22). Matthew could have seen the rending of the veil as both a judgment upon Israel and the supersession of the holy of holies by Jesus Christ. This would accord with Jesus' word about building a new temple in the place of the old.

That ***the earth shook, and the rocks were split*** are probably to be understood as pointing to the cosmic significance of the death of Jesus (cf. Rom. 8:19–23).

Two points may be stressed with respect to the raising of the dead. First, ***many bodies*** (*sōmata*) ***were raised. Resurrection*** is more than immortality. The idea of immortality is a widely held view that the soul or spirit is the true self and the body its tomb or prison from which it is released by death. In the biblical doctrine of creation, body belongs essentially to what man is, and death is seen to be the enemy to be overcome, not the friend that frees soul from body. In the pagan doctrine of immortality there is no place for body. In the biblical doctrine of resurrection, body is included in redemption. Of course, "body" (*sōma*) in Greek, as in English, is used sometimes for person, as in "somebody." But resurrection always implies the full self, including body.

The second point with respect to the raising of the ***many bodies*** is that they came ***out of the tombs*** and made their appearance ***after his*** (i.e., Jesus') ***resurrection.*** Matthew's concern was probably to affirm the priority of Jesus in the ***resurrection,*** that he is "the first fruits of those who have fallen asleep" (1 Cor. 15:20) or "the first-born from the dead" (Col. 1:18). ***The saints*** could hardly be other than Israelites who had died and been entombed near Jerusalem.

Greek grammar leaves open the question of the response of ***the centurion*** (officer over a hundred soldiers) and those with him. ***Filled with awe*** could be rendered "they feared greatly" (KJV); and since there is no article with "son," it could be rendered ***a son of God,*** i.e., a hero to their pagan thinking. Although grammatically possible, this rendering is unlikely. The Greek phrase is literally "God's Son" (*theou huios*), and the Greek article is not required for definiteness. The recognition of the deity of Jesus Christ in the Gospel of Matthew is not dependent upon this verse, and it must be observed that in the Lukan parallel the centurion says only that "this was a righteous man" (23:47, KJV). It is highly probable, however, that Matthew intends to contrast this Gentile's acclaim of Jesus as ***son of God*** with the scoffing of the high priests and elders as well as to dramatize the fact that the lowly and despised crucified one is indeed God's Son (Lohse, *Die Geschichte*, p. 102).

All three Synoptics report that certain women who had followed Jesus from Galilee witnessed the crucifixion ***from afar.*** Matthew and Mark both include ***Mary Magdalene.*** Matthew's ***Mary the mother of James and Joseph*** is probably the same as Mark's "Mary the mother of James the younger and of Joses." ***The mother of the sons of Zebedee*** in Matthew is probably the same as "Salome" in Mark. Luke gives no names, referring rather to all Jesus' "acquaintances" and the women who had followed from Galilee. John (19:25 f.) reports that Jesus' mother, his mother's sister, Mary Magdalene, and the "beloved disciple" were at the cross in speaking distance. Matthew's mention of the women ***looking on from afar*** probably was not to rebuke them for being at a distance but to credit them with at least being within sight of the crucifixion. Possibly he saw them as guarantors of the tradition (cf. Johnson, p. 611).

3. *The Burial of Jesus* (*27:57–66*)

(1) *The Burial* (*27:57–61*)

[57] When it was evening, there came a rich man from Arimathea, named Joseph, who also was a disciple of Jesus. [58] He went to Pilate and asked for the body of Jesus. Then Pilate ordered it to be given to him. [59] And Joseph took the body, and wrapped it in a clean linen shroud, [60] and laid it in his own new tomb, which he had hewn in the rock; and he rolled a great stone to the door of the tomb, and departed. [61] Mary Magdalene and the other Mary were there, sitting opposite the sepulchre.

It was not only the Jewish custom to bury on the day of death but the Law required that the body of one who had been crucified be buried the same day (Deut. 21:22 f.). Both Mark and Luke specify that it was Friday, just before the sabbath, and this would be additional reason for a hasty burial of Jesus (cf. John 19:31). ***Evening*** signifies the approach of the sabbath, which began at sunset.

Joseph of Arimathea is named in all four Gospels as the one who buried Jesus. Mark knew him as "a respected member of the council," presumably the Sanhedrin. He does not call him a disciple but reports that he was "looking for the kingdom of God" (15:43). Luke adds that he was "a good and righteous man" and that he had not consented to the council's purpose and deed (23:50–51). Matthew names him ***a disciple of Jesus,*** and John adds "but secretly, for fear of the Jews" (19:38). Matthew alone says that Joseph was "rich."

Being a man of prominence and wealth would give Joseph access to Pilate with minimum risk. His real risk would be in offending his fellow Jews. Wrapping the ***body*** in ***clean linen*** was in keeping with rabbinical custom. John adds that Nicodemus brought the customary spices for the burial (19:39). Although from Arimathea (possibly the Ramathaim-zophim of 1 Sam. 1:1), Joseph had moved to Jerusalem, for he had prepared his own tomb there. Tombs were ***hewn in the rock,*** as was Joseph's, or improvised from caves. Whether the burial of Jesus in Joseph's tomb was intended to be temporary or permanent, Joseph would not be permitted to use it for family burial, for rabbinical law forbade one to bury his family in a tomb where an executed man had lain.

The ***great stone*** which was rolled before the ***door of the tomb*** was flat and circular. A groove or trench would serve as a track upon which it could be rolled. Such stones may yet be seen at Jerusalem in the Garden Tomb and the Tomb of the Kings. Mary Magdalene and ***the other Mary,*** presumably "Mary the mother of Joses" (Mark 15:47), watched the burial. No mention is made of the twelve or the immediate family.

(2) *The Guard at the Tomb* (*27:62–66*)

[62] Next day, that is, after the day of Preparation, the chief priests and the Pharisees gathered before Pilate [63] and said, "Sir, we remember how that impostor said, while he was still alive, 'After three days I will rise again.' [64] Therefore order the sepulchre to be made secure until the third day, lest his disciples go and steal him away, and tell the people, 'He has risen from the dead,' and the last fraud will be worse than the first." [65] Pilate said to them, "You have a guard of soldiers; go, make it as secure as you can." [66] So they went and made the sepulchre secure by sealing the stone and setting a guard.

Preparation (*paraskeuē*) designated the day just before the sabbath, and it came to mean Friday, as in modern Greek. The day after would be the sabbath. Why Matthew avoids calling it the sabbath is not apparent.

Much debate continues to this day over the authenticity of Matthew's story, but two important factors emerge, however assessed. Both Jews and Christians believed that the tomb in which Jesus had been buried was found empty. Jews claimed that the body was stolen, and Christians claimed that Jesus was risen, but no one claimed that the body remained in the tomb.

A second important factor is that, to Jew and Christian, resurrection necessarily meant the raising of the body. The empty tomb did not and could not prove the resurrection. All that an empty tomb necessarily proved was that it was empty. Christian faith rested upon the appearance of the living Lord, not upon the empty tomb. Even the disciples first believed the body to have been stolen. But although the empty tomb did not prove the resurrection, had the body been found, neither Jew nor Christian would have believed that Jesus had arisen. Resurrection meant "bodily resurrection," not just immortality or "a sense of Christ's presence," despite today's modernizing tendencies, however sophisticated. One may believe or disbelieve the story of Jesus' resurrection, but to "spiritualize" it is to depart from the New Testament claim.

The high priests and Pharisees asked Pilate that the tomb *be made secure until the third day.* Jews believed that after three days the body had reached a stage of decomposition and the spirit had departed so that there was no chance of return to life. In other words, after three days the fact of death was established. Pilate's contempt for the Jewish leaders is reflected in his curt answer, putting a Roman guard at their disposal. A cord fastened by seals at each end to the stone and the rock tomb would guarantee its security. *The last fraud* feared by the Jews was belief in the resurrection of Jesus, *the first* being belief that he was Messiah.

4. The Resurrection and Appearances of Jesus (28:1–20)

The resurrection of Jesus belongs to the very foundation of Christian faith and proclamation (cf. 1 Cor. 15:12–19). By resurrection no New Testament writer means simply a vision of Christ or a "purely spiritual" survival (cf. Cox, pp. 166 f.). They meant a bodily resurrection, whatever the transformation of that body may have been. No sharp distinction was drawn between the "material" and the "spiritual," as is true today. There is something with continuity known as "body" which survives the constant, daily change or displacement of its atomic substance, a continuity of body along with the discontinuity in its atomic substance. The mystery of this bodily "continuity in change" foreshadows the heightened mystery of resurrection, but resurrection is necessarily "bodily" resurrection.

The Gospels and Paul build faith upon something that happened "on the third day," not the second or the fourth. The appearances were such as could be named and numbered (cf. 1 Cor. 15:3–8), beginning "on the third day" and concluding on the day of the ascension. Christ's presence with us today is real, but that is not what New Testament writers meant by "raised on the third day" or "last of all . . . he appeared also to me" (1 Cor. 15:8).

(1) Appearance to the Women (28:1–10)

**1 Now after the sabbath, toward the dawn of
the first day of the week, Mary Magdalene and
the other Mary went to see the sepulchre.
2 And behold, there was a great earthquake;
for an angel of the Lord descended from
heaven and came and rolled back the stone,
and sat upon it. 3 His appearance was like
lightning, and his raiment white as snow. 4 And
for fear of him the guards trembled and became like dead men. 5 But the angel said to the
women, "Do not be afraid; for I know that you
seek Jesus who was crucified. 6 He is not here;
for he has risen, as he said. Come, see the
place where he lay. 7 Then go quickly and tell
his disciples that he has risen from the dead,
and behold, he is going before you to Galilee;
there you will see him. Lo, I have told you."
8 So they departed quickly from the tomb with
fear and great joy, and ran to tell his disciples.
9 And behold, Jesus met them and said, "Hail!"
And they came up and took hold of his feet
and worshiped him. 10 Then Jesus said to them,
"Do not be afraid; go and tell my brethren to
go to Galilee, and there they will see me."**

It is not clear whether Matthew means by *the dawn of the first day of the week* Saturday evening, after sunset, or Sunday morning. Mark 16:1 f., Luke 24:1, and John 20:1 clearly place the visit of the women to the tomb at daybreak on Sunday. If Matthew is following Mark at all, he is also guided by another source. What emerges from all the narratives is that Mary Magdalene and at least one other woman visited the tomb after the sabbath and found it empty. In Matthew it seems that the stone was not rolled away by the angel until the approach of the women. So understood, the stone was not rolled away to let Jesus out but to let the women in. The detail that the angel ***sat upon*** the stone is probably added as a note of triumph. The *fear* of the guards is a further reflection of the awesomeness of the event.

The proclamation of the angel to the women catches up two important elements in early Christian faith: the empty tomb and the resurrection: ***He is not here; for he is risen.*** Although the empty tomb did not of itself convince friend or foe that Jesus was risen, it was an important factor to friend and foe, despite modern tendencies to obscure the point. The women were invited to see the place where Jesus had lain. But the real persuasion that Jesus was risen came only with his appearance to his followers (cf. John 20:13–16).

That the women were to ***tell his disciples*** implies that they were yet in Jerusalem. The fact that only the sabbath had intervened since the crucifixion would in part account for their not already having returned to Galilee. ***Going before you*** (*proagei*) could be rendered "he leads you," leaving room for appearances in Jerusalem; but the statement that follows seems to imply that in Galilee the disciples would first see him. To "go before" is a biblical expression for a shepherd's leading of his flocks (cf. Mark 10:32; John 10:4).

As the women ran in ***fear and great joy,*** Jesus himself met them. It was ***Jesus*** who ***met them,*** the name employed being that of the one whom they had known in the flesh. Jesus and the risen Lord were one and the same to Matthew and to the other New Testament writers. The "resurrection" is not just something that happened to the faith of the disciples; it was something that happened first to Jesus. Käsemann well states it:

"The Easter faith was the foundation of the Christian kerygma but was not the first or only source of its content. Rather, it was the Easter faith which took cognizance of the fact that God acted before we became believers, and which testified to the fact by incapsulating the earthly history of Jesus in its proclamation . . . we cannot do away with the identity between the exalted and the earthly Lord without falling into docetism and depriving ourselves of the possibility of drawing a line between the Easter faith of the community and myth" (*Essays,* p. 34).

Jesus greeted the women with an ordinary term, used daily. ***Hail*** (*chairete*) could be rendered "rejoice," or simply "hello." If this sounds too mundane, it may at least help to recover the fact that it was Jesus, not an other-worldly counterpart, who appeared to the women. They ***took hold of his feet*** (cf. John 20:17) ***and worshiped him.*** Before them was one in a body which they could touch, but they recognized him as one to be worshiped, that which is due God alone. Jesus repeats the command about a meeting in Galilee, but he shifts from disciple to the yet warmer term ***brethren.*** He yet claimed those who had so miserably failed him in his hour of greatest suffering and need.

(2) *False Report of the Guards (28:11–15)*

[11] While they were going, behold, some of the guard went into the city and told the chief priests all that had taken place. [12] And when they had assembled with the elders and taken counsel, they gave a sum of money to the soldiers [13] and said, "Tell people, 'His disciples came by night and stole him away while we were asleep.' [14] And if this comes to the governor's ears, we will satisfy him and keep you out of trouble." [15] So they took the money and did as they were directed; and this story has been spread among the Jews to this day.

The guards seem to be Roman soldiers, but Pilate had assigned them to the chief priests and Pharisees for their purpose. This would account for their reporting to ***the chief priests*** rather than to Pilate. The fact that matters would require to be squared with the governor implies that ***the soldiers*** were actually Roman and not Temple guards. The chief priests and elders would most fear the reaction of the ***people*** to the news of the empty tomb. If the body could have been produced, that would have solved their problem, but that was beyond their power. All that they could do was bribe the soldiers to report that the disciples had stolen the body while they ***were asleep.*** Sleeping soldiers would be poor witnesses to what happened!

The soldiers' fears would relate to Pilate, not the people. The powerful priests and elders promised to ***satisfy*** Pilate and keep the soldiers out of trouble if the report that they had failed in their duty, through going to sleep on assignment, reached the ears of Pilate.

To this day refers to a period some time after A.D. 70. The story that the body of Jesus was stolen by his disciples continued to circulate for another century (cf. Justin Martyr, *Dialogue with Trypho*, 108; and *Gospel of Peter*, 11:46–49). What is most certain and most significant is that Jews and Christians accepted as fact the empty tomb, however they may have explained it.

(3) *The Commissioning of the Disciples (28:16–20)*

16 Now the eleven disciples went to Galilee,
to the mountain to which Jesus had directed
them. 17 And when they saw him they wor-
shiped him; but some doubted. 18 And Jesus
came and said to them, "All authority in
heaven and on earth has been given to me.
19 Go therefore and make disciples of all na-
tions, baptizing them in the name of the Father
and of the Son and of the Holy Spirit,
20 teaching them to observe all that I have
commanded you; and lo, I am with you always,
to the close of the age."

Matthew alone places Jesus' first appearance to the eleven in Galilee (cf. Luke 24:33–43; John 20:19–29), but Mark 14:28 and 16:7 may imply the same. Again, details are impossible to correlate, but the basic fact of the appearance of Jesus to his followers is solidly attested in the Synoptics, John, and Paul. The ***mountain*** in Galilee is not identified nor the time when Jesus designated it as the place for their meeting.

When the eleven saw Jesus ***they worshiped him; but some doubted.*** Greek grammar is not decisive as to the identity of those who doubted, but there is no hint that the doubters were persons other than from the eleven. Luke reports that the apostles discredited the report of the women, looking upon it as "an idle tale" (24:12). He reports that even when Jesus appeared among the eleven there were "questionings" in their hearts and "they still disbelieved for joy" (24:38,41). John tells of the doubting of Thomas, who declared that he would not believe unless he could see the nail prints and the wound in Jesus' side (20:24 f.). The transparent honesty of the Gospels is reflected in these forthright confessions of the doubts of the apostles, and the case for the fact of the resurrection and subsequent appearances is thereby strengthened. The disciples had not expected to see Jesus again, and both the reports of his appearances and his actual presence among them were almost too good to be true.

The relationship between seeing and believing is important to Matthew, just as it is of primary importance in the Gospel of John (cf. 4:48; 6:30; 20:8). The appearances of Jesus had evidential value (cf. John 20:8) and are a part of the early Christian witness, but physical sight alone did not compel faith. ***Some doubted*** even though they ***saw him.*** The high priests misunderstood faith when they demanded Jesus' descent from the cross, saying "that we may see and believe" (Mark 15:32). Seeing may contribute to believing, but the deeper New Testament view is that if one will believe he will see (cf. John 11:40). Jesus declared the greater blessing to be upon "those who have not seen and yet believe" (John 20:29). It is significant that Matthew in the last paragraph of his Gospel brought out the fact that the physical appearance of Jesus left some in doubt. Vision is more dependent upon faith than is faith upon sight.

The Great Commission serves as a summary of basic themes in Matthew as well as a dramatic and forceful conclusion. The one who was introduced as "the son of David, the son of Abraham" and placed in a Jewish genealogy is now declared to have ***all authority in heaven and on earth.*** Crucified as King of the Jews, he is indeed sovereign over ***all nations.*** The covenants with Abraham and David (see Introduction, pp. 63–64), with the promise of a universal and everlasting kingdom in a sovereignty of righteousness is now fulfilled in Jesus Christ.

All nations are to be brought under his discipline (teaching and rule). Some take *ta ethnē* to refer to Gentiles, not to "the nations" (Hare, p. 148), holding that to Matthew the Jews are excluded as ones who irrevocably have rejected Christ (cf. Walker). The emphasis probably is upon the Gentiles, but Jews are not excluded. The key verb is ***make disciples,*** an imperative in Greek. ***Go*** is a participle which may have imperative force, but probably it is subordinate to ***make disciples.*** Accordingly, the idea is, "As you go, bring all nations under my discipline [teaching and rule]." Jesus had almost restricted his personal ministry to "the lost sheep of the house of Israel," but he now commissions his disciples to a world mission.

Baptizing in the name or "unto the name" (*eis to onoma*) of ***Father, Son,*** and ***Holy Spirit*** is to immerse in water those who now have come into the possession and protection of God, known as Father, Son, and Holy Spirit. This is the earliest known explicit Trinitarian formula, although it is approached in the earlier writings of Paul (cf. 1 Cor. 12:4–6; 2 Cor. 13:14). The earliest formula used by the church seems to have been "in the name of the Lord Jesus" (cf. Acts 2:38; 8:16). It is significant that although a Trinitarian formula is employed, ***name*** is singular. Although God came to be known as Father, Son, and Holy Spirit, he remained one God. ***Name*** in biblical usage stands for the person himself.

The ***teaching*** commanded involves instruction, but that is not the emphasis. The command is to teach obedience—***to observe all that*** Jesus ***commanded.*** This gathers up the major emphasis throughout Matthew upon the demand which belongs to salvation. The emphasis is not upon doctrine or study but upon actual obedience to Jesus' commands.

Matthew's Gospel closes on the note sounded from the start in the preaching of John the Baptist (3:2) and of Jesus (4:17) and maintained throughout this Gospel. It is the demand for righteousness, set forth in an eschatological context (Strecker, pp. 184–88). ***The close of the age*** is the Parousia. Although future, its force is felt already through the presence, ***I am with you,*** of the risen Lord Jesus. Just as the inbreaking of the kingdom of heaven was a call to repentance (3:2; 4:17), so at the close of the Gospel, ***all authority in heaven and on earth*** is behind the demand for obedience to the commands of Jesus. Moral and ethical demand (cf. 5:48) is thus kept foremost throughout this Gospel, which also leaves no hope for salvation except to sinners who receive it as the gift of God (cf. 11:28–30).

The book closes with a beautiful reassurance which reaches back to the beginning of the Gospel. ***I am with you*** is a near equivalent to Emmanuel, "God with us" (1:23). The risen Lord gave assurance of his continuing presence ***to the close of the age.*** This means until the completion of history, but the emphasis is upon its consummation and not its termination. The risen Lord is with us until ***the age*** is brought to its consummation, i.e., until history is brought to its goal.

The Gospel of Matthew closes with the Great Commission, but its center of gravity is more often missed than seen. The conclusion to Matthew's Gospel (vv. 18–20) is christological, not anthropocentric. That is, its focus is upon Christ and not upon the nations. It is not so much a preoccupation with a lost world—as much as that concerns this whole Gospel—as a call to the world to acknowledge its Lord and obey him. It is not basically soteriological (salvation-centered) but christological, commissioning disciples to bring the nations under the authority of Christ. In this submission to Christ is man's salvation.

The middle point of verses 18–20 is not the commission but Christ. It sums up what the whole Gospel is about and gives us the key to its interpretation (cf. 28:19*a* with

10:5 ff.; 28:19*b* with 3:11; and 28:20 with 1:23).[54] This represents the fulfilment of Daniel 7:13 f., the promise of dominion or a glorious kingdom for the Son of man, an everlasting kingdom under which all nations are to be brought.

Observing the Christocentric emphasis of the Commission is not only a matter of sound exegesis, but it is decisive for missions. It is only as soteriology is subordinated to Christology that it is truly salvation. The gospel is first of all a call to men to submit to the kingdom of God (cf. 10:5 ff.). When missions or evangelism becomes primarily a concern for man, the end result is religious egocentricity, a mere sublimation of man's basic sin problem. Man is saved only when he "loses himself" to Christ. Matthew's Gospel closes with a commission concerned not first of all with man's salvation but that ***all nations*** be brought under Christ's discipline and be taught to obey ***all*** that has been ***commanded*** by the one to whom ***all authority*** has been given and who is with us (cf. Emmanuel in 1:23) ***always,*** the very presence of God (the *Shekinah*) ever present to bring to completion what he came to do.

[54] See Otto Michel, "Der Abschluss des Matthäusevangeliums," *Evangelische Theologie,* 10 (1950–51), pp. 21 f.

Mark

HENRY E. TURLINGTON

Introduction

The gospel of Jesus Christ was being proclaimed for decades before the writers of Mark, Luke, Matthew, and John set their pens to scrolls. Jesus' ministry was virtually confined to the tiny lands of his birth and boyhood. By the time the first Gospel was written, there were communities of faith in Jesus Christ scattered widely through the Roman Empire.

The 12 apostles, the 120 of Acts 1:15, and the "more than five hundred" witnesses of the resurrection (1 Cor. 15:6) were Jews. At least for a time they continued to think of themselves as Hebrew in faith, they continued to worship in the Temple in Jerusalem, and they participated in the life of their synagogues.

Not so the churches which first read the Gospels: they were increasingly separated from Judaism, and they were more and more dominated by people of Gentile origin. Even though the custom of the early missionaries had been to go first to the synagogues with their witness to Jesus, the stories in Acts and the content of the Epistles reflect the inevitable dominance of non-Jews in the churches of the Gentile world. It was in connection with the discipleship and worship of these churches that nearly all of the New Testament was written.

The Gospels were composed, therefore, in the midst of the tensions and questions that assaulted the young Christian congregations. It was no easy thing to be faithful to Jesus Christ in a culture that was alien to the gospel and both ignorant and suspicious of the new faith. The Epistles generally brought doctrinal and ethical guidance to these churches by attacking directly their problems and questions. The lordship of Christ was always asserted, but very little of his action or teaching was cited. The cross and the resurrection are exceptions (cf. 1 Cor. 11:23–26; 7:10).

Unlike the Epistles, however, the Gospels focused on the central figure of Jesus of Nazareth. Who was Jesus? Why had not the Jews accepted him? Did God mean for this to happen? What does Jesus' life and word mean for us?

Always the Gospel writers stand on the Easter side of Jesus' life: he is to them, as he was to their churches and as he is to us, the risen Lord. They write of Jesus of Nazareth, the man who went about doing good. But there is always evident the imprint of their faith: the Jesus of whom they speak is Christ the Lord. They do not write simply because the story is interesting. They write because the story is significant, the most significant thing that ever happened.

It is quite accurate, therefore, to point to a basic unity in the Gospels. They all affirm one central motif, that the coming of Jesus was *the* crisis in the world's history. All four of the Gospel writers hold that in Jesus a new order has arrived, bringing victory over evil, judgment, and the inauguration of a new people of God (cf. Davies, pp. 136–46).

For most of the Christian era the four

Gospels were studied together, on the assumption that they simply and independently supplemented one another in the telling of Jesus' life. Commentaries were written from time to time on Matthew, Luke, and John, because blocks of material in these Gospels did not appear in the others. Nearly every line in Mark was to be found also in either Matthew or Luke. There seemed to be no great reason to study with equal care the shortest and, it was assumed, least distinctive of the "lives of Jesus."

All this has changed. Early in the nineteenth century students began applying the methods of literary and historical criticism to the study of the Bible. Instead of concentrating on the similarities and parallels of the Gospels, they began noting the differences, asking questions about the variations in chronology, and subjecting the accounts to more recent philosophical viewpoints. Recognizing that the Gospels were written some time after Jesus had lived, scholars began to concentrate on discovering the difference between the "real, historical Jesus" and the Christ who was later preached as Lord.[1]

To many of these scholars, Mark—more nearly than the other Gospels—appeared to be a simple record of Jesus' word and deed. Although this judgment has been superseded, another conclusion to which their study led has endured. For it finally became clear that Mark had preceded both Luke and Matthew and had been one of their principal sources. Studies in Christian origins had to begin with Mark and proceed to the later, more "theological" Gospels.

Recently, the pendulum of theological concern has swung sharply back to the "Christ of faith," that is, to the nature of the gospel as it was proclaimed in the early Christian communities. Unlike what the casual observer might expect, however, this has in no sense dulled interest in Mark.

[1] For a commentary on current views see the excellent work by Hugh Anderson, *Jesus and Christian Origins* (New York: Oxford University Press, 1964); also J. M. Robinson.

The recognition of the priority of Mark had led to intensive study, and had borne an unexpected fruit. It was now clear that Mark, like the other Gospels, is no mere record of Jesus' word and deed. Here also is found a testament of faith, an affirmation of the Christian understanding of "Jesus Christ, the Son of God" (1:1).

The study of the Gospel according to Mark, then, requires much more than a knowledge of the Galilean and Judean environment in which Jesus lived. We must also seek to understand what the author of this book believed about Jesus. How had Jesus fulfilled his ministry? Who was he, and how did men come to know who he was? How could it be that he was crucified? We must inquire why this book was written, and how the author sought to fulfil his purpose.

The answers to these questions must be sought, for the most part, in the Gospel itself. The book is anonymous, yet we must try to know as much as possible about who wrote it. Nothing is said in the book about its intended readers or their circumstances, but we must seek some solution to this problem. To know the *when* and *where* and *who* of a document is very helpful in defining *why*.

I. Authorship, Place of Writing, Date

Fortunately, the traditions concerning the writing of Mark are very old and fairly consistent. The earliest of these is from Papias, Bishop of Hierapolis, who was writing about A.D. 140. His writings are no longer extant, but they are quoted at pertinent points by Eusebius, the fourth-century church historian. Although Papias never had the opportunity of knowing any of the apostles, he claims to have retained carefully what their pupils had passed on.

Papias said that the elder John had spoken to him about Mark:

"Mark, indeed, having been the interpreter of Peter, wrote accurately, howbeit not in order, all that he recalled of what was either said or done by the Lord. For he neither heard the Lord, nor was he a follower of His, but, at a later date (as I said), of Peter; who used to adapt his instructions to the needs [of the moment], but not with a view to putting together the Dominical oracles in orderly fashion: so that Mark did no wrong in thus writing some things as he recalled them. For he kept a single aim in view: not to omit anything of what he heard, nor to state anything therein falsely."[2]

The ancient references to the second Gospel all ascribe the writing to Mark, and they all claim that Mark's information came from the apostle Peter. A second-century prologue to the Gospel, referring to Mark as Peter's interpreter, asserts that he wrote the book in Italy but after Peter's death. Irenaeus' testimony (*ca.* A.D. 180) is quite similar and connects the Gospel with Rome. Clement of Alexandria (*ca.* A.D. 200) gives a similar witness, except that he supposes the Gospel to have been written during Peter's lifetime.[3]

The Christians of the second century believed, then, (1) that the Gospel was written by a man named Mark; (2) that this Mark was a disciple of Peter and that he wrote after Peter's death (Clement's testimony is the first to hold otherwise); and (3) that the book was composed especially for the Christians in and near Rome.

The best of the tradition does not clearly identify Mark except as the interpreter of Peter. Mark (Marcus) was about as common a name among the Romans as is William or Edward among us. We are not certain that the Mark of 1 Peter 5:13 is the same man as Barnabas' kinsman of whom we read in Acts. Probably "Babylon" should be understood as Rome, in which case the verse is in accord with the tradition that Peter was put to death during Nero's persecution. The verse also fits well with the tradition that Mark wrote his Gospel in Rome after Peter's death.

We should like very much to have more biographical data on the author. Some scholars think he was Mark of Jerusalem; others, like F. C. Grant in "The Interpreter's Bible," count it very unlikely that the author could have lived in Jerusalem. On this question our evidence is inadequate.

If one should conclude that Mark was the kinsman of Barnabas and did live in Jerusalem, it still does not follow that he was also a disciple of the earthly Jesus. The Mark known to us in Acts was probably a very young man when he left home to travel with Barnabas and Paul (Acts 12:25), and this was perhaps 15 years after the resurrection. During Jesus' ministry he would probably have been a small child.

We ought also to note that the tradition reflects some criticism of the second Gospel. Papias said Mark wrote accurately, although not in order. Perhaps he was replying to some who may have belittled Mark's composition. Also, the differences between Mark's order and that of the other Gospels, especially John, were obvious; and by Papias' time, Matthew, Luke, and John were all more widely used than Mark.

That Mark derived all his materials from Peter is very unlikely. Mark would hardly have omitted an incident in Jesus' life of which he knew and which suited his purposes just because he had not received it from Peter. Paul had been influential in the Roman church, and we ought not to suppose that traditions which he and his co-workers had passed on would have been ignored in the writing of the Gospel. These co-workers of Paul probably included the author himself (Col. 4:10; 2 Tim. 4:11). We must remember that second-century Christians would have wanted to emphasize the connections of the Gospel's author with one of the twelve.

On the other hand, the tradition is quite credible that the book was written in (or near) Rome at a time when the church there was experiencing (or had undergone) heavy pressures and persecution. If we can-

[2] Eusebius, *Ecclesiastical History*, III, 39. A careful appraisal of the tradition from Papias is to be found in B. W. Bacon, *Is Mark a Roman Gospel?* (Cambridge: Harvard Univ. Press, 1919).

[3] Taylor (pp. 1–8) provides a convenient and detailed presentation of the evidence from these and other early Christian writers.

not be certain of other details about Mark, it is reasonable to conclude that he was a disciple of Peter and a leading Christian in Italy. And if we do not suppose that all, or even most, of the materials of the Gospel of Mark are Petrine, we may still believe that Peter had told in Rome many stories of Jesus, and that some of them are found in the Gospel of Mark.

We cannot with assurance give an exact date for the composition of Mark. However, if it was from Rome and after the death of Peter, it must have been written no earlier than A.D. 65. If it was used by the authors of Matthew and Luke, as is generally acknowledged, it cannot be much later than A.D. 70.

II. Roman Christians and Purpose of Mark

We do not know who it was who first brought the gospel to Rome, nor can we say with precision when the church there was established. We do have reason to believe that there were Christians among the Jewish community in Rome by about A.D. 45. Suetonius reports that the Emperor Claudius commanded the Jews to leave the city because of the disturbances that arose over one *Chrestos* (Cl. 25). Priscilla and Aquila left Rome in connection with this edict, and it seems likely that they were already Christians (Acts 18:2).

The Christian community in the imperial city was not destroyed, however, and came to have an appreciable number of Gentile adherents. Paul's letter to the Romans must be dated near A.D. 55, and could not have been written for Jewish Christians only (cf. especially Rom. 9—11). By the end of that decade Paul had been brought as a prisoner to Rome. On the way he found Christians at Puteoli, and other Christians from Rome came to the Forum of Appius and Three Taverns to meet the apostle (Acts 28:13–15). He then preached in Rome "quite openly and unhindered" for two years, though he was during that time kept in custody at his own expense (28:30 f.).

Peter's connection with the Roman church is less certain. Tradition from I Clement and Ignatius (from 30 to 50 years after Peter's supposed martyrdom), plus the cryptic reference to Babylon in 1 Peter 5:13, support the conclusion that Peter did reach Rome and was probably put to death there under Nero. There is no inkling of Peter's presence in Rome for any extended period, certainly not when Paul wrote his epistle to that church or while Paul himself was there.

The first major persecution of Christians in the Gentile world took place in A.D. 64, when Rome was ravaged by a terrible fire. Rumor had it that Emperor Nero himself had ordered the fire started to provide space for his building program. Tacitus tells us that he diverted this rumor by blaming "the mob called Chrestians" (*Annals*, XV, 44). Tacitus' description of the Christians reflects the general ignorance about their tenets but also that their number had grown enough for them to gain attention. The persecution itself was fierce. Some Christians were dressed in skins of wild animals so that the dogs would attack them. Others were crucified and set afire in Nero's gardens.

We do not know how Mark escaped, but the Christian community survived the tragedy. If the Gospel of Mark was written at this time, as we believe, it is in some sense, as Robert M. Grant says, "a product of Nero's reign." [4]

In the first place, the deaths of Paul, Peter, and other able and mature Christian leaders would have threatened a vacuum in the intimate knowledge of the church about Jesus' life and work. The first generation of Christians had virtually passed away. Their legacy of the knowledge of Jesus must not be lost. It is reasonable to assume that Mark gathered the available written stories of Jesus, together with the traditions he already knew so well, partly for the simple purpose of preserving them.

However, the Gospel of Mark is no simple collection of stories of Jesus. It has particular viewpoints and interests which would

[4] See his article on "Nero," *Interpreter's Dictionary of the Bible* (Nashville: Abingdon, 1962), III, 537 f.

have been of special concern to the Christians of his day. The end of the world had not come with the persecution they had undergone. Neither did it come with the terrible carnage of the Jewish revolt, which began in A.D. 66 and resulted in the destruction of Jerusalem in A.D. 70, though at least a pocket of resistance persisted at Masada till A.D. 73. Because of the wording of Mark 13:14–20, some think Mark was not written until after the Temple had been destroyed, but this is uncertain. What is evident is that Christian thinking about last things had intensified, and their major interest lay in the figurative apocalyptic traditions as recorded in Mark 13.

Most of all, the Gospel of Mark was written in a way that would serve to strengthen and guide the disciples of Mark's day in their situation of grief and doubt, of danger and persecution. This is clearly seen in the exhortation to the discipleship of self-denial and the taking up of one's own cross (8:34). It is the burden of the whole book. Christians must follow Jesus.

The Gospel of Mark, then, deals with Jesus as the example for his disciples. How utterly inadequate this would have been, however, had Jesus been merely a good example of moral living! Mark tells of Jesus in a way to remind his contemporaries of Jesus' identity as God's strong Son, of Jesus' confrontation with every kind of evil power that besets man, of Jesus' triumph over everything that blinded and warped manhood could do to him.

The disciples of Mark's day were men whose friends had become martyrs and who lived in a society hostile to their Christian commitment. They must have been asking, Why is it necessary for a man to die for his faith? Mark answers them by wrestling with the prior questions for a disciple: What about Jesus? Why did he have to die?

There is no doubt that this problem had occupied Mark's mind, and by his arrangement and presentation he offers three discerning answers. His answers take into account Jesus' own character, the nature of evil in men's lives, and God's purpose in his Son.

Jesus was put to death because of the unreasoning anger and hardness of heart he encountered in the Jewish leaders. He was crucified because men are that evil and because evil is that callous and unyielding.

Jesus died also because he was great in the only way his disciples could be great. He was a good servant of men who needed him. He was the kind of servant who gave "his life as a ransom for many" (10:45).

Finally, but not separately from the other answers, Jesus died because it was God's will. It had to be. God had sent the kind of Son he was into the kind of world this is. It was required of the Son of man that he suffer and be killed. But this necessity of his death is always coupled by Mark with the inevitable outcome of victory: death will be overcome, he will rise again (cf. especially 8:31; 9:31; 10:33 f.)

Here for Roman Christians, and for us as well, was example, challenge, assurance, and hope. Here was comfort and strength for their day, here was understanding of sin's power, here was promise of victory. Here again was Jesus' invitation, follow me.

III. Content and Structure

When Mark began to plan his account of Jesus, as far as we know he had no outline to follow nor any extended written materials. Part of the Gospel's importance is its own service as a major source book for Matthew and Luke. Mark is the first man of whom we know, and probably the very first of all, to write a major account of the ministry of Jesus.[5]

A survey of the whole book gives first of all the impression of a series of incidents which have been linked together to form one book. Mark's paragraphs do not begin with the same formula each time, but there is a certain similarity in his simple transi-

[5] A number of theories have been presented suggesting that there was a Palestinian gospel (*Ur-Markus*) which preceded our present writing. It is supposed that this book was very simple in theology and narration and was expanded and edited for churches of the Gentile world. However, most scholars today explain the data of Mark and the interrelationship of the Synoptics in other ways. Cf. S. E. Johnson, "The Interpreter's Bible," VII, 236 ff., and the article by Ray Summers in this COMMENTARY.

tions from one story to another (cf. 1:16, 21,29,35,40; 2:1,13,18,23; 3:1; 4:1).

It is reasonable to agree with modern scholars generally that the stories of Jesus first circulated orally and in self-contained units. By Mark's time some of these may have been written down. The length of these separate incidents varies little enough so that, as H. A. Guy theorizes, each one could have been recorded on a separate sheet of papyrus. A collection of these sheets then would have formed the material which Mark had at his disposal.[6]

However, the remembered voice of an apostle or the oft-repeated parable applied by the Christian teacher in the congregation would also have been treasured. Paul's reference to "the traditions" he handed down (1 Cor. 11:2,23) is most naturally understood as oral. Even though Mark was composed more than a decade later, it is very unlikely that each incident had been set down in writing. Some stories were probably recorded by Mark with no written source before him.

This conclusion is strengthened by a comparison of stories. Some are so vivid in detail that they may well have come directly from an eyewitness like Peter (cf. 1:16–20; 1:35–38; 4:35–40; 5:21–43; 9:2–8; 14:66–72). In some of these cases only a very limited number of people could have narrated the incident, and Simon Peter, one of the inner circle of the apostles, was present on each occasion. Mark may have sometimes recalled the story in his own words. In other narratives we seem to have the words of the witness himself, whether or not Mark was the first to record them.

Other parts of Mark's material are given in well-rounded form but with little of the detail that is distinctive of the eyewitness. Examples would include 2:18–20; 3:31–35; 11:27–33; 12:18–34. Teachers and evangelists must have been repeating these incidents ever since Pentecost. Sometimes words of interpretation were added which we must understand as interpretive for early Christians. How else would one understand the parenthetic, "Thus he declared all foods clean" (7:19)? Cf. also 2:28, which could be so interpreted, but which RSV quotes traditionally as from Jesus; and note the discussion in this volume of the interpretation of the sower (4:13–20). It is undoubtedly true that the mission and message of Jesus, as our Lord no doubt intended and as the Holy Spirit would have led, became intertwined with the mission and message of the church.

It would be wrong to conclude that Mark received all of his source materials in very brief units. The block of parabolic teaching in 4:1–34, the "little apocalypse" of chapter 13, and the succession of stories in the passion narrative probably came to him very much as he hands them on to us. It is common judgment among modern New Testament scholars that the incidents of the passion narrative were the first to be assembled into a connected account.

The simple truth we must bear in mind is that Mark did not write in a vacuum. He was both participant and heir in the life and mission of the people of God in his own day. There is probably not an incident in the entire Gospel which Mark himself had not recounted on behalf of his Lord, for whom he was a witness.

We have said that it is reasonable to suppose that one reason for the writing of the Gospel was to preserve many of the accounts which the first generation of Christian preachers had been able to tell so vividly from their own knowledge. But the further hopes of Mark to serve the needs of his fellow Christians influenced the order and presentation of the whole narrative.

The style of Mark in putting together the various accounts he narrates is sometimes rough, but always brief and to the point. Luke and Matthew were both abler men as far as literary usage is concerned. Nevertheless, the materials in Mark are certainly put together in no haphazard manner. They cohere, and they build toward the climax of the crucifixion of Jesus.

Roy Harrisville, in his attractive little book *The Miracle of Mark* (Minneapolis:

[6] *Origin of the Gospel of Mark* (New York: Harper & Bros., 1955).

Augsburg, 1967) treats the whole of the Gospel as a sermon on the death of Christ. In doing so, he has partly followed Willi Marxsen. Marxsen also regards the book as a sermon in which the history of Jesus and the situation of the disciples have become contemporary. Whether Mark's Gospel be sermon or no, it certainly has some of the sermon's traits, and includes every facet of C. H. Dodd's well-known kerygma (the primitive gospel proclamation), though its contents are primarily the events of Jesus' life.

Perhaps Mark began with the passion narrative and arranged his materials from the climactic event back toward the beginning of the ministry. In any case, the finished Gospel falls naturally into two (or perhaps three) main divisions. In addition, an introduction includes the prophetic expectation culminating in John the Baptist, and a conclusion testifies to the empty tomb and the risen Lord.

The first major division (1:14—8:30) presents Jesus, the strong Son of God, in whom the kingdom of God has drawn near. He defeats the enemies that alienate man from God and man's own best self. But around Jesus there remained a measure of mystery, so that his deeds brought conflict (2:1—3:6), so that he was not adequately understood (4:1–34), and so that he was often rejected and opposed. However, his disciples came finally to the open conclusion, voiced by Peter, "You are the Christ" (8:29).

This confession serves as Mark's starting point for Jesus' open and repeated theme that the Son of man must suffer. This theme has its preludes all through the first half of the Gospel, most obviously in the anger of Jesus' enemies and their plots against him (3:1–6,22). Note also the passages relating to John the Baptist (1:14; 6:14–29). But the death of Jesus is above all anticipated by the constant references to the moral and spiritual blindness and the intellectual dullness of men (cf. especially 3:5; 4:10–12; 6:6). The disciples share with other men a measure of this hardness of heart; and one of them, the betrayer, never did overcome it.

The second half of the Gospel deals with the way to the cross, not merely physically and geographically but also spiritually. Jesus is impelled by divine necessity toward a confrontation with the evil and hardness of alienated men. Coupled constantly with the theme of conflict and suffering by the Son of man is Jesus' encouragement to a discipleship patterned after the same fashion (8:31—9:1; 9:30–37; 10:32–45). The struggle between Jesus and the religious authorities grows in intensity. Jesus' claims concerning himself become ever clearer and more objectionable to their way and their status.

The culmination of Jesus' ministry is narrated in detail in chapters 14—15. To the very end there were real difficulties for the twelve. Judas betrayed Jesus, Peter denied him, three could not watch with him during the garden experience, and "all the disciples" fled at his arrest. The women who were the first witnesses to his resurrection were terrified (16:8). With true appraisal of the situation for disciples in his own day, Mark has described (without overt application) some of the pitfalls that will befall Christian people of faith and courage in every epoch.

That Jesus was, and claimed to be, the Christ, the Son of God, is part of the divine climactic event. See especially his answer to the high priest's charge (14:61 f.). Jesus died as Messiah, the King of Israel, but he died with the title regarded as ridiculous by the people who should have been willing to receive him. On the other hand, the army officer, the representative of Rome who witnessed the scene, recognized Jesus in his death as really God's Son (15:39).

Mark does not dwell on the theme of the resurrection. It is the event that demonstrates the victory of Jesus over the worst that men could do. But the crowning work of the Son of God, the terrible but necessary event, had been the death on the cross. The resurrection was the sure sign that God's mighty work was done, that men were right to believe in Jesus and to be his disciples (16:1–8).

IV. Theological Ideas

Although the Gospel of Mark is not oriented toward theological ideas in any systematic fashion, the content of the book is the heart of the Christian faith and message. Mark's thesis may be stated briefly: in Jesus Christ, the Son of God, God's expected kingdom has drawn near to bring salvation to man. Although the very power of God was active in him in the accomplishment of his work, it was necessary for him, in the struggle, to defeat the enemy forces of evil assailing man, to suffer, and to die. However, there is hope, for man may look ahead to that final and glorious day when Jesus will come again in power and judgment, and will gather his waiting and watching disciples to himself. Indeed, even the cross did not bring the Son of God to an end, for he has risen from the grave!

From this summary it is obvious that Markan theology is primarily Christological. Who was Jesus? The titles given him are taken up at appropriate places in the body of the commentary. The most important are Son of God (cf. 1:1,11; 14:61; 15:39); Son of man (cf. 2:10; 8:31; 13:26); and Christ, or Messiah (8:29). Mark does consider Jesus to be Lord, but does not characteristically call him by this title (note, however, 1:3; 7:28).

These titles which were applied to Jesus all have, in Mark's approach, a certain mystery in them. The readers all understand from the beginning who Jesus was; so also do powers that have discernment beyond the human. The demons recognize him and call him by appropriate titles, though Jesus' power is far stronger than their own (1:24, 34; 3:27; 5:7). But Jesus forbids the demonic spirits to make him known. As for man, warped and hardened in his sin and blindness, he often does not recognize Jesus, but opposes him with growing fierceness. Some men hearken, but many do not.

None of the principal names applied to Jesus in Mark would have been necessarily clear and illuminating to his audience. What would "Son of God" have meant to Galileans? A godly man? A man with God's power expressing itself in him? Would it have meant—blasphemy of blasphemies!—genuine deity? Jesus did call himself "Son of man." What did this name mean? Simply man? This is its meaning in Ezekiel. Did it mean the heavenly Son of man, who would come with glory? So Daniel. But Jesus identified the Son of man as one who must suffer and die. "Christ" was a title Jesus accepted, but he would not allow its use. What it meant to Simon Peter in 8:29 could hardly be what Jesus conceived as his role.

The mystery of Jesus' identity is a major motif in Mark. In 1901 William Wrede concluded from his study of Mark that Jesus' ministry had not been regarded as messianic until after the resurrection. Most Markan students since Wrede have taken contrary positions (R. Bultmann is a notable exception), but with varying conclusions.[7]

The position taken in this treatment is that the mystery in Jesus' identity, together with the dullness or blindness of his contemporaries, explained for Mark and his readers why so many did not believe or follow Jesus. Moreover, a similar situation in Mark's own day is present with the same consequences: only the Christian people understand the true meaning of Jesus and know who he really is.

The phrase kingdom of God is not used often in Mark. It would not have been meaningful to Christians in Rome except to the extent of their Jewish heritage. Here again discussion of the concept has been taken up in the body of the commentary (cf. especially 1:15).

The student must bear in mind that the concept of the kingdom was always in some sense eschatological, something at once sig-

[7] For a survey of views on this question see J. M. Robinson (ch. 1), and, by the same author, "The Recent Debate on the 'New Quest,'" *Journal of Bible and Religion*, XXX, 3 (1962), 198–208. See also the excellent article by L. S. Hay, with which I find myself in substantial accord: "Mark's Use of the Messianic Secret," *Journal of the American Academy of Religion*, XXXV, 1 (1967), 16–27.

nificant and ultimate. Mark believed that the kingship of God was very real and active in Jesus and, in derived fashion, in his disciples (e.g., 6:7). The kingdom therefore has already been inaugurated. Nevertheless, Mark also expected a Parousia, a triumphant coming in the future, probably (in his thinking) the near future, though not even the Son knew the hour (13:32). Mark does not directly connect the idea of the second coming with the resurrection. That he might have done so in an ending now lost to us is as uncertain as it is speculative.

V. The Text of Mark

Modern students of the Bible are recipients of a remarkable heritage of scholarly research in the present critical texts of the New Testament. There are comparatively few textual questions of significant interest in this Gospel, and where appropriate these are taken up in the treatment of the text.

The only major textual problem with which we must concern ourselves at this point deals with the ending of the book. Mark 16:9–20 is definitely a later addition, though by a consecrated Christian writer who draws heavily from our other three canonical Gospels. One ancient Armenian text ascribes the ending to the presbyter Aristion. The verses are not present in the oldest and best manuscripts of Mark, and the best informed Christian scholar of antiquity, Eusebius (*ca.* 325), tells us that in the oldest and best manuscripts known to him, the conclusion of the Gospel was, "for they were afraid" (16:8).

After careful examination of the evidence, B. H. Streeter concluded that either Mark did not live to finish the Gospel (martyred under Nero?) or that the Gospel was very early mutilated and its original ending lost.[8]

Some (e.g., E. Lohmeyer, R. H. Lightfoot, W. C. Allen) have argued that the original text was meant to end with 16:8, with Jesus having risen but with fear and awe still very present in the hearts of his followers. However, there is no parallel in ancient literature for a book to end, as does the Greek of Mark 16:8, with a conjunction such as *gar* (for). Moreover, this Gospel obviously intended to exalt the strong Son of God whom Mark and his readers believed would yet come "in clouds with great power and glory." It is incredible, as Taylor says, that Mark intended such a conclusion.

The original ending was lost, it must be supposed, very shortly after it was written. Perhaps, as Streeter suggests, the end of the scroll was torn off in some way in connection with the harassment of Christians in Rome. However, even if all that remains from Mark himself ends with 16:8, we have his testimony to the reality of the resurrection of our Lord.

VI. Design and Limitations

The COMMENTARY of which this treatment of Mark is a part is directed toward ministers and lay students who have an earnest desire to know the meaning of the biblical revelation. It is designed not chiefly for academic study but for interpretation, instruction, and witness.

However, the contemporary study of Mark has so many facets that are of significant interest for the serious student of the Bible that the task of writing a commentary appears overwhelming. In a work of this scope, one is forced to choose between emphases. One might concentrate, for example, on the questions concerning the Jesus of history: if Mark wrote a generation after the crucifixion, how well does his portrayal of Jesus accord with the life of Jesus as his Galilean contemporaries had seen it? Or, one might work through the text of Mark studying the development of early Christian faith and thought as reflected in the Gospel narratives.

This treatment gives most of its attention to the meaning of the Gospel to Mark and his own contemporaries. How did they understand the life and words of Jesus as they had received them? I have attempted, however, in the text, or occasionally by footnotes, to call attention to some of the keen

[8] *The Four Gospels* (rev. ed.; London: Macmillan, 1930), 338–44.

insights and some of the still disputed questions discussed by scholars who have approached Mark in another fashion.

The limitations present in a commentary are not all of the author's choosing, nor of the particular design suggested by editors, nor of space, nor even of the writer's competence. The study of Scripture, and specifically Mark, is a continuing discipline. Every decade in this century has brought new questions, or old ones set forth in new and productive ways.[9]

An Outline of Mark

I. The beginning of the good news 1:1–13
  1. The keynote 1:1
  2. John and Jesus 1:2–11
    (1) The prophetic expectation 2,3
    (2) John the baptizer 4–8
    (3) The baptism of Jesus 9–11
  3. The temptation of Jesus 12–13

II. The ministry of Jesus: mystery and revelation 1:14—8:30
  1. The beginning of the Galilean ministry 1:14—3:6
    (1) A summary of Jesus' teaching 1:14–15
    (2) Calling the first disciples 16–20
    (3) The new teaching and immediate fame 21–45
    (4) Controversies with the scribes 2:1—3:6
  2. The expanding ministry and instruction of the twelve 3:7—5:43
    (1) The crowds by the lake 3:7–12
    (2) The appointment of the twelve 13–19*a*
    (3) The charges against Jesus: madness or demonic power 19*b*–30
    (4) The true family of Jesus 31–35
    (5) Instruction by parables 4:1–34
    (6) Instruction by mighty works 4:35—5:43
  3. Rejection and recognition of the Christ 6:1—8:30
    (1) Unbelief and rejection at home 6:1–6*a*
    (2) Ministry through the twelve 6*b*–13
    (3) Herod's appraisal of Jesus and the death of John the Baptist 14–29
    (4) The return of the twelve and the feeding of the five thousand 30–44
    (5) Walking on the water 45–52
    (6) The healings at Gennesaret 53–56
    (7) Ritual washing: the command and the tradition 7:1–13
    (8) The nature of real defilement 14–23
    (9) The healing of the Gentile girl 24–30
    (10) The healing of the deaf and dumb man 31–37
    (11) The feeding of the four thousand 8:1–10
    (12) The Pharisees' demand for a sign from heaven 11–13
    (13) A warning to disciples against dullness of mind 14–21
    (14) The healing of a blind man 22–26
    (15) The recognition of the Christ 27–30

III. The way to the cross: secret Christ and revealed Son of man 8:31—13:37
  1. The expected passion and the meaning of discipleship 8:31—10:52

[9] In this connection one current example in Markan studies is that by Best. He asks not, What did Jesus teach? Or, What did Jesus himself think of the meaning of his life and death? He asks, "What does Mark hold to have been achieved by the life, death and resurrection of Jesus the Christ?" (p. ix). He examines what he calls the Markan "seams" and "explanatory additions" and Mark's selection of materials. The methods being utilized by such men as H. Conzelmann, J. M. Robinson, and others have much in common with Best, and will surely provide many new insights in the years ahead. For a survey of current viewpoints and trends, cf. Anderson, and C. E. Braaten, *New Directions in Theology Today*, Vol. II, "History and Hermeneutics" (Philadelphia: Westminster Press, 1966).

(1) The Son of man to suffer (I) 8:31–33
(2) The difficult choice of discipleship 8:34—9:1
(3) The transfiguration 9:2–8
(4) Elijah's return and the rising of the Son of man 9–13
(5) The healing of the epileptic boy 14–29
(6) The Son of man to suffer (II) 30–32
(7) True greatness in discipleship 33–37
(8) The inclusiveness of discipleship 38–41
(9) The necessity for faithful discipleship 42–50
(10) The question about divorce 10:1–12
(11) Blessing the children 13–16
(12) The hazard of wealth to discipleship 17–31
(13) The Son of man to suffer (III) 32–34
(14) Selfish ambition versus great discipleship 35–45
(15) The healing of Bartimaeus 46–52

2. The arrival in Jerusalem and the conflict with the religious leaders 11:1—12:44
   (1) The claims of Jesus in parabolic acts 11:1–19
   (2) Encouragement to faith and true prayer 20–25 (26)
   (3) The counterattack upon Jesus and his defense 11:27—12:27
   (4) The question about the chief commandment 28–34
   (5) The question about David's relationship to the Christ 35–37
   (6) The contrast in stewardship: scribes and the poor widow 38–44
3. The apocalyptic discourse: the importance of alert discipleship 13:1–37
   (1) The doom of the Temple and the disciples' questions 13:1–4
   (2) Warnings of false christs, great disturbances, and harsh troubles for disciples 5–13
   (3) The terrible time of the desolating sacrilege 14–23
   (4) The triumphal coming of the Son of man 24–27
   (5) The necessity for perceptive alertness 28–37

IV. The culmination of the ministry: death on the cross and resurrection from the tomb 14:1—16:20
1. The conspiracy against Jesus 14:1–2
2. The anointing at Bethany 3–9
3. The betrayal of Judas 10–11
4. The preparation for the Passover 12–16
5. The Passover meal 17–25
   (1) The prophecy of betrayal 17–21
   (2) The bread and the cup 22–25
6. The prophecy of denial 26–31
7. The agony and prayer in Gethsemane 32–42
8. The arrest of Jesus 43–52
9. The hearing before the high priest 53–65
10. Peter's denial 66–72
11. The trial before Pilate 15:1–15
    (1) The governor's question 1–5
    (2) The release of Barabbas and the sentencing of Jesus 6–15
12. The scornful torment by the soldiers 16–20
13. The crucifixion of Jesus 21–32
14. The death of Jesus 33–41
15. The burial by Joseph 42–47
16. The empty tomb and the announcement of the resurrection 16:1–8
17. The longer ending: resurrection appearances and the ascension 16:9–20

Selected Bibliography

Reference is made in the text to a few of the monographs, introductions, and reference works which have been consulted. More comprehensive bibliographies are given in the books listed by V. Taylor, E. Best, and C. E. B. Cranfield.

BEST, ERNEST. *The Temptation and the Passion: The Markan Soteriology*. Cambridge: University Press, 1965.

BRANSCOMB, B. H. *Gospel of Mark*. ("Moffatt New Testament Commentary.") New York: Harper & Bros., n.d.

BRATCHER, R. G., and E. A. NIDA. *Translator's Handbook on the Gospel of Mark*. Leiden: E. J. Brill, 1961.

BURKILL, T. A. *Mysterious Revelation: an Examination of the Philosophy of St. Mark's Gospel*. Ithaca: Cornell University Press, 1963.

CARRINGTON, PHILIP. *According to Mark*. Cambridge: University Press, 1960.

CRANFIELD, C. E. B. *Gospel According to Mark*, ("Cambridge Greek Testament Commentary.") Cambridge: University Press, 1966.

DAVIES, W. D. *Invitation to the New Testament*. Garden City, New York: Doubleday & Co., 1966.

FARRER, AUSTIN. *A Study in St. Mark*. New York: Oxford University Press, 1952.

GRANT, F. C. *Gospel According to St. Mark*. ("The Interpreter's Bible," Vol. VII.) Nashville: Abingdon Press, 1951.

JOHNSON, S. E. *Gospel According to Mark*. ("Black's New Testament Commentaries.") London: Adam and Charles Black, 1960.

LIGHTFOOT, R. H. *The Gospel Message of St. Mark*. Oxford: Oxford University Press, 1962.

MAJOR, H. D. A.; T. W. MANSON; and C. J. WRIGHT. *The Mission and Message of Jesus*. New York: E. P. Dutton & Co., 1938.

MINEAR, PAUL S. *Gospel According to Mark*. ("Layman's Bible Commentary," XVII. Richmond: John Knox Press, 1957.

MOULE, C. F. D. *The Gospel According to Mark*. ("Cambridge Bible Commentary on NEB.") Cambridge: University Press, 1965.

NINEHAM, D. E. *Saint Mark*. ("Pelican Gospel Commentaries.") Baltimore: Penguin Books, 1963.

RAWLINSON, A. E. J. *St. Mark*. 7th ed. London: Methuen & Co., 1949.

ROBINSON, J. M. *The Problem of History in Mark*. ("Studies in Biblical Theology," No. 21.) Naperville, Ill.: Alec R. Allenson, 1957.

TAYLOR, VINCENT. *The Gospel According to Mark*. 2d ed. New York: St. Martin's Press, 1966.

Commentary on the Text

I. The Beginning of the Good News (1:1–13)

1. The Keynote (1:1)

[1] The beginning of the gospel of Jesus Christ, the Son of God.

The title, "The Gospel According to Mark," like those of our other three canonical Gospels, was attached to the book during the second century and gives evidence of the church's belief at that time about its origin. Nevertheless the Gospels are anonymous, and the word gospel was previously applied not to a form of literature but to God's activity through Jesus.

The first verse is not merely a title. It is a keynote for the book as a whole. Austin Farrer calls the opening words a "seed out of which the following sentences are to grow."

In Mark, the work of God in John the Baptist is considered the beginning of the divine action expressed fully in Jesus. In Luke, John is regarded as the last prophet of the old epoch. Luke would say, "The law and the prophets were until John; since then the good news of the kingdom of God is preached" (16:16). Luke even tells of John's imprisonment before saying that Jesus was baptized (3:18–22). Mark, however, treats John's ministry more nearly as an introductory phase of the gospel. It is even possible to translate, "The beginning of the gospel . . . was John the baptizer."

In earlier usage among the Greeks, "gospel" meant the reward given to one for bringing good news. By the first century, however, it was applied to the good news itself. Christians in Rome may very well have been familiar with the way devotees of the emperor cult used the word. An inscription at Priene (dated 9 B.C.) speaks of the birthday of the god (the Emperor Augustus) as bringing "gospels" to the world.

However, Mark was writing for Christians, and the word gospel had a special connotation for the followers of Jesus. The meaning must be considered in the light of the Old Testament and the expectations of Israel. The great prophet of the Exile, sometimes called the Second Isaiah, brought a message of hope to the people. He looked forward to the end of the captivity, to the return of the people, and finally to a new age. In that new age God would be victorious over Israel's foes, and his reign would be established on the earth. A messenger would come, a herald of good news, to foretell the event. See especially Isaiah 40:1–11; 52:7–10.

When the word gospel was applied to God's action in Jesus, it meant that the decisive and long-awaited victory over God's foes had been accomplished. Jesus had fulfilled the hope of Israel and a new epoch had dawned. The good news was that God had visited the world in Jesus to defeat the powers of evil and to establish his divine rule.

The contrast between the good news of God's salvation in Jesus and the good news or benefits from the emperor would be very vivid to Christians who lived in Rome under Nero's rule. But it is very doubtful that the Roman Christian of the seventh decade A.D. would ever have dreamed of calling anything under Nero good news! For Christians generally, and so also for Mark, the term gospel had a distinctive meaning. It was applied uniquely to Jesus' life and work.

Brief summaries of the gospel are to be found in several of the speeches in Acts, especially those of Peter and Paul. An analysis of the content of Acts 10:34–43, for example, almost provides an acceptable outline for Mark. God who had promised help by the witness of the prophets had sent the good news of peace to Israel by Jesus. He was anointed by God and went about doing good and overcoming evil powers. Nevertheless, he was put to death. Yet God raised him from the dead, and he appeared to his followers as risen Lord and the one ordained by God to judge all mankind.

The words ***Jesus*** (the Lord saves) and ***Christ*** (the anointed one), as used in this opening verse, have become for Mark simply the proper names by which the church speaks of her Lord.

Some of the oldest manuscripts do not include the words ***the Son of God.*** It is impossible to know whether they were originally present. They are, however, singularly appropriate to the Gospel of Mark. In addition to the acknowledgment by the demonic powers (cf. 3:11; 5:7), the Roman centurion confesses Jesus as "the Son of God" (15:39). The voice of God himself calls Jesus his Son both at his baptism (1:11) and at the transfiguration (9:7). Although Jesus does not in Mark use this title of himself, the phraseology in 12:6; 13:32, and 14:61 f. is close.

For Mark, ***the Son of God*** describes essentially who Jesus is: the mighty one from whom God's power goes forth, the true one to whom they must listen, the suffering one who was obedient to the Father even to the point of dying on the cross (12:1–11; 14:36).

2. *John and Jesus (1:2–11)*

(1) The Prophetic Expectation (1:2–3)

2 As it is written in Isaiah the prophet,
"Behold, I send my messenger before thy face,
who shall prepare thy way;
3 the voice of one crying in the wilderness:
Prepare the way of the Lord,
make his paths straight—"

For Christians the coming of Jesus into the world was (as it remains) the decisive event of history. If Jesus was indeed God's Son, then his coming could not have been an accident.

Who was the God of whom Jesus was the Son? All the Christians in this early period identified him, as Jesus himself had, with the God of Israel, the Giver of the Law, the God whose message the prophets had brought. As Jesus' followers, Christians believed themselves to be the true Israel, the heirs of the divine promises. Accordingly, they searched the Scriptures not only for guidance but also for passages that confirmed or illumined the place and work of Jesus in the divine purpose.

Along with the early church of which he was a part, Mark believed that John the Baptist was an integral part of the holy plan. John had been a messenger sent to announce the coming of one greater than himself and to prepare for his ministry. This is the way John's ministry was interpreted, and Scriptures that confirmed this conclusion were readily discerned and quoted.

The quotations in our text are from Malachi 3:1 and Isaiah 40:3.[10] The first of these is almost identical with Exodus 23:20 (read "messenger" for "angel"; the words are identical in both Hebrew and Greek). Among the Hebrews, the writings of the prophets were considered authoritative as comments on or interpretations of the Law of Moses. Perhaps the earliest use of these passages together was by Jewish Christians expressing their faith as they worshiped in their synagogues.[11]

In Exodus the messenger is to go before Israel, but in Malachi before the Lord God himself. Similarly, in Isaiah 40 "the way of the Lord" is the way of God. When Mark asserts that John fulfilled these prophecies, he clearly means to identify Jesus with the Lord of whom the prophet spoke.

(2) *John the Baptizer* (*1:4–8*)

4 John the baptizer appeared in the wilderness,
preaching a baptism of repentance for the for-
giveness of sins. 5 And there went out to him
all the country of Judea, and all the people of
Jerusalem; and they were baptized by him in
the river Jordan, confessing their sins. 6 Now
John was clothed with camel's hair, and had a
leather girdle around his waist, and ate locusts
and wild honey. 7 And he preached, saying,
"After me comes he who is mightier than I, the
thong of whose sandals I am not worthy to
stoop down and untie. 8 I have baptized you
with water; but he will baptize you with the
Holy Spirit."

To the Christians, and perhaps to the prophet himself, the primary work of John was as the forerunner of one greater than himself. He was, nevertheless, a powerful and influential religious figure in his own right. The dilemma of the chief priests and scribes in Mark 11:27–33 reflects the esteem in which John was held. After his death his disciples continued to proclaim his message of repentance and to baptize. Apparently these followers were numerous and became widely scattered.[12]

John was known as ***the baptizer.*** Although repeated ceremonial washings were practiced among the Jews, the closest parallel to John's action was the baptism of Gentiles when they were submitting to the Hebrew faith. No confession of sin was required of proselytes who submitted to this baptism nor did their baptism mean repentance. The proselytes did receive careful instruction in the Jewish commandments and bound themselves to observe Jewish laws and religious customs.

John came as a prophet from God, demanding repentance on the part of God's people. Mark does not give us very much of his message. According to Luke 3:7–14

10 The RSV is surely right in reading "in Isaiah the prophet" instead of "in the prophets" (AV). The textual evidence is conclusive. Whether the passage from Malachi was inserted by an early copyist or was taken by Mark from a collection of OT passages in which the verse had already been linked with Isa. 40:3 is uncertain.

11 The Essenes of the monastic community at Qumran believed that they were fulfilling the prophecy from Isaiah 40 by preparing in the wilderness the Lord's way. Cf. 1QS VIII, 12–15. Qumran was on the edge of the wilderness from which John came out to preach. There are similarities between John and the people of the Dead Sea Scrolls, but we have no direct evidence of contact between them. The comparisons are instructive. The Essenes also practiced ablutions, but unlike them, John went out preaching to the people and calling on them to submit to a baptism of repentance. John's emphasis was on right living and impending judgment; the Essenes were greatly concerned with ritual purity. Neither did John seek to establish a monastic community, though he was an ascetic and he did reject sharply the ways of the religious institutions of his day.

12 Paul baptized some of John's disciples in Ephesus (Acts 19:1–6), and Apollos had known only the baptism of John (Acts 18:25). See C. H. Kraeling, *John the Baptist* (New York: Scribner, 1951) and Charles H. H. Scobie, *John the Baptist* (Philadelphia: Fortress, 1964).

(cf. Matt. 3:7–10), the repentance he called for involved both negative and positive elements in a very practical way. Men must not steal or extort from their fellows. They are to share with those in need of food and clothing. Their evil is part of their inheritance, but they are continuing to poison society by their lives and attitudes (they are a "brood of vipers"). Judgment is coming from God, and they must change their allegiance and commit themselves to a different and godly way.

The baptism meant therefore an open confession of sin and a public declaration of the person's intent to live a new life. Since he is a messenger from God, John's call for repentance is part of the divine command to the people. So also is the promise that those who genuinely repent will surely be forgiven. Immersion in the river does not accomplish either the repentance or the forgiveness; but the baptism signifies and affirms both.

"Baptize" means to dip, to immerse. Precisely how this may have been done we cannot be sure. In the Jewish proselyte baptism, the candidates immersed themselves (cf. Mishnah, Pesahim 8:8). The verb ***they were baptized by him*** could mean they were baptizing themselves in the prophet's presence. But the language here, as elsewhere, favors the interpretation that John himself administered the baptism.

We need not take literally the assertion that ***all the people*** submitted to John's baptism. Mark wishes us to understand that John's preaching was highly effective, that he had a mighty impact upon the multitudes.

His desert garb and diet are reminiscent of the prophet Elijah, who had worn "a garment of haircloth, with a girdle of leather about his loins" (2 Kings 1:8). By living so simply, John dramatized his contempt for the plush living and extravagance of some of his wealthy contemporaries. He was ridiculed for this (Matt. 11:18; Luke 7:33), but he must have struck responsive chords in the lives of many of his fellow Jews. Ascetic practices like John's are often a means of effective protest against the gross luxuries of unconcerned people. As the example of Jesus clearly shows, however, extremes of self-denial in daily living are not in themselves vital to the Christian way.

Several species of locusts were edible, and the Law permitted their use as food (Lev. 11:22). John's diet may not have been confined to ***locusts and wild honey,*** but the wilderness afforded only meager choice for one's diet.

The only part of John's message which Mark repeats is that which directly pertains to Jesus. However great the people may have thought John to be, he was announcing the coming of another vastly superior to himself. So great would he be that John said he was not worthy to serve him in the most menial of tasks.

John said, the one coming is ***mightier than I.*** Jesus will be the "strong" one, so mighty that Satan and all the forces of evil will be unable to resist his authority and power. The Gospel of Mark is indeed the gospel of the strong Son of God, who "binds the strong man" (3:27) and takes for himself those whom evil has dominated. He will even share with the twelve the "authority" from himself to free men from the yoke of the evils (moral or physical) that enslave them (3:15; 6:7,13).

John's own service to men was limited, even though his message was from God. He called men to a self-dedication to godly living, but his emphasis was on the human commitment and endeavor. What was needed was that power from God that John could not bestow. John's message is that God is about to give men this divine aid. The one who is coming will baptize them ***with the Holy Spirit.***

The outpouring of God's Holy Spirit was expected in the last times (cf. Joel 2:28 f.; Acts 2:17 f.; Ezek. 36:26 f.; Isa. 44:3). Christians would probably have thought of Pentecost, and certainly of the presence of the Holy Spirit in themselves. The parallels in Luke 3:16 and Matthew 3:11 add that Jesus will baptize also "with fire." But Mark is content to emphasize the power of God which brings victory to and within man and not the divine judgment.

What distinguishes the new covenant from the old is what was anticipated by Jeremiah: "I will put my law within them, and I will write it upon their hearts; and I will be their God, and they will be my people" (31:33). Ultimate victory, according to John's word, depends upon the entry of God's power into the lives of repentant men. John cannot give this victory; the coming one will do so.

(3) *The Baptism of Jesus (1:9–11)*

9 In those days Jesus came from Nazareth of Galilee and was baptized by John in the Jordan. 10 And when he came up out of the water, immediately he saw the heavens opened and the Spirit descending upon him like a dove; 11 and a voice came from heaven, "Thou art my beloved Son; with thee I am well pleased."

In those days, i.e., about the time John was speaking of him and the coming baptism with the Holy Spirit, ***Jesus came from Nazareth.*** Mark says nothing of Bethlehem, nothing of Jesus' childhood, nothing of his descent from David (but cf. 12:35–37). He does identify him later as "the carpenter" and speaks of members of his family by name (6:2–3). Mark's account of the work of God in his Son begins here at the Jordan.

There is nothing distinctive about the way Jesus was baptized. Mark describes the baptism as taking place ***in the Jordan*** (literally "into") and says that ***he came up out of the water.*** It is apparent that John's baptism was consistently by immersion. Not the mode but the experience of Jesus at the baptism was unique.

Why was Jesus baptized? Mark does not raise the question at all. That the one who called for repentance from sin should have baptized the sinless Redeemer may have been a problem for some early Christians (cf. Matt. 3:15). According to Mark, Jesus certainly believed the baptism of John was from God (11:30) and wished to identify himself with the wilderness prophet. That Jesus joined with "all the country of Judea, and all the people of Jerusalem" (v. 5) in being baptized is equally true and appropriate. In a very real sense, he was identifying himself with the people he came to save.

The difference between the baptism of others and the baptism of Jesus lies in the special events that occurred. By the coming of the Spirit and the voice from the heavens, Jesus was identified uniquely with God himself.

The distinctive happenings at Jesus' baptism and temptation were not something totally foreign to the Jewish expectations. There are striking similarities with Mark's account to be found in the contemporary Hebrew literature, especially in passages that spoke of the last days and of God's triumph over evil.[13]

As Jesus arose from the water, ***he saw the heavens opened.*** This is no mere parting of literal clouds or blue atmosphere. In Hebrew idiom, God's throne is far above the highest heaven, in light unapproachable. Thus it was out from a cleft in the heavens that God's powerful words and deeds had to come. The phrase means that the whole world of spiritual power and truth was unveiled before Jesus.

The Spirit that descended out of the heavens is, of course, God's Spirit. He came down upon Jesus in a dovelike manner. Mark does not indicate, as Luke does (cf. also John 1:32), that the event would have been visible to others. Perhaps all that is meant by the phrase ***like a dove*** is gently or quietly, but there may well be an allusion to the story of creation in Genesis 1:2.

[13] E.g., Testament of Levi 18:1–12: "Then shall the Lord raise up a new priest. And to him all the words of the Lord shall be revealed: and he shall execute judgment upon the earth for a multitude of days. . . . The heavens shall be opened, and from the temple of glory shall come upon him sanctification, with the Father's voice as from Abraham to Isaac. . . . In his priesthood the Gentiles shall be . . . enlightened through the grace of the Lord: In his priesthood shall sin come to an end, and the lawless shall cease to do evil. . . . And he shall open the gates of paradise, and shall remove the threatening sword against Adam. And he shall give to the saints to eat from the tree of life, and the spirit of holiness shall be on them. And Beliar shall be bound by him." R. H. Charles, *The Apocrypha and Pseudepigrapha of the Old Testament* (Oxford: Clarendon, 1913), II, 314 f.

There we are told that the Spirit of God was "moving over" the face of the waters. Certainly, the Christians of Mark's generation knew that by the power of God's Son endued with the Spirit a "new creation" had come into being (cf. 2 Cor. 5:17).

Through the opened heavens, as the rabbis conceived the case, God might speak. But the divine message would be heard on earth only as the echo of a voice (or, as they would put it, "daughter of a voice"). This echo of a voice was sometimes identified with the voice of the Holy Spirit (Rawlinson). Generally, as here, the words of the voice were taken from the Scriptures (cf. the similar event in Mark 9:7).

Thou art my beloved Son is an echo from Psalm 2:7. These words indicate that God is crowning his King, who will rule over all the nations and kings of earth. Perhaps the word beloved has become a messianic name (cf. Eph. 1:6). Or it may be, as has been suggested by some scholars, that the word beloved here means only or unique, and the phrase would be equivalent to the "only Son" of John 1:14 and 3:16.

With thee I am well pleased are the echoing words from Isaiah 42:1. In that passage, it is the servant of the Lord who was addressed. The divine promise of a better day of justice and peace was to come through the suffering of this chosen Servant.

Neither clause of the echoing voice is a precise quotation from the passage named. The language has close affinities also with other Old Testament phrases (cf. Gen. 22:2; Isa. 44:2). As Taylor has noted, Jesus is not addressed here as "the Christ" but in terms no less Hebraic that express a new and vital relationship to the Father-God.

As Mark has described it, the baptismal experience was for Jesus an assuring word concerning his sonship to God, an anointing for his divinely appointed task, a bestowal of power to accomplish the work given him to do. The task would include the defeat of every form of evil that besets man from without or within. It also would include Jesus' own death in obedience to the divine will and in full acceptance by Jesus of his own role as a man living among blinded and evil men. For Mark's readers it was specifically a word that assured them that God's Son had come and their own baptism was indeed with the power of the Holy Spirit which had rested upon Jesus.

3. *The Temptation of Jesus (1:12–13)*

12 The Spirit immediately drove him out into the wilderness. 13 And he was in the wilderness forty days, tempted by Satan; and he was with the wild beasts; and the angels ministered to him.

The account of the temptation experience in Mark is remarkably brief. In Matthew and in Luke, Jesus is portrayed as resisting Satan's appeal to do his own task in ways that would be appealing to men of the world but grossly inadequate for his spiritual purpose. However, in each of the Synoptic accounts the baptismal and temptation experiences are closely related.

The Spirit immediately drove him out. The verb is strong, and emphasizes the control exercised in Jesus by the Spirit which had come upon him so signally. It is the same verb used to tell us that Jesus "cast out many demons" (1:34).

It was according to God's will, Mark is asserting, that Jesus was tested without delay. That the difficult period should have come immediately after his wonderful and assuring experience at baptism provided also warning and encouragement to new Christians who might read this book.

Why would God's Spirit drive Jesus into this conflict? God did not send his Son into a world of tranquillity and peace, within or without. It was necessary that the powers of evil be defeated. Here in ***the wilderness,*** traditionally the haunt of demons, the battle is joined. ***Forty days*** is perhaps a figurative expression for a considerable period of time. We are reminded of Moses and Elijah (cf. Ex. 34:28; 1 Kings 19:8). However, for them it was a time with God, not with the prince of evil.

Mark does not tell us in so many words the outcome of Jesus' struggle with Satan, at least not at this point. Ernest Best argues persuasively that Mark does tell us later, in the parable in which the stronger man (Jesus) has already bound the strong man (Satan) and is proceeding to despoil his house (3:27). The struggle with those forces which oppose man (not necessarily moral, but including demon-possession, disease, and discordant elements) continues throughout Jesus' ministry. Best holds that (in Mark) the war with Satan was won at the temptation experience, that Belial (another name for Satan) was bound there, and that authority over Satan's minions was established.

However, Best regards most of the problem of evil with which Jesus has to contend (still according to Mark) as being from man to man, or within a man's own self, and not with the prince of evil. It is certainly true that the stories of casting out demons dwindle in number and Jesus' encounters with the moral evils of men dominate the last chapters. The cross is a judgment especially upon these moral evils. On the positive side, Jesus' blood is shed for others, and his life brings them with forgiveness and joy into the new community formed in accord with his teaching and his self-giving.

Whether we are able to accept the divorce Best makes between Satan as tempter and man's own spirit as author of evil, we are surely right in concluding with him that in the wilderness, driven by the Spirit, Jesus established conclusively his own victory over Satan. From now on the reign of God has drawn near in Jesus' own person.[14]

The presence of ***wild beasts*** could simply emphasize the loneliness and dangers of the wilderness. Also, sometimes wild beasts were associated with evil powers. Perhaps, however, the reference to wild beasts was made because of the decisiveness of this time in God's purpose, because a cosmic victory had been won. Could men dare to hope that at last the long awaited time of peace was on the way? See, for example, such a hope as is expressed in Isaiah 11: 6–9: "The wolf shall dwell with the lamb, and the leopard shall lie down with the kid, . . . They shall not hurt or destroy in all my holy mountain."

In the longer accounts of the temptation, it is the voice of the tempter which calls to mind Psalm 91:11–12. Had not God promised his chosen One that his angels would protect him? Here in Mark, in quite different fashion, it is asserted that God's angels did indeed care for his needs and protect him. Incidentally, in verse 14 of the same psalm there is promise of victory over the lion and the venemous snake.

In these first few sentences Mark has left no doubt about the identity of Jesus. Every reader will understand that he was indeed God's Son, endowed with the Holy Spirit. Jesus himself has been victor over the existing powers and by the baptism of that Spirit he extends that triumph to men.

On the other hand, both Mark and his readers are aware that Jesus walked as a man among men and was not readily acknowledged to be the Christ of God. In Mark's presentation of Jesus' ministry it will be seen that the disciples only gradually became aware of Jesus' true identity. For the many, and especially for the Jewish religious leaders, the truth remained undiscerned. For them the fact that Jesus was indeed the Messiah remained a mystery, impenetrable and unacceptable.

II. *The Ministry of Jesus: Mystery and Revelation (1:14—8:30)*

1. *The Beginning of the Galilean Ministry (1:14—3:6)*

(1) *A Summary of Jesus' Preaching (1: 14–15)*

14 Now after John was arrested, Jesus came into Galilee, preaching the gospel of God,
15 and saying, "The time is fulfilled, and the kingdom of God is at hand; repent, and believe in the gospel."

14 Best (pp. 18–23) gives a very instructive analysis of Robinson's *The Problem of History in Mark.* In contrast with Best, Robinson views the whole of the Gospel of Mark in terms of the cosmic struggle between the Spirit and Satan.

The fourth Gospel speaks of a parallel ministry of John and Jesus in Judea (3:22–30). Mark assumes that his readers know what has happened to John, and withholds his description of the event until 6:14–29.

The verb ***was arrested*** hints that John may have been betrayed, for it is used also of Judas' act (14:18,21). Mark does not quote Jesus' word, "Blessed are you when men . . . persecute you . . . for so men persecuted the prophets who were before you" (Matt. 5:11–12; cf. Luke 6:22–23). Yet the prophet John did suffer in this way; and so did Jesus.

Mark probably intends for his readers to think of John as the forerunner not only of Jesus' ministry but also of his suffering.[15]

If the composition of the book has a background of Nero's persecution of Roman Christians, as we believe, then the first readers would think anew about the dangers of their own spiritual commitments. Did not their sufferings have worthy precedents?

Mark treats John's work as finished. The Christ has come; the work of John is concluded. It is as though God has brought to an end one chapter in his work in history and now begins the climactic epoch.

The setting of the major part of Jesus' ministry is in ***Galilee.*** Mark does not take us to Nazareth at first, as does Luke (cf. Matt. 4:13). Except for Jesus' excursion to "the region of Tyre and Sidon" (7:24), Mark's narrative through 9:50 centers Jesus' work either in Galilee proper or in other districts close by the Sea of Galilee.

Jesus came preaching ***the gospel of God.*** John's preaching had been full of warning, like a word from Amos, announcing the time of judgment. Cf. Amos 5:18–20: "Woe to you who desire the day of the Lord! . . . Is not the day of the Lord darkness, and not light?" But Jesus brought good news about God. His proclamation sounded the joyous note of Isaiah 52:7: "How beautiful upon the mountains are the feet of him who brings good tidings, who publishes peace, who brings good tidings of good, who publishes salvation, who says to Zion, 'Your God reigns.' "

What was Jesus' good news? The essence of what he taught and what he did, and even who he is, is summarized in this one verse.

The time is fulfilled: that is, the decisive hour of God's saving action in history has now come. ***Time*** means the fitting or right time. In Galatians 4:4, "when the time had fully come," a different word is used, which often refers to chronological time. However, Mark's understanding, like Paul's, would be that the right time would be the divinely chosen and prepared stage in man's continuing history.

The kingdom of God means God's reign, the divine sovereignty. In one sense God's rule was considered to be eternal and absolute. Everything and everyone ultimately belong to God: as the devout Jews sang, "The earth is the Lord's and the fulness thereof, the world and those who dwell therein" (Psalm 24:1; cf. 47:7; and all of Psalm 2).

However, Satan was regarded as the prince of this world, and the nations and peoples were thought of as subject to his power. It was perfectly clear that God's reign and will were often ignored and opposed. When will evil be defeated and God's rule openly established? That will be God's day, the Hebrews understood, the "afterward" of Joel's hope (2:28), the new covenant-time of Jeremiah's prophecy (31:31–34).

Jesus' word, then, must be understood as eschatological, having to do with the ultimate victory of God. He says, God's rule ***is at hand,*** literally, "has drawn near." What has been vague and blurred in the distance has invaded our sight. The verb does not quite say the kingdom has come and is fully realized now. C. H. Dodd goes too far in insisting that the verb means "has ar-

[15] See H. D. Knigge, "The Meaning of Mark," *Interpretation,* Vol. 22, No. 1 (January, 1968) pp. 68 f. He is persuaded that Mark has here and elsewhere (in his insertion of the story of John's death in ch. 6, and, more enigmatically, in 3:6; 8:28; 9:11–13) conflated the fate of the Baptist with Jesus and oriented the story of Jesus to his passion from the very beginning.

rived." But the triumph of God is now so close that the powers of evil are being opposed successfully, and the reign of God is seen clearly in his Son.

It would be natural for the disciples (as well as the Christians of the early churches) who accepted this teaching from Jesus to believe that the end of all things was near. But the words of Jesus and of Mark do not go this far. The announcement claims that God's new order has broken significantly into history in Jesus. However, the old order has not yet passed away, and the struggle continues. There is still a call to ***repent, and believe.***

Davies illustrates this point very clearly by recalling an incident of World War II. As he was walking home one Sunday from church, a friend hailed him with the news that Hitler had invaded Russia. "Then the allies," Davies responded, "have won the war." The struggle continued for many months, as we know: but something decisive for an allied victory happened when Hitler ventured to fight on two fronts. In the same way, though no one can know when the struggle will end, something final and decisive happened for man in the life and work of Jesus (Davies, p. 162).

Repent, and believe in the gospel. Both verbs call for continuing action. The repentance and faith required are no single event but an enduring attitude and characteristic. To ***believe in the gospel*** reflects the Aramaic idiom and should be understood simply as to believe—accept and live by—the gospel (cf. on 1:1).

Repent does mean to change one's mind, and naturally to turn from evil to what is good. Jesus' word is quite consonant with John's. In this context, however, there is a special significance. God's reign is no faroff thing; it is a reality that has drawn near to man. Repenting is not separable from believing this good news: it means to open one's being to a different King, to accept God's sovereignty for oneself, to let the glad tidings of divine, royal power over every evil being or thing be the faith by which one lives.

(2) *Calling the First Disciples (1:16–20)*

16 And passing along by the Sea of Galilee,
he saw Simon and Andrew the brother of
Simon casting a net in the sea; for they were
fishermen. 17 And Jesus said to them, "Follow
me and I will make you become fishers of
men." 18 And immediately they left their nets
and followed him. 19 And going on a little
farther, he saw James the son of Zebedee and
John his brother, who were in their boat mend-
ing the nets. 20 And immediately he called
them; and they left their father Zebedee in the
boat with the hired servants, and followed him.

God's rule can never be understood as existing in a void. To speak of the reign of God in the world implies a people living in faith and submission to that reign. If in Jesus the divine reign has drawn near and is to be clearly in evidence, and if Jesus is calling for men to open their own selves to God's kingship, it is altogether appropriate that Mark should speak next of some notable recruits.

In the Gospel of John we are told that some of the disciples of Jesus first followed the Baptist. Among them was certainly Andrew, and the story is that he told Simon about Jesus (John 1:35–42). We need not suppose, accordingly, that this paragraph in Mark narrates Jesus' first contact with these men. It is apparent that Mark's readers will need no introduction to their names. Simon is, of course, the apostle known as Peter (3:16).

The ***Sea of Galilee*** is about eight miles wide and thirteen long. Its fresh water still abounds in fish. The brothers were ***casting*** a circular net, working at the occupation which provided their livelihood.

Jesus' call was strong and demanding, similar to a military order. The personal nature of the call, ***Follow me,*** would have been especially appropriate to disciples of an imprisoned John: their prophetic leader is no longer here, and the one mightier than he claims their allegiance.

The old use of the metaphor to catch men was generally applied to trapping them, or nabbing them for judgment (e.g., Jer. 16:16; Hab. 1:15–17). Here (as in Luke 5:10) the call to discipleship is joined with an invitation to help Jesus in the task of capturing men out of the powers of evil and judgment so that they too may rejoice in God's new dominance over their lives.

The primary task of the Jewish teachers was to study and meditate upon the law of Moses. Afterwards, they were exhorted to "raise up many disciples" to pass on their learning and traditional practices. Jesus' disciples were called to participate with their Master in leading men into God's kingdom.

The response of the fishermen was immediate. They left their old vocation and became disciples. The verb ***followed*** was widely used to describe the acceptance of Jesus' invitation to learn his way and to heed his teaching. Cf. Luke 9:57–62.

The call of these two pairs of brothers may very well have been remembered by Mark from Peter's preaching. The references to casting and mending the nets are quite vivid; so also is the note about Zebedee and the hired servants. But the placing of the story at the very beginning of the ministry would be Markan.

For sons to leave the business of their father with only ***hired servants*** points both to the urgency of Jesus' call and to the radical commitment required of the disciples. There is deliberate emphasis on the personal sacrifice involved.

(3) *The New Teaching and Immediate Fame* (*1:21–45*)

a. Teaching and Healing in a Synagogue (*21–28*)

21 And they went into Capernaum; and immediately on the sabbath he entered the synagogue and taught. 22 And they were astonished at his teaching, for he taught them as one who had authority, and not as the scribes. 23 And immediately there was in their synagogue a man with an unclean spirit; 24 and he cried out, "What have you to do with us, Jesus of Nazareth? Have you come to destroy us? I know who you are, the Holy One of God." 25 But Jesus rebuked him, saying, "Be silent, and come out of him!" 26 And the unclean spirit, convulsing him and crying with a loud voice, came out of him. 27 And they were all amazed, so that they questioned among themselves, saying, "What is this? A new teaching! With authority he commands even the unclean spirits, and they obey him." 28 And at once his fame spread everywhere throughout all the surrounding region of Galilee.

With the four disciples whom he had invited to be with him, Jesus began his ministry in Capernaum's synagogue. Capernaum was located at the site known to us as Tell Hum, on the northwest shore of the Sea of Galilee. It was apparently the home of Simon and Andrew (v. 29), and perhaps others of the twelve. Ruins of a synagogue have been identified at Tell Hum, but its date is acknowledged to be a century or more after Jesus' ministry.

The synagogues of Jesus' day were primarily centers for instruction. ***On the sabbath*** the services included the reading from the sacred scrolls of the Hebrew Bible, with a rather free interpretation into the Aramaic language of the people. There were also prayers and blessings said, and perhaps a psalm. The preaching was done by any competent man present. He would be invited to speak by the ruler of the synagogue (sometimes more than one shared this office), who was responsible for leading the worship. There were no sacrifices offered, nor were a priest's services required at the synagogue. (The priests ministered at the Temple in Jerusalem, regarded by devout Jews as the only place adequate for the full worship of God.) [16]

It was not strange that Jesus, an outspoken Hebrew man already regarded as a teacher, should be invited to teach in the synagogue. Neither ought we to suppose that the things Jesus taught, taken one by one, were astonishing to devout Hebrews. Parallels to many of the teachings of Jesus may be found in the sayings of the great rabbis.

Nevertheless, the people ***were astonished at his teaching.*** If they were amazed at what he taught, it would be because he claimed the kingdom of God had drawn

[16] The synagogue service was quite naturally a forerunner of the worship services practiced in the early Christian meetings. None is described in detail in the NT, but cf. 1 Cor. 14:26–33.

near (v. 15). This claim is evident in the healing of the man with an unclean spirit. But probably we ought to understand that they were astonished because he spoke "like an authority, not like the scribes" (Moffatt).

The scribes were men trained in the knowledge of the Old Testament and its interpretations. In one dialect the title is paraphrased well as "those who knew the Jews' ways" (Bratcher and Nida). The scribes characteristically documented their teaching with the traditions passed down to them. Like the famous scribe Hillel, Jesus often appealed to the Scriptures: see, for example, 2:25–26. Still, Jesus did not hesitate to go beyond the Old Testament words or the customary interpretation of them. Matthew 5:17–48 is a clear example of his independence, and of his confidence that God's truth was being spoken in his teaching.

Mark gives no illustration of Jesus' teaching in the synagogue except in the healing of ***a man with an unclean spirit.*** No distinction seems intended between persons possessed with demons (v. 32) and those with unclean spirits. Something unclean alienates a man both from God and from God's people. An unclean spirit was thought of as a power hostile to man and to God's rule, possessing a man so he is not the person God intended him to be.[17]

The cosmic struggle was joined. The afflicted person—or, rather, the affliction within him—shrieked out, "Why dost thou meddle with us, Jesus of Nazareth?" (Rawlinson). The unclean spirit identified himself with all the demonic world. Only by insight beyond man could one recognize Jesus, and be able to say, ***I know who you are, the Holy One of God.***

It was commonly believed that if one knew the name of the demonic power, he might exorcise it. Was the unclean spirit attempting this in reverse, by calling out who Jesus was?

[17] A brief, penetrating discussion of the exorcism narratives in Mark is found in J. M. Robinson, pp. 33–42.

Jesus had indeed come to destroy the powers that kept man alienated from God and from his fellows. He did not, however, rely on special formulae or names to cast out demons (but cf. 5:8–10). His victory over them came simply, with a command. ***Be silent*** (literally, be muzzled), ***and come out,*** he ordered. Not without one last struggle, the spirit departed, and the man was evidently whole.

The assembly was ***amazed,*** quite naturally. What was happening among them? Who is this Jesus? Here is ***a new teaching,*** and it is stamped ***with authority.*** Probably the words ***with authority*** should be read with the preceding exclamation. Mark's readers would understand that the new teaching was not simply how to cast out demons. It was that the rule of God had manifested itself in Jesus.

Without further discussion Mark simply reports that Jesus' fame began to spread widely and immediately.

b. The Healings at Simon's Home and a Widening Ministry (1:29–39)

**29 And immediately he left the synagogue,
and entered the house of Simon and Andrew,
with James and John. 30 Now Simon's mother-
in-law lay sick with a fever, and immediately
they told him of her. 31 And he came and took
her by the hand and lifted her up, and the
fever left her; and she served them.
32 That evening, at sundown, they brought to
him all who were sick or possessed with demons. 33 And the whole city was gathered together about the door. 34 And he healed many
who were sick with various diseases, and cast
out many demons; and he would not permit
the demons to speak, because they knew him.
35 And in the morning, a great while before
day, he rose and went out to a lonely place,
and there he prayed. 36 And Simon and those
who were with him followed him, 37 and they
found him and said to him, "Every one is
searching for you." 38 And he said to them, "Let
us go on to the next towns, that I may preach
there also; for that is why I came out." 39 And
he went throughout all Galilee, preaching in
their synagogues and casting out demons.**

The events described in 21–34 are treated as taking place on one sabbath day. For the Jews the day's end was not at midnight but at sundown. The people would naturally think of Jesus as one who observed the religious scruples and so did not bring their sick to him until the sabbath was past.

Simon and Andrew apparently had a house together in Capernaum. Was it the typical home—one room, dirt floor? Perhaps the brothers had spoken to Jesus of the elderly woman's illness before he came into their dwelling, and they quite probably hoped he would help her. It is plain that discipleship had not involved any absolute rejection of family relationships or responsibilities.

The woman ***lay sick with a fever.*** We have no knowledge whatever of its nature. Branscomb suggests that this woman and many others cured by Jesus were suffering from hysteria. Who can accurately diagnose an ancient illness, with no more data than is given here? In Luke 4:38 we are told that she was suffering "with a high fever," and that Jesus "rebuked" the fever—just as he would a demon he was casting out. But Luke was apparently interpreting Mark's account.

He ***lifted her up*** is similar to an Aramaic idiom which would mean he healed her. That ***she served them*** the evening meal provides no evidence that Simon was a widower (cf. 1 Cor. 9:5), but an expression of her gratitude and (for the readers) proof of her cure.

At the close of this memorable day, the crowds came. If he has healed one, can he not heal all our sick? The line formed and grew longer, we may imagine. If ***the whole city*** is an exaggeration, it is probably less so than the hyperbole of 1:5 ("all the people of Jerusalem"). Those who had no sick would have come to see. One of Mark's major emphases in this section is the rapidly multiplying fame of Jesus (cf. 1:37,45).

Mark usually distinguishes between those ***who were sick with various diseases*** and the demon-possessed. In the Greek, to be sick translates the very vivid "having [something] badly."

Unlike Matthew, who omits regularly the phrases about the demons' recognizing Jesus, Mark pointedly asserts that Jesus would not let the unclean spirits identify him openly. Did Jesus wish to keep his messiahship a secret? Or did he reject this identification because of its source? It does seem clear that during his ministry Jesus did not publicly and explicitly refer to himself as the Christ. He knew who he was and exercised the powers given to him, but he rejected the use of the title Messiah or Christ.

The messianic secret, if it may be properly so termed, has its counterpart in Mark with a kind of progressive revelation of Jesus' identity. Our Lord himself clearly understood his sonship at his baptism. The demonic world realized his unique nature (the "Holy One of God," 1:24) in the temptation experience and in these triumphs over unclean spirits for the control of persons. There follows (though with some limitations) the revelation to the disciples, specifically to Peter (8:29) and those with him at the transfiguration (9:7). Jesus himself ultimately discloses the truth about himself to the Jewish court (14:61–62). Finally, the Roman centurion is enabled to discern something of his true nature just as Jesus dies: he is truly the "Son of God" (15:39).[18]

Jesus found time for prayer. Mark's portrait of Jesus is of a man busy and unable by day to escape the long and tiring demands of people in need. Victorious over Satan and his minions, healing every kind of disease, Jesus was nevertheless a man in need of prayer. Was his especial anxiety at this time his concern not to be known simply as healer and exorciser?

The disciples were excited by the immediate popularity of Jesus, and wished their Teacher to take full advantage of it. Perhaps there is some hint of local pride, which assumed Jesus would or should make his home in Capernaum. They ***followed him*** or more literally, they "hunted him down,"

[18] See Curtis Beach, *The Gospel of Mark* (New York: Harper, 1959), p. 46. He points out how the other Gospels have no comparable concept of a "messianic secret," nor is knowledge withheld from various groups. In Luke, however, the demons are also forbidden to speak.

to bring him back to the crowd.

Jesus' calling was too wide to be confined to one city. Mark does want his readers to think of the growing fame of Jesus, but we need not suppose he thinks of Jesus' going to other towns just to escape the pressure of the crowds. The only preaching of Jesus described so far is the opening summary in 1:15. He proclaimed that God's long-awaited time had come and that men were to repent and believe. The casting out of demons was evidence of the truth of his proclamation: a higher power is present in Jesus.

c. *The Cleansing of a Leper (1:40–45)*

**40 And a leper came to him beseeching him,
and kneeling said to him, "If you will, you
can make me clean." 41 Moved with pity, he
stretched out his hand and touched him, and
said to him, "I will; be clean." 42 And immediately the leprosy left him, and he was made
clean. 43 And he sternly charged him, and sent
him away at once, 44 and said to him, "See that
you say nothing to any one; but go, show
yourself to the priest, and offer for your cleansing what Moses commanded, for a proof to
the people." 45 But he went out and began to
talk freely about it, and to spread the news, so
that Jesus could no longer openly enter a town,
but was out in the country; and people came to
him from every quarter.**

The Law's instructions concerning leprosy are given in Leviticus 13—14. The name leprosy is used today specifically of Hansen's disease, but in the Law the description of symptoms is applicable to several skin diseases. Leprosy was not regarded as hopelessly incurable. Careful instructions were given the priests to determine whether the unclean ailment was healed. The priests were responsible both for diagnosis and the declaration of cleanness.

The leper himself was a pitiful spectacle. The Law ordered that the diseased person shall wear torn clothes and let the hair of his head hang loose, and he shall cover his upper lip and cry, 'Unclean, unclean.' He shall remain unclean as long as he has the disease; he is unclean; he shall dwell alone in a habitation outside the camp" (Lev. 13:45–46). Shut off from family and neighbors, excluded from society and consequently from work and worship, the lepers were a wretched lot. What this treatment would do to a man's spirit might well be tragic. Perhaps the ingratitude of the nine lepers of Luke 17:17 is understandable, even if there could be no adequate health in their spirits unless they could be grateful.[19]

The leper knelt not in worship but in entreaty. He did not doubt Jesus' ability to heal. He did doubt whether any man—or God himself—was concerned with his plight.

Jesus was ***moved with pity*** for this miserable castaway.[20] His response with his hand was as kind as his word: he ***touched him.*** By this little act Jesus identified himself with the leper; it made him a partner in the man's ritual defilement. This man was forbidden by custom and law to come into a house like Simon's to seek help, or to touch one like Jesus along the roadside. But Jesus touched him, and spoke healing words.

The word ***immediately*** is used often and loosely by Mark, and we may not press the meaning too literally. Jesus followed the Law's teaching by requiring the man to go before a priest for examination and to offer the proper gift, a testimony or proof that the cure was complete. Mark upholds the kind of freedom in relation to the Law which Paul advocates in Galatians and Romans. The discussions in the next two chapters make this clear. But he also would agree that "the law is holy, and the commandment is holy and just and good" (Rom. 7:12).

The verb ***sternly charged*** is very strong, and often indicates anger or violent dis-

19 Branscomb (pp. 37–40) does point out that some synagogues had special booths for those afflicted with leprosy, and that they were not forbidden to enter the unwalled towns. On the other hand, one rabbinic view (not mentioned or supported by Mark) was that leprosy was a form of punishment from God for the worst sins.

20 Some ancient mss have "moved with anger" instead of "moved with pity." If this reading is correct, as it may be, Jesus' anger would have been directed against the customs that so often without mercy and with hardness of heart compelled a fellow human being to live in such circumstances.

pleasure. We need not suppose that, because Jesus had compassion on him, the man was "worthy" or in any way a model of gratitude. However, the demand Jesus made of the healed suppliant was only for silence, at least until after he was pronounced clean in the proper and lawful way.

The command was not obeyed. The man added his voice to the growing clamor about Jesus. Now the former leper could go anywhere, in and out of the cities freely. But the one who healed him ***could no longer openly enter a town*** without the immediate crush of a crowd. Even though he customarily stayed away from the cities, the people were coming to him ***from every quarter.***

(4) *Controversies with the Scribes* (*2:1—3:6*)

a. *The Paralytic: to Forgive and to Heal* (*2:1–12*)

1 And when he returned to Capernaum after some days, it was reported that he was at home. 2 And many were gathered together, so that there was no longer room for them, not even about the door; and he was preaching the word to them. 3 And they came, bringing to him a paralytic carried by four men. 4 And when they could not get near him because of the crowd, they removed the roof above him; and when they had made an opening, they let down the pallet on which the paralytic lay. 5 And when Jesus saw their faith, he said to the paralytic, "My son, your sins are forgiven." 6 Now some of the scribes were sitting there, questioning in their hearts. 7 "Why does this man speak thus? It is blasphemy! Who can forgive sins but God alone?" 8 And immediately Jesus, perceiving in his spirit that they thus questioned within themselves, said to them, "Why do you question thus in your hearts? 9 Which is easier, to say to the paralytic, 'Your sins are forgiven,' or to say, 'Rise, take up your pallet and walk'? 10 But that you may know that the Son of man has authority on earth to forgive sins"—he said to the paralytic— 11 "I say to you, rise, take up your pallet and go home." 12 And he rose, and immediately took up the pallet and went out before them all; so that they were all amazed and glorified God, saying, "We never saw anything like this!"

Up to this point Mark has recounted stories that have demonstrated the rising fame of Jesus and his appeal to great crowds of people. There is no change in this regard: rather, Jesus continued to attract the multitudes. But now begins a strong new note, discordant and mounting in anger. Jesus begins to face the major opposition of Jewish leaders, especially the religious teachers or scribes.

The first incident in these "conflict" narratives tells of the healing of a paralyzed man. Interwoven with the miracle of healing is a sharp dispute over Jesus' right to forgive sins.

In accord with his assertion that Jesus "could no longer openly enter a town" (1:45), Mark implies that he quietly slipped back into Capernaum after some days' interval. ***He was at home:*** this translation is probably correct. From this phrase it is possible, but not certain, to conclude: that Jesus made Capernaum his headquarters for a Galilean ministry; that the home was that of Simon Peter (cf. 1:29); and that the story of this healing was recalled from the preaching of the apostle.

How vivid the description of the crowd! The little house crammed and the doorway jammed with people: there was no room anywhere. Jesus was ***preaching the word to them.*** Mark has yet given no sample of Jesus' teaching except the summary statement in 1:15.

How could the plight of a paralyzed man ever be brought to Jesus' attention? Four men had carried the paralytic to the house. Others (for example, his parents) may very well have come with them; this is the natural interpretation of the language. But the entranceway was blocked.

The house had, no doubt, the common external stairway leading to a flat roof. The construction of the roof was probably of poles across the space between the walls, with smaller sticks and reeds forming a network across them. This was covered with some kind of matting and hardened earth. (Luke 5:19 assumes a different kind of construction, with which he would likely have been more familiar.) To tear open the roof would not have been difficult to do, nor would the task of repair have been major. We may well assume that the crowd below made some room because of the shower of debris descending upon them.

The paralytic had been brought to Jesus in hope that he would be healed. Healing and forgiveness are in the Gospel accounts often specifically related to faith. Nor is the faith spoken of always the faith of the person in need of healing: compare 7:24–30; 9:14–29.

Your sins are forgiven. This is a strange word from Jesus, compared to the other incidents of healing. It is so unexpected and different from accounts of his other cures that many have concluded that verses 5*b*–10 were a separate story. If this is true, as it may be, the reason for uniting the two stories would have been the interest of the early Christian communities in the Master's example and authority as they might be applied to contemporary and acute spiritual needs.[21]

According to the commonly held Hebrew viewpoint, one needed to seek divine forgiveness before he could expect to be cured. It was even said that no one got up from his sickbed until all his sins were forgiven. However, there is no indication that Jesus' healing was on this basis.

The rabbis believed that God was forgiving and merciful. They held that (1) only God could forgive and that (2) God would forgive any man who was truly sorry for his sin, confessed it, and turned away from it to act in accord with God's righteousness. However, they did expect evidence of this repentance. John the Baptist seems to have preached in accord with this principle (cf. Luke 3:10–15), but Mark gives no sample of John's preaching of repentance).

The guardians of acceptable religious teaching took offense at the words of Jesus. He was daring to claim the prerogatives of God. The claim innate to Jesus' word is that through Jesus God is speaking and acting. Here is no prophet saying, The word of the Lord came to me. Here is one speaking as though his own voice is that of God, forgiving a sinner without even waiting for evidence of repentance.

To the scribes this was ***blasphemy.*** The word commonly refers to slanderous or abusive language in general. Here the scribes believed that Jesus had wrongly assumed for himself what belongs to God and therefore had spoken blasphemously. What could be more slanderous than for a man to speak as though authority which is God's alone belongs really to himself?

Mark would have us know that Jesus did have this divine authority—and so power over the demonic realm and the prerogative to heal the breach between God and man. But he wanted his readers also to understand that the religious teachers of the Jewish people did not perceive the true nature of Jesus, nor could they accept his claims. This motif is recurrent in the Markan presentation; its most comprehensive expression is in 4:10–12.

The utter disapproval of the scribes was unspoken, but Jesus was perceptive enough to recognize their objection. His answer was also a question: ***Which is easier,*** to tell this man he is forgiven or to heal him?

The question was rhetorical. If the words were but empty sounds, mirages to encourage and then stifle a man's spirit, of course it would be easier to say, You are forgiven. But if they are true and real!

Yet this account is very different from the usual accounts of Jesus' healings. Elsewhere Jesus refused to give signs to the people in order to prove who he was and that he had the right to act and speak as he did (Matt. 12:38–42; Luke 11:29; cf.

[21] Cf. especially Taylor, pp. 191 f.; and Rawlinson, p. 25. F. C. Grant in *The Interpreter's Bible* on Mark agrees, but confesses that without 5*b*–10 the story loses in dramatic quality. William Manson, *Jesus the Messiah* (Philadelphia: Westminster, 1946), pp. 66–68, suggests that Jesus forgave the man's sins according to the original story (which would be 1–5, 12), and that as a result of the forgiveness his paralysis was cured. On the question of the rabbinic doctrine of forgiveness, see G. F. Moore, *Judaism,* I, 500–20.

Mark 8:11–12). Here the recovery of the man becomes a proof of Jesus' authority to forgive sins. The telling of the story in this way, however, would be most forceful in preaching the truth about Jesus. Certainly the disciples regarded the miracles as proofs of Jesus' identity. Certainly also the word of forgiveness is thoroughly consonant with Jesus' nature.

Jesus here calls himself *the Son of man.* The use of this title might very well have been understood as meaning simply "man," an ordinary person (cf. Ezek. 2:1; 3:1). But Mark understood the name to mean the heavenly Son of man spoken of in Daniel 7:13–28. In Mark, the Son of man will come with the clouds of heaven to execute judgment (8:38), and he has during his ministry on earth the full authority of God to forgive and to blame. In 14:62, Jesus' reply to the high priest identifies the Son of man with "the Christ, the Son of the Blessed."

Not to the early Christians, then, but to the crowds who heard Jesus, the name *Son of man* would have borne a certain mystery. They would have been baffled by Jesus' use of this title as descriptive of himself. Most of the Markan occurrences of the title are concerned with Jesus' teaching that he must suffer, that he will be rejected and put to death, and that he will be raised (8:31; 9:31; 10:33,45; 14:21,41). In regard to Jesus' passion, the Old Testament background is more nearly that of the Suffering Servant in Isaiah 40—66 than the passages about the Son of man in Daniel.

Jesus' authority to forgive sins was signaled by the healing of the paralytic. The cured man arose, picked up his pallet, and the crowd made an aisle for him to leave. Nothing is said further of the scribes at this point; Mark is building toward the angry climax of 3:6, where a plot to destroy Jesus has its beginning.

The people *were all amazed.* The verb is very strong, the same one translated in 3:21, "He is beside himself." How could what they had seen really have been? Mark insists that they *glorified God,* but he does not imply that they perceived Jesus' claims with any clarity.

b. The Tax Collector: to Seek and to Befriend (2:13–17)

13 He went out again beside the sea; and all
the crowd gathered about him, and he taught
them. 14 And as he passed on, he saw Levi the
son of Alphaeus sitting at the tax office, and he
said to him, "Follow me." And he rose and
followed him.
15 And as he sat at table in his house, many
tax collectors and sinners were sitting with
Jesus and his disciples; for there were many
who followed him. 16 And the scribes of the
Pharisees, when they saw that he was eating
with sinners and tax collectors, said to his
disciples, "Why does he eat with tax collectors
and sinners?" 17 And when Jesus heard it, he
said to them, "Those who are well have no
need of a physician, but those who are sick; I
came not to call the righteous, but sinners."

The story of the call of the first four disciples (1:16–20) has a notable number of parallels with the call of Levi, the tax collector. A statement of Jesus' teaching, a place by Galilee, the invitation, and the response are all very similar.

There is one marked difference. The first men were more suitable disciples from the point of view of Jewish religionists. It is true that they were common people. They did not keep the law fully or know all its requirements. Their act of pulling grain on the sabbath was probably born of habit, not deliberate violation (2:23).

On the other hand, the tax collector was regarded as grossly irreverent and unsuited for godly discipleship. For Jesus to invite such a person to become an intimate disciple was a sharp departure from accepted conduct.

Levi the son of Alphaeus is identified in the Gospel of Matthew as being that Matthew who was one of the twelve (cf. 9:9; 10:3). Mark apparently has no such information, for he includes Matthew (but not Levi) in his listing (3:16–19), and in no way identifies the two. James the son of Alphaeus is also one of the apostles, but Mark gives no hint of any kinship with Levi, nor does the Gospel of Matthew

Some of our questions must remain unanswered.

The tax office was probably one which collected dues from those transporting goods to and through Capernaum. The collectors would have been serving under Herod Antipas, the tetrarch of that area. The translation "publicans" (KJV) is more accurately applied to a different and more affluent office, for *publicani* were men to whom tax collections were farmed out. That the tax collectors often took unfair advantage is evident from the preaching of John (Luke 3:12–13) and the confession of Zacchaeus (Luke 19:8).

When Levi ***rose and followed*** Jesus, like Simon and Andrew he did not ignore his home and old relationships. To his house (at least as Luke understands it; the text of Mark is ambiguous) he invited Jesus, the other disciples, and many people who had much in common with himself. Many of these tax collectors and sinners, Mark tells us, were among the throngs which crowded Jesus. The word ***followed*** clearly affirms a relationship of disciples to Teacher.

The name ***sinners*** when coupled with tax collectors probably meant simply irreligious people, persons who ignored or consistently violated the religious regulations of the stricter Jewish people. The emphasis in the word here is not on morals, though neither the word nor the habits of tax collectors can possibly exclude this idea. Of course, many of these people were dishonest and corrupt. But the bitter alienation from the scribes and Pharisees came because they ignored the synagogue, together with the Mosaic Law and its interpretation, and because they cooperated with oppressive and heathen foreigners. To the orthodox Jew they were people who said in their hearts, "There is no God" (Psalm 14:1).

The scribes of the Pharisees were the Jewish teachers who subscribed to the viewpoints of the Pharisaic party. This party was by far the most influential among the Jewish people in Jesus' day, even though the high priesthood is identified with the Sadducees. The party arose in the second century B.C. Pharisees were the spiritual descendants of the people known as the Hasidim, who had successfully aided the Maccabean revolt and who stood for strict upholding of the Law of Moses and against any compromise with other religious influences.

In general, the Pharisaic influence remained dominant in the synagogues, and the New Testament throughout reflects the continuing difficulties between the emerging Christian churches and the Jewish congregations. Some Pharisees became believers in Christ, but they found it very difficult to accept Gentiles, tax collectors, or sinners on an equal basis, with genuine brotherhood and without strict enforcement of the Old Testament law. See especially Acts 15:5 ff.; Galatians 2:11 ff.; and Acts 10:44–48.

The Pharisees believed that God's will had been expressed fully in the Law as they interpreted it. They treated the tax collector and the sinner as religious outcasts, and could not understand why Jesus would eat with such people. Yet they, too, would have said, God will forgive any of these who will repent. Repentance to them would have meant evidence of change and the adherence to the Law's regulations.

What, then, is the difference between their concepts and the good news that Jesus brought? A. M. Hunter has put it clearly: "The new thing in Christianity is not the doctrine that God saves sinners. No Jew would have denied that. It is the assertion 'that God loves and saves them *as sinners* without waiting for them to become righteous and deserving of salvation.' "[22]

The scribes from their viewpoint could not help but ask, ***Why does he eat with tax collectors and sinners?***

If, as they held, man owes unquestioning obedience to God, and if, as the Old Testament clearly taught, God's commands included tithing and ritual cleanness, how could a true and godly man eat at Levi's house? Dining with tax collectors involved the risk of eating food which had been (ac-

[22] *The Gospel According to St. Mark* (New York: Collier, 1962), pp. 41 f.

cording to the Law) improperly prepared and/or on which no tithes had been paid. Moreover, they considered that close contact with these sinners might very well infect their own desires, and even a Pharisee might be tempted to be like these men who ignored God's will.

Jesus' conduct and his defense reflected a very different view of the call and mercy of God. The God of the Lord Jesus is opposed to the "social and religious ostracism" (Branscomb) which is inherent in the Pharisees' way of life. No matter how secular or evil a man might be, he is nonetheless within God's concern and in need of God's rule. Jesus' invitation was for sinners. The kingdom which was now at hand in Jesus was surely for them too.

Whether the question was expressed openly or not, the scribes would have to inquire, Who does he think he is, that he treats the Law so lightly and its precepts as morally insignificant? Jesus' answer to their unspoken question was not merely the setting forth of a new moral principle or a fresh interpretation of the divine purpose. When he identified himself as a ***physician*** for ***those who are sick*** and said ***I came . . . to call . . . sinners,*** he was giving voice to the new situation that in God's providence had come. The time was fulfilled. The kingdom had drawn near. The calling of sinners was part of the good news, and it was part of the work of God's King to redeem them from evil's power.

When Jesus said that he ***came not to call the righteous,*** we ought not to suppose he was praising the scribes as being righteous. There was irony in his use of the word.[23] To him it was the grossest misunderstanding of God's mercy to ostracize men who were regarded as sinners, or to suppose God had ceased to care for them.

[23] Nineham (pp. 97 f.) disagrees, and insists on taking the phrase literally. He thinks the words may be "a comment of the early Church referred back to the life of Jesus." He points out that but few of the righteous people of the Jewish nation (Pharisees, scribes, etc.) became Christians, while his followers were mainly of the people called "sinners." However, the Gospel accounts show that Jesus ate also in the homes of Pharisees, and he taught regularly in the synagogues where their ideas were dominant. He surely counted them also as in need of his message and power.

c. The Custom of Fasting: New Cloth and New Wine (*2:18–22*)

**18 Now John's disciples and the Pharisees
were fasting; and people came and said to him,
"Why do John's disciples and the disciples of
the Pharisees fast, but your disciples do not
fast?" 19 And Jesus said to them, "Can the
wedding guests fast while the bridegroom is
with them? As long as they have the bridegroom with them, they cannot fast. 20 The days
will come, when the bridegroom is taken away
from them, and then they will fast in that day.
21 No one sews a piece of unshrunk cloth on an
old garment; if he does, the patch tears away
from it, the new from the old, and a worse tear
is made. 22 And no one puts new wine into old
wineskins; if he does, the wine will burst the
skins, and the wine is lost, and so are the skins;
but new wine is for fresh skins."**

Fasting was enjoined by the Law only once a year, on the Day of Atonement (Lev. 16:29–30). Among the more religious Jews the custom was much more in evidence. In the parable of the Pharisee and the publican Jesus included in the Pharisee's proud boast, "I fast twice a week."

From the original connection of fasting with the Day of Atonement, it is obvious that fasting was regarded as an expression of sorrow for sin. The custom was also followed by many during periods of mourning. Mark does not have any details of the setting of this incident, but a particular period of fasting was apparently going on. Some commentators suggest that John's disciples (in the original context) were mourning because of the arrest or the death (narrated later) of their teacher. But it is quite likely that John's disciples followed the customs of the Pharisees.

Jesus nowhere requires of his followers that they fast. He did denounce the use of fasting as a public display of piety and instructed his disciples, whenever they might fast, to be sure they were motivated by a godly purpose (Matt. 6:16–18).

Perhaps the Christians for whom Mark

was writing fasted on occasion. The concluding word in verse 20 ***then they will fast in that day*** may reflect the custom in the churches he knew. We know that the Christians of the early second century practiced fasting. In the Didache (or Teaching of the Twelve Apostles), Christians are instructed to fast as well as pray for their enemies, and to fast also in connection with baptism. The spirit of Jesus' teaching is surely missed, however, in the Didache's further warning not to fast on Mondays and Thursdays with the hypocrites (i.e., the Jews), but on Wednesdays and Fridays! (1,7,8)

The phrase ***disciples of the Pharisees*** is strange, for not the ordinary Pharisees but only their teachers would have disciples. It seems best to understand the phrase as meaning the people who followed the Pharisaic practice in fasting, whether or not they were actually members of the party.

The question put to Jesus sought to know why his disciples did not follow the well established religious custom of his day. The attack is directed at his disciples, and is the more cutting for this reason. It is as if they say, What you do yourself may be your business, but how dare you lead your disciples into such careless habits? Jesus' answer is a parable, using the figure of the prolonged feasting that preceded a wedding. A wedding period is a time of joy. It would be utterly inappropriate to mourn and fast during such an occasion. Normally, of course, the wedding guests would not mourn after the marriage either!

However, ***the bridegroom*** who was ***with them*** in this instance was Jesus himself. Whatever the original context, this is surely the meaning here. The Davidic king is sometimes pictured as a bridegroom (see especially Psalm 45). Mark's readers would perhaps understand the allusion in this way. They would surely understand also that the words, ***The days will come, when the bridegroom is taken away from them,*** were fulfilled in his death. The King has come announcing forgiveness of sins, acceptance into God's kingdom, good news; there will come a day of atonement, a time of sorrow, a time when the King dies "for our sins in accordance with the scriptures" (1 Cor. 15:3).

The two parables which follow in verses 21–22 speak to the larger problem raised by the question in verse 18. Why did Jesus' followers not observe the religious customs of their contemporaries? Jesus' answer was that his new message was too vibrant and different to be fitted into the old patterns or institutions. He did not so much condemn the old as treat it as having passed its useful period.

New cloth which has not been preshrunk cannot make a satisfactory patch for a torn garment that has been washed over and over. No more did Jesus, who had come preaching that the kingdom of God has drawn near, intend merely to patch up existing institutions. The continuity of Jesus with the old covenant was not in its patterns of expression. The continuity is present in the nature of the God who revealed himself through Israel and who seeks man's freedom from evil and allegiance to himself.

Wineskins were made from whole goat hides: similar containers are still in use today. The animal was skinned from the neck, by severing the legs. The openings were tied off, and the skin was tanned properly. Naturally, old skins would be brittle and would burst under the pressure of fermentation. Jesus' word is like ***new wine;*** their traditions so rigid and rutted were like brittle wineskins. The two are not compatible.

When Jesus first told these parables, they would have been applied to such customs as fasting and various requirements of the oral law, including perhaps some aspects of sabbath observance. By Mark's time Christians might well understand them also to apply to such matters as circumcision, eating of certain foods, Temple worship, or worship with non-Christian Jews in the synagogues.

The truth of these parables must not be limited to other times and circumstances.

The nature of the message of Jesus requires fresh wineskins in every generation. These parables affirm that there is nothing untouchable in custom or tradition, or in the structure of an institutional church. Nothing must be so sacred as to hamper the forgiveness of a merciful God or restrain the practice of Christian love toward one's fellowmen.

The phrasing of these parables makes their message a warning. "The point of these parables," says Branscomb, "seems rather to be the damage which the new does to the old than the opposite." So if we try to fit the freedom and calling of Jesus into our old patterns and institutions, we shall not only miss what Jesus would do for us, we shall destroy also what we have had before. It is true that the old garment and the aged wineskin had in the nature of things already served their useful time. But no one can become a true disciple if he tries also to hold on to his old life (8:34–35).

d. Sabbath Observance: Man's Need and God's Purpose (*2:23–28*)

23 One sabbath he was going through the grainfields; and as they made their way his disciples began to pluck ears of grain. 24 And the Pharisees said to him, "Look, why are they doing what is not lawful on the sabbath?" 25 And he said to them, "Have you never read what David did, when he was in need and was hungry, he and those who were with him: 26 how he entered the house of God, when Abiathar was high priest, and ate the bread of the Presence, which it is not lawful for any but the priests to eat, and also gave it to those who were with him?" 27 And he said to them, "The sabbath was made for man, not man for the sabbath; 28 so the Son of man is lord even of the sabbath."

Much more significant to Judaism than fasting was the observance of the sabbath. The sacredness of the day was traced back to God's creative work (Gen. 2:1–3), and the charge to keep the sabbath day holy is one of the Ten Commandments (Ex. 20:8–11).

What the written Law required for sabbath observance was expressed in rather general terms. There were detailed rules interpreting the Law, making exact what was and what was not a violation. These rules were part of the oral law, the sacred tradition handed down through the scribes. The scribes themselves acknowledged this fact. In the Mishnah, the second-century codification of these traditions, it is confessed that the rules about sabbath observance are "as mountains hanging by a hair," because the pertinent teaching in the Law is so scanty and the rules so many.

The observance of the sabbath had been maintained by the Jewish people at heavy cost. In the second century B.C. pious Jews in defense of their faith refused to bear arms on the sabbath, even to protect themselves (1 Maccabees 2:32–38). Keeping the sabbath became both religious and patriotic. The penalties for its violation were very severe: excommunication from the sacred community of Israel or even death (Ex. 31:14), though we are uncertain how often enforcement may have been by capital punishment. Sometime prior to A.D. 70 violators of the sabbath were allowed to make amends by the sacrifice of a sin offering.

In the oral law there were 39 kinds of labor prohibited on the sabbath, with a multitude of regulations under each. While the number is overwhelming and the burden of keeping them all seems intolerable to modern ears, it was nevertheless true that for many of the Jewish people sabbath observance was a joyful custom. Fasting (a sign of mourning) was prohibited on the sabbath. Yet for others of the Hebrew people—the demon-possessed (1:23), persons afflicted like the man with a withered hand (3:1), the hungry, the wretched, the needy, and to some degree those who were classified as "sinners"—the sabbath day could hardly have signified rest and thanksgiving.

As the disciples ***made their way*** (along a path, for the words do not imply careless trampling of grain) they pulled a little ripened wheat or barley to eat. The Law expressly allowed this (see Deut. 23:25), for there was no real damage to the crop and the Law often made special provisions for the poor or those who might be in need. However, by plucking the grain on the sabbath they were "reaping," one of the 39 kinds of labor forbidden on the holy day. By rubbing in their hands what they had pulled they violated a second rule, for this was a form of "threshing." To the Jew devoted to his nation and its heritage, the disciples' action was irresponsible and irreverent, because it was contrary to their understanding of the sabbath.

Jesus defended his disciples by reference to the action of David, who had led his men to eat bread which had been offered in sacrifice and was reserved for the priests (1 Sam. 21:1–6). The high priest at the time was Ahimelech, not Abiathar. No entirely satisfying explanation for this discrepancy has been set forth: it may have been an error of a very early copyist, for the name of Abiathar would have been better known than that of his father.

The point of the scriptural analogy is that the Law was rightly broken for the sake of men in need. David had not been wrong to do so; nor had the hungering disciples. The Law was intended, from Jesus' point of view, to be helpful and redemptive for man, not restrictive of his joy and fulfilment. The teaching about the sabbath was given for man's sake. Man in his need must not be defrauded by adherence to a law which was intended by God to help man.

T. W. Manson thinks that Jesus and his disciples were engaged in the missionary work of the kingdom, and were not simply taking "a quiet Sabbath afternoon stroll." He is confident that Jesus did not break the sabbath lightly, "but because 'the King's business required haste'; because the service of the Kingdom of God and the warfare against the kingdom of Satan must go on day in and day out; because the business on which God had sent Him was the most important business in the world." [24]

[24] Major, Manson, and Wright, pp. 481 f. For further discussion of the sabbath see the article by J. Morgenstern, "Sabbath," in *The Interpreter's Dictionary of the Bible,* IV, 135–41.

We cannot know whether Jesus' remarks in verses 27–28 were made in connection with this particular incident. Rawlinson and Taylor both think these words were added to the narrative because they are concerned also with the sabbath. Rawlinson thinks that verse 28 is best understood as a Christian interpretive addition (cf. Mark 7:19). Certainly verse 27 is an appropriate statement in general principle of the truth expressed in Jesus' use of the Scripture about David: ***The sabbath was made for man, not man for the sabbath.*** It summarizes a dynamic attitude toward religious practices.

The concluding verse goes beyond this, and asserts the lordship of the Son of man over the sabbath. ***Son of man*** in this context in Jesus' day would be understood to mean simply a man, or a representative man. But for the early Christians and according to Mark's usage in general the title Son of man refers only to Jesus, and to him as the heavenly Son of man anticipated in Daniel (cf. above on 2:10). We must conclude therefore that, in Mark's understanding, Jesus claimed for himself, as Son of man, authority over the sabbath, just as he claimed authority to forgive sins in healing the paralytic (2:7–10).

We may further judge that the people of the early churches, for whom Mark wrote, found in this statement support for turning away from the sabbath observances of the Jewish people and also freedom to concentrate their worship on the first day of the week. There is a specific allusion to the Lord's Day in the New Testament (Rev. 1:10), but the first clear and absolute rejection of the sabbath in favor of an observance of the Lord's Day is found in Ignatius' *Epistle to the Magnesians* (*ca.* A.D. 110). Too often in those early years the practice of the Lord's Day was patterned after the scribal teaching about the sabbath rather than after Jesus' own spirit. To transfer the sabbath rules to the Lord's Day is forbiddingly similar to pouring new wine into old wineskins. If he is Lord of the sabbath, is not the Son of man Lord also of his own day?

e. Sabbath Observance: to Do Good and to Save Life (3:1–6)

1 Again he entered the synagogue, and a
man was there who had a withered hand.
2 And they watched him, to see whether he
would heal him on the sabbath, so that they
might accuse him. 3 And he said to the man
who had the withered hand, "Come here."
4 And he said to them, "Is it lawful on the
sabbath to do good or to do harm, to save life
or to kill?" But they were silent. 5 And he
looked around at them with anger, grieved at
their hardness of heart, and said to the man,
"Stretch out your hand." He stretched it out,
and his hand was restored. 6 The Pharisees
went out, and immediately held counsel with
the Herodians against him, how to destroy him.

In the preceding paragraph, it has been affirmed that (1) sabbath laws must be regarded as secondary to man's needs and that (2) as Son of man Jesus had full authority over the sabbath. But it had been the disciples and not Jesus who had defied the sabbath laws by plucking the grain. Now the offended Pharisees looked for clear evidence of Jesus' own guilt.

When the sabbath came, Jesus again ***entered the synagogue.*** Perhaps the synagogue in Capernaum is intended; but the definite article is not present in some of our best manuscripts. Taylor is probably right in interpreting the phrase as parallel to our idiom, He went to church. Perhaps the man ***who had a withered hand*** had come to the synagogue in hope of seeing Jesus and gaining his help. We cannot know. It is also plausible that the man came regularly to that synagogue. We have no reason to suppose that the afflicted person was party to the vindictive plans of those hostile to Jesus.

According to the Gospel to the Hebrews, the man had been a stonemason. "I was a mason seeking a livelihood with my hands: I pray thee, Jesus, to restore me mine health, that I may not beg meanly for my food." [25]

[25] M. R. James, *The Apocryphal N. T.* (Oxford: Clarendon, 1945), pp. 4 f. The word withered (in v. 1, not v. 3) is in form a perfect passive participle, and its use implies that the defect was not present at birth (the hand "had become withered").

They watched him. The verb is particularly vivid and may carry the connotation to watch with ulterior and malicious motive. In any case, they were keeping a very close eye on him.

Who were ***they?*** The subject has no clear antecedent, but because of the purpose expressed (***so that they might accuse him***) we are surely justified in understanding it to refer to the Pharisees (cf. v. 6) and their associates. They were actually watching in hope that he would heal on the sabbath and damn himself by his lawbreaking.

Healing on the sabbath was regarded as lawful only when life itself was in danger. Otherwise, physicians were required to confine their services to the other six days (cf. Luke 13:14).

Interest in this story is centered on three points. The first is, of course, the healing of the unfortunate man. The second is more focal: Jesus taught that it is right to do good on the sabbath. The third, however, is the chief emphasis. Opposition to Jesus, so strong as to put his life in jeopardy, came because of men's ***hardness of heart.*** They were blinded to the good news; they were bound hopelessly captive in the ruts of their own minds and in the hardness and evil of their own hearts.

No question was raised about whether Jesus could heal the man. ***Come here*** (literally, "rise into the midst"), he ordered; and, afterwards, ***Stretch out your hand.*** The hand was restored. Unlike the previous stories of healing, however, there was no word of praise to God, no amazement in the crowd, no joy expressed—only the cold, calculating hostility of Jesus' enemies.

What did Jesus teach as he healed this man on the sabbath? To do good, rather than harm, and to save life, rather than to kill? Swete and Rawlinson consider the whole story and reason from verse 6 that Jesus was accusing his enemies of breaking the sabbath, rather than himself. Were they not plotting to do harm and even to kill?

As the story is told, however, the teaching of Jesus is simply that it cannot be against God's law to do good, even on the sabbath. Moreover, to let the opportunity to do good slip by is itself an evil—would this not be to do harm? (Cf. James 4:17.) True, the man's life does not appear to have been in danger; but his livelihood and his sense of usefulness were surely in jeopardy. What does it mean ***to save life*** if it does not mean to redeem a man to a meaningful existence?

The onlookers' response to Jesus was only silence. His questions did not suggest any answer they were willing to give, and their own questions remained exasperatingly unanswered. Does this man consider himself above Moses and the law of God? By what right does he dare to ignore the law and custom of the holy sabbath? Does not any man who would wilfully break the sabbath deserve the enmity of every God-fearing person?

Jesus looked at the hostile eyes around him ***with anger.*** This is the only place in the Gospels in which this quality is ascribed to Jesus. "Wrath" (the Greek word used is identical) is spoken of in connection with future judgment (Matt. 3:7; Luke 3:7; cf. Luke 21:23) and also in terms of that living death present in the man who rejects the lordship of Jesus (John 3:36). The wrath of God as described in Romans 1:18—2:11 is a present reality and it culminates in future ruin: it is not, however, a personal emotion but a moral principle at work in man and in the world.

Matthew and Luke, who follow Mark's narrative at this point, leave out the word anger, apparently because they were unwilling to ascribe this emotion to Jesus (Taylor). We need not suppose that Jesus lost his temper. Neither ought we to ignore his oneness with us as human beings. But what word is more appropriate than "wrath" to describe what Jesus must have felt within himself because of the callous but self-righteous indifference of man toward his fellowman?

The word ***anger*** must be understood in connection with the following words: Jesus was ***grieved at their hardness of heart.*** According to the passage in Romans 1:18–32, the wrath (or anger) of God followed this pattern: (1) men who knew God nevertheless did not honor him but followed their own wilful thoughts; (2) this resulted in futile thinking: "their senseless minds were darkened" (v. 21); (3) God gave them up to themselves, their own choices, their own baseness; (4) they received "in their own persons the due penalty for their error" (v. 27); and (5) they came finally, no matter what they may have understood earlier to be right, blindly to approve of evil (v. 32). This description of the workings of God's wrath is also a description of ***hardness of heart.***

The heart was the seat of understanding as the ancients spoke of it. ***Hardness*** etymologically is from the verb which means to petrify. But J. A. Robinson, in his *Commentary on Ephesians* (pp. 264–74), has shown that ***hardness of heart*** should be understood as intellectual blindness. Still, it is that kind of blindness which wrongly but consistently claims, We see, we see! (Cf. John 9:40–41.)

The mystery of Jesus' identity remained hidden from these people because of this very hardness of heart. (See Mark 4:10–12.) This blindness is at the core of the struggle of God's Son with all the powers of evil. Even the disciples are not totally exempt (8:17).

In 2:1—3:6 Mark has narrated five stories of conflict between Jesus and the Pharisaic scribes. In every case the opposition to Jesus rested on a fundamental inability to discern who Jesus was, that in him the kingdom of God had drawn near, and that he was truly sovereign over the revered Law and custom. If 3:6 is the close of the story of Jesus' healing on the sabbath, it is also the conclusion of the entire section. As far as Mark is concerned, it is their hardness of heart, their blindness, which led them to oppose Jesus even unto death.

The Pharisees went out from the synagogue and ***held counsel with the Herodians*** against Jesus. We do not know precisely who the Herodians were. They may have been influential supporters of Herod Antipas, but if so would not have been normally allied with the Pharisees. As Taylor notes, however, common hostility creates strange unions. The ancient Jewish historian Josephus referred to "men who were thoughtful of Herod's interests," but whether this was a specific and continuing group after his death (the Herod referred to died in 4 B.C.) is unproved.

2. *The Expanding Ministry and Instruction of the Twelve* (*3:7—5:43*)

(*1*) *The Crowds by the Lake* (*3:7–12*)

7 Jesus withdrew with his disciples to the sea, and a great multitude from Galilee followed; also from Judea 8 and Jerusalem and Idumea and from beyond the Jordan and from about Tyre and Sidon a great multitude, hearing all that he did, came to him. 9 And he told his disciples to have a boat ready for him because of the crowd, lest they should crush him; 10 for he had healed many, so that all who had diseases pressed upon him to touch him. 11 And whenever the unclean spirits beheld him, they fell down before him and cried out, "You are the Son of God." 12 And he strictly ordered them not to make him known.

The Markan development of the gospel story has many facets, and they overlap with one another so that no attempted outline is entirely satisfying. What must always be in the mind of the reader is the first summary of Jesus' preaching: the decisive hour in history has come, for the kingdom of God has drawn near in the person of Jesus (1:14–15). The motifs of the first section (1:14—3:6)—the authority manifest in Jesus, his growing fame, and the hardening opposition—continue unabated into the following chapters. As Rawlinson puts it, "The more the scribes opposed our Lord, the more the people flocked to him."

In the section that begins with 3:7 the Galilean ministry reached its height. Much more of the teaching of Jesus is recorded, both in response to his enemies and in the parables. The twelve especially began to comprehend more clearly who Jesus was. However, the blind hostility of the scribes increased, and the shallow understanding of the multitudes became more and more evident.

The multitude that followed came from a much larger area than had been suggested earlier. Jesus' fame had spread. They were not only Galileans but people from ***Judea and Jerusalem*** (cf. the description of the Baptist's crowd in 1:5). They came from Idumea too, the homeland of the Herods, which lay south of Judea. Idumeans were not always regarded as truly Jewish, because their forebears had been forced by the Maccabean king John Hyrcanus to accept circumcision and the Hebrew faith (*ca.* 110 B.C.). Some of the multitude came ***from beyond the Jordan,*** i.e., from Perea to the east, and others ***from about Tyre and Sidon,*** the lands to the north. Nothing is said of Samaria: Johnson suggests that (unlike Luke and John) Mark did not know of a Samaritan mission. But Mark's description seems intended only to describe the crowd as huge and as including persons from afar.

In response to his request his disciples had a small boat ready for his use, so that he might have some relief from the crowd's pressure.

The people who were diseased were anxious ***to touch him.*** See 1:40–41, where Jesus touched the leper; and the story of the woman who touched Jesus' garment (5:24–34). In Luke's parallel passage (6:19), the explanation is that "power came forth from him." Another Markan summary (6:53–56) reflects the same understanding about his healings: people brought their sick to "the market places, and besought him that they might touch even the fringe of his garment; and as many as touched it were made well."

The word translated ***diseases*** in verse 10 (plagues in KJV) is from a root that means to whip or scourge. In the Greek Old Testament it sometimes referred to sufferings sent from God. But the word by now had become a general term for illnesses, and there is no hint of their presence being caused by any divine punishment. On the contrary, Jesus was constantly at war with these human afflictions.

The ***unclean spirits,*** just as formerly, recognized Jesus and succumbed to his authority. (See discussion on 1:23–26,34.) Their previous name for Jesus had been the Holy One of God. Now they fell down before the authority of one they identified as ***the Son of God.*** It is doubtful that Mark intended any special distinction between the two titles.

Carrington refuses to "take seriously the 'theology' of these demented souls," though he acknowledges Mark's emphasis on their homage. But it seems perfectly clear that Mark regarded their outcries as a genuine witness to the divinity of Jesus. Jesus was at war with them and their chief, as is clear from 3:20–30. Their power is one symptom of the evil that enslaves men, and only the power of God, with whom they were identifying Jesus, was able to overcome them. Carrington insists that Jesus did not accept "the popular views about demon-possession." On the contrary, all the evidence shows that Jesus never hinted at correcting these views but always exercised his ministry within the world view of the first century (cf. Carrington, pp. 80 f.).

(2) *The Appointment of the Twelve* (3:13–19a)

[13] And he went up into the hills, and called to him those whom he desired; and they came to him. [14] And he appointed twelve, to be with him, and to be sent out to preach [15] and have authority to cast out demons: [16] Simon whom he surnamed Peter; [17] James the son of Zebedee and John the brother of James, whom he surnamed Boanerges, that is, sons of thunder; [18] Andrew, and Philip, and Bartholomew, and Matthew, and Thomas, and James the son of Alphaeus, and Thaddaeus, and Simon the Cananaean, [19] and Judas Iscariot, who betrayed him.

The training of the twelve is an important element in all four Gospels. For the Synoptic writers a climax in the disciples' development was reached at Caesarea Philippi with the confession of Jesus as Christ. (Cf. 8:27–30; Matt. 16:13–20; and Luke 9:18–22. In John 6:66–71 note similarities with the Synoptic passages.) Jesus' work in teaching his followers continued after that event. Indeed, Luke holds that Jesus' instruction was considerable and distinctive during his resurrection appearances (Luke 24:32,44–49; cf. Acts 1:3).

According to Mark, Jesus already had called certain men as disciples (1:16–20; 2:13–14). Now he recounts Jesus' calling of the twelve men who will occupy a special place in his company.

He went up into the hills. This is probably the best translation, even though the Greek text literally means "the mountain." The statement is more than a casual geographical note: the mountaintop is traditionally the setting for solemn, divine acts. Mount Sinai is only the best known of many examples; compare God's revelation of himself on Mount Carmel in answer to Elijah's prayer. Nineham correctly reminds us of our Lord's "involvement in the thought-forms of his day." Something significant was about to occur, something of importance to the divine purpose. Luke 6:12 makes this point more explicit by telling us that Jesus prayed all night before choosing the twelve.

Jesus invited ***those whom he desired.*** The initiative lay not with the disciples but with the Master. Verse 13 reminds us that we must think of many more disciples than the inner circle Jesus was about to choose. The twelve will be his closest associates; we may suppose that the others were in his company often but not continually.

The old translation "ordained" (KJV) has connotations in English that are not present in the Greek. ***He appointed twelve.***[26] The verb itself is not the usual word for appoint but one found often with this meaning in the Greek translation of the Old Testament. Taylor calls this usage "translation Greek." It certainly reflects the Palestinian origin of Mark's material, no matter if he is writing in far-off Italy.

Why ***twelve?*** Most commentators agree

[26] Some of our best ancient manuscripts add "whom he named apostles," and TEV follows this text. However, most commentators believe the words are those of an early copyist who has taken them from Luke 6:13. The verb "to be sent out" in verse 14 has the same root, but would denote only a function, not an office.

that the number was selected to correspond with the twelve tribes of Israel. Johnson warns us that the number may be coincidental, rather than purposeful. But there is no question that the early church regarded these men as symbolic leaders in the new Israel (cf. Matt. 19:28; Luke 22:30).[27] The choice of twelve also has a parallel in the *Manual of Discipline* of the Qumran community (1QS 8:1).

The reasons given for Jesus' calling of the twelve are two. First of all, he wanted them ***to be with him.*** Jesus' way of thinking, his understanding of God's attitude toward sinful man, his compassion—his whole character was in sharp contrast to that of the religious leaders of his day. But men such as these disciples had a very difficult time erasing the old influences and entering fully into Jesus' way. This was not achieved before Calvary in any case. The progress that the disciples did make while Jesus was on earth would surely have been far less had they not lived with him so constantly.

In the second place, Jesus wanted these men to share in his mission. They made possible a wider dissemination of his message. The gospel they preached included the open evidence that God's reign had come near to man, and the divine rule would overpower the evil forces that alienated man from his true personhood. As was true of their Master, an inseparable portion of their preaching was the casting out of demons by the authority of their king. The first record Mark gives of their being sent out is in 6:7; he refers to them as "apostles" in 6:30.

The list of the twelve which follows is also given in Matthew 10:2–4; Luke 6:14–16; and Acts 1:13 ff. The first named is always ***Simon,*** whom Jesus ***surnamed Peter.*** The Greek name for Peter (like its equivalent Aramaic form Cephas: cf. John 1:42; Gal. 1:18) means stone, and is a tribute to the strength of character he would come to possess.

James and John (cf. 1:19) also received a surname, ***Boanerges,*** which Mark translates as ***sons of thunder.*** It has been suggested that Mark 9:38 and Luke 9:54 show the appropriateness of this name: but in that case the name, unlike Peter, would be applicable to them because of limitations of their Christian love. We simply do not have enough information to draw any certain conclusions.

Most of the disciples are only names to us, because we know so little of their later lives and contributions. This may very well have been true for the Gospel writers also. The later traditions about their work may have some historical basis, but we have very little record of these men in the New Testament itself. ***Andrew*** was Simon's brother (1:16); we know little more about this appealing man except for the brief references in 13:3 and in John 1:40–41; 6:8; 12:22.

Bartholomew (son of Tolmai) is usually identified with Nathanael, whom Philip brought to Jesus (cf. John 1:43 ff.). The name is incompletely given; but it is usually paired with ***Philip*** (not together in Acts 1:13). Concerning Philip himself, we have little information except for the tantalizing references in John 6:5–7; 12:21 f.; 14:8 f.

Matthew is identified in the first Gospel with the Levi of Mark 2:14, though our Gospel of Mark gives no hint of such identification. ***Thomas*** means twin, just as the word Didymus also does (John 11:16). He is remembered especially for his insistence on seeing the risen Lord for himself (John 20:24–28). There are Christians in India today who trace the conversion of their forebears back to Thomas.

The name of ***James the son of Alphaeus*** is given in longer form to distinguish him from ***James the son of Zebedee.*** Was he a brother of "Levi the son of Alphaeus" (2:14)? Was the Mary of 15:40 his mother? We simply cannot be certain. About ***Thaddaeus*** (some manuscripts read Lebbaeus)

[27] Farrer (pp. 79–81) points out that Levi was not included among the twelve (cf. Mark 2:13 f.), just as the ancient Levi was not one of the twelve tribes but the thirteenth. Joseph's sons Ephraim and Manasseh were numbered with their uncles. However, the degree of correspondence and typology on which Farrer insists has not met with general acceptance.

we know even less. His name is given as Judas, the son of James, in Luke 6:16 and Acts 1:13.

Since ***Simon*** was called ***the Cananaean,*** we have a substantial clue to his character. The Cananaeans were Zealots (cf. Luke 6:15; Acts 1:13). How thoroughly developed this party was in the third decade of the first century we are not able to say. The Zealots advocated armed revolt against the Roman overlords and succeeded in rousing nationalistic fervor to such a high pitch that the Palestinian Jews united in rebellion against Rome in A.D. 66. That Jesus warned against this whole spirit is clear in such passages as Luke 13:1–5. Barabbas was also a man with a violent nationalistic fervor (15:7). Such men had a great appeal to the Cananaeans. That Jesus should have succeeded in enlisting and transforming Simon was a remarkable accomplishment.

Judas the betrayer was called ***Iscariot.*** Some have tried to identify this title with the Sicarii, the "dagger men" or assassins, who were a kind of left wing of the Zealot party. More often it has been interpreted as "man of Kerioth," a town in Judea. If this is correct, Judas was the only one of the twelve who was not a Galilean. Mark does not interpret the name, and Dalman believed it quite plausible that any distinctive meaning of Iscariot was already unknown to the evangelist.

(3) *The Charges Against Jesus: Madness or Demonic Power* (*3:19b–30*)

**Then he went home; 20 and the crowd came together again, so that they could not even eat.
21 And when his friends heard it, they went out to seize him, for they said, "He is beside himself."
22 And the scribes who came down from Jerusalem said, "He is possessed by Beelzebul, and by the prince of demons he casts out the demons."
23 And he called them to him, and said to them in parables, "How can Satan cast out Satan?
24 If a kingdom is divided against itself, that kingdom cannot stand.
25 And if a house is divided against itself, that house will not be able to stand.
26 And if Satan has risen up against himself and is divided, he cannot stand, but is coming to an end.
27 But no one can enter a strong man's house and plunder his goods, unless he first binds the strong man; then indeed he may plunder his house.**

**28 "Truly, I say to you, all sins will be forgiven the sons of men, and whatever blasphemies they utter;
29 but whoever blasphemes against the Holy Spirit never has forgiveness, but is guilty of an eternal sin"—
30 for they had said, "He has an unclean spirit."**

As A. T. Robertson's *Harmony of the Gospels* points out, the events of Mark 3:19—5:20 were narrated as taking place in one day. After the choosing of the twelve, Jesus returned ***home.*** Compare 2:1 and also 1:29; possibly the place is the home of Simon and Andrew in Capernaum. The Greek idiom does not distinguish as clearly as the English between "house" and "home."

The crowd came again to be with Jesus. They filled the place and would not leave, so that there was no way possible to prepare and eat a meal in that house. In addition to the twelve, these people formed the first group present in 3:20–35. They had been attracted by his words and deeds and were eager to hear him further. One need not suppose they had all become disciples.

The second group involved in the story were Jesus' own people. ***His friends*** came to take him away, because they had concluded, ***He is beside himself.*** Mark's other uses of this word are all figurative: see 2:12; 5:42; 6:51.

Who were the persons making this charge? The phrase translated ***his friends*** (lit., the ones from beside him) was used to refer to one's family, to a larger group including one's family, to one's followers, or to one's envoys or agents. In view of their charge against Jesus, the disciples were surely excluded. Moreover, they had come ***to seize him;*** that his followers would not have wanted to do. The only reasonable understanding of the words is that Jesus' family, and perhaps some neighbors who had known him in earlier years, believed that their loved one was beset by some religious ecstasy, was endangering himself, and needed their protection. That Mark intended his readers to think this seems clear from 3:31, where his mother and brothers arrived and tried to call him out from the crowd.[28]

However mistaken or apologetic the word of his relatives, it was not a malicious and hostile word. To accuse Jesus of being in league with the devil was another matter altogether. It is like the difference between saying, He is ill, but will be better; or saying, He is criminally insane, and will destroy us if we do not get rid of him.

The scribes who came down from Jerusalem may have come to Galilee to encourage their northern compatriots in upholding the Law. They were probably Pharisees, and would have been disturbed by such words and actions as Mark recorded about Jesus in 2:1—3:6. Johnson reminds us that the Pharisees in Jesus' time had not yet established their control over the Jews of Galilee. This partly accounts for the continuing support many Galileans gave our Lord.

Beelzebul served as one name, not otherwise known to us, for a prince of the evil powers. The name itself means lord of the dwelling (as translated from Aramaic) or less probably lord of dung. If "lord of the dwelling" is correct, there might have been originally a play on words in Jesus' answer in verse 27: Jesus would be the true "lord of the house" and replace the false and evil "lord." But Mark's readers, following his Greek, could hardly have understood this. In the Ras Shamra tablets (*ca.* 1400 B.C.) one of the gods is called "Zebul, baal of the earth." "Beelzebub" (KJV, but not found in our best ancient MSS) means lord of flies and was god of Ekron (2 Kings 1:2). The Hebrews apparently degraded the gods of the foreigners around them to the status of demons.

To be ***possessed by Beelzebul*** meant that the demon of that name had taken over a man's body and will and was gaining his evil objectives through that mortal. If one translates, "He has Beelzebul," the charge would be that Jesus had gained control over this demonic power and therefore was able to do remarkable (but fundamentally evil) deeds.[29] Jesus was accused of being in criminal league with Satan, and was therefore bent on the utter ruin of the people he would lead or help. If he casts out demons, they said, it would only be for a more powerful evil spirit to wreak worse tragedy upon the subject mortals.

Jesus' answer was given ***in parables.*** The Markan (and Synoptic) use of this term derives from its Hebrew parallel and includes not only comparisons and illustrative stories but maxims, taunts, and proverbs. (See on 4:2,10–13.) The problem was certainly not always whether Jesus' teaching was lucid enough but whether men would accept within themselves what he said.

The first part of Jesus' answer (vv. 23–26) dealt with their false assumption concerning Satan. However evil the prince of demons might be, he was certainly not stupid, as they apparently assumed him to be. Why should Satan war against himself? demanded Jesus. If it be granted that the prince of demons has a kingdom, or a ruling house with many underlings, he would surely not foster revolution among his minions. If Satan were to loose his great power against himself, he would be seeking his own destruction. Therefore Jesus, who indeed has been casting out demons, cannot sensibly be accused of collusion with them!

[28] Some have held either that "they said" is impersonal and must refer to people other than Jesus' friends or relatives (Streeter); or that the text has been tampered with and the charge of madness must be attributed to the "scribes and the rest" (E. Lohmeyer, F. C. Grant). But John 7:5 also asserts that Jesus' brothers did not believe. All that this incident implies, as Taylor says, is that with Jesus' own people, "Deep personal concern for Jesus is combined with a want of sympathy for His aims and purposes." The other accounts include no such charge by Jesus' friends: cf. Matt. 12:22 ff.; Luke 11:14–26.

[29] Johnson, p. 81. Cf. KJV ("He hath Beelzebub") and TEV ("He has Beelzebul in him"). Taylor does not make this distinction; he does, however, think that Mark differentiated between Beelzebul and the prince of demons (p. 238). Nowhere in Jewish literature is Beelzebul given as a name for Satan. But Markan sources probably retained a Hebrew parallelism, and Matt. and Luke both identify Beelzebul as the prince of demons (Matt. 12:24; Luke 11:15). Moreover, Jesus' answer in the following verses refers directly to Satan.

The second part of Jesus' answer was a strong claim by our Lord that the power of God's Spirit was operating through him. In Luke 11:20 this is spelled out: "If it is by the finger of God that I cast out demons, then the kingdom of God has come upon you." Mark simply gives the pithy parable about plundering a strong man's house.

Like most parables Jesus used, this one was employed to argue a point forcibly. No person of ordinary physical prowess would ever try to force his way into a house occupied by a muscular giant. Only a man able to control decisively the occupant would dare do so. No one else could ever successfully pillage that house. That is all: let the illustration make its own point! There was no need to add that someone stronger than Satan has come or to say (picking up again the first part of Jesus' answer) the powers of evil are being defeated. Man, too long under evil dominion, has a new sovereign!

The casting out of the evil forces was of the essence of Jesus' good news. The kingdom of God is at hand in him, and men need to turn to the new sovereign in faith (1:15).

It is apparent in this passage, as elsewhere, that the earthly Jesus accepted a world view of Satan and his kingdom that was contemporary with the years of his ministry. Taylor is quite convincing in his argument that this belief was not simply an accommodation to current ideas, but a necessary condition to a real incarnation. "The modern Christian," he writes, "is not bound to take the same view. His attitude to the doctrine of Satan will be determined by his philosophy of evil and his interpretation of the fact of life and religious experience" (p. 239).

The first two parts of Jesus' response to the charge of Satanic alliance demolished the accusation and asserted a more powerful (divine) alliance as the true explanation of his conduct. The third part (28–30) was the severest condemnation of persons who would make so evil a judgment. If these verses existed as a separate saying of Jesus, as many recent commentators think, they are nevertheless appropriate to this context. But the pronouncement is recorded in a different context in Luke 12:10.

Truly, I say to you are words used to introduce the most solemn of Jesus' statements. The phrase was characteristic of Jesus, occurring about 70 times (in some form) in the Gospels and nowhere else in the New Testament. As scholars generally have observed, the phrase called special attention to the emphatic words which follow. More important than this, however, was the claim innate in the words: Jesus had the right to speak, for he possessed the truth. But the judgments of Jesus which customarily were marked by this phrase were judgments about which only God himself, the ultimate Wisdom, could have known. The adverb ***truly*** translates amen. In Revelation 3:14, our risen Lord is referred to as "the Amen," which is explained as "the faithful and true witness, the beginning of God's creation."

God's forgiveness, asserted Jesus, is remarkable in its scope. ***All sins*** and ***whatever blasphemies*** need not alienate men permanently from the merciful God. The verb translated "shall be forgiven" means to remit, to cancel, and in this context to set aside any obstacle to full fellowship. Blasphemies were slanderous or scurrilous words. When spoken against ***the sons of men***—and we should understand this to include Jesus, the Son of man (cf. Luke 12:10)—they might be erased by the divine mercy. It was surely understandable that many should fail to recognize the dignity of one who had "emptied himself" and was found "in human form" (Phil. 2:7 f.).

Blasphemy ***against the Holy Spirit,*** however, stands in a different category. The man who does this is ***guilty of an eternal sin;*** he ***never has forgiveness.*** In verse 30 Mark made clear his interpretation of this specific blasphemy: it was to attribute the good and redemptive acts of help and healing done by the Spirit's power to the agency of Beelzebul. As Johnson puts it, it meant "ascribing to Satan what is perhaps the greatest gift of the Holy Spirit, that of rescuing those who are in Satan's power." One who does this not only rejects moral values but reverses them. It is as though he says in his heart, "Evil, to me you are what is good!"

It is certainly true that such a Satanic viewpoint must utterly block any hope for fellowship with God. There is, however, some disagreement about (1) the meaning of the word translated ***eternal*** and (2) whether Jesus spoke literally or in hyperbole. The noun from which eternal is derived may mean (in addition to related ideas) either all of the time to come, i.e., eternity, or a segment of time, as the present age (Arndt and Gingrich). ***An eternal sin*** thus might mean a sin outlasting time, or it might mean, as Johnson suggests, a sin that leaves man guilty "so long as this age lasts." But the second interpretation dilutes the otherwise strong language of Jesus, and Taylor is surely right in asserting that this sin is described as a "permanent barrier" raised by man between himself and God.

Branscomb points to parallel sayings in the Mishnah, listing those who are excluded from the future world: those who deny a resurrection from the dead, those who deny that the Law of Moses is from God, and those who are heretics. These ought not, he says, to be interpreted as "a fixed limitation of the divine grace," but as "a warning against a too great trust in God's mercy." In the same way, he believes, Jesus spoke in hyperbole. He meant only to emphasize that blasphemy against the Holy Spirit was a most terrible evil and would earn God's fullest condemnation.

This interpretation is possible but not altogether plausible. The contrast between sins loses its force. Moreover, no word of explanation followed. Compare the figurative word in Mark 10:25; verse 27 makes clear the limitations of Jesus' statement. A camel cannot go through the eye of a needle, but by God's help a rich man may enter the kingdom.

Nevertheless, the Gospels consistently emphasize the possibility of repentance and the broad scope of God's mercy. Was the act of the scribes in saying about Jesus, "He is possessed by Beelzebul," sufficient to condemn them forever? This is difficult to believe. Indeed, Jesus continued to work with Pharisees and scribes throughout his ministry.

If we do not weaken the truth of this saying and yet bear in mind the great power of divine forgiveness, how then are we to understand it? The sin can hardly be just any railing or angry word against the work of God's Spirit—in Jesus or through any Spirit-led man. Persons committing such evils are surely often attracted to the way of our Lord and are capable of repentance.

The sin against the Spirit which brings permanent alienation must be not one act or series of acts, but a perversion of one's self which utterly denies and defies moral values and characteristically thinks of good as evil and light as darkness. For the scribes to identify Jesus with Satan was evidence that their attitudes were at the very least pointing to this spiritual danger in themselves. They had better be warned: their lives were pursuing a way in which they could become so terribly lost and entangled that they could never return to the true and living way.

(4) *The True Family of Jesus* (3:31–35)

31 And his mother and his brothers came; and standing outside they sent to him and called him. 32 And a crowd was sitting about him; and they said to him, "Your mother and your brothers are outside, asking for you." 33 And he replied, "Who are my mother and my brothers?" 34 And looking around on those who sat about him, he said, "Here are my mother and my brothers! 35 Whoever does the will of God is my brother, and sister, and mother."

Mark placed at this point the story of Jesus and his true family because of the charges he cited in verse 21, and it is quite appropriate to his message. At the conclusion of Jesus' answer to the charges leveled against him, Mark properly wanted to emphasize to his readers Jesus' divine sonship and the nature of the true brotherhood that is of the very essence of discipleship.

However, it is most probable that 3:31–35 had been a separate unit of gospel narrative. That Mary was among the "friends" of verse 21 is an unlikely and unnecessary conclusion, as I see it. It is true that Mark displays no evidence of any knowledge of the virgin birth, but this passage must not be used as evidence that Jesus' mother opposed his mission. Mary is referred to in 6:3, but only in this paragraph does she appear directly in Mark's narrative.

The simplest and best explanation of the identity of Jesus' ***brothers*** is that they were sons of Joseph and Mary, and younger than Jesus. The idea that they were sons of Joseph by a former wife goes back at least to the apocryphal Gospel of Peter (*ca.* A.D. 140–150). In the late fourth century Jerome pressed the hypothesis that they were cousins, a possible but unlikely translation of the word "brothers" used here and in 6:3. The fact that the husband and father of the family is unmentioned during Jesus' ministry suggests that Joseph had died some years earlier.

The members of Jesus' family ***sent to him and called him.*** These words mean only that they asked to see and talk with Jesus. The Markan arrangement has linked their request with the concerned fear of his "friends" that he was "beside himself." The ***crowd*** around Jesus apparently included his disciples but may very well have contained many unpersuaded people. We may assume that we do not have a full account of what took place. There is no reason to suppose that Jesus refused to see his blood relations. The message which was needed by the Christians of the apostolic age generally, and by Mark's readers in particular, dealt not with what Jesus said to his mother and brothers but with the question and answer that Mark did record in verses 34 f.

Who are the true family of Jesus? Mark has just made clear again that Jesus claimed an intimate relationship with God and that his power in doing good was from God. Mark does not often refer to God as Father to the disciples (but cf. 11:25), nor does he include such phrases as "that you may be sons of your Father who is in heaven" (Matt. 5:45). His understanding of Jesus' teaching, however, is identical with the other Gospels on this point. God's true family includes all those who identify themselves with Jesus by doing "the will of God."

Have they left father or mother to do God's will? Then they are surely Jesus' kin. They need not fear isolation: their family has multiplied (10:29–30), and they are parents and brothers and sisters of Jesus, and so of one another. This is what God's kingdom is about. It is no abstract idea, nor is it a fixed theological belief. As Branscomb puts it, the reign of God as Jesus conceived it centered in "a personal fellowship with men and women who do the will of God."

(5) *Instruction by Parables* (*4:1–34*)

a. Parable of the Sower (*4:1–9*)

**1 Again he began to teach beside the sea.
And a very large crowd gathered about him, so
that he got into a boat and sat in it on the sea;
and the whole crowd was beside the sea on the
land. 2 And he taught them many things in
parables, and in his teaching he said to them:
3 "Listen! A sower went out to sow. 4 And as he
sowed, some seed fell along the path, and the
birds came and devoured it. 5 Other seed fell
on rocky ground, where it had not much soil,
and immediately it sprang up, since it had no
depth of soil; 6 and when the sun rose it was
scorched, and since it had no root it withered
away. 7 Other seed fell among thorns and the
thorns grew up and choked it, and it yielded
no grain. 8 And other seeds fell into good soil
and brought forth grain, growing up and increasing and yielding thirtyfold and sixtyfold
and a hundredfold." 9 And he said, "He who
has ears to hear, let him hear."**

Mark had a preference for recording the actions rather than the discourses of Jesus. He did, however, group some of Jesus' parables in 4:1–34. We cannot be certain that this material came to Mark as a unit. It is unlikely that the settings given are original for each of these parables. Nevertheless, we have every reason to suppose that (1) Jesus often taught ***beside the sea;*** (2) the crowds were often so large that he taught from ***a boat,*** with the people standing about on the shore; (3) the multitudes would have included the curious and the casual, the hostile and the friendly; and (4) his characteristic teaching method was the parable.

As we have noted, some of the parables are pithy, provocative illustrations that argue or clarify a point in the briefest imaginable way (e.g., 2:21–22). The term parable is broad enough to include the metaphor and the figurative saying, but it is most often applied to the expanded simile (the mustard seed, the leaven), the simple story (the sower, the seed growing secretly), or the full-length tale (the good Samaritan, the prodigal son).

Most of the time the parable's meaning must have been obvious. Sometimes, however, Jesus' point was more subtle, and might be missed completely by men whose ways and thoughts were so foreign to those of Jesus and too rigid or programmed to allow fresh ideas.

Mark has received the parables in the context of his own life. He has repeated them for his own audience, in order to portray to them the teaching of the risen Lord. Mark's readers did not live in Galilee, so they were not directly acquainted with the Pharisee, the Zealot, the scribe, or others who regularly had listened to Jesus' words. The truths of the parables remained for Mark's audience, as also they abide for us today. But only occasionally does the pointed argument, the devastating cutting edge of the original story, strike with equal force the people so removed from Jesus' milieu.

Nevertheless, it will not do to interpret the parables without constantly being reminded that men killed Jesus because they could not endure what he did and taught. His most forceful teachings and his most unanswerable arguments were set forth in parables. The clearest example of this in Mark is in 12:1–12, where Jesus' enemies wanted to arrest him, "for they perceived that he had told the parable against them."

The command, ***Listen!*** is most important for Mark's message in chapter 4. The verb means not only to hear but to act—to hearken to what is heard. See verse 9: if ears are made for hearing, men must use them for this purpose.

The story of the ***sower*** may seem strange to the modern wheat or barley farmer. However, from the leather bag he tied to his waist, the Galilean farmer sowed before he plowed.[30] He ***sowed*** on ***the path*** and where ***the thorns*** had been because he expected to work that surface afterwards. The ***rocky ground*** (Palestine has an abundance of rocks!) was that in which limestone was covered only thinly by the soil. The sower did not carelessly waste his seed.

Where villagers had hardened a path across the field, the seeds were most exposed and least likely to be covered. The percentage lost to birds, hunting for sustenance, would be very high. Warmed from the sun and also from its reflected heat in the rock hidden just below the surface, some unfortunate seed germinated rapidly but could not produce lasting roots that would allow the plants to reach maturity. What seemed at first so full of promise simply dried up.

Other seed fell among thorns. Apparently the thorns which had previously grown on this field had been cut down and burned. Instead of being eradicated they grew back stronger and more troublesome than ever. By the time the wheat or barley came up, so had these unwanted thorns. No harvest here! The verb ***choked*** is very strong and the description apt.

Most of the seed fell, as the farmer purposed, ***into good soil.*** Mark's account of the parable makes this clear, although neither Matthew nor Luke is careful to do so. In the first three instances a singular form for seed was used, which RSV has rendered ***some seed*** and ***other seed;*** but in verse 8 a plural form was employed. It has been translated inadequately ***other seeds,*** though

[30] Cf. J. Jeremias, *The Parables of Jesus,* tr. by S. H. Hooke (New York: Scribner, 1955), 9 f.

only a paraphrase could make the contrast clear. These seeds were productive indeed, some of a fine harvest—*thirtyfold;* some of a great harvest—*sixtyfold;* and some of an amazing harvest—*a hundredfold.*

As the parable stands, and without yet taking into consideration the interpretation given in 13–20, what was its meaning? Jeremias insists that the parable must have originally been eschatological in meaning. The coming of the kingdom is compared to a harvest: in spite of the hungry birds, the thorns, and the weather, with all the frustrations, God will have his great harvest—and his hour is approaching.

T. W. Manson (*Teachings of Jesus,* p. 76) believes that the parable is one about parabolic teaching. The result of the sowing depends not on the seed but on the soil in which it lodges. So the effectiveness of the parables depends not on the parables as such but on the character of those who hear Jesus speak. This interpretation is pertinent to the statements in 4:10–12 and appropriate to the expanded explanation in 13–20. But the parable's climax of a great harvest is minimized.

Rawlinson and Menzies assert that the parable is of the experience of Jesus himself as he proclaimed the good news of the kingdom. Not everyone would heed him and there were many discouragements, but there was enough response and understanding to make his work worth the investment of his life. So the purpose of the parable would include a warning to his listeners but would aim especially at encouraging them in their discipleship.

The latter interpretation recognizes that the disciples, even with attentive listening, would not have thought readily of such expanded meanings of birds, rocky ground, or thorns as are given in 13–20. Nevertheless, these dramatic elements in the story do reflect the experiences of Jesus and point to the necessity for open and acquisitive hearing (v. 9). The differences in the soils and the promise of a great harvest in spite of some losses—these are both central features in the story. In the first is *warning,* in the second is *hope.* As the story is told, the emphasis is clearly directed toward hope, with the warning itself providing some encouragement and invitation.

b. Understanding the Parable (4:10–20)

**10 And when he was alone, those who were
about him with the twelve asked him concerning the parables. 11 And he said to them, "To
you has been given the secret of the kingdom
of God, but for those outside everything is in
parables; 12 so that they may indeed see but
not perceive, and may indeed hear but not
understand; lest they should turn again, and be
forgiven." 13 And he said to them, "Do you not
understand this parable? How then will you
understand all the parables? 14 The sower sows
the word. 15 And these are the ones along the
path, where the word is sown; when they hear,
Satan immediately comes and takes away the
word which is sown in them. 16 And these in
like manner are the ones sown upon rocky
ground, who, when they hear the word, immediately receive it with joy; 17 and they have no
root in themselves, but endure for a while;
then, when tribulation or persecution arises on
account of the word, immediately they fall
away. 18 And others are the ones sown among
thorns; they are those who hear the word,
19 but the cares of the world, and the delight in
riches, and the desire for other things, enter in
and choke the word, and it proves unfruitful.
20 But those that were sown upon the good soil
are the ones who hear the word and accept it
and bear fruit, thirtyfold and sixtyfold and a
hundredfold."**

The function of the parables (*4:10–12*).—The scene has shifted. Jesus was no longer addressing the whole multitude but only *those who were about him with the twelve.* The circumstances were informal, and it must have been natural to pursue further questions raised by Jesus' teaching.

The people in Mark's day probably required some explanation why so many failed to recognize and heed the Teacher whom they knew as Lord. But the question would not have been new. The first disciples must have been intensely aware of the rejection Jesus received from so many.

If the disciples understood to any degree the meaning of the parable as we have suggested, they may well have inquired about those who rejected true discipleship. Mark says that they asked Jesus about ***the parables,*** not only about the sower but others as well. The discussion of the meaning of the sower (13–20) is a further elucidation of Jesus' answer in 4:11–12. These words of Jesus may very well have been applied originally to Jesus' teaching as a whole, as Taylor and others believe, and not to parables alone.

The word ***secret*** or "mystery" is found most often in the writings of Paul. There it represents that which once was not clear but has now been made known by God. So to Paul the good news is that God was in Christ reconciling the world to himself—this is a mystery—this is what God has now made known to his people. So also is the healing of the rift between Jew and Gentile when both come to the cross: the inclusion of these peoples is a wonderful mystery from God, a secret now open (cf. Rom. 11:25; Eph. 1:9; 3:3,9; 1 Cor. 4:1; 1 Tim. 3:9).

Nowhere in the New Testament does the term secret correspond to esoteric knowledge and rites as in the so-called mystery religions of the Roman Empire.

Here in Mark the ***secret*** is the mystery ***of the kingdom of God.*** To the followers of Jesus, whose ears were open and who hearkened to him (v. 9; cf. v. 12), God has given a measure of insight and obedience to the reign of God. In their case, God was helping them to accept fully the divine sovereignty and live in that faith.

What was true for the disciples was not true in the case of ***those outside.*** This term must include not only those hostile to Jesus, but those described in verses 14 f. To them ***everything*** was ***in parables.*** The temptation to translate this word as "riddles" at this point is very real. The corresponding Hebrew word sometimes carried this meaning.

The difficulty is that the natural interpretation of the words that follow is that Jesus told the parables in order to hide the truth, not to make it lucid. The Greek word rendered "so that" usually denotes purpose, sometimes result.

What sorts of solutions have been offered for this problem? Some have argued that this saying of Jesus was related to the teaching ministry of Jesus, but that Mark, by placing it in this context, has made it refer to the purpose of the parables (T. W. Manson, Taylor). Others have urged some solution predicated on a Markan misinterpretation of the word translated "so that." For example, Hunter accuses Mark of mistranslating an Aramaic word and insists that he should have used a relative pronoun instead. By this means, Hunter concludes that Jesus was here saying that the parabolic method was necessary for the multitude *who* (not so that or in order that) were lacking in spiritual insight.

Why these objections to the most natural meaning of the text? These scholars are right in their premise: *the purpose of the parables was certainly not to conceal the truth.* Jesus did not practice the proverbial wisdom of "men who know the way to wrap in fog the things they say." Would Jesus have couched the truth in terms not understandable by closed and malicious minds, lest they be stirred to quick and vicious opposition? On the contrary, just as the purpose of a lamp is to give light (v. 21), Jesus must have had a positive motive in his teaching.

Yet what happened during the teaching of Jesus? Men heard him but did not heed him. They saw his works, but they did not perceive that he must be from God and not Satan (3:20–30). The gospel called for repentance and faith, but they were unwilling to accept their need or make the necessary commitment. The arguments and the warnings of Jesus were most forceful in parables. However, the result, which was to be expected because of the sinfulness of man and his "hardness of heart" (cf. 3:5), was that many did not submit willingly to God's sovereignty.

This experience of Jesus has close theological parallels in Paul's letters. As the apostle described God's wrath, he pointed out that man deliberately turned to his own way and ignored what he knew of God. God did not force him away from this path but gave man up to his own evil, and the evil was allowed to run its full and tragic course in man's life (cf. Rom. 1:18–32). In Romans 9–11, Pharaoh and the nation of Israel were described as victims of the divine wrath, whom God gave up to their own rebellious choices. However, Paul says that God's purpose in all of this was still mercy: "For God has consigned all men to disobedience, that he may have mercy upon all"—that is, every step down the path to ruin is from God a call to repentance and to the acceptance of his forgiveness (Rom. 11:32).

The purpose of the parables was to call men to repentance and discipleship. This was the result also for those who opened their minds to the good news, or, to express it differently, for those to whom God gave receptive lives. For those outside, in one sense the purpose was the same—to make clear, to correct, to invite. But the result (the conjunction in v. 12 is better expressed for us in this way) was an increasing spirit of rejection and antagonism.

The words of Jesus are very close to those of Isaiah 6:9–10, which are quoted in this context in Matthew 13:14–15. We must remember that the Scriptures speak sometimes of God's hardening a Pharaoh's heart or (as here) closing a man's ears. However, God does not initiate the sinfulness. He simply gives a man up to his own disobedience and its consequences (Rom. 1:24,26, 28).

However clearly Jesus made such people ***see***, they still would ***not perceive***. However lucid Jesus' teaching, they still would not understand. They were unwilling to ***turn again***, acknowledging their need and wrongness, and accept the divine forgiveness Jesus offered.

In this short paragraph Mark has expressed something of his own understanding of the reasons men did not follow Jesus. Even the disciples continued to need additional explanations and guidance. They only gradually came to see who Jesus was and his overwhelming significance. Nevertheless, they were open to the truth, and Jesus was able gradually to convey to them ***the secret of the kingdom of God***. To their more accessible minds he kept adding truth (cf. 4:33–34). For the others the secret of the kingdom remained hidden.

An interpretation of the parable of the sower (4:13–20).—In the explanation of the parable, only Mark records that Jesus rebuked his own disciples for their dullness. Luke simply records the explanation (8:11) but Matthew (13:16 f.) contrasts the alert and discerning open-mindedness of the disciples with the obstinate dullness of others. The slowness even of the disciples to discern Jesus' teaching serves a special function in Mark. It heightens the sense of mystery about Jesus' identity. Mark's readers, though themselves aware of his divine lordship, were led to see how the disciples only gradually recognized the Messiah and how so many persons never did discern who Jesus was.

The interpretation of the parable in 14–20 must have been preached in the early churches and, as Rawlinson says, surely seems to be "rather the way in which the parable was currently applied when Mark was written than any authentic word of Jesus." On the other hand, the biblical account of this parable's meaning has protected it to a great degree from the wild and uncontrolled allegorical interpretations of many of the other parables for which no application is recorded.

We ought to assume that Jesus customarily discussed his own teaching, including the parables, with his disciples. Is this not a mark of good teaching? On the other hand, we need not assume that the discussion would be limited solely to the original point of a parable. In the interpretation of the sower in 14–20 more emphasis is placed on the character of the listeners and the temptations to which they fall prey than on the promise of the harvest and the significance of work that does not meet with complete success. If there is doubt that Jesus' discussion of the parable was preserved just as he spoke it, still there is nothing here that could not have been nurtured from what he did say and appropriately applied in fresh ways among the early Christians.

To Jesus ***the word*** was that the kingdom had drawn near for man (1:15). To the man who knew him as risen Lord, ***the word*** was that God had visited his people in Jesus the Christ and was reconciling them to himself through this crucified and risen Lord. Cf. Acts 8:4: "Now those who were scattered went about preaching the word." The ***sower*** himself is not identified with Jesus specifically; he is any preacher of the good news.

The identification of ***the seed*** with ***the word*** is not followed through with precision. In general the seed and/or the soils on which it falls represent four classes of persons who hear God's messengers.

Satan (cf. 1:13; 3:23) is the prince of evil, the power against God. The name is Aramaic and, along with several others (e.g., Beliar, Sammael), is one of the devil's titles. The allegorical pattern is not pressed, and whether Satan is equated with the birds is not clear. What is plain is that these people are those whose receptivity to the good news is like that of a beaten down path to seed falling upon it. Long before God's word could penetrate their hard and unyielding minds. Satan would have stolen it from their consciousness.

In verse 16 the seed is identified not with the word of the gospel but with persons who have heard the good news. Seed sown on thin soil with underlying rock may spring up, but it will have no root. In the same way, men may give open affirmation of the gospel and appear to be promising citizens of God's kingdom and yet be totally unprepared for the consequences. Their faith is ***for a while,*** that is, for the season when everything is easy and joyful.

However, in the realities of life in Christ, ***tribulation*** does come: the word means pressure—the distress that comes from being caught in a crushing squeeze. These persons could not endure pressure. The strength of the kingdom is not in them. ***Persecution*** comes, too, as it came upon Jesus and as he warned it would come upon his disciples. Persecution means harassment; the verb from which it is derived means to pursue, to keep hounding someone.

The cause of the pressure and harassment vanishes if one turns back to the ordinary patterns of life about him, for the cause is ***the word*** itself. Every Christian for whom Mark wrote would be thinking of the difficulties, the derision, the rejection, the danger he had to endure if he followed Christ faithfully. Some men simply were not willing to do this, and their commitments gave way to pressures.

The verb ***fall away*** is derived from a noun which meant the bait stick in a trap. The verb means either to trap (here passive, to be trapped), or to stumble (mg., RSV). In either case, the result is as TEV paraphrases, "So when trouble or persecution comes because of the message, they give up at once."

Other hearers of the message are like seed ***sown among thorns.*** These persons try to serve both God and mammon, and it cannot be done (Matt. 6:24). They are like the man "who puts his hand to the plow and looks back" (Luke 9:62).

The cares of the world are the anxieties and worries of the present age. "Care" suggests a mind torn in different directions. The two phrases which follow should not be divorced from this one: they are in effect commentaries on it.

The ***delight in riches*** is characteristic of the world, the age and environment in which man lives. English has no one word parallel to the Greek, for ***delight*** may properly be translated deceitfulness (KJV) or pleasure. When this word is used, the pleasure is that kind which involves one in sin. Arndt and Gingrich suggest we translate here, "the seduction that comes from wealth."

In the Hebrew-Christian tradition, unlike Buddhism, ***desire*** is not necessarily evil, and the word for desire is sometimes used in the best sense (cf. Luke 22:15; 1 Thess. 2:17). But the word is also used (as a verb) in the Greek translation of the commandment, "Thou shalt not covet." Disciples of

Jesus must have different goals, e.g., "his kingdom and his righteousness" (Matt. 6:33) from the world's concern with wealth and ***other things.*** The latter phrase is so general that it includes every kind of desire which is alien or inimical to the gospel.

When interests and goals which are not subject to the word ***enter in*** the lives of those who had been attracted by the claims of the gospel, the result is tragic. What might have been is choked and the word bears no fruit at all. How appropriate the warning must have been to the early Christians! No church can ever fulfil its calling if its membership becomes enamored with the life and success-goals of the society in which it exists.

Those that were sown upon the good soil are the ones who . . . bear fruit. This discussion of the meaning of the parable has centered on the seed that were lost, the people whose eyes did not see and whose ears did not hear. Nevertheless, there are those who respond to the word, and marvelous things happen through them. The key word in verse 20 is ***accept.*** In verse 16 some ***receive*** the word ***with joy;*** i.e., they seize the message, delighted with its promises. The word ***accept*** implies that the people believe and welcome the word so that they understand it and submit themselves to its guidance. Only in such persons does Jesus' teaching find fulfilment.

c. *Parabolic Sayings: the Lamp, the Measure (4:21–25)*

21 And he said to them, "Is a lamp brought in to be put under a bushel, or under a bed, and not on a stand? 22 For there is nothing hid, except to be made manifest; nor is anything secret, except to come to light. 23 If any man has ears to hear, let him hear." 24 And he said to them, "Take heed what you hear; the measure you give will be the measure you get, and still more will be given you. 25 For to him who has will more be given; and from him who has not, even what he has will be taken away."

Whether these sayings about the lamp and the measure were in this context in Mark's sources, we cannot know. Matthew (5:15; 7:2) has included with somewhat different applications the words of 4:21, 24. See also Luke's parallel passage in 8:16–18 and the very similar words of Luke 12:2–3. Mark may have been heir to a written collection of Jesus' sayings independent of Q, believed by most scholars to have been a major source utilized by Matthew and Luke.

The meaning of these sayings in Mark, like that of the preceding verses, deals with man's receptivity to and understanding of the word of the gospel. In the context of Jesus' life as recorded here, the specific reference was to the understanding of the parables and of the secret of God's kingdom.

In verse 21 there are really two questions, the first insistently calling for the answer no, the second equally demanding the answer yes. If we paraphrase a little we read, "Is a lamp brought in to be placed under a bushel? Of course it's not, is it? It is brought in to be placed on a lampstand, isn't it?" By ***lamp*** we should probably understand the simple clay lamps of that day, of which many samples have been preserved. The ***bushel*** was a measuring vessel which would hold almost exactly two gallons. By ***bed*** (a different word from the pallet of 2:4) may be meant the couch on which they reclined at meals. The lamp ***stand*** was probably a slight ledge in the wall designed for that purpose. The translation "candle" (KJV) reflects the practice of seventeenth-century England and not the ways of first-century Galilee.

What then is the parable's application? The divine purpose in Jesus' ministry must not be construed to be confusion or any deeper ignorance for man. Just as the purpose of a lamp is to give light, so the ultimate reason for Jesus' teaching must be made clear. However true the saying in verses 11–12 and whatever may be the immediate results of Jesus' word and ministry, nevertheless the realities cannot forever remain hidden. True, the kingdom of God is a secret, a mystery, concealed from many for a time. But it would not have been concealed at all ***except to come to light.*** The words "except to" translate a very strong adversative conjunction together with a conjunction expressing purpose: the meaning is, "not for some other reason, but for this purpose only."

Some interpreters translate the verb in verse 21 with its more common meaning of come. Does a lamp come? is the awkward result in English. But Johnson, for example, thinks the saying should be so understood and that Mark's readers would think of Jesus' final coming. However, it is both lexically and contextually sound to translate this verb ***is . . . brought*** and to understand that Mark was thinking of the ministry of Jesus. Jesus may have originally been speaking of the Law and the way it had become hidden with scribal interpretations in spite of its divine purpose. In this case, Mark's application would be quite different but also quite consonant with what Jesus had taught and what the gospel meant to Mark's own generation.

The repetition of the exhortation (v. 9) to listen closely and comprehendingly to these words points again to the importance of what has been said.

Take heed what you hear means, Pay attention to what you are listening to! The warning is not directed against hearing other things but is aimed at deeper understanding of the words that are being spoken to them.

The context of Jesus' word in verse 24 makes the saying more difficult than that in Matthew 7:2, where it applies to judging others. Taylor calls it "an unnatural connexion," which Mark must have taken from a collection of sayings. As it stands here, the saying probably means, "What you provide and do (on the basis of your response to the word) will be the measure of what you will receive; and you will receive additional blessings and responsibilities." (Cf. Swete and Cranfield.) Or the application of the verse may be applied only to teaching: if a follower of Jesus listens with understanding, he will be given added insights (Johnson).

Hunter calls the paradoxical saying of verse 25 "the parable of the talents (Matt. 25:14–30) in a nutshell." The verb ***has*** may mean either possesses or is getting. If a man keeps responsive to the way and word of Jesus, he is given more and more. If not, his mind is hardening, God's wrath (cf. above, 4:11–12) is operative, and the limited spiritual insight he once had will be lost. Note how closely this lesson compares with verses 15–19.

d. The Parable of the Seed Growing Secretly (4:26–29)

26 And he said, "The kingdom of God is as if
a man should scatter seed upon the ground,
27 and should sleep and rise night and day, and
the seed should sprout and grow, he knows not
how. 28 The earth produces of itself, first the
blade, then the ear, then the full grain in the
ear. 29 But when the grain is ripe, at once he
puts in the sickle, because the harvest has
come."

The kingdom of God is not compared to a ***man*** or ***seed*** or growth or ***harvest*** or ***sickle,*** but to this story as a unit. The theme of the story is what Johnson has called "patience with delay." Just as seed sown cannot be forced quickly to harvest time, but nevertheless in its own mysterious way moves toward the purpose for which it was made and planted, God's kingdom has drawn near and his purpose in it moves toward fulfilment. But no man possesses the power to determine its time, for that is in God's hands.

The common nineteenth-century view was that the parable affirmed the gradual but inevitable evolution of the kingdom. This interpretation depended heavily upon the Greek word which could be transliterated into our "automatic" and for which the RSV has ***of itself.*** However, there is promise in the parable only of God's ultimate victory; there is no promise of inevitable progress for the whole world.

With the concentration among early twentieth-century theologians on eschatology, many have interpreted the parable with almost exclusive emphasis on the ***harvest:*** the main idea then becomes that the kingdom will soon break in upon us. Verse 29 partly quotes Joel 3:13, in which the language and the emphasis are on the triumphant justice of God. Mark's readers, living uneasily in Nero's Rome, would surely have treasured this hope.

The quotation from Joel gives us some hint of an appropriate context for the parable during Jesus' life. Some among his enthusiastic listeners were eager to accomplish God's will in a hurry, and in God's name to fight and overthrow the enemy. One of Jesus' chosen twelve was a Zealot (cf. above on 3:18). The context in Joel 3 includes words which would readily have been cited by these impatient advocates of "godly (!)" violence.

To men of violence who thought to work God's wrath for him Jesus' parable spoke in rebuke. The kingdom is unlike the fanatical spirit of the Zealot. You cannot force the kingdom; you can only live according to its ways and share your understanding of God's rule. The final outcome is with God. His times and seasons are beyond us.

The parable affirmed too what was declared in 1:15, that the kingdom had drawn near to man in Jesus. How this could be true and how the course Jesus chose in life could accomplish God's triumph was a mystery (man "knows not how"). But the nature of the kingdom is derived from the providence of God (***The earth produces of itself***), and men must patiently depend upon God.

Yet in the parable there was for the Zealot, as for Mark's readers and ourselves, some emphasis upon fulfilment. Along with the correction of Zealot ideas, Jesus must have been calling men into discipleship offering difficulties, calling for patience, offering help. There may even have been an identification of the time of sowing with the time of the Baptist's preaching of repentance, so that the harvest time was already upon them. In this case, the saying in Luke 10:2 (Matt. 9:37; cf. John 4:35–38) would be quite apt: "The harvest is plentiful, but the laborers are few; pray therefore the Lord of the harvest to send out laborers into his harvest."

e. The Parable of the Mustard Seed (4:30–32)

30 And he said, "With what can we compare the kingdom of God, or what parable shall we use for it? 31 It is like a grain of mustard seed, which, when sown upon the ground, is the smallest of all the seeds on earth; 32 yet when it is sown it grows up and becomes the greatest of all shrubs, and puts forth large branches, so that the birds of the air can make nests in its shade."

The mustard plant which grows from the tiny seed spoken of by Jesus has been identified as the *sinapis nigra.* It sometimes grows wild in that area, and when it is cultivated may attain a height up to 12 feet. Although an herb or shrub, because of its size it would sometimes loosely have been called a tree (Luke 13:19) with branches (Matt. 13:32) providing ***shade*** in its foliage.

The formula with which the parable begins (v. 30) is very similar to the words used by other Jewish teachers of Jesus' day when introducing their parables. As in the preceding parable, we must understand that this whole similitude tells us something (not everything) about the kingdom: we ought not to attempt to equate the kingdom with seed or plant or birds. Jeremias helpfully suggests that we should translate, "It is the case with the Kingdom as with the grain of mustard seed."

The contrast in the parable between the tiny beginning (the seed) and the tremendous growth (the huge shrub) is central to the meaning of the parable. Although the seed is not literally ***the smallest of all the seeds on earth,*** its size and that of the plant from which it comes make the hyperbole entirely apt. The disciples ought not to be anxious because of their insignificant number or status in the world. Who would guess the magnitude of the mustard plant from its seed?

C. H. Dodd believed that the emphasis on the smallness of the seed was not from Jesus, though it may have been in the material which Mark was using. He insisted that the prevailing idea originally was "that of growth up to a point at which the tree can shelter the birds." A tree sheltering the birds was symbolic of the protection given to subject peoples by a great empire. The allusion to Old Testament passages does seem clear at this point (cf. Dan. 4:10–12; Ezek. 17:22 f.; 31:6). Dodd concluded that the parable asserts that in Jesus the kingdom with its blessings has become available to all men. The kingdom has arrived, he says: "the birds are flocking to find shelter in the shade of the tree." [31]

As the parable stands in Mark, however, the contrast between seed and plant is certainly primary, and there is no question but that the original text of Mark spoke of the smallness of the seed. Nevertheless, it is true that the clear allusions to the broad and inclusive scope of the kingdom are also a part of the parable. This would have been true for Jesus' first disciples and also for Mark's readers.

For Mark's harried Christian congregations, therefore, the parable must have spoken of promise being fulfilled, not of promise already fully attained. They were still small in the world and needed to look to God for the accomplishment of his purposes. Yet Jesus their Lord was indeed King of kings, and had they not found a refuge and home under his saving lordship? Moreover, did this parable not also hint that there was room for all men and nations in the kingdom? Here was encouragement to patient endurance and to missionary zeal.

f. Summary: Special Instruction to Disciples (4:33–34)

33 With many such parables he spoke the word to them, as they were able to hear it; 34 he did not speak to them without a parable, but privately to his own disciples he explained everything.

These two verses are quite obviously the work of the Gospel writer. For this reason they reveal more explicitly than any of the preceding Mark's personal understanding of Jesus' use of parables. We should note four salient points.

First, Jesus used parables to speak ***the word*** to all. As has been noted, ***the word*** to Mark's readers would have meant the whole gospel, including Jesus' death and resurrection, the proclamation of God's victory over all evil forces. This concept of ***the word*** does not represent any change from its earlier meaning, except the inevitable change wrought by the further climactic events that were God's work in Christ. ***The word*** was still the message of God's rule, it was whatever Jesus, God's Son upon whom the Spirit had descended, had taught and done. ***The word*** continued to be God's promised deliverance from the powers of evil, calling men to repentance and faith.

Second, the ***parables*** narrated were samples of the kind that Jesus used. We do not know how many of these Mark could have recorded, but he was aware that Jesus had told many of them. These parables included instruction, sharp warning, and exhortation; they were from Jesus' Palestinian context and were directed, in the first instance, to his listeners as a whole. It does seem significant that the parables chosen by the evangelist for this chapter should all have a special emphasis on the spread of the gospel (Rawlinson).

Third, the parables were spoken as Jesus' audiences ***were able to hear.*** It is impossible to suppose that Jesus deliberately intended to befuddle the minds of most of his hearers by speaking in parables. We must understand the controversial passage above in 4:10–12 in accord with verse 33: if the people who were in Jesus' audience did not understand him, the responsibility was their own; the biblical view that the way they listened was within the purpose of God depended on the concept of a permissive as well as a causative divine will. By God's will in a permissive sense a man may be given up to his own disobedience and evil. See 4:10–12 discussion of God's wrath.

Other interpreters, however, sometimes offer very different explanations. Branscomb, for example, thinks verse 33 must have been

[31] *The Parables of the Kingdom* (London: Nisbet, 1946), pp. 190 f. For a summary of other views, cf. Taylor, p. 269.

"the ending of the original document used by Mark." He says that verse 33 agrees with verses 2 and 9, but that verses 11 and 34 represent a different and Markan viewpoint!

Fourth, Jesus was perfectly aware that the kingdom was remaining a mystery to many. However, to those who were receptive to him he had the custom of expounding all his teaching in more detail. It is implied that the disciples themselves were by no means perfect in their receptivity (cf. above v. 13). In the very next story Jesus rebuked the disciples for the meager nature of their faith.

(6) *Instruction by Mighty Works (4:35—5:43)*

a. The Calming of a Storm (4:35–41)

35 On that day, when evening had come, he
said to them, "Let us go across to the other
side." 36 And leaving the crowd, they took him
with them, just as he was, in the boat. And
other boats were with him. 37 And a great
storm of wind arose, and the waves beat into
the boat, so that the boat was already filling.
38 But he was in the stern, asleep on the cush-
ion; and they woke him and said to him,
"Teacher, do you not care if we perish?"
39 And he awoke and rebuked the wind, and
said to the sea, "Peace! Be still!" And the wind
ceased, and there was a great calm. 40 He said
to them, "Why are you afraid? Have you no
faith?" 41 And they were filled with awe, and
said to one another, "Who then is this, that
even wind and sea obey him?"

Throughout his narrative Mark displays an obvious interest in the miracles performed by Jesus. Up to this point, however, the telling of the wonders has been less detailed, and the emphasis has been on some particular lesson or claim from Jesus. See, for example, 2:10–12 and 3:2–5. In the recounting of the four miracles in this section, however, Jesus is presented as the one empowered beyond all men, the doer of good and mighty works beyond all human conception.

The instruction that came to the twelve through these activities of Jesus was in the nature of a challenge to faith in their Master. The movement in the narrative is toward the confession in 8:29. The retelling of the miracles must have been also a stimulus to the trust of Mark's contemporary Christians: surely he who had shown power over the elements, demons, disease, and death was worthy of their commitment in the midst of the perils they faced.

The story of Jesus' calming the storm is unusually vivid and detailed. Mark connects the time very closely with what has preceded. If we had not had notes such as those of verses 10 and 34, we might readily suppose that Jesus had taught from the boat throughout the whole day. In any case, ***when evening had come*** (i.e., after sunset, but before dark) Jesus proposed that they cross the lake, from the Galilean shore to the eastern or Perean side. Mark does not say explicitly that they did this in order to get away from the crowd, but this must have been one reason. Another suggestion is that Jesus wished to preach in areas not yet visited (cf. 1:38).

The boat in which Jesus had been teaching would likely have been one of the fishing boats. None of these would have been large. Of shallow draft and varying size, all of these boats were small enough to be dragged up on the shore of the lake. If Jesus and all the twelve were aboard, it was surely filled to capacity.

They took him with them, just as he was —i.e., without his going ashore (Swete). At first a few from the crowd were not left behind, for other boats went along. What happened in their case we have no way of knowing. The note adds a vivid detail to the story, but nothing else. Taylor persuasively insists that this detail, along with the precise time given, the reference to the cushion, the fact that the trip was made at Jesus' suggestion and that he did not go ashore, and especially the strong reproach called to Jesus by his disciples (v. 38) reflect the primitive nature of the story and offer some support to the possibility that it came from the apostle Peter.

The squalls that fall upon Lake Galilee are often sudden and severe. On the east shore the mountains rise quickly to a height two thousand feet above the lake's surface. When the wind is channeled through ravines that descend through those heights, the danger to an overloaded little fishing boat becomes fearsome indeed. When this happened to the disciples, they must have exercised all their skill and bailed as fast as they could, but still the high waves and wind brought them to the brink of disaster.

And where was Jesus? Back at the stern, sleeping through it all! Matthew and Luke both soften the disciples' outcry, so that they do not appear to reproach Jesus (Matt. 8:25; Luke 8:24). But Mark's account, from which the others were apparently drawn, has the disciples complaining, Don't you even care if we are about to drown? This is a cry of fear, of irritation, perhaps even of anger. The tense used in the participle translated ***asleep*** and in the verb ***woke*** ordinarily denotes durative action, and may imply that Jesus was so at peace in his sleep that they had difficulty rousing him.

When Jesus ***awoke,*** he ***rebuked the wind.*** He spoke also ***to the sea, Peace! Be still!*** More literally, though less smoothly, the words could be translated, "Stop this noise! Be as though you have been muzzled!" The words rebuked and be muzzled are the same verbs used to describe Jesus' casting out the demon in 1:25. At Jesus' command the wind abated, and calm settled over the sea.

Then Jesus turned to his disciples. The RSV text of his words to them is much better supported than the longer KJV: compare the parallels in Matthew 8:26 and Luke 8:25, which are not so blunt or strong as Mark's account. The ***faith*** which the disciples have not shown is that which would answer their fear: it means trust and reliance on God for help and safety.

It is impossible that this faith should be unconnected with Jesus' own person, as far as Mark and his readers were concerned. Since Jesus was still at work doing what God had sent him to do, and the power of the divine Spirit was upon him, the forces of nature would surely not be able to destroy him. The later generation derived from this story encouragement and hope in facing their own perils as Jesus' followers.

For the twelve, the prior and as yet unsettled question of Jesus' identity was raised by this wonder. If even the wind and the sea were obedient to him, and (it was assumed) nature's works are but vehicles of divine power, who then was Jesus? Whether or not Jesus ever used his extraordinary powers to persuade men to believe on him, their impact upon those around him was surely an incitement to confession of faith. The disciples were rebuked for their lack of faith in God. But the stilling of the storm would have incited faith in Jesus himself as the agent of divine power.

Questions concerning the historicity of this story have been numerous and the solutions proposed have been imaginative, though sometimes strained. For example, it has been suggested that two passages in the Psalms (89:9; 106:9) provided trustful early Christians with the idea that Jesus must have calmed one of nature's storms. Narratives about other nature miracles in contemporary sources have sometimes been cited, though the parallels are not very convincing (one of those suggested is the story of Jonah).

The real problem, however, does not lie in the historicity of the account in Mark. The basic question is theological. As Taylor says, "It depends on our interpretation of the *manner* of the Incarnation in its historical manifestation." Even though it is difficult for us to think of one addressing the wind and the sea in the manner of Jesus, the confidence of Jesus that nature was indeed a vehicle of the divine power and providence was perfectly natural for him. Of course, the story was told in popular language and in contemporary thought-forms. But it was not inevitable that miracle stories should cluster around the name of a great religious figure: no such stories were told of John the Baptist, in the Bible or elsewhere. We can only agree with Rawlinson that Jesus' contemporaries and close associates certainly believed that he worked miracles. Who is yet able to discern the limitations or the possibilities suggested by the incarnation?

In his concluding word about the disciples, Mark says ***they were filled with awe.*** Literally, in an idiom obviously influenced by the Aramaic, "they feared a great fear." Then in the wake of the marvel they began to ask one another who Jesus was. For them the miracle was opening their minds to the truth that Jesus was the Christ and (as they finally would realize) was Lord of all.

b. The Healing of the Gerasene Demoniac (5:1–20)

**1 They came to the other side of the sea, to
the country of the Gerasenes. 2 And when he
had come out of the boat, there met him out of
the tombs a man with an unclean spirit, 3 who
lived among the tombs; and no one could bind
him any more, even with a chain; 4 for he had
often been bound with fetters and chains, but
the chains he wrenched apart, and the fetters
he broke in pieces; and no one had the
strength to subdue him. 5 Night and day among
the tombs and on the mountains he was always
crying out, and bruising himself with stones.
6 And when he saw Jesus from afar, he ran and
worshiped him; 7 and crying out with a loud
voice, he said, "What have you to do with me,
Jesus, Son of the Most High God? I adjure you
by God, do not torment me." 8 For he had said
to him, "Come out of the man, you unclean
spirit!" 9 And Jesus asked him, "What is your
name?" He replied, "My name is Legion; for
we are many." 10 And he begged him eagerly
not to send them out of the country. 11 Now a
great herd of swine was feeding there on the
hillside; 12 and they begged him, "Send us to
the swine, let us enter them." 13 So he gave
them leave. And the unclean spirits came out,
and entered the swine; and the herd, number-
ing about two thousand, rushed down the steep
bank into the sea, and were drowned in the
sea.**

**14 The herdsmen fled, and told it in the city
and in the country. And people came to see
what it was that had happened. 15 And they
came to Jesus, and saw the demoniac sitting
there, clothed and in his right mind, the man
who had had the legion; and they were afraid.
16 And those who had seen it told what had
happened to the demoniac and to the swine.
17 And they began to beg Jesus to depart from
their neighborhood. 18 And as he was getting
into the boat, the man who had been possessed
with demons begged him that he might be with
him. 19 But he refused, and said to him, "Go
home to your friends, and tell them how much
the Lord has done for you, and how he has
had mercy on you." 20 And he went away and
began to proclaim in the Decapolis how much
Jesus had done for him; and all men marveled.**

Mark's account is much more vivid and detailed than the parallels in Luke 8:26–39 and Matthew 8:28–34. Matthew has two fierce demoniacs instead of one, and identifies the place as the country of the Gadarenes rather than Gerasenes. Both were cities of the Decapolis (v. 20), but Gerasa (now called Jerash) was 30 miles and Gadara 6 miles from the lake. A ruin much nearer the shore and called Khersa has been discovered and may have been in the district subject to Gadara. Transliteration may account for some variations in spelling. We have no reason to assume that Mark knew in detail the geographical boundaries of the territory: if he was from Jerusalem it was unlikely that he would have had occasion to travel through the Decapolis.

The story as told may be divided into four parts. In 1–10 the man and his initial encounter with Jesus are described. In 11–13 there is the strange account about the demons and the swine. What happened as far as the herdsmen were concerned is given next (14–17), and finally the healed man, though wanting to go with Jesus, was sent back to his own people (18–20).

When Jesus and his disciples stepped on shore they were in a territory predominantly Gentile. Certainly the swineherds were not Jews, and probably the demon-possessed wretch was also Gentile. However, Mark makes no mention of this.

The man now lived in ***the tombs.*** These were cave-like rooms hewn out for burials, or generally used for that purpose (either in earlier or contemporary times). It was popularly believed that cemeteries might be haunted by demons. But this man lived there, an alien from his people and all society, because he was so utterly violent and unmanageable. People had tried to control him, but he was unusually strong and did not spare his own body in order to break whatever bonds with which they tried to restrain him.

In verse 3 the words translated ***no one could bind him any more*** contain three strong Greek negatives, as strong an expression as imaginable. How he could have ***wrenched apart*** the ***chains*** and crushed the ***fetters*** until they fell to pieces must have been a remarkable and frightening thing to those who heard of it.

In verse 4 the word ***subdue*** is used normally of taming wild animals. Day and night made no difference to him, for he was heard to shriek at any hour and at any place and was constantly bruised and cut by what he did to himself. Mark uses the imperfect tense of the verbs cry out and bruise to accent the unrelieved misery of the man.

If we had only verse 2 we might suppose that the man ***met*** Jesus antagonistically, for sometimes that verb is so used. However, in verse 6 we are told that ***he ran and worshiped him.*** If we understand the conjunction ***for*** in verse 8 to be explanatory of the preceding two verses we may have some insight into why he did this. Even a wild man is a child of his own day. He must have supposed in his demented condition that by prostrating himself before Jesus, by asking him not to meddle with him, by identifying him as ***Jesus, Son of the Most High God,*** and by his plea in God's name not to torment him, maybe Jesus would leave him alone. (Cf. the parallels in the words of the demoniac in 1:24.)

Jesus had been saying (the verb is imperfect) to the unclean spirit, ***Come out of the man.*** However, the deep distress of the man was not readily banished. So Jesus began asking him (again the verb is imperfect and implies some repetition), ***What is your name?*** The response of the man and the unclean spirit are not separable. We must remember that, according to first-century understanding of this man's tragic condition, the demon controlled the man and spoke through his mouth. If the name of the demon was known to the exorciser, it was believed that the exorciser could then control the demon. Perhaps the demon-possessed man tried to defeat Jesus by calling *him* by name (v. 7)! It was therefore probably a help to the man's reliance upon Jesus for our Lord to address by name the demon who possessed him.

The name ***Legion*** did represent ***many*** for a Roman legion numbered about six thousand men. Having told his name, the unclean spirit(s) began to plead for mercy. Moffatt was probably right to translate verse 10, "They begged him earnestly not to send them out of the country." The verb ***begged*** allows either a singular subject (as RSV) or a neuter plural subject; and the words for demon and spirit are both neuter.

The symptoms of the demon-possessed persons described in the Gospels have often been closely examined for similarities with known disorders today. However, the details given are hardly adequate for careful diagnosis by modern physicians. In this case, it has been suggested that verses 3–5 describe "the manic stage of a manic-depressive psychosis." The man was indeed hyperactive, destructive, unable to control himself, or to subject himself to control.

In any case, Jesus did not in his choice of words or in some other discernible way reject the language and presuppositions of the people whom he sought to help. To do so would have been confusing and probably would have clouded their way toward faith. (See above on 1:23 f.; 3:11.)

The ***swine*** that covered the slopes nearby must have been of special concern to the demon-possessed man. Did he in some demented way connect them with his own malady? Mark does not imply this. He speaks only of the demons and their request (through the poor soul whom they dominated) to be allowed to enter the hogs. Neither does Mark say that Jesus sent them into the herd, only that ***he gave them leave.*** That the swine became demon-possessed must have been concluded from what happened to them. Did the demon-possessed man in one last untamed act vent his rage wildly upon the (hated?) hogs and stampede them? Were the herdsmen equally frightened by this notoriously strong and uncontrolled person?

The story abounds with difficulties, but not all our questions can be answered. What we have is a report of what happened from men who spoke in the thought-forms of the first century. Modern interpreters of this event must reach their conclusions on the basis of what they believe about the demonic realm and how they interpret the incarnation. It is most precarious to conclude, for example, that Jesus cared nothing for the hogs: our Lord himself asserted that God is concerned even for sparrows (Luke 12:6). On the other hand, the references by Jesus to God's care for lower forms of life are regularly employed to emphasize his overwhelming concern for man (cf. Matt. 6:26).

When the fleeing herdsmen told what had taken place, the people hurried out to see for themselves (v. 14). We may suppose that the herdsmen had left without waiting to see what finally happened to the demon-possessed man, upon whom they may first have laid the blame for the loss of the swine (v. 16 need not imply that they witnessed everything). However, no such debacle had taken place before Jesus and his disciples appeared on the scene, and it was easy to conclude that their association with the tomb-dweller had precipitated the whole event.

Even the loss of the hogs was not so unbelievable as the change that had taken place in the demoniac. Mark's use of the Greek tenses in verse 15 is unusually vivid. The people see the man who used to be demon-possessed now sitting calmly; he had dressed himself and was now in full and continuing control of his faculties, though he had been under the control of *Legion;* and they got scared. Here was present an awesome power they did not understand. If they had not been so frightened, they might have attacked the intruders, especially the one through whose power this incredible thing had happened. But their fear made them suppliants, and they only begged him to leave.

The final scene in the story is of the man who had been healed (18–20). Like his countrymen, he became a suppliant; but he was begging to be allowed to join the band of disciples. Jesus refused and sent him to his own people to tell of his experience of the Lord's mercy. ***Your friends*** (v. 19) is more precisely "the your" (people), a more inclusive expression than family and close acquaintances. ***The Decapolis*** was originally a league of ten cities lying generally east of Galilee and the Jordan.

Why Jesus' instruction to this man was so different from that to the healed person in 1:44 is not made explicit. (Cf. also 3:12; 5:43.) Since Jesus' own ministry was generally in a different region, fame in this new territory would not constitute a problem for him. Jesus' command was for the man to tell what *the Lord* (i.e., God) had done for him. But the man, according to Mark, made no distinction between God's deed and that of Jesus. The missionary emphasis would not be lost upon Mark's readers.

The focus of the story, however, is not on the spread of Jesus' fame but on the miracle itself. Although nothing similar to 4:41 is expressed, the story points to the unique, divine power that issues through Jesus. The Markan account is progressing toward the question of Jesus in 8:29, "But who do you say that I am?"

c. *The Healing of the Woman with a Flow of Blood (5:21–34)*

**21 And when Jesus had crossed again in the
boat to the other side, a great crowd gathered
about him; and he was beside the sea. 22 Then
came one of the rulers of the synagogue, Jairus
by name; and seeing him, he fell at his feet,
23 and besought him, saying, "My little daughter is at the point of death. Come and lay your
hands on her, so that she may be made well,
and live." 24 And he went with him.**

**And a great crowd followed him and
thronged about him. 25 And there was a woman
who had had a flow of blood for twelve years,
26 and who had suffered much under many
physicians, and had spent all that she had, and
was no better but rather grew worse. 27 She
had heard the reports about Jesus, and came
up behind him in the crowd and touched his
garment. 28 For she said, "If I touch even his**

garments, I shall be made well." 29 And immediately the hemorrhage ceased; and she felt in
her body that she was healed of her disease.
30 And Jesus, perceiving in himself that power
had gone forth from him, immediately turned
about in the crowd, and said, "Who touched
my garments?" 31 And his disciples said to him,
"You see the crowd pressing around you, and
yet you say, 'Who touched me?'" 32 And he
looked around to see who had done it. 33 But
the woman, knowing what had been done to
her, came in fear and trembling and fell down
before him, and told him the whole truth.
34 And he said to her, "Daughter, your faith
has made you well; go in peace, and be healed
of your disease."

The first verses of this section are the introduction to the recounting of two mighty works. The stories are uniquely interwoven and probably came to Mark in this form. As in the two preceding narratives, the interest lies in the miracles themselves and consequently on Jesus' power over disease and death. There is also a strong emphasis on faith as either present or needful (vv. 34–36), and the contrast with what happened (or did not happen) at Nazareth is anticipated (cf. 6:1–6). The parallel accounts are Matthew 9:18–26 and Luke 8:40–56.

After crossing the sea, Jesus was again in familiar Galilean surroundings. The crowds quickly thronged about him again, in contrast with the people on the eastern side who were afraid of his presence. Here Jesus' deeds were well known, and the hope of help drew two distraught persons to call upon him.

The first of these is identified as ***one of the rulers of the synagogue.*** His name is given as ***Jairus*** (though Taylor thinks this note is a scribal addition from Luke 8:41). A synagogue ruler was naturally a very prominent person in the congregation, though his leadership was chiefly administrative rather than spiritual.

Jairus prostrated himself at Jesus' feet and began begging him on behalf of his ***little daughter.*** The diminutive form probably denotes affection and accents the plea for help; it occurs in the New Testament only here and in the similar circumstance of 7:25. A sick person is described as one "having [something] badly" (1:32); the little girl "has [her disease] in the last stages." Will not Jesus come and place his hands on her, Jairus pled, ***so that she may be made well*** (as in v. 34 the verb used is the same one often translated "be saved") and not die?

Jesus turned to go with Jairus, and the crowd ***thronged about him.*** The verb is very strong, and the tense used is again the descriptive imperfect of which Mark is so fond. They kept pressing together on him, or they were crowding him at every step and from every side.

In the throng a second suppliant pressed toward Jesus with single-minded purpose. Her malady had been with her for long years, and her existence must have been miserable. Along with the discomfort her particular problem made her ceremonially unclean. The Law read, "If a woman has a discharge of blood for many days, not at the time of her impurity, or if she has a discharge beyond the time of her impurity, all the days of the discharge she shall continue in uncleanness." (Lev. 15:25); and this uncleanness was regarded as transmissible to others. Mark's account of her long, pathetic quest for help from many doctors and her reduction to worse physical condition as well as utter poverty is very graphic. Compare Luke 8:43, where the account is much kinder to physicians.

She ***touched his garment*** (Matthew and Luke have "fringe of his garment"). She did this because she had heard of Jesus' healings (v. 27) and because she shared the ancient view that the healer's own person was potent and that his clothing or even his shadow could serve as bearers of his power. For New Testament examples, note the incidents of Acts 5:15 and 19:12. When she had successfully fought her way through the crowd, near enough to touch Jesus' robe, she felt that the flow had stopped and her body had finally been healed.

If the woman had hoped to maintain her anonymity she failed. More likely she had not thought further than her objective already achieved. There would have been strict Jews nearby who would have resented this unclean and so estranged woman endangering their own acceptable status. However, she must have known that Jesus had been unusually willing to reach out to persons from whom her more rigid compatriots turned away—the leper, the tax collector, the sinner.

Mark tells us that Jesus turned immediately to find out who touched him, because he perceived ***in himself that power had gone forth from him.*** In biblical usage the word here translated ***power*** usually denoted some mighty work that manifested God's activity (cf. 6:2,5; 9:39 where RSV so translates it), or else the active power of the living and personal God. The faith that lies behind this verse claims that in Jesus' person there dwelled the power of God over the maladies that beset men. The Spirit of God had descended upon Jesus (1:10). Now, as at other times since then, ***power*** had indeed ***gone forth from him.***

It has often been remarked that the disciples' curt answer to Jesus reflects the primitive nature of Mark's account (cf. 4:38). It also testifies to the comprehensive nature of the incarnation and to the limitations of the disciples' own faith in their Teacher at this point. Jesus did not know who had sought help from him (v. 32), though he had intuitively realized that someone had done so (v. 30). Calvin thought Jesus did know already who she was, and that he asked only to make her confess her faith. But the event is more naturally explained by Jesus' desire to draw her imperfect faith away from any diluting superstitions about his robe to a more personal commitment to himself.

The woman was grateful and courageous. In the hearing of that crowd to tell ***the whole truth,*** including the confession that she had rendered Jesus ceremonially unclean according to the Law, required courage. However, the ***fear*** and ***trembling*** which were her uncontrollable experience came upon her because she realized what had happened to her body. This at least is Mark's explanation—***knowing what had been done to her;*** Luke's account is different (cf. 8:47).

Jesus accepted the woman's explanation, and the woman herself. ***Daughter*** is of course not to be interpreted literally, but nevertheless in terms of full acceptance into Jesus' "real" family (3:35). The meaning of ***faith*** must not be narrowed to an attitude entirely dependent on the woman's mind. As Taylor says, New Testament faith consistently derives its strength and content from its object. Faith in God, although a venture of the human spirit, becomes real and powerful through the divine inworking (cf. 9:24; 11:22). The trust of the woman was welcomed by the power present and working through Jesus.

Go in peace was the usual Hebrew word of farewell. Perhaps Jesus intended the rich heritage of the Hebrew parallel to be understood; in that case, peace means wholeness, soundness, rather than simply the absence of strife. The adieu would be a calming answer to the woman's fear and trembling. Nida translates into Shilluk dialect, "Go with sweet insides," and in Tzeltal, "Go and sit down in your heart."

d. Healing Jairus' Daughter (5:35–43)

**35 While he was still speaking, there came
from the ruler's house some who said, "Your
daughter is dead. Why trouble the Teacher any
further?" 36 But ignoring what they said, Jesus
said to the ruler of the synagogue, "Do not
fear, only believe." 37 And he allowed no one
to follow him except Peter and James and John
the brother of James. 38 When they came to the
house of the ruler of the synagogue, he saw a
tumult, and people weeping and wailing
loudly. 39 And when he had entered, he said to
them, "Why do you make a tumult and weep?
The child is not dead but sleeping." 40 And
they laughed at him. But he put them all
outside, and took the child's father and mother
and those who were with him, and went in
where the child was. 41 Taking her by the hand
he said to her, "Talitha cumi"; which means,
"Little girl, I say to you, arise." 42 And immediately
the girl got up and walked; for she was
twelve years old. And immediately they were
overcome with amazement. 43 And he strictly
charged them that no one should know this,
and told them to give her something to eat.**

Before Jesus had finished talking with the woman (perhaps the interruption hurried his farewell), some of Jairus' household broke through the crowd to tell the distraught father that his daughter had died. Since there is obviously nothing anyone can do now, ***Why trouble the Teacher any further?*** But the power of God in Jesus, Mark is about to say, called for no such resignation. The rule of God which had drawn near in Jesus (1:15) and which is mightier than storm, or host of demons, or tenacious disease, wielded control also over death.

The idea that the little girl did not die but was in a coma has its roots in the philosophical viewpoint that a resurrection of a dead body is contrary to the nature of reality. Jesus' denial of her death (v. 39) has been seized upon to support this view, as indeed that particular statement does permit. Compare the parallel accounts in Matthew 9:24 and Luke 8:52. We cannot be dogmatic on this point. We must recognize, however, that Jesus did not speak in the manner of a physician, nor as a diagnostic specialist: he spoke as the Son in whom God's power was perfectly manifest. The writers of the Gospels certainly believed Jesus could and did raise the dead.[32]

Jesus could hardly have helped overhearing the message from the ruler's house. The word translated ***ignoring*** in RSV may also mean overhearing, and Luke (8:50) so understood it. ***Do not fear, only believe*** may be paraphrased, "Stop being afraid, only keep trusting." John 14:1 is a close parallel; see also Mark 6:50.

The bulk of the crowd was sent away, and only the three disciples who seem to have been a kind of inner circle were allowed to go along with Jesus and the girl's father. This action may have been taken to allow them to hurry, or perhaps to avoid unwanted publicity (cf. v. 43).

Those in the house were loudly wailing, according to the custom of that day. Probably some were professional mourners, whether or not they had already been employed for that purpose. In the Mishnah even the poorest were encouraged to employ at least two flutists and one "wailing woman." When Jesus told them the child was ***not dead but sleeping,*** their reaction was scornful, mocking laughter (the verb form describes continuous or repeated scoffing).

What did Jesus mean by saying the girl was ***sleeping?*** Does he mean only that, although the girl may be dead from man's point of view, he will raise her and so her death is no more permanent than a sleep? The problem is complicated by the customary use of the verb sleep to describe death (1 Thess. 5:10; John 11:4,11–14; also in LXX; Dan. 12:2; Psalm 87:6). Mark's readers, of course, would be reminded of their hope, even in the presence of death.

The derisive mourners were banished from the house, and only the three disciples and the parents of the girl witnessed what happened. ***Talitha cumi*** is transliterated from Aramaic and simply means, as Mark tells us, ***Little girl*** (or lamb), ***arise.*** The use of foreign words was common in miracle stories of ancient times, as R. Bultmann, M. Dibelius, and others have pointed out. But Mark's use here and elsewhere seems rather to reflect the Aramaic origin of his narrative than any special reference to his healings (3:17; 7:11; 14:36).

The girl answered Jesus' command by standing up and beginning to walk again. The note concerning her age is simply to tell us that she was no little infant. Our Lord's concern for the girl's need of food was intended to bring the group in the room back to earthly reality. Perhaps also the simple business of feeding the girl would help them to calm themselves and to obey his strict order not to go telling everybody about the miracle. Who would understand what had happened anyway, except men whose minds were open and who had come to believe? (See 4:10–12; 5:36.)

32 See A. Richardson, *The Miracle-Stories of the Gospels* (London: SCM, 1941); R. H. Fuller, *Interpreting the Miracles* (Philadelphia: Westminster, 1963); D. S. Cairns, *The Truth That Rebels* (London: SCM, 1954); and the brief, excellent summary in Cranfield, *Mark,* pp. 82–86.

3. *Rejection and Recognition of the Christ (6:1—8:30)*

(1) *Unbelief and Rejection at Home (6:1–6a)*

**1 He went away from there and came to his
own country; and his disciples followed him.
2 And on the sabbath he began to teach in the
synagogue; and many who heard him were
astonished, saying, "Where did this man get all
this? What is the wisdom given to him? What
mighty works are wrought by his hands! 3 Is
not this the carpenter, the son of Mary and
brother of James and Joses and Judas and
Simon, and are not his sisters here with us?"
And they took offense at him. 4 And Jesus said
to them, "A prophet is not without honor,
except in his own country, and among his own
kin, and in his own house." 5 And he could do
no mighty work there, except that he laid his
hands upon a few sick people and healed them.
6 And he marveled because of their unbelief.**

Jesus' instruction of the twelve continues through the next section. However, the Markan emphasis shifts more and more to the question, Who do men think Jesus is? Before the climax of recognition in 8:27–30, Mark describes how both Jesus and John were rejected, how the crowds marveled but did not really perceive, how Jesus separated his own outlook from that of the Jewish teachers, and how the disciples were slow to understand but finally recognized the Messiah. There is no sharp break in the narrative, either grammatically (it begins, "He went away from there . . .") or in Mark's concern with Jesus' ***mighty works*** (v. 2) and man's faith or unbelief (v. 6).

By Jesus' ***own country*** is meant his "home town" (TEV). Mark knew that this was Nazareth (1:9,24). Perhaps he used the less precise term because, writing to Roman Christians, he wished to symbolize Jesus' rejection by most of the Hebrew people. That Jesus had used this word in the saying quoted in verse 4 may also have influenced Mark's choice.

In Luke's account, Jesus visited Nazareth very early in his ministry, and what he read and spoke in the synagogue there served as a definitive theme for Jesus' work as a whole (4:16–30). Robertson thinks that Jesus was giving the Nazarenes another opportunity to hear and accept him. The pattern of amazement and offended rejection are common to both, however, and the order in which other events are recounted in the Gospels varies widely.

Jesus went to the ***synagogue*** and was teaching there. Mark does not speak again of Jesus' using the synagogue as a center for his work (cf. 1:21; 1:39; 3:1).

The reaction of the citizens of Nazareth was first one of amazement (v. 2), then of indignation (v. 3), and is summed up in the word ***unbelief*** (v. 6). How could this ordinary looking man from such an ordinary home be the agent of such extraordinary ***wisdom*** and ***mighty works?*** Wisdom and power ("mighty works" translates the word powers; cf. 5:30) correspond to word and deed in biblical usage and are especially applicable to divine guidance and activity. See the description of wisdom in Proverbs 8:12–31. Wisdom and power are coupled in the description of the root of Jesse (Isa. 11:2), and of the Messiah in the noncanonical Psalms of Solomon (17:24 f.). Paul called Christ God's power and wisdom (1 Cor. 1:24).

Jesus was called ***the son of Mary.*** If this is the correct reading, this may well have been a slurring, insulting remark by the men of Nazareth, meaning, Who was his father? But Mark gives no hint that he understood the phrase in this way, and the common explanation that Joseph was dead may be adequate. Matthew, however, calls Jesus "the carpenter's son," a more natural Hebrew description even if Joseph had died. Johnson and Taylor, with some strong evidence, consider that the original Markan text corresponded with Matthew.

The word translated ***carpenter*** was applied to any artisan. In the second century Justin Martyr wrote that Jesus did "carpenter's jobs" and made plows and yokes. It is altogether probable that Jesus would have worked with Joseph, but only here in the New Testament is he specifically described as a carpenter; and, as just noted, the correct text may read "son of the carpenter." Mark's point is still clear: to the people of Nazareth Jesus may have seemed unusually gifted, but his heritage was utterly ordinary. They might have been offended by Nathanael's question, "Can anything good come out of Nazareth?" but the ironic parallel with their own feelings is all too evident (John 1:46).

The brothers of Jesus are named only here (and in Matt. 13:55). We do not know the names of any of his sisters. Of James and Judas (or Jude) we have some later word: James was an early leader of the church in Jerusalem (Gal. 1:19), and two of the letters in the New Testament were credited to these two brothers. The "brothers of the Lord" are also referred to by Paul as doing missionary work (1 Cor. 9:5). See comment on 3:31.

The people of Nazareth ***took offense at him;*** i.e., they were unable to bring themselves to believe that God might be at work among them, particularly in one of such humble origin. For an instructive parallel use of this verb see Matthew 11:6.

The saying of Jesus compares his own experience to that of the prophets. As John wrote (1:11), "He came to his own home, and his own people received him not." His work was limited among his own people by their inability or unwillingness to trust him.

Mark's account is remarkable for its candor in affirming that Jesus ***could do no mighty work there*** except to heal a few people and that he was surprised at the people's opposition to himself. Faith on the part of the one being healed was not the source of Jesus' power. The power had to be in Jesus himself. The girl in 5:31–43 could not have had prior faith (cf. 9:14–29). Burkill thinks that Mark 6:5–6 was not primarily concerned with Jesus' supernatural power as such, but was meant to illustrate the privations which result from lack of faith. Accordingly, he suggests that Mark's report owes its form to the disappointment of many early Christians in their witness to Jews. However, Taylor is probably right in regarding the difficulties of these verses as marks of the genuineness of Mark's sources.

(2) *Ministry Through the Twelve* (*6:6b–13*)

And he went about among the villages teaching.

[7] And he called to him the twelve, and began to send them out two by two, and gave them authority over the unclean spirits. [8] He charged them to take nothing for their journey except a staff; no bread, no bag, no money in their belts; [9] but to wear sandals and not put on two tunics. [10] And he said to them, "Where you enter a house, stay there until you leave the place. [11] And if any place will not receive you and they refuse to hear you, when you leave, shake off the dust that is on your feet for a testimony against them." [12] So they went out and preached that men should repent. [13] And they cast out many demons, and anointed with oil many that were sick and healed them.

Jesus' training of the twelve had by now come to the point that he could send them out to spread his teaching. He himself continued to work from village to village, but the voices of his disciples could multiply his ministry. According to 3:14, part of his purpose in choosing the twelve had been so that he might send them out to preach and share in a desired way his authority over all the powers of evil.

That Jesus ***began*** to send out his disciples means only that he had not done so before. Whether they all left at the same time is not clear. See verse 30: had he appointed a set time for their return, or did he keep in touch with their progress? In any case, Jesus always seems to have sent them in pairs (cf. Luke 10:1), and the early church followed this practice as well (Paul and Barnabas, Barnabas and Mark, Paul and Silas).

Itinerant religious teachers were not foreign to the Eastern scene of the day. Heathen preachers, equipped with staff and wallet and not much else, travelled about speaking their messages. Pairs of Jews were sent out similarly, but they were normally sent out as collectors of alms. The disciples, however, were forbidden to ask alms: they were not to take a ***bag*** (the word is used for the begging bag of the itinerant preachers), nor were they to have ***money in their belts.*** Coins were normally carried in a man's girdle; the word for money here means copper or brass, which would refer to coins of least value.

They could take ***a staff*** (for protection?) and ***wear sandals.*** These two items were denied the disciples according to Matthew 10:10 and Luke 9:3. Taylor and Cranfield are among the recent interpreters who believe that the stricter version is more original, but would have been difficult for those in the western part of the empire, for whom Mark wrote, to understand.

They were not to put on ***two tunics.*** The tunic was the shirt worn next to the body. The parallel accounts simply forbid taking along a change in tunics.

Hospitality was regarded as a duty among the Hebrew people, and it could be taken for granted that the disciples would be given food and lodging. However, they were not to be looking for more comfortable quarters to which they might move! The disciples were to seek a hearing in every appropriate way, but they were not to force themselves or their message on anyone.

To ***shake off the dust that is on your feet*** was a symbolic act. It meant that the place was unresponsive to the word of God, that it was heathen, whether or not it was by heritage a Jewish town (Swete, T. W. Manson). Not a curse, the symbol was in the nature of a warning. It was ***for a testimony against them;*** Moffatt translates it "as a warning to them." Compare the instruction to the watchman in Ezekiel 33:1–9; and note the similar actions in Acts 13:51 and 18:6. (The KJV has an additional clause about Sodom and Gomorrah, but it is original in Matt. 10:15 and Luke 10:12, not in Mark.)

Why did Jesus give his disciples such instructions? One obvious reason, applicable in Mark's day also, was that Jesus knew that men could bring the gospel into disrepute by taking advantage of the opportunities for profit. The commands of Jesus were not consonant with upper-middle-class living: they required frugality. His missionaries must not be greedy or grasping. The Teaching of the Twelve Apostles reflects how seriously these instructions needed to be taken.

"Let every apostle, when he cometh to you, be received as the Lord; but he shall not abide more than a single day, or if there be need, a second likewise; but if he abide three days, he is a false prophet. And when he departeth let the apostle receive nothing save bread, until he findeth shelter; but if he ask money, he is a false prophet." [33]

We should also note that Jesus' commands had a note of urgency in them. The heralds were to take only the barest essentials, with no preparatory packing and no luggage to slow them down. They were to travel lightly, stop briefly, hurry on to find persons receptive to the message.[34]

On their mission the disciples preached repentance (cf. on 1:15), and through their hands the presence of divine power was manifested in healing. The tense of the verbs used implies that the casting out of demons and the acts of healing occurred from time to time.

Olive oil was widely used in medicinal practice of that day. With the disciples, to anoint with oil was probably also a symbolic religious act. Later miracles were done "in the name of Jesus" (Acts 3:6). See, how-

33 The translation is from J. B. Lightfoot, *The Apostolic Fathers* (London: Macmillan, 1926), p. 233.

34 The urgency evident in Jesus' instructions was not dwelled upon by Mark. Schweitzer's interpretation of Jesus' ministry hinged heavily upon his theory that Jesus expected an apocalyptic inbreaking of his kingdom, the coming of a heavenly Son of man. His key verse was Matt. 10:23: "You will not have gone through all the towns of Israel, before the Son of man comes." This is not in Mark; the closest parallel is 8:38—9:1. Taylor thinks Schweitzer was right in concluding that Jesus altered his understanding of the kingdom and the role of the Son of man at this time, though Taylor's understanding of Jesus' concept of the kingdom is quite different. "A crisis was imminent," he writes; "it was the eve of expected events. . . . [This was no] simple evangelistic tour. . . . They were heralds of the swift advent of the kingdom of God." *Life and Ministry of Jesus* (New York: Abingdon, 1955) p. 114. However, in his commentary, Taylor recognizes that in Mark's account the mission of the twelve is only an extension of Jesus' teaching ministry (p. 302).

ever, the instruction in James 5:14, when prayer and anointing with oil are coupled in the church's healing ministry. Anointing with oil is not mentioned elsewhere in the New Testament, except in the parable of the good Samaritan (Luke 10:34).

(3) *Herod's Appraisal of Jesus and the Death of John the Baptist* (*6:14–29*)

14 King Herod heard of it; for Jesus' name had become known. Some said, "John the baptizer has been raised from the dead; that is why these powers are at work in him." 15 But others said, "It is Elijah." And others said, "It is a prophet, like one of the prophets of old." 16 But when Herod heard of it he said, "John, whom I beheaded, has been raised." 17 For Herod had sent and seized John, and bound him in prison for the sake of Herodias, his brother Philip's wife; because he had married her. 18 For John said to Herod, "It is not lawful for you to have your brother's wife." 19 And Herodias had a grudge against him, and wanted to kill him. But she could not, 20 for Herod feared John, knowing that he was a righteous and holy man, and kept him safe. When he heard him, he was much perplexed; and yet he heard him gladly. 21 But an opportunity came when Herod on his birthday gave a banquet for his courtiers and officers and the leading men of Galilee. 22 For when Herodias' daughter came in and danced, she pleased Herod and his guests; and the king said to the girl, "Ask me for whatever you wish, and I will grant it." 23 And he vowed to her, "Whatever you ask me, I will give you, even half of my kingdom." 24 And she went out, and said to her mother, "What shall I ask?" And she said, "The head of John the baptizer." 25 And she came in immediately with haste to the king, and asked, saying, "I want you to give me at once the head of John the Baptist on a platter." 26 And the king was exceedingly sorry; but because of his oaths and his guests he did not want to break his word to her. 27 And immediately the king sent a soldier of the guard and gave orders to bring his head. He went and beheaded him in the prison, 28 and brought his head on a platter, and gave it to the girl; and the girl gave it to her mother. 29 When his disciples heard of it, they came and took his body, and laid it in a tomb.

The spread of Jesus' call to repentance by the disciples' preaching, together with the wonders accompanying their work, brought much wider fame to Jesus himself. One of those who now gave attention was *King Herod.* This ruler was Herod Antipas, tetrarch of Galilee and Perea from 4 B.C. to A.D. 39; he was the son of Herod the Great (Matt. 2:1) and Malthace. From Josephus we learn that his ambition for the title "king" led finally to his banishment with Herodias to Gaul.

Speculation about who Jesus might be was rife everywhere. The disciples preached Jesus' message, but they did not (yet) call him Christ. Nevertheless, 6:14 anticipates the disciples' confession in 8:27–30. We must bear in mind that Jesus did not assert openly to the crowds about him his specific identity.

Herod's own fearful conclusion was that John, the man he had put to death, must have come back to life. A. Loisy did not believe that Herod was so superstitious as this, but that he probably meant by such words that Jesus would bring to his domain the same kind of trouble that John had brought. John and Jesus were both popular leaders, calling for change (repentance) and speaking of the kingdom of God (words which in themselves might or might not be fomenting rebellion). Josephus reported that John was put to death for political reasons. Publicly, Antipas would surely have given these reasons rather than the personal problem to which Mark ascribes his motives for beheading John.

Herodias had been married first to a half-brother of Antipas whose name was Philip. This Philip is not to be confused with the grandson of Herod the Great, Philip II, who was currently tetrarch of Iturea, Trachonitis, and Gaulonitis. Philip II eventually married Salome, Herodias' daughter. Herodias herself was a granddaughter of Herod the Great: her father was a half-brother of Antipas and Philip I, who was put to death by his suspicious father.[35]

In order to marry Herodias (already the

[35] A good, brief treatment of Herod's family relationships is found in M. Unger, *Bible Dictionary* (Chicago: Moody, 1957), pp. 470–79. Josephus' account of John's death is found in *Antiq.* XVIII, v. The historical problems are still not fully resolved because of the limitations of the ancient records. Mark's account seems to be the popular explanation of events. Also see article by Smith on p. 1.

wife of his brother) Herod Antipas divorced his first wife, who was the daughter of Aretas IV of Nabatea. Eventually this act led to war, and Herod was decisively beaten (A.D. 36). The judgment of the common people was that God in this way was punishing Herod for his sin in killing John. John the Baptist, perhaps in answer to the questions of common people at first, had denounced Herod's marriage as a breach of God's law (cf. Lev. 18:16; 20:21).

The narrative does not seem unduly hard on Herod. It does reflect his fearfulness and his interest in religion. But Herod was also subject to other pressures about him, whether from his wife, from the opinions of those who might think him weak, or from his own careless promises. The angered Herodias would have had John put to death sooner. The text is very vivid: she "had it in for him" and "was constantly seeking" his death. However, she had no power herself to order the execution. Herod knew that John ***was a righteous and holy man*** and kept protecting him and even listening to him.

Josephus says that John's imprisonment was at Machaerus, a strong castle high above a ravine near the eastern shore of the Dead Sea. It has been suggested that detention near Tiberias would better accord with Mark's account of the feast and the execution, as well as with Herod's own interest in hearing John (Rawlinson, Johnson, Taylor). The evidence is inadequate for any sure conclusion.

Herod ***was much perplexed*** by John (KJV has a less well attested text, "he did many things"). The sense of Mark's account is that Herod liked to listen to John, but whenever he did he was much disturbed. Herod could find no way to remain who he was and as he was and still change in the ways John must have been suggesting.

Herodias' long-coveted opportunity came on Herod's birthday when the tetrarch gave a great feast for all the aristocracy of his territory (v. 21). For Herodias' daughter to dance before this assembly, where so much wine must have been imbibed, is evidence of the utter corruption of Herod's court. Johnson suggests that Salome must have been born about A.D. 10, and that she may already have been married to her much older uncle, Philip II.

Antipas' vow to the girl (v. 23) must have been given loudly, under the influence of his drink and spurred by the lustful delight of the feasters. There is good textual support for the reading that he repeatedly voiced his promise to her (TEV reads, "With many vows"); in any case, the word oaths in verse 26 is plural.

The girl turned the promise over to her mother, and Herodias, who already had what money could buy for her, wanted most of all to be rid of her meddling enemy, John the Baptist. Was he not the voice of the barbs that kept her husband's conscience bleeding and her own life disturbed? Now, before her weak husband changed his mind, she wanted John beheaded. It may well have been, as Mark's account allows, that the gruesome details of the request were added by Salome: Bring me at once (before this assembly?) John's head on a platter!

Herod was sorry then that he had made such an oath, but it was easier for him to accede to her request than to withdraw his vow before his guests. Compare Pilate's predicament in 15:6–15. Mark may have given this story in such detail partly because of this parallel.

What the girl asked was done, and the party must have broken up with its spirit of careless debauchery changed by the ghastly scene. Mark tells us only that the girl took the gift she had requested and gave it to her mother. Then he adds that John's disciples came and gave the body of their teacher proper burial. (Of John's disciples at this time we know little; cf. 1:5; 2:18; John 3:22—4:3.)

(4) *The Return of the Twelve and the Feeding of the Five Thousand (6:30–44)*

30 The apostles returned to Jesus, and told him all that they had done and taught. 31 And he said to them, "Come away by yourselves to

a lonely place, and rest a while." For many
were coming and going, and they had no leisure even to eat. 32 And they went away in the
boat to a lonely place by themselves. 33 Now
many saw them going, and knew them, and
they ran there on foot from all the towns, and
got there ahead of them. 34 As he landed he
saw a great throng, and he had compassion on
them, because they were like sheep without a
shepherd; and he began to teach them many
things. 35 And when it grew late, his disciples
came to him and said, "This is a lonely place,
and the hour is now late; 36 send them away, to
go into the country and villages round about
and buy themselves something to eat." 37 But
he answered them, "You give them something
to eat." And they said to him, "Shall we go and
buy two hundred denarii worth of bread, and
give it to them to eat?" 38 And he said to them,
"How many loaves have you? Go and see."
And when they had found out, they said,
"Five, and two fish." 39 Then he commanded
them all to sit down by companies upon the
green grass. 40 So they sat down in groups, by
hundreds and by fifties. 41 And taking the five
loaves and the two fish he looked up to heaven,
and blessed, and broke the loaves, and gave
them to the disciples to set before the people;
and he divided the two fish among them all.
42 And they all ate and were satisfied. 43 And
they took up twelve baskets full of broken
pieces and of the fish. 44 And those who ate the
loaves were five thousand men.

The remainder of Mark 6 is told as a closely knit unit, as though neither Jesus nor his disciples had opportunity even to sleep. We may assume that Matthew, who was following Mark's order at this point, was partly correct in assuming that Jesus' withdrawal from Galilee at this time was to get out of Herod's territory (Matt. 14:13; cf. Luke 13:31). However, the only reason that Mark explicitly gives is that Jesus was hoping to have some leisure and quiet time with the twelve. According to Mark's arrangement, Jesus was in this respect unsuccessful, for the crowd that pursued him numbered ***five thousand men*** (6:44), and the weary disciples were still battling the wind on the lake at "the fourth watch of the night" (6:48).

Mark begins with the return of the twelve, whom he here, and only here, calls ***apostles.*** During the time of Jesus this name would have signified "missionaries" (Rawlinson), but Mark's readers would readily have thought of the responsibility and authority of their later position in the early church.

When the disciples had reported ***all that they had done and taught,*** Jesus must have desired the opportunity to instruct them further—on the basis of their experiences. They were hungry and tired: after involvement with the crowds, which their teaching must have excited, they were likely very glad to seek ***a lonely place.*** The word used is commonly translated "desert," but RSV has correctly interpreted here. They were hunting an isolated spot where the green grass of that springtime would be inviting (cf. v. 39). Luke reports that they went to Bethsaida (i.e., Bethsaida Julias), but he also assumes a place in the open country (9:10–12).

As they often did, they traveled by boat. However, the lake is not so large that their direction could not be judged by people ashore. Many of these recognized the band and journeyed around the lake, spreading the word of Jesus' presence. Mark tells us ***they ran there on foot from all the towns*** and arrived ahead of Jesus and the twelve. A less worthy person might have been exasperated—perhaps the disciples were—but Mark's record reports Jesus' reaction as compassion.

The people who had followed Jesus had not thought of his (or his disciples') weariness. The root of Jesus' compassion lay in the fact that he did consider why they had come. Were they not as shepherdless ***sheep?*** (Cf. Matt. 9:36.) ***A shepherd*** would keep his flock together, he would lead them to water and pasture, he would protect them (cf. Psalm 23). The people needed a sense of unity, they needed purpose, and they needed leadership that would not exploit them but guide them aright.

The feeding of the five thousand is the only mighty work of Jesus recorded in all four Gospels (cf. Matt. 14:13–21; Luke 9:10–17; John 6:5–13). Except for John, where the discourse given hinges on the meaning of this great sign, no teaching is recorded except what the miracle itself implies. But certainly some of the meaning given to the "sign" by John was intended by Mark for his own readers.

As the day drew to a close, the disciples interrupted the teaching that had been going on for so long and suggested the crowd be dispersed to the nearby settlements to procure food for themselves. Jesus' response was, ***You*** [the pronoun is emphatic] ***give them something to eat*** (v. 36). What could they do? It would have cost ***two hundred denarii*** to buy bread for such a throng. A denarius was a Roman silver coin, worth about 18 cents by weight. This amount is misleading to Americans living in a different economy: one denarius represented the full day's wages of a day-laborer (cf. Matt. 20:2). The band of disciples would surely have had no such sum.

The discussion concerning the bread needed and the cost involved is but "window dressing" for the main event which is to follow. John's account states openly that Jesus knew what he would do (6:6). John also is the only writer to mention Philip and Andrew by name and to say that the five loaves and two fish were secured from a lad in the crowd. The Synoptics are not explicit at this point, but without other information we would have assumed that the bread and fish were all that was left of the disciples' store (v. 38).

With this little bit of food at hand (the fish would have been small and ready to eat), Jesus instructed the crowd ***to sit down by companies upon the green grass.*** The word sit down is often used for reclining at a banquet table. They arranged themselves by fifties and hundreds so that they appeared as "garden plots" (RSV has ***groups***) on the verdant landscape.

Thereupon, Jesus, taking the bread and the fish, ***looked up to heaven.*** The verb here denotes an act of prayer, especially thanksgiving. We are reminded of the Jewish blessing: "Blessed art thou, O Lord our God, King of the world, who bringest forth bread from the earth." So Jesus blessed the loaves and broke them up for distribution to the people by the disciples. The two fish were similarly divided for all.

The phrasing in verse 41 is so closely similar to that of 14:22 that Mark obviously is thinking of what happened later at the institution of the Lord's Supper.

And they all ate and were satisfied. The verb is the same as in Matthew 5:6, but here it means their physical hunger was fully satisfied. That Mark (and the others) do not understand the word in some figurative sense is emphasized by how much was left over. These ***baskets*** were wicker baskets, varying in size and use; a different word for baskets is used after the four thousand are fed (8:8).

The nature and meaning of this event have been widely debated. It is an interesting fact that nothing is said of the amazement or wonder of the crowd. But this silence does not mean their amazement was not being roused. Why, for example, did Jesus compel his disciples to leave, "while he dismissed the crowd" (v. 45)? Even if so large a crowd had not been able to watch closely what happened, the disciples had surely done so. Is not John's account most reasonable in reporting that the crowd wanted Jesus to accept kingship over them? (Cf. 6:14–15.) Is it not likely that the disciples encouraged this acclaim, perhaps even leading the crowd in its misunderstanding of what kind of King-Messiah God had purposed? Still, the meaning of the story to Mark and his readers is more likely to be found in the teaching implied by the event than in the mighty work itself.

The explanations of the passage may be divided into four groups (cf. Major, Manson, and Wright, 90 f.).

The first group view the story as pure myth, created by the early believers, perhaps in imitation of the miraculous feeding by the prophet Elisha (cf. 2 Kings 4:42–44). The contrasts in amount of food and the number who ate would of course point to the greater power of Jesus.

The second group view the story as an allegory. The five loaves are the Law (five books), while the fish represent the sections of the Hebrew Bible—the Prophets and the Writings. But the people are hungry until Jesus comes with adequate nourishment. Others have allegorized the passage according to what Major calls "the Gospel of the Christian Socialist": Jesus first fed men's moral and spiritual wants, and then more than satisfied their economic needs. Such allegorical methods often set forth a truth, but who can seriously believe that Mark intended his account to be treated in such fashion? In John, however, Jesus did compare himself to the heavenly manna (6:51).

Third, other interpreters accept the narrative as historical, but because of their view of nature's laws and of the incarnation do not believe that the bread and fish were actually multiplied. A. Schweitzer and W. Sanday, for example, think the entire story true except for the one particular, that all had enough to eat! It has been suggested that the miracle lay in the fact that Jesus by his action induced all to share what they had, so there was enough for all; or that Jesus, by the force of his person, banished the physical pangs of those who shared but tiny morsels.

Finally, the traditional interpretation of the narrative as miracle is still accepted by many. Cranfield, for example, adopts this view, though he believes that only the disciples were aware of what happened. He emphasizes the simplicity of the fare provided by Jesus, and points out that its austerity has much in common with the divinely provided manna in the wilderness (Num. 11:6 f.) but not with the eschatological feast described by Isaiah (25:6).

We must remember that the Bible of Mark's readers was the Old Testament, and that the great event of the Old Testament was the Exodus—God's deliverance of his people from bondage. The Jewish people traditionally expected the coming Redeemer to provide manna anew for his own.[36] The miracle would surely have come to mean to Christians that the Redeemer had indeed come from God and the promises of deliverance were to be fulfilled.

It is in full accord with this that Mark also has in mind the Last Supper, as it was instituted and as the early Christians shared it. The parallels in word and event between 6:40–42 and 14:18–32 are too close to suppose otherwise. In their own circumstances the Christians whom Mark was addressing would have drawn a paralled between Jesus and his guests at the meal in the wilderness, and the thankful table-fellowship which they celebrated with one another and the risen Lord when they observed the eucharistic meal. The catacombs contain very early Christian frescoes in which bread and fish are symbols of the Lord's Supper. The fish mosaics preserved on the traditional site of the miracle are another (but later) example.

In our interpretation of this passage, we are not required to believe that the disciples understood the meaning of the miracle as Mark expected his readers to do. We are specifically told that they did not, for they were still under the unyielding influence of their earlier religious concepts (v. 52). Mark's contemporaries were not restricted in this way, and were always conscious of what later happened to Jesus. The twelve were still struggling, not yet recognizing Jesus. Mark's presentation gives us both mystery and revelation at the same time.

(5) *Walking on the Water (6:45–52)*

45 Immediately he made his disciples get into the boat and go before him to the other side, to Bethsaida, while he dismissed the crowd. 46 And after he had taken leave of them, he went into the hills to pray. 47 And when evening came, the boat was out on the sea, and he was alone on the land. 48 And he saw that they were distressed in rowing, for the wind was against them. And about the fourth watch of the night he came to them, walking on the sea. He meant to pass by them, 49 but when they saw him walking on the sea they thought it was a ghost, and cried out; 50 for they all saw him, and were terrified. But immediately he

[36] Cf. Cranfield, p. 222. OT background pasages include Ex. 16, 1 Kings 17:8–16, and 2 Kings 4:42–44. Cf. also 2 Baruch 29:8; and the *Mekilta* on Exodus 16:25 (quoted by Cranfield), "Ye shall not find it (i.e., the manna) in this age, but ye shall find it in the age that is coming."

spoke to them and said, "Take heart, it is I; have no fear." [51] **And he got into the boat with them and the wind ceased. And they were utterly astounded,** [52] **for they did not understand about the loaves, but their hearts were hardened.**

The geographical notes in this and the preceding section, with the parallels in the other accounts are difficult to follow with any precision. If the disciples were to go ***to the other side, to Bethsaida,*** and if Luke 9:10 is taken seriously, then Jesus and the disciples must have put to shore earlier than planned, perhaps because they saw the crowd following. Bethsaida is probably Bethsaida-Julias, east of the river as it flows southward into the Sea of Galilee. Gennesaret (v. 53) was the name of a small plain close by Capernaum. Did they need to "cross over" to get there? John 6:17, in contrast with Mark 6:45, has the disciples going from the place where the five thousand were fed directly to Capernaum.

Mark's arrangement is careful and purposeful, affirming for his readers the significance of Jesus. In 4:1–41 the Jesus who taught the secrets of the kingdom is Lord over the storm. In 6:34 Jesus the teacher and shepherd feeds his people and walks on the water: is he not Lord of space and time and all the elements? If the disciples still did not understand (v. 52), Mark's readers could rejoice in the fulness of faith that had come to themselves.

As was suggested above, Jesus apparently found it necessary to compel his disciples to leave, so that he could dismiss the five thousand. However, this inference is drawn from John's account and from the circumstances described. Mark reports only that Jesus ***dismissed the crowd,*** bade ***them*** farewell (either the crowd or the disciples: the Greek is ambiguous), and ***went into the hills to pray.***

When evening came: the hour was already late before the five thousand were fed (v. 35). (Cf. v. 48.) The fourth watch of the night would be no earlier than 3:00 A.M. The wind on the sea must have given the disciples great trouble. ***Distressed*** translates a verb whose usual meaning is tortured or tormented. Thus, Bratcher suggests, "They were straining at the oars."

When the disciples saw Jesus, he was ***walking on the sea.*** The rationalization that he was merely in shallow water, or that he but appeared to be walking on the water, is certainly not in accord with what Mark has written. And if we remove this detail of the story, there remains no point to the narrative at all.

According to Mark, the event was more awesome than instructive for the disciples. ***They thought it was a ghost, and cried out,*** for they ***were terrified*** and ***utterly astounded.*** The word for ***ghost*** here is not spirit but the word from which fantasy is derived.

When what they had supposed to be an apparition spoke, the disciples thought they were going utterly out of their minds. ***They were . . . astounded*** (v. 51) translates a descriptive imperfect form of the verb used by Jesus' "friends" (3:21), when they said, "He is beside himself." Both what had happened at the feeding of the five thousand and this strange appearance of Jesus were contrary to any rational explanation of which they were capable.

The hardness of heart ascribed to hostile Pharisees in 3:5 and "to those outside" in 4:10–12 was shared in measure also by the disciples (v. 52). See 8:17, and also Peter's response, after his confession of Christ, to Jesus' teaching about the Son of man (8:29–31). In this respect, Mark's presentation is sharply different from that of Matthew 14:32–33. It is also in Matthew alone that we have the story of Peter's walking on the water.

The last part of verse 48 is peculiar to Mark. ***He meant to pass by them.*** The natural inference is that he would have done so had they not seen him and become frightened. Perhaps this is only what appeared to be the case from the disciples' point of view. It is a difficult passage. Moffatt translates, "He could have passed them by," and Swete offers several suggestions, including, "He was on the point of passing by them."

Of all the narratives of Jesus' mighty works this one is as difficult as any to explain. Our Gospels do not depict Jesus as a wonder-worker, doing miracles for no apparent and significant reason. What he did helped persons in need, or at least taught something very graphically. Our Master's original purpose in doing this mighty work is not clear. Was it simply to heighten the faith of the disciples?

Perhaps the story was popular among Mark's Roman readers, and they were already interpreting it very figuratively. Rawlinson suggests that it must have appeared to Christians in Rome, after Peter, Paul, and others of them had been martyred, that even ***the wind was against them,*** that they were abandoned with little hope. Yet their Lord came to them, in the darkest part of their own night, and gave them encouragement by his presence, so very real in their hearts.

Jesus' first word to the disciples when he spoke to them was, ***Take heart, it is I.*** The verb ***take heart*** is found also in 10:49 and John 16:33—"be of good cheer." In Acts 23:11 the verb "take courage" is a word of the Lord that came to Paul one night in his distress.

It is I, literally, "I am," may mean no more than the English words imply. But it is altogether possible that Mark intended his readers to identify Jesus with the Lord, the divine I AM of Exodus 3:14. The phrase occurs often in John, and with theological overtones (cf. 6:35; 8:12; 10:7; 11:25; 14: 6). Mark uses the phrase two other times, in 13:6 and 14:62.

(6) *The Healings at Gennesaret* (*6:53–56*)

53 And when they had crossed over, they came to land at Gennesaret, and moored to the shore. 54 And when they got out of the boat, immediately the people recognized him, 55 and ran about the whole neighborhood and began to bring sick people on their pallets to any place where they heard he was. 56 And wherever he came, in villages, cities, or country, they laid the sick in the market places, and besought him that they might touch even the fringe of his garment; and as many as touched it were made well.

This paragraph provides a summary and a transition. As in 3:7–12, the healings are not described in any detail but are similar to those already given. The period of time involved is indefinite, and Gennesaret is but the place ***they came to land,*** not one in which they tarried. They brought their sick to Jesus ***to any place where they heard he was . . . villages, cities, or country***—a combination that omits no collection of dwellings (Swete). Nothing is said in this summary of the demon-possessed or of raising the dead.

The ***fringe of his garment*** was probably the blue tassel worn by every devout Jewish male on the corners of his robe. This was required in Numbers 15:37–41 (cf. Deut. 22:12) to remind God's people of their responsibility to obey the Lord's commandments. Their overemphasis on such symbols probably resulted in the same sort of disobedience reflected in 7:9–13. The healings that were wrought when the sick touched his garment must have been similar to that of the woman with the flow of blood (5: 25–34).

The enthusiasm of the Galilean crowds was in sharp contrast to the hostile spirit of the strict Pharisees and the teachers (scribes) to whom they listened. Jesus had to break the grip of scribal tradition within his own disciples, a task which was not easy (7:17–18). Even after Peter had long been a successful evangelist, he would have qualms about eating with Gentiles (Gal. 2:11 f.).

(7) *Ritual Washing: the Command and the Tradition* (*7:1–13*)

1 Now when the Pharisees gathered together to him, with some of the scribes, who had come from Jerusalem, 2 they saw that some of his disciples ate with hands defiled, that is, unwashed. 3 (For the Pharisees, and all the Jews, do not eat unless they wash their hands, observing the tradition of the elders; 4 and when they come from the market place, they do not eat unless they purify themselves; and there are many other traditions which they observe, the washing of cups and pots and vessels of bronze.) 5 And the Pharisees and the scribes asked him, "Why do your disciples not

live according to the tradition of the elders, but eat with hands defiled?" [6] And he said to them, "Well did Isaiah prophesy of you hypocrites, as it is written,

'This people honors me with their lips,
but their heart is far from me;
7 in vain do they worship me,
teaching as doctrines the precepts of men.'

8 You leave the commandment of God, and hold fast the tradition of men."

9 And he said to them, "You have a fine way of rejecting the commandment of God, in order to keep your tradition! [10] For Moses said, 'Honor your father and your mother'; and, 'He who speaks evil of father or mother, let him surely die'; [11] but you say, 'If a man tells his father or his mother, What you would have gained from me is Corban' (that is, given to God)—[12] then you no longer permit him to do anything for his father or mother, [13] thus making void the word of God through your tradition which you hand on. And many such things you do."

Mark gives no clear connection between this section and the preceding one. He begins with the simple connective *and,* which TEV ignores and RSV treats as a simple particle ***now.*** This section does complete a description of the precarious situation of Jesus in his ministry. Rejected at Nazareth (6:1–6), connected by the political ruler with John whom he had put to death (6:14–29), and still enduring the meager faith and dull-mindedness of his disciples (6:45–52), he now confronts the open denunciation of the Jewish religious leadership.

The Pharisees and scribes were Jesus' opponents in the series of controversies in 2:1—3:6, and many of their attitudes have been noted. Their basic position with regard to the written Law was that it had been divinely given to Moses; but this was also their view about ***the tradition of the elders*** (v. 3). The Mishnah teaches that Moses received the tradition at Sinai, and it had been passed down, unmarred, by the prophets to the "men of the Great Synagogue," and so on down through authorized teachers or elders (Aboth 1:1). The tradition commanded the scribes "to make a fence about the law," and so the tradition grew to include specific instructions about almost every human action. The scribes' premise and procedure accordingly put the oral traditions on an equal footing with the Law itself. Moreover, this treatment gave a legalistic cast to the Law, so that it was the "letter" and not the "spirit" which was emphasized.

The disciples were caught in an infraction of the oral law: they were eating ***with hands defiled.*** Modern sanitation was not what the Pharisees had in mind. ***All the Jews*** (i.e., the strict observers of the traditions) washed ***their hands*** when they came in ***from the market place,*** because they might have been in contact with ritually unclean persons or things. Under these circumstances they were required to ***wash*** away the profane, and ***purify*** themselves. The oral tradition was connected with Lev. 22:1–16; what was applied there to the priests came to be applied to all the holy people.

The word translated ***defiled*** means common, or, in Jewish religious context, the opposite of holy, and so profane or impure as far as the worship of God was concerned.

Verses 3 and 4 are explanatory to Gentiles, though we cannot be sure whether they were composed first by Mark or were already present in his source. In verse 3, the word omitted by RSV (see marginal note) means literally "with the fist." Whether we should understand that they scrubbed thoroughly, or purified themselves by washing up to the wrists, we do not know. Perhaps the meaning was that a fistful of water would be adequate. There are other suggested readings, some ancient, but none with adequate support. In verse 4 the word baptize (marginal reading) has almost as strong attestation as ***purify,*** and the word used for ***washing of cups*** and other utensils is indeed the word for baptizing or dipping.

The question of the Pharisees and scribes in verse 5 is answered in three parts. The first two are given directly to the hostile Jewish leaders (6–8; 9–13), and the third to the people, with added explanation to his disciples (14–23).

Why did Jesus' ***disciples not live according to the tradition of the elders?*** Because, replied Jesus, the keeping of the traditions was a means of external praise to God without any commitment of the heart to true worship. The traditions are not actually from God but are ***precepts of men*** and are useless, ***in vain,*** as far as purifying a man before God.

This is the substance of Jesus' first response, but the sharp bite is found in the way Jesus hurls at his enemies the words of the prophet and then accuses the accusers of forsaking the very commandment of God. In verse 6 the adverb ***well*** could be translated, "How beautifully did Isaiah speak of you hypocrites!" What irony! (Jesus' first word in verse 9 is identical, but translated ***a fine way***).

Were they conscious of their hypocrisy? In any case, the scribes were inviting men to maintain proper relationship with God by way of external rules. Their guidance was therefore contrary to reality—no man comes to God by such means—and their action was indeed what Isaiah 29:13 described. The quotation is very close to the wording of the Greek Bible (LXX), and the Hebrew (which RSV follows in Isaiah) is somewhat different. Still, as A. S. Peake, Taylor, and others have pointed out, the same condemnation can be derived from the Hebrew text: men had learned their religion by rote and had no intelligent interest in their faith.

In order to keep your tradition: if the commandment of God is rejected with this end in view, then it is obvious that the tradition is merely human and is opposed to God's purpose. Jesus cites one example, though he adds that there are ***many such things*** which they do.

The law of Moses is cited concerning one's responsibility to his parents, *to honor* them and not *to speak evil of them.* (Cf. Ex. 20:12; Deut. 5:16; and Ex. 21:17; Lev. 20:9; Mark has again followed the LXX.) Then Jesus points to the traditional rule of ***Corban.*** The word itself means, as Mark says, gift, but the RSV has correctly understood it to mean a gift ***to God,*** and particularly a Temple offering. According to Josephus (*Against Apion,* I, 22), ***Corban*** was a form of Jewish oath. Jesus himself cited the tradition that an oath that was sworn "by the gift that is on the altar" was especially binding (Matt. 23:18). Was not God more important than parental obligations?

We are not able to reconstruct the situation precisely with assurance, but the general result is clear. Jesus may have been referring to a particular and well-known incident. Apparently a man could avoid supporting his parents (and obeying God's instruction) by vowing to make a gift to the Temple treasury. However, arrangements might include that either the income from the gift or the actual use of the money would remain with the donor. Thus he would be able to use his money for himself and deny his obligation to his parents; and at the very same time he would be widely praised for his generosity and his piety! It might even become a matter of religious pressure for his parents to renounce their own right and join in the praise.

Jesus realized of course that religious defilement is moral and spiritual, and that the fulfilment of scribal tradition could never fulfil true righteousness (Matt. 5:20; cf. also Paul in 1 Cor. 13:1–3.) Traditions such as ***Corban*** permitted a man to erect a religious wall against moral responsibility. They made ***void the word of God.***

Some of the regulations given in the rabbinic literature suggest that the Jewish traditions were stricter in Jesus' day than they were a century or more later. C. G. Montefiore maintains, with some justification, that the rabbis of the Mishnah and the Talmud are on the side of Jesus concerning ***Corban,*** and that they follow his very argument. Is it possible that the legacy of Jesus did have some substantial impact upon the Jewish religious leadership who opposed him? It is good to remember that the spiritual vitality of the Law was not always lost on every Jewish teacher.

The strong language used in this and the following section may well reflect not only the situation Jesus faced but also the continuing friction between church and synagogue in Mark's day. The vine of Jewish tradition may have been cut at its root by Jesus' emphasis on the inward and the spiritual, but it was a long time before its hardened tentacles were pulled away from the people who claimed to be Israel's true heirs. Questions about uncleanness and circumcision and observance of special days did not disappear automatically, as Acts 15; 22; Galatians 2; 5; and Colossians 3 plainly assert. (Cf. also Romans 14:5 f.) It is altogether probable that some of the material in each of the Gospels was preserved and widely used because of this very problem.

(8) *The Nature of Real Defilement* (7:14–23)

**14 And he called the people to him again,
and said to them, "Hear me, all of you, and
understand: 15 there is nothing outside a man
which by going into him can defile him; but
the things which come out of a man are what
defile him." 17 And when he had entered the
house, and left the people, his disciples asked
him about the parable. 18 And he said to them,
"Then are you also without understanding? Do
you not see that whatever goes into a man
from outside cannot defile him, 19 since it enters, not his heart but his stomach, and so
passes on?" (Thus he declared all foods
clean.) 20 And he said, "What comes out of a
man is what defiles a man. 21 For from within,
out of the heart of man, come evil thoughts,
fornication, theft, murder, adultery, 22 coveting,
wickedness, deceit, licentiousness, envy, slander, pride, foolishness. 23 All these evil things
come from within, and they defile a man."**

Nothing outside a man can defile him, whether contact with evil people or profane things. The verb *defile* is, in its root, the same word as the adjective translated *defiled* in verse 2, and its import is the same. Nothing from an external source can of itself alienate a man from God. Only what comes from within the man's own being can mark a man as defiled and prevent him from true worship.

Rawlinson thinks Jesus meant only that "pollutions from within are more serious than pollutions from without." He points out that the Hebrew mind did not think in terms of comparative degrees, but only in terms that are black or white, never gray. Consequently, by their inordinate emphasis on avoiding ceremonial pollutions from without, the scribes were in danger of distorting their own moral judgment and giving too little attention to the defilements of sin.

What Rawlinson says is true enough, and it is in accord with the words of Jesus, for example, Matthew 5:17–20 and 23:23 f. However, his interpretation is surely inadequate for Jesus' words to his disciples in verses 18 f.: ***whatever goes into a man from outside cannot defile him*** is an absolute statement, and Mark certainly understands the statement absolutely. His parenthetic conclusion in verse 19 makes this quite clear.

Note how Mark continues his emphasis on the slowness of the disciples to perceive in depth the nature and teaching of Jesus. The use of the word *parable* here is almost equivalent to "figurative teaching" or "enigmatic saying." (Cf. above on 4:2, 10–12.) The teaching of Jesus which follows is stated simply and plainly, and must have been quite useful in the instruction of young Christians. It expands and applies the principle stated in verse 15.

The wording of verse 19 seems so blunt that RSV has tempered it for modern readers. But Jesus (and his contemporaries) could speak of the natural processes without offense. The Greek text says that food eaten does not have to do with the ***heart*** (i.e., the mind and thought) of a man; it merely passes through his ***stomach*** and out into the latrine. Therefore, Mark concludes, we have Jesus' authority for saying that the food we eat or reject neither commends us nor disqualifies us before God.

What, then, is it that marks a man as defiled? Only that which ***comes out of a man***—out of what he is, his mind, his inmost self, his ***heart.*** No evil in the world, real or supposed, erects a wall between a person and God, save that evil which is at home in the person himself (v. 23).

Thoughts (v. 21) translates a word that includes both what a man is thinking and what he plans to do. ***Evil thoughts,*** therefore, encompasses the whole of the list of the twelve sins which follow. Bratcher divides these into two parts. The first six are plural in form in the original and refer to "acts" of evil which have their source in the inner man. The other six are singular and refer to the vices fostered by the man's own spirit. But some of the terms seem to refer both to acts and attitudes.

There is no comparable list of sins given in any of the Gospels except the shortened list in Matthew 15:19, which was derived from Mark. Only three of the terms are used elsewhere by Mark (***murder,*** 15:7; ***deceit,*** 14:1; and ***slander*** in 3:28). One must turn to such passages as 1 Peter 4:3; Romans 1:29–31; Galatians 5:19–21 for anything comparable in the New Testament. Nevertheless, the list may not be of Pauline (or early Gentile Christian) origin, as Taylor holds, for eleven of the terms are found in the LXX, and there is a similar list in the *Manual of Discipline* (1QS 4:9–11).

Fornication is a more inclusive term than ***adultery*** and may refer to every kind of sexual vice. ***Coveting*** connotes avarice or greed, and probably here means "acts of cupidity" or even "deeds of lustfulness" (Cranfield). The word is often associated with sexual violations. Moffatt translates it here as lust. ***Wickedness*** is a general term for all kinds of evil deeds.

Deceit, translated "stealth" in 14:1, is cunning or treachery. ***Licentiousness*** is wantonness—something shocking to public decency, open and shameless in its evil. ***Envy*** renders two words which mean literally an evil eye. But the idea is not of one who casts a malignant spell over another. See Matthew 20:15, where "Do you begrudge my generosity?" correctly paraphrases, "Is your eye evil because I am good?" It is a greedy, grasping spirit that is condemned.

Slander is literally "blasphemy" (3:28), though it is unclear whether the word refers here primarily to one's attitude toward God or toward man. ***Pride*** (here only in NT, though the adjective is present in Luke 1:51; Rom. 1:30; 2 Tim. 3:2, James 4:6; 1 Peter 5:5) combines the ideas of haughty arrogance and self-centeredness. ***Foolishness*** is the "out-of-mind-ness" of the man who rejects any reverence for God and for reasonable moral judgment (see the description of the fool in Psalm 14).

In verses 1–23 it is most obvious that Jesus challenged the authority of the oral law. What must not be overlooked is that he also challenged the letter of the written Law. Precepts concerning food were not merely oral, and the early Gentile Christians clearly understood Jesus to have set them free from these regulations (v. 19). It must be realized that Jesus claimed authority over the Law itself. Just as he is Lord over the sabbath (2:28), he is Lord also over the laws concerning uncleanness.

Jesus emphasized the morality of a free human spirit submitted to the purposes of God. He does not discount moral teaching, as the catalog of sins indicates. Neither does he ever treat the Law lightly. Rather, as Cranfield has analyzed it, Jesus speaks as one who knows himself to be the "end of the law" (Rom. 10:4), the one in whom the Scriptures find their fulfilment.

The implications of Jesus' teaching were not fully realized by the disciples at once, as Peter's experience later confirms (Acts 10). But this also is part of the mystery of Jesus—who he was and is, and what the kingdom of God which has drawn near in him means for man.

(9) *The Healing of the Gentile Girl* (*7:24–30*)

**24 And from there he arose and went away to
the region of Tyre and Sidon. And he entered a
house, and would not have any one know it;
yet he could not be hid. 25 But immediately a
woman, whose little daughter was possessed by
an unclean spirit, heard of him, and came and
fell down at his feet. 26 Now the woman was a
Greek, a Syrophoenician by birth. And she
begged him to cast the demon out of her
daughter. 27 And he said to her, "Let the children first be fed, for it is not right to take the**

children's bread and throw it to the dogs."
[28] But she answered him, "Yes, Lord; yet even
the dogs under the table eat the children's
crumbs." [29] And he said to her, "For this saying
you may go your way; the demon has left your
daughter." [30] And she went home, and found
the child lying in bed, and the demon gone.

Jesus ***went away to the region of Tyre and Sidon,*** i.e., to the north, away from Galilee. As Rawlinson points out, we have no solid reasons from the text to assume that Jesus fled Galilee to avoid arrest, although there is no question his enemies would have desired this. Perhaps he sought a time and place for more intimate dialogue with his disciples; or, perhaps he was looking only for an opportunity for some respite from the strenuous, unrelieved pressures of the crowds, of hostile questions, and of those seeking aid (cf. 6:31). Mark says only that Jesus would have liked to remain unnoticed, but his fame had become so widespread that ***he could not be hid.***

We do not know how long the journey lasted, nor can we be sure that Mark has placed these events in true chronological order. When we consider the context of the story in Mark, however, we note readily his shift from our Lord's Jewish mission to a ministry to non-Jews. We have had the feeding of the five thousand, a healing ministry in Galilee, and the question about defilement. Now we have two stories of healing among the Gentiles, and the feeding of the four thousand, apparently in territory foreign to the Jews.

One other connecting link with the preceding controversy should not be overlooked, for it would be especially obvious to Mark's audience. The story about defilement seemingly has to do strictly with Jewish tradition and law. However, every Gentile was aware that, according to the same Jewish tradition, contact with Gentiles might be just as defiling as any other "uncleanness" one might pick up in the market place. Note the parallels also with Peter's experience recorded in Acts 10: first, the awareness that food does not determine a man's status with God; then, the realization that God shows no partiality because of race or cultural background.

Among the people most desperate for help and from whom Jesus ***could not be hid*** was a mother ***whose little daughter*** (5:23) was afflicted with ***an unclean spirit.*** The nature of the child's problem is in no way discussed: Mark's emphasis is entirely on who the woman is and Jesus' response to her importunate words of humility and faith. She is ***a Syrophoenician by birth;*** i.e., Syrian rather than Carthaginian. She is called ***a Greek,*** which here may refer either to her religion or to the language she is accustomed to use.

The parallel passage in Matthew (15:21–28) calls her a "Canaanite." While this is not a contradiction in terms, the accounts vary to such a degree that it is reasonable to suppose Matthew had the story from another source in addition to Mark. Matthew is following Markan order in this section, but puts much more emphasis on Jesus' reluctance (if that is the correct word) to help the woman, and also on the disciples' reaction.

We must remember that the Markan story was written primarily for Gentile Christians, who had much in common with this woman. The fact was obvious to them that Jesus worked primarily among the Jews; only in this one story does Mark tell of a healing by Jesus of a person clearly designated as a Gentile. (Cf. Matt. 8:5–13 and Luke 7:1–10; Luke does not repeat this story from Mark, perhaps because of the seeming harshness of Jesus' word to the Gentile woman.) Mark apparently is confident that his readers accept the positions we think of as Pauline and Johannine. The gospel "is the power of God for salvation to every one who has faith, to the Jew first and also to the Greek" (Rom. 1:16; cf. John 4:22 f.

Let the children first be fed. The word ***first*** corresponds to Paul's statement cited above, because the designation ***children*** must here refer to the Jewish people. This designation is common enough in the Old Testament (cf. Ex. 4:22; Deut. 14:1; Hos-

1:10; Isa. 1:2; 63:8) and in Jewish literature generally, including both the Apocrypha (Wisdom of Sol. 16:21) and the Mishnah (Aboth 3:20: "Beloved are Israel, which are called the sons of God").

If ***children*** refers, as it must, to Israel, then ***the dogs*** must refer to Gentiles. That the Jewish people occasionally referred to Gentiles as "dogs" is acknowledged by Jewish and Christian scholars generally. Jesus does use the diminutive form for ***dogs,*** and thereby softens its harshness. Johnson points to evidence that diminutives were used loosely in the Greek of this period, and he thinks that therefore the figure remains harsh and severe. However, the dogs of the courtyard or street would not have been welcomed at the children's ***table.*** The woman's rejoinder seems to imply that she understands the dogs to be the little household pets.

The woman's reply—even the little dogs ***eat the children's crumbs***—is responsive, even witty. It shows that the woman was not offended by Jesus' reply. No more must Gentiles be offended that God in his own mysterious way had chosen to make himself known in history through a particular nation. Neither must they resent the fact that Jesus had come among the Jews and had primarily ministered to them. For it is also true that in this way other people also are heirs of God's help.

As Cranfield says, the woman simply appealed to the kindness of Jesus unconditionally. Her ***Yes, Lord*** may have meant only "Yes, Sir," when the words were spoken. To the Christian people they meant more, for they expressed the basic Christian confession of Jesus as Lord.

In the course of the efforts of modern scholars to recover the historical Jesus (as over against the Christ of faith) it has been suggested that the woman's reply to Jesus was to him a revelation from the Father that his mission was wider than that to the Jews (so Bacon; cf. Johnson, p. 137). But there is no evidence that the course of Jesus' ministry was in fact altered toward work directly among other nations. He continued to live and work mostly among the people of Israel.

For this saying: Jesus acknowledged and welcomed the woman's faith, and therefore (***for*** means because of) assured her that her daughter had been relieved of her demonic affliction. Taylor accepts the wording as probably meaning that Mark believed a cure had been wrought by Jesus, but thinks the words might refer only to a kind of "telepathic awareness" of what was taking place at a distance. However, Mark's understanding of Jesus' power in controlling demonic forces is quite consistent with the natural interpretation of this event as miracle.

(10) The Healing of the Deaf and Dumb Man (7:31–37)

31 Then he returned from the region of Tyre, and went through Sidon to the Sea of Galilee, through the region of the Decapolis. 32 And they brought to him a man who was deaf and had an impediment in his speech; and they besought him to lay his hand upon him. 33 And taking him aside from the multitude privately, he put his fingers into his ears, and he spat and touched his tongue; 34 and looking up to heaven, he sighed, and said to him, "Ephphatha," that is, "Be opened." 35 And his ears were opened, his tongue was released, and he spoke plainly. 36 And he charged them to tell no one; but the more he charged them, the more zealously they proclaimed it. 37 And they were astonished beyond measure, saying, "He has done all things well; he even makes the deaf hear and the dumb speak."

Jesus ***then*** (the Greek is "and again") departed Tyrian territory and ***went through Sidon to the Sea of Galilee.*** Mark says that he went either ***through*** or "into" (Arndt and Gingrich) ***the region of the Decapolis,*** which generally lay east and even south of Galilee and its lake (cf. 5:1,20). ***The Decapolis*** was, as has been noted, predominantly a non-Jewish territory; but we do not know its boundaries in detail. Mark is not really clear about whether Jesus remained in Gentile territory, though he seems to have done so. Sidon is 20 miles north of Tyre, and the description implies a circuitous journey. (Cf. Matt. 15:29).

A man was brought to Jesus ***who was deaf and had an impediment in his speech.*** It is interesting to note how often others bring a person in need to Jesus' attention. The phrase ***an impediment in his speech*** translates one Greek word, a rather rare one, for it occurs but this one time in the New Testament. It is found in the Old Testament only in Isaiah 35:6 (LXX), where there is a promise of God's coming help for his people: "then shall the lame man leap like a hart, and the tongue of the dumb sing for joy." Perhaps an allusion is intended. In any case, the healing is a sign of God's victory over yet another enemy of man's fulfilment and another evidence that the kingship of God has invaded this tangled world in Jesus (cf. Isa. 29:18 and Wisd. of Sol. 10:21).

Jesus healed the man ***privately,*** though apparently the disciples and the man's friends were present (***aside from the multitude,*** but ***he charged them to tell no one***). Jesus was still attempting to keep some semblance of privacy, and he was still aware that the nature of his messiahship had not been accepted nor even made clear. The people ***were astonished beyond measure,*** and they praised him without reserve. The sad truth was that they knew not him whom they praised.

In the healing itself, Jesus' method arrests our attention. Is not the putting of ***his fingers into his ears*** and the touching of his own saliva on the man's ***tongue*** as eloquent a word and as tangible a call to faith as he could offer? ***He sighed,*** or groaned: this seems to be a description of his prayer as he is so cognizant of the man's wretched condition. Arndt and Gingrich think the verb is used here "as an expression of power ready to act." Jesus' only word was in Aramaic, and Mark translates its import as ***Be opened.***

The parallels between this account and other ancient healing accounts have often been noted. Johnson remarks that the use of saliva, the healer's groan or sigh, and a mystery word from the healer's original language have their counterpart in other ancient miracle stories (cf. also John 9:6 f). However, Jesus' sighing is in conjunction with his ***looking up to heaven,*** i.e., in prayer. As Taylor puts it, "only a love for the bizarre" would find in this sigh of Jesus anything foreign to his own deep compassion for the victim.

In verse 37, Jesus is praised for doing ***all things well; he even makes the deaf hear and the dumb speak.*** The phrasing makes more probable the understanding of this incident as an allusion to fulfilment of God's promised help. In addition, it points up starkly the dull-mindedness of the disciples noted again in 8:14–21. One should note too the parallels between the healings of the senses—the ear with the voice, and the eyes (8:22–26)—and the opening of the minds of the disciples to see who Jesus is (8:29).

(11) The Feeding of the Four Thousand (8:1–10)

[1] In those days, when again a great crowd had gathered, and they had nothing to eat, he called his disciples to him, and said to them,
[2] "I have compassion on the crowd, because they have been with me now three days, and have nothing to eat; [3] and if I send them away hungry to their homes, they will faint on the way; and some of them have come a long way." [4] And his disciples answered him, "How can one feed these men with bread here in the desert?" [5] And he asked them, "How many loaves have you?" They said, "Seven." [6] And he commanded the crowd to sit down on the ground; and he took the seven loaves, and having given thanks he broke them and gave them to his disciples to set before the people; and they set them before the crowd. [7] And they had a few small fish; and having blessed them, he commanded that these also should be set before them. [8] And they ate, and were satisfied; and they took up the broken pieces left over, seven baskets full. [9] And there were about four thousand people. [10] And he sent them away; and immediately he got into the boat with his disciples, and went to the district of Dalmanutha.

In those days (cf. 1:9) is a rather indefinite note of time; neither is the ***great crowd*** more specifically identified, and the place (***in the desert***) is equally imprecise. The details in this narrative are fewer and less vivid than those in the feeding of the five thousand ("lonely place," "by hundreds and by fifties," "by companies" or garden beds, etc.). Mark does not tell us that the crowd was Gentile, although he apparently means to leave that impression; the story is in a "Gentile context," beginning from 7:24.

The differences between the stories in 8: 1–10 and 6:32–44 should be noted. Among these, in the feeding of the five thousand, Jesus had compassion, but because the people were as sheep without a shepherd, not simply because they had nothing to eat. All the events in the case of the five thousand were in one day; here, the crowd had been following Jesus ***now three days.*** Instead of five loaves and two fish we have ***seven loaves*** and ***a few small fish*** (equally ready for eating). Before, there were twelve baskets of leftovers, now there were ***seven,*** and the word for "basket" is different. (The word in v. 8 usually means vegetable basket and is also the word used for Paul's escape vehicle over the Damascus wall. Cf. Acts 9:25.)

With all these differences, however, the stories remain very similar. Many scholars have considered the two narratives a "doublet," i.e., two varying accounts of the same incident. This conclusion is reached with varying subsidiary arguments, but depends basically on one point. How, it is asked, could the ***disciples*** have witnessed the feeding of the five thousand and then asked the kind of question attributed to them in verse 4? This, it is argued persuasively, is psychologically unintelligible. If Jesus fed one crowd with multiplication of bread, he could do so again.

The differences in the accounts, however, seem clearly to indicate that Mark received and employed them as two separate incidents. If the stories are not a doublet, we must judge that they came to Mark through two different lines of the Christian teaching-tradition and were told with no reference to each other. Probably the disciples' question in verse 4, which was generally representative of their outlook, would have been included in this story, narrated independently, to heighten the emphasis on the greatness of Jesus' power. The stories would have been used the same ways in preaching.

Why, then, did Mark not note the inappropriateness of the disciples' question in his continuing account and modify it himself? First, because he tended to use his sources as they came to him, with only modification enough to allow a measure of continuity; and second, because of his own desire to point up the dullness of the disciples, their hardness of heart and slowness to perceive who Jesus was. As should be perfectly clear now, this is a major motif in Mark (cf. 8:14–21). Who is there who understands who Jesus is and can believe in him as Christ and as God's Son? How difficult for the disciples, and how hard for the church! But impossible for those (e.g., scribes or Pharisees) whose hearts remain hardened!

The words and implications of this passage have in large part been noted in the previous story in 6:32–44. In verse 6, as in 14:23, we have a word translated ***having given thanks.*** The meaning is partly identical with, partly supplementary to, the verb ***having blessed*** in verse 7 (also in 6:41 and 14:22). That Jesus ***blessed them*** (***the little fish***) means that he blessed God for them. See 1 Corinthians 10:16, which should be interpreted "the cup of blessing for which we bless God's name" (Cranfield). Here again we have a fellowship meal with overtones and words that would immediately bring Mark's readers to think of the Lord's Supper as Mark will record it and as they regularly observed it in fellowship, thanksgiving, and faith.

If the feeding of the five thousand be understood as Jesus' invitation to the Jewish people to fellowship and to sharing his life, then the feeding of the four thousand should be understood as Jesus' inclusion of the Gentiles equally in full fellowship and divinely shared life. So think Bacon and, more hesitantly, Rawlinson. Mark does not make any direct assertion about the racial makeup of the crowd; perhaps he did not know. What he was sure of was that Jew and Gentile both were provided for by God in

Jesus Christ. Accordingly, Mark has placed this story in a Gentile context, and it complements the story in 6:32–44.

Whether Mark associated the twelve baskets full of remnants with the whole of Jewish Israel and the ***seven baskets full*** here with the whole number of other nations is uncertain. (If seven is symbolic, it would signify completeness.) The use of numbers in symbolism was so common among the Jews (cf. Rev. 1:4,12) that the number must have been sometimes preached as symbolic when the story was told in the early churches. However, we need to guard against reading into the text more than the Gospel writer intended to say.

After the meal, Jesus ***sent them away***, and went across the sea with his disciples ***to the district of Dalmanutha.*** We suppose this to be in Galilee, on the western side of the lake, opposite the region of Decapolis (v. 13). However, so far we have found no positive identification of any place by this name; perhaps further archaeological search will bring us some definite information.

(12) *The Pharisees' Demand for a Sign from Heaven (8:11–13)*

11 The Pharisees came and began to argue with him, seeking from him a sign from heaven, to test him. 12 And he sighed deeply in his spirit, and said, "Why does this generation seek a sign? Truly, I say to you, no sign shall be given to this generation." 13 And he left them, and getting into the boat again he departed to the other side.

If we observe the parallelism in Mark's order, then just as 6:32–44 corresponds to 8:1–9, 6:45–56 matches 8:10, and 7:1–23 matches this paragraph. Afterward, 7:24–30 (the children's bread) pairs with 8:14–21 (the Pharisees' leaven), and finally the healing of the deaf and dumb in 7:31–37 corresponds to the healing of the blind in 8:22–26. We have every reason to suppose that the Markan arrangement is his own and by his design. One of the results has been an emphasis on the inclusion of Gentiles along with the Jews.

The present paragraph, though brief, reverts again to an illustration of the utter and impenetrable blindness of the Jewish religious leaders. The disciples need not only to be defended when assailed from the viewpoint of scribal approach to the Law; they need to beware of what this spirit, and the spirit of a Herod, can do within themselves (8:15).

The Pharisaic spirit was expressed on this occasion by their desire to ***argue*** and to ***test*** Jesus. If he were indeed from God, they demanded that he prove it with ***a sign from heaven.*** The parallel passages (Luke 11:29–32; 12:54–56; Matt. 16:1–4; Matt. 12:38–42) are apparently from different lines of tradition (i.e., from the source called Q). Of course, this sort of demand may have been repeated. Luke and Matthew both say no sign shall be given "except the sign of Jonah." But Luke interprets this sign to mean the preaching of repentance (11:32), while Matthew thinks also, with his fellow believers, of the resurrection of the Son of man (12:40).

Jesus' fundamental preaching was that the kingdom of God had drawn near. Many devout Jews, influenced by apocalyptic tradition, expected this eschatological victory from God to be heralded by supernatural signs. ***A sign*** from Jesus would have required some sure evidence of the presence and power of God, a clear token of his identity as God's agent. But Jesus consistently refused to do any mighty work merely to prove who he was.[37]

The blinded Pharisaic mind must have continued to attribute Jesus' works to Beelzebul (3:22). The disciples still would anticipate signs in the future (13:4). The real reason ***no sign*** could ***be given to this generation*** was the futility of the action. If, as Luke records it (16:31), people would not

37 On the meaning of *signs* in the Gospels and in the early church, see the note in Rawlinson's *Commentary* (pp. 257 f.). He holds that in the early church the two "signs" most emphasized were the resurrection and the observance of the Lord's Supper, and correctly points to their similarity in meaning. He believes this is the reason for Matthew's interpretation of the "sign of Jonah" as resurrection, and that Mark's meaning in this and the succeeding passage (cf. 8:17–21) is that men should have understood the sign in the feeding of the multitudes.

heed Moses or the prophets, neither would they repent even if one rose from the dead.

This generation should be understood in this context, not as including everybody, but as referring to those whose spirit and attitudes were like those of the Pharisees. So fixed and warped in mind were they that they could not in any case have recognized a sign. See "this generation" in 8:38 and 9:19; also Matthew 11:16; Acts 2:40. Nevertheless, even the disciples were still infected to some degree by the same spirit, as the next paragraph again will charge.

(13) A Warning to Disciples Against Dullness of Mind (8:14–21)

**[14] Now they had forgotten to bring bread;
and they had only one loaf with them in the
boat. [15] And he cautioned them, saying, "Take
heed, beware of the leaven of the Pharisees
and the leaven of Herod." [16] And they discussed it with one another, saying, "We have
no bread." [17] And being aware of it, Jesus said
to them, "Why do you discuss the fact that you
have no bread? Do you not yet perceive or
understand? Are your hearts hardened?
[18] Having eyes do you not see, and having ears
do you not hear? And do you not remember?
[19] When I broke the five loaves for the five
thousand, how many baskets full of broken
pieces did you take up?" They said to him,
"Twelve." [20] "And the seven for the four thousand, how many baskets full of broken pieces
did you take up?" And they said to him,
"Seven." [21] And he said to them, "Do you not
yet understand?"**

This paragraph is closely connected by Mark with the preceding incident, in Jesus' thought if not in the disciples'. It appears that as soon as they got into the boat (v. 13), the disciples forgot all about the Pharisaic demands just made upon their Teacher, and devoted their attention to food. ***They had forgotten to bring bread.***

Jesus attempted to bring their minds back from their hungry lament by warning his followers against ***the leaven of the Pharisees and the leaven of Herod.*** What blindness and cruelty their attitudes of mind could produce! ***Leaven*** is almost always, when used figuratively, employed with evil connotations: it permeates the whole lump, spreading its corrupting tentacles everywhere and remaking the character of the dough (1 Cor. 5:6; Gal. 5:9; Luke 12:1; Matt. 16:6,11–12). If the Pharisees were corrupted in moral insight by their addiction to legalism, Herod was equally blinded by his own bent to worldliness (6:14 ff.). His character made him an adulterer and a murderer, even while he displayed some interest in John's teaching. Herodians and Pharisees are also grouped in 3:6.

He cautioned them. The Greek verb is strong, and its tense is vividly descriptive: "he kept laying it down as an order"; "he repeatedly stressed this warning." However, the disciples were so preoccupied with their own problems (and, probably, who was to blame for them!) that they were giving no close attention to Jesus' teaching. There is a textual problem in verse 16, and the correct meaning may well be: They were quarreling with one another because (or, over the reason why) they had no bread.

Jesus retorted to their dullness: ***Do you not yet perceive?*** Are ***your hearts,*** like the Pharisees', ***hardened?*** Verse 18 recalls 4:10–12, and is clearly an allusion to Isaiah 6:9 f. (cf. Jer. 5:21; Ezek. 12:2).

The reminder of the two great meals which Jesus had served was hardly intended to promise the disciples a meal at any time they complained of hunger. The point is rather that they would not have been so preoccupied with their own frustrations and worries if they had remembered and understood what Jesus had done (Cranfield). If they were now unable to hearken to him, they must not have comprehended Jesus' message in these two events (as, naturally, Mark's readers have).

In the feeding of the two multitudes, Jesus had offered himself as true guide and teacher (shepherd). He had gone beyond legalism concerning defilement (the second meal was with Gentiles); he had with thankfulness and divine blessing broken bread with all, in holy fellowship. Although the open prediction of the death and resurrection of the Son of man has not yet been spoken (8:31), every Christian reader will understand that, in a very real sense, "signs" have already been given of what is to come and what their own holy and commemorative meals together signify. Perhaps also Mark means for his readers to consider with some measure of sympathy how hard it was for the disciples to come to fulness of faith and understanding. Yet, as the Gospel of John puts it, Jesus himself was "the living bread" and whoever ate of that bread would never hunger nor die (6:47–51).

Do you not yet understand? Phrased as it is, Jesus' question anticipates the answer yes. Nevertheless, there is in fact still no answer from the disciples, though Peter's confession will not now be long in coming.

(14) *The Healing of a Blind Man (8:22–26)*

22 And they came to Bethsaida. And some people brought to him a blind man, and begged him to touch him. 23 And he took the blind man by the hand, and led him out of the village; and when he had spit on his eyes and laid his hands upon him, he asked him, "Do you see anything?" 24 And he looked up and said, "I see men; but they look like trees, walking." 25 Then again he laid his hands upon his eyes; and he looked intently and was restored, and saw everything clearly. 26 And he sent him away to his home, saying, "Do not even enter the village."

Having crossed the lake, ***they came to Bethsaida.*** For the place, cf. 6:45. Like the deaf and dumb man (7:31–36), this ***blind man*** was ***brought*** by friends to Jesus. The blind man asked Jesus ***to touch him.*** Again, Jesus took the man away from the crowd (***out of the village;*** cf. 7:33) and again used contemporary physical means to build faith and confidence in the afflicted person (***spit on his eyes and laid his hands upon him***).

In this context it is impossible to view Mark's telling of this story as meaning simply that Jesus had compassion on a blind man. That Jesus was concerned for a man without physical sight, we need have no doubt. But the current theme is of disciples who are still without understanding (v. 21).

This miracle is not only a healing of one poor blind man: it is also a parable of what Jesus was doing for the disciples. Children of their own age, afflicted by the blindness of the warped Pharisee or the worldly Herod, the eyes of the disciples' minds need to be opened.

The blindness is lifted in stages. First, the person being healed sees ***men; but they look like trees***—though now visible, still indistinct. They must be ***men,*** for (unlike trees) they are ***walking.*** Finally, when Jesus had for the second time ***laid his hands upon his eyes,*** the man ***looked intently*** (a little stronger word than ***looked up*** in v. 24, though from the same root) ***and was restored*** (as the man with the withered hand in 3:5). Now fully healed, he could ***clearly*** distinguish ***everything;*** not only "men" (KJV) but all objects.

Only this once do we have any record that Jesus in healing required two treatments. Grant suggests that neither Matthew nor Luke includes this story because the man's sight was not restored at once. Perhaps he is right in this surmise, though this can hardly be judged fatal to the account's accuracy. In any case, the parallel with the disciples' slowness to understand is most apt. They did not understand who Jesus was from the first: did not his identity appear to them "as a tree walking"?

Mark has now set the stage for the next events of his narrative. Peter will have a partial vision, by which he will recognize Jesus as Christ but not understand that the Christ must suffer. Then the experience of the transfiguration will take place (9:2–8), enlarging his vision. In Mark, however, the vision of the disciples is never absolutely clear, at least not before the resurrection. With the book's present ending (16:8), the resurrection has become reality, but the disciples' vision is still not full. It is altogether probable that the original ending (as the one we presently have appended 16:9–20 does to some degree) spoke in some manner of the disciples' confident faith.

(*15*) *The Recognition of the Christ* (*8:27–30*)

[27] And Jesus went on with his disciples, to the villages of Caesarea Philippi; and on the way he asked his disciples, "Who do men say that I am?" [28] And they told him, "John the Baptist; and others say, Elijah; and others one of the prophets." [29] And he asked them, "But who do you say that I am?" Peter answered him, "You are the Christ." [30] And he charged them to tell no one about him.

This brief section and the next (31–33) comprise the major transitional paragraphs in Mark. They are divided in outline here because the first half of Mark achieves its climax in the confession of Jesus as the Christ. On the other hand, the confession by Peter provided the necessary occasion for Jesus to interpret to the disciples the nature of his own role as the suffering Son of man.[38]

The villages of Caesarea Philippi: Jesus has led his disciples again away from Galilee, probably in hope of achieving some time alone with them. They apparently did not go to the city, but remained in the sparsely settled regions nearby, not far from Mount Hermon and the sources of the Jordan. Caesarea Philippi, enlarged and renamed by Herod Philip for Tiberius Caesar, was earlier called Paneas, because of the famed grotto nearby where the god Pan was revered. The contrast between the heathen cult and the recognition of Jesus as God's Christ is sharp. It is tempting to imagine that the discussion of other religious beliefs offered the original occasion for Jesus' question, ***Who do men say that I am?*** The question itself, however, was basic to Jesus' hopes for his disciples. He wanted them to recognize him as the Christ and comprehend his own understanding of his role.

There must have been considerable speculation about Jesus' identity and role (cf. 6:14–16). ***John the Baptist*** and ***Elijah*** are identified in 9:11–13; see the commentary on that passage. The use of their names to identify Jesus means at least that there was messianic excitement, for Elijah was expected to prepare Messiah's way, and John had claimed to be fulfilling the prophecy in Isaiah 40:3–4. But the concept of Jesus as one of these, or as an unnamed prophet, is far from the concept which Jesus had of himself or desired from his disciples.

The question was now put bluntly to the disciples: As for ***you*** (the pronoun is quite emphatic: the multitude does not know him), ***who do you say that I am? Peter*** was the one who responded, ***You are the Christ.*** Jesus apparently accepted this title, but he did not use it, and he forbade the disciples to do so (v. 30). The word ***Christ*** means anointed, and translates the Aramaic term Messiah. What did the confession mean?

In the Old Testament, persons who were specially consecrated for some particular task, and who were regarded as divinely chosen and endowed for its accomplishment, were often anointed with oil. This was true of priests and kings, and also occasionally of prophets (cf. 1 Kings 19:16, Isa. 61:1 ff.). It is used of the Gentile leader Cyrus (Isa. 45:1), of the whole of Israel, and of the patriarchs, though the use is figurative: they were not actually anointed, but consecrated by God for a given task.

The expectation of Israel seems especially to have looked for an anointed one, a Messiah, who would be the ideal ruler, a new David. He would rule for God, restore Israel's greatness, establish God's ways. Some

[38] The self-understanding of Jesus has been widely discussed by scholars in recent years, and opinions have varied widely. An extreme and negative view is held by R. Bultmann, who rejects Peter's confession and Jesus' subsequent description of himself as without historical grounds; he holds that these are Christian ideas and that they were born only in the context of the Easter experience of the disciples. But most recent scholarly opinion is more optimistic and acknowledges a historical basis behind the Gospel narrative. We may assume that in the handing down of tradition and in its preaching there was considerable freedom and variety, as the differences in the Synoptic Gospels illustrate (Matt. 16:13–23; Luke 9:18–22). The Gospel of John has no comparable climax in Jesus' ministry (but cf. 6:66–71). On the questions involved in this passage, see Taylor, 374 f.; for more comprehensive discussion, see e.g., R. H. Fuller, *The Mission and Achievement of Jesus* (London: SCM, 1954); J. W. Bowman, *The Intention of Jesus* (Philadelphia: Westminster, 1943); M. Dibelius, *Jesus* (Philadelphia: Westminster, 1949); G. Bornkamm, *Jesus of Nazareth* (New York: Harper, 1960); T. W. Manson, *The Servant Messiah* (Cambridge: Univ. Press, 1961); and William Manson, *Jesus the Messiah* (Philadelphia: Westminster Press, 1946).

of the pertinent passages are found in the Psalms (e.g., 2; 78; 89), others in the prophets (Isa. 9; 11; 49; Hag. 2; Zech. 4; etc.). That some of the words of anticipation should be more specific and clearer than others is natural enough. This hope in Israel continued into New Testament times. (Cf. especially Psalms of Solomon 17:23–29; 18:1–10; and the expectation of both a priest-messiah and a king-messiah in the *Manual of Discipline* from Qumran, 9:11.) Sometimes it is an earthbound hope, but always there is the triumph of God through his Christ.

It seems clear that this expectation of a Davidic Christ is dominant in Peter's confession. Mark at least customarily speaks in terms consonant with this idea (cf. 10:47; 11:9,10; 12:35) and the disciples' anticipation of greatness in the kingdom (9:33–37 and 10:35–45). Peter's objection to Jesus' interpretation of himself as a suffering Son of man comes because, according to his understanding, the (Davidic) Christ would rule victoriously—not be killed (vv. 31–33).

Nevertheless, for Peter to call Jesus ***the Christ*** must have meant more to him than that Jesus was of lineal descent from David or would be a king over Israel. The Davidic Christ was God's chosen one (his anointed one), and would do the chosen work God had consecrated him to do. He would restore God's chosen people to the great destiny God had chosen for them. He would be the ideal ruler, and his coming would mark a true inauguration of God's kingdom. There is a note of expected victory from God, a note of eschatological finality, a note of wonder and awe in the confession. With all of this, Jesus' understanding of himself is in full accord. But he knows he will not be a ruler of the type of the first David.

Dull the disciples may have been, and slow to comprehend. But one of their number has now voiced his thinking. That the others were in agreement, however awed into silence, is evident from Jesus' command to all of them ***to tell no one about him.*** It was a necessary order. When the time of the trial came, Jesus was charged with claiming to be "the King of the Jews" (15:2,12,18).

III. The Way to the Cross: Secret Christ and Revealed Son of Man (8:31—13:37)

1. The Expected Passion and the Meaning of Discipleship (8:31—10:52)

(1) The Son of Man to Suffer (I) (8:31–33)

31 And he began to teach them that the Son of man must suffer many things, and be rejected by the elders and the chief priests and the scribes, and be killed, and after three days rise again. 32 And he said this plainly. And Peter took him, and began to rebuke him. 33 But turning and seeing his disciples, he rebuked Peter, and said, "Get behind me, Satan! For you are not on the side of God, but of men."

The conclusion of the disciples that Jesus was the expected Christ was one at which they could have arrived by growing spiritual insight—but see Matthew 16:17 and Jesus' commendation of Simon. That it was inevitable that Jesus should ***be rejected*** and ***killed,*** and that he should ***rise again*** was a conclusion that was utterly foreign to their mind-set. So Jesus ***began to teach them.*** According to Mark's account, Jesus repeated three times and quite ***plainly*** this warning about his own fate (8:31–33; 9:30–32; 10:32–34), yet they still had trouble reconciling this concept with their confession of Jesus as ***Christ.***

Son of man as Jesus' name for himself is found twice earlier (2:10,28); it will be used much more often in the latter half of Gospel (12 times). Like the name Christ, ***Son of man*** is a term which has commanded great attention from New Testament scholars. As the note on 2:10 indicates, Mark's concept has close kinship with the heavenly son of man spoken of in Daniel 7:13–28. Still, the meaning of the name is seen "through a glass darkly," because in Daniel the son of man is a victorious figure.

However, we do not have to turn to the latter part of Isaiah to find the note of suffering in God's cause. In Daniel, the one "like a son of man" represented God's true people, "the saints of the Most High" (7:18, 22). The forces of evil—four kings, the fourth beast, the horn—utterly defeated the saints, who became martyrs rather than betray their faith. However, their loyalty even to death brought them final and lasting victory in God's kingdom, and it is the "son of man" who has dominion in that eternal glory (Moule). It is beyond doubt that the early Christians identified Jesus with the Suffering Servant of God in Isaiah 40—66; but the vision in Daniel 7, which originally concerned the faithful Hebrews during the seemingly hopeless years of the Maccabean revolt, also had an ultimate fulfilment in Jesus, the true Son of man.

If Jesus was ***the Christ***, then, as Peter recognized, he was the key figure in God's kingdom. But Jesus now says that his dominion must be established not by military force or human achievement but by his loyalty and obedience to God, even to the cross. Such complete submission to God's will always arouses suspicion, threat, anger, retaliation: cf. the disciples' experiences in Acts 4:1–22; 5:17–39; 6:8—7:60; 8:3. It was bound to happen in Jesus' case, though the purpose of God was to be accomplished through it. Indeed, it was already happening (3:1–6,22; 6:1–6; 7:1–13; 8:11–13).

What does the man loyal to God do under such circumstances? Compromise with the opposition by adopting their methods or expectations? Protect his own life by modifying who he is and what he does in favor of the status quo? This was one of the temptations to Jesus, according to both Matthew 4:8–10 and Luke 4:5–8. It now appears in Peter, though he would not have realized the implications of his position when he ***began to rebuke*** Jesus for anticipating his suffering.

Jesus knew very well, however, that compromise with the forces of a worldly viewpoint would defeat God's purposes in himself. He was already aware how hard it was to shake his disciples from that pattern of thought (8:14–21): should he blur that distinction now? No, he could not, though he could see very clearly that God's way would lead to conflict and death. The voice of ***Satan*** tempted again in Peter's rebuke: he was ***not on the side of God, but of men.***

That the ***Son of man*** would ***rise again*** is also part of Jesus' insight into God's way to victory. Taylor doubts that Jesus was quite so explicit about his resurrection as he was his death; but he acknowledges that Jesus must also have spoken in terms of "victory" and "exaltation." Matthew 16:21 and Luke 9:22 both modify ***after three days*** to the more precise "on the third day." When Jesus said it, the meaning was "an indefinite expression for a short time." [39]

(2) *The Difficult Choice of Discipleship (8:34—9:1)*

[34] And he called to him the multitude with his disciples, and said to them, "If any man would come after me, let him deny himself and take up his cross and follow me. [35] For whoever would save his life will lose it; and whoever loses his life for my sake and the gospel's will save it. [36] For what does it profit a man, to gain the whole world and forfeit his life? [37] For what can a man give in return for his life? [38] For whoever is ashamed of me and of my words in this adulterous and sinful generation, of him will the Son of man also be ashamed, when he comes in the glory of his Father with the holy angels."

[1] And he said to them, "Truly, I say to you, there are some standing here who will not taste death before they see the kingdom of God come with power."

For himself, Jesus did not attempt to show that he chose the way of the cross because of the benefits it would bring, but because it was the Father's will. It was the

[39] Cranfield, p. 278. Some scholars doubt whether Jesus spoke so clearly about the death, resurrection, and coming of the Son of man as these verses and others (9:31 f.; 10:33 f.; 13:26 f.) would indicate. Perhaps the words do not go back to Jesus in their present form; nevertheless they may well be authentic redactions of what he did say. In addition to the works cited on the self-understanding of Jesus, cf. H. M. Teeple, "The Origin of the Son of Man Christology," JBL 84 (1965), 213–50; E. Schweizer, "The Son of Man," JBL 79 (1960), 119–29. In any case, it is certain that Mark thinks of Jesus both as the Son of man who suffered and as the exalted Son of man whose coming they expected.

path on "the side of God" (v. 33). Although he is the Christ, the Son of man, his disciples—and whoever will become his disciples—must choose the same way of the cross.

That Jesus ***called to him the multitude with his disciples*** probably indicates that the sayings which follow had a different context (or stood alone) when Mark received them. Jesus had apparently been with only his disciples before, and he took but three with him in 9:2–8. On the other hand, as far as the teaching of Jesus is concerned, Mark showed deep insight in choosing his order at this point. Not for the twelve only, but for disciples in his and every age, the hard principles set forth in Jesus' example are the necessary steps to the victorious life.

The prerequisites to true discipleship are two. First, ***let him deny himself.*** The basic idea in this word (it is not merely an exhortation, but a command) is simply to say *no!* "To deny oneself is to disown, not just one's sins, but one's self, to turn away from the idolatry of self-centeredness" (Cranfield). This is not the kind of "self-denial" by which one chooses to give up smoking or movies for a period of time: it requires submission to a new King in one's life, replacing the selfishness inherent in our persons. Cf. the discussion of "repent" in 1:15.

The second requirement is the twin of the first: ***take up his cross.*** The cross was never merely a burden or trouble to the Jew of Jesus' day, or to the Roman of Nero's time. The victim was required to carry his own cross to the place of his own execution. To take up one's cross therefore requires an absolute commitment, even to death.

Follow me means, because of the form of the verb, make it your habit to follow my example. It is a supporting command rather than a third requirement. It encompasses and interprets the first two, which explain what it means to be disciples. ***Follow*** is Mark's usual word in connection with discipleship (cf. 1:17,18,20; 2:14).

"Whoever cares for his own safety is lost; but if a man will let himself be lost for my sake and for the Gospel, that man is safe." So eloquently does NEB translate verse 35. If one's moral and spiritual outlook is subject to change because of one's fears or because of outside pressures, there is no lasting health in him. Yet no kind of self-abandonment except that which finds a new and determining commitment can avail. What is this commitment? It is an utter dedication to Jesus (not as Christ only but as Son of man, with his loyalty to God's will) and to the good news that is true because of his obedience and victory.

Is the cost of this discipleship too much? No, because the man who seeks to save himself may ***gain the whole world:*** but in the final analysis ***his life*** is not safe but ***forfeit.*** The word translated ***life*** in verses 35–37 is always the same in the original, though KJV uses "soul" part of the time. Here it means the man himself, his being, that which he really is. The underlying assumptions are, of course, that only what a man really is can last, and that God, who is ultimately in charge, will receive to himself those who are genuinely his own. As John would put it, they "have eternal life" (though John 3:36 uses another word for life). To deny oneself is not to despise one's own life. It is the only avenue to what life ought to mean and be.

Will anyone be ***ashamed*** of Jesus ***in this*** evil-dominated ***generation?*** Would Simon, should Jesus be crucified (v. 32)? Would James and John, should there be no places of high honor in his kingdom (10:35–40)? Would some of the people at Rome, called Christians, but now under pressure, deny their allegiance to Jesus? Then, according to the nature of discipleship and of life, they ***forfeit*** their lives, as the time of judgment (when the ***Son of man . . . comes***) will reveal. The either/or is before men: one either chooses to deny himself and walk in the way of the Son of man; or one compromises with ***this adulterous and sinful generation,*** hopelessly lost while trying to preserve his own hollow life.

Mark may have been responsible for placing 9:1 in this context; but both Matthew and Luke follow his order here, though with some notable variations in wording (Matt. 16:28; Luke 9:27). The meaning of the verse is clear enough in one respect: some of ***the multitude*** or of the ***disciples*** (v. 34) would still be alive in this world to observe that ***the kingdom of God*** had ***come*** (perfect participle in form) ***with power.*** But when they would ***see*** this great event realized—if indeed they did ***see*** it—has been much disputed.

Among the most notable and helpful suggestions about the meaning of the passage we mention only four.

(1) Some think the passage refers to the final coming of the Son of man in glory. However, this prophecy had still not been fulfilled, certainly not literally, by Mark's own time, though some of those who had been present were still living. Moreover, Jesus claimed *not* to know the time of the Parousia (13:32).

(2) The reference is to the truth that the kingdom of God had already come, and that finally some of those present would perceive the truth. This is what is called "realized eschatology." But see the note on 1:14 f.

(3) The reference is to the transfiguration (9:2–8). This is an old and widely supported interpretation: what the three disciples saw was a kind of preview of the resurrection and the glory of the Christ. Perhaps this is what Mark had in mind in placing the saying at this point.

(4) The reference is to the triumph of the Son of man over the cross with its shame and death. Was this not clearly the central event in the establishment of Christ's kingship? It is not necessary to suppose that Jesus had already anticipated every facet of the disciples' experience during the resurrection and the pentecostal events that followed; but never was God's power manifested more completely than at that time.

It is likely that suggestions one, three, and four all would have had their advocates among Mark's readers from the first. But this is as much as to say that there remained a certain mystery about Jesus even for the church. Moreover, all of these four suggestions, and most other suggestions offered, recognize that something final and ultimate has happened or is about to happen in Jesus. He himself, as Christ and Son of man, is not simply one important name in a continuing history. He is according to God's providence an eschatological figure. "In many and various ways God spoke of old . . . but in these last days he has spoken to us by a Son" (Heb. 1:1 f.).

(3) *The Transfiguration (9:2–8)*

2 And after six days Jesus took with him Peter and James and John, and led them up a high mountain apart by themselves; and he was transfigured before them, 3 and his garments became glistening, intensely white, as no fuller on earth could bleach them. 4 And there appeared to them Elijah with Moses; and they were talking to Jesus. 5 And Peter said to Jesus, "Master, it is well that we are here; let us make three booths, one for you and one for Moses and one for Elijah." 6 For he did not know what to say, for they were exceedingly afraid. 7 And a cloud overshadowed them, and a voice came out of the cloud, "This is my beloved Son; listen to him." 8 And suddenly looking around they no longer saw any one with them but Jesus only.

After six days: this is the only precise note of time given by Mark outside of the passion narrative (cf. 14:1). In this way he has carefully connected Peter's confession, Jesus' anticipation of suffering and glory, and perhaps also 9:1 with this paragraph.

The three disciples he took with him are the same who were singled out in 5:37. They are the three whose difficulty in accepting the prospect of Christ as suffering is particularly noted (***Peter,*** 8:32; ***James and John,*** 10:35 ff.). Mark emphasizes that Jesus arranged to be alone with these three. The ***high mountain*** is probably not the traditional Mount Tabor, which is not high nor near Caesarea Philippi (8:27). It may have been Mount Hermon, or one of its spurs or another of the rather lofty peaks southeast of the city.

He was transfigured before them. The verb is used to describe the transformation which is to come about in the Christian' character (Rom. 12:2), and also (2 Cor. 3:18) to speak of the reflected glory of the Lord which is said to "transfigure" us into his very likeness. Here, part of what the disciples saw is described in verse 3: ***his garments became glistening, intensely white,*** beyond the ability of man to ***bleach them.*** It is strange that Mark does not even attempt to describe Jesus' face in any way (cf. Ex. 34:29, where the face of Moses is described after he had been with God). One cannot help but believe that Mark considers the transfiguration experience something of a preview for the three disciples of the exalted Son of man.

There appeared then to the disciples ***Elijah with Moses.*** In Luke's account (9:28–36) we are told that they spoke with Jesus about his death, and the impression is given that the experience was at least partly to confirm to Jesus his understanding of his role as suffering Son of man. In Mark, however, the experience seems especially to have been given for the sake of the disciples.

Elijah is representative of the prophets, ***Moses*** of the law which God had given to Israel. The transfiguration experience, therefore, affirms the continuity of Jesus' work with those who had been God's spokesmen in other days and ways. Perhaps Elijah was given priority by Mark (cf. Matt. and Luke) because of his identification, at least in role, with John the Baptist (cf. below, v. 13). As the Son of man will be before long, the Baptist has already been killed because of his loyal obedience to God.

Modern ideas about what exactly took place have varied widely. Some have considered that the whole event has no historical basis, but owes its existence to a kind of early Christian theological art and is purely symbolic in the presentation of the faith. Others consider it a resurrection story read back into the lifetime of Jesus. Still others think it a straightforward account of the actual event, and that Jesus' true form was thus early revealed to chosen disciples. Some think the story historical but that the experience itself was in the form of a vision.

Such details as the ***six days,*** the names of the disciples, and the emphasis on solitude and place are most reasonably explained by accepting the story as historical. How much Mark understood to have been vision and how much more tangible reality, who can say? The verb ***appeared*** (v. 4) and the sudden disappearance of Moses and Elijah (v. 8) support the vision concept (cf. Matt. 17:9).

Nevertheless, the story is primarily theological in its impact. The ***cloud*** certainly signified to Mark and his readers (as to the three disciples surely after they considered the matter) the very presence and guidance of God. The ***cloud*** also served to veil the divine glory (cf. Ex. 13:21 f.; 14:19 f.; and Num. 9:15–23). Even the verb ***overshadowed*** is found in this connection in Exodus 40:35.

Just as Moses "entered the cloud" to go up the mountain to seek God's direct guidance, so the divine ***voice came out of the cloud*** to instruct the disciples. (Cf. the note on 1:11, where the voice is directed toward Jesus.) Perhaps there is also intended an anticipation of the revelation of the Son of man (Mark 13:26; 14:62; Acts 1:9–11).

This is my beloved Son. Jesus is more than "the Christ" (8:29). The disciples must realize that Jesus is God's own Son. ***Listen to him:*** that is, hear and obey him, for he will rightly interpret his divine Father. In this context, therefore, the specific burden of the divine voice is to assert the rightness of Jesus' interpretation of himself and of what it means to follow him. It confirms Jesus' word in calling himself Son of man, and anticipates the tragedy and exaltation to come.

Peter indeed ***did not know what to say*** (v. 6). ***Master*** translates "Rabbi," hardly the name that would have been chosen by men composing the story later. Probably we should understand ***it is well that we are here*** as meaning that the three disciples could minister to the needs of Jesus and his remarkable guests. Peter offered their services in providing some shelter.

As Mark tells the story, Peter's suggestion may reveal an eager spirit for service, but it also reinforces a motif characteristic of the whole Gospel: the disciples are learning, but they have a terribly difficult time understanding who Jesus is. On the other hand, Mark's readers again have an open affirmation that Jesus is God's Son.

(4) *Elijah's Return and the Rising of the Son of Man* (*9:9–13*)

**9 And as they were coming down the moun-
tain, he charged them to tell no one what they
had seen, until the Son of man should have
risen from the dead. 10 So they kept the matter
to themselves, questioning what the rising from
the dead meant. 11 And they asked him, "Why
do the scribes say that first Elijah must come?"
12 And he said to them, "Elijah does come first
to restore all things; and how is it written of
the Son of man, that he should suffer many
things and be treated with contempt? 13 But I
tell you that Elijah has come, and they did to
him whatever they pleased, as it is written of
him."**

If the three disciples who had been there did not clearly comprehend the import of what they had seen in the transfiguration, the others would not greatly have benefited from their telling it. So Jesus *charged them to tell no one* until the time when the great experience would have more meaning for all. *The Son of man* is again identified both as one who is to suffer and one who is to be exalted.

The disciples obeyed Jesus by not spreading their versions of what happened. However, their own *questioning* continued. The words of Jesus plus the experience on the mountain would have kept them from being content with the concept of Jesus as the Christ they had expected. But they were apparently still unable to be satisfied in their own minds about how his words about *rising from the dead* could be construed.

Moreover, *the scribes* taught that *Elijah must come* before Messiah. (Cf. Mal. 4:5–6.) Were they wrong, since Messiah has already come? Or, how can Jesus be what he appeared to be in the transfiguration, since Elijah still has not prepared the way?

Jesus' reply was that the scribes were right in their expectation, but that *Elijah* had already *come* and men had done to him what men (hardened in heart and under the control of evil) had *pleased* to do. Note again Mark's parallel between the fate of John the Baptist and Jesus. In Matthew 17:13 the identification of John as Elijah is spelled out.

The Scriptures referred to by Jesus in verse 12, showing that *the Son of man* would undergo suffering, must have included Isaiah 49:7 and 53:3, where the same verb (treat with contempt) occurs either in LXX or another ancient Greek translation. Perhaps Psalms 22:6 and 123:3 were also mentioned; and Jesus may have spoken in some detail of Daniel 7. Mark does not help us much with this question. Perhaps the Christians for whom he was writing already had special collections of Old Testament passages that were understood by them to refer to Jesus.

(5) *The Healing of the Epileptic Boy* (*9:14–29*)

**14 And when they came to the disciples, they
saw a great crowd about them, and scribes
arguing with them. 15 And immediately all the
crowd, when they saw him, were greatly
amazed, and ran up to him and greeted him.
16 And he asked them, "What are you discussing with them?" 17 And one of the crowd answered him, "Teacher, I brought my son to
you, for he has a dumb spirit; 18 and wherever
it seizes him, it dashes him down; and he
foams and grinds his teeth and becomes rigid;
and I asked your disciples to cast it out, and
they were not able." 19 And he answered them,
"O faithless generation, how long am I to be
with you? How long am I to bear with you?
Bring him to me." 20 And they brought the boy
to him; and when the spirit saw him, immediately it convulsed the boy, and he fell on the
ground and rolled about, foaming at the
mouth. 21 And Jesus asked his father, "How
long has he had this?" And he said, "From
childhood. 22 And it has often cast him into the
fire and into the water, to destroy him; but if
you can do anything, have pity on us and help
us." 23 And Jesus said to him, "If you can! All
things are possible to him who believes."
24 Immediately the father of the child cried out
and said, "I believe; help my unbelief!" 25 And
when Jesus saw that a crowd came running**

together, he rebuked the unclean spirit, saying to it, "You dumb and deaf spirit, I command you, come out of him, and never enter him again." [26] **And after crying out and convulsing him terribly, it came out, and the boy was like a corpse; so that most of them said, "He is dead."** [27] **But Jesus took him by the hand and lifted him up, and he arose.** [28] **And when he had entered the house, his disciples asked him privately, "Why could we not cast it out?"** [29] **And he said to them, "This kind cannot be driven out by anything but prayer."**

The parallel accounts in Matthew 17:14–21 and Luke 9:37–43 are much shorter than that of Mark. The story is so detailed in Mark that it has been suggested that this is one of the narratives Mark derived from Peter. The connection in verse 14 indicates that Mark considered his order of events here to be chronological.

The other *disciples* were surrounded by a crowd, and *scribes* were *arguing with them,* perhaps about the power of exorcism or the necessary procedures for attempting to help the boy who had been brought to them. The *crowd* and, we may assume, *the disciples* with them were surprised to see Jesus. *Greatly amazed* is normally a stronger word than surprised, but we have no evidence that Jesus' countenance was still affected by the transfiguration—verse 9 indicates the contrary.

Jesus' question in verse 16 may have been directed to the nine disciples, or even to the scribes, but it was answered by the man whose distress had precipitated the whole matter. He had *brought* his *son* to Jesus, and when he was unable to reach the Master himself he had *asked* his *disciples* for help. The disciples on previous occasions had indeed "cast out demons" (6:13), but they had been unable to heal this time. Were they surprised at their failure? (Cf. verse 28.)

The boy's affliction seems clearly to have been epilepsy, and Matthew 17:15 so names it. In Mark, the father describes his son's trouble as coming from *a dumb spirit,* i.e., one that will not speak, so that it is as one deaf and dumb (cf. vv. 17,25). The problem is recurrent and causes the boy to fall, sometimes in places that endanger his very life (v. 22). *He foams and grinds his teeth and becomes rigid*—all these are symptoms of the epileptic.

Faithless generation emphasizes lack of faith rather than lack of dependability. We should probably understand Jesus' exclamation as directed toward the crowd as a whole, though some think it confined to the disciples (cf. 6:6). Mark's treatment quite often encourages us to think of how much Jesus' patience must have been tried by men's dullness of mind and slowness to believe in him.

Jesus' conversation with the father centers also on the question of faith and power. The disciples *were not able* ("strong") to help (v. 18), and the father, distraught by their failure and the degeneration of attempts to help into arguments of one kind and another (v. 14), pleaded, *If you can do anything . . . help us* (v. 22). The man is also of the generation that could or would not believe. Mark and his readers anticipate that the strong Son of God will exercise his proven authority over the power assailing the boy.

Jesus repeated the father's phrase, *If you can!* He was therefore calling for faith on the part of the father, and the father so understood him. *I believe,* he cried; *help my unbelief!* How well does his confession reflect the difficulties of every man's faith in God! The life of faith is no tranquil experience, without doubt and without turmoil. And this is especially evident in times of personal crisis.

All things are possible to him who believes (v. 23): this probably does not mean that with faith one can do anything he chooses; but, as Rawlinson says, that the man who has faith will set no limit for God's power. In this story the clear inplication is that the disciples' faith was also lacking (v. 28). With their limited faith, they had failed to be truly in communion with God's Spirit and so with his power (v. 29).

The *crowd* was swelling rapidly (v. 25). Jesus wished to help the afflicted boy but not to have any more public display of his authority than required. He commanded the ***spirit*** to ***come out*** and to leave the boy permanently. The boy's malady showed its fierceness for one final time, but this made his healing more obvious to all.

We must never minimize the importance of Mark's teaching about Jesus' compassion, as it is shown again in this story. But we ought especially to note that Mark's twin emphases continue to be on Jesus' power, and consequently on his unique authority and on the limitations of the disciples' faith.

In verse 29, a great many ancient manuscripts, though not some of the most reliable, add "fasting" as a prerequisite, along with ***prayer,*** for the accomplishment of such works of healing. Its inclusion must reflect the practice of many early and devout Christians (cf. the note on 2:18 ff. and also Acts 13:2; 14:23). However, Jesus certainly did not encourage his disciples to fast during his ministry. The additional words might have been added (but hardly omitted) by an early copyist influenced by contemporary practice. The text of RSV rather than KJV has more to commend it. There is no evidence that Jesus anywhere taught that ascetic habits increase spiritual power.

(6) *The Son of Man to Suffer (II) (9:30–32)*

30 They went on from there and passed
through Galilee. And he would not have any
one know it; 31 for he was teaching his disci-
ples, saying to them, "The Son of man will be delivered into the hands of men, and they will kill him; and when he is killed, after three days he will rise." 32 But they did not understand
the saying, and they were afraid to ask him.

From there . . . through Galilee: the journey according to Mark is in a southeasterly direction back into the territory in which Jesus had spent most of his ministry and in which he and the twelve were best known. Probably because he was concentrating on his instruction to ***his disciples,*** he was attempting to keep his presence secret.

For Jesus' prediction of his passion, see above on 8:31 f. There is a third similar statement in 10:32–34. Perhaps Mark's phrasing of Jesus' teaching in the three passages is all derived from a single tradition. But it is quite reasonable to assume that Jesus kept instructing his disciples about his role and its expected outcome.

The verb ***will be delivered*** is especially interesting. It is the same word that described the arrest of John the Baptist (cf. above on 1:14) and Judas' betrayal of Jesus (14:10). It is used also of handing down traditions (1 Cor. 11:2), of risking one's life (Acts 15:26), or of commending a person to God's grace for the accomplishment of a task (Acts 14:26). Although translated by RSV as future, the verb here is in form a present, and more likely describes something that is already taking place. God is already giving ***the Son of man*** over ***into the hands of*** (hardened in heart) ***men.*** The death of Jesus has its source in God who sent his Son into the world, but the cause of his death is to be found in the nature of men among whom he lived.

The disciples ***did not understand:*** cf. 4:13; 6:52; 8:17–21; 9:10. Both this verb and the next (***they were afraid***) are imperfect in form and are descriptive of the continuing situation among the followers. Perhaps their fear was of being reprimanded again for dullness of mind; but they apparently could not adjust their thinking to the idea that the Christ might die or that suffering might lead to victory.

(7) *True Greatness in Discipleship (9:33–37)*

33 And they came to Capernaum; and when he was in the house he asked them, "What were you discussing on the way?" 34 But they
were silent; for on the way they had discussed with one another who was the greatest. 35 And
he sat down and called the twelve; and he said to them, "If any one would be first, he must be last of all and servant of all." 36 And he took a
child, and put him in the midst of them; and taking him in his arms, he said to them,
37 "Whoever receives one such child in my name receives me; and whoever receives me, receives not me but him who sent me."

Each of the predictions of the passion is followed immediately by a section of Jesus' teaching on the nature of discipleship. In these verses (and in 10:35–45) the subject is greatness in the kingdom, for the problem is the lingering self-centered ambition present in the disciples. They were having great difficulty in accepting the idea that God's Messiah should be humiliated by his enemies, much less be exalted and triumphant through the way of the cross.

Perhaps *the house* in *Capernaum* is again the home of Simon and Andrew (1:29). When Jesus inquired about the nature of the disciples' discussion along *the way*, no one was willing to speak. At least they realized that their own motivations would be subject to his rebuke. He *sat down*, we assume simply because they had finished their journey; some, however, think he was following the custom of a teacher to sit while he was instructing (cf. Matt. 5:1).

The word *first* was used often of rank or degree and meant most prominent or most important. Some of the Hebrew scribes occasionally said something similar to Jesus' saying here. Hillel, for example, used to say, "He who [seeks to] exalt his name destroys his name" (Mishnah, Aboth 1:13). But the teaching with Jesus is central to his outlook and spirit. Who is great in the kingdom? Not the man who wants to be chief, but the man who has no selfish care for his own advancement, and is a *servant* even to the lowliest of his fellowmen.

If we interpret verses 36–37 in this context, as Mark apparently did, then to *be last of all and servant of all* would be illustrated by one's care for and ministry to even a *child*. To receive a child in Jesus' *name* probably meant to receive and help him, because this is what Jesus would do for a person who is immature and unable to find answers for his own need. The *child* is a concern to Jesus, so he must be a concern to any disciple. To express one's care for the child, therefore, is also to receive Jesus. When one does this, he is embracing the humility and service characteristic of Jesus, "the man for others"; and so he is also receiving the Father (*him who sent me*), after whose life the character of Jesus is patterned.

Perhaps the sayings of Jesus in 9:33–50 came to Mark in separate units. More likely they may already have been joined together as a catechetical device. As Johnson has remarked, the theme of the whole is "little ones." In verses 33–37 they are children; in verses 38–41 they are those who, though not discerning disciples, nevertheless use Jesus' name with reverence and try to serve persons in need; and in verses 42–50 they are those whose littleness or weakness makes them an easy prey to temptation. The phrase *in my name* (or something very similar) is also recurrent in the passages and would have been an aid to memorization.

(8) *The Inclusiveness of Discipleship* (*9:38–41*)

[38] John said to him, "Teacher, we saw a man casting out demons in your name, and we forbade him, because he was not following us." [39] But Jesus said, "Do not forbid him; for no one who does a mighty work in my name will be able soon after to speak evil of me. [40] For he that is not against us is for us. [41] For truly, I say to you, whoever gives you a cup of water to drink because you bear the name of Christ, will by no means lose his reward.

It was *John*, one of the three who witnessed the transfiguration, one of the two who are specifically named as being jealous for high position (10:35 f.), and one of the two who wanted to burn an inhospitable Samaritan village (Luke 9:54), who self-righteously told Jesus that they *forbade* a man to use Jesus' name. *Forbade* is an imperfect in form: they tried to stop the man from using Jesus' name, but he probably kept on doing so.

The man described would have been called a magician, or someone great, who sought to cast *out demons* by using every name he knew that might be effective in his exorcism. The magical papyri afford many examples of formulae used by these persons, and the long list of "divinities" often include Israel's God, or Abraham,

Isaac, and Jacob; occasionally the name of Jesus also appears (cf. Luke 11:19; Acts 8:9 ff.; 13:6 ff.; 19:13 ff.).

Jesus abruptly rejected John's spirit of intolerance. ***Do not forbid him*** means, You are wrong: stop hindering him. Why? Because, although he is not now one of us, his mind is at least favorably disposed and open: if ***a mighty work*** (the word used of Jesus' own acts) be done ***in my name,*** the man who used it will surely not be quick ***to speak evil of me.*** The man has taken no hostile position like that of the scribes (3:22). So far he is friendly toward us, and we should accept him in this light.

It is difficult to understand how some (including Nineham) can ascribe the origin of this story to the early church. ***He that is not against us is for us*** is perfectly consonant with Jesus' spirit, but the temptation among immature Christians, in the first century as today, has always been toward exclusiveness and intolerance.

In Luke 11:23 (cf. Matt. 12:30) Jesus is quoted as taking apparently the opposite of this tolerant position. However, as long as men have not reached any final decision about Jesus, the Master was disposed to treat them as persons who may with openness of mind become his followers. On the other hand, when a decision concerning Jesus has to be made, persons who determine to stay neutral or agnostic are equally aligned with others against Jesus.

The point in verse 41, as it stands in this context, is that one who does even the smallest act of kindness toward God's people will find that God honors and values that token of faith and Christlike character. (Matt. 10:42 has this saying in a different context.)

The name of Christ: is it not unlikely that Jesus would have used this title of himself? Cf. above on 8:27–30. There is some evidence for "in my name" being the original text. If the name ***Christ*** had been used here by Jesus, he would likely have been quoting the title which the exorcist had used of him.

Unlike the probability in verses 38–40, the person commended in verse 41 is spoken of in terms of helping one in the Christian fellowship. This would have been especially meaningful to Roman Christians, for whose non-Christian friends every gesture of support may have carried some threat of reprisal. Throughout the New Testament, Christians are urged to do good to all people; but there is an especial obligation to care for those in the Christian fellowship (cf. Matt. 5:43–48; John 15:12–17; Gal. 6:9–10).

(9) *The Necessity for Faithful Discipleship (9:42–50)*

[42] "Whoever causes one of these little ones who believe in me to sin, it would be better for him if a great millstone were hung round his neck and he were thrown into the sea. [43] And if your hand causes you to sin, cut it off; it is better for you to enter life maimed than with two hands to go to hell, to the unquenchable fire. [45] And if your foot causes you to sin, cut it off; it is better for you to enter life lame than with two feet to be thrown into hell. [47] And if your eye causes you to sin, pluck it out; it is better for you to enter the kingdom of God with one eye than with two eyes to be thrown into hell, [48] where their worm does not die, and the fire is not quenched. [49] For every one will be salted with fire. [50] Salt is good; but if the salt has lost its saltness, how will you season it? Have salt in yourselves, and be at peace with one another."

For the connection of the various parts of this paragraph with the preceding verses see the final note on verses 33–37. The fundamental burden of the whole, so relevant to Mark's readers, concerns the enormous importance of being faithful in discipleship.

The verb ***causes . . . to sin,*** or "causes to stumble," is translated "they fall away" in 4:17 and "they took offense" in 6:3 (see the notes there.) ***One of these little ones*** may have referred to little children when Jesus first spoke (so T. W. Manson, Nineham), but it is also appropriately applicable to weak or immature Christians (Rom. 14–15; 1 Cor. 8—10; 3:1 ff.). The fault lies in tempting someone to do what he understands to be evil, not in doing something which "offends" (KJV) someone because he does not approve of the action.

A great millstone is literally a "donkey millstone," i.e., one so large it had to be turned by a donkey (rather than the smaller one which was usually turned by a woman). To bind a person to such a stone and throw him into deep water was a Roman form of capital punishment. The meaning of verse 42, then, is that a man had better be drowned than to lead simple Christians into paths that are destructive of spiritual health.

Moreover, a man must guard himself from commitments, however pleasurable, that alienate him from true discipleship. If ***your hand . . . your foot . . . and if your eye causes you to sin:*** if what you desire to do, or the places you long to frequent, or the things you are greedy to possess (see "envy" on 7:22, a word which translates "evil eye") would entice you into a path departing from the way of the cross, whatever sacrifice is necessary must be made. This is no command for mutilation of the body. But there cannot be two masters in life; either you "deny yourself" and accept a new master ("follow me"), or you lose your life. (Cf. above on 8:34 f. and also the note on meaning of "repent" in 1:15.)

Hell with its unquenchable ***fire*** is "Gehenna," not merely Hades, which would mean only the abode of the dead. Gehenna historically was a valley at the western edge of Jerusalem. Used at one time by worshipers of Molech as a place where their sons or daughters were offered in sacrifice, the valley was defiled during King Josiah's religious reformation (2 Kings 23:10; cf. Jer. 7:31; 19:5 f.,; 32:35). Since that time it had been used as a dump for all kinds of refuse. Therefore it was correctly described as a place where maggots continually fed and multiplied (***their worm does not die***) and where fire was always smoldering (***the fire is not quenched***).

Just as heaven was thought of always in the most beautiful and wonderful terms (cf. Rev. 21:1—22:5), so the imagery describing the fate of the wicked was comparably horrible: hell was like Gehenna. (In our best manuscripts vv. 44,46 are omitted; but they are in any case identical with v. 48. There are also variant readings in v. 49, but RSV follows the best supported text.)

The connection between verses 49–50 with the preceding seems almost entirely verbal, the key word being ***fire.*** Taylor is right in rejecting the suggestion that verse 49 means that the fires of Gehenna were only for purifying. The idea set forth by LaGrange is even more speculative and less possible: he thinks verse 49 indicates that the fire in Gehenna preserves the departed and wicked occupants and that in this way their terrible punishment will continue. It is far more likely that the saying ***every one will be salted with fire*** was understood to mean that the disciples would have to be "seasoned and purified," or "preserved" (***salted*** could be used for either figure) through the persecution and suffering they would need to endure.

In verse 50 ***salt*** has become a figure for the good qualities of life, that "season" it. Pure salt never loses its strength, but the people who spoke of salt in this way did not realize that the sodium chloride they used might well be mixed with less soluble salts which were similar in appearance. Under these circumstances what had appeared to be salt might become no longer useful in making things salty; and there was naturally no way successfully to season foods with it again.

The disciples should nurture the things that make life fine and good. The selfish ambitions of the disciples in 33–37 and the excluding spirit expressed by John in verse 38 are not good seasoning for life. Jesus apparently meant, If you possess ***salt in yourselves,*** as disciples must, you will have those qualities of life that make for ***peace with one another.*** Both commands are linear: keep striving for the salt qualities and in this way keep working to create a healthful fellowship among yourselves.

(10) The Question About Divorce (10:1–12)

[1] And he left there and went to the region of Judea and beyond the Jordan, and crowds gathered to him again; and again, as his cus-

tom was, he taught them.
2 And Pharisees came up and in order to test
him asked, "Is it lawful for a man to divorce
his wife?" 3 He answered them, "What did
Moses command you?" 4 They said, "Moses
allowed a man to write a certificate of divorce,
and to put her away." 5 But Jesus said to them,
"For your hardness of heart he wrote you this
commandment. 6 But from the beginning of
creation, 'God made them male and female.'
7 'For this reason a man shall leave his father
and mother and be joined to his wife, 8 and the
two shall become one.' So they are no longer
two but one. 9 What therefore God has joined
together, let not man put asunder."
10 And in the house the disciples asked him
again about this matter. 11 And he said to
them, "Whoever divorces his wife and marries
another, commits adultery against her; 12 and if
she divorces her husband and marries another,
she commits adultery."

Beyond the Jordan means the territory east of that river, apparently southern Perea. The original setting may have been on a journey from Judea toward Galilee. However, in the Markan plot, Jesus is moving ever closer to the time and place of his death.

The question posed by the Pharisees (cf. above on 2:16; 7:1) concerned ***divorce.*** In Matthew 19:3, the form of the question is somewhat different: "Is it lawful to divorce one's wife for any cause?" The followers of two great rabbis, Shammai and Hillel, took extremely divergent views on this matter. Shammai's followers were very strict in interpreting Deuteronomy 24:1–4: for them, "some indecency" could only mean acts of unchastity. The disciples of Hillel were much more lenient, giving as examples such things as careless preparation of meals or some other unsatisfactory quality in a wife. But neither Shammai nor Hillel encouraged divorce: it was a matter of interpretation of Scripture. The question may have been asked originally in the form it is cited by Matthew, because there really was no doubt about whether the law actually permitted divorce.

However, the interest of Mark and his readers would not have been in the rabbinical dispute but in Jesus' teaching about God's will. ***Is it lawful?*** should be understood to mean, Is it according to God's instruction? In any case, the question answered is not whether divorce (or remarriage) is legal, but whether it is in accord with the divine purpose.

Moses allowed: the name of Moses was virtually a title for the collection of Scriptures from Genesis through Deuteronomy. Under the Mosaic code a man might ***divorce his wife,*** though no provision was made for a wife to divorce her husband. The wife who was being put away was entitled to ***a certificate of divorce,*** which would indicate her status. The law obviously was an attempt to promote some order and restraint in the society to which it was first given.

Jesus' answer goes directly to the heart of the matter. The reason for the law was adequate enough. ***Hardness of heart,*** Jesus describes it: i.e., the people were set on doing what they thought and desired; they were blind and unteachable as far as God's will for them was concerned. This particular word (***hardness of heart***) occurs only here (cf. Matt. 19:8) and in 16:14 in the New Testament; but the idea, as we have seen, is a central one in Mark. See 3:5; 8:17.

However, just because a law is necessary and appropriate under our human circumstances, it does not follow that its provisions are what God desires for man. Citing pertinent passages from the creation narrative in Genesis 1—2, Jesus drew the conclusion that the institution of marriage was in the purpose of God; that in the marital relationship a new home was established with a new unity; and that it was not according to God's purpose for so sacred a relationship to be severed by God's creatures.

This is an absolute teaching. That we may have failures in marriage because of immaturity or misrepresentation or some other reason can never make the failures a good thing, nor change what God would have purposed for marriage. As in early Hebrew society, in the course of our human existence, divorce may sometimes be the lesser of two evils. ***Hardness of heart*** is not a sin confined to antiquity.

Laws can, and ought, to aid in building an orderly society and establishing justice. But no law, Mosaic or modern, can lift us to God's full purpose for life. Nor should we understand Jesus' teaching here as "law" in any rigid sense. It is an exhortation to seek God's will, but it is not a legalism. It is the ideal expressed in God's purpose as Jesus interprets it: lifelong and exclusive faithfulness.

In Matthew 5:32 and 19:9, unchastity is treated as a legitimate ground for divorce. But this evil is also symptomatic of ***hardness of heart***, and is specifically that kind of act which by its very nature mars union in marriage. Mark's word (not Matthew's) is the one cited by Paul in 1 Corinthians 7:10–15, but Paul does not treat it as a binding law for non-Christian marital situations. He does insist that any Christian marriage partner shall always behave in appropriate Christian fashion and seek to uphold and not to destroy the marital bond.

With the high ideal Jesus had set before them ***the disciples asked him*** further about the matter. (Cf. Matt. 19:10: "If such is the case of a man with his wife, it is not expedient to marry.") Jesus simply reinforced his previous words. He probably assumed a person divorced would likely remarry. For most women who were divorced there was little real choice except to enter upon marriage again (Johnson), and the husband who had divorced his wife generally took another. However, said Jesus, this divorce and remarriage mars the previous union and fails the ideal present in God's purpose.

We have no word from Jesus at this point about many questions raised in our modern culture. We may be sure that the purposes of God for marriage do not change. We may be equally sure that the divine character, offering forgiveness and restoration, remains for those also who have failed in marriage.

According to Jewish rabbinical law, a man might commit adultery against another married man, or a wife might commit adultery against her husband. But a woman's status was so inferior that an unfaithful husband was not regarded as having committed adultery against his wife. (Some manuscripts, and their reading is accepted by Taylor and others, have the woman "leaving," rather than "divorcing," her husband, but nevertheless marrying another. Herodias' marriage to Herod Antipas—cf. above on 6:17—is suggested as the specific example at issue.)

In verses 11–12 Jesus speaks of man and woman in identical terms; neither is distinction in status implied in verse 6 (cf. Gal. 3:28). The matter is not pressed here, but it is apparent that the early Christians, on the basis of their Master's teachings, accorded to wives a status well above that given them in Judaism.

(*11*) *Blessing the Children* (*10:13–16*)

13 And they were bringing children to him, that he might touch them; and the disciples rebuked them. 14 But when Jesus saw it he was indignant, and said to them, "Let the children come to me, do not hinder them; for to such belongs the kingdom of God. 15 Truly, I say to you, whoever does not receive the kingdom of God like a child shall not enter it." 16 And he took them in his arms and blessed them, laying his hands upon them.

They were bringing children to him. No clear connecting link with the preceding narrative is given; ***they*** is impersonal, and certainly might include fathers or friends as well as mothers. The word used for ***children*** would be appropriate to any up to about twelve years of age. The purpose of asking Jesus to ***touch them*** would have been to obtain his blessing. (See Taylor, who cites Gen. 48:14, and refers to modern parallels.)

The disciples seem to have supposed Jesus would not wish to waste his time with little children, and ***rebuked*** those who brought them for imposing on their Teacher. Jesus ***was indignant***—a strong word, so strong that neither parallel account repeats it (Matt. 19:13–15; Luke 18:15–17). It is the only time the word is used of Jesus; see comment on anger in 3:5.

Do not hinder, or better, stop hindering ***them.*** The verb ***hinder*** is often found in baptismal contexts in the New Testament (cf. Acts 8:36; 10:47; 11:17); Matthew 3:14 has a variant form of this word. But we have no reason to suppose that Mark (much less Jesus) intended any such application of this incident as approving baptism for little children.

Nevertheless, Jesus welcomed ***the children.*** Mark and his readers would understand the appropriateness of ***to me:*** was not Jesus the King of the kingdom? Let them bring the children to Jesus, ***for to such belongs the kingdom.*** The kingdom does not belong to the mighty, the strong, the influential; it belongs to the weak, the insignificant, the unimportant.

The words must not be construed as meaning that the kingdom consists of little children (or, the weak and the helpless). But no one can enter the kingdom unless he receives it ***like a child.*** Can anyone ever earn his place in the kingdom? Jesus' teaching here is parallel in meaning to that in Matthew 11:25 f. and to the Beatitude about the poor in spirit (Matt. 5:3). (Cf. 1 Cor. 1:26 ff.) Mark, like the rest of the New Testament, holds that the favor of God's kingship is a gift, not something which is given on merit.

Jesus did more than he was asked. He lifted the children into ***his arms and blessed them, laying his hands upon them,*** according to the custom of one asking God's favor upon a person.

The verb ***shall not enter*** is used with the very strong Greek double negative. The meaning is not that there are two kingdoms, one present here and one coming; but that, unless one receives the kingdom as one in need, who cannot merit its blessings, he never will enter it at all. To put it in another Markan term, one cannot enter the kingdom with a hardened heart—a rutted and proud intellectual and moral blindness: he must come as a teachable, humble person, and accept it. The kingdom cannot be forced (4:26–29), and it is not dependent on wealth or status (10:17–31).

(12) *The Hazard of Wealth to Discipleship (10:17–31)*

**17 And as he was setting out on his journey, a
man ran up and knelt before him, and asked
him, "Good Teacher, what must I do to inherit
eternal life?" 18 And Jesus said to him, "Why
do you call me good? No one is good but God
alone. 19 You know the commandments: 'Do
not kill, Do not commit adultery, Do not steal,
Do not bear false witness, Do not defraud,
Honor your father and mother.' " 20 And he
said to him, "Teacher, all these I have observed from my youth." 21 And Jesus looking
upon him loved him, and said to him, "You
lack one thing; go, sell what you have, and
give to the poor, and you will have treasure in
heaven; and come, follow me." 22 At that saying his countenance fell, and he went away
sorrowful; for he had great possessions.**

**23 And Jesus looked around and said to his
disciples, "How hard it will be for those who
have riches to enter the kingdom of God!"
24 And the disciples were amazed at his words.
But Jesus said to them again, "Children, how
hard it is to enter the kingdom of God! 25 It is
easier for a camel to go through the eye of a
needle than for a rich man to enter the kingdom of God." 26 And they were exceedingly
astonished, and said to him, "Then who can be
saved?" 27 Jesus looked at them and said,
"With men it is impossible, but not with God;
for all things are possible with God." 28 Peter
began to say to him, "Lo, we have left everything and followed you." 29 Jesus said, "Truly,
I say to you, there is no one who has left house
or brothers or sisters or mother or father or
children or lands, for my sake and for the
gospel, 30 who will not receive a hundredfold
now in this time, houses and brothers and
sisters and mothers and children and lands,
with persecutions, and in the age to come
eternal life. 31 But many that are first will be
last, and the last first."**

A man ran up and knelt: the story in Mark does not tell us that he was young (v. 20; cf. Matt. 19:16–22) or that he was a ruler (Luke 18:18–24). It was not customary to kneel to a rabbi, so the act was one of some reverence. To address anyone as ***Good Teacher*** was most unusual. The man may have used *good* in some flattering way. Jesus' response repeats the same word with obvious reference to moral attributes; and only God is *good* (perfect) in that sense.

Whatever may have been the man's original intention in addressing Jesus as *good,* Mark and his readers would readily have applied the word to the risen Lord without hesitation. There are some scholars, however, who think that some contrast was intended between God's "absolute goodness" and that of Jesus (Taylor, Rawlinson, H. R. Mackintosh). The words allow this, and passages such as Hebrews 4:15; 5:8 are cited in support of the concept. Mark nowhere else hints at any limitation or lack of goodness in Jesus, and it is unnecessary so to understand this passage. Mark's readers would have understood the Son of God to be like God, and this would include full moral goodness.

The man sought ***eternal life.*** In the Gospel of John, to have eternal life is virtually equivalent to entering the kingdom of God: but it refers to quality of life which is eternal because of its very nature. From the lips of the man who approached Jesus, however, it meant to ***inherit*** (i.e., to win) participation in the age to come. So also verse 30.

Jesus answered by quoting much of the second half of the Decalogue. One other command is added, ***Do not defraud,*** perhaps as special emphasis on one phase of ***Do not steal,*** or in place of "Do not covet." It was singularly appropriate to men of wealth, whose opportunities for (sometimes legally) depriving or defrauding less fortunate persons were considerable. The verb was used, for example, of holding back the wages of hired help, or not returning goods or money at the appropriate time. There is no implication that the second part of the Commandments is more important than the first; all of them were considered to be from God and derived from his will.

The man was disappointed in Jesus' reply. Was it not the same thing he had always been told, and even in the same language? The depths of meaning in the Commandments he had never probed: he was probably more naïve than dishonest in saying he had ***observed*** them from his ***youth.*** The rabbis believed man possessed the ability to keep all the Commandments of God (Cranfield, Strack, and Billerbeck). But Jesus demanded a righteousness that was inward as well as externally obedient, so that a man's very being was in accord with the Heavenly Father's will and character (Matt. 5:17–48).

In any case, Jesus' reply—we may suppose intentionally—provoked the man to speak further. He must have come to Jesus because his keeping of the laws left him inadequate and unassured as far as eternal matters were concerned. Was there nothing more for him?

Jesus ***loved him:*** probably we should understand the verb (*agapao*) to include here some idea of attraction and affection. (So Taylor, Bratcher, J. Moffatt, but not Cranfield; Matt. and Luke both omit this word.) However, the basic meaning of the word is certainly present: it is that kind of love which, regardless of affection or worthiness, seeks deliberately to help, to meet another's need. It is a central quality Jesus called for in Christians and is expected in relation not only to God and neighbor but even to one's enemy (Mark 12:28–34; Matt. 5:43 f.).

You lack one thing. Jesus does not tell him exactly what that ***one thing*** is, but he tells him what is necessary for the ***one thing,*** in his case, to become a reality. ***What you have,*** said Jesus, stands between you and your quest. Do not keep it: ***sell*** it, and ***give*** it ***to the poor.*** It is as Mark's Gospel has been saying: God takes note of a man's kind and unselfish act (9:41), and sometimes a man must cut off that which is dearest to him if he would enter the kingdom (9:43,45,47).

Obviously Jesus understood this man to be a victim of the concepts of success and "the good life" and security which were prevalent in his day. (Of course, there are parallel ideas in modern culture.) What meant most to him, that which he relied on for safety, the kind of life which he enjoyed and found comfortable, had insulated the man from true and absolute commitment to God. How could he break through to a new way? How could he come to trust genuinely upon God? It was necessary for him to do away with the things which prevented a single-hearted faith, and to begin again by following Jesus.

Treasure in heaven is a Jewish expression, but should be understood neither as something earned nor as some special wealth. In the teaching of Jesus the phrase is contrasted with the impermanence and false security of wealth in this life (cf. Matt. 6:19 ff.). ***Treasure in heaven*** refers simply to the things that God counts significant.

Verse 22*a* is translated idiomatically in the RSV: the verb means either that he became gloomy or (less probably) that he was shocked by what Jesus said. That the man ***went away sorrowful*** is the only ray of hope expressed in the story, and it offers only the faintest hope. Would the man ever change? The reason for his going remained too dominant in his person: ***he had great possessions.*** Only here in the Gospels is a command by Jesus to follow him clearly rejected.

The rest of the conversation is with the disciples, but it is closely related to the problem raised by the man's inquiry and his affluence. The Jewish people considered wealth to be a sign of God's blessing. But Jesus realized fully how difficult it is for a man humbly to seek God's way and to let his life be determined by God's will, if he has other values more tangible and on which he has learned to rely. No wonder ***the disciples were amazed*** at Jesus' words, for they were still too much disciples of their Jewish culture and not fully aware of all the contrasts between their heritage and Jesus' teaching.

Jesus' response to his disciples' perplexity was first of all to broaden the scope of his saying in verse 23: it is ***hard*** for anybody ***to enter the kingdom.*** The words "they that have riches" (KJV) are not in our best manuscripts. But it is especially difficult for those for whom wealth has been a formative factor in life.

To hammer home this truth, Jesus resorted to the strongest kind of hyperbole. The ***camel*** was the largest animal commonly seen in the land, and ***the eye of a needle*** the smallest opening of which they commonly spoke. Of course, no camel could really go through a needle's eye: Jesus was saying, it is impossible for a rich man to enter the kingdom. But the "impossible" figure is given, not to be taken literally, but to emphasize how hard it is! [40]

He qualifies his own word by saying it is really not impossible with God (v. 27), but he must have successfully captured his disciples' minds with his point. At least, this is part of what may be inferred from Peter's response in verse 28.

What, then, is the reward of those who do meet the qualifications and become disciples? This would have been the practical question of the twelve, but it was a question that would not be diluted in interest for early Christians. It is possible that the wording of Jesus' reply was altered slightly because of the experience of the early Christians: ***for my sake and for the gospel*** (v. 29), and ***with persecutions*** are in accord with Jesus' teachings in general, though especially appropriate to Mark's readers (cf. Matt. 19:29; Luke 18:29 f.).

The rewards of discipleship are both ***in this time*** and ***in the age to come.*** In the present the reward is found in membership in the family of God, a fellowship of sharing. Compared to what one is and has, the new relationship in God's family is superior by ***a hundredfold.*** After this age, the true disciple will receive what the rich man was seeking (v. 17), ***eternal life.***

The statement about the ***first will be last, and the last first*** occurs in other contexts also (Matt. 20:16; Luke 13:30). It implies that there will be some surprises in the matter of eternal rewards (men's judgments

[40] Cf. W. O. E. Oesterley (tr.), *The Sayings of the Jewish Fathers* (London: S.P.C.K., 1919), p. 53, who cites a Midrash (Shir Rabba, v. 2) which has a similar metaphor: "Open for me a gateway of repentance as big as a needle's eye, and I will open for you gates wide enough for chariots and horses." The translation "rope" (instead of "camel") depends on a hypothetical alteration of the text. A so-called "needle's eye" gate, said to be a small entrance, open after night, large enough for a camel only with burden removed and down on its knees, is a fanciful figment of fifteenth-century imagination (Grant, Taylor).

—as Peter's, for example—are naturally infected by earthly considerations). Grant suggests that Mark's persecuted readers might think of themselves as "among the last to be called" and find encouragement here to believe that some of them might be first in the kingdom.

(13) *The Son of Man to Suffer* (III) (*10: 32–34*)

32 And they were on the road, going up to
Jerusalem, and Jesus was walking ahead of
them; and they were amazed, and those who
followed were afraid. And taking the twelve
again, he began to tell them what was to
happen to him, 33 saying, "Behold, we are
going up to Jerusalem; and the Son of man will
be delivered to the chief priests and the
scribes, and they will condemn him to death,
and deliver him to the Gentiles; 34 and they
will mock him, and spit upon him, and scourge
him, and kill him; and after three days he will
rise."

This is the third prediction of the passion: cf. the notes on 8:31–33 and 9:30–32. (The parallel passages are Matt. 20:17–19 and Luke 18:31–34.) As the last it is the most specific and detailed.

The story of what actually happened at Jerusalem was naturally well known to all the early Christians, and most recent commentators think their knowledge after the event influenced considerably their repetition of Jesus' prophetic words. Cranfield, however, rightly warns us against too readily assigning this paragraph to the creative understanding of early Christians. Jesus did anticipate his death, and the details given would be common in the case of a death sentence.

More than before, Jesus appears on this occasion to be active in bringing to pass his own hard destiny (Nineham). He walks ***ahead of them*** toward the city whose leaders he anticipated would put him to death. ***They were amazed*** probably means the twelve. ***Those who followed*** is a larger group, but the verb probably implies some measure of discipleship; these were frightened by the course of events and by Jesus' determined path.

The details in verses 33–34 have some Old Testament parallels: cf. especially Isaiah 50:6 and Psalm 22. Mark may have been cognizant of these. However, Minear is probably closer to Mark's intent when he describes these verses as picturing the baptism with which Jesus would be baptized (v. 38). What would happen to Jesus was of the essence of what it meant to be great in the kingdom of God. Note again how intimate is the relationship between each of Jesus' predictions of his suffering and his call to full and obedient discipleship.

(14) *Selfish Ambition Versus Great Discipleship* (*10:35–45*)

35 And James and John, the sons of Zebedee,
came forward to him, and said to him,
"Teacher, we want you to do for us whatever
we ask of you." 36 And he said to them, "What
do you want me to do for you?" 37 And they
said to him, "Grant us to sit, one at your right
hand and one at your left, in your glory."
38 But Jesus said to them, "You do not know
what you are asking. Are you able to drink the
cup that I drink, or to be baptized with the
baptism with which I am baptized?" 39 And
they said to him, "We are able." And Jesus
said to them, "The cup that I drink you will
drink; and with the baptism with which I am
baptized, you will be baptized; 40 but to sit at
my right hand or at my left is not mine to
grant, but it is for those for whom it has been
prepared." 41 And when the ten heard it, they
began to be indignant at James and John.
42 And Jesus called them to him and said to
them, "You know that those who are supposed
to rule over the Gentiles lord it over them, and
their great men exercise authority over them.
43 But it shall not be so among you; but
whoever would be great among you must be
your servant, 44 and whoever would be first
among you must be slave of all. 45 For the Son
of man also came not to be served but to serve,
and to give his life as a ransom for many."

James and John believed Jesus to be the Christ and they expected his exaltation (9: 2–8); but, as Mark recounts the story, they were still woefully unable to grasp the meaning and significance of Jesus' servanthood. (Cf. 9:33–37.) Still absorbed by the standards of greatness they had envisioned from childhood, they asked for the two places of honor (seats, or thrones, one on the king's ***right hand and one*** on his ***left***) when Jesus would come into power. ***In your glory*** must refer to Jesus' messianic glory, as in 8:38 (cf. Matt. 20:21). However, Jesus' ***glory*** is still compatible in the disciples' minds with a kingdom like the kingdoms of this world. Their request is somewhat parallel to a request for appointment to be Secretary of State and Secretary of Defense in the President's cabinet.

Jesus' response was first to James and John (vv. 38–40) and afterward to the indignation of the other disciples (vv. 42–45). Greatness in Jesus' kingdom would require that they ***drink*** his ***cup*** and undergo his ***baptism.*** To drink one's ***cup*** meant to endure one's lot and to accept one's destiny: the figure of the ***cup*** was used sometimes of joy (Psalms 23:5; 116:13), but also, as here, of suffering (Isa. 51:17–22; Psalm 75:8 f.; Jer. 25:15). ***Baptism*** was also used figuratively, especially of trouble or suffering that floods and overwhelms a person or city. (Moulton and Milligan cite examples from the papyri.) To Mark's readers reference to the meaning of Christian baptism and of the Lord's Supper was inevitable.

The ***cup*** is one Jesus is already drinking, and the ***baptism*** is one which is also being experienced: this is the most natural interpretation of the verb forms. (So Taylor; but many, including Cranfield, Bratcher, Lagrange, think they refer only to what is soon to happen.) The ***cup*** will not be drained until he is taken from the cross. And John's ***baptism*** of Jesus was the initiatory rite marking Jesus' dedication to his work as God's strong Son (cf. notes on 1:9–11). The task begun will not be finished until the world in conflict with the freedom and integrity expressed in the Son has done its worst by killing Jesus.

James and John did not even yet ***know what*** they were ***asking:*** the suffering would not be confined to Jesus. Could they endure and be faithful? They replied, ***We are able.*** James was indeed put to death as an apostle of Christ (Acts 12:2). One tradition claims that John was martyred like his brother. But the evidence is better that John was still alive when Mark was written and that as an old man he lived peacefully in Ephesus.

We need not suppose that Jesus referred by ***cup*** and ***baptism*** simply to martyrdom. The Christian's cup and baptism involve the denial of self and the taking up of one's own cross; i.e., they mean to follow Jesus without reservation (cf. on 8:34 f.). Sometimes a Christian's destiny through which he is required by his faith to live may be more difficult than death itself.

Mark's use of the figures of ***baptism*** and the ***cup*** reflect the deep seriousness with which the two sacred ordinances were received by Roman Christians. Cf. Paul's word in Romans 6:3. They were well aware of what their commitment might cost them.

In verse 40, Jesus tells his two apostles that he has no authority to grant their request in any case. ***It is for those for whom it has been prepared*** means that the prerogative is with God.

The indignation of ***the ten*** was to be expected. They were probably equally ambitious for position. Jesus seized the opportunity to tell them again the way to greatness in his kingdom. It is not the way of the people who do not reverence and follow God, i.e., ***the Gentiles. Supposed to rule*** does not mean that they do not in fact rule over others as men speak of ruling; but Jesus does not regard their position as great or their power as making them free. They do control others, and they suppose this fact sets them apart as men of stature.

For the followers of Jesus, ***it shall not be so.*** The great ***must be*** (lit. "shall be") ***your servant*** and the chief, ***slave of all.*** Not the exercise of power, but the spirit and practice of ministering to one's fellowmen marks greatness.

The supreme example is Jesus. His own dedication was to a life of unselfish ministry. ***The Son of man*** did not come to be great as men count greatness; instead he sought ***not to be served but to serve.*** The supreme example of Jesus' own service was the giving of ***his life,*** and in this way he served ***as a ransom for many.***

The word ***ransom*** occurs in the Gospels

only here and in the Matthean parallel (20:28), although kindred Greek words (translated redeem, redemption, redeemer) are rather common in the Greek Bible. A ***ransom*** was the price of release paid for the manumission of a slave. In the Old Testament, especially when God is considered the Redeemer, the emphasis is not on the price paid, but on the freedom and restoration to divine favor that is achieved. Neither is there any necessary connotation that someone had to be paid the price for release—God paid no price to Pharaoh when Israel was redeemed from slavery, nor did Jesus pay any power of evil to ransom mankind. The figure cannot be pressed in this way. The word asserts only that Jesus' gift of self is the means of redemption.

The ransom is ***for many.*** The preposition usually means "in stead of," though it sometimes is used in the sense of "on behalf of." The language here would to the Hebrews carry sacrificial connotations, and the preposition implies that Jesus did something for the many they could not do for themselves. The phrase, as Rawlinson says, sums up the thought of Isaiah 53. However, the Markan emphasis remains upon Jesus as exemplary Servant.

F. J. Taylor considers that verse 45 summarizes the character and purpose of Jesus' ministry. Jesus here asserts, he says, (1) that his sacrifice of himself was deliberate and voluntary; (2) that what he did required his life; (3) that something was done for the many which they could not do, but which was necessary for them to have any hope; and (4) that what was done was done for *many* (i.e., for men without any partiality; the word does not exclude the idea of all).[41]

41 F. J. Taylor, "Redeem" in A. Richardson, *Theological Wordbook of the Bible* (New York: Macmillan, 1951), pp. 185–87. The literature on this verse and the questions raised here concerning the atonement is voluminous. See especially J. Knox, *The Death of Christ: The Cross in NT History and Faith* (New York: Abingdon, 1958); V. Taylor, *Jesus and His Sacrifice* (London: Macmillan, 1937); J. Denney, *The Death of Christ,* rev. ed. by R. V. G. Tasker (London: Tyndale, 1951).

(15) The Healing of Bartimaeus (10: 46–52)

46 And they came to Jericho; and as he was
leaving Jericho with his disciples and a great
multitude, Bartimaeus, a blind beggar, the son
of Timaeus, was sitting by the roadside. 47 And
when he heard that it was Jesus of Nazareth,
he began to cry out and say, "Jesus, Son of
David, have mercy on me!" 48 And many re-
buked him, telling him to be silent; but he
cried out all the more, "Son of David, have
mercy on me!" 49 And Jesus stopped and said,
"Call him." And they called the blind man,
saying to him, "Take heart; rise, he is calling
you." 50 And throwing off his mantle he sprang
up and came to Jesus. 51 And Jesus said to him,
"What do you want me to do for you?" And
the blind man said to him, "Master, let me
receive my sight." 52 And Jesus said to him,
"Go your way; your faith has made you well."
And immediately he received his sight and
followed him on the way.

Jericho lay just north of the Dead Sea and on the western side of the Jordan River. It is the oldest continuously inhabited site of which we know, as excavations in recent years have ascertained. It was a fine city during the period of Jesus' ministry, and a principal road to Jerusalem began its climb from that point.

Bartimaeus means ***son of Timaeus:*** was his name remembered because he became a prominent disciple (v. 52), or for some other reason? Mark alone gives us his name (cf. Matt. 20:29–34; Luke 18:35–43).

Probably every blind man in the land had heard of ***Jesus of Nazareth.*** Whatever others had concluded, Bartimaeus believed him to be the expected Messiah, for he addresses him as ***Son of David.*** This is the first time Jesus accepts such an identification without rebuke or an injunction to silence. The incident anticipates that Jesus will enter Jerusalem as Messiah (11:1–11).

As in the case of the little children (10: 13–16), many tried to silence Bartimaeus and protect Jesus (or themselves?) from interruption. The people may have thought he was asking only for alms. In any case, the man was persistent, and Jesus summoned him. So much detail may reflect a personal reminiscence, perhaps of Peter.

Jesus' words, ***Your faith has made you well,*** show the Master's response to the personal trust of the man. The story is the concluding one before Jesus enters Jerusalem, and it brings into focus Jesus' service to the many for whom he is giving his life (v. 45). The ***blind beggar*** is one of these, and the words ***has made you well*** could as readily be translated "has saved you." It is possible that for Mark the story is not only historical but a parable of what Jesus does for those who find it so hard to see (cf. 4:10–12), but nevertheless put their faith in him.

2. *The Arrival in Jerusalem and the Conflict with the Religious Leaders (11:1—12:44)*

(1) *The Claims of Jesus in Parabolic Acts (11:1–19)*

a. *The Entry into Jerusalem (11:1–11)*

**1 And when they drew near to Jerusalem, to
Bethphage and Bethany, at the Mount of Olives, he sent two of his disciples, 2 and said to
them, "Go into the village opposite you, and
immediately as you enter it you will find a
colt tied, on which no one has ever sat; untie it
and bring it. 3 If any one says to you, 'Why are
you doing this?' say, 'The Lord has need of it
and will send it back here immediately.'"
4 And they went away, and found a colt tied at
the door out in the open street; and they untied
it. 5 And those who stood there said to them,
"What are you doing, untying the colt?" 6 And
they told them what Jesus had said; and they
let them go. 7 And they brought the colt to
Jesus, and threw their garments on it; and he
sat upon it. 8 And many spread their garments
on the road, and others spread leafy branches
which they had cut from the fields. 9 And those
who went before and those who followed cried
out, "Hosanna! Blessed is he who comes in the
name of the Lord! 10 Blessed is the kingdom of
our father David that is coming! Hosanna in
the highest!"**

**11 And he entered Jerusalem, and went into
the temple; and when he had looked round at
everything, as it was already late, he went out
to Bethany with the twelve.**

Both by injunctions to silence and by speaking of himself in other terms, Jesus had tried to stifle talk about himself as the Christ, Son of David, the King of Israel. He did not allow the voices of the demon-possessed to continue to identify him (3:11 f.), and he warned his disciples not to use the title Christ (8:29 f.). Now as his ministry draws toward the close he is clearly anticipating, he deliberately provokes the crowd in their speculation about himself.

It is difficult to interpret Jesus' entry into Jerusalem in any other way than as a symbolic act, a lived-out parable, by which he asserted his identity. Jesus rode into Jerusalem not as the Christ-King many expected, but in a manner that accorded with his own understanding of his role. He is "chief," or "King," or "Messiah," but he is always servant, a man of peace, meek and lowly. Because his action was in no way a rallying of political agitators, the Roman officials seem to have paid little attention. Mark makes no mention even of the opposition of some religious stalwarts (cf. Luke 19:39–44).

Questions concerning Jesus' identity must have been already rampant among the worshipers in the city. If even a blind beggar was calling Jesus the *Son of David,* we may be sure others were excited about the possibility that Jesus might be the coming King. Luke 19:11 asserts that some expected the kingdom "to appear immediately."

The closest parallels with Jesus' activity in his coming to Jerusalem are found in Zechariah 9–14. Jesus had from the beginning of his ministry identified himself with the purposes of the God of Moses and the prophets. Mark does not quote Zechariah here as do other Gospel writers. Nevertheless, Jesus seems deliberately to have identified himself with much of this prophecy, and in this sense to have offered himself as its fulfilment and so as Israel's king.[42]

[42] Cf. R. Grant, *A Historical Introduction to the NT* (New York: Harper, 1963), pp. 305 f. Grant also thinks that Jesus, like his disciples, expected the kingdom to come when he went up to Jerusalem. But this is an unnecessary conclusion in any case, and is certainly wrong if Jesus was anticipating his own suffering and death.

However the early Christians may have come to understand the entry, Jesus' action was in fact not an immediately clear and unmistakable claim to be the Christ. He himself said little, and his action is not mentioned in the trial accounts that follow. We must understand his action as parable or symbol. "Those outside" and even his disciples would not have understood clearly (cf. Mark 4:10–13; John 12:16).

Bethany is southeast of Jerusalem, further from the city than the suburb ***Bethphage,*** which, according to Jewish sources, was within a sabbath day's journey. Apparently Jesus sent from Bethany to secure the colt. The description ***on which no one has ever sat*** might have suggested to a Christian student of the Scriptures a sacrificial animal, or at least one that was fit for a holy purpose (cf. Num. 19:2; Deut. 21:3). But it may have been originally the only animal available.

Jesus ***sent two of his disciples*** to get the ***colt,*** with instructions to say to any questioners, ***The Lord has need of it.*** It would be impossible for the Christians of a Roman church not to think of Jesus as their Lord, risen and exalted, at the time these words were penned. But the Greek word translated ***Lord*** means also owner or master, and it is difficult to believe (if Greek was indeed spoken) that bystanders would have understood the word as referring to deity or even to Jesus. The parallel accounts, especially Luke 19:31 f., show it was the "owners" (the word equals "the lords") who asked, "Why are you untying the colt?"

The most probable conclusions to be drawn are (1) that Jesus had arranged for the colt with its owner and agreed on a kind of password identification (the owner could have been a friend currently following in Jesus' company); (2) that Mark is thinking of Jesus as Lord, and did not consider the simple historical question. The remainder of Jesus' instruction to his disciples (***will send it back here immediately***) varies widely in the accounts: Luke omits it and Matthew changes its meaning completely.

The disciples prepared the colt for riding by throwing their outer ***garments on it,*** apparently in lieu of a saddle. The homage given to Jesus in this act is reminiscent of 2 Kings 9:13, in which royal homage was being given to Jehu. The ***leafy branches*** (the word is also applied to mattresses made of straw, leaves, etc.) were found in fields nearby, and ***spread*** also in homage to Jesus. Palm branches are mentioned only in John 12:13, but the account here in Mark is also reminiscent of the triumph of the great Maccabean hero Simon, who entered the citadel in Jerusalem "with praise and palm-branches" (1 Macc. 13:51).

Those who went before and those who followed: the crowd is one, all of them surrounding and acclaiming Jesus. ***Hosanna*** literally would be a cry for help, and in Psalm 118:25 (cf. 2 Sam. 14:4; 2 Kings 6:26) is correctly translated "save." But Psalm 118 was sung at the Feasts of Tabernacles and Passover, and so could be used popularly as a welcome and acclamation to people coming to the Temple. Mark's readers probably understood ***Hosanna*** to mean simply "Hail!" or some word of praise. If it is more than a cry of praise or thanksgiving here, we should understand it to mean "God save him" in verse 9 and "God in heaven save him" in verse 10 (so C. C. Torrey and Taylor).

Blessed be he who comes in the name of the Lord. The ***Lord*** here means God. The line is from Psalm 118:26 (LXX) and may have been acclaimed antiphonally with the next line, ***Blessed be the kingdom of our father David that is coming!*** It is most natural to understand ***he who comes*** as a messianic title (cf. Matt. 11:3; but it was certainly not commonly used). In any case, these words of the crowd anticipate the messianic victory. However, it remains obvious that the crowd did not comprehend the nature of Jesus' role as the suffering Son of man.

Riding on the colt, not as a warring conqueror but as a man of peace, Jesus entered the city. Both Matthew and Luke have him cleansing the Temple immediately, but Mark says simply that ***he went into the*** *temple; and . . . looked round at everything.* Then he went out of the city to spend the night at *Bethany* with his disciples.

b. The Cursing of the Fig Tree (11:12–14)

[12] On the following day, when they came from Bethany, he was hungry. [13] And seeing in the distance a fig tree in leaf, he went to see if he could find anything on it. When he came to it, he found nothing but leaves, for it was not the season for figs. [14] And he said to it, "May no one ever eat fruit from you again." And his disciples heard it.

This is the single "curse miracle" attributed to Jesus in the canonical Gospels. On first reading it appears so out of character for Jesus that many compare it to the stories in the apocryphal gospels. (In the later "gospels" there are even stories of the boy Jesus cursing those who have acted cruelly, so that they die—totally out of character for the Jesus we know in the canonical books.) Some scholars think the story was no miracle at all, but that it is a miracle story probably created from the parable in Luke 13:6–9 (Johnson, J. Weiss, Branscomb, Taylor).

Mark certainly thinks of the story as historical—the details given are too precise to suppose otherwise—but its meaning was for him symbolic. In this paragraph it relates to the failure of God's people to recognize God's Son and their King, and so to their uselessness for God's purposes. In verses 20–25 Mark also connects it with prayer and faith and forgiveness.

On the following day: this would have been Monday. We must remind ourselves that not every word or incident recorded in the passion narratives took place in the order given, and perhaps not even during the last week or at passion time. For example, in Luke and Matthew the Temple was cleansed on Sunday, and in John early in Jesus' ministry: but in Mark, Jesus did this on Monday. The entry into Jerusalem (11:1–11) may actually have occurred at another feast. But for all the Gospel authors its meaning was best set forth in connection with Jesus' death, for he died as Israel's rejected King of peace.

It was probably early as Jesus returned to Jerusalem from *Bethany.* Perhaps hunger was awakened in Jesus by the sight of the *fig tree in leaf.* The sense of hunger did not depend on whether it was *the season for figs,* which do not ripen normally at Jerusalem before June. Jesus nevertheless sought to *find anything* to eat on it, but there was nothing.[43]

Jesus then, with his disciples listening, spoke to the tree, *May no one ever eat fruit from you again.* In verse 20 we are told that the next time the disciples saw the tree it had "withered away to its roots."

Nothing more is said at this point. But since the preceding event saw Jesus offering himself as King of peace, but being misunderstood; and, since the next event has Jesus cleansing the Temple of those who would dispossess its rightful occupant and change its purpose from God's desire to their own profit; and, since Israel as the people of God was often spoken of as a tree, plant, or vine (Jesus' parable in Luke 13:6–9 compares Israel to a fig tree; see below on Mark 12:1–12), it is most reasonable to conclude that the tree suggested to Jesus an Israel who would not bear the fruit it should have produced. For the so-called people of God, hardened in heart, would not recognize God's strong Son. They would not hear or heed his message.

The fig tree gave an appearance of health and usefulness, like Jerusalem with its Temple, the center of the worship of God. Actually the religious life of Israel was barren and unperceptive. Was not Israel like the fig tree? Let it die! It has forfeited its religious leadership.

[43] The difficulties in this phase of the story are illustrated in Carrington, p. 237, who at first judged the event as having taken place at the Feast of Tabernacles and that the phrase "not the season for figs" was a Markan addition. "I do not feel very happy about this suggestion now," he writes. "Was Mark explaining the action of Jesus in the story, or was he dealing with a difficulty which was caused by the placing of the story?"

c. The Cleansing of the Temple (11:15–19)

**[15] And they came to Jerusalem. And he en-
tered the temple and began to drive out those
who sold and those who bought in the temple,
and he overturned the tables of the money-
changers and the seats of those who sold pigeons; [16] and he would not allow any one to
carry anything through the temple. [17] And he
taught, and said to them, "Is it not written,
'My house shall be called a house of prayer for
all the nations'? But you have made it a den of
robbers." [18] And the chief priests and the
scribes heard it and sought a way to destroy
him; for they feared him, because all the multitude was astonished at his teaching. [19] And
when evening came they went out of the city.**

Only in ***Jerusalem*** at ***the temple*** did the faithful Hebrews believe God could be worshiped adequately. Here, but not in their synagogues, they could offer the Law's prescribed sacrifices. Here, but not in Galilee or other distant centers of Jewish life, the priesthood served and led the worship of the devout.

There is no question but that true and earnest worship was carried on in the Temple: the stories in Luke 1–2 concerning the humble priest Zechariah and devout Simeon and Anna are fair examples. Obviously caravans of worshipers like that which included Jesus' own family came for appropriate reasons to worship in Jerusalem. The Jewish teachers at the Temple were giving attention to the Jewish boys who came plying them with questions (Luke 2:41–50).

However, the authority over the Temple and its revenues was vested in the high priest and his priestly aides. They and their families were not Pharisees, but Sadducees (cf. on 12:18–27). They fed well at the trough of Temple revenues, but they were not extolled for their generosity or kindness. According to Josephus, only a few years after Jesus' death the priestly leaders seized all the tithes for themselves, and some of the poorer priests were left to starve (*Antiq.*, XX, 8:8; 9:2). We have from the Essenes of Qumran, as well as from rabbinical writings, evidence of the general opinion of the people that the Sadducees charged extortionate prices for the doves sold for sacrifice, and generally abused the purposes of the Temple by their greedy practices.

Jesus' cleansing of the Temple is his clearest parabolic act. His deed is parallel to the symbolic acts of the great prophets: Isaiah went naked and barefoot to dramatize God's message (Isa. 20:1–6); Ezekiel shaved off his hair and beard, and dramatically divided and used them to express God's word (Ezek. 5:1–12); and the Christian Agabus bound Paul with his belt as a divine warning (Acts 21:11 f.). Jesus would not have been so naïve as to suppose that the commercial traffic in the Temple would stay banned by his action. Still, his prophetic act would hardly have been possible if ***the multitude*** who had come to the Temple had not been so sympathetic to Jesus and eagerly listening, ***astonished at his teaching*** (v. 18).

What did Jesus do? He began by driving ***out those who sold and those who bought***, i.e., those engaged in selling and buying the larger sacrificial victims, and the oil, salt, and wine. He ***overturned the tables of the money-changers:*** the ordinary Greek or Roman money could not be used in connection with the worship, so pilgrims were required to exchange their money for Tyrian or Jewish coins. The poor were allowed to use ***pigeons*** for their sacrifices. Like the other merchants serving the Sadducean priesthood, the bird-sellers also had been transforming the holy place into a mere center for business.

We do not know for what period of time, but for as long as he stayed there on this one day, Jesus appears to have been in full charge in the court of the Gentiles, where the merchandising commonly was carried on. ***He would not allow any one to carry anything through the temple.*** This prohibition surely met with approval from the devout, for the use of the Temple as a shortcut or ordinary road was a denial of its holiness. Jesus was not objecting to the use of the Temple as the center of God's worship. He objected to its abuse and misuse, especially to the commercialism and the materialism which were so blatant.

Jesus' teaching centered around the words of two prophets. From Isaiah 56:7, he reminded the people, ***My house shall be called a house of prayer for all the nations. Nations*** is the same word as Gentiles; the only place foreigners were allowed to worship in the Temple precincts had been clogged with all sorts of things inimical to true worship.

Jeremiah had prophesied against the false worship in the Temple and the false supposition that God would protect it from destruction. As men had ***made it a den of robbers*** then, so Jesus charges, you have again done (cf. Jer. 7:1–15). The word for ***robbers*** is very strong, meaning not merely thieves but brigands, bandits. If the Temple has become a ***den of robbers,*** then they have not merely polluted it by stealing from those who came to worship. In effect, they have stolen the house of the Lord God for their own criminal home.

What did Jesus by his action say to the people? That he was reclaiming the Temple for its rightful owner. That the true worship of God can happen only when materialism and commercialism are purged away. That the God of the prophets speaks with authority in the Nazarene who stands in their midst. As he is Lord of the sabbath, he is Lord also of the Temple.

The chief priests and the scribes heard Jesus and began seeking (this is the force of the verb ***sought***) a way to get rid of him. ***They feared him*** as a threat to their own authority and way of life. But they wanted no open trouble, especially not from the ***multitude*** of worshipers who were crowding the city and providing their revenue. So they bided their time. But what happened at this incident is no doubt the basis of their charge against Jesus at his trial (cf. 14:58).

(2) *Encouragement to Faith and True Prayer (11:20–25) (26)*

**20 As they passed by in the morning, they
saw the fig tree withered away to its roots.
21 And Peter remembered and said to him,
"Master, look! The fig tree which you cursed
has withered." 22 And Jesus answered them,
"Have faith in God. 23 Truly, I say to you,
whoever says to this mountain, 'Be taken up and cast into the sea,' and does not doubt in his heart, but believes that what he says will come to pass, it will be done for him.
24 Therefore I tell you, whatever you ask in prayer, believe that you receive it, and you
will. 25 And whenever you stand praying, forgive, if you have anything against any one; so that your Father also who is in heaven may forgive you your trespasses."**

No explanation of Jesus' curse on the fig tree was given by Mark in 11:12–14. Not until the tree actually withered were questions raised by the disciples. But it would be wrong to connect Jesus' words in 20–25 only with the fig tree and not with the somewhat related meanings of Jesus' entry into the city on the colt and his cleansing of the Temple. In Mark these actions of Jesus speak of basic truths: Israel has rejected God's King and God's way, and her religious leadership has perversely transformed the focal point of God's worship. Change from God must come. God's use of Jewish religious leadership is not eternal but temporal, not permanent but dying, not necessary but conditional.

These concepts may be put bluntly and in simple historical terms. In the following sections they are reinforced and more clearly expressed. However, they are in Christian thought of the very essence of God's nature and purpose in declaring his kingship in Jesus Christ, the Son of man. By expressing ideas in symbolic acts, Jesus intended (just as he had in his sayings and parables earlier) to express more truth than would be fully and immediately grasped. This, at least, is true of Mark's presentation: the Christians who read would understand more readily and adequately because they have become aware of Jesus' full identity.

According to verse 20, the conversation of Jesus with his disciples took place on the next ***morning*** when they were returning to Jerusalem (v. 27). The ***fig tree*** which Jesus had ***cursed*** (the words of the curse are in v. 14) had died, and the disciples assumed a causal relationship. They were bound to have been thinking about Jesus' dangerous take-over of the Temple courtyard the day before, and the fact that they were going back. What would happen? To Jesus? To themselves? Even to the Temple?

Have faith in God, Jesus encouraged them. The power which belongs to Israel's chief priests and Temple leaders (or even to Roman authorities) is earthly and not insuperable; they must not despair. How appropriate to the needs of Mark's readers! Minear suggests that the "implacable hostility" of the Jewish leaders in Roman synagogues was the most difficult barrier to the gospel they had to face.

Prayer is an expression of faith. The figure of a ***mountain*** being ***cast into the sea*** is a hyperbolic and thoroughly Hebrew way of saying that the seemingly impossible tasks are not too difficult for God and those who genuinely trust him. ***Peter*** and the other disciples must not despair because of the coming confrontations and dangers: ***whatever*** in ***prayer*** a man of faith asks, God will give him. ***Believe that you receive it*** means "have faith that you have (already) received it." That is to say, God is already with you (cf. Matt. 7:7 f., Luke 11:9 f.).

A miracle which causes a fig tree to wither and die is hardly an example of the faith to which Jesus encourages the disciples. But its meaning, like that of the cleansing of the Temple, calls for trust in God. What faith achieves by God's power is not the accomplishment of a curse but the facing of reality. Can the disciples' trust in God endure through what is happening to Israel's religious leadership, and through what the old leadership will do to Jesus?

Some interpreters regard Mark's arrangement of Jesus' words in this paragraph as artificial and the exhortation to faith inappropriate. But if we are nearly correct in our understanding of the symbolism, the words are appropriate enough here. Mark probably did attach these sayings to each other and to these symbolic acts of Jesus. There is no adequate reason to question their genuineness, and they were pertinent to the needs of the twelve at the time, and to the needs of Roman Christians also.

This teaching of Jesus about ***prayer*** and faith does not stand in isolation, and must not be interpreted to mean that every prayer of faith is answered in the terms which the man of faith might prefer. See Jesus' own prayer in Gethsemane (Mark 14:35 f.): he would not have regarded the answer to his prayer as a failure of faith or of God; but he did not wish the cross either.

The greatest test of true faith in time of difficulty is whether the spirit of forgiveness is present. To ***stand praying*** was the usual posture for prayer by the Jews and also by the Greeks (Johnson; cf. Matt. 6:5; Luke 18:11). That the forgiveness of God requires a man to ***forgive*** those who have inflicted wrong is not only present in Jesus' teaching but is also found in the Jewish literature. For example, Ecclesiasticus 28:2 reads, "forgive your neighbor . . . , and then, when you pray, your sins will be forgiven." (Cf. also Test. of Gad, 6:3–7; on forgiveness, cf. comment on 2:5.)

In verse 25, the phrase ***your Father . . . in heaven*** is unique in Mark. Jesus occasionally referred to God as his Father (8:38; 13:32; 14:36), but this is the only passage in Mark in which it is assumed that the disciples are to think of God as their ***Father . . . in heaven.*** The sentence may reflect, as Rawlinson suggests, that the Lord's Prayer was in use at Rome at the time of writing, and that it was in the Matthean form. Verse 26 is not present in the best Markan texts, but is original in Matthew 6:15.

(3) *The Counterattack Upon Jesus and His Defense* (*11:27—12:27*)

a. The Question of Authority (*11:27–33*)

27 And they came again to Jerusalem. And as he was walking in the temple, the chief priests and the scribes and the elders came to him, 28 and they said to him, "By what authority are you doing these things, or who gave you this authority to do them?" 29 Jesus said to them, "I will ask you a question; answer me, and I will tell you by what authority I do these things.

**30 Was the baptism of John from heaven or
from men? Answer me." 31 And they argued
with one another, "If we say, 'From heaven,'
he will say, 'Why then did you not believe
him?' 32 But shall we say, 'From men'?"—they
were afraid of the people, for all held that
John was a real prophet. 33 So they answered
Jesus, "We do not know." And Jesus said to
them, "Neither will I tell you by what authority I do these things."**

When Jesus cleansed the Temple, although it was a prophetic act (cf. above, 11:15–19), it was also a high-handed one. The recognized authorities in God's house were the men whom God had appointed from of old. Even if Jesus were right about the corruption in the use of the holy place, did he suppose that his was the rightful privilege of judging and controlling conduct in God's Temple? Was he putting himself above the words of the law of Moses, who had assigned this authority to the sons of Aaron?

The supreme court of the Jewish people, called the Sanhedrin, was composed of ***the chief priests and the scribes and the elders*** (whether Pharisees or Sadducees). See below, on 14:53. A representative delegation —hardly the entire court of seventy persons —met Jesus in the Temple to examine his credentials. It is entirely probably that the motives of the questioners were mixed, for revenues from Temple business were highest at feast times, and Jesus had disrupted their normal course. But the question itself was religious: What kind of ***authority*** did Jesus possess, and ***who gave*** him the right to act as he had?

As Jesus often had done before (2:9,19, 25 f.; 3:4; 10:3), he replied with a question. Johnson notes that he might have replied as the ancient prophet Amos had to the priest in charge at Bethel, that God had sent him. As it was, Jesus appealed (by question) to the authority of the prophet John the Baptist. The people, at least, had recognized John's word and deed as from God: what did the religious authorities say about this? ***Was the baptism of John from heaven;*** i.e., something God sent him to do —or, was it merely his own, human idea? The marks of the prophet were present in John's life. Did not Jesus carry, in even more undeniable fashion, the marks of genuine, divine authority in his own person?

The debate among the distinguished delegates must have been recounted with relish by Jesus' followers. They never wrestled with the question Jesus asked, but they did reflect their own subservience to popular support and to their own pride of face. They tried to play chess with Jesus by anticipating his response to their answer. They concluded that the least damaging thing they could say would be, ***We do not know.*** After all, they had not accepted John as a prophet, and on the other hand they did not want the crowd of worshipers to become angry with them. Who could tell what that kind of crowd might do next? These people might disrupt the business in the court of the Gentiles again!

However, when the religious leaders confessed their inability to judge whether John was from God, did they not also confess their inadequacy to serve as judges of such questions? Was it not of the essence of their calling to lead people to God? How could they do so if they could not tell whether God was at work in a prophet? Jesus refused to tell them whence his authority, because by their own words they admitted they lacked the insight to recognize God's prophets when they did appear.

b. The Parable of the Wicked Tenants (12:1–12)

**1 And he began to speak to them in parables.
"A man planted a vineyard, and set a hedge
around it, and dug a pit for the wine press, and
built a tower, and let it out to tenants, and
went into another country. 2 When the time
came, he sent a servant to the tenants, to get
from them some of the fruit of the vineyard.
3 And they took him and beat him, and sent
him away empty-handed. 4 Again he sent to
them another servant, and they wounded him
in the head, and treated him shamefully. 5 And
he sent another, and him they killed; and so
with many others, some they beat and some
they killed. 6 He had still one other, a beloved
son; finally he sent him to them, saying, 'They
will respect my son.' 7 But those tenants said to**

one another, 'This is the heir; come, let us kill him, and the inheritance will be ours.'
8 And they took him and killed him, and cast him out of the vineyard.
9 What will the owner of the vineyard do? He will come and destroy the tenants, and give the vineyard to others.
10 Have you not read this scripture:
'The very stone which the builders rejected
has become the head of the corner;
11 this was the Lord's doing,
and it is marvelous in our eyes'?"
12 And they tried to arrest him, but feared the multitude, for they perceived that he had told the parable against them; so they left him and went away.

This section is attached closely by Mark to the preceding verses. We must remember that the chapter divisions we use were accepted more than one thousand years after Mark wrote. The parable is directed toward the representatives of the religious establishment, who had answered Jesus so carefully but unwisely. No question is raised (as in 4:10–12) about whether these men understood Jesus: on the contrary, ***they perceived that he had told the parable against them*** (v. 12).

In verse 1 the allusions to Isaiah 5:1–7 are unmistakable. There the ***vineyard*** so carefully tended was "the house of Israel" and the "men of Judah," and the Lord himself was owner and provider.

The ***hedge*** or "wall" may have been of unmortared stones; the ***tower,*** perhaps a leaf-covered booth on a high place. Both were provided for protection of the vineyard from wild animals or marauders, and the tower afforded not only a lookout point but shelter for the ***tenants.*** The ***pit*** was the vessel or trough into which the juice was filtered as the grapes were trodden in the ***wine press.***

Tenants commonly rented the ***vineyard*** for a share of the crop. In this case they were no doubt considered to be men experienced as vinedressers. The owner ***went into another country:*** this phrase translates but one word and may mean simply that he went on a journey (so Moulton and Milligan, Bratcher). The other parts of the story make it likely that he lived in another part of the empire.

Naturally the owner expected to receive his rightful return, so he sent for his share ***when the time came.*** But the tenants did not honor their contract. They even mistreated the owner's messengers, and in a progressively cruel and vicious way. They killed the third servant (v. 5). Some think that verse 5*b* is a later addition to the story, as Christians in the retelling were reminded of how many times God had warned his people (cf. Heb. 11:32–40). It must be admitted that verse 5*b* is not as realistic as the rest of the story, or as Jesus generally was in his parables. But a parable is not bound absolutely by historical realism: it is bound by its purpose, however unusual its details. It is of course true that no father would be likely to send his ***son*** on such a dangerous errand (v. 6).

The owner then sent his ***beloved son,*** supposing that he would command the respect of the vicious tenants. Mark's readers would not miss an identification of ***beloved son*** with Jesus, who was identified as God's beloved Son at the baptism (1:11) and the transfiguration (9:7). The chief priests or scribes could not have made this precise connection, and ***beloved*** may have been added to the story by Christian preachers, to help hearers to interpret the parable.

That the tenants should suppose they would become owners of the vineyard by destroying ***the heir*** seems to us foolish. Jeremias points out that a large part of the Galilean uplands was owned by foreign landlords. He calls attention to a law by which the property of a proselyte who died without a will would be considered ownerless property; and whoever was in possession of the property at that time had a prior claim. He thinks the tenants assumed, when the son arrived, that the owner (who had been a foreign absentee landlord) had already died.[44]

What will the owner (the word is iden-

[44] *Op. cit.*, pp. 58–60; cf. Dodd, pp. 125–32; but D. O. Via, *The Parables* (Philadelphia: Fortress, 1967), pp. 132–36, disagrees, and follows W. Michaelis in holding simply that the owner, "for a reason not given," was unable to come back to his property.

tical with "Lord," cf. above on 11:3) *do?* Matthew 21:41 has the audience answering the question, and so making initial application of the parable. In any case, the answer had to be that such tenants deserved the worst, and would be utterly destroyed.

All the Synoptic Gospels interpret the parable somewhat allegorically. As it has come down to us, however, the elements of the story (wine press, tower, pit) are part of the realism of the story: they are not allegorical. Why should Jesus not have alluded to a famous passage like Isaiah 5:1–7, with the inevitable result that the religious hierarchy present would understand the barb of the story as directed at themselves? As to Jesus' identifying the religious leaders with those who had stoned God's prophets, compare Matthew 23:29–37. It is reasonable to conclude that the reference of the parable to that religious leadership, to the messengers from God, and to himself as a last and significantly superior messenger would have been intended by Jesus and understood by his audience.

Later, the church's teachers would very naturally have, as Dodd says, dotted the *i*'s and crossed the *t*'s of the original application. Christian people would have thought first of what these people had actually done to God's beloved Son, and that he, the rejected ***stone***, had ***become the head of the corner*** (v. 10). But the emphasis in the original story must have been on the mounting and utterly incorrigible wickedness of the tenants; the religious leaders were rejecting any of the limitations which might be laid upon them by the God whom they were supposed to serve and whose was the Temple and the worship therein. They ***killed*** and ***cast*** the heir ***out of the vineyard.***

By implication, therefore, Jesus did answer their original question in 11:28. His authority is from God, but they are so grossly wicked they do not recognize him. They attempt to steal for themselves everything that belongs to God. Moreover, they care not how many human beings may be trampled down in the process of their triumph. Nevertheless, the Lord is going to have his way, they will be destroyed, and (as Christians understood the fulfilment of Psalm 118:10–11) Jesus would yet reign. Yes, the disciples would sing, ***this was the Lord's doing, and it is marvelous in our eyes.***

They tried to arrest him: how direct the attempt at this time is difficult to say. The verb ***tried*** means "they were making the attempt," or, perhaps, "they were about to attempt" the arrest. But because they wanted no uproar and were afraid of what the multitude might do, they ***went away*** and bided their time. It must not be supposed that the crowd embraced Jesus' teaching as a whole, particularly that on humility and greatness, or on taking up one's cross. But ***the multitude*** in the Temple obviously would have loved his ability and courage to stand up to and confound the wealthy and hypocritical representatives of the religious establishment.

c. The Question About Paying Taxes to Caesar (12:13–17)

13 And they sent to him some of the Pharisees and some of the Herodians, to entrap him in his talk. 14 And they came and said to him, "Teacher, we know that you are true, and care for no man; for you do not regard the position of men, but truly teach the way of God. Is it lawful to pay taxes to Caesar, or not? 15 Should we pay them, or should we not?" But knowing their hypocrisy, he said to them, "Why put me to the test? Bring me a coin, and let me look at it." 16 And they brought one. And he said to them, "Whose likeness and inscription is this?" They said to him, "Caesar's." 17 Jesus said to them, "Render to Caesar the things that are Caesar's, and to God the things that are God's." And they were amazed at him.

Some ***Pharisees*** and quite possibly some ***Herodians*** were numbered among the members of the Sanhedrin. The subject of ***sent,*** as far as syntax is concerned, may be impersonal. In view of 11:27–33 and 12:12, however, it is natural to understand Mark to mean that they were ***sent*** by the Jewish religious leaders. If this be true, the plan to trap Jesus was carefully rehearsed, and they hoped his answer would afford opportunity for his arrest (v. 12). For ***Pharisees,*** see on 2:16 and 7:1 ff.; for ***Herodians,*** see comment on 3:6 and 8:15.

Both ***Pharisees*** and ***Herodians*** were nationalistic in bent, though neither so radical as the Zealots who later instigated the Jewish revolt against Rome. They were not natural allies. The Herodians must have been interested in replacing the Roman governors (as Pilate) with one of the Herods (by heritage Idumean, but the Idumeans had been forced to accept circumcision and become Jews more than a century earlier). Roman rule would have continued, but less directly and with a king or tetrarch more acceptable to Jewish people. The Pharisees' differences with Jesus, as has been illustrated, stemmed from his authoritative stance with regard to the law of Moses and the customs they followed.

Although Mark does not assert this, the Herodians must have regarded a leader of Jesus' caliber as a threat to their own hopes. Mark has named the two groups together earlier (3:6), but it is a reasonable guess that the Sadducean leaders of the Sanhedrin encouraged their union at this time.

The verb ***entrap*** in the papyri means to take or catch by hunting or fishing (Moulton and Milligan). The words addressed to Jesus were, as far as the questioners were concerned, mere flattery, not compliment. But they were obviously designed to prevent Jesus from evading their question. If he is ***true,*** and if he cares ***for no man*** (i.e., he will not be anxious about what anyone will say about his answer), they can depend on him to give a straightforward reply. He will not be afraid to ***teach the way of God*** in this matter. Just as Jesus had done in the Temple (11:29–31), they probably made certain that the crowd heard the question as they posed it: they were trying to make it impossible for Jesus to avoid the hook in their question.

The question itself was a burning one, for it roused all the religious and nationalistic fervor of the multitude against the foreign and heathen oppressors from Rome. ***Is it lawful?*** means, "Is it according to the way of God?" (Cf. on 10:2, where the same verb is used.) ***Taxes*** may here be a general term, as RSV renders it, but its more specific application was to a kind of poll tax which was particularly obnoxious to nationalistic groups. ***Caesar*** was Tiberius, an emperor whom no Jew could consider a godly or righteous. man. Should not the people of God, out of loyalty to their faith, refuse to pay tribute to that kind of government?

If Jesus answers yes, pay Caesar, the people will reject him as a coward, a man who does ***regard the position of men*** and who fears for his own welfare. If he answers no, do not pay the tax, then it will be simple enough to have him arrested by the Romans.

Jesus not only did not dodge the question, he called attention to it by dramatically asking for a silver ***coin.*** He was about to teach something very important, and he wanted them all to hear. The ***coin,*** a denarius, had inscribed on one side (in abbreviated Latin) Tiberius Caesar Augustus, son of the Divine Augustus; on the other, *Pontifex Maximus,* or chief priest. The engraved image of Tiberius was also on the coin. ***Bring me a coin*** implies (probably very truly, though Luke 20:24 makes no such point) that none of these careful representatives had this kind of money in the Temple and had to go over to a table of the money changers to get one.

Render to Caesar means "pay back to Caesar." It is a debt. You owe some allegiance and support to the government whose coinage you use; the coin is an evidence of the civil order under which you live. Certainly, then, it is lawful—according to the way of God—to give appropriate support to the civil government. Jesus never supported any party which advocated violent overthrow of the civil government of his day. This saying was in perfect harmony with the later statements of Paul (Rom. 13:1–7) and Peter (1 Peter 2:13 f.). Obligations to the state are within the design of God for mankind.

With Jesus, however, the claims of God were all-embracing. One must also give back

to God the things that are God's. Allegiance to the state, even to a Caesar, is one of these things. This saying should not be construed as meaning that the world of religion and politics can rightly be divorced. Both deal with man and his needs, with problems of living together, with justice as well as order. On the other hand, no disciple—and no Jew—could have understood this saying as permitting a man to obey Caesar, or any other man, in opposition to God. The disciple would always have to choose the cross rather than disobey God. He must always adhere to the first commandment of all (see 12:29 f.), regardless of the personal cost (cf. 1 Peter 4:12 ff.).

The questioners ***were amazed:*** the verb (here only in the NT) is a compound of the word in 5:20, and stronger in meaning. However grudgingly, they must have admired his answer. Mark cuts off the story abruptly at this point in order to describe the next approach by Jesus' enemies (cf. Luke 20:26; Matt. 22:22).

d. The Question About Resurrection (12: 18–27)

18 And Sadducees came to him, who say that there is no resurrection; and they asked him a question, saying, 19 "Teacher, Moses wrote for us that if a man's brother dies and leaves a wife, but leaves no child, the man must take the wife, and raise up children for his brother.
20 There were seven brothers; the first took a wife, and when he died left no children; 21 and the second took her, and died, leaving no children; and the third likewise; 22 and the seven left no children. Last of all the woman also died. 23 In the resurrection whose wife will she be? For the seven had her as wife."

24 Jesus said to them, "Is not this why you are wrong, that you know neither the scriptures nor the power of God? 25 For when they rise from the dead, they neither marry nor are given in marriage, but are like angels in heaven. 26 And as for the dead being raised, have you not read in the book of Moses, in the passage about the bush, how God said to him, 'I am the God of Abraham, and the God of Isaac, and the God of Jacob'? 27 He is not God of the dead, but of the living; you are quite wrong."

The chief priests (11:27) generally belonged to and dominated the religiopolitical party known as the ***Sadducees.*** Only here does this name occur in Mark, and, similarly, the Gospel of Luke uses it only in the parallel passage (but cf. Acts 4:1; 5:17; 23:6 ff.). The party's importance is stressed much more in Matthew. John (who usually writes "the Jews" for Israel's religious leadership) does not mention the Sadducean party. The Roman Christians would likely have been familiar with the name only through the traditions about Jesus which they had been taught.

The nature of the Sadducees' question was, like that asked by Pharisees and Herodians, quite hypocritical. The Sadducees asked about a ***resurrection*** in which they did not believe; the earlier question was prefaced by premises to which the enemies of Jesus could not have subscribed.

The intention of the Sadducees' question was not to find out anything about the resurrection, but to illustrate at Jesus' expense how absurd was the belief in any such doctrine. They intended to demonstrate that Jesus was not a worthy but a fallible and foolish teacher, and thus to drive a wedge between him and his popular following.

The opposition of Sadducees was ominous. Although the first-century historian Josephus rightly notes their unpopularity with the multitudes (*Antiq.*, 18,1), they were very wealthy and their influence with Pilate must have been significant. Their open and vicious opposition to Jesus, at least as far as Mark recounts it, solidified when he interfered with the Temple business which they controlled.

The approach to Jesus was in accord with rabbinic style and method. Jesus was addressed as ***Teacher*** (which translates "Rabbi"), a law of ***Moses*** is cited, an example given in which the law should be applied, and a pertinent question raised. The passage referred to is a free rendering of Deuteronomy 25:5 ff. The phrase "if brothers dwell together" is not present in the quote, but Jesus' response takes no notice of this fact. (The best known OT story of levirate marriage is that of Boaz and Ruth; but cf. also Gen. 38:8. There is no evidence of the practice of this law in Jesus' time.)

The story itself, with its humorous twist, had probably been used by the Sadducees before to confound the Pharisees. That Jesus believed in a resurrection, as the Pharisees did, was assumed. However, belief in a bodily resurrection is not explicitly taught in the Old Testament except in passages which are generally regarded as late (Dan. 12:2; Isa. 26:19; cf. 25:8; Job 19:25–27 and Psalm 73:24 f. reflect a budding hope, but a concept of resurrection is not clear). The Sadducees recognized as fully inspired Scriptures only the books of Moses.

In the resurrection whose wife will she be? The doctrine of the resurrection, which was assumed by the question, included the premise that resurrection bodies must be the same or similar to our earthly bodies and that our present human relationships will continue. Probably most of the Pharisees at this time believed this. Second Baruch 50 reflects this naïve view and insists that the earth will restore the dead body, preserved perfectly, with no change in its form. Enoch 10:17 promises that the righteous will live till they beget thousands of children.

Jesus' reply (1) corrected the false concept about the nature of the resurrection, pointing (as Paul did in 1 Cor. 15:35 ff.) to ***the power of God*** to provide a different and appropriate body for the resurrection life; and (2) cited Scriptures from the Law which supported the idea of resurrection.

When they rise from the dead: Jesus did teach, then, that there will be a resurrection. However, human relationships will be superseded, and the question of the Sadducees is irrelevant, for in that life they do not ***marry.*** That they ***are like angels in heaven*** gives no precise picture, but suggests a wider and more wonderful fellowship in the family of God. Life after death cannot be described in words bound to earthly images, and the ***power of God*** is far greater than man's concepts of joy and hope might suppose.

Have you not read? See 2:25 and 12:10 for similar phrases. Jesus always spoke with deep regard for the Scriptures. ***The passage about the bush*** is Exodus 3:1–6. The passage says nothing directly of resurrection, it is true, but God there identified himself as the God of Abraham, Isaac, and Jacob. If the living God was their God, then the patriarchs must also be living.[45]

The basis of faith in the resurrection is faith in the power of God. The Living One who has called man into a relationship with himself does not permit death to break that relationship. One may say that the passage about the bush was not written to affirm life after death. Nevertheless, here was faith that the God who had fellowship with the revered patriarchs is a living God, whose power and providence do not wane. Here is a letter of hope and faith upon which the resurrection of Jesus places the stamp of God's answering assurance.

The story ends even more abruptly than the previous one. ***You are quite wrong,*** said Jesus. The verb is apparently interpreted as middle in voice (RSV): they have been leading themselves completely away from God's truth.

(4) *The Question About the Chief Commandment (12:28–34)*

28 And one of the scribes came up and heard them disputing with one another, and seeing that he answered them well, asked him, "Which commandment is the first of all?" 29 Jesus answered, "The first is, 'Hear, O Israel: The Lord our God, the Lord is one; 30 and you shall love the Lord your God with all your heart, and with all your soul, and with all your mind, and with all your strength.' 31 The second is this, 'You shall love your neighbor as yourself.' There is no other commandment greater than these." 32 And the scribe said to him, "You are right, Teacher; you have truly said that he is one, and there is no other but he; 33 and to love him with all the heart, and with all the understanding, and with all the strength, and to love one's neighbor as oneself,

45 To speak of God as "living" was characteristic of the Hebrews, as NT examples reflect: Matt. 26:63; Rom. 9:26; 2 Cor. 3:3; 6:16; Heb. 9:31. In 4 Maccabees 7:19 (first century?) it is affirmed by the Jewish writer that Abraham, Isaac, and Jacob did not die, but live unto God.

is much more than all whole burnt offerings and sacrifices." 34 And when Jesus saw that he answered wisely, he said to him, "You are not far from the kingdom of God." And after that no one dared to ask him any question.

Mark's next story of the confrontation in the Temple is of a scribe who had been listening to Jesus' answer to the previous question. Whether or not this event actually occurred at a different time, Mark has woven the stories together very rationally. (Cf. Luke 10:25–37; but T. W. Manson insists that the stories are no doublet, that they tell of two distinct occasions.) The scribe was quite apparently a Pharisee, for he was pleased and impressed by Jesus' response to the Sadducees. We must remember the tension and scornful prejudice that often were present between these two parties, specifically on the question of resurrection (cf. Acts 23:6 ff.).

Seeing is translated "perceive" in 4:12; for the adverb ***well,*** describing Jesus' answer, see its use in 7:6 and note again in verse 32. Neither the scribe's question nor his spirit, which Jesus commends, reflects any animosity toward Jesus. The question about the most important (i.e., *first,* or chief) commandment was one which the scribes themselves debated: they commonly discussed which law was relatively weightier than another. The best known scribal answer is Hillel's to a would-be proselyte: "That which is hateful to thy self, do not do to thy neighbor; this is the whole law and the rest but commentary." Rabbi Akiba (second century) chose Leviticus 19:18, the one Jesus calls ***second.***

The student of the New Testament must not forget the fine quality of much of the scribes' teaching, nor that the Old Testament was so highly regarded by Jesus.

Jesus' answer was bold and absolute. The ***first*** commandment was the one with which the Shema began and which the devout Hebrew was expected to recite three times a day. (Cf. Johnson, p. 203; the Shema included Deut. 6:4–9; 11:13–21; Num. 15:37–41.) ***Hear*** translates the Hebrew word *shema.*

The Lord our God, the Lord is one is difficult to translate either from the Greek, as here, or from the Hebrew. NEB has "The Lord your God is the only Lord;" and note the scribe's interpretive response in verse 32 (careful, like a good Hebrew, not to use the terms Lord and God unnecessarily). In any case, the current understanding of the words did not emphasize only that God was Israel's Lord but also a genuine monotheism. Although the first clause is not a command in itself, the obligation to love God stems from the fact of his oneness, and from the fact that ***Israel*** was chosen by him in covenant-love (Cranfield).

Love for God must be supreme. In the New Testament, emphasis usually falls on God's love for man, and on man's love for others in accord with this divine, unselfish, outgoing quest for good. But genuinely to desire and to seek God's will and way is in full accord with the meaning of this word, and this is central to Jesus' teaching. One must love him, therefore, ***with*** (Arndt and Gingrich say the preposition here means the inner source from which something proceeds) ***all*** that one is.

The ***heart*** is, in Hebrew idiom, the center for man's thinking. The ***soul*** is thought of as the fount of man's will and feelings. The word translated ***mind*** means understanding or intelligence (it is often used interchangeably with heart, but does not occur in the LXX of Deut. 6:5). ***Strength*** emphasizes the physical power and being of a person. The quotation is not precise, but it is quite in accord with the original commandment. These nouns may be accented separately if one chooses, but the use of the four terms was intended to mean, You must love the Lord with your whole self, without reservation.

The second commandment (Lev. 19:18) follows the LXX exactly. Jesus' concept of ***neighbor*** was certainly much broader than that of many scribes, as Luke 10:25–37 shows. The passage involved applied originally to Israelites and to the strangers who sojourned among them (Lev. 19:34). There is no special exhortation by Jesus to love oneself: he could assume that one did care for his own person. But a man must love others in the same way.

The scribe was again happy with Jesus' answer, and adds his own conviction that obedience to these commands is far more important with God than the observance of the prescribed sacrificial offerings such as one made in the Temple. The scribe was not repudiating the sacrificial system however. Neither did the Christians at first, for after Pentecost they continued to include worship at the Temple in their practice for some time. The break came partly from growing opposition among the Jewish leaders, partly from rising convictions such as those expressed in Stephen's address (Acts 7), at the Council of Jerusalem (Acts 15), and in 1 Peter and Hebrews.

Jesus spoke appreciatively of the scribe's answer, for he had replied *wisely*—intelligently. He had an alert and responsive mind, his spirit partook of that which Jesus called "blessed" in Matthew 5:3–6. Therefore, he was ***not far from the kingdom;*** i.e., he appeared prepared to receive it, or to enter it. If the kingdom has drawn near in Jesus (1:15), this man has in turn drawn near to the kingdom. The idea of ***the kingdom*** here is hardly eschatological, in the sense that this man will be ready when it arrives; it is concerned with the realm in which God's will is understood and followed. The Roman Christians would recognize the importance of what had been said and the depth of the compliment to the scribe.

Verse 34*b* may have been added here by Mark; Matthew places it after the next question (cf. 22:46), and Luke (who does not tell this story) after the Sadducees' question (20:40).

(5) *The Question About David's Relationship to the Christ (12:35–37)*

35 And as Jesus taught in the temple, he said,
"How can the scribes say that the Christ is the
son of David? 36 David himself, inspired by the
Holy Spirit, declared,
'The Lord said to my Lord,
Sit at my right hand,
till I put thy enemies under thy feet.'
37 David himself calls him Lord; so how is he
his son?" And the great throng heard him
gladly.

If we could know the original and larger context of these verses it might prove very helpful. The question of the identity of Jesus and his relationship to the prophets and the Messiah must have been of great interest to the people at the feast in Jerusalem. The conversation must in some way have derived from their speculation.

It is unlikely that the story comes out of Christological debates in the early Palestinian church (so Johnson, following R. Bultmann, J. Weiss), for the church hardly needed convincing that Jesus was the Christ and of Davidic descent. Cranfield follows the attractive suggestion of R. P. Gagg (in *Theologische Zeitshrift,* VII, 18–30) that what we have is genuine, but that a question about whether Jesus taught that the Messiah was David's son was part of his opponents' attack. Perhaps they were attempting to get him to incriminate himself with the Romans by his answer. However, if Gagg's hypothesis is correct, the opponents' question had been forgotten.

Jesus did not accept, as we have seen, the ordinary expectation of the Jewish people about the Christ (cf. on 8:29). Neither does he deny in these verses that he himself is of Davidic descent, nor that he is the Christ.

The scribes held as standard doctrine that ***the Christ is the son of David.*** Among the Scriptures used were Isaiah 9:2–7; 11:1–9; Jeremiah 23:5 f.; Ezekiel 34:23 f.; and many others. That Jesus cited Psalm 110:1 here makes probable that this passage was also so used, but there is no rabbinic evidence until two hundred years afterwards. (The rabbinic scholars, H. L. Strack and P. Billerbeck, think this was because the early Christians used it so often concerning Jesus that mention of this passage was suppressed.)

If the Christ were simply a descendant of David, then one should think of him as

David's inferior. Jesus, arguing in rabbinic fashion (whether or not he brought up the subject), cited Psalm 110 as showing that David called him Lord. God was expected to exercise his power in putting *all thy* (Messiah's) *enemies under thy feet.* In the Hebrew psalm the first word for *Lord* is the name of God; the second is the usual word *Lord.* The meaning is, The Lord God said to my Lord. The LXX and the NT quotation of it do not clearly make this distinction, though the absence of the article with the first *Lord* implies that it was so understood.

Inspired by the Holy Spirit: this is a clear affirmation of the divine inspiration of the psalm's author, that is, that he spoke as God's prophet or messenger. Many think that the psalm was actually written in the second century B.C. with reference to Simon Maccabeus; an acrostic of his name is found in the initial lines of the Hebrew in the Psalm's first four verses. However, Davidic authorship of the Psalms generally was assumed in first-century Israel.

The conversation (we have only the words from Jesus) breaks off abruptly with the question in verse 37. Mark displays no interest in Jesus' genealogy, here or elsewhere. The Roman Christians were not oriented to be so interested in Jesus' earthly lineage as his Jewish contemporaries were. And Mark was surely right in his emphasis that Jesus' true nature was not adequately expressed by calling Christ David's son. To Mark, the Christ is better described as the exalted Son of man and the strong Son of God.

(6) *A Contrast in Stewardship: Scribes and the Poor Widow (12:38–44)*

**38 And in his teaching he said, "Beware of
the scribes, who like to go about in long robes,
and to have salutations in the market places
39 and the best seats in the synagogues and the
places of honor at feasts, 40 who devour widows' houses and for a pretense make long
prayers. They will receive the greater condemnation."**

**41 And he sat down opposite the treasury,
and watched the multitude putting money into
the treasury. Many rich people put in large
sums. 42 And a poor widow came, and put in
two copper coins, which make a penny. 43 And
he called his disciples to him, and said to them,
"Truly, I say to you, this poor widow has put
in more than all those who are contributing to
the treasury. 44 For they all contributed out of
their abundance; but she out of her poverty
has put in everything she had, her whole living."**

The scribes and other opponents withdrew (v. 34), but the "mass of the people" (Moffatt) continued to listen to him with delight (v. 37). The denunciation of the scribes is much expanded in Matthew 23 (probably from the source Q), but the author's audience and purpose were not Mark's. Perhaps the incident in verses 41–44 is recorded here because it occurred at this time (Lagrange). In any case, it is appropriate because Mark wished to show the contrast in worship and commitment between the scribes Jesus denounced and the widow he praised.

Beware of the scribes, said Jesus, not all of them (this is the implication of the syntax used here, and 12:28–34 described a different kind of man), but those ***who like to go about in long robes, and to have salutations . . . the best seats . . . the places of honor.*** The vanity of these scholarly men, so expert in God's law, was a symptom of their own unworthiness.

The *long* robe was the *tallith,* and was supposed to signify piety and scholarship. The *salutations* in this case meant deferential greetings: Jesus was saying such men liked to have others bow low before them, and especially ***in the market places*** where there were crowds. ***In the synagogues*** the "seats for distinguished persons" were on the bench just in front of the ark that contained the sacred scrolls. ***The places of honor at feasts*** were the couches next to the host (cf. Luke 14:7).

If vanity were all, it would have been bad enough. But Jesus asserted that their vanity was matched by their greed. This was not true, of course, of some of the scribes; their fellow scribes warned against this sin. The Mishnah (Aboth 1:13) reflects that some were guilty, for it asserts that the man who serves himself for gain from the Torah will perish. It was also true of some of the unscrupulous, wealthy priests, and the saying in verse 40 may have originally been directed against both chief priests and some of the wealthy scribes. (V. 40 begins with a break in the syntax, and perhaps had a somewhat different context in the beginning. Any distinction between chief priests and scribes who were hypocrites and who opposed Jesus would in any case be blurred among Roman Christians reading Mark.)

To ***devour widows' houses*** meant to exploit their goods, either by their position as religious leaders (Lagrange) or in other ways equally greedy and evil. ***Houses*** here stands for goods, fortunes—whatever they may possess.

For a pretense may mean either for the sake of appearances (Bratcher) or to cover up their evil purposes (Goodspeed). Their ***prayers*** are long, extensive; see comment on Jesus' teaching in Matthew 6:7.

Because of their hypocrisy—because they claim to be committed to God and his law but actually exploit their positions to feed their vanity and their banks—***they will receive the greater condemnation*** on the day of God's judgment.

Religious leaders of Pharisees and Sadducees were not the only persons present in the Temple. God had his faithful adherents. One of these was a ***widow,*** whose poverty was not—as that of the scribes just condemned—a poverty of the spirit. Hers was a poverty of the material.

The treasury is often identified with one of the 13 collection boxes, shaped like trumpets with narrow openings, placed at the colonnade of the Court of the Women. However, the word could refer to a room in which the Temple treasures were stored, and in this case we must suppose some means of depositing gifts there.

In contrast with the size of the gifts of wealthy men, ***a poor widow*** made her contribution of ***two copper coins.*** As a poor widow in that culture the woman could not have had much hope for a major reversal in her economic status. Her two copper coins were *lepta,* the smallest coin in circulation. The penny was a *quadrans,* a Roman coin with which Mark's readers would have been familiar. The value suggested was not exact, but gave the Romans some general idea. The two coppers together were worth only a fraction of one cent in our coinage.

Jesus considered the lesson to be learned a crucial one, and so called attention to his own words, ***Truly, I say to you.*** Her gift was greater than the magnificent, valuable offerings of all the others. (If taken literally, the words mean more than all others combined.)

How could this be? Because they gave ***out of their abundance.*** Nida points to ways in which Bible societies have translated this phrase into languages with limited vocabulary: "they gave money which they didn't need," or "they contributed the leftover money." The widow, however, made her gift out of her own need. Neither vain nor avaricious, she committed her very livelihood in trust to God.

3. *The Apocalyptic Discourses: the Importance of Alert Discipleship (13:1–37)*

The discourse in chapter 13, often called the "Little Apocalypse," is the last and most controversial block of teaching recorded by Mark. It is especially necessary here to keep in focus the perspective of the author and his readers, for their situation was very different from that of the disciples who listened to Jesus on the Mount of Olives.

To the Christians of Rome, the resurrection of Jesus was not a mysterious event which was still to be disclosed, but something wonderful which had already happened. Though the twelve did not understand Jesus' teaching at the time about his resurrection (9:30–32), the people of the church were bound to think about and look for the further victory and manifestation of the power of God.

Moreover, the Christians around Mark had already been experiencing the hardest kinds of persecution. The disciples with Jesus heard and then later participated in experiences like some of those Jesus anticipates. But in Rome much had already happened. Brother had delivered up brother, and because they were known by the name Christian they were distrusted and hated (cf. 13:12 f.). It would have been impossible for those who had endured or were enduring Nero's attacks to hear these words of Jesus as if in the environment of far-off Jerusalem.

Again, some of the language of Mark 13 is *apocalyptic*, i.e., language which is highly figurative, symbolic, and even extravagant. Apocalyptic means unveiling, or revelation, and is a technical term for writings which claimed to offer a glimpse behind the curtain which veils the purposes and activities of God. In the Bible most of Daniel and the Revelation of John are the clearest examples. There was also a multitude of nonbiblical apocalypses, and apocalyptic style has influenced books as different as Joel and 2 Thessalonians.

However common apocalyptic writing may have been among the Jews, its language could not have been so readily understood by an audience in Italy. Note the warning in verse 14 (presumably inserted into the tradition by Mark or a predecessor), "Let the reader understand."

Nevertheless, apocalyptic style was the literary form in which the confident expectations—sometimes desperate hopes—of God's people were often expressed. Mark 13 does look to the future, to ***the Son of man coming in clouds with great power and glory.*** He will ***gather his elect*** (vv. 26 f.). The risen Lord has not abdicated, and we must be alert for his coming. These promises were very precious and meaningful to Christians who might otherwise have despaired.

It is quite true, of course, that the early Christians sometimes overemphasized or even misinterpreted these hopes expressed in apocalyptic writing. For example, we know that Paul had to correct a situation in the church in Thessalonica, in which some members of the church had even quit working because they anticipated the day of the Lord (2 Thess. 2:2 ff.; 3:6 ff.).

More than a century ago T. Colani set forth the thesis that Mark 13 did not come from Jesus at all; that what we have is a summary of the views held by early Jewish Christians; that the document from which it has been taken might well be identified with an apocalyptic oracle, spoken of by Eusebius, the fourth-century Christian historian, which was delivered in Jesus' name and which warned the Christians to flee from a doomed Jerusalem. (More recently, this hypothetical document has been judged to have come from the time of the Emperor Caligula [38–42], who ordered his statue placed in the Temple in Jerusalem: so, for example, Johnson, p. 209.)

With various modifications, this view has been accepted in whole or in part by many scholars since that time. Some have concluded that the chapter contains many genuine sayings of Jesus but that Jesus was not responsible for the pattern in which they have come down to us. Still others have concluded that the teachings came to Mark (and so to us) in substantially the way Jesus spoke.[46]

The chief difficulties in the chapter, as Moule has observed, are two in number. First, can we believe that Jesus, who usually spoke in such a different vein, thought of the future in terms of fantastic signs in the heavens and the cataclysmic end of history in one single event (13:24–27)? Second, would not the reader of the chapter normally understand that everything prophesied would take place in that generation, now 19 centuries ago? It is said, of course, that the precise moment was not known to Jesus (v. 32), but if these were his words (vv. 13,23,30,32 f.), was he not mistaken in his expectation?

In regard to the first difficulty, it can be answered that apocalyptic language was

[46] For a careful history of this discussion and an excellent study of the meaning of the chapter, see G. R. Beasley-Murray, *Jesus and the Future* (London: Macmillan, 1954), and his *Commentary on Mark Thirteen* (London: Macmillan, 1957).

never meant to be taken literally. It partakes more of the exaggerated figures of the editorial cartoon (e.g., in which the donkey stands for the Democratic Party, or the Statue of Liberty for freedom or the Bill of Rights: cf. Rev. 1:20) than it does of the ordinary simile or metaphor. See below on 13:24 f. Apocalyptic language provided a convenient way of speaking of inexpressible power and activity beyond the human, while still using words that were in common use. It would be surprising indeed if Jesus had not said anything of God's invading presence in the future, and should be equally startling if he had never used apocalyptic language with which the people of his own country were so familiar.

As to the second difficulty, we have to acknowledge, first of all, that Jesus confessed his own lack of information as to the day and hour (v. 32). That he did not anticipate that it would be so many centuries as have already elapsed should not be surprising, nor should it be a problem. The prophets viewed clearly the moral and spiritual trends of their times and envisioned what must be coming, inexorably, from God. Yet it was characteristic of them to telescope the future, to bring it closer to present reality. If it be objected that Jesus was more than a prophet, that is something we judge by faith to be true. But we also judge that our Lord became genuinely a man, and Mark quoted him as saying he did not know the time of the end.

It is quite possible that the readers of Mark would have interpreted this chapter to mean that the end of time was indeed very near. How greatly it would help our understanding if we could have all that Jesus may have said on this occasion, or on other occasions when he used apocalyptic language or spoke of man's hope under God! But we do need to bear in mind that neither Matthew 24 nor Luke 21:8–36 follows Mark 13 precisely, and that Peter uses almost the same words as 13:24 f. to describe what happened at Pentecost (Acts 2:19 f.).

As it now stands, and as it likely came to Mark, the chapter is arranged in rather standard apocalyptic fashion, with a beginning of sufferings (5–13), a time of great tribulation (14–23), and the end (24–27). Nevertheless, the burden of the chapter is not apocalyptic, but warning and encouragement and exhortation. The eschatology is present, but it is a vehicle to speak of faith and obedience. Unlike other apocalyptic writing, moreover, there is no reference to Satan, no dwelling on the destruction of evil forces, no drawn-out description of final judgment.

While there is very little in the discourse that cannot plausibly be attributed to Jesus, it is reasonable to suppose that what is recorded may well have been spoken on different occasions (cf. 9:39–50). It is equally fair to suppose that early Christians should have at some appropriate occasion put the chapter in approximately its present form, perhaps adding warning or explanatory phrases for clarification.

(1) *The Doom of the Temple and the Disciples' Questions* (*13:1–4*)

1 And as he came out of the temple, one of his disciples said to him, "Look, Teacher, what wonderful stones and what wonderful buildings!" 2 And Jesus said to him, "Do you see these great buildings? There will not be left here one stone upon another, that will not be thrown down."

3 And as he sat on the Mount of Olives opposite the temple, Peter and James and John and Andrew asked him privately, 4 "Tell us, when will this be, and what will be the sign when these things are all to be accomplished?"

The ***stones*** of the Temple walls were indeed ***wonderful.*** The ***buildings*** at which the disciple was looking had been begun by King Herod almost half a century earlier (John 2:20). Intermittent construction was still going on. Josephus described the lovely white stones, dressed and fitted, as being 25 cubits long, 8 high, and 12 in breadth. The eastern face of the holy of holies was covered with plates of gold. As the disciples walked eastward toward the Mount of Olives, the view must have been magnificent.

Jesus' response must have been startling. The Temple was the center of the worship of God for all of Israel: it seemed unreasonable that utter destruction could come upon so sacred and so apparently strong a place. The prophecy, however, was almost totally fulfilled in A.D. 70. A few stones, notably at the Wailing Wall, can still be seen. However, the destruction of the Temple was first by fire, of which no hint is given. Jesus gave no precise blueprint of events, but he did see all too clearly the tragic end of the course being pursued by the Jewish leadership.

Four of the disciples, apparently drawing Jesus apart from the others, asked him about his words. ***When will*** the destruction of the Temple ***happen? What will be the sign*** that will warn us?

In Matthew 24:3 the question is transformed so that the disciples are said to have asked, "What will be the sign of your coming and of the close of the age?" (cf. Luke 21:7). When we consider Jesus' answer in Mark, we see that he actually dealt with both questions. Judging from Mark's account, we must conclude that, from the point of view of the disciples, the destruction of the Temple would be such a signal disaster, such an unthinkable event, that it was assumed to be related intimately to the end of the age.

The infinitive ***to be accomplished*** translates a verb form of the same word as the noun in Matthew 24:3 which is translated "close of the age." The verb itself means to bring things together in a final consummation or achievement. The question in Matthew is thus an interpretation of Mark, dependent not only on the answer given by Jesus but also on Mark's phrasing of the original question.

(2) *Warnings of False Christs, Great Disturbances, and Harsh Troubles for Disciples (13:5–13)*

5 And Jesus began to say to them, "Take heed
that no one leads you astray. 6 Many will come
in my name, saying, 'I am he!' and they will
lead many astray. 7 And when you hear of wars
and rumors of wars, do not be alarmed; this
must take place, but the end is not yet. 8 For
nation will rise against nation, and kingdom
against kingdom; there will be earthquakes in
various places, there will be famines; this is
but the beginning of the sufferings.

9 "But take heed to yourselves; for they will
deliver you up to councils; and you will be
beaten in synagogues; and you will stand be-
fore governors and kings for my sake, to bear
testimony before them. 10 And the gospel must
first be preached to all nations. 11 And when
they bring you to trial and deliver you up, do
not be anxious beforehand what you are to say;
but say whatever is given you in that hour, for
it is not you who speak, but the Holy Spirit.
12 And brother will deliver up brother to death,
and the father his child, and children will rise
against parents and have them put to death;
13 and you will be hated by all for my name's
sake. But he who endures to the end will be
saved.

In answer to his four most intimate disciples, Jesus began with a warning to ***take heed.*** Throughout the chapter there is a repeated exhortation to be alert, to be careful in their interpretations of words and events. The final command in the discourse is in the same vein (cf. v. 37). Jesus regarded it as a grave possibility that his disciples might be misguided in the face of false claims and unexpected and fearful upheavals.

There would be special danger, he said, when persons came claiming to speak ***in my name, saying, I am he!*** By itself ***in my name*** need only mean "on my authority," i.e., one who would claim to speak for Jesus. See above on 9:38; and the story of the seven sons of Sceva in Acts 19:13 ff. The added phrase, however, requires us to understand the claim to be the Son of man himself. For ***I am he,*** see above on 6:3, and note also 14:62.

Evidence of "false Christs" during the period from Jesus' resurrection to the writing of Mark is admittedly slim. Note however Simon Magus' description of himself in Acts 8:9–11, also Gamaliel's references to Judas and Theudas (Acts 5:33 ff.). The first known messianic pretender was Bar Cochba (A.D. 132).

Wars and rumors (reports) ***of wars*** were

frequently associated with the end-time in Jewish apocalypse, as were ***earthquakes*** and ***famines.*** Indeed, the use of these words in prophetic expectation was common also in early Old Testament prophecies. See, for example, Isaiah 19:2 ("city against city, kingdom against kingdom," though the oracle concerned Egypt); 8:21 and 14:30 ("famine;" cf. Acts 11:28); 13:13 (earthquake). Compare also the later description of the four horsemen of the Apocalypse of John (6:1–8). The Roman Christians would think of such historical events as the troubles with Parthia, the uprising of the Jews (A.D. 66), earthquakes at Laodicea (A.D. 61), and the volcanic destruction of Pompeii (A.D. 62).

Four phrases in verses 7 f. call for special notice. ***Do not be alarmed*** means "do not be frightened." Why not? Because these things are sure to happen, in view of man's inclinations and deeds and God's way of dealing with them. So ***this must take place:*** it is "bound to be," just as Jesus' suffering is bound to be (cf. on 8:31), and just as God's wrath is bound to be operative (cf. on 4:10–12).

The phrase ***this must take place*** should not be interpreted as meaning God initiates wars and other tragedies that curse mankind, much less that we should not strive for peace between nations. The disciples need not fear that God has deserted them, though the world caves in or explodes about them. But neither should they suppose that dreadful calamities bring on the end, for ***the end is not yet;*** i.e., the final consummation of this age does not hinge on the time or occurrence of some tragedy in history, it is "not at this point."

What are these things then? They are ***but the beginning of the sufferings. Sufferings*** translates the word for birth pangs. In apocalyptic literature, this is apparently the technical phrase for "the terrors and torments that precede the coming of the Messianic age" (Bratcher). It is a word singularly fitting for a description of both pain and promise.

The dangers described in verses 5–8 were from outside pretenders or events that might ***lead*** them ***astray.*** In verses 9–13 the disciples were warned again, ***take heed to yourselves,*** because heavy pressures would be brought to bear to force them to renounce their allegiance to Jesus.

Deliver you up may mean arrest (1:14) or betray (3:19); the word occurs three times in this paragraph. ***Councils*** were local courts or sanhedrins, with 23 members each, located in Jewish communities other than Jerusalem. Paul was beaten five times, according to 2 Corinthians 11:24, presumably on the orders of such courts.

Governors and kings were non-Jewish authorities. Mark uses the word king loosely (Herod Antipas did not actually possess the title, though it was used of him in 6:14), and the word may have referred to the Herodian rulers (Acts 12:1; 25:13), though clearly applicable to Nero. The governors would include procurators, proconsuls, and perhaps even magistrates (Acts 16:20 ff.). To ***stand before*** them means to be tried before them.

Why would this happen? ***For my sake,*** said Jesus, a phrase which here means because of your faithfulness to me (cf. 8:35). Yet the purposes of God would be served even in their trials and persecutions. What happened would be a ***testimony before them,*** either of the power of the gospel in the disciples, or the proclamation of the good news itself, or, more probably, both. Perhaps there is also a note of warning: they may not believe you, but you will have faithfully testified to them, and they will have to answer to God.

It is possible to take the phrase ***to all nations*** (i.e., all the Gentiles) with verse 9. The reading of the RSV is, however, a reasonable interpretation of the Greek text; and even if the alternative translation be preferred, Mark obviously understood Jesus to teach that the gospel will be preached to Gentile peoples.

The gospel must first be preached. Perhaps ***first*** has no reference to time and simply means most important: so the "chief" necessity would be that the gospel be proclaimed. Nevertheless the adverb normally has a temporal meaning in Mark, and quite plausibly answers to verse 7, "the end is not yet" (W. G. Kümmel, Beasley-Murray).

The Holy Spirit will be with disciples wherever they, having been faithful servants, face trial and persecution. Therefore they need ***not be anxious beforehand***, because he will help them to testify. ***Do not be anxious beforehand*** means, do not be worriedly dividing your attention between your preaching and their threats about what may happen to you. This is an exhortation parallel to "take up your cross." A disciple's commitment must be full, no matter what the cost. And God's Spirit will be with him to strengthen and guide even his words.

The division within families will be so sharp and so tragic that faithful disciples will find themselves betrayed by their closest of kin, even when they are aware that betrayal will mean death. This was part of the apocalyptic expectation (Enoch 99:5; 2 Esdras 6:24; 2 Baruch 70:6; cf. Micah 7:6). Such incidents undoubtedly occurred, because the pressures spoken of in verses 9 f. must have been terrible. The Roman historian Tacitus describes Christians as hated for their abominations; cf. again 1 Peter 4:12–16. We do not know how soon they were persecuted for the ***name*** itself, but we do know it was not long in coming.

The suffering, however, would be but "preliminary to glory" (Beasley-Murray). ***Saved*** refers to more than physical life here, though Johnson would so confine it; on the contrary, it is evident that the physical life may be snuffed out (v. 12). To ***be saved*** —in this context—means to have life, resurrection, continuing relationship with the Lord. This term, in other instances, may mean the initial commitment of a person to the Lord or his growth in the Christian life, by God's grace. The verse need not mean that the end of the age would come before their deaths. To endure means to remain faithful to the name, no matter what may come; it means not to "fall away" (Matt. 24:10) but to bear witness, relying on the Holy Spirit.

(3) *The Terrible Time of the Desolating Sacrilege* (*13:14–23*)

**14 "But when you see the desolating sacrilege
set up where it ought not to be (let the reader
understand), then let those who are in Judea
flee to the mountains; 15 let him who is on the
housetop not go down, nor enter his house, to
take anything away; 16 and let him who is in
the field not turn back to take his mantle.
17 And alas for those who are with child and
for those who give suck in those days! 18 Pray
that it may not happen in winter. 19 For in
those days there will be such tribulation as has
not been from the beginning of the creation
which God created until now, and never will
be. 20 And if the Lord had not shortened the
days, no human being would be saved; but for
the sake of the elect, whom he chose, he
shortened the days. 21 And then if any one says
to you, 'Look, here is the Christ!' or 'Look,
there he is!' do not believe it. 22 False Christs
and false prophets will arise and show signs
and wonders, to lead astray, if possible, the
elect. 23 But take heed; I have told you all
things beforehand.**

The desolating sacrilege is a phrase from Greek translation of the apocalypse of Daniel. The pertinent passages are Daniel 11:31; 9:27; 12:11. The Hebrew phrase would be better translated "the appalling horror." It described the awful abomination against the Hebrew faith and people which was done when Antiochus Epiphanes attempted to stamp out the worship of the Lord. His forces covered God's altar with a heathen altar and sacrificed swine meat to the Olympian Zeus. This was in 168 B.C., and it triggered the Maccabean revolt (1 Macc. 1:41–64; the same phrase "desolating sacrilege" occurs in 1:54).

What does the phrase mean here in verse 14? It certainly looks to the future, not the past. It may refer to Antichrist, for (1) the participle translated ***set up*** is masculine in form, not neuter (like sacrilege), and probably refers to a person; and (2) it is often considered that 2 Thessalonians 2:3–10 supports the identification of ***desolating sacrilege*** with Antichrist, or the "man of lawlessness."

It is difficult to decide to what degree Mark here understands the phrase to refer to a future eschatological event, and to what degree he connects it with the destruction of Jerusalem. In verses 24–27 Jesus is surely referring to the end-time; in verses 5–12 he is surely referring to events of history; in verses 14–23 most of what is said is applicable to the destruction of the Temple and of Jerusalem.

The constant struggle and hope of the disciples (and of Jewish apocalypse), however, would hardly have allowed them to divorce so tragic and symbolic an event as the destruction of the Temple from the conviction that God would be intervening were such a thing to happen. Luke, writing after the catastrophe, clearly finds the fulfilment of Jesus' words here in the Roman conquest and destruction of Jerusalem (21:20–24). Cranfield is probably right in concluding that Jesus did speak of the approaching disaster in some relation to the final events, but that he left "room for the possibility" that the impending destruction of the Temple might be followed by other crises in history before the final day.

Let the reader understand is obviously from an interpreter of Jesus' words, whether Mark or someone earlier. As has been pointed out, it need not mean that Mark 13 as a whole is constructed from some other source than Jesus' teaching. It is an exhortation to be careful, to put one's mind to work on this matter, for the phrase just used was cryptic; it held a certain mystery.

What is said in the remainder of verses 14–20 is specifically applicable to the tragedies of the Jewish revolt against Rome, A.D. 66–70. The city offered no refuge, and it was safer to hide in the caves in ***the mountains.*** Eusebius tells us that the Christians did not attempt to find safety in Jerusalem, but fled and established the church in Pella.

The man ***on the housetop,*** perhaps resting on the flat roof, would have time only to escape. He was not to ***go down,*** i.e., to risk trying to save his goods. Neither should the man at work ***in the field*** (i.e., outside the walls of his town) attempt to return home even to get ***his mantle*** or outer cloak, which would be needed at night.

The times will be so difficult that it will be especially tragic for the woman who happens to be burdened with the carrying of an unborn child, or one which she must feed at her breast (cf. Luke 23:29). Any season would be hard, but to have to hide in ***the mountains*** in the winter's cold would be unbearable.

The ***tribulation*** will be the worst the world has ever experienced. The description might well apply to the time of the Jews' defeat, if we allow for hyperbole. Yet this frightful experience was anticipated in prophecy and apocalyptic also in connection with the end. Note Jeremiah 30:7 and Daniel 12:1. It was also anticipated that God would care for his own. Jesus' assurance is that God, ***for the sake of the elect,*** had already provided that the ***days*** be ***shortened*** ("amputated"). The promise is in the style of the prophets: the word of God is so certain that one may look on his promise as already fulfilled.

The elect (vv. 20,22) means God's chosen people. The term does not imply that God is partial and plays favorites, for God's choice corresponds in appropriate measure to man's response. They have answered God's call, not to safety or to some earthly or eternal security, but to serve God's will. There is no promise of protection from pain, or from being led off in error, though God does not forget them. God's call is wider than his election, for the religious leadership of the Hebrew people undoubtedly was considered to have been called (cf. Matt. 21:43). But their refusal of the role of servants of mankind, their utter rejection of Jesus, and their attitudes toward other peoples (including the Romans) led to the doom of Jerusalem itself. Mark's readers would of course identify ***the elect*** in their day as those who had responded affirmatively to the gospel.

With verse 21 should be compared Luke 17:20 ff., as well as verses 5–6 above. ***Then*** connects the verse with what precedes, though it can mean "at that time" (i.e., the time of 14–20), or at some future time, or at the time following that just described (cf.

Arndt and Gingrich). As was indicated above, the first full-blown messianic pretender of whom we know was Bar Cochba some sixty years later. But ***false Christs and false prophets*** are sufficiently indefinite terms to include many who announced that they were speaking for God.

Signs and wonders, deeds that gave an appearance of being from God or exercising divine power, would be performed by these false claimants. Cranfield points out that the powers of evil would in this way "exploit . . . the natural craving of the disciples to escape from [the painful difficulties and uncertainties of faith] into the comfortable security of sight."

In verse 23, the pronoun ***you*** twice occurs in the Greek in emphatic form. "As for *you* (i.e., the four disciples of verse 3, though Mark's readers would probably think of themselves), take heed; I have told *you* all things beforehand." ***All things*** should not be pressed to imply that Jesus gave, intended to give, or even could have given a detailed history of coming events. The sentence should be understood to mean only that they have been fully and adequately warned.

(4) *The Triumphal Coming of the Son of Man (13:24–27)*

24 "But in those days, after that tribulation, the sun will be darkened, and the moon will not give its light, 25 and the stars will be falling from heaven, and the powers in the heavens will be shaken. 26 And then they will see the Son of man coming in clouds with great power and glory. 27 And then he will send out the angels, and gather his elect from the four winds, from the ends of the earth to the ends of heaven.

The language and ideas expressed in these verses derive from the Old Testament. The apocalyptic writers, of course, also freely employed the same sources and the same figures. We must not suppose that each time a given figure of speech occurs it refers to the same event or means precisely the same thing: but its usage elsewhere does furnish indispensable clues to meaning.

For some of the passages that employ phrases used here, cf. Isaiah 13:10; 34:4; Amos 8:9; Joel 2:10,30 f.; Ezekiel 32:7 f. For the same pictorial language utilized in apocalypse, cf. 1 Enoch 80:2–7; 2 Esdras 5:4 ff.; Assumption of Moses 10:5; and Revelation 6:12–14.

In those days was a phrase that usually pointed in Jewish idiom to the end-time (cf. Jer. 3:16; Zech. 8:23). The adversative ***but*** separates this event from what precedes, as does ***after that tribulation*** (see v. 19). Nevertheless, the language used would not imply to the Roman reader that there could be no connection between the anticipated events of 14–23 and those of 24–27. See below on verse 29.

We are not required to interpret all the figurative phrases which follow as predictions of objective events. But they dramatically assert that God is over all his universe, that the ultimate changes and outcome are in his hands (who but God could darken the sun?). They mean that evil does not have final dominion (even though nothing is said directly concerning judgment), for ***the Son of man*** will come for his own.

Great changes will be taking place—described in terms of ***the sun*** being blacked out, ***the moon*** no longer shining, ***the stars*** falling. ***The powers in the heavens*** may refer to the elemental spirits or forces that were commonly spoken of as ruling the stars and influencing the world (cf. Col. 2:8,20; Eph. 6:12; Rom. 8:38 f.; Gal. 4:3; 2 Peter 3:10–12). However, the verb ***will be shaken*** favors an interpretation parallel to the first three figures, a change so dramatic that it can be described as an earthquake in the heavens.

The coming of ***the Son of man*** will take place ***then.*** (We must not, however, suppose that this is the only time or way in which Christians might think of his coming: cf. 8:38—9:1 and notes there.) He will come ***in clouds with great power and glory.*** (Cf. Dan. 7:13 f., where much of the same language is used.) The figure here is of a "superhuman person invested with divine authority and clothed with heavenly light" (Taylor). ***Clouds*** were often symbolic of the very presence of God, upon whom man could not look directly. (Cf. 9:7; and Ex.

16:10; 33:9; Num. 11:25; but the figure would have been less dramatic in Rome than in Jerusalem where a cloud is a rare phenomenon from May through September.)

Mark thinks of this ***coming*** of ***the Son of man*** as the end-event. So also Matthew 24: 29–31, but less surely Luke 21:25–28 ("when these things begin to take place, look up and raise your heads, because your redemption is drawing near"). ***They will see*** is impersonal and does not imply that everyone will see. But the effect will be worldwide. ***Angels*** (messengers on a divine errand) will be sent out. That ***his elect*** would be scattered and would need to be gathered from the whole earth is a common Old Testament idea (Deut. 30:4; Isa. 11:11; Zech. 2:6–12), though it would be an especial solace to beleaguered Christians in Rome.

The four winds here means simply the four directions or points of the compass. Similarly, ***from the ends of the earth to the ends of heaven*** must mean "from everywhere," though the first phrase may refer particularly to all the land mass east of Palestine, and the second to the horizons of the west, where lay the blue waters of the Mediterranean.

What is promised in this paragraph was not intended to shift the center of our faith from this age to the next. The entire chapter, with its warnings and exhortations, is a rejection of an "otherworldly" religion. However, the promise of the Son's triumphant coming offered God's people hope and encouragement. It affirmed that God is in charge and that he has not forsaken his people. He will claim and gather his own. Whatever men may do to the disciple, in whatever age, must not take away the faith by which we live and cannot destroy the hope by which we are sustained. The Son will reign!

(5) *The Necessity for Perceptive Alertness (13:28–37)*

28 "From the fig tree learn its lesson: as soon as its branch becomes tender and puts forth its leaves, you know that summer is near. 29 So also, when you see these things taking place, you know that he is near, at the very gates. 30 Truly, I say to you, this generation will not pass away before all these things take place. 31 Heaven and earth will pass away, but my words will not pass away.

32 "But of that day or that hour no one knows, not even the angels in heaven, nor the Son, but only the Father. 33 Take heed, watch; for you do not know when the time will come. 34 It is like a man going on a journey, when he leaves home and puts his servants in charge, each with his work, and commands the doorkeeper to be on the watch. 35 Watch therefore —for you do not know when the master of the house will come, in the evening, or at midnight, or at cockcrow, or in the morning— 36 lest he come suddenly and find you asleep. 37 And what I say to you I say to all: Watch."

The concluding section of the chapter emphasizes three things: (1) the disciples should be able to discern the coming of these prophesied events, for they would be as clear as the signs of spring and would happen within that generation; (2) nevertheless, the time of the end is known only to the Father; and (3) the disciples must be constantly alert and prepared.

What happens regularly to ***the fig tree*** in the spring provides a ***lesson*** (lit., "parable") for the disciples. When it shows signs of renewal, everybody knows winter is past and ***summer*** is on the way. Similarly, the disciples should take courage. Even the divisive and unjust and cruel tragedies that come are but birth pangs of a new day from God (see v. 8). It is true, as Jeremias and others have pointed out, that the parable may originally have been given in a different context, and that the fig tree's changes are more parallel to the good signs of salvation (the resurrection, the preaching of the gospel, the spread of the faith) than to the horrors that had to be faced. But the point to Mark and his readers is, as Beasley-Murray says, that the disciples can be absolutely certain, when they see the happenings of which Jesus has spoken, that God is with them and the summer of their salvation is close at hand. ***He is near*** is translated "the end is near" in NEB: the subject is not specified in the original.

Do ***these things*** in verse 29 and ***all these things*** in verse 30 refer to all that is said in

5–27 or only to the events of 5–23? That is, does the phrase include the coming of the Son of man, or does it not? In answer, we must observe that the events of 24–27, unlike those of the earlier verses, are expressed in terms of events beyond the earth, or else of the actual end itself. Therefore, it is quite possible to take ***these things*** to refer specifically to the events up to 5:23. However, it would be difficult, in view of the normal and inclusive meaning of ***all these things,*** not to understand that when these visible events occur, the coming of the Son of man may be then expected at any time.

This generation has been said to refer to the Jewish people; to this kind of generation i.e., to evil men who would perpetrate such horrors as were to be expected; to disciples, to Christians generally; or to the human generation (race) as a whole. Beasley-Murray is quite persuasive in insisting that it must be understood in its normal sense, that is, that ***this generation*** refers to Jesus' own contemporaries. In any case it appears clear that Jesus viewed his own fulfilment of his calling (including his death and resurrection, his giving of his life as a ransom for the many, cf. 10:45) as making certain the issues of history. His coming in clouds would but be the final triumph.

At least in this passage as it is recorded in Mark, Jesus appears to have telescoped the whole of the future into a very brief period of time. But in verse 32 he qualified his own prophecy: the Son does not know of that day and hour—***only the Father.*** Moreover, the exhortation to ***watch,*** and to do so expectantly, is pertinent to Christians of every age.

On what permanent realities can man rely? Not on ***heaven and earth,*** which ***pass away,*** but on Jesus, whose word is sure and eternal (v. 31). The Hebrew—and so the Christian— will understand such a claim to mean that his word is of God. They can depend therefore on the promise of the Spirit's presence (13:11) and on the ultimate providence and triumph of God. However, the time of that ultimate end is reserved to God's providence: it does not belong to man or even to the supreme one of God's representatives (v. 32).[47]

In verse 33, for the fourth time in this discourse, we have the exhortation ***take heed*** (cf. 5,9,23). Here it is reinforced by the command, ***watch.*** The verb occurs only here in Mark; the noun built on the same root is used by Paul to describe his sleepless nights (cf. 2 Cor. 11:27). The further command to ***watch*** in verses 35,37 is another word, meaning "be alert." All these commands are in the present imperative: they call for constant watchfulness, constant care, constant expectation. Mark's understanding of Jesus' teaching on things to come accents this single point. The disciples are to live always in anticipation of difficulty and pressure and at the same time in confident and expectant hope of the sovereign triumph of God. (Many ancient manuscripts add the command to pray in v. 33; it would be appropriate enough, for prayerfulness is one expression of taking heed. Cf. 14:38. Nevertheless, the evidence favors the text followed by RSV.)

A reason for alertness is that the disciples ***do not know when the time will come.*** This is true of chronological time also, but the word for ***time*** here means "the fit time," the appropriate occasion which God in his providence chooses. The little parable in 34 ff. has parallels with all three of the longer stories in Matthew 25. However, the emphasis here is on the responsibility of

[47] This saying in v. 32 is acknowledged by most biblical scholars as being genuinely Jesus' own. It was naturally used by Arius and his followers as indicating the Son's inferiority to the Father, so that some of the more orthodox in the fourth century denied its genuineness! In recent times many scholars, including A. T. Cadoux, R. Bultmann, and A. Loisy, have suggested that the verse is not original; the usual reason given for its existence is that it provided the church with an explanation of why the Parousia had not occurred. But it is more natural and more appropriate to recognize that the reality of the incarnation "involved such ignorance on the part of Jesus during his earthly life" (Cranfield). Besides, the emphasis in the verse is not on Jesus' not knowing but on the ignorance of everyone save the Father. It is therefore a verse that accents the command to watch. Cf. Beasley-Murray, pp. 261–64.

the doorkeeper (the guard at the gate), who must stay awake and ready. All the *servants* are *in charge,* i.e., they have some stated authority and responsibility. But one part of that responsibility is constant alertness.

The four watches of the night, according to the Roman system, are listed in verse 35. *The evening* watch was 6:00 P.M. to 9:00 P.M.; the *midnight,* 9:00 P.M. to 12:00; the *cockcrow* (etymologically "the crowing of the rooster") was from midnight to 3:00 A.M.; and *the morning* or "dawn" watch from 3:00 A.M. to 6:00 A.M.

The warnings against relaxation of spiritual alertness must have been needful to the Christians for whom the Gospel of Mark was written. In verse 3 only four disciples addressed Jesus, but his response to them must not be considered as an answer for them alone. Mark therefore assured his readers that what Jesus had been saying was applicable to all. The promise of the Son's coming and their uncertainty as to God's appointed time were to be to them encouragement and impetus for faithful Christian living in a world distressed by evil.

IV. The Culmination of the Ministry: Death on the Cross and Resurrection from the Tomb (14:1—16:20)

1. The Conspiracy Against Jesus (14:1–2)

[1] It was now two days before the Passover and the feast of Unleavened Bread. And the chief priests and the scribes were seeking how to arrest him by stealth, and kill him; [2] for they said, "Not during the feast, lest there be a tumult of the people."

In chapter 13 Mark has recorded the prophetic assurance of Jesus that God is sovereign, and that the Son of man will ultimately accomplish the full salvation of his people, even though they must endure dire trouble and unprecedented affliction. He now takes up again the story of the tragedy that was already upon the disciples, the betrayal and crucifixion of Jesus. Mark has made sure that his readers understand who Jesus is, and that they will read of his death in the full knowledge that he is yet and will be Lord. What will happen takes place because of the cruel blindness of the Jewish religious leaders, but it will happen within the divine purpose for the Son.

The Hebrews reckoned their days from sunset to sunset. *The Passover* took place on Nisan 15 of the Jewish calendar. The paschal lambs were offered in the Temple on the afternoon of Nisan 14, and the Passover meal was prepared and eaten that very evening, which would by Jewish reckoning be the next day, Nisan 15. *The feast of Unleavened Bread* lasted from Nisan 15 through 21.

Leaven, the substance used in dough to cause it to rise, was generally made from bread flour which had been kneaded without salt and saved until it fermented; it was therefore ordinarily secured from the dough of the previous baking. In eating unleavened bread for a week at this festival, the devout symbolized their break with the past, especially its evil, and a fresh start in godly living. *The Passover* itself reminded the people that God in triumph had delivered their forebears from slavery in Egypt, and was a festival of hope and expectation that God would again redeem them.

Two days before the Passover is sometimes interpreted as two full days before the feast. But by Jewish reckoning, if we understand that the Passover meal was eaten on a Thursday evening, this probably means that an (informal?) meeting of *the chief priests and the scribes* took place sometime on Wednesday. For *chief priests* and *scribes* see 11:18,27; the word elders would probably be included had Mark meant the entire Sanhedrin.

These religious leaders were already *seeking* a way to destroy Jesus. They prepared to act *by stealth* (this is the word translated "deceit" in 7:22), because they did not wish to have any disturbance among the people, particularly while the city was thronged with worshipers. Jeremias is probably correct in interpreting the phrase *not during the feast* to mean not in the presence of the multitude who had come to the feast.[48]

As far as Mark is concerned, these ***chief priests and scribes*** were less concerned about their own possible violations of scribal rules (cf. on 14:53 f.) than they were with getting rid of Jesus, but without precipitating ***a tumult of the people.*** Since they ***were*** already ***seeking*** to destroy Jesus, we should understand that they probably hoped to do so before ***the feast*** began. It is unnecessary to suppose (as do H. B. Swete and A. Plummer) that they had planned to wait until after the feast and that Judas' defection precipitated their action at once. From Mark's standpoint, Judas' betrayal provided only the way to ***arrest*** Jesus ***by stealth.***

2. *The Anointing at Bethany (14:3–9)*

**3 And while he was at Bethany in the house
of Simon the leper, as he sat at table, a woman
came with an alabaster jar of ointment of pure
nard, very costly, and she broke the jar and
poured it over his head. 4 But there were some
who said to themselves indignantly, "Why was
the ointment thus wasted? 5 For this ointment
might have been sold for more than three
hundred denarii, and given to the poor." And
they reproached her. 6 But Jesus said, "Let her
alone; why do you trouble her? She has done a
beautiful thing to me. 7 For you always have
the poor with you, and whenever you will, you
can do good to them; but you will not always
have me. 8 She has done what she could; she
has anointed my body beforehand for burying.
9 And truly, I say to you, wherever the gospel
is preached in the whole world, what she has
done will be told in memory of her."**

From 11:11 f. and from this paragraph it appears that Jesus and his disciples were spending their nights ***at Bethany.*** However, Judas led the arresting posse to Gethsemane on the Mount of Olives (14:26–44). Compare Luke 21:37: "At night he went out and lodged on the mount called Olivet." ***Bethany*** is not far from that place. We know nothing more of ***Simon the leper;*** we surmise that he may be one whom Jesus' power had healed.

[48] *The Eucharistic Words of Jesus*, rev. ed. (New York: Charles Scribner's, 1966), pp. 71 f. Cf. the use of "feast" in John 7:11, and the phrase in Luke 22:6, "in the absence of the multitude."

The story in Luke 7:36–50, though a woman anoints Jesus (i.e., his feet) at the home of a man called Simon (a very common name), is too different to be identified with Mark's account. In that case the woman is identified as "a sinner," and the anointing was a sign of gratitude for forgiveness.

There are differences also with the story given in John 12:1–8. There the householder is not named, but Martha serves the table and Mary does the anointing; Mary anointed his feet, wiped them with her hair; but the woman in Mark is said to have anointed Jesus' ***head.*** Only Mark says the woman ***broke the jar;*** this was the custom when anointing a body for burial. However, in both accounts the woman is criticized for her waste of the precious ointment; and in both, Jesus accepts the act as anticipating his burial (v. 8; note that in 16:1 ff. the women intended to anoint his body, but the resurrection had already taken place). John places this incident six days before the Passover; here in Mark (as in Matthew, who is following Mark) it is inserted later. Both Mark and John are capable of arranging their materials to set forth more clearly who Jesus is and what he means to the world. This is apparently what has happened in this case. It is a little strange that Mark does not name the woman, even though he affirms that ***what she has done will be told in memory of her.***

The ***alabaster jar*** may have been of alabaster, or an "alabastron" of something less valuable; it would have been a "long, tubelike flask" (Johnson). ***Nard*** oil was extracted from the root of a plant native to India (*Nardostachys jatamansi*). It is described as ***pure,*** but the meaning of the adjective is uncertain, and it quite possibly describes the oil of the pistachio nut which was used as a base for perfumes.

She ***poured it over his head.*** The anointing of the head did not necessarily imply more than courtesy or kindness: cf. Luke 7:46. But Mark's readers would surely understand it to mean more. Bacon, half a century ago, suggested that she meant to anoint him as the Christ, and that Jesus' reply in verse 8 meant that no throne awaited him, only a martyr's death. To Mark's readers, since the anointing of the head often implied a royal dignity, the act of the woman might well affirm, in symbol, Jesus as the Christ—the King.

The reaction among some other guests, so inadequately aware of the meaning of the person and events involved, was—not surprisingly—vexed. The expensive perfume, costly enough to pay a laborer's hire for a full year, used up in one short moment! What a waste! (For denarius, cf. on 6:37.) In John 12:4 f., Judas Iscariot is identified with this view, and John reflects on his insincerity. Matthew identifies the objectors as disciples.

Jesus defended the woman's deed. It was true, of course, that the poor could have used help; this is always true. But the woman had ***done a beautiful thing*** to Jesus: was it not an expression of generous love? And in view of the occasion the action was especially fitting, for he was about to be put to death. Jesus would not interpret the anointing as referring to royal dignity, but as an anticipation of his burial.

The passage must not be taken to imply that the care of the poor is either unimportant or casual (i.e., to be undertaken only at our convenience); but that no one had any right to ***trouble her*** (the Greek idiom literally means "provide her difficulties") for taking advantage of an opportunity more significant than she herself realized. That Jesus said ***the poor*** are ***always*** present in society is not to say that poverty is of God any more than is war, or some other social evil (cf. 13:7). On the contrary, we must struggle against these evils. The verse means that the disciples will have oppportunity and responsibility for ministering to needy persons.

In verse 9 we again have an affirmation of the universality of the gospel and the missionary imperative. Many commentators think this verse must have come not from Jesus but from the early church's convictions. Rawlinson thinks that the kernel of this saying may be authentic "though the wording has been recast" into the language used in early Christian preaching. Much depends on whether we believe that Jesus thought of the end as being very near, and whether such sayings as 13:10 are also from Jesus. It is perfectly clear that Mark understands that the gospel was universal from the first. The fully appropriate statement here that the woman's act would ***be told in*** her ***memory*** and the characteristic ***truly, I say to you*** lend some support to the conclusion that the statement is essentially from Jesus and that Mark's understanding was accurate.

3. The Betrayal of Judas (14:10–11)

10 Then Judas Iscariot, who was one of the twelve, went to the chief priests in order to betray him to them. 11 And when they heard it they were glad, and promised to give him money. And he sought an opportunity to betray him.

The story of the anointing, perhaps inserted into the tradition at this point by Mark, interrupted the narration of the plot against Jesus' life. However, it may well be that Jesus' rebuke of the woman's critics triggered the action of ***Judas.*** Did he understand, perhaps more clearly than some of the other disciples, that Jesus really did reject any concept of an earthly Christ and really did expect to die? Together with the sting of Jesus' response (in v. 6; cf. John 12:4–7), the realization that Jesus expected to be put to death at once may have driven him to divorce himself from his Master and go ***to the chief priests.***

Judas' offer provided the enemies of Jesus with the hoped-for opportunity of arresting him without any tumult (v. 2). Naturally, ***they were glad,*** and they ***promised*** payment for his action. But it is doubtful that the lure of money was in itself sufficient to cause Judas to betray Jesus. Mark simply gives no explanation; Matthew 26:15 has Judas inquiring how much they will pay him; Luke says that "Satan entered into" Judas, and he decided to betray Jesus. Compare John 13:27.

We really know very little about *Judas Iscariot.* Mark mentions him by name only three times (cf. 3:19; 14:43). Many suggestions as to Judas' motives have been made. Was he trying to force the hand of God, to reveal Jesus' messiahship and vindicate him by some miracle? Or was Judas himself deceived into the belief that the religious leaders would not harm Jesus? We can only speculate. It does seem most reasonable that Judas was, as Taylor puts it, "the victim of disillusionment, doubt, and despair."

4. The Preparation for the Passover (14:12–16)

12 And on the first day of Unleavened Bread, when they sacrificed the passover lamb, his disciples said to him, "Where will you have us go and prepare for you to eat the passover?" 13 And he sent two of his disciples, and said to them, "Go into the city, and a man carrying a jar of water will meet you; follow him, 14 and wherever he enters, say to the householder, 'The Teacher says, Where is my guest room, where I am to eat the passover with my disciples?' 15 And he will show you a large upper room furnished and ready; there prepare for us." 16 And the disciples set out and went to the city, and found it as he had told them; and they prepared the passover.

The first day of Unleavened Bread, if the words be strictly interpreted, was not the same day *they sacrificed the passover lamb* (cf. on 14:1 f.). The lamb was killed on the afternoon of Nisan 14, and eaten on that night, by Jewish reckoning Nisan 15. Strack and Billerbeck cite some evidence that Nisan 14 was sometimes loosely referred to among the Jews as *the first day of Unleavened Bread,* as Mark has done here; this would have been a natural variation in usage, particularly with persons who lived in a society in which others thought of days as ending at midnight.

Verse 12 clearly indicates that Mark treats the institution of the Lord's Supper as having occurred at a Passover meal. This is in accord with the other Synoptics, which are following Mark at this point, but is in contrast with John, which has the death of Jesus occurring at the hour the Passover lamb was slain. (See especially John 19:14, 31.) Both the Synoptic Gospels and John would have the meal on Thursday night, with the resurrection early on Sunday, after the sabbath was past. It has been noted often that John's dating is a means of affirming the theological truth that Jesus is our "passover lamb," and that his death delivers his people from bandage. (Cf. Paul's words in 1 Cor. 5:7.) But it must be recognized that the institution of the Lord's Supper at the Passover meal is almost equally capable of the deep and similar symbolic expression of the Christian faith.[49]

In answer to the disciples' question, Jesus *sent two of his disciples* (Luke 22:8 identifies them as Peter and John) to prepare for the Passover meal. It was unusual (though not unheard of) for a *man* to be *carrying a jar* (i.e., an earthenware vessel) *of water.* Since this was "woman's work," the disciples would be able to identify the man and follow him to the place Jesus had apparently already reserved. Compare the account of the entry into Jerusalem in 11:1–11: much of the phrasing is the same. The impression is that Jesus had prearranged both the place and the means by which his disciples might locate it, and that he did so because he wished this meal to be undisturbed by his enemies. Johnson and Grant

49 For thorough discussion of the questions involved and proposed solutions, cf. Jeremias, *The Eucharistic Words of Jesus,* pp. 1–88. Cf. also Cranfield, pp. 420–22, who holds that the Lord's Supper was indeed instituted at a Passover meal. In contrast, Grant, *Interpreter's Bible,* VII, 872 f., 876 f., believes it impossible for the trial and execution of Jesus to have taken place after the Passover had begun. P. Carrington, pp. 307–10, thinks the meal was "the preparatory meal on the previous night" (Nisan 14), that the supper at Bethany had taken place on Nisan 13, and that Jesus died as the passover lamb on Nisan 14, in accord with John 19:14. Another hypothesis, that Jesus and his disciples celebrated the Passover on Tuesday night, three days before the crucifixion, assumes that Jesus followed the practice of the Qumran community in this regard: but our accounts of Jesus reflect no close connection on his part with the Essenes, and their practice with regard to sacrifices in the Temple remains somewhat obscure. The *Manual of Discipline* contains no reference to Temple or sacrifice except in figurative expressions; cf. M. Burrows, *The Dead Sea Scrolls* (New York: Viking, 1955), pp. 237 f.

believe that Jesus may indeed have made these arrangements, but that Mark treats Jesus as having a "supernatural perception." Mark himself simply narrates what happened: it is unlikely that what Jesus had or had not done beforehand was preserved in the account that came to him. However, ***my guest room*** should normally be understood as "the room I have reserved."

Furnished ("spread out") ***and ready*** would mean only that there were rugs and cushions, perhaps a low table, and that it was not otherwise occupied. It was by religious custom incumbent on Jerusalem house-owners to show hospitality to festal pilgrims. This was particularly true for the Passover meal, which had to be eaten in the city itself or within a very limited, prescribed distance.

The room itself is described as an ***upper room,*** i.e., a room upstairs, and as ***large,*** which was needful for such a company. It has been suggested that this was the home of friends of Jesus (which is quite likely), and some have identified it as the home of John Mark's parents (which is purely speculative).

5. *The Passover Meal (14:17–25)*

(1) *The Prophecy of Betrayal (14:17–21)*

17 And when it was evening he came with the twelve. 18 And as they were at table eating, Jesus said, "Truly, I say to you, one of you will betray me, one who is eating with me." 19 They began to be sorrowful, and to say to him one after another, "Is it I?" 20 He said to them, "It is one of the twelve, one who is dipping bread in the same dish with me. 21 For the Son of man goes as it is written of him, but woe to that man by whom the Son of man is betrayed! It would have been better for that man if he had not been born."

When it was evening means after sunset, and so, according to Jewish reckoning, now on Nisan 15. The Passover meal included the lamb (roasted), wine, unleavened bread, bitter herbs, and a special sauce into which the bread (perhaps with herbs) was dipped. The meal was normally a festive but holy occasion, with special blessing to God for his redemption of the people from Egypt; and the head of the household was expected to review the nation's history at this sacred repast.

Neither the clause, ***who is eating with me,*** nor, ***one who is dipping bread in the same dish with me*** would have singled out Judas. All of them dipped their bread in the common dish. From the question of the disciples, and from Jesus' response in verse 20, it is perfectly clear that Mark does not consider that Jesus identified the betrayer to the others. Compare Luke 22:23. Matthew 26:25 (unless, as A. H. McNeile suggested, the words were whispered) is somewhat in contrast, as John 13:27 would be if the writer had not expressly stated that the other disciples did not understand the remark. The fact is that the disciples seem all to have been so astonished by Jesus' charge of coming betrayal that each one thought only to clear himself of any suspicion.

The question ***Is it I?*** more literally is, "It is not I, is it?" or, as NEB translates, "Not I, surely?" Jesus' reply accents the horror that would be felt that any one associated in table fellowship at this holy meal should be guilty of treachery.

For ***the Son of man,*** cf. on 2:10 and 8:31. ***Goes,*** or "goes his way," describes, in Taylor's phrase, "a voluntary act of home-going." In the providence of God for his people, as the (unspecified) Scriptures have indicated, his death was bound to happen. But this is not to say that Jesus did not voluntarily choose to follow the path that God intended for him. Nor dare we conclude that the betrayer bears no responsibility. What happened by and to Judas was not some irresistible and remorseless fate. ***Woe*** is not a curse; it is more nearly a cry of sorrow and compassion. How deep his tragedy! ***Better . . . if he had not been born!***

The phrase ***as it is written of him*** is not very intelligible unless we recognize, as Mark has affirmed before (8:31; 9:31; 10:33), that Jesus had been teaching this and had connected his role as ***Son of man*** with God's Suffering Servant.

(2) *The Bread and the Cup (14:22–25)*

22 And as they were eating, he took bread, and blessed, and broke it, and gave it to them, and said, "Take; this is my body." 23 And he took a cup, and when he had given thanks he gave it to them, and they all drank of it. 24 And he said to them, "This is my blood of the covenant, which is poured out for many. 25 Truly, I say to you, I shall not drink again of the fruit of the vine until that day when I drink it new in the kingdom of God."

The other accounts of the institution of the Lord's Supper are found in Matthew 26: 26–29, which relies on Mark; 1 Corinthians 11:23–25, which is very similar; Luke 22: 15–19, which the writer apparently derived from another tradition, for he does not follow Mark's order. (The text in Luke is uncertain, but RSV is probably right in following the shorter text, which omits v. 20.) The Lukan order (first the wine, then the bread) was followed in at least part of the early churches, as the second-century Didache (9:1–4) confirms. We cannot be certain which order is original. Four cups were actually taken during a Passover meal.[50]

Mark's account is rather clearly Palestinian in origin (Taylor) and is quite brief. It contains fewer interpretative words than Paul's, even though the apostle had written at least a decade earlier. Phrases such as "which is broken for you" are often considered to have been additional explanation for the churches. Luke and Paul's inclusion of a command to repeat the observance is probably also interpretative, but Cranfield thinks Mark may have omitted this phrase because he thought it could be taken for granted.

As they were eating, i.e., during the main course; this came after the memory of God's previous redemption of Israel had been recalled. Whether the meal was the Passover or not, we must so construe it here, for Mark does. The lamb was being served during this course, and its sacrifice must have been in the minds of all present. The ***bread*** would have been the unleavened loaf provided for the meal (though the word used for bread does not usually carry this meaning). The blessing may have been similar to one still used in Judaism: "Blessed art thou, O Lord our God, king of the world, who hast brought forth bread from the earth." But Jesus perhaps modified the blessing for this special occasion, then ***broke*** the loaf, and himself ***gave*** it to his disciples. See comment on the feeding of the five thousand, 6:41.

This is my body, explained Jesus. This conforms to the language of sacrifice. Portions of most of the offerings prescribed in the Old Testament were eaten by the worshipers. None of these offerings, however, was considered to be transformed into a different substance when sacrificed, nor should the words here ever have been so construed. Moffatt was right to paraphrase, "Take this, it means my body." Jesus is saying that those who shared the broken pieces of bread also were to share in the power and meaning of his self-sacrifice. They will live in the way he has taught them, they will bear their own crosses.

Since, according to Mark, Jesus is God's unique Son who announces the divine victory and calls redeemed men into the kingdom (1:11,15); and since he is also the Son of man who must, in accord with the divine purpose, suffer and be killed in his conflict with that evil spirit characterized by hardness of heart (8:31 ff.; 3:5 f.); we must understand the ***bread*** (and the ***cup,*** which means ***the blood of the covenant***) in terms of participation in God's ***kingdom.*** This participation cannot mean simply being saved in some future time: it involves the reign of God in place of whatever tyrant or power controls human life. And the single emphasis most obviously present in this passage is the mutuality of their participation; they ate from one loaf, ***they all drank*** from the one ***cup.*** The disciples are not merely individual kingdom-men. They are one fellowship, participants together in the way of

[50] Jeremias, *ibid.*, pp. 85 f., lists carefully the stages of the meal. If the cup was drunk after the bread was eaten, it was either the "cup of blessing," or, less probably, the *hallel* or "praise" cup.

Christ. And it is Christ's life which they share and which makes this a reality.

The covenant of Israel was no ordinary covenant between equals. It was a covenant made by God and on his terms. He would be their God, and they would be his people —voluntarily obedient to his commands. The language chosen is very close to that of Exodus 24:6–8; cf. also Zechariah 9:11, where the "blood of the covenant" was sometimes identified in Jewish interpretation with the blood of circumcision, sometimes with that of the Passover lamb.

The covenant of which Jesus speaks is to be ratified, or established, by Jesus' blood, i.e., his death. To drink the cup (analogous to being sprinkled by blood in Ex. 24:8) means to share in the obligations and benefits of Jesus' covenant. The ***cup*** and the ***covenant*** are ***for*** the ***many:*** as in 10:45, ***many*** does not mean some, but not all; it means those present, and many others as well. The term itself is broad enough to include all.

Verse 25 is expressed in the form of a Nazirite vow, and with it Jesus consecrates himself openly to his own life-offering (Cranfield, K. Barth; cf. John 17:19). ***The fruit of the vine*** is wine such as they have shared from the one cup. The ***day*** spoken of may be the period of the resurrection appearances, or it may refer to the messianic feast. (See above on 9:1.) His work done, they may look forward to the day of deeper fellowship and joy in ***the kingdom of God.***

6. The Prophecy of Denial (14:26–31)

26 And when they had sung a hymn, they went out to the Mount of Olives. 27 And Jesus said to them, "You will all fall away; for it is written, 'I will strike the shepherd, and the sheep will be scattered.' 28 But after I am raised up, I will go before you to Galilee." 29 Peter said to him, "Even though they all fall away, I will not." 30 And Jesus said to him, "Truly, I say to you, this very night, before the cock crows twice, you will deny me three times." 31 But he said vehemently, "If I must die with you, I will not deny you." And they all said the same.

At the conclusion of the Supper, Jesus and the band of disciples made their way through the gate of the city, down the Kidron ravine, and began to ascend ***the Mount of Olives.*** The ***hymn*** sung at the close of the Passover meal was from Psalms 115–18, the second part of the Hallel.

Jesus was thinking—how could it have been otherwise!—of his coming death; of Judas' betrayal; of the inadequacy of his disciples' commitment. We may suppose that Mark's account here derived from Peter. It is surely unwarranted to think that either this paragraph or the next, in which the disciples fail to watch with Jesus, would have been invented by a church led by apostles.

Jesus' thoughts again found expression in terms of the prophetic expectations in the Old Testament, specifically Zechariah. It is unnecessary to suppose, as some do, that the connection between the events and the Scriptures was here the later discovery of disciples, unless we deny that Jesus regarded himself as the suffering Son of man who was fulfilling God's eternal purposes. If he deliberately interpreted himself as fulfilling Zechariah 9:9 (cf. Mark 11:1–11), it is natural enough to conclude that (1) he anticipated the scattering of his disciples in terms expressed in Zechariah 13:7 (the quotation is somewhat free); (2) he may also have been thinking of the words in Zechariah 13:6, though with new meaning in his own circumstance: "The wounds I received in the house of my friends;" and (3) he recognized, with Zechariah 13:9, that the disciples needed to undergo their own trials and difficulties before their commitment could become adequate.

Fall away is the same verb that occurs in 4:17; 6:3; and 9:42,45,47: they will all "stumble into the trap" of fear and despair. Nevertheless, ***after I am raised up*** (cf. 8:31; 9:31; 10:34), ***I will go before you to Galilee.*** To ***go before*** may mean to lead, to walk in front of them (so J. Weiss in this context, concluding that this was unfulfilled); or it may simply mean to precede them, as in 6:45. (See 16:7.)

Peter's response was very insistent. He was sure Jesus could depend on him. He would not *fall away* (same word as in v. 27), whatever the others might do; he would die with Jesus, *he said vehemently,* rather than *deny* (disown) him. (Peter is not identified in 14:47 as the disciple who began to fight the arresting officers.) But Jesus warned him most emphatically and precisely that this day (so KJV, and with much evidence in support), *this very night, before the cock crows twice,* Peter would disown him. Perhaps the cock crow referred to the bugle call at the beginning of the fourth watch; but the more likely explanation is the ordinary one.

Mark's account (which Matthew follows rather closely here) emphasizes not only Peter's defection but the weakness of *all* the disciples. Were they not still affected by some hardness of heart (8:14–21), some selfish ambition (10:35–45), some fear of what the authorities might do to them? It is so much simpler to assert loyalty and faith than to maintain it in the face of terrible adversity.

7. *The Agony and Prayer in Gethsemane (14:32–42)*

**32 And they went to a place which was
called Gethsemane; and he said to his disciples, "Sit here, while I pray." 33 And he took
with him Peter and James and John, and began
to be greatly distressed and troubled. 34 And he
said to them, "My soul is very sorrowful, even
to death; remain here, and watch." 35 And
going a little farther, he fell on the ground and
prayed that, if it were possible, the hour might
pass from him. 36 And he said, "Abba, Father,
all things are possible to thee; remove this cup
from me; yet not what I will, but what thou
wilt." 37 And he came and found them sleeping,
and he said to Peter, "Simon, are you asleep?
Could you not watch one hour? 38 Watch and
pray that you may not enter into temptation;
the spirit indeed is willing, but the flesh is
weak." 39 And again he went away and prayed,
saying the same words. 40 And again he came
and found them sleeping, for their eyes were
very heavy; and they did not know what to
answer him. 41 And he came the third time,
and said to them, "Are you still sleeping and
taking your rest? It is enough; the hour has
come; the Son of man is betrayed into the
hands of sinners. 42 Rise, let us be going; see,
my betrayer is at hand."**

One of the traditional spots for Gethsemane is a small grove of ancient olive trees on the slope near the Kidron ravine. *Gethsemane* itself probably means "oil press." The word *place* means simply "piece of land" or field; it is called a garden in John 18:1. Most of the disciples were instructed to stay at one point (near the entrance to prevent or signal any interruption?) until he had prayed.

Peter, James, and John were the three disciples who seem to have been closest to Jesus, and who shared, as the larger group did not, some of the most intimate experiences of their Lord (cf. 5:37–43; 9:2–8). Once Andrew was with them (cf. 13:3).

The experience in Gethsemane was unique. Nowhere else is Jesus said to have undergone such emotional stress as here. The infinitives, *to be greatly distressed and troubled,* are very difficult to translate. The first verb occurs in early Christian literature only in Mark (also in 9:15; 16:5); it implies amazement and shock. The second (in NT elsewhere only in Matt. 26:37; Phil. 2:26) means to be in anxiety, uncertain as to which way to turn. Attempts to translate these feelings of Jesus into our language are difficult: Moffatt has, "to feel appalled and agitated"; TEV renders it, "Distress and anguish came over him."

That Jesus *began* to be so disturbed must mean that here, with only the three close disciples, he gave way to the pent-up stress boiling within himself. *My soul is very sorrowful, even to death* were words which would hopefully convey to his friends the depth of his feelings. *My soul* here means my very self, my whole being. His anxious grief seemed so terrible that it threatened to destroy him. If we think of Jesus as strong and serene during his trial and even his crucifixion, here in Gethsemane the curtain of his very human self was drawn back for the three disciples.

Mark (his account from Peter?) will not let us suppose that the three comprehended his distress or entered into the experience in any full way. The cost of Jesus' full obedience to God was vivid before the Master, and he had to endure it all the way. It must have been easier for Jesus to view his own death at a distance, as at earlier times (8: 31, et al.) he had spoken of his coming suffering. Now the terrible final deed is upon him. But the disciples could not have slept had they been able to identify with him in his distress. He craved their presence and comfort, but their own understanding was too distant from his to afford what he needed.

Remain here, and watch. By this request Jesus was probably seeking some measure of human companionship in his stress. He went only a little distance farther, then ***fell on the ground.*** This was the ultimate physical gesture in prayer. His prostration marked in a physical way the intensity with which Jesus sought divine strength.

The hour is a much more common expression in John (cf. 2:4; 7:30; 12:23,27; 17:1). It was an eschatological expression (Dan. 8:17,19; 11:40, 45 LXX), and in this New Testament context marked the appropriate time for fulfilment of the destiny of the Son of man. Verse 35 simply states in indirect form the prayer Jesus offered in verse 36.

Abba is Aramaic for father. Whether Jesus repeated the address in both languages is doubtful, of course. It is more likely that the *Abba* of Jesus was retained in memory and use by the early Christians, who in their prayers would say *Abba* together with their own word for ***father*** (here, Greek *pater;* cf. Rom. 8:15; Gal. 4:6). ***This cup*** means the cup of suffering. See above on 10:38 f.: two of the three disciples nearby had been challenged as to whether they could endure to drink his ***cup.***

Jesus, then, even in the midst of his personal torture in Gethsemane, continued to think of God as his Father. And the greatness of his prayer lies in this, that in spite of his own anxiety and his wish not to undergo the horrors ahead, his deepest desire remained unchanged. Surmounting everything else, the Father's will should be done. Obedience to God was not questioned, nor was God's way of dealing with sinful men challenged, though that way meant that the evil in men's lives would destroy the Son of man.

The answer to Jesus' prayer came not at once, and his restless prayer was repeated (v. 39). Mark never gives us any hint of any answer that ever did come to Jesus, except that he was able to face with unequalled serenity the events that followed, and to endure most of them without the presence of a human friend.

Though we read elsewhere of Jesus' praying for long periods of time (Luke 6:12; cf. Mark 1:35; 6:46), he was restless and filled with deep emotion as he prayed in Gethsemane. He kept returning to the three disciples, but ***found them sleeping.*** Apparently he woke Peter—here called Simon, for he was no rock (*Petros*) of strength at this hour—and reminded him of his weakness. Not that Peter did not mean what he had said earlier (cf. 14:29,31), but that he did not know his physical and spiritual limitations. Jesus' prayer and his exhortation to Peter have close parallels with the Model Prayer Jesus had earlier taught his disciples (cf. Matt. 6:9–13).

When Jesus returned from prayer again, Simon had once more joined the others in sleep. ***They did not know what to answer him*** means not that Jesus had asked them something but only that they were unable to respond appropriately to Jesus' need in this situation.

The translators of RSV and NEB take the first part of verse 41 as a question. If right, is the question rhetorical; or does it mean, "Are you going to sleep and be at ease?" The words can also be read as a statement, or as a command (KJV, RV, ASV).

The words ***It is enough*** are difficult to interpret. The one Greek verb which they translate was the word commonly used on receipts, meaning "paid in full." Perhaps the meaning is that the time for full payoff had arrived, sin's hardening of heart had reached its final act in Jesus' life. We may dismiss the suggestion that it refers to Judas' having received his betrayal money! But it remains most likely that the word simply refers to their sleeping, and called the disciples to awake.

The Son of man had been ***betrayed into the hands*** of men who are here named ***sinners.*** It ought to be noted that the word ***sinners*** was ordinarily applied to people who were careless about the keeping of the law (cf. 2:15,17). Moule thinks that ***sinners*** here refers (as it sometimes does) to Gentiles, and speaks of the irony that "the one who is at the very heart of the truest Jewish loyalty is betrayed to Gentiles!" However, Mark has already made perfectly clear who are the real protagonists of evil (cf. especially 7:1–23; 12:38–40): insofar as ***sinners*** here refers to a particular group, it must mean the chief priests and scribes. They are Gentiles only in the sense that they know not God!

8. The Arrest of Jesus (14:43–52)

43 And immediately, while he was still speaking, Judas came, one of the twelve, and with him a crowd with swords and clubs, from the chief priests and the scribes and the elders.
44 Now the betrayer had given them a sign, saying, "The one I shall kiss is the man; seize him and lead him away safely." 45 And when he came, he went up to him at once, and said, "Master!" And he kissed him. 46 And they laid hands on him and seized him. 47 But one of those who stood by drew his sword, and struck the slave of the high priest and cut off his ear.
48 And Jesus said to them, "Have you come out as against a robber, with swords and clubs to capture me? 49 Day after day I was with you in the temple teaching, and you did not seize me. But let the scriptures be fulfilled." 50 And they all forsook him, and fled.

51 And a young man followed him, with nothing but a linen cloth about his body; and they seized him, 52 but he left the linen cloth and ran away naked.

Perhaps some of the disciples who had been left near the entrance to Gethsemane (v. 32) had called a warning. In any case, the arresting party was likely to be hurrying lest the one they sought should escape. ***Judas*** is identified again as ***one of the twelve,*** which in his tragic case becomes an accent of reproach.

The ***crowd with swords and clubs*** may have been mainly Temple police (as in Luke 22:52), who were subject to the leaders of the Sanhedrin (cf. 11:27). But there was at least one ***slave of the high priest*** among them. The word for ***swords*** can mean "knives," and ***clubs*** can refer to any kind of wooden cudgel. The term soldiers in John 18:3 would imply men of the Roman garrison. Mark's description of the crowd could readily apply to any hastily gathered posse. The words of Jesus in verse 49 would be better suited if the arresting party were composed chiefly of members of the Sanhedrin with the Temple police.

Sign means a prearranged signal: the Greek word occurs here only in the New Testament. The ***kiss*** was a customary form of greeting, particularly of a rabbi. (The early Christians were encouraged to assert their fellowship by greeting with a "holy kiss"; Rom. 16:16; 1 Cor. 16:20; etc.). ***Seize*** is a verb often used for arrest or apprehend. The precaution to ***lead him away safely*** was apparently given in fear that Jesus might attempt to escape. This time there was to be no questioning, no discussion (cf. 11:27—12:27; John 7:25–31).

Judas addressed Jesus as ***Master,*** that is, "Rabbi," and identified him by kissing him. The verb for kiss in verse 45 is a compound of the word in verse 44, and has sometimes been interpreted as "repeatedly kiss" or "kiss very affectionately." However, the probable meaning is that Judas prolonged the kiss somewhat, so that the sign could be observed by all and they could be sure of arresting the right person. See 2 Samuel 20:9 f. for a similar hypocritical greeting of Amasa by Joab.

One of those who stood by would have fought to help Jesus escape, or at least avenge the indignity done him. John 18:10 identifies the man as Peter, but Mark gives no hint of this. His words would allow us to think that it may have been someone other than a disciple, perhaps one who had heard what the crowd was about to do and sought to prevent it. ***The slave of the high priest*** is named as Malchus in John 18:10. That Jesus healed him is recorded only in Luke 22:51. Matthew's account (26:51–54) shows special interest in answering the question of whether Jesus could have called for divine help (cf. John 18:5–6). Mark, however, lets the Gethsemane scene serve: what happens is in accord with the Father's will.

Jesus protested in appropriate (and dignified) terms about the manner of arrest. He had not been in hiding, but ***day after day*** (the phrase implies Jesus had been in or near Jerusalem longer than the short period Mark records) he had been ***in the temple teaching.***

The ***scriptures*** to be ***fulfilled*** are not named, though the early church, as we know, would have thought of Isaiah 53 and other passages commonly used in connection with the death of Jesus. The most pertinent suggestions are Psalm 41:9 and Zechariah 13:7 (cf. Mark 14:27).

After Jesus had been taken, the disciples ***fled,*** leaving Jesus in the hands of his enemies. The word ***all*** is emphatic. What would have happened to them had they lingered is indicated by the attempted arrest of the ***young man*** mentioned in verses 51 f. They did catch him, but he was able to twist out of the ***linen*** garment by which they were holding him and to make good his escape. The word translated ***naked*** should probably be taken with utter literalness, though it was sometimes used of persons wearing only an undergarment, and so being not decently clothed.

The cloth left behind was of ***linen,*** more expensive than the usual outer covering of wool. To forfeit such a fine garment would have been no small loss for most persons. Was he a member of a well-to-do family? Had he heard of the treachery, and hurriedly wrapped himself only in his good cloak in a vain effort to warn Jesus? Was he a son of a member of the Sanhedrin? Or, as has often been suggested, is this the hidden signature of John Mark, the author? (See the Introduction; Mark was probably a very small child at this time.) We cannot do more than speculate.

9. *The Hearing Before the High Priest (14:53–65)*

**53 And they led Jesus to the high priest; and
all the chief priests and the elders and the
scribes were assembled. 54 And Peter had followed him at a distance, right into the courtyard of the high priest; and he was sitting with
the guards, and warming himself at the fire.
55 Now the chief priests and the whole council
sought testimony against Jesus to put him to
death; but they found none. 56 For many bore
false witness against him, and their witness did
not agree. 57 And some stood up and bore false
witness against him, saying, 58 "We heard him
say, 'I will destroy this temple that is made
with hands, and in three days I will build
another, not made with hands.' " 59 Yet not
even so did their testimony agree. 60 And the
high priest stood up in the midst, and asked
Jesus, "Have you no answer to make? What is
it that these men testify against you?" 61 But he
was silent and made no answer. Again the high
priest asked him, "Are you the Christ, the Son
of the Blessed?" 62 And Jesus said, "I am; and
you will see the Son of man sitting at the right
hand of Power, and coming with the clouds of
heaven." 63 And the high priest tore his mantle,
and said, "Why do we still need witnesses?
64 You have heard his blasphemy. What is your
decision?" And they all condemned him as
deserving death. 65 And some began to spit on
him, and to cover his face, and to strike him,
saying to him, "Prophesy!" And the guards
received him with blows.**

The ***high priest*** at this time (A.D. 18–35) was Caiaphas, though Mark does not name him, and though his father-in-law, whose name was Annas, seems to have been regarded similarly as high priest in spite of his removal from that office some years earlier (cf. Luke 3:2; John 18:13,24). The high priest and 71 of the ***chief priests and the elders and the scribes*** formed the Sanhedrin (cf. on 11:27). The words ***all*** in verse 53 and ***whole*** in verse 55 are not in emphatic position (as "all" is in v. 50), and we need not suppose that every member was present (cf. Luke 23:50 f., though it is not clearly stated whether Joseph was present).

Verse 53–54 are really introductory to the two remaining sections of this chapter, respectively. Peter had fled with the other disciples, then followed unobtrusively to see what might happen to Jesus. The high priest's palace would have been built around an open courtyard, and Peter and at least one other disciple were able to get inside (cf. John 18:15 f.). It was still night, and it appeared unlikely he would be given close scrutiny. Apparently he sat too close to the fire! The word translated ***fire*** in verse 54 is the word meaning "light," but the phrase must mean something like "in the glow of the fire." Only Peter could have told the story in 66–72. The account of the trial itself is not so vivid or marked by detail.

The ***council*** means the court, the Sanhedrin. The procedure described by Mark has been strongly questioned because it violated the rules known to us from the Mishnah (Sanhedrin 4–7). Among other things, a trial had to be conducted during the daylight hours; a conviction could be reached only by a majority of two or more, and not until the following day; a trial could not be held on a feast day, or on the day before the sabbath, both of which provisions were, according to Mark, ignored. Jesus was charged by the high priest with ***blasphemy*** (v. 64), but the penalty of stoning was not to be carried out unless the guilty party spoke the Name itself.

It must be remembered, however, that the Mishnaic rules were codified in the second century and may not all have been in force. Moreover, the rabbinic scholars H. Danby and (to a lesser degree) I. Abrahams considered that the rules were "ideal" or "theoretical" and not strictly enforced. What is described in 14:55–64 may have been a kind of judicial inquiry, something similar to a grand jury investigation rather than a trial. In any case, the court met again after daybreak (15:1). C. G. Montefiore reminds us that we have always had instances of illegal trials, and that any flimsy legal form has been adequate to dispose of a feared or hated enemy. Finally, whatever the Sanhedrin agreed to, and however careless they were with their own rules, they arranged for the final sentence to be pronounced by Pilate, and the crucifixion was carried out by Roman soldiers.[51]

The ***council*** was unsuccessful in securing satisfactory evidence to support their purpose to destroy Jesus. That ***many bore false witness against*** Jesus should not be surprising; the witnesses were aware that these powerful men wanted to get rid of Jesus. Apparently, however, in the rush of things their testimonies were crude and unrehearsed and could not be made to agree (literally, "were not equal").

One charge the rulers hoped to fasten upon Jesus was that he claimed he would ***destroy*** the old ***temple*** and replace it with ***another, not made with hands.*** The question here was whether Jesus had claimed the prerogatives and power of God himself, and so had blasphemed. Some current Jewish literature anticipated that God himself in that new day coming would provide a glorious temple in the place of the one in which they worshiped (Jubilees 1:17,27 f.; Enoch 90:28 f.). According to Mark 13, Jesus had indeed anticipated the destruction of the Temple, and, however much sorrow he may have shared with other Hebrews over its ruin, he certainly did look beyond that tragedy to the divine victory and continuing worship of God. The Christians for whom Mark was writing would have rejoiced in the truths hidden in these charges. See John 2:19–22; Acts 7:48; and Hebrews 9—10.

The high priest was unable to get Jesus to testify against himself in regard to the Temple. In connection with Jesus' silence, note Isaiah 53:7. It is clear that Mark anticipated that his readers would be aware of many matters (whether tradition, as about the Temple, or Scripture) on which he does not elaborate.

The Blessed was God himself: this was

[51] On the trial of Jesus, cf. J. Blinzler, *The Trial of Jesus* (Westminster, Md.: Newman Press, 1959); P. Winter, *On the Trial of Jesus* (Berlin: De Gruyter, 1961). For summary statements, cf., S. Johnson, pp. 240–44; V. Taylor, pp. 644–46.

one way the Hebrews had of speaking of God without using the divine Name. (Cf. the scribe's words in 12:32 f.; in the NT the word here translated "blessed" is always used of God.) The ***Christ*** of David was not thought of as deity, and to claim to be the Christ was not in itself blasphemy. Neither would the words ***Son of the Blessed*** have meant to the chief priests a unique claim to deity, but only that the one saying this would in a chosen and remarkable way have claimed to be God's servant.

However, the words would not have been so limited for Mark and his readers. To them Jesus was indeed the Christ, the unique and beloved Son of God. He was also the divine ***Son of man***, who was ***sitting at the right hand of Power*** (i.e., God, whose power is exercised through the Christ), and who would come ***with the clouds of heaven.*** (Cf. 13:26; 8:38—9:1. On ***Son of man***, see above also on 2:10 and 8:31; on Christ, 8:29; and on Son of God, 1:1,11; 3:11; 9:7; 15:39.)

Mark is probably following the tradition as he received it, and some have questioned whether the high priest would have connected ***Son of the Blessed*** with ***the Christ.*** It is difficult to be sure of the precise words used at this hearing; the disciples probably received their own information from one of the high priest's servants, or perhaps from some member of the Sanhedrin who became a disciple. But there is no question that, for Mark, Jesus is condemned for claiming to be ***the Christ*** and the divine ***Son of man.*** For the words ***I am***, and the possibility that they would suggest to the Christian community more than a simple affirmation, see above on 6:50.

The high priest tore his mantle—a sign of mourning (he must have been glad!) because he had heard ***blasphemy.*** As far as he was concerned, something irrevocable and dreadful had taken place, for Jesus had dared claim more than any man might dare to be and do. The council agreed forthwith that he deserved to die. Nothing is said of any formal sentence.

The ugly indignities now heaped upon Jesus were probably done by the servants and guards. Every sadistic impulse was loosed, and Jesus was spat upon, mocked, and beaten. ***Prophesy*** in this context means, use your divine knowledge to reveal who strikes you.

10. Peter's Denial (14:66–72)

**66 And as Peter was below in the courtyard,
one of the maids of the high priest came;
67 and seeing Peter warming himself, she
looked at him, and said, "You also were with
the Nazarene, Jesus." 68 But he denied it, saying,
"I neither know nor understand what you
mean." And he went out into the gateway.
69 And the maid saw him, and began again to
say to the bystanders, "This man is one of
them." 70 But again he denied it. And after a
little while again the bystanders said to Peter,
"Certainly you are one of them; for you are a
Galilean." 71 But he began to invoke a curse on
himself and to swear, "I do not know this man
of whom you speak." 72 And immediately the
cock crowed a second time. And Peter remembered
how Jesus had said to him, "Before the
cock crows twice, you will deny me three
times." And he broke down and wept.**

Of all the stories in the Gospel, this one has most claim to be a reminiscence of Peter. ***Below in the courtyard*** (apparently the Sanhedrin was meeting upstairs), he was waiting to find out what would happen to Jesus. The maid (the word is applicable either to a slave or a hired girl) is identified in John 18:17 as the one who kept the door. She was curious, perhaps suspicious, about the stranger and ***came*** and ***looked at him*** carefully in the light of the moon and the fire. Then she made her accusation directly to Peter, probably loud enough for some around to hear. The ***you*** is emphatic, and the position of the term ***the Nazarene*** make it likely that she spoke the words with contempt (cf. John 1:46; but cf. also Mark 16:6).

Peter's position was precarious. If he was really the one who in the garden had drawn his sword, he had even more reason to fear for his own safety. He might have reasoned, What help could I possibly be to Jesus if I myself am arrested? But he probably blurted out his denial without pausing to rationalize. His words may be translated as RSV has them, or they may be paraphrased, "I don't have any idea what you are talking about. What do you mean?" ***Know*** and ***understand*** probably should not be distinguished here, the second only accenting the first. He moved away from the warmth and light of the fire, back ***into the gateway,*** or vestibule leading from the gate. Some of our manuscripts here insert the note that the cock crowed: cf. 14:30,72.

The same girl came again (Matt. 26:71 thinks of a different servant: the point is not crucial, but Mark's version is psychologically more likely, especially if the maid was responsible for keeping the entrance), and this time spoke ***to the bystanders,*** accusing Peter of being one of Jesus' band. ***Again he denied it:*** the tense of the verb (unlike in v. 68) is linear, and means he kept disowning Jesus. Indeed, he talked so much that ***the bystanders*** noted his ***Galilean*** accent, and concluded that the maid must have been right. The difference between the language of Jerusalem and Galilee was probably somewhat parallel to the difference between the speech of people from Boston and Birmingham.

In protest against their accusation, Peter ***began to invoke a curse on himself*** to attempt to convince them of his innocence and noninvolvement. The word ***curse*** is correctly interpreted by RSV, and should not be understood merely as foul language. Peter now had explicitly and vehemently disowned any relationship with Jesus. ***And immediately the cock crowed a second time.*** The evidence of the manuscripts is strongly for the inclusion of the words ***a second time,*** whether or not the first time had been as early as verse 68. There were chickens kept in Jerusalem, and we are probably right to understand this as literal rather than the sounding of a Roman watch (cf. on 13:35; 14:30).

Peter had been defending himself from outside accusers, but now the memory of Jesus' warning flooded his soul. ***He broke down*** is an effort to translate a participle whose precise meaning in this context is elusive. It may mean, "he thought about" (what he had done); or "he covered over" (his head with his robe); or "he answered" (the situation, i.e., by weeping). But most recent translators, supported by references cited by Moulton and Milligan, agree with RSV; cf. NEB, "And he burst into tears." It is a sad but vivid story.

What a contrast! Jesus, though innocent, was condemned by his own confession. Peter, though guilty (not of a crime, but of what the maid affirmed), was allowed to remain free by his own denial (Minear). For harassed and threatened Christians in Rome, this story of the failure of the esteemed apostle would have served as stirring warning and exhortation.

11. The Trial Before Pilate (15:1–15)

(1) The Governor's Question (15:1–5)

[1] And as soon as it was morning the chief priests, with the elders and scribes, and the whole council held a consultation; and they bound Jesus and led him away and delivered him to Pilate. [2] And Pilate asked him, "Are you the King of the Jews?" And he answered him, "You have said so." [3] And the chief priests accused him of many things. [4] And Pilate again asked him, "Have you no answer to make? See how many charges they bring against you." [5] But Jesus made no further answer, so that Pilate wondered.

Morning having come, a formal meeting of the Sanhedrin could be held more legitimately, though the fact that it was on the first day of Unleavened Bread (according to Mark 14:12, cf. John 18:28) still violated what we know to be the later rule. See above on 14:43 ff. At this meeting, according to the text followed by RSV, they ***held a consultation.*** (Important evidence supports the text followed by NEB, "having made their plan . . . [they] put Jesus in chains." The RSV reading has the better support, and can more easily be harmonized with Luke 22:66—23:1.)

The *council* decided to take Jesus before Pilate and accuse him of fomenting rebellion. What to the council was blasphemy could be made to sound like sedition to the

Roman governor.

Pilate was the Roman procurator of Judea A.D. 26–36. He was described in a letter from Agrippa I to the Emperor Gaius Caligula as inflexible, self-willed, and relentless, vindictive and cruel, guilty of repeated executions without trial (so Philo, *Embassy to Gaius,* 299–305). The gospel accounts are not so hard on Pilate as Philo, or even Josephus, who tells us of Pilate's removal from office because of his wanton killing of a band of Samaritans (*Antiq.*, 18,4). Mark excuses no one of guilt in what happened to Jesus, though he especially emphasizes the sin, or hardness of heart, seen in the betrayer, in the Jewish religious leaders, and even in his disciples—Peter who disowned him, and the other disciples who fled. But Pilate, the crowd calling for blood (15:11 ff.), and the Roman soldiers (15:16–20) are also treated as participants in the outrage.

Pilate's residence was normally in Caesarea. He came to Jerusalem during the Passover, when the city was so crowded, presumably to maintain order. In Jerusalem it is uncertain whether he stayed in Herod's palace or in the fortress of Antonia.

Mark's account is so brief and omits so many data that it becomes obvious that he considers the facts well known to his readers (Taylor). He does not even bother to say here that Pilate was governor: he can assume they are well aware of his identity. His account of the trial before ***Pilate*** differs considerably from John's, who describes a measure of philosophical discussion between Jesus and the Roman (John 18:28–38). Neither does Mark say anything of Jesus' being sent before Herod (Luke 23:6–12), nor does he speak of the dream of Pilate's wife and of Pilate's symbolic handwashing, as does Matthew 27:19,24 f.

On the charge made against Jesus before the governor, however, the Gospels are in accord. He claimed to be King of the Jews. Luke 23:2 elaborates this, the chief priests charging Jesus with "perverting our nation," with "forbidding us to give tribute to Caesar," and with calling himself "Christ a king." Mark merely adds that they heaped up accusations against him (v. 3).

Pilate's question about the charge puts special emphasis on the pronoun ***you.*** Probably it is contemptuous: how absurd that someone like ***you*** claims to be ***King of the Jews!*** But the pronoun may merely express Pilate's surprise.

What irony in the charge! Jesus really is Christ the King in a spiritual sense (John 18:36), but he has refused every pressure to enforce his kingship politically (cf. Mark 6:45; John 6:15). Now, after the religious leaders had condemned his claim to kingship as blasphemy, they accused him of trying to be the very kind of king he had refused to become, a military and political insurrectionist.

Jesus' answer to Pilate, ***You have said so,*** is deceptively simple. It is more nearly a yes than a no. At the same time, the answer probably means, This is *your* way of saying who I am; but it is not mine. Nothing more would Jesus add, Mark tells us. No wonder Pilate realized that the man before him was no ordinary, frightened peasant. Cf. again Isaiah 53:7.

(2) *The Release of Barabbas and the Sentencing of Jesus* (*15:6–15*)

[6] Now at the feast he used to release for them one prisoner whom they asked. [7] And among the rebels in prison, who had committed murder in the insurrection, there was a man called Barabbas. [8] And the crowd came up and began to ask Pilate to do as he was wont to do for them. [9] And he answered them, "Do you want me to release for you the King of the Jews?" [10] For he perceived that it was out of envy that the chief priests had delivered him up. [11] But the chief priests stirred up the crowd to have him release for them Barabbas instead. [12] And Pilate again said to them, "Then what shall I do with the man whom you call the King of the Jews?" [13] And they cried out again, "Crucify him." [14] And Pilate said to them, "Why, what evil has he done?" But they shouted all the more, "Crucify him." [15] So Pilate, wishing to satisfy the crowd, released for them Barabbas; and having scourged Jesus, he delivered him to be crucified.

We know nothing of Pilate's custom of releasing ***any one prisoner*** at the ***feast,*** except what the Gospels tell us. ***Barabbas*** is described here as ***among the rebels*** who had ***murdered*** some persons during ***the insurrection.*** John 18:40 says he "was a robber," an additional charge of which the rebel band would likely have been guilty. His other name may have been "Jesus," as some manuscripts indicate in Matthew 27:16 f. Had he claimed to be a savior from God? We do not know. What Mark describes is how it happened that a man guilty of insurrection was set free, and how Jesus Christ, innocent as he was, was crucified as an insurrectionist.

Who composed ***the crowd*** that asked ***Pilate*** to follow his usual custom and release a prisoner? It is highly improbable that it was composed of Galileans (Herod Antipas ruled Galilee), even less likely that they were the same crowd that had welcomed Jesus to Jerusalem (11:8–11). On the contrary, they may even have been friends of ***Barabbas*** who had come to ask for his release. This would be, as Rawlinson says, a "strangely dramatic historical coincidence," but it accords with what happened. In any case, the disciples were nowhere in evidence; as far as Mark is concerned, they had fled (14:50).

Pilate suggested the release of ***the King of the Jews.*** Whether or not he used the words cynically, Mark's readers would be again reminded of who Jesus was and is. The ***chief priests,*** either capitalizing on the crowd's original purpose or instigating the idea, deigned to mingle with the rabble to foil Pilate's apparent hope to let Jesus go. And the crowd asked for Barabbas.

Pilate was quite right in recognizing that ***the chief priests*** were motivated, at least in part, by ***envy.*** If Jesus had not had such a popular following, and if his claims and teaching had not so contradicted their own, the Sadducean leaders might not have joined the rabbis of the Pharisees in seeking Jesus' death.

Mark clearly implies too that the governor would have liked to foil the purpose of the chief priests. There is, however, no hint that his efforts were made for the sake of justice. After all, by his judicial authority he could have released Jesus. The explanation that he was cynically trying to play the crowd against their bloodthirsty religious leaders is much more probable. He does not appear to have cared what happened either to Barabbas or Jesus.

In fact, there is a hint that Pilate might have released both prisoners, if the crowd had only asked him (v. 12). The repeated and growing cry, ***Crucify him,*** ended any such hope. (On crucify, cf. below on 15:22,24.) A mob was satisfied, a criminal ***released,*** and Jesus was ***scourged*** and ***crucified.***

Scourging was a horrible punishment inflicted on slaves, sometimes on ordinary provincial people, never on Roman citizens (cf. Acts 22:25 ff.). Whips of leather with bits of metal or bone were used, often with the victim stretched and bound to a pillar. It was usually done to those about to be crucified.[52]

12. The Scornful Torment by the Soldiers (15:16–20)

16 And the soldiers led him away inside the palace (that is, the praetorium); and they called together the whole battalion. 17 And they clothed him in a purple cloak, and plaiting a crown of thorns they put it on him. 18 And they began to salute him, "Hail, King of the Jews!" 19 And they struck his head with a reed, and spat upon him, and they knelt down in homage to him. 20 And when they had mocked him, they stripped him of the purple cloak, and put his own clothes on him. And they led him out to crucify him.

The ***soldiers*** were Pilate's men. Perhaps they belonged to the Second Italian Cohort, as Johnson suggests. Such a military unit (***battalion***) had a normal complement of six hundred men, one-tenth of a legion (cf. on 5:9), though probably only a detachment was present at this time. The word

[52] Cf. Livy, *Ab Urbe Condita,* 33, 36, who writes of slave insurrectionists' being "scourged and crucified." Josephus, *Wars of the Jews,* 2:14, describes similar treatment of citizens of Jerusalem by the procurator Florus. John 19:1 seems to place the scourging of Jesus before the final sentence was handed down.

court is translated *palace* by RSV; this is a possible meaning, and the *praetorium* would be understood to mean Pilate's headquarters. Traditionally this would be at the Tower of Antonia, where the excavated paving stones still show markings used for gambling games indulged in by the Roman military garrisons. However, the site could have been Herod's palace (cf. above on 15:1).

The soldiers dressed him "royally," probably using some soldier's *pudamentum*, a scarlet military cloak (Rawlinson). The ***crown of thorns*** likely resembled the laurel wreath worn by the emperors, but it could have been intended as a king's diadem. The ***reed*** may have been a scepter at first (cf. Matt. 27:29), but was snatched away and used for striking ***his head.*** They mocked his kingship with salutes and repeated gestures of obeisance, accenting their contempt by covering him with their spit.[53]

How keenly ironic this story is! Jesus enters the ***palace,*** is robed, crowned, and even reverenced as "king," all with vulgar and sadistic humor. Yet, beset by taunts, ridiculed, and utterly humiliated, the suffering Son of man is being enthroned as the true King. Minear suggests that the Christians of Mark's day would have read his passion narrative "with one eye on Psalm 2." The Lord himself will have them in derision!

When the preparations which had to be made for the execution had been completed, the soldiers again dressed Jesus in ***his own clothes.*** Then, according to the usual practice, a centurion with a detachment of four men ***led him out*** to put him to death.

13. The Crucifixion (15:21–32)

21 And they compelled a passer-by, Simon of
Cyrene, who was coming in from the country,
the father of Alexander and Rufus, to carry his
cross. 22 And they brought him to the place
called Golgotha (which means the place of a
skull). 23 And they offered him wine mingled
with myrrh; but he did not take it. 24 And they
crucified him, and divided his garments among
them, casting lots for them, to decide what
each should take. 25 And it was the third hour,
when they crucified him. 26 And the inscription
of the charge against him read. "The King of
the Jews." 27 And with him they crucified two
robbers, one on his right and one on his left.
29 And those who passed by derided him, wag-
ging their heads, and saying, "Aha! You who
would destroy the temple and build it in three
days, 30 save yourself, and come down from the
cross!" 31 So also the chief priests mocked him
to one another with the scribes, saying, "He
saved others; he cannot save himself. 32 Let the
Christ, the King of Israel, come down now
from the cross, that we may see and believe."
Those who were crucified with him also reviled
him.

Jesus apparently was too weak by this hour ***to carry his*** own ***cross,*** at least not all the distance (John 19:17). Heavy beams or even trees used for the purpose would already have been at the place of execution. A criminal sentenced to crucifixion would carry only the crosspiece which was to be attached to the upright stake. A wooden block or support of some kind near the base of the upright beam would bear some of the body's weight, but also would prolong the period of intense suffering.

The soldiers ***compelled . . . Simon of Cyrene,*** probably a Jew who had lived in that place, to perform the humiliating task of carrying the crosspiece on which Jesus was to be nailed. ***Compelled,*** or "forced into service," is also used in Matthew 5:41. We have no reason at all to suppose that Simon had previously known Jesus. The fact that his name and those of his two

[53] Philo, *In Flaccum,* 36–40, describes imaginative cruelty of Alexandrians mocking Herod Agrippa I, who had been appointed by Caligula as a petty king over part of the old Jewish kingdom. Using Carabas, a wretched but docile "lunatic," they put him on an improvised throne, made him a paper crown, chose a rug for a robe and a papyrus reed for a scepter. Some of their young men put rods on their shoulders, and mimicked a bodyguard. All of this was done to express contempt for the Jews in their own midst, though directed specifically at Agrippa.

This ancient story and others concerning mocking practices at Saturnalia and the Babylonian *Sacaea* have been cited either to cast doubt on the historicity of the story of Barabbas or to warp the religious irony so eloquently expressed in it. Cf. the helpful note in Taylor's *Commentary,* 646–48. "The industry with which parallels are gathered," he writes, "is not commensurate with the value of the results gained." We must concur with his conclusion that the actions and mockery of the soldiers were in accord with a long history of similar practices. Mark's account is realistic and requires no defense.

sons are recorded suggests that they became members of the Christian community. Moreover, the sons' names would hardly have been mentioned in this fashion had they not been well known to Mark's readers. See Romans 16:13, where the ***Rufus*** named may have been one of these sons of Simon.

The site of the crucifixion is not known. The traditional place within the present Church of the Holy Sepulcher is probably not right (though the tradition dates from the fourth century), but neither are more modern guesses likely to be correct (Rawlinson). ***Golgotha*** is, as Mark says, Aramaic for ***skull.*** (Calvary is derived from the Latin translation of this word.) Perhaps the contour of the place did bear some resemblance to a ***skull.*** It was probably near one of the city gates where many people constantly passed. Such terrible and public execution was intended to make witnesses fear the wrath of their rulers.

Wine mingled with myrrh would have dulled the senses (and so the suffering), and was probably offered Jesus by friends or sympathizers, or by women of Jerusalem who customarily did this kindness, rather than by the soldiers. Since he refused it, we assume that he was avoiding any loss of consciousness.

They crucified him. The victim's hands were commonly spiked to the crosspiece, though sometimes the feet were not nailed similarly. In Jesus' case, cf. Luke 24:39 f. and John 20:20,25, though some suggest the influence of Psalm 22:16 upon the narrative at this point. The detail of soldiers who had the task of execution could take for themselves whatever possessions the condemned man might still have on his person. Before they actually ***crucified him,*** accordingly, ***they stripped him*** and cast ***lots*** for ***his garments*** (cf. Psalm 22:18). So hurriedly had it all been done that it was only ***the third hour,*** i.e., 9:00 A.M.

The charge against the criminal was customarily posted for all to see. Jesus was guilty, the ***inscription*** read, of being ***The King of the Jews.*** The truth, the "crime," and the glory, all in one placarded phrase! The alienation and contempt which Pilate felt toward the chief priests and leaders of the Jews were expressed also in the words, for he must have known they would regard the words as insulting. (Cf. John 19:18–22. The variations between the Gospels in the phrasing of the charge are insignificant in most respects.)

Two robbers were ***crucified*** at the same time. Mark records no conversation of Jesus with either of them, except to say that they also ***reviled him*** (v. 32). Matthew 27:44 follows Mark, but Luke 23:39–43 tells of the kind word and petition of one of the two; John records nothing at all of the attitude or words of the robbers. That Mark should tell us that one was crucified ***on his right*** and the other ***on his left*** may well have been intended by the author to remind his readers of the petition of James and John—and of Jesus' reply (10:37–40). The ***King*** was "drinking his cup," enthroned on a cross. But at what cost were two men on either side!

The coarse derision of those who passed by was expressed both in gestures and in loud taunts. ***Wagging their heads*** was an open expression of contempt (cf. Isa. 37:22; Psalm 22:7; and especially Lam. 1:12 and 2:15, which Mark may have had in mind.) With the reference to destroying ***the temple,*** cf. 14:58; the ordinary Jew would have considered such a claim, which they supposed Jesus made, as both ridiculous and blasphemous. Yet again the scornful words express for Christian readers the profound truth, and Jesus (who is ***the temple*** in the sense that in him we meet God) is the true ***King of Israel,*** who indeed would have ***saved*** them, and even yet offered them salvation. Mark groups them all together—the casual onlookers, the ***chief priests,*** the ***scribes,*** and ***those . . . crucified with him.*** See Isaiah 53:12: "[He] was numbered with the transgressors." (This OT allusion is quoted in some manuscripts as 15:28; but it is not original here, though it is in Luke 22:37.)

14. The Death of Jesus (15:33–41)

33 And when the sixth hour had come, there was darkness over the whole land until the

ninth hour. 34 And at the ninth hour Jesus cried
with a loud voice, "Eloi, Eloi, lama sa-
bachthani?" which means, "My God, my God,
why hast thou forsaken me?" 35 And some of
the bystanders hearing it said, "Behold, he is
calling Elijah." 36 And one ran and, filling a
sponge full of vinegar, put it on a reed and
gave it to him to drink, saying, "Wait, let us
see whether Elijah will come to take him
down." 37 And Jesus uttered a loud cry, and
breathed his last. 38 And the curtain of the
temple was torn in two, from top to bottom.
39 And when the centurion, who stood facing
him, saw that he thus breathed his last, he
said, "Truly this man was the Son of God!"
40 There were also women looking on from
afar, among whom were Mary Magdalene, and
Mary the mother of James the younger and of
Joses, and Salome, 41 who, when he was in
Galilee, followed him, and ministered to him;
and also many other women who came up with
him to Jerusalem.

Mark's notes of time on the day of crucifixion are rather full (cf. 15:1,25,33,42). The ***sixth hour*** was noon, and the ***ninth*** was 3:00 P.M. The darkness could not have been an eclipse, for the moon was full at Passover. Various suggestions have been offered, including the possibility of a very intense "black sirocco," i.e., a dust storm (M. Lagrange). Mark's description is as straightforward and simple as the rest of his crucifixion narrative. And it is probable that the darkness was, in his understanding, a literal, supernaturally caused phenomenon.

Many scholars think the darkness is figurative, with theological meaning. Certainly it was the hour in which darkness ruled (cf. Luke 22:53). Nowhere else is it more evident, or more damning, that "men loved darkness rather than light, because their deeds were evil" (John 3:19). The darkness is as appropriate as the inscription (v. 26) in describing the significance of the event, and neither Mark nor his readers could or would have confined the meaning to a mere recital of events.

The one saying of Jesus from the cross recorded by Mark (or Matthew) is from Psalm 22:1. The transliteration in our text is predominantly Aramaic. That in Matthew, which is closer to the Hebrew, is more likely original, for *Eli* would sound more like "Elijah" than would ***Elōi.*** The very difficulty we have in believing that God could ever have forsaken Jesus is evidence that the lonely cry is authentic. Luke, and perhaps John, must have felt the same difficulty we do—neither included this word—and, as M. Goguel says, the saying is in sharp contrast with the perfect communion the Gospels indicate was characteristic of Jesus' relationship with the Father.

Why hast thou forsaken me? How can anyone say that, had he had strength, Jesus would have expressed the triumphant faith with which Psalm 22 ends? Not that he had lost his faith—M. Dibelius says sharply that one does not quote Scripture in prayer when he gives up his faith! But the experience Jesus was undergoing made him cry out in utter desolation. Why, indeed? Was it not that his complete identification with sinful man, his abandonment of himself to the spiritual and physical penalties wrought in this world by the evils of man's hardness of heart, broke heavily upon him in his tortured condition? Did he not feel that God in his will had abandoned him to his tragic cup of destiny (14:36)?

Nevertheless, not one of Mark's readers would have felt really that God had ***forsaken*** Jesus. (The verb forsake means abandon, or desert.) On the contrary, as this whole narrative, with its irony and its sad mockery, makes so eloquently clear, the true King was doing God's will. By his obedience even to death, he was offering salvation from man's sin and hardness of heart to a newly established relationship with God. But the way of salvation can never avoid the way of the cross (cf. above, 10:45; and cf. 2 Cor. 5:21; Gal. 3:13; 1 Peter 2:24).

Ancient legends about ***Elijah*** reflect a popular belief that he often came to help God's people in distress. It was a natural misunderstanding of the unexpected outcry. The ***vinegar,*** or "sour wine," may have been from what the soldiers had brought for their own use. Since the soldiers would hardly have permitted a bystander to give Jesus anything, perhaps it was one of the soldiers who put the sponge to Jesus' lips. According to Mark, it was the same man who said,

"Wait, let us see whether Elijah will come." (Contrast Matt. 27:49; but one of the soldiers could have been familiar with the Jewish legends about the fabled prophet.)

Many interpreters take the offering of the wine as an act of rough kindness to Jesus. But the text of Mark by no means makes this clear. More probably the ***bystanders'*** words in verse 35 had added to the taunts, and pushing the sponge to Jesus' face may well have been a soldier's way of joining in the ugly mockery. The words, ***Wait, let us see*** should probably be translated, Do let us see ***whether Elijah will come.*** (So Moulton and Milligan, Taylor, Johnson, NEB; but not TEV; the verbal construction is late Greek, but is identical with that in Matt. 7:4, "Let me take.")[54]

The crucified man who was near death would normally be too weak and exhausted to utter ***a loud cry.*** Usually the torment on a cross would be more prolonged than six hours. "Intense spiritual suffering must have led to the embolism, if such it was, which was the immediate cause of death" (Taylor). Both the centurion (v. 39) and Pilate (v. 44) were surprised that Jesus so soon had died.

The ***curtain of the temple*** hung thickly at the entrance to the holy of holies (Ex. 26:31–37). Into this place the high priest was to go once a year, on the Day of Atonement, when he offered the sacrifice to remove the guilt of the people (cf. Heb. 9:7; and Lev. 16). Here in the holy of holies was God's presence considered to be. For the ***curtain*** to be ***torn in two*** meant that the death of Jesus opened to all men freely the way to God. ***From top to bottom*** meant that not man but God himself had made this true. We have no extra-biblical evidence that the veil was physically torn at this time: whether the event be literal or symbolic, it expressed eloquently the truth that Jesus had made the way open for man to approach God.

The ***centurion,*** who was supervising the execution, must have been moved by Jesus' demeanor throughout the day. The mockery of the people passing by, and even of chief priests and scribes who would not ordinarily have stopped there, had been concentrated on Jesus. Jesus, however, had endured his suffering without the usual cursing and screaming. The last outcry of Jesus, followed so abruptly by his death, moved ***the centurion*** to speak.

Truly this man was the Son of God. In themselves, all that the Greek text has to mean is that ***the centurion*** thought Jesus was a really noble human being, a man of outstanding quality, perhaps a person with a spark of divinity. That is why NEB and earlier RSV editions translate "a son of God." However, Mark surely understood them in a much deeper sense. He is ending his story of Jesus with a confession that matches 1:1 and 1:11, and his readers would think of the words of the centurion in terms of what they themselves would mean by their use. Jesus was for them the strong Son of God.[55]

The ***women*** who were present Mark now lists, apparently reminding his first readers of names with which they are familiar. Their introduction here serves the literary purpose of preparing for their part in the events to follow. ***Mary Magdalene*** is spoken of again in 15:47 and 16:1; Magdalene means she was from Magdala. In Luke 8:2 (cf. Mark 16:9) we are told that from her "seven demons had gone out." We have no warrant, however, for identifying her with the unnamed woman of Luke 7:36–50.

Another Mary is identified as ***the mother of James the younger and of Joses.*** See 15:47 and 16:1. She is called "the wife of Clopas" in John 19:25 (though "wife" is an interpretive insertion in the English

[54] The suggestion by M. Goguel (following Renan) that giving something to drink to a man being crucified was popularly thought to hasten death is interesting and attractive, but too little evidence supports it. Cf. his *Life of Jesus*, tr. O. Wyon (London: Geo. Allen & Unwin, 1958), pp. 543 f. Cf. Psalm 69:21, to which there may be an allusion: "They gave me poison for food, and for my thirst they gave me vinegar to drink."

[55] Cf. the note by R. G. Bratcher in *The Expository Times*, Vol. 68, No. 1 (Oct., 1956), 27 f.

text). *James* and *Joses* must have been well-known names among early Christians, but we know little or nothing about them. Some think *James* may be the one called "the son of Alphaeus" in 3:18 (Taylor, Cranfield). The word *younger* is literally "little," but appropriate evidence shows the rendering in RSV to be idiomatic.

Salome may have been to Mark an unusually well-known name, or only a name preserved in the tradition. Matthew 27:56 does not list Salome, but if the accounts are brought together we may conclude that she was the mother of two leading disciples, James and John.

These women had *ministered* to Jesus (and presumably his disciples) while he had been in Galilee. See Luke 8:1–3, in which it is said that certain women (including Mary Magdalene) "provided for them out of their means." Little is said in the Gospels of what these women did day by day, but brief words such as these suggest that they were among Jesus' most steadfast and valuable disciples.

15. The Burial by Joseph (15:42–47)

42 And when evening had come, since it was the day of Preparation, that is, the day before the sabbath, 43 Joseph of Arimathea, a respected member of the council, who was also himself looking for the kingdom of God, took courage and went to Pilate, and asked for the body of Jesus. 44 And Pilate wondered if he were already dead; and summoning the centurion, he asked him whether he was already dead. 45 And when he learned from the centurion that he was dead, he granted the body to Joseph. 46 And he bought a linen shroud, and taking him down, wrapped him in the linen shroud, and laid him in a tomb which had been hewn out of the rock; and he rolled a stone against the door of the tomb. 47 Mary Magdalene and Mary the mother of Joses saw where he was laid.

When evening had come should be understood to mean not long before sundown, for ***the day of Preparation*** would end at that time, and ***the sabbath*** begin (cf. above on 14:1,12,17). Taylor suggests it was about 4:00 P.M.

Joseph is described by Mark as a native ***of Arimathea*** (perhaps the "Ramathaim" spoken of in 1 Maccabees 11:34, a town near Lydda) and ***a respected member of the council.*** The word ***respected*** was interpreted in Matthew 27:57 as "rich"; in itself it means "of assured social position." The word translated ***member of the council,*** i.e., the Sanhedrin, was applied in Rome to senators; but cf. Luke 23:50 f., where it is added that Joseph "had not consented" to the Sanhedrin's decision.

That Joseph was ***looking for the kingdom of God*** would have led Mark's readers to count him as one of themselves. Matthew's description of him as a "disciple" may be, as Rawlinson says, "perhaps rather too much." But cf. John 19:38, where he is called a secret follower.

Mark considered that it ***took courage*** (the word is "dared") to ask a man like Pilate ***for the body.*** However, the Romans did not always leave the bodies of crucified victims to rot away on the cross. They sometimes gave them to petitioning relatives or friends for burial, and if asked, they may even have respected the Jewish religious customs on this matter. Deuteronomy 21:22 f. required that the bodies of hanged men should be buried the same day.

Pilate wondered if he were already dead: the Greek idiom probably means, as NEB has it, "Pilate was surprised to hear that he was already dead." In any case, he checked the matter with ***the centurion*** before granting Joseph his request. The marginal reading in verse 44, "whether he had been some time dead," has as much support as the one in the text; and is followed by NEB and TEV.

The ***linen shroud*** (the Greek text has no word for shroud, but it would have been a cloth for that purpose, not a garment as is perhaps implied in 14:51 f.) was purchased for Jesus' body. This might have required some special effort or influence on a Passover day, but would not have been impossible (Taylor).

Probably some of Joseph's servants helped him in his task. John tells of Nicodemus' aid also, but Mark does not mention him and apparently knows nothing of the myrrh and aloes which he contributed (cf. John 19:39 f.). Mark tells the story as if Joseph had had no time to arrange for anointing the body and left the task to be performed later by the women who attended the burial.

The *tomb* itself, described as *hewn out of the rock,* is said by John and Luke to have been new and unused. (In many tombs there was space for a number of bodies.) Matthew tells us that it was Joseph's own tomb.

16. The Empty Tomb and the Announcement of the Resurrection (16:1–8)

**1 And when the sabbath was past, Mary
Magdalene, Mary the mother of James, and
Salome bought spices, so that they might go
and anoint him. 2 And very early on the first
day of the week they went to the tomb when
the sun had risen. 3 And they were saying to
one another, "Who will roll away the stone for
us from the door of the tomb?" 4 And looking
up, they saw that the stone was rolled back; for
it was very large. 5 And entering the tomb, they
saw a young man sitting on the right side,
dressed in a white robe; and they were
amazed. 6 And he said to them, "Do not be
amazed; you seek Jesus of Nazareth, who was
crucified. He has risen, he is not here; see the
place where they laid him. 7 But go, tell his
disciples and Peter that he is going before you
to Galilee; there you will see him, as he told
you." 8 And they went out and fled from the
tomb; for trembling and astonishment had
come upon them; and they said nothing to any
one, for they were afraid.**

When the sabbath was past, i.e., on Saturday evening after sundown, the women *bought spices* to *anoint* Jesus' body. The names of the women were first given in 15:40, and at least two of them had witnessed the burial (15:47). The repetition of the names probably reflects the separate circulation and use of the traditions Mark is now following. It did not occur to the godly women to break the sabbath to perform their work of love. The *spices* purchased were probably perfumed oils (Taylor); cf. Luke 23:56, "spices and ointments."

The notes of time in verse 2 have been variously interpreted. *Very early* (exceedingly early) is almost as strong as the expression in 1:35 ("in the morning, a great while before day"), and stronger than that in 15:1. It would usually mean a time earlier than sunrise. Probably, however, F. C. Burkitt and Rawlinson are right to conclude that Mark's meaning is something like, "As early the next morning as they possibly could."

The tomb was probably hewn in an exposed rock face, and its *door* would have been perpendicular to the ground. The *stone* which covered the entrance, if it was similar to some pointed out in Jerusalem today, would have been set in a groove so that it could be rolled in front of the entrance and effectively seal the tomb. Then with effort it could be rolled to the side again to admit another body. Mark describes the tomb as *very large,* and it may well be that Joseph expected that his own family would be buried also in the same place (cf. on 15:46).

When they found *the stone* already *rolled back,* the women entered *the tomb* itself. Matthew's account is somewhat different, partly because he has included a story about a guard of soldiers; according to him the women do not enter the tomb. Compare also Luke 24:3; John 20:1 f.

Mark's description of the *young man* is a not uncommon way of describing an angel. One may compare 2 Maccabees 3:26,33. Johnson suggests the possibility of a counterpart in the *young man* of 14:51 f., but we have no *white robe* nor amazement. Matthew (28:2) thinks of an "angel" and Luke also: "two men stood by them in dazzling apparel" (24:4). Mark lays little stress on the supernatural elements implied in his story, but he does say the women *were amazed.* This verb is difficult to translate; in the New Testament, only Mark uses it (9:15; 14:33; and in vv. 5–6 here). Mark means that they were unusually upset, for what had taken place was so far beyond their understanding.

The young man told them Jesus had *risen.* It is therefore perfectly clear that Mark knew about and affirmed the cardinal Christian tenet that Jesus had triumphed over the grave. The tomb is empty: ***see,*** he said to the women, ***the place where they laid him.***

The message he gave to the women for the ***disciples*** was that Jesus was ***going before*** them ***to Galilee,*** and that they would ***see him*** there, ***as he told you.*** This accords with 14:28, but leaves unanswered any questions we may have about appearances said by our other sources to have happened in or near Jerusalem. Compare Luke 24 and John 20, though John 21 pictures the risen Lord also in Galilee. Matthew elaborates on Mark's story, but does affirm a meeting of Jesus with his disciples in Galilee (28:16). We simply do not have enough data adequately to interpret the differences in the accounts that have been preserved in the Gospels, in Acts 1:3–11, and in 1 Corinthians 15:3–11. Nevertheless, we must conclude from Mark's wording that the disciples had not yet left the environs of Jerusalem.

Peter was singled out by the ***young man*** in the message to the women. This must have been because he had so completely disowned his relationship with Jesus (14:66–72). Mark clearly means for his readers to think of this apostle as fully restored to the fellowship: probably in the original ending an event was recorded which demonstrated this fact. The oldest written account we have does speak of an appearance of Jesus to Peter (1 Cor. 15:5).

You will see him. E. Lohmeyer has claimed that this verb refers especially to the Parousia, not to resurrection appearances; and also that ***Galilee*** (not Jerusalem) is for Mark the land of eschatological fulfilment. But the verb translated ***see*** is a common one, and it is difficult to agree that it had become a technical term used in connection with Jesus' final coming. Nor is the supposed meaning of ***Galilee*** to Mark (i.e., as the place where Jesus would come again) any more clearly affirmed by the evidence.

It is better to conclude either that Mark knew only of appearances in ***Galilee*** (so Taylor); or else that (in an original ending) he affirmed a personal appearance of Jesus in Judea, perhaps to Peter, or to Mary Magdalene. This incident would then logically follow the description of the women who had ***fled,*** and who ***said nothing to any one.***

It is hard to believe that Mark would have ended his Gospel with such a clause as ***for they were afraid.*** His book concerns the strong Son of God, who was fully subject to the Father's will, who finished the Father's work, and who will come with the clouds in heaven. The last clause leaves too much unaffirmed and unfinished.

17. The Longer Ending: Resurrection Appearances and the Ascension (16:9–20)

9 Now when he rose early on the first day of the week, he appeared first to Mary Magdalene, from whom he had cast out seven demons. 10 She went and told those who had been with him, as they mourned and wept. 11 But when they heard that he was alive and had been seen by her, they would not believe it.

12 After this he appeared in another form to two of them, as they were walking into the country. 13 And they went back and told the rest, but they did not believe them.

14 Afterward he appeared to the eleven themselves as they sat at table; and he upbraided them for their unbelief and hardness of heart, because they had not believed those who saw him after he had risen. 15 And he said to them, "Go into all the world and preach the gospel to the whole creation. 16 He who believes and is baptized will be saved; but he who does not believe will be condemned. 17 And these signs will accompany those who believe: in my name they will cast out demons; they will speak in new tongues; 18 they will pick up serpents, and if they drink any deadly thing, it will not hurt them; they will lay their hands on the sick; and they will recover."

19 So then the Lord Jesus, after he had spoken to them, was taken up into heaven, and sat down at the right hand of God. 20 And they went forth and preached everywhere, while the Lord worked with them and confirmed the message by the signs that attended it. Amen.

On the textual problem, see the Introduction. These verses have close affinity with the other canonical accounts, especially with

Luke. Because their composition is later and by another hand than Mark's own, the student of the resurrection appearances will normally wish to concentrate on the conclusions recorded in the other Gospels.

Verses 9–11 have a rather close parallel in Luke 24:10 f. One will wish to compare also Matthew 28:8–10 and John 20: 14–18. Verses 12 f. summarize the remarkable story of Jesus' appearance to the two despondent disciples trudging toward Emmaus; but here we have only a prosaic affirmation, nothing of Luke's vivid narrative (24:13–35).

Verse 14 (***he appeared to the eleven***) is perhaps closer to Luke than to the other Gospels, though all of them (and 1 Corinthians 15 also) speak of appearances to the original disciples. No temporal note is given, nor is the place named. The ***unbelief and hardness of heart*** spoken of are appropriate themes to Mark (cf. 3:5; 6:6; 10:5).

The narrative element in the appearance to the eleven is sparse indeed. More attention is given to his injunctions to them. In verses 15 f. we have words parallel to the Great Commission in Matthew 28:19 f. Mark, however, has ***preach*** (i.e., "proclaim") ***the gospel*** where Matthew has a verb meaning to make disciples; also Matthew has "all the nations," or "all the Gentiles," while Mark has ***the whole creation.***

Coming to ***believe*** and to be ***baptized*** were regularly connected in the thinking of Christians from the very beginning. See, for example, Acts 2:38–41; 8:36–38, including the confessional addition in v. 37; and 16:31–33. This did not mean that the act of immersion was regarded as essential for salvation; but the witness and confession which baptism expressed were (and are) of the very essence of Christian faith. For the tragedy of unbelief, cf. John 3:18,36; and 20:22–31.

Signs were believed to accompany the work of God in the world, particularly that done through the apostles (Acts 4:16,30; 5:12; Rom. 15:18 f.; 2 Cor. 12:12). See John 14:12: "greater works than these will he do, because I go to the Father." The sign of speaking in ***tongues*** was often evidence of the coming of the Spirit, according to the narrative in Acts; compare also 1 Corinthians 14:22. Casting ***out demons*** had already been part of the experience of the disciples (6:13).

To ***pick up serpents*** was not characteristic of the early Christians as far as we know. However, the apostle Paul, according to Acts 28:2–6, was bitten by a viper; and, when he suffered no harm, the incident was regarded by the people of Malta as a sign of divinity. Luke 10:19 may have been intended figuratively, but by the compiler of Mark 16:9–20 the verse must have been read with simple literalness. The drinking of deadly poisons with no ill effects is not mentioned in the New Testament. Eusebius (III, 39) attributes to Papias (second century) the story of Justus Barsabbas' drinking poison with no harm to himself. Writers such as James also anticipate healing miracles (James 5:14 f.), and the twelve had already experienced the joy of this ministry (Mark 6:13).

To verse 19 compare Luke 24:50 f., including the added words (margin, RSV) "and was carried up into heaven." Acts 1:9–11 also gives an account of the ascension. That Jesus was ***at the right hand of God*** was affirmed by Stephen, the martyr (Acts 7:56). See also Psalm 110:1, and its citations by New Testament writers (Matt. 22: 44; Mark 12:36; Luke 20:42 f.; Heb. 1:13).

They went forth, presumably from Jerusalem, for the author has paid little or no attention to 16:1–8. Clement of Rome, about A.D. 95, tells of the apostles' "preaching everywhere," after they had been assured through the resurrection of Jesus and the coming of the Holy Spirit (Letter to Corinthians, 42). That ***the Lord*** continually was working with them (the tense is linear) was a part of the faith of the author of this reverent addition to the Gospel.

A shorter ending, which occurs in a few manuscripts, is also recorded in the RSV margin. It is equally reverent, and equally reflects the faith of Christians who shared Mark's commitment to Jesus Christ our Lord.